Hawaii For Dummies, 3rd Edition

W9-AYD-204

Waikiki

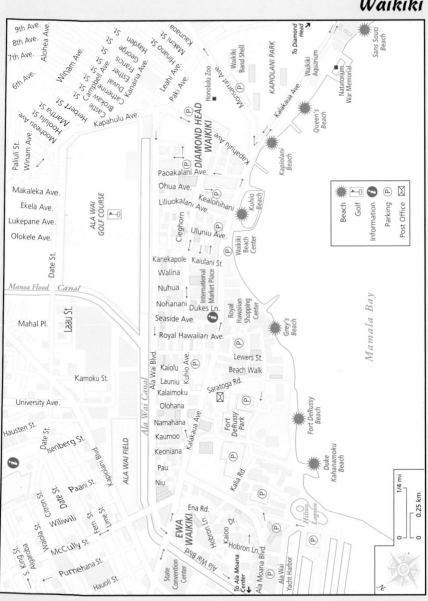

Honolulu

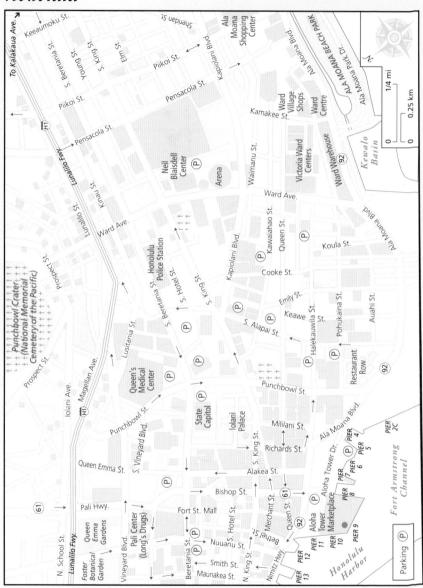

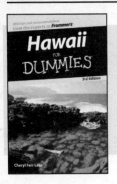
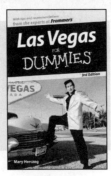

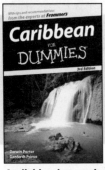
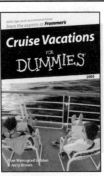

Hawaii
FOR
DUMMIES®
3RD EDITION

by Cheryl Farr Leas

WILEY

Wiley Publishing, Inc.

Hawaii For Dummies®, 3rd Edition

Published by
Wiley Publishing, Inc.
111 River St.
Hoboken, NJ 07030-5774
www.wiley.com

WILEY

About the Author

Cheryl Farr Leas may live on the mainland, but she's a Hawaii girl at heart. She fell in love with Diamond Head, aloha wear, and mai tais in 1994 and has had trouble staying away ever since. Whenever she's not in the islands, she and her husband, Rob, call Phoenix, Arizona home.

Before embarking on a writing career, Cheryl served as senior editor at Macmillan Travel (now Wiley) where she edited the *Frommer's Hawaii* travel guides for the better part of the 1990s. Now happy to be a globetrotting author and consultant, Cheryl also writes *Maui For Dummies.*

Dedication

This book is for Rob, for loving Hawaii as much as I do.

Publisher's Acknowledgments

We're proud of this book; please send us your comments through our Dummies online registration form located at www.dummies.com/register/.

Some of the people who helped bring this book to market include the following:

Editorial

Editors: Kelly Ewing, Project Editor; Amy Lyons, Development Editor

Cartographer: Anton Crane

Consumer Editorial Supervisor and Reprint Manager: Carmen Krikorian

Editorial Assistant: Melissa S. Bennett

Senior Photo Editor: Richard Fox

Cover Photos: © SIME s.a.s./eStock

Cartoons: Rich Tennant, www.the5thwave.com

Composition

Project Coordinator: April Farling

Layout and Graphics: Lauren Goddard, Joyce Haughey, Barry Offringa, Lynsey Osborn, Stephanie D. Jumper, Heather Ryan

Proofreaders: John Greenough, Leeann Harney, Joe Niesen, TECHBOOKS Production Services

Indexer: TECHBOOKS Production Services

Publishing and Editorial for Consumer Dummies

Diane Graves Steele, Vice President and Publisher, Consumer Dummies

Joyce Pepple, Acquisitions Director, Consumer Dummies

Kristin A. Cocks, Product Development Director, Consumer Dummies

Michael Spring, Vice President and Publisher, Travel

Brice Gosnell, Associate Publisher, Travel

Kelly Regan, Editorial Director, Travel

Publishing for Technology Dummies

Andy Cummings, Vice President and Publisher, Dummies Technology/General User

Composition Services

Gerry Fahey, Vice President of Production Services

Debbie Stailey, Director of Composition Services

Contents at a Glance

Maps at a Glance

Table of Contents

Introduction

I'm here to spread the good news: Hawaii really lives up to its heady promise. These islands of *aloha* offer all the ingredients of a carefree beach vacation. (*Aloha* is an all-purpose greeting meaning hello, welcome, or goodbye, but its meaning runs much deeper. Aloha is the Hawaiian concept of unconditional love.)

One of Hawaii's most magical and winning qualities is its ability to fulfill everyone's own island dream — whether you're 6 or 60, single or the head of a growing family, the *Survivor* type or a newly minted millionaire living the luxe life. Enjoyment is just a matter of knowing what you want from your island vacation — and how to make it happen.

Planning a Hawaii vacation is easy — too easy, in fact. Far too many people head off to Hawaii blindly without exerting the little bit of effort that it takes to tailor a mass-market vacation to their own needs, tastes, and desires. So just knowing that you want to look before you leap puts you well ahead of the pack.

And picking up this guidebook shows that you have the right instincts about your vacation planning.

About This Book

Hawaii For Dummies, 3rd Edition, cuts the wheat from the chaff — or the husk from the pineapple, as it were. An island vacation, after all, is supposed to be easy and fun, and planning your trip to should be easy and fun, too.

I've done the legwork for you, and I want you to benefit accordingly. I'm not afraid to take a stand to help you decide what to include in your island vacation — and, even more important, what *not* to include. I understand that you work hard to set aside a few precious weeks of vacation time, and that money doesn't grow on trees — no matter how much you have, you don't want to waste it. After all, the time to figure out this stuff is now, in the planning stage, not when you get to Hawaii.

No one right answer exists for everyone, of course — that's why you're here. This book gives you the tools you need — *just* what you need, not too much — so that you can make smart decisions about what works for you and what doesn't. I've tried to give you the clearest picture of your options so that you can make informed decisions easily and efficiently. Because this book is a reference guide, you can start reading at any point and concentrate on finding out exactly what you want to know at any given time.

Dummies Post-it® Flags

As you're reading this book, you'll find information that you'll want to reference as you plan or enjoy your trip — whether it be a new hotel, a must-see attraction, or a must-try walking tour. Mark these pages with the handy Post-it® Flags included in this book to help make your trip planning easier!

Building your Hawaii vacation is like putting together a jigsaw puzzle. This book helps you assemble the right puzzle pieces so that they interlock smoothly, and the finished product reflects the picture *you* want, not somebody else's image of what your island paradise should be.

Conventions Used in This Book

The structure of this book is nonlinear: You can dig in anywhere to get information on a specific issue without any hassles. Hotels and restaurants are listed alphabetically with actual prices and frank evaluations.

In this book, I include lists of hotels, restaurants, and attractions. As I describe each one, I often include abbreviations for commonly accepted credit cards. Take a look at the following list for an explanation of each card:

> AE: American Express
>
> DC: Diners Club
>
> DISC: Discover
>
> MC: MasterCard
>
> V: Visa

I include some general pricing information to help you as you decide where to unpack your bags or dine on the local cuisine. I use a system of dollar signs to show a range of costs for one night in a double room in each hotel or a typical meal at a restaurant (included in the cost of each meal is an appetizer, main course, dessert, one drink, tax, and tip — per person). Check out the following table to decipher the dollar signs:

Cost	Hotel	Restaurant
$	Less than $100	Less than $15
$$	$100–$175	$15–$25
$$$	$175–$250	$25–$40
$$$$	$250–$375	$40–$70
$$$$$	More than $375	More than $70

Foolish Assumptions

As I wrote this book, I made some assumptions about you and your needs as a traveler:

✔ You may be an experienced traveler who hasn't had much time to explore Hawaii and wants expert advice when you finally do get a chance to enjoy some time in the sun.

✔ You may be an inexperienced traveler looking for guidance when determining whether to take a trip to Hawaii and how to plan for it.

✔ You're not looking for a book that provides all the information available about the Hawaiian islands or that lists every hotel, restaurant, or attraction available to you. Instead, you're looking for a book that focuses on the places that offer the best or most unique experiences in Hawaii.

If you fit any of these criteria, then *Hawaii For Dummies,* 3rd Edition, gives you the information you're looking for!

How This Book Is Organized

Hawaii For Dummies, 3rd Edition, contains seven parts. You can read each chapter or part without reading the one that came before it — no need to study up on Oahu or Kauai if you're only heading to Maui and the Big Island, for example — but, as you read, I may refer you to other chapters of the book for more information on certain subjects.

Part 1: Introducing Hawaii

This first part gives you an overview of what Hawaii is like, so you can start getting excited about all the fun that lies ahead. It includes

✔ An easy-to-scan list of the very best of the best — my personal picks of Hawaii's top hotels, restaurants, beaches, golf courses, and more

✔ A quick overview of Hawaiian history and culture

✔ An introduction to each of the Hawaiian islands, plus a fun quiz that helps you decide which islands suit your fancy and which ones you'd rather leave for the next trip

✔ Time-tested advice on how to divide your time between the islands you want to visit

✔ The scoop on when to go

Part II: Planning Your Trip to Hawaii

In this part, I get down to the serious trip preparation, including

✔ How much you can expect your trip to cost and how to save on costs if money is a concern

✔ The pros and cons of planning your trip on your own, using a travel agent, and buying an all-inclusive package deal

✔ The ins and outs of flying to Hawaii, and how to travel between the islands after you're there

✔ Special considerations for families, seniors, travelers with disabilities, and gay and lesbian travelers

✔ A how-to guide for couples who want to tie the knot in the Aloha State

Parts III through VI: Being There — The Islands

These parts form the bulk of the book and cover the destinations that you may visit in hands-on detail. Each part is dedicated to one of the major Hawaiian islands — Oahu (Part III), Maui (Part IV), the Big Island (Part V), and Kauai (Part VI)— and offers all the specific details and recommendations you need while you're there, including

✔ Settling in

✔ Staying in style

✔ Dining out

✔ Enjoying the island

Part VII: The Part of Tens

Every *For Dummies* book has a Part of Tens. If Parts III through VI are the main course of a travel meal, think of these fun top-ten-list chapters as dessert. Chapter 19 tells you how to ditch the tourist look and act like a local, with tips on everything from how to pronounce those tongue-twisting Hawaiian place names to getting to know a few points of island-style etiquette. Chapter 20 focuses on one of everybody's favorite topics — food! Use it to familiarize yourself with common island food terms and local dishes, so that after you arrive, you'll know whether you want the *saimin,* the *poke,* or the *opakapaka* — and whether you want to save room for a little haupia for dessert.

In back of this book, I include an appendix — your Quick Concierge — containing lots of handy information you may need when traveling in Hawaii, like phone numbers and addresses of emergency personnel or area hospitals and pharmacies, lists of local newspapers and magazines, protocol for sending mail or finding taxis, and more. Check out this appendix when searching for answers to lots of little questions that may come up as you travel. You can find the Quick Concierge easily because it's printed on yellow paper.

Icons Used in This Book

Think of the following icons as signposts. I use them to highlight especially useful advice, to draw your attention to things that you won't want to miss, and to introduce a variety of topics.

 The Best of the Best icon highlights the best the destination has to offer in all categories — hotels, restaurants, attractions, activities, shopping, and nightlife.

 Keep an eye out for the Bargain Alert icon as you seek out money-saving tips and/or great deals.

 Watch for the Heads Up icon to identify annoying or potentially dangerous situations such as tourist traps, unsafe neighborhoods, budgetary rip-offs, and other things to beware.

 Find out useful advice on things to do and ways to schedule your time when you see the Tip icon.

 Look to the Kid Friendly icon for attractions, hotels, restaurants, and activities that are particularly hospitable to children or people traveling with kids.

 The Local Know How icon indicates well-guarded *kamaaina* (local) advice that I let out of the bag, so that you can have the edge over *Malihini* (newcomers) who don't know better.

Where to Go from Here

As you read through this book and start to formulate your vacation, remember this: The planning really *is* half the fun. Don't think of choosing your island destinations and solidifying the details as a chore. Make the homebound part of the process a voyage of discovery, and you'll end up with an experience that's that much more rewarding, enriching, and relaxing — *really*. Have a blast with it. Happy planning!

Part I
Introducing Hawaii

The 5th Wave   By Rich Tennant

HAWAII'S ESCALATOR FALLS

In this part . . .

This part of the book introduces you to the wonders of Hawaii. You discover why so many people are drawn to these islands of aloha, and you begin to shape the basic outlines of your trip. I preview each island one by one and offer tips of planning an itinerary. Then I help you figure out when to go, with information on Hawaii's climate, the least crowded (and expensive) seasons, and a full calendar of special events.

Chapter 1

Discovering the Best of Hawaii

In This Chapter
▶ Scoping out Hawaii's top accommodations
▶ Uncovering the top dining establishments and luaus
▶ Exploring the best beaches and attractions

*T*he most marvelous thing about Hawaii is that every day is a slice of paradise. Hawaii is such a breathtakingly beautiful place and exudes such a generous spirit of genuine aloha, that just about every island experience offers something special.

It doesn't take a lot of cash or elaborate planning to get to the heart of Hawaii. Hawaii is at its best when you experience its simple pleasures in their purest form. Here, everybody can feel like royalty: A simple beach apartment can be your castle, a fresh papaya and a cup of robust Kona joe can be your princely breakfast, and a joyous aloha shirt can be your royal robe.

But if you're looking for more worldly luxuries, that's great, too — because vacation is about having what you want. These islands don't lack the kind of pamper-yourself experiences; you'll run out of time before you exhaust your cash supply.

Whether you prefer the simple pleasures of life or are in the market for island luxury at its finest, you'll find it in Hawaii. This chapter is designed as an at-a-glance reference to the absolute best — the Best of the Best — that Hawaii has to offer. I discuss each of these places and experiences in detail later in this book; you can find them in their indicated chapter, marked with — what else? — a "Best of the Best" icon.

The Best of the Best Luxury Resorts

In the market for a little luxury — or a lot of it? Hawaii's your place. These islands are home to some of the world's finest resorts. The following are the best of the best:

- ✔ **Halekulani** (Oahu): The finest hotel on Waikiki Beach is the epitome of graciousness and elegant aloha. The white-on-white rooms are gorgeous, the service is impeccable, SpaHalekulani is a pampering oasis, and the restaurants are the best on the beach. Ask for a room with a Diamond Head view, and the world is yours. See Chapter 11.

- ✔ **Grand Wailea Resort & Spa** (Maui): Many tout the reserved understatement of the neighboring Four Seasons, but I'm underwhelmed. Instead, I prefer this grand beach palace, with its exclusive tropical theme park vibe, big and beautiful guest rooms, and over-the-top treat at every turn. Hawaii's best pool complex awaits your (very lucky) kids, and you can indulge in the island'sfinest spa. The luxurious Napua Tower offers such extra amenities as personalized concierge service. See Chapter 13.

- ✔ **Hotel Hana-Maui** (Maui): Rejoice — for the Hotel Hana-Maui is glorious once again. After years in the doldrums, this breathtaking resort at the end of the "heavenly" Hana Highway has been reborn as a luxurious haven of genuine Hawaiiana thanks to the folks behind Big Sur's Post Ranch Inn. This elegant hideaway is reason enough alone to cruise to the remotest end of the island. See Chapter 13.

- ✔ **Four Seasons Resort Hualalai** (Big Island): You'll want for nothing at this elegantly understated resort, Hawaii's best. Ask for a room with an open-air lava-rock shower for the ultimate in natural-style luxury. A stunning oceanfront pool with a graceful wooden deck stands center stage, while a second comes stocked with friendly stingrays. Service is impeccable, the restaurants are among the island's finest, and the superb Jack Nicklaus–designed golf course is for guests only. See Chapter 15.

- ✔ **Kona Village Resort** (Big Island): Hawaii's only all-inclusive resort is the polar opposite of its sophisticated neighbor, the Four Seasons Hualalai (see preceding entry). Whereas that resort offers every cutting-edge luxury, this South Seas paradise of tropical cottages offers something else really special: blissful escape, *Gilligan's Island* style, where your "Do Not Disturb" sign is painted on a coconut and in-room entertainment is your glorious ocean view. However long you plan to stay, stay longer — it still won't be long enough. See Chapter 15.

- ✔ **Hyatt Regency Kauai Resort & Spa** (Kauai): From start to finish, this crown-jewel Hyatt is one of Hawaii's most satisfying resorts. Situated on Kauai's sunny south coast, the resort boasts a genuine tropical vibe with big, beautiful rooms; a terrific pool complex that pleases both kids and adults alike; a brilliant spa with open-air treatment rooms; and service that exudes the most genuine aloha. I'd move in if I could afford it. See Chapter 17.

✔ **Princeville Resort Kauai** (Kauai): If it weren't for the fact that guest rooms lack open-air lanais, this stunning North Shore resort would be perfect; as it is, it comes *very* close. Situated on the Garden Isle's most breathtaking coast, the resort offers spectacular views in every direction, while just out the back door is one of the island's finest beaches for snorkeling and sunbathing. The views alone are reason to come — but you won't be disappointed with elegant appointments and attentive service, either. See Chapter 17.

The Best of the Best Accommodations Values

Don't have limitless cash? No worries. Get the most for your accommodations dollar by booking into one of these fine establishments:

✔ **Waikiki Beach Marriott** (Oahu): This freshly renovated hotel sits just across the street from Waikiki's best stretch of sand. Its attractive style and full-service amenities — including Spa Olakino, one of Hawaii's finest relaxation palaces — make it feel like a much more expensive hotel. Yet rates are lower than you'd expect, quickly shaping this hotel into one of Hawaii's consistently best-value hotels. See Chapter 11.

✔ **Waikiki Beachcomber** (Oahu): Looking for Waikiki's best accommodations bargain? This attractive and well-located hotel — just 297 steps from the beach! — is usually it. What the Beachcomber lacks in cutting-edge style, it more than makes up for with first-rate packages and a wealth of online discounts for travelers of every stripe. See Chapter 11.

✔ **Fairmont Kea Lani** (Maui): Sure, this fanciful Moorish palace on the sand is pricey, but it gives you so much more for your money than Maui's other luxury resorts. For the same price as a standard hotel room at other places — and sometimes less — here you'll enjoy a large one-bedroom suite with a complete entertainment system (including stereo and DVD) and a huge marble bathroom. See Chapter 13.

✔ **Kaanapali Beach Hotel** (Maui): This charming, older beachfront hotel is the last hotel left in Hawaii that gives you a real resort experience at a moderate price. The resort brims with genuine aloha spirit and good value — and the on-the-beach location can't be beat. See Chapter 13.

✔ **Noelani Condominium Resort** (Maui): This top-notch oceanfront condo complex is both an excellent value and a really enjoyable place to stay. Every unit — from the value-minded studios for two to the family-friendly two- and three-bedroom apartments — boasts an ocean view and all the comforts of home. See Chapter 13.

✔ **Waikoloa Beach Marriott, an Outrigger Resort** (Big Island): Want a beachfront resort with all the perks, but without the hefty price tag? Try this pleasing — and pleasantly affordable — resort, situated on one of the sunny Kohala coast's finest beaches. A prime location, a genuine tropical feel, and activities galore, all for a fraction of its ritzier neighbors. See Chapter 15.

✔ **Kona Billfisher** (Big Island): Some say you have to have a bundle to benefit from a Hawaii vacation, but the Kona Billfisher begs to disagree. This simple, straightforward condo complex is the place to stay on the Big Island if you want a good, clean apartment with all the comforts of home for less than $100 a night. Bring the kids, too — even two-bedroom units are a bargain. See Chapter 15.

✔ **Nihi Kai Villas** and **Waikomo Stream Villas** (Kauai): These wonderful condo complexes on Kauai's sunny south shore, both managed by Grantham Resorts, offer the best accommodations values on the Garden Isle. Waikomo Stream's one- and two-bedroom apartments are ideal for families who want all the comforts of home at bargain-basement prices. Nihi Kai's one-, two-, and three-bedroom apartments are closer to the beach and a bit more upscale, but offer equally good value. See Chapter 17.

The Best of the Best Restaurants

Attention, foodies: You'll have no trouble dining well in Hawaii. Whether you're looking to celebrate a special occasion or mapping out a culinary calendar for the length of your stay, don't overlook these fabulous restaurants:

✔ **Alan Wong's Restaurant** (Oahu): If there is one master of Hawaii Regional cuisine above all others, it is Alan Wong. His warmly contemporary and tropical Honolulu dining room is the ideal showcase for his fine-dining twists on the local culinary tradition. Don't miss this dining experience. See Chapter 11.

✔ **Chef Mavro** (Oahu): While Alan Wong stays true to his island ingredients, James Beard award-winning chef George Mavrothalassitis brings the flavors of his native Provence to Hawaii's table. Every dish dazzles, and the dining room is a paragon of elegant simplicity. Alan Wong's may be the best choice if you have only one fine-dining night and want maximum local style, but Chef Mavro offers an equally fine dining experience that's a tad more romantic. See Chapter 11.

✔ **Mama's Fish House** (Maui): The increasingly sophisticated Valley Isle is coming perilously close to surpassing Oahu as the fine-dining island of choice for vacationing gourmands. My absolute favorite in this well-stocked sea is this delightful seafooder, which offers a magical combination of food, ambiance, and service. Sure, prices are high, but the tiki-room setting is an archetype of timeless Hawaii cool, and fresh island fish simply doesn't get any better than this. See Chapter 13.

✔ **Brown's Beach House** (Big Island): On the Big Island, it's a neck-and-neck race between this elegant open-air restaurant at the Fairmont Orchid and the Four Seasons's supremely elegant Pahui'a. I hate to choose between these divine dining rooms, but if forced to, I opt for Brown's. Chef Etsuji Umezu has created an East-meets-West cuisine that fuses Japanese culinary arts and French cooking traditions for maximum effect. Reserve a table close to the spotlit surf for the ultimate in tropical romance. See Chapter 15.

✔ **Kaikodo** (Big Island): This Hilo newcomer has wowed the rainforest city with chef Mike Fennelly's inspired and innovative East-meets-Southwest cooking, which the young star brought from Santa Fe and adapted to local ingredients with breathtaking success. The gorgeous setting — an impeccably renovated historic building brimming with light and art — enhances the culinary magic. See Chapter 15.

✔ **Roy's Poipu Bar & Grill** (Kauai): Star chef Roy Yamaguchi is the Babe Ruth of Hawaii Regional Cuisine. His chain of Roy's restaurants have brought island-style fine dining to cities across the world, but his best successes remain those closest to home. More casual than the other Roy's throughout Hawaii, torch-lit Roy's Poipu is my favorite of the famous chain — and my favorite way to dine here is family style from the tapas-style appetizer menu, which offers the best variety of taste sensations. See Chapter 17. (If you're not visiting Hawaii, I recommend sampling Roy's on another island, each of which has an outpost; see Chapters 11, 13, and 15.)

The Best of the Best Beaches

The world's finest surf and sands fringe the shores of Hawaii's islands. The best of the best are these breathtakingly beautiful beaches.

✔ **Waikiki Beach** (Oahu): This beach is the most famous one on the planet for a perfectly good reason: It lives up to its reputation in every way. The world's biggest and best beach party actually inhabits a string of stunning beaches fringing crystal clear, turquoise blue waters. There's something for everybody, whether you want to learn to surf, play in the waves, or just bask in the glory of it all. See Chapter 12.

✔ **Hanauma Bay** (Oahu): Without exception, this sunken volcanic crater on Oahu's sunny southeast coast is Hawaii's premier snorkel spot for beginners and experts alike. The bay is preserved as a marine life conservation district, and the fish seem to know it — they'll practically come up and stare into your mask. Even non-swimmers can wade in, look down, and see a whole new kaleido-scopic side of Hawaii. See Chapter 12.

✔ **Waimea Beach Park** (Oahu): This legendary surf spot is my favorite place to watch big-wave riders in action in the winter months. It's a nonstop rollicking beach party when the surf's up and the daredevils are in the water. The rolling waves leave a placid pool behind in summer; that's when everybody can jump in to frolic in the surf. See Chapter 12.

✔ **Kaanapali Beach** (Maui): This fabulous, crescent-shaped beach is reminiscent of the Waikiki of yesteryear, before the entire world made it their destination of choice. There's something for everyone here: crystal-clear snorkeling, thrilling wave jumping, golden sands inviting hours of sunbathing, even beachfront bars for enjoying that perfect middle-of-the-day mai tai. See Chapter 14.

✔ **Hookipa Beach Park** (Maui): Come to watch the world's best wind-surfers pirouette over white-capped waves at this glorious north shore beach. Surfers have eminent domain in the mornings, while the colorful windsurfers take over in the afternoons. The action is equally breathtaking at any time of day, especially when the winter waves are in top form. See Chapter 14.

✔ **Hapuna Beach** (Big Island): Don't let anybody tell you that the volcanic Big Island doesn't have any good beaches. Copiously endowed with delicate white sands and gorgeous turquoise waves, this beauty isn't just the star of the Big Island — it just may be the most beautiful beach in all of Hawaii. Great facilities are the icing on the cake. See Chapter 16.

✔ **Kahaluu Beach Park** (Big Island): This roadside salt-and-pepper beach isn't much to look at, but its shallow, protected waters offer some of the finest snorkeling in the islands. If you can't get to Hanauma Bay (see entry earlier in this list), don't miss Kahaluu. See Chapter 16.

✔ **Anini Beach** (Kauai): This secret north shore beach is one of the most beautiful — and one of the safest — swimming beaches on Kauai. The golden sands and shallow waters are protected by an offshore reef even when rough winter waves pound other north shore beaches, making this an ideal snorkel spot. An always peace-ful feeling at this beach makes it ideal for quiet contemplation, too. See Chapter 18.

✔ **Poipu Beach Park** (Kauai): This south shore beach is Kauai's favorite family playground. There's something for everybody here: White sands for sunbathing, grassy lawns for picnicking, shallow pools for little ones to play in, reefs for good snorkeling, and waves for boogie boarders. Lots of great facilities round out the perfect beach day. See Chapter 18.

The Best of the Best Activities and Attractions

If all you want is an oceanfront hammock and a mai tai, Hawaii's your paradise. But part of the beauty of Hawaii is that it has a bounteous menu of rich experiences to offer if you're motivated to do more. These activities and attractions are Hawaii's finest:

- ✔ **Touring the USS *Arizona* Memorial** (Oahu): There's hardly a more moving site than this stark memorial to the nearly 1,200 who lost their lives in the Japanese air raid on Pearl Harbor on December 7, 1941, which launched the United States into World War II. Arrive early for the best experience and pair your visit with a tour of the **Battleship *Missouri* Memorial,** also in Pearl Harbor, for a tragedy-to-triumph view of World War II. See Chapter 12.

- ✔ **Visiting the Bishop Museum** (Oahu): If you're intrigued by Hawaii's vibrant culture, the best place to get a little background is at this captivating museum, rich with the treasures of Hawaii's past. Pair a visit with a trip to **Iolani Palace,** the official royal residence of Hawaii's last monarchs, for a surprisingly riveting history lesson. See Chapter 12.

- ✔ **Whale-watching with the Pacific Whale Foundation** (Maui): Whale-watching is a premier activity in the islands from mid-December until mid-March; in some lucky years, the great humpbacks remain in Hawaii's warm waters into April. Boats are available to take you whale-watching from every island, but I love the Pacific Whale Foundation for its excellent naturalist guides and its nonprofit commitment to protecting whales in Hawaii. And if you don't want to splurge on an expensive cruise, you don't need to — the foundation also operates a **Whale Information Station** on the road to Lahaina where you can spot humpbacks from the shore with an expert for absolutely free. The Pacific Whale Foundation also takes you out on terrific snorkel cruises year-round, even when the whales aren't in town. See Chapter 14.

- ✔ **Diving Molokini** (Maui): This sunken volcanic crater is one of Hawaii's top dive spots thanks to calm, clear, protected waters; an abundance of marine life, from reef dwellers to manta rays; and exciting viewing opportunities for every level of diver — even first-timers. You don't dive, or you're not ready to learn? No worries — Molokini offers excellent viewing for snorkelers, too. Molokini is only reachable by boat, so see Chapter 14 for recommended outfitters.

- ✔ **Driving the "Heavenly" Road to Hana** (Maui): Hawaii's most spectacular drive is well worth a day of your vacation. For 52 winding miles, this blissful highway takes you past flowering gardens, spectacular waterfalls, and magnificent ocean vistas. Start early and keep in mind that it's all about the drive, not about getting to the end of the road. Rent a convertible for maximum effect. See Chapter 14.

✔ **Snorkeling Kealakekua Bay** (Big Island): This magical marine life preserve, reachable only by watercraft, is my absolute favorite snorkel spot in Hawaii. The coral is the most beautiful I've ever seen, and the calm, clear waters teem with a kaleidoscope of colorful reef fish, octopuses, and sea turtles, plus playful spinner dolphins who often swing by to see what all the fuss is about. My favorite way to get there is with **Fair Wind Snorkel Cruises & Orca Raft Adventures,** although experienced kayakers can rent and paddle their way in. See Chapter 16.

✔ **Exploring the Big Island with Hawaii Forest & Trail** (Big Island): Nobody shows you Hawaii's natural wonders like this terrific nature guide company. You may have seen owner Rob Pacheco on the Travel Channel; Rob and his troupe of well-trained guides take you into the remote valleys of the rainforest, as well as help you scale the star-studded crest of Mauna Kea, and burrow through hidden lava tunnels. You can see a side of Hawaii that few others do — don't miss it! See Chapter 16.

✔ **Visiting Hawaii Volcanoes National Park** (Big Island): In my book, if you do one nonbeach-related activity in Hawaii, this should be it. Hawaii Volcanoes National Park is the only national park that's home to a live, lava-pumping volcano. Witness the yin/yang magic of the oozing red stuff as it leaves destruction in its landscape — and shapes new virgin land. See Chapter 16.

✔ **Stepping back in time at Puuhonua O Honaunau National Historical Park** (Big Island): The most compelling historic attraction in the islands is this awesome place. This ancient "city of refuge" is guarded by fierce ancient totems just like it was back in the day, when defeated warriors and *kapu* (taboo) breakers who managed to make it within the walls were forgiven all transgressions. The archeological excavations and restorations are fascinating, and the ancient sanctuary city is just downright fun to explore. See Chapter 16.

✔ **Touring Kauai's Na Pali Coast State Park** (Kauai): Hawaii's most majestic coastline is a 22-mile stretch of green-velvet fluted cliffs that wraps around the northwest shore of Kauai. It's all but inaccessible to man, who can only reach it by sailing by, flying over, or hiking in. The effort is well worth it. Hook up with a boating company to sail by, which offers majestic vistas and excellent snorkeling opportunities, plus up-close-and-personal whale-watching in winter. Rugged types can hike in; even the first 2 miles (the only part of the trail accessible without a permit) offer a spectacular taste of the park. Helicopter tours offer the easiest access. See Chapter 18 for details on all options.

✔ **Exploring the Allerton & McBryde Gardens** (Kauai): These sister National Tropical Botanical Gardens highlight the breathtaking botanical beauty of the Garden Isle. Even those who don't think they have a passion for horticulture marvel at the natural majesty of these two slices of paradise. I recommend starting with the more manicured Allerton Garden, a turn-of-the-century private estate, and then returning to tour the McBryde Garden if you're itching to see more — which you just may be. Check the schedules in advance and plan accordingly. See Chapter 18.

✔ **Learning to surf** (Oahu, Maui, and Kauai): Believe it or not, surfing is easier than it looks — and there's hardly a feeling finer than conquering a wave. A number of good surfing schools guarantee that you'll be hanging ten in a single two-hour lesson. My favorites are **Hans Hedemann Surf School** on Oahu, the **Nancy C. Emerson School of Surfing** on Maui, and Kauai's **Margo Oberg's Surfing School.** See Chapters 12, 14, and 18.

✔ **Hitting the links** (Oahu, Maui, Big Island, and Kauai): If you love golf, don't miss the opportunity to play at least one of Hawaii's premier courses. All the islands boast championship courses designed to make 18-hole memories, but you'll find the most spectacular challenges on the neighboring islands; others may argue, but I think the Big Island boasts the most breathtaking selection of courses. Book before you leave home to guarantee tee times. See Chapters 12, 14, 16, and 18.

✔ **Getting a bird's-eye view of the islands of Aloha** (Maui, Big Island, Kauai): Touring Hawaii by helicopter gives you a perspective on these islands that others simply can't enjoy. Helicopter tours give you access to each island's otherwise inaccessible heartland, where nature has been unspoiled by modern man. Each island offers special perks from the sky: On Maui, you can scale the desolate peak of Haleakala National Park and enjoy a breathtaking view of the road to Hana that takes an hour instead of a day; on the Big Island, you fly over the heart of the bubbling volcano; and on Kauai, you can explore the lush virgin canyons that give the Garden Isle its well-deserved nickname. It's expensive but worth it. See Chapters 14, 16, and 18.

The Best of the Best Luaus

The best luaus are in high demand, so book your spots before you leave home to ensure access:

✔ **Old Lahaina Luau** (Maui): Hawaii's most authentic and acclaimed luau is justifiably celebrated, and a real treat to experience. Come early to watch craftspeople at work in the lovely oceanfront setting; you can also watch as the luau pig is unearthed from its underground oven, where it's been slow-cooking all day. The live hula show is dazzling. You simply can't do better than this one. See Chapter 13.

✔ **The Feast at Lele** (Maui): The folks behind the Old Lahaina Luau (see preceding entry) also operate this interesting twist on a traditional luau. The Feast at Lele is an excellent alternative for romance-seeking couples, or anyone who would prefer a luau with a more upscale demeanor, a more intimate setting, and/or a fine-dining twist. The multicourse meal and thrilling performance troupe reach beyond the Hawaii tradition to celebrate the food and culture of the South Seas as well, and the beachfront setting can't be beat. See Chapter 13.

✔ **Kona Village Luau** (Big Island): The Big Island's best luau is offered on Fridays only, so plan accordingly. The luau grounds aren't oceanfront, but the South Seas–style setting of grass-roofed huts and swaying palms offers ambiance in excess. The food is excellently prepared, and the stage show is a delight. The entertainment embraces broader Pacific traditions in order to justify a fire dancer (native Hawaiians weren't nearly so foolhardy), and his set is a showstopper. See Chapter 16.

Chapter 2

Digging Deeper into Hawaii

In This Chapter

▶ Discovering the fascinating story of Hawaii's past
▶ Marveling at Hawaii's spectacular natural landscape
▶ Experiencing the joys of island-style dining
▶ Mastering a few key Hawaiian words and phrases

*I*t's been a stressful day at the office. Or the kids have been driving you crazy, and you realize that everybody in the family needs a break. Or maybe you've just had it with gray skies and gloomy weather.

Then the idea comes, and it's a gem: Hawaii. Ahh, *Hawaii.*

Just thinking about a Hawaii vacation warms the soul, doesn't it? Turquoise waves, white sand, toasty sun. Palm trees swaying in the breeze as emerald-green cliffs rise up to meet a sweet blue sky. The fragrance of orchids filling the air as the music of a slack-key guitar carries you into tropical reverie. . . .

Vacation has long been the ultimate antidote to the stresses and strains of daily life — and no destination is more relaxing and restorative than the exquisite Hawaiian Islands. Don't just take it from me — take it from Mark Twain, who lauded Hawaii as "the loveliest fleet of islands that lies anchored in any ocean." Renewal calls for total escape to this idyllic tropical paradise, where days of soaking up the island sun are interwoven with easygoing adventuring and plenty of friendly *aloha* (an all-purpose greeting meaning hello, welcome, or goodbye).

History 101: The Main Events

Hawaii's historic tapestry is far richer than what can be recreated in these few pages. If you're interested in the whole story, pick up *Shoal of Time: A History of the Hawaiian Islands* (University of Hawaii Press) by Gavan Daws. Both definitive and delightful to read, *Shoal of Time* is the ideal one-volume history of Hawaii. From the geological formation of the islands through statehood, the Hawaii story is so well told that it reads like a novel. It's so rich with detail that the characters who shaped Hawaiian history come alive in its pages.

A.D. 700: The first Hawaiians arrive

The first Hawaiians arrived by canoe nearly 3,000 years ago. They came from Tahiti and the Marquesas Islands, some 2,500 miles to the south, as part of a greater Polynesian migration. They likely arrived at the southernmost Big Island first; what they found was a pristine and blessedly empty island, roiling with fire from the volcanoes at its heart. An entire Hawaiian culture grew from these first settlers. As islanders migrated throughout the chain, each island became its own distinct kingdom. The inhabitants built temples, fish ponds, and aqueducts to irrigate taro plantations. Sailors became farmers and fishermen. The *alii* (high-ranking chiefs) created a caste system and established taboos. Ritual human sacrifices were common. Life was both vicious and blissful — just like the islands' breathtaking landscapes.

1778: The "modern" world arrives

For 2,000 years, no Hawaiian ever imagined that an outsider would appear in these remote "floating islands." But in 1778, Captain James Cook sailed into Waimea Bay on Kauai on his ship the *Resolution* and was welcomed as the Hawaiian god Lono.

Cook stumbled upon the Hawaiian Islands quite by chance. He named them the Sandwich Islands, for the Earl of Sandwich, a great friend and first lord of the British admiralty, who had bankrolled the expedition. The Big Island would ultimately be the death of the world-famous explorer — but not before stone-age Hawaii entered the age of iron, and the West forged a permanent foothold. Gifts were presented and objects traded: nails for fresh water, pigs, and the affections of Hawaiian women. The sailors brought syphilis, measles, and other diseases to which the Hawaiians had no natural immunity.

The islands were united as one kingdom by Kamehameha I in 1810; he used guns seized from a British ship to establish his iron-fisted rule. The door was open, and the new Hawaiian monarchy welcomed the West with open arms. In April 1820, the first missionaries arrived from New England. Victorian mores overtook island style, and eventually subsumed it; hula was abolished in favor of reading and writing, and neck-to-toe dress became the norm. At the same time, missionaries also played a key role in preserving island culture. They created the 13-character Hawaiian alphabet, and began recording the islands' history. Until this time, history was only passed down from generation to generation orally, in memorized chants.

The children of the missionaries became the islands' business and political leaders. They married Hawaiians and stayed on in the islands, causing one astute observer to remark that the missionaries "came to do good and stayed to do well." More than 80 percent of all private land was owned by non-natives within two generations. Sugar cane became big business, and planters imported immigrants by the thousands to work the fields as contract laborers. The first Chinese came in 1852, followed by Japanese in 1885, and Portuguese in 1878. These immigrants would have a lasting and influential impact on island culture that persists in the present day. King David Kalakaua — known as the "Merrie Monarch" for the elaborate parties he threw — ascended to the throne in 1874, marking the beginning of the end of the short-lived Hawaiian monarchy. He performed a few acts of note, however: He built Iolani Palace in 1882; lifted the prohibitions on the hula and other native arts; and gave Pearl Harbor to the United States. In 1891, King Kalakaua visited chilly San Francisco, where he caught a cold and died. His sister, Queen Liliuokalani, assumed the throne.

1893: Paving the way for tourism and statehood

On January 17, 1893, a group of American sugar planters and missionary descendants, with the support of U.S. Marines, imprisoned Queen Liliuokalani in her palace, where she penned "Aloha Oe," the famous song of farewell. The monarchy was dead. Hawaii was now an American territory ruled by the powerful sugar cane planter Sanford Dole. He and his cohorts — known as the Big Five — controlled the entire economic, social, and political life of the islands. Sugar was king, and the native Hawaiians became a landless minority.

The first tourists to the islands were hard-core adventure travelers — among them Mark Twain — who came to the Big Island in the late 1800s to see the roiling Kilauea volcano. But the new industry didn't stick until transportation improved, and the sugar industry became too expensive to support. In 1901, W. C. Peacock built the elegant Moana Hotel (now the Sheraton Moana Surfrider) on Waikiki Beach. After a concentrated marketing effort in San Francisco, 2,000 tourists came to Waikiki in its first big tourism year, 1903. Tourism came by steamship; the sailing took almost five days. By 1936, visitors could fly to Honolulu from San Francisco on the *Hawaii Clipper,* a seven-passenger Pan American plane; the flight took 21 hours, 33 minutes. Modern tourism was born and was doing brisk business — until the Japanese arrived, that is.

On December 7, 1941, a Japanese air raid wreaked havoc on the American warships parked at Pearl Harbor, drawing the United States into World War II.

1959: Setting the stage for today's Hawaii

The harsh realities of war gave way to the lighthearted culture of *Blue Hawaii,* Trader Vic's, and Arthur Godfrey. Hotels sprouted along the curvaceous beach at the food Diamond Head known as Waikiki. In 1959, this blossoming paradise became the 50th state of the United States. That year also saw the arrival of the first jet airliners. Postwar Americans had disposable cash, and now Hawaii was an easy flight away. Visitors began to arrive in droves — and tourism as we know it was off the ground, surpassing sugar as the premier industry of the islands.

Tired of the plastic aloha that had supplanted genuine island culture, Hawaiian elders started making a concerted effort to integrate traditional hula, chant, visual arts, and values into the vast array of visitor experiences. Tourism and hospitality employees are now educated in Hawaiian history, culture, and genuine aloha spirit. The culture that was once clipped at the root has now come back in full bloom — and, thankfully, it's stronger than ever.

Building Blocks: Local Architecture and Design

Thanks to blessedly mild weather that includes cooling year-round trade winds and temperatures that don't vary by more than 15 degrees Fahrenheit from January to July, Hawaii thrives on open-air living. A seamless blend of indoors and out is the prevailing architectural style. Why put up a wall when you don't have a reason to keep out the weather — or the dazzling view?

The local architectural style is called kama'aina, or native born. Kama'aina is a style rich in beautiful simplicity and island tradition. True kama'aina architecture is generally open plan, keeping with the importance of multigenerational family living and the strength of the community spirit — and to capitalize on those gentle ocean breezes. Decoration is simple but beautiful, generally focused on the shapes, materials, and hues of nature. My favorite example of a kama'aina house is the **Holualoa Inn.** You can enjoy this open-air, native wood home, nestled in the Big Island's Kona coffee country, as a romantic accommodation (see Chapter 15).

The finest homes are fitted with natural woods, such as *ohia* floors and gleaming koa furnishings. Koa is a gorgeous slow-growth hardwood that has been a favorite of local artisans for centuries thanks to its deep palette and rich grain. Crafts and furnishings made from the wood are increasingly expensive, simply because koa is a slow-growth wood that takes decades to replenish. If you can afford a piece to take home — perhaps a jewelry box or a hand-turned calabash — you'll likely treasure it as a family keepsake for generations to come, as island families do.

Not all native materials must be necessarily expensive, however. Some of the most beautiful and tropically evocative home furnishings are crafted of simple, light materials like bamboo and rattan. Most floor coverings are woven mats, soft and cool on the bare feet. The finest are tightly woven *Lauhala,* crafted from pandanus leaves by talented artisans. The best place to find Lauhala in the islands is just down the road from the Holualoa Inn at **Kimura Lauhala Shop** (see Chapter 16).

The beautiful shapes and hues of Hawaii's bold fauna have woven their way into the island's favorite fabrics, too. Boldly hued tropical barkcloths — nubby cotton fabrics that wear well and say "Old Hawaii" with their large-leafed tropical and storytelling patterns — are famously suited to the furnishings of the islands. Vintage fabrics can often be found at two delightful Kauai shops, **Bambulei** and **Yellowfish Trading Company;** if you want newly woven fabrics on the bolt, you'll find a sea of possibilities at **Vicky's,** also on Kauai (see Chapter 18).

Despite its glitz and glamour as a tourist destination, Hawaii is fundamentally a farming and fishing community — and the story is abundant in its streetscapes. Simple plantation cottages were built to house the workers brought in from all over the world to farm the islands' abundant sugar, pineapple, and taro fields; now, plantation style is the most pervasive architectural style in the islands, especially on the still-rural neighbor islands. With their single-story style, bright facades, and sloping roofs (many still crafted of corrugated aluminum), plantation cottages embody the simple beauty of island life. A more elaborate, multistoried style originated as the plantation manager's home.

You can experience the simple beauty of old Hawaii — without the backbreaking labor, of course — at **Waimea Plantation Cottages** (see Chapter 17). This charming collection of restored 1930s plantation workers' cottages, nestled in a gorgeous beachfront grove of coconut palms on Kauai's south shore, is now available as vacation rentals for families of all shapes and sizes. Maui's **Best Western Pioneer Inn** (see Chapter 14) offers a like-kind experience with a seafaring bent.

Ranch life predominates in the cool upcountry of the Big Island and Maui, where plantation life gives way to *paniolo* (cowboy) style. Paniolo style is built for somewhat cooler weather; as a result, you're likely to find it to be a bit more familiar. Expect ranch-style homes with island touches such as brightly painted exteriors and broad porches. Grander buildings take on Victorian details and the aura of the Old West. The bayfront storefronts along the city of **Hilo's Kamehameha Drive,** on the Big Island's lush east coast, and the city's charmingly Victorian **Shipman House Bed & Breakfast Inn** (Chapter 15) are excellent examples. Experience paniolo style in its full glory by visiting **Parker Ranch,** one of America's largest working cattle ranches, in the Big Island's misty upcountry (Chapter 15).

The Victorian influence on Hawaii even hit the beach. One of the most excellent examples of the adaptation of European architecture to island living is the **Sheraton Moana Surfrider,** Waikiki's very first hotel (see Chapter 11). This genteel clapboarded gray lady looks like it could have been displaced from Nantucket from street side — but stroll through the structure to the ocean-facing verandah, and the style is all Hawaii.

Hawaii is roughly halfway between Asia and the mainland United States, so the Asian influence is pervasive in island architecture and design. Pagoda-style influences are evident in residential and commercial architecture throughout the islands, especially in areas that absorbed the wealth of Chinese and Japanese immigrants who came to work in the fields generations ago and stayed. Oahu's **Chinatown** offers the most concentrated examples.

A Taste of Hawaii: Local Cuisine

Hawaii has lured some of the world's finest chefs to its kitchens. About a dozen or so years ago, Hawaii Regional Cuisine was born. Local chefs were tired of turning out a stodgy menu of continental fare that was unsuited to Hawaii living. So they began to celebrate the bounty of the islands, emphasizing the use of fresh locally grown (often organic) produce, tropical fruits, the freshest seafood, and island-raised beef. Their light, creative combinations often feature Asian accents as a nod to Hawaii's multicultural heritage.

This type of cuisine is often disguised under other names — Euro-Asian, Pacific Rim, Indo-Pacific, Pacific Edge, Euro-Pacific, Island Fusion, and so on — but it all falls under the jurisdiction of Hawaii Regional Cuisine. Although there are variations, you can expect the following keynotes: lots of fresh island fish; Asian flavorings (ginger, soy, wasabi, seaweed, and so on) and cooking styles (searing, grilling, panko crust, wok preparations) galore; and fresh tropical fruit sauces (mango, papaya, and the like).

Thanks to Hawaii's proximity to the Pacific Rim and its large Asian population, the islands boast a wealth of fabulous Chinese, Thai, Vietnamese, and Japanese restaurants. And if Asian fare isn't your thing, you'll find plenty of other options, from the French classics to good ol' ranch-raised, fire-grilled steaks. Hawaii's cooks have even managed to put their own spin on some of the world's most revered foods — pizzas, burgers, and burritos — with rousing success.

Seafood lovers, rejoice: Hawaii offers you an astounding array of fresh-caught fish. In fact, you may find yourself puzzling over lists of unfamiliar fish on island menus. See Chapter 20 for a handy list of definitions that will help you decide what to try.

Lest all this unfamiliar food talk make you think otherwise, remember that the majority of Hawaii islanders are red-blooded, flag-waving Americans — and they love a good burger just as much as your average mainlander. Real local food is generally starchy and high in calories, so the Atkins crowd will want to skip the traditional plate lunch, which usually consists of a main dish (anything from fried fish to teriyaki beef), "two scoops rice," an ice-cream-scoop serving of macaroni salad, and brown gravy, all served on a paper plate. Plate lunches are cheap and available at casual restaurants and beachside stands throughout the islands.

A Word to the Wise: The Local Lingo

Everyone in Hawaii speaks English, of course, but a number of Hawaiian words and phrases regularly pop up in everyday conversation. You probably already know the Hawaiian word *aloha* (a-LO-ha), which serves as an all-purpose greeting — hello, welcome, or goodbye. It's a warm and wonderful word that expresses the sense of peace and hospitality that epitomizes the islands. You'll definitely need to learn the word *mahalo* (ma-HA-low), which means "thank you" and is used extensively throughout Hawaii.

Here's a handy list of other words you may encounter:

- ✔ **Hale** (HA-lay): House

- ✔ **Haole** (HOW-lee): Foreigner or caucasian (literally "out of breath" — pale, or paleface); a common reference, not an insult (usually)

- ✔ **Hula** (HOO-lah): Native dance

- ✔ **Kamaaina** (ka-ma-EYE-nah): Local person

- ✔ **Kapu** (KA-poo): Anything that's taboo, forbidden

- ✔ **Keiki** (KEH-kee): Child

- ✔ **Lanai** (LAH-nigh): Porch or veranda

- ✔ **Lei** (lay): Garland (usually of flowers, leaves, or shells)

- ✔ **Luau** (LOO-ow): A celebratory feast

- ✔ **Muumuu** (moo-oo-MOO-oo): A loose-fitting dress, usually in a tropical print

- ✔ **Ono** (OH-no): Delicious

- ✔ **Pau** (pow): Finished or done

- ✔ **Pupu** (POO-poo): Starter dish, appetizer

Say what? How to pronounce Hawaiian words

The Hawaiian language has only 12 characters to work with — the five vowels (*a, e, i, o,* and *u*), plus seven consonants (*h, k, l, m, n, p,* and *w*). Consequently, Hawaiian words and names tend to be long and difficult, with lots of repetitive syllables. The vowels are pronounced like this:

a	*ah* (as in father) or *uh* (as in above)
e	*eh* (as in bed) or *ay* (as in they)
i	*ee* (as in police)
o	*oh* (as in vote)
u	*oo* (as in too)

Almost all vowels are sounded separately, although some are pronounced together, as in the name of Waikiki's main thoroughfare, Kalakaua Avenue, which is pronounced "Kah-lah-COW-ah."

The simplest way to pronounce a Hawaiian word or name is to approach long words or names as a collection of short syllables. Accents almost always fall on the second-to-last syllable. All syllables end with vowels, so a consonant always indicates the start of a new syllable.

The Hawaiian language actually has a 13th character: the glottal stop, which looks exactly like a single opening quotation mark (') and is meant to indicate a pause. I've chosen not to use the glottal stop throughout this book; it's often omitted in printed Hawaiian and on things like store and street signs. Although serious Hawaiian-language students insist on using the glottal stop, you don't need to worry about it as a visitor; just ignore it when you see it.

Background Check: Recommended Books and Movies

Studying up on Hawaii can be one of the most fun bits of "research" you'll ever do. If you'd like to find out a bit more about the islands before you go — which I encourage — these books and movies are an enjoyable way to do it.

Books

One of my all-time favorites is *Hawaii* (Random House) by James Michener, the epic, Pulitzer Prize-winning novelist who loved the islands, heart and soul. Michener's novel charts a similar course to Daws' book, but this fictionalized account has the style — and the can't-put-it-down appeal — of a beach read. This book is a great way to get a real feel for the past without delving into serious nonfiction.

Another intriguing work of fiction that tells the story of Hawaii, albeit on a smaller scale, is Kiana Davenport's *Shark Dialogues* (Plume).

Want to learn the stories of Pele and the other gods and supernatural creatures, both fiery and benevolent, that comprise Hawaii's mystical backstory? Check out *Hawaiian Mythology* (University of Hawaii Press) by Martha Warren Beckwith and Katharine Luomala. Hundreds of books tell the personal stories of the great figures of Hawaiian history.

One of my favorites chronicles the life — and bloody Big Island death — of the great, devastating seafarer, James Cook, who introduced Hawaii to the western world: *Farther Than Any Man: The Rise and Fall of Captain James Cook* (Simon & Schuster) by Martin Dugard. Only a sliver of the book is about Hawaii, but it articulates the British colonial mindset beautifully.

University of Hawaii Press's richly illustrated *Atlas of Hawaii* is a fascinating source for everything you ever wanted to know about Hawaii's physical geography, weather patterns, population, and the like. It's an ideal gift for natural science buffs who want to delve deeper.

Albert J. Schutz's *All About Hawaiian* (University of Hawaii Press) is a great pocket-sized reference for those who would like to know just a bit more about the Hawaiian alphabet and language, including how to pronounce all those funky place names.

Want to bask in the glory of Hawaii as innocent vacationland, in the days of Matson Cruise Lines, Duke Kahanamoku, and Don Ho crooning "Tiny Bubbles," when Waikiki really was paradise? *Leis, Luaus and Alohas: The Lure of Hawaii in the Fifties* (Island Heritage) by Fred E. Basten and Charles Phoenix, is the book for you. This vibrant coffee-table book will really put you in the mood for a mai tai.

Some beautiful illustrated books tell the story of the aloha shirt in all of its silky, full-color glory. Best of the bunch is *The Aloha Shirt: Spirit of the Islands* (Beyond Words Publishing) by Dale Hope and Gregory Tozian. Broader in its reach — but no less beautiful — is Linda B. Arthur's *Aloha Attire: Hawaiian Dress in the 20th Century* (Schiffer Publishing).

Both craft and horticulture fans will find Ronn Ronck's *A Pocket Guide to the Hawaiian Lei: A Tradition of Aloha* (Mutual Publishing) to be an easy-to-carry reference to Hawaii's most visible and popular creative ritual: lei making and wearing.

If you can manage to find it, no book exudes the genuine spirit of living in Hawaii like Jocelyn Fujii's *Under the Hula Moon* (Crown Publishing Group), a gorgeous blend of photos and text with an introduction by Paul Theroux.

Hawaii culture is predicated on the wisdom of its elders, passed down through the generations. *Voices of Wisdom: Hawaiian Elders Speak* (Booklines Hawaii Ltd.) by MJ Harden features interviews with 24 respected island elders, gorgeously illustrated with black-and-white portraits by photographer Steve Brinkman. This beautiful and easy-to-read book is a perfect primer for anyone who wants to embrace Hawaii's rich heritage and the cultural renaissance the islands have experienced over the last two decades.

If you have a hard time finding any of these books — or if you want additional suggestions from Hawaii's rich library — two Big Island bookstores serve as particularly good resources: **Basically Books** (☎ **800-903-MAPS** or 808-961-0144; www.basicallybooks.com) and the **Kohala Book Shop** (☎ **808-889-6400**; www.kohalabooks.com). Both offer online catalog browsing and ordering services.

Movies

Gorgeous Hawaii has served as a backdrop for countless TV shows and movies, from *Hawaii Five-O* ("book 'em, Dano") to *Pearl Harbor*. Here are just a few of my favorites, all available on DVD.

The epic Academy Award winner *From Here to Eternity* (1953), starring Montgomery Clift, Frank Sinatra, Burt Lancaster, and a bevy of other Hollywood big names, tells the story of the attack on Pearl Harbor with gravity and intimacy — and the location shots are gorgeous, even in black-and-white.

Blue Crush (2002) is a silly surf movie that nevertheless captures the genuine heart of Oahu's North Shore surf culture. The stunning photography alone is worth putting up with the plot — you'll feel like you're riding the waves yourself. (*Note:* The hotel that the girls work at in the movie is the JW Marriott on Oahu.)

Breathtaking Kauai hosts the dinosaur-dotted jungle of *Jurassic Park* (1993). Of course, Spielberg didn't exactly discover Kauai; Hollywood had discovered the Garden Isle's silver screen magic decades before. For the best retro views, check out Elvis in *Blue Hawaii* (1961) and *South Pacific* (1958), filmed on the north shore of Kauai, whose stunning Bali Hai mountains shape the film's stunning backdrop. And even flying Elvises can't upstage the gorgeous scenery when *Honeymoon in Vegas* (1992), starring Nicolas Cage and Sarah Jessica Parker, move to Kauai.

One of my absolute favorite movies about Hawaii is the little-seen *Picture Bride* (1994), which tells the story of a young Japanese girl who sails to Hawaii in 1918 to marry a man — a laborer in the sugar cane fields — whom she has never met. This stirring and beautiful movie is well worth seeking out.

Chapter 3

Choosing Where to Go

● ●

In This Chapter

▶ Introducing the islands: Oahu, Maui, the Big Island, and Kauai
▶ Deciding how many islands to visit

● ●

*H*awaii isn't just one place — it's an entire island chain comprising eight major islands and 124 islets. Together, they form a 1,500-mile crescent that slices a lush, volcanic swath through the sparkling Pacific waters just above the equator (in the North Pacific Ocean, not the South Pacific, as many believe).

The Hawaiian Islands are just a hair's breadth larger, in total land mass, than the state of Connecticut — but oh, what glorious square miles they are. The islands are actually the summits of underwater volcanoes that have grown tall enough, in geologic time, to peek above the waves. (All the volcanoes are dormant except for two on the Big Island, Mauna Loa and Kilauea, part of Hawaii Volcanoes National Park. See Chapter 16 for more information.) A volcanic core gives each island a breathtakingly rugged mountainous heart.

Most of the island development is at sea level, along the sunny coastal fringe of each island. Thanks to Hawaii's proximity to the equator, those coastal areas experience near-perfect weather year-round: temperatures in the high 70s or low 80s, clear skies, and gentle trade winds.

Introducing the Hawaiian Islands

The eight main islands are *Oahu* (oh-WA-hoo), the hub of the Hawaii island chain, and the "neighbor" islands: *Maui* (MOW-ee); *Hawaii,* or the *Big Island,* as it's commonly called; *Kauai* (ka-WAH-ee); *Molokai* (mo-lo-k-EYE); *Lanai* (la-NAH-ee); *Niihau* (nee-EE-how); and *Kahoolawe* (ka-ho-ho-LA-vay). These islands make up more than 99 percent of the state's land mass. Of these, the first six are prime tourist destinations, each with its own personality, attractions, and tropical appeal. (Niihau is a privately owned island with a tiny population, and Kahoolawe is an unpopulated island that was formerly a U.S. military bombing target.)

Of the six islands that are open to tourists, four are ideal choices: Oahu, Maui, the Big Island, and Kauai — these are the islands covered in this book. Molokai and Lanai are much less developed and offer fewer places to stay; they're worth visiting, but I generally recommend waiting until you've already gotten to know the four major islands more intimately.

The Gathering Place: Oahu

Oahu is the most developed of the Hawaiian Islands and its greatest population center — about 75 percent of Hawaii's residents (about 875,000 people) live on this gateway island. About three-quarters of Oahuans reside in Honolulu, the only real big city in the state. Hawaii's most famous district is the area of Honolulu called Waikiki, an urban beach resort that stretches along the south coast of the island to the landmark crater known as Diamond Head. A compact city of concrete and high-rises, Waikiki is the most densely built of Hawaii's beach resorts.

Oahu is a wonderful destination. It's home to some of Hawaii's best sightseeing, including the **USS *Arizona* Memorial** in **Pearl Harbor,** the most moving tribute to World War II in existence; the best little museum in the Pacific, the **Bishop Museum;** the world's best cultural theme park, the **Polynesian Cultural Center;** and much more. Oahu also boasts the state's finest restaurants and shopping, as well as, believe it or not, some of Hawaii's finest off-the-beaten path adventures.

And **Waikiki Beach** really is fabulous, which is why travelers from around the world regularly converge on this sunny little haven. In the last few years, formerly kitschy Waikiki has been reinvented along more sophisticated lines, mainly as a result of its popularity with Japanese honeymooners who love to shop the couture boutiques (hello, Prada!) along the main drag, **Kalakaua Avenue.** The Outrigger hotel company also has a fabulous multi-million-dollar development underway around Waikiki's Beach Walk that will add additional shops, dining, and entertainment, as well as hotel rooms and timeshare units. A multimillion-dollar beachfront beautification project has already been a spectacular success, and the old seediness is pretty much ancient history. (Lest you think it sounds all too kitsch-free, Don Ho still sings "Tiny Bubbles" nightly, folks.)

Still, Waikiki maintains some of Hawaii's best moderately priced hotels; you're even likely to score some of the best luxury-hotel rates here, too. In addition, a comprehensive, easy-to-use public transportation system makes Oahu the one-and-only choice for those who don't want to rent a car.

Leave Oahu off your itinerary if your singular goal is to get away from it all; head to the Big Island or Kauai instead. But if you're up for endless diversion and don't mind a few crowds with your aloha — if you're the type who revels in the glitz and energy of it all — justifiably world-famous Waikiki is the place for you.

The Hawaiian Islands

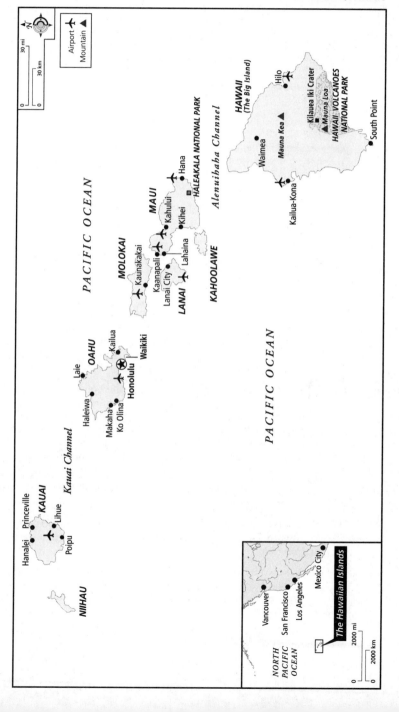

Many newcomers who visit *only* Waikiki leave with the wrong idea about Hawaii — that it's more crowded, overbuilt, and urbanized than a real tropical paradise should be. So if you want to go home without feeling like you missed out on the magic, the best strategy is to pair a stay on Oahu with a visit to at least one of the neighbor islands. I also highly recommend that you dedicate a day to visiting Oahu's Windward Coast and North Shore (the epicenter of Hawaii's surf culture), which offer some of the most gorgeous territory in the state.

Here are some of Oahu's pros and cons:

- ✔ Yes, Waikiki beach is overbuilt and crowded — but it's still pure magic. If you want some alone time, idyllic Windward Coast beaches like Lanikai and Kailua are just a short drive away.

- ✔ If you just want to sit around and do nothing, why hassle with Honolulu? Head to a neighbor island instead.

- ✔ Budget seekers should know that Waikiki now has the cheapest average room rate in Hawaii (about $120 a night) and boasts a surprising number of reasonably priced hotels right on — or a stone's throw from — the sand, including any number of centrally located Outrigger and Ohana hotels.

- ✔ Oahu is home to Hawaii's most famous snorkel spot, Hanauma Bay. Sure, it gets crowded — but a whole new world awaits you underwater here. Waikiki is a great place to learn to surf, outrigger canoe, or boogie board, and the windward beaches are great for wanna-be windsurfers. Another reason to keep Oahu on your agenda: The magical dolphin-watching cruises offered by Dolphin Excursions.

- ✔ This island is the birthplace, and still the epitome, of surf culture. If you want to learn to surf, you already know how, or you just like to watch, this is the island for you — no question. Waikiki's beach boys swear that they can teach anyone to surf (or stand up, anyway). Come in winter and point your rental car to the North Shore to see the big kahunas hang-ten in legendary style.

- ✔ The whole family will enjoy the multitude of kid-friendly sightseeing attractions and parks including Waikiki Beach, the perfect kiddie playland.

- ✔ Honolulu may not fulfill your dreams of Eden, but the gorgeous Windward Coast may well do the trick. Still, you will have to go in search of it.

- ✔ With Sea Life Park, the Honolulu Zoo, the Waikiki Aquarium, Hawaiian Waters Adventure Park, Hawaiian Ocean Thrills, the Polynesian Cultural Center, Waimea Valley Adventure Park, and even more to choose from, you're certain to find a theme park or island-themed attraction to suit your fancy.

- ✔ Oahu is the destination for serious shoppers. The finest collection of alfresco malls in the country is home to everything from Prada and Versace boutiques to first-rate department stores to one-of-a-kind shops carrying top-quality aloha shirts, surf gear, island-accented homewares, and more.

✔ Oahu offers a large quantity of bars, dancing, and live entertainment venues, plus the best sunset hula and cocktails in the islands at the Halekulani's House Without A Key.

The Valley Isle: Maui

When people think Hawaiian paradise, they usually think Maui. Almost everyone who comes here falls in love with this island, and for good reason: It offers the ideal mix of unspoiled natural beauty and tropical sophistication, action-packed fun, and laid-back island style. In fact, the readers of *Condé Nast Traveler* have voted Maui "Best Island in the World" for eight years running, and "World's Best Travel Destination" five years in a row.

The Valley Isle is more like the mainland than any other place in Hawaii (yes, even Honolulu). The highways and L.A.-style traffic jams and mini-malls will look comfortingly familiar, or annoyingly so — it all depends on your perspective. (Because Maui generally has only one main road going in each direction, traffic is actually worse on the Valley Isle than it is on Oahu.) Although hotels have a bit more breathing room on Maui than they do in Waikiki, the shoulder-to-shoulder resort development is far more dense than what you'll find on the Big Island or Kauai. Also, Maui's status as Fantasy Island means that it has the most high-profile population of relocated mainlanders; a quicker pace of living prevails, which can make Maui feel more like Southern California than Hawaii, especially in the resort areas.

Despite the mainland-style development, Maui really is a tropical paradise, with golden beaches, misty tropical cliffs, and countless waterfalls along the **Heavenly Road to Hana,** one of America's most spectacular drives. Offshore are two of Hawaii's finest snorkel and dive spots. Onshore, at the summit of one of the island's two great mountains, is **Haleakala National Park,** a wild, otherworldly place that's hugely popular with hikers, bicyclers, and sunrise-watchers. Hawaii's finest luau, a new theater, and an energetic party vibe in Lahaina make Maui the best choice for those who enjoy after-dark activities.

Maui's attractions are no secret — so expect to battle a few crowds and pay for the privilege of visiting. I've heard an increasing number of complaints about overdevelopment and crowds in the last couple of years. And thanks to the rules of supply and demand, Maui tends to be more expensive than other islands, and booked-to-capacity hotels can be less than willing to reduce rates; the high cost of all those available activities doesn't help matters. What's more, the tacky heart of Hawaii now beats in the old whaling town of Lahaina (which has superceded newly refined Waikiki as a cheesy tourist center), and Kihei's dominant architectural style is high strip mall. Still, nothing can dull the sheen on Maui, which oozes sex appeal and sports enough excitement and activity to keep even the most go-go-go travelers constantly on their toes.

Here are some of Maui's pros and cons:

- ✓ The Valley Isle scores for abundant, wide, breathtaking beaches.

- ✓ Maui is a winner for the sheer variety of great snorkel, dive, and learn-to-surf spots. One caveat: Molokini, a sunken offshore crater that's world famous for snorkeling and diving, no longer equals the Big Island's Kealakekua thanks to a shoulder-to-shoulder snorkel boat population and a worn-down reef.

- ✓ Despite its popularity and high resort rates, Maui has a decent number of beachfront bargains. If you don't want to go condo, try the Kaanapali Beach Hotel, one of my midpriced faves.

- ✓ Maui has enough world-class golf courses to keep club-wielders happy for a good, long time.

- ✓ The windsurfers at Maui's Hookipa Beach are a blast to watch.

- ✓ Maui is the humpback's favorite place to hang offshore; if you show up during prime whale season (January through March), you're bound to see them, even if you don't head out to sea.

- ✓ This action-packed island wins for its wealth of kid-friendly condos and beaches, plus activities galore, from snorkel cruises to hikes to family-fun luaus. Your kids will wonder why you haven't come here before.

- ✓ Outdoor fun is the name of the game here. There's something new to do around every corner, from riding a bike down a volcano to taking a snorkel cruise.

- ✓ If you have a yen to frolic among waterfalls, do not pass go, do not collect $200 — head straight to Maui. The drive to Hana is chock-full of fabulous falls, and at the end of the road is the granddaddy of 'em all, Oheo Gulch.

- ✓ Maui has the most innovative dining scene in the islands these days, from casual to chic — and with a wealth of beautifully situated oceanfront restaurants to boot.

- ✓ Attention, shoppers: Maui has an increasingly excellent specialty boutique and gallery scene, especially in Paia and Upcountry.

- ✓ Maui has surpassed Oahu as the nightlife capital of Hawaii. A party mood characterizes Lahaina town; the resorts offer lots of after-dark fun; and the Old Lahaina Luau is Hawaii's absolute best. This island even boasts the state's best live theater in the form of the Cirque du Soleil-goes-to-the-islands show *'Ulalena,* plus a couple of excellent ongoing magic revues.

The Big Island: Hawaii

Salt-and-pepper beaches, primal rainforests, stark lava fields as far as the eye can see — this otherworldly island simply may not be your idea of a tropical paradise. But travelers with a passion for adventure, an eye for the unusual, or a taste for luxury will think that they've found heaven on earth.

The island that gave the entire island chain its name is the largest in the bunch — twice the size of all the others combined — and a real study in contradictions: Don't be surprised if you spot snow atop the nearly 14,000-foot peaks while you're deep-sea fishing off the legendary **Kona Coast** — considered the Sportfishing Capital of the World — or snorkeling in some of the warmest waters in the Pacific. North of Mauna Kea is vast ranchland, complete with herds of beef cattle and its own *paniolo* (cowboy) culture.

The left (Kona-Kohala) side is hot, dry, and studded with expansive, ultradeluxe beach resorts that add up to the finest collection of luxury resorts in all Hawaii. The **Kona-Kohala coast** is one of the finest watersports playgrounds there is for divers, snorkelers, and kayakers, while sun worshippers love white-sand **Hapuna Beach,** one of Hawaii's finest.

The right (Hilo-Volcano) side is lush, wet, green, and fragrant with tropical flowers. **Hilo** is the prettiest city in the Pacific, and **Volcano Village** puts you right in the heart of a tropical rainforest.

In between are two of the tallest mountain peaks in the Pacific, **Mauna Kea** and **Mauna Loa;** the summit of Mauna Kea offers some of the world's finest stargazing. At the heart of the island is **Kilauea volcano,** the world's largest active volcano, currently in the midst of recorded history's longest-ever uninterrupted volcanic eruption. Most people think of volcanic activity as solely destructive, but Kilauea's eruptions have actually been productive, adding more than 20,000 acres of new land (and counting) to the Big Island since January 1983. Needless to say, **Hawaii Volcanoes National Park** is one of the coolest — excuse me, hottest — places you'll ever have a chance to visit in your lifetime. If you like weird places, you won't want to miss it.

The Big Island can, however, dash expectations. It's jaw-droppingly spectacular — force me to choose, and I'll name it as my favorite of the islands — but it falls short of some people's tropical-island fantasies. Rugged chocolate-brown lava fields in every direction greet visitors flying into Kona Airport. Sure, you can experience a traditional tropical idyll on picture-perfect white-sand beaches as wide as a football field, or revel in the scent of wild orchids in flowering rainforests, but you may have to go out of your way to find them. Also, this is rural Hawaii, so nightlife is scarce.

Still, this island is so big that you're likely to have the place to yourself after you arrive. With lots of room to spread out, the Big Island has a more laid-back, quieter vibe than what you find on Oahu or Maui — and, much of the time, you'll also find relatively lower prices at all but the ultraluxury resorts. A nice selection of affordable, family-friendly condos are on hand (although most require a drive to a swimmable beach). And B&B lovers will discover the island's best collection of inns, most offering an excellent base for visitors looking for something other than the average beachfront resort or affordable condo experience. Just remember that the sheer size of this extra-large island makes for longer driving times; either plan on spending a week or limit yourself to one coast.

Here are some of the Big Island's pros and cons:

- You'll find some unusual beaches here, including a number of striking black-sand ones.

- The Big Island is the place to park yourself in style. You'll find a string of terrific megaresorts along the Kona-Kohala coast, where all have plenty of room to spread out.

- These spectacular championship resort golf courses, each an oasis of manicured green surrounded by a sea of black lava, are simply wild.

- The big kahuna is rich with one-of-a-kind sightseeing opportunities, including Hawaii Volcanoes National Park.

- Kealakekua Bay is the best snorkeling and dolphin-watching spot in all Hawaii, hands down, and the whole coast is tops for sea turtle spotting. It offers great offshore diving, too. And the icing on the cake? The Big Island's a sportfisher's mecca.

- Oahu scores big for its WOW! factor. From fantasy megaresorts to that amazing volcano, the Big Island should keep your kids dazzled for awhile. You'll also find some affordable family condos here.

- The fabulous resorts make great wedding locations — and you're on your honeymoon as soon as you cut the cake. On the other side of the island, lush rainforests and romantic B&Bs make great places to hide from the rest of the world.

- You'll find lots of activities here to keep you busy, including visiting the phenomenal Hawaii Volcanoes National Park — but plan on increased driving time getting around.

- Also known as the "Orchid Isle," the Big Island earns deserved points for beautiful rainforest lushness around Hilo and Volcano Village — but the dry, arid Kona-Kohala coast is the antithesis of some folks' island dreams.

- The Big Island offers a very respectable slate of restaurants in both the moderate and expensive price ranges, but the driving distance between them puts a strain on your nightly choices.

    ✔ An abundance of natural resources makes this island tops for quality shopping of island art and crafts. Expect to go on the hunt for the best galleries, though.

    ✔ The Big Island is much quieter than Oahu and Maui, with a low-key waterfront bar scene in Kailua-Kona and some chic cocktail spots at the resorts — but if Kilauea's spouting red-hot lava, there's no better after-dark show around.

The Garden Isle: Kauai

Of all the Hawaiian Islands, Kauai is the one that comes closest to embodying the Hawaiian ideal — it's the ultimate in tropical romance and beauty. Even Hollywood thinks so, which is why Kauai has had starring roles as Paradise in movies ranging from *Blue Hawaii* and *South Pacific* to *Jurassic Park*. The island landscape doesn't get any more spectacular than what you'll find on Kauai. Every time I visit, I'm newly wowed by how exquisite it is. Kauai boasts the kind of natural beauty that cameras can't really capture, and that even mere memory can't conjure up.

Kauai is the perfect place to leave the modern world behind. Gardenlike Kauai is quieter and less developed than its sister islands; in fact, you can count the number of full-fledged resorts on one hand. (This lack of choice makes it important to book well in advance if you plan on staying at one of the resorts.) Don't come expecting Cancun-style nightlife or St. Thomas-worthy shopping. Discover instead the oldest of the Hawaiian Islands, an unspoiled place boasting wind-carved cliffs, fertile valleys rich with taro, powder-fine white-sand beaches, and gorgeous vistas in every direction. It's an ideal setting for some well-deserved relaxation time: The North Shore is the most tranquil and beautiful shoreline in all Hawaii, and the South Shore's **Poipu** (poy-EE-poo) **Beach** is a fabulous, family-friendly playground that's the ideal place to kick back and paddle around in the waves for days on end.

Kauai is great for adventurous souls, too. The island boasts two remote natural wonders: the jagged emerald cliffs of the **Na Pali Coast,** and **Waimea Canyon,** called the "Grand Canyon of the Pacific" for its remarkable resemblance to the multicolored Arizona crater. The otherwise inaccessible Na Pali Coast, in particular, is a tropical dream-come-true for hikers, but you can also see these magical cliffs on a day cruise along the coastline or on an eye-popping helicopter tour.

It takes a lot of rain to keep Kauai so lush, fertile, and flower-fragrant; consequently, the weather on Kauai is a little less reliable than on the other islands. Kauai is the one island where a week of rain can quash your fun-in-the-sun plans. This is most likely to happen in winter, but it's happened to me even in May. (Conversely, I've enjoyed a rain-free March on the Garden Isle, and I've enjoyed sunny Kauai when it was raining everywhere else in the islands, so the weather is always anybody's guess.) Kauai's **Mt. Waialeale** is actually the wettest spot on earth, commanding an average annual rainfall of 444 inches; luckily, the coasts stay substantially drier. Still, stick to the South Shore if you have your heart set on a string of sunny days. The superlush North Shore is best for summer vacations, when the wild winter surf has calmed down and the days tend toward dry and sunny. (See Chapter 4 for more information on Hawaii's weather.)

Here are some of Kauai's pros and cons:

✔ It's home to the powdery-white, palm-lined, postcard-perfect beaches you fantasize about — and you're likely to have them virtually all to yourself as soon as you get here.

✔ Robert Trent Jones, Jr., called Kauai "the best island for golf there is."

✔ It has great snorkeling, spectacular underwater sightseeing, with a kaleidoscopic collection of marine life (although snorkeling is not safe in winter).

✔ Although this island is mostly for the relaxation-minded, Kauai does have condos, and Poipu Beach is fun for kids.

✔ No question — Kauia is the undisputed winner in the **romance** category.

✔ Kauia is the best island for catching up on relaxation time — but you'll have lots to do if you want it, from movie tours to world-class golf to ocean activities galore.

✔ The Garden Isle is the closest you'll come to the realization of the tropical dream — it's simply stunning. Don't miss the North Shore, even if you drive up for only a day.

✔ Kauai has less dining variety than the other islands. However, Poipu is home to my favorite branch of Roy's, the temple of Hawaii Regional Cuisine; the Coconut Coast boasts the only remaining (and the original) outpost of the wonderful A Pacific Cafe; and the island features some of Hawaii's best wallet-friendly restaurants (including Duane's Ono Char-Burger — yum!!).

✔ The shopping is minimal in terms of quantity, but excellent for quality, especially if you like retro looks.

The most Hawaiian isle: Molokai

Sleepy Molokai is a rural island that's largely untouched by modern development (although, as residents like to boast, they do have a KFC restaurant now). This lean, funky, scruffy little place is often called the most Hawaiian island because it's the birthplace of the hula, and it has a larger native Hawaiian population than any other in the chain. Although it offers some lovely, secluded beaches, the island's most famous site is Kalaupapa National Historical Park, a world-famous 19th-century leper colony that can only be reached by mule, prop plane, or helicopter.

I don't really cover Molokai in this book because I don't recommend making it part of your first visit to Hawaii. It's worth seeing eventually for its unsullied beauty and true Hawaiian spirit, but you should fully explore the other islands before you devote a significant amount of time to Molokai. The island has plenty of aloha, no question, and is working on its image as a tourist destination, but facilities for visitors are minimal: a few condos, a handful of B&Bs, and one adventure-resort spread with a lodge and upscale camping called **Molokai Ranch Lodge & Beach Village.** I find it to be overpriced for what you get so I don't recommend that you spend your time and money there. If you're interested in checking it out, however, call ☎ **888-627-8082** or visit www.molokairanch.com online.

If your heart is set on dedicating a chunk of your vacation to Molokai, check out *Frommer's Hawaii, Frommer's Hawaii from $60 a Day,* or *Frommer's Maui,* all of which include complete coverage of the island. Or contact the Molokai Visitors Association (☎ **800-800-6367,** 808-553-3876; www.molokai-hawaii.com). The Maui Visitors Bureau can also provide you with island information because Molokai is part of Maui County. See the Quick Concierge in the appendix for complete contact info.

The private island: Lanai

This tiny island (pop. 3,500) is featured on a few packages, but I don't recommend spending time here until you conquer the other islands. Staying on Lanai is less a Hawaiian experience and more a generic park-yourself-at-a-resort vacation, which you can do with more local flavor elsewhere in the islands. For this reason, I don't cover Lanai in detail in this book.

 If you're committed to visiting Lanai, you don't need me or this book, anyway — this island is where you go to *really* get away from it all. Formerly dedicated to pineapple production, Lanai is not particularly beautiful, nor does it offer much in the personality department. There's little or nothing to do here, which is the entire idea of this getaway island. Just about everything that *is* here is completely handled through the two mega-expensive resorts that have taken over this humble little place: the English manor-house-style Lodge at Koele, which sits on the cool, misty peak of the island, and the more what-you'd-expect-from-Hawaii beachfront Manele Bay Hotel. Both hotels are slated to become members of the ultraposh Four Seasons chain — arguably the finest hotel and resort brand in the world — sometime in 2005, which will certainly enhance the Lanai experience for those looking for a leave-it-all-behind luxury escape. For the latest details, call Four Seasons at ☎ **800-819-5053** or visit www.fourseasons.com.

If you visit Lanai, plan on eating every meal at the two sister resorts, and otherwise being entirely at their mercy. Still, Lanai has fans who love the total pampering and utter solitude. (Bill Gates booked up the entire island, so that he could get married here beyond the prying eyes of the media and public a few years back.) Golfers also like its two world-class courses.

I prefer visiting Lanai for a day of beachgoing, snorkeling, and sightseeing on one of Trilogy Excursions' day and overnight cruises from Maui; I tell you how to sign up in Chapter 14. Golfers may also consider flying over for the day to hit the links, which is what many locals do.

If you really want to make Lanai a more substantial part of your vacation, see *Frommer's Hawaii* or *Frommer's Maui* (both published by Wiley), both of which include complete coverage of the island. Or contact Destination Lanai at ☎ 800-947-4774 or www.visitlanai.net. You can also contact the Maui Visitors Bureau because Lanai is part of Maui County (☎ 800-321-4666; www.lanairesorts.com). See the Quick Concierge in the appendix for more contact information.

Visiting More than One Island

Most Hawaii vacationers visit more than one island, which I highly recommend you do. But don't try to see all the islands, or even the four major ones, unless you have a month of vacation time to do it. About a week per island is a good general rule — or you end up spending what feels like your entire vacation in the airport, at the car-rental counter, and checking in and out of hotels. Trust me: Nonstop packing and unpacking can really put the kibosh on relaxation and the laid-back pace that should be the crux of any Hawaii vacation. And increased security at the airports — which not only demands earlier arrival at the airport but also lengthens the time it takes to pick up your rental car on the other end because all cars have been moved offsite — has turned every half-hour flight between the islands into a three-hour-or-more affair.

As you plan your itinerary, keep the following tips in mind:

 ✔ **Try to fly directly from the mainland to the island of your choice.** Doing so can save you a two-hour layover in Honolulu and another plane ride on an interisland carrier — a process that can add four or five hours to your total travel time. Oahu, the Big Island, Maui, and Kauai all receive multiple direct flights from the mainland. However, mainland flights to the neighbor islands can be more expensive and less frequent than those that arrive in Honolulu, so be sure to compare prices if money matters.

 ✔ **Remember the one-week, one-island rule.** It's smart to allot a week per island. For a two-week vacation, three islands is max — and that's only if you're the kind of traveler who can't handle more than three days amid the hustle and bustle of Waikiki.

 ✔ **If you have two weeks and your heart is set on seeing three islands, consider the following:** Arrive in Honolulu and spend three days seeing the highlights. Then head to Kauai to kick back on the beach for four or five days and recover from the time you spent running around Honolulu. After that, head to the Big Island, which easily has a week's worth of activities to keep you busy.

✔ **Pass on seeing a third island if you're committed to visiting both Oahu and Maui in two weeks.** Believe me, these two powerhouse islands have more than enough to offer to keep you busy for two months, much less two weeks.

✔ **Never budget fewer than five days on the Big Island.** The Big Island is the size of Connecticut, and just about everything is located on the island's coastline; therefore, you're going to be spending plenty of time in the car if you really want to see everything. If you book yourself fewer than five days for serious sightseeing and lots of activities, too much of your time will be eaten up by driving — which would be a major disappointment on this fabulous island.

✔ **Don't overplan your itinerary or try to do everything.** If relaxing is No. 1 on your agenda, work plenty of do-nothing time into your travel plans. Keep your days loose and go with the flow; don't plan your time the way you would on a sightseeing tour of Europe. A Hawaii vacation is less about seeing everything and more about letting go with the island flow — and a big part of the experience is just taking things as they come. Don't feel guilty that you're not doing or seeing enough — you do enough the other 50 weeks out of the year, don't you?

✔ **Leave at least one day per island to chance.** Don't book a big activity for every day of your vacation. Leave at least one day on each island for whatever strikes your fancy, whether it be sightseeing or shopping or just sitting on your condo's oceanfront lanai, soaking up a beach read and the laid-back vibe. I can't say it enough: A Hawaii vacation is about leaving the conventions of regular life — including a hardcore commitment to time — behind. Make the most of these few carefree weeks in your life.

✔ **If you're dividing your day between land and sea activities, make mornings your ocean time.** Beaches tend to be less crowded, and the surf and winds tend to be calmer in the morning hours — especially in winter. Always take the first snorkel and dive cruise of the day, when conditions are calmest and clearest; there's a reason why outfitters offer discounts on their afternoon sails.

✔ **Keep an eye on the weather and plan accordingly.** Don't be a slave to your schedule — watch the local weather reports and keep your plans flexible enough to make the most of great weather.

✔ **Book extra-special activities before you leave home, so that you won't miss out.** Many of Hawaii's best activities can book up weeks in advance, so read this book and call ahead to reserve a few select adventures before you leave home. After all, it's not every day you get to Hawaii — and I wouldn't want you to miss out on the best luau in the islands or the eco-tour of a lifetime. For tips on those activities that you may want to book before you arrive, see Chapter 10.

Chapter 4

Deciding When to Go

. . . .

In This Chapter

▶ Understanding Hawaii's climate

▶ Decoding the secrets of the travel seasons

▶ Zeroing in on special events you may want to catch

. . . .

Situated in the North Pacific just 1,470 miles above the equator, the Hawaiian Islands enjoy fabulous weather all year-round. Winter is virtually nonexistent. Severe storms are a rarity. Even those times considered the "off-season" — spring and fall — are gorgeous, which means that those of you on a budget can save a bundle if you choose the right dates.

Still, some times are better than others — especially if you prefer to avoid crowds. This chapter tells you when everybody else comes to Hawaii, so that you can either join the party or avoid it like the plague.

Revealing the Secret of the Seasons

Hawaii's high season is during the winter months, from the second half of December through mid-April, when people flee the cold, snow, and gray skies of home for the warm sun of Hawaii. During this winter high season, prices go up, and resorts can be booked to capacity. This scenario is especially true during the holiday season; book far in advance for a trip during this period and expect to pay the highest prices. Although not nearly as bad as Christmastime, Easter week can also be crowded, as West Coast families flock to the islands for a few days of sunshine over spring break.

Summer (mid-June through August) is a secondary high season in Hawaii. Because so many families travel over the summer break, you won't find the bargains of spring and fall — but you may still do better on accommodations, airfare, and packages than you would in the winter months.

Hawaii's off-seasons have traditionally been spring (from mid-April to mid-June) and fall (from Labor Day to mid-December) — which, para-doxically, also happen to be the best seasons in Hawaii in terms of reliably great weather. Herein lies the secret of the seasons: In spring and fall, hotel rates typically drop, package deals abound, airfares are often at their lowest rates of the year (sometimes as cheap as $400 round-trip from the West Coast, or less), and you can expect consistently clear skies and 80°F days after you arrive.

Because the weather is relatively constant year-round, the decision on when to visit Hawaii is ultimately up to you and your schedule. It's a good bet that you can arrive at any time of year and enjoy prime island conditions. It really boils down to how much you want to spend, how important it is to escape a harsh winter back home, how willing you are to deal with crowds, and what's available.

Understanding Hawaii's climate

Hawaii lies at the edge of the tropics, so it really has only two seasons: warm (winter) and warmer (summer). Temperatures generally don't vary much more than 15 degrees or so from season to season, depending on where you are. The average daytime summer temperature at sea level is 85°F, and the average daytime winter temperature is 78°F.

Temperatures stay even steadier when you consider the coastal areas alone: At Waikiki, the average summer high is 87°F, and the average winter high is 82°F — not much difference. Nighttime temps drop about 10 to 15 degrees — less in summer, a little more in winter. August is usually the warmest month of the year; February and March are the coolest months. Almost-constant trade winds bring a cooling breeze even in the hottest weather.

Each of the islands has a *leeward* side (the west and south shores of the islands), which tends to be hot and dry, and a *windward* side (the east and north shores), which is generally cooler and wetter. For sun-baked, desertlike weather, visit the leeward side of an island. When you want lush, junglelike weather, go windward.

 Locals like to say that if you don't like the weather, just get in the car and drive — you're bound to find something different. That's because each island also has many microclimates, which are highly localized weather patterns based on a region's unique position and topography. On the Big Island, for example, Hilo gets 180 inches of rainfall annually, which makes it the wettest city in the nation — yet only 60 miles away is desertlike Puako, which gets less than 6 inches of rain per year.

Generally speaking, each island has a mountain (or mountains) at its center. The higher you go in elevation, the cooler it gets. Thus, if you travel inland and upward, the weather can change from summer to winter in a matter of hours. If you visit Maui's Haleakala National Park, for example, you climb from sea level to 10,000 feet in just 37 miles — and it's not uncommon for the temperature to be 30 to 35 degrees cooler at the summit than it is at the beach.

In general, November to March marks Hawaii's rainy season, and summer is considered the dry season. The weather can get gray during this season, but, fortunately, it seldom rains for more than three days in a row. Winter isn't a bad time to go to Hawaii; the sun's just a little less reliable, that's all.

The good news about Hawaii's rainy season is that it's almost never raining *everywhere* on an island, even in winter. So if it's raining on your parade, just get in the car and drive — you'll likely reach a sunny spot in no time. (The south and west coasts are usually your best bet.)

If you want guaranteed sunshine year-round — or, at least as close as you can get to a guarantee — base yourself in one or more of the following regions:

- ✔ Waikiki, on Oahu
- ✔ Maui's south coast (Kihei and Wailea)
- ✔ The Big Island's Kona-Kohala coast
- ✔ The south and southwest coasts of Kauai (Poipu Beach and Waimea)

Charting sea changes

Hawaii's ocean waters stay warm year-round. The average water temperature is a warm 74°F, and reaches a jump-right-in 80°F or so in summer.

Wave action, though, varies greatly between winter and summer, and from coast to coast. All Hawaii's beaches tend to be as placid as lakes in the summer and autumn months. In winter, the islands' north-facing beaches are hit with swells, and the surf goes wild, especially in places like Oahu's North Shore, where daredevil surfers with a death wish hang-ten on monster curls that can reach 50 feet. South-facing beaches like Waikiki generally remain calm and friendly to swimmers and snorkelers of all ages and abilities throughout winter, although spring and early summer bring south swells right about the time North Shore waves flatten out.

If the waves are too powerful for you, seek calmer conditions by taking a short drive to another beach that's more sheltered. In the island sections later in this book (Parts III through VI), I recommend the best local beaches, including the safest for inexperienced swimmers. When in doubt on where to go, ask one of the staff at your hotel or call the local tourist office for recommendations — and watch for warning flags and posted beach conditions at the beach.

A few important words about ocean safety: Never turn your back on the ocean when you're at the beach. A big wave can come out of nowhere before you can say aloha. Always watch the surf, even if you're just taking a casual stroll along the shoreline. Also, ocean conditions can change dramatically in a matter of hours — surf that was safe for swimming one day can develop a dangerous undertow the next. Get out of the water when the big swells come.

Avoiding the crowds

Yes, there are times when coming to Hawaii is a bad idea if you're allergic to crowds. At the very least, you should know what you're getting into.

The entire nation of Japan basically shuts down during Golden Week, which falls annually in late April or early May and encompasses three Japanese holidays. Japanese tourism to Hawaii has generally slipped in the last five years or so, but you'd never know it during Golden Week — especially in Waikiki, the favored destination among Japanese travelers. Be sure to book hotels, interisland air reservations, and car rentals well in advance.

The Big Island's Kona-Kohala coast fills up during Ironman week (which leads up to the Saturday closest to the full moon in October). Hotels book to capacity, rental cars sell out, and you'll pay top dollar for everything. People flock to Hilo during the Merrie Monarch Hula Festival, the week after Easter; plan well in advance if you're coming for these events.

On Maui, Halloween in Lahaina is a major event; up to 20,000 people come for the festivities. Booking your Lahaina hotel room a year or more in advance isn't too early. You shouldn't have a problem elsewhere on the island, though.

Additionally, more than 30,000 runners descend on Oahu for the week before the Honolulu Marathon (usually the second Sunday in December).

And keep in mind that the islands are at maximum capacity during the Christmas holidays; spring break and Easter week can also be crowded. Stay at home during these seasons if you don't want to fight crowds or pay top dollar.

Perusing a Calendar of Events

Here's a rundown of the top events that take place annually throughout the Hawaiian Islands. This list is merely a drop in the bucket, of course; for a complete rundown, as well as the latest event information, visit www.calendar.gohawaii.com. For details on the events on a given island, your best bet is to contact the local visitor's bureau directly. See the Quick Concierge at the back of this book for contact information.

Many of the following events absolutely require significant planning before you leave home. Calling ahead before any event is always best as tickets may be required, details may have changed, and so on.

✔ **January and February:** 'Tis the season for world-championship golf in paradise. The season kicks off with the first PGA event of the year, the **Mercedes Championships** at Maui's Kapalua Resort (☎ **808-669-2440**), followed almost immediately by the **Sony Open** at Oahu's Waialae Country Club (☎ **808-734-2151** or 808-523-7888). On the senior tour, there's the **MasterCard Championship** at the Big Island's Four Seasons Hualalai (☎ **800-417-2770** or 808-325-8000), and the **Wendy's Champions Skins Game** at Wailea, Maui (☎ **808-875-7450**). Expect top-ranked talent at every event. Check www.pgatour.com for complete details on each event, including how to purchase tickets.

✔ **January through April:** These months are Hawaii's prime **whale-watching season,** when humpback whales — the world's largest mammals — make their way from frigid Alaska to the balmy waters of Hawaii. Because whales prefer water depths of less than 600 feet, these endangered gentle giants come in relatively close to shore. You can see them regulary from the beach in prime season, spouting and *spyhopping* (peeking above the waterline to "spy" on what's going on). They often prefer the west, or leeward, sides of the islands.

Maui is particularly terrific for whale-watching because the giants love to frolic in the channel separating the Valley Isle from Molokai and Lanai. The best on-shore vantage is West Maui's MacGregor Point, a large pullout on the ocean side of Highway 30, halfway between Maalaea and Lanai. The nonprofit Pacific Whale Foundation operates a **Whale Information Station** there that's staffed by friendly naturalists daily from 8:30 a.m. to 3:30 p.m. from December through April. Just stop by — they even have high-powered binoculars you can use — or call ☎ **800-WHALE-1-1** (800-942-5311) or 808-249-8811 for more details.

If you happen to be in the islands during whale season, you won't want to miss seeing these remarkable behemoths. For the best views, take any one of the variety of whale-watching cruises that are offered from each island; I recommend the best ones later in Parts III through VI.

✔ **Mid-January or early February:** The annual **Hula Bowl Maui All-Star Football Classic** features America's top college teams competing at Maui's newly renovated War Memorial Stadium. The all-star event is preceded by **Hula Fest,** a week full of football-oriented fun. Ticket orders start being processed on April 1 for next January's game, so be sure to call ☎ **808-874-9500** well in advance of kickoff time (or visit www.hulabowlmaui.com, where you can find out more details and order tickets online).

✔ **Late January through early February:** Help ring in the **Chinese New Year** in Honolulu's historic Chinatown, on the island of Oahu. New Year's events include a pageant, lion dances through the streets of Chinatown, a narcissus and bonsai exhibition, cooking demonstrations, live entertainment, and a festival bazaar. Call ☎ **808-533-3181** for this year's schedule and dates. Always ready for any excuse to party, Maui's Lahaina is another excellent place to celebrate the Chinese New Year; events include a traditional lion dance in front of the historic Wo Hing Temple, plus food, music, fireworks, Chinese crafts, and much more. Call ☎ **888-310-1117** or 808-667-9175 or go online to www.visitlahaina.com. February 9, 2005, ushers in the year of the rooster.

✔ **First Sunday in February:** The National Football League's best pro players get it on in the **NFL Pro Bowl.** This annual all-star game takes place at Oahu's Aloha Stadium. Call ☎ **808-486-9300** or visit www.nfl.com/probowl well in advance for ticket information for next year's game. A week's worth of gridiron-oriented fun usually precedes the big event.

✔ **Early February:** Honolulu's most prestigious private school hosts the **Punahou School Carnival,** and it's well worth seeking out. This huge two-day fun fair features everything from high-speed thrill rides to art shows by island artists to traditional Hawaiian food booths. Excellent island-style fun! Call ☎ **808-944-5711** or visit www.punahou.com for this year's schedule of events.

✔ **Mid-February:** The Pacific Whale Foundation honors the majestic humpback whale with the **Great Maui Whale Festival,** a full winter-long calendar of events that culminates in mid-February with a parade, a regatta, special whale-watching events, the annual Whale Day Celebration (usually held on the third Saturday of the month), and much, much more. Call the foundation at ☎ **800-942-5311** or 808-249-8811 or go online to www.greatmauiwhalefestival.org for details.

✔ **Mid-March:** The second humpback-themed celebration of the season rules Maui during the **Ocean Arts Festival,** Lahaina's own two-day series of special events honoring the island's most high-profile visitors, including whale-watching, an outdoor arts festival, games, and a touch-pool exhibit for kids. Call ☎ **888-310-1117** or 808-667-9193 for this year's schedule.

✔ **Easter Weekend:** Maui's annual **Ritz-Carlton Kapalua Celebration of the Arts** is the premier interactive Hawaii arts and culture festival. Well-known artists give free hands-on lessons in hula, chant, Niihau shell lei-making, tapa cloth-making, primitive clay firing, and more. Events include a traditional luau, kids' activities, and live entertainment of the highest order. Call ☎ **800-262-8440** or 808-669-6200 or visit www.celebrationofthearts.org for this year's schedule and reservations.

✔ **Easter Sunday:** Since 1902, people from near and far have been gathering for the **Easter Morning Sunrise Services** at Honolulu's National Cemetery of the Pacific, in Punchbowl Crater. Call ☎ **808-532-3720.**

✔ **Week following Easter:** Hawaii's biggest annual cultural event is the **Merrie Monarch Hula Festival,** which sweeps the misty city of Hilo on the Big Island for a full week in spring, usually the week following Easter Sunday. The islands' largest and most prestigious hula festival features four nights of modern and ancient dance in honor of King David Kalakaua, the "merrie monarch" who revived the dance, which had been all but forgotten with the coming of Western ways to the islands. Tickets sell out by late January, so reserve early; some events are free, however, and a limited number of returned tickets may be available at the last minute. Competitions wind down with a festive parade on the final Saturday of the event. Call ☎ **808-935-9168** or visit www.kalena.com/merriemonarch for details — and plan to stay away from booked-solid Hilo during festival week if you don't plan to participate.

✔ **May 1:** May Day is **Lei Day** in Hawaii — and cause for big-time rejoicing. At Oahu's Kapiolani Park, Hawaii's most colorful and fragrant holiday is celebrated all day with lei-making contests and exhibits, art-and-crafts fairs, food booths, and more; you can even meet this year's Lei Queen. The crowning event is the big **Lei Day Concert by the Brothers Cazimero,** kings of the Hawaiian music scene, at the Waikiki Band Shell; it's a magical, aloha-filled event well worth planning your trip around. Tickets usually go on sale in early April. Call ☎ **808-692-5118** for details on Kapiolani Park's Lei Day events and ☎ **808-597-1888** for concert information.

✔ **Mid-May:** Oahu's Polynesian Cultural Center hosts the weeklong **World Fire-Knife Dance Competition,** literally the world's hottest competition, in which fire dancers of all ages gather from around the globe to compete for the title of world champion fire-knife dancer. It's all part of the annual **We Are Samoa Festival,** celebrated with authentic Samoan food and festivities. Contact the Polynesian Cultural Center at ☎ **800-367-7060** or 808-293-3333 for this year's details or go online to www.polynesia.com.

✔ **Memorial Day:** There's no better place to honor past war heroes than at the **USS *Arizona* Memorial,** in Honolulu's Pearl Harbor; call ☎ **808-422-2771** or 808-422-0561 for the program of events. At 9 a.m., the armed forces also hold a ceremony recognizing the brave men and women who died for their country at the **National Cemetery of the Pacific** at Punchbowl Crater, the final resting place of 35,224 victims of three American wars fought in Asia and the Pacific; call ☎ **808-532-3720** for further details.

✔ **Mid-June:** The **Maui Film Festival at Wailea** is Hawaii's very own version of Sundance, with five days and nights of premiere screenings, parties, and celebrity appearances, plus Hawaiian cultural events for island flavor. Call ☎ **808-579-9244** or 808-572-FILM, or visit mauifilmfestival.com, for complete program information.

✔ **June 11 (or nearest weekend):** In honor of the great chief who united the Hawaiian Islands, **King Kamehameha Day** — Hawaii's longest-running holiday, since 1871 — is celebrated as a statewide holiday, with massive floral parades, slack-key guitar concerts, Hawaiian crafts shows, and lots of partying. Probably the best event is the celebratory parade through Maui's old Lahaina town, which concludes with a food and craft fair, demonstrations of ancient warrior skills, and other entertainment; call ☎ **808-667-9193** for details. Contact the individual island visitor center (see the Quick Concierge in the appendix) for the full calendar of local celebrations or visit www.state.hi.us/dags/kkcc.

✔ **Last weekend in June:** Oahu becomes a gourmand's paradise during **Taste of Honolulu,** a three-day food and wine festival held at Honolulu's Civic Center. After paying the $3 admission fee, you buy a roll of tickets at the gate, which you can exchange for tasting portions of yummy delights from dozens of the island's best restaurants. The fun also includes beer and wine tastings, cooking demonstrations, activities for kids, top-quality Hawaiian entertainment, and more. Best of all, proceeds benefit islanders with disabilities through Easter Seals Hawaii. Call ☎ **808-536-1015** or visit www.taste808.com for more info.

✔ **Late June or early July:** See demonstrations of traditional Hawaii arts-and-crafts making, sample traditional island foods, watch Hawaiian royal court living-history reenactments, and even learn to shake your hips to the hula at the two-day **Annual Hawaiian Cultural Festival,** which takes place at Puuhonua o Honaunau National Historical Park — one of Hawaii's most well-preserved and fascinating cultural landmarks — on the Big Island's South Kona Coast. Call ☎ **808-328-2288** or visit www.nps.gov/puho.

✔ **Early July:** World-famous winemakers and chefs gather (along with appreciative gourmands) on Maui annually for the highly acclaimed — and appropriately grand — **Kapalua Wine & Food Festival.** This festival is a bounteous weeklong series of wine tastings, cooking demonstrations, and gourmet meals prepared by celebrity chefs. The event is well worth attending if you fancy yourself a foodie. Make your arrangements well in advance because this event is hugely popular. Call ☎ **800-KAPALUA** or visit www.kapaluamaui.com and click "Events" for details.

✔ **July 4:** Each island celebrates **Independence Day** with a variety of star-spangled accompaniments. But the best event of all is Turtle Independence Day at the Big Island's Mauna Lani Bay Hotel, in which scores of 3- and 4-year-old endangered green sea turtles, all raised in the shelter of the resort's historic fishponds, are released from captivity. Watching their race to the sea is a sight to behold — an epic celebration of freedom. Call the Mauna Lani at ☎ **808-885-6622** for this year's details.

✔ **July 4:** Discover Hawaii's buckin' bronco side at the **Parker Ranch Rodeo and Horse Races,** a full day of cowboy-themed fun in Waimea, heart of the Big Island's cattle country. Barbecue and foot-stompin' entertainment accompany the traditional rodeo events and relay horse races, where you'll see real-life *paniolos* (Hawaiian cowboys) in action. Call ☎ **808-885-2303** or go to www.parker ranch.com.

✔ **Third weekend in July:** The one-day **Prince Lot Hula Festival,** held annually at Honolulu's Moanalua Gardens, features authentic performances of ancient and modern hula, plus craft demonstrations, traditional island games, live music, and food vendors. This festival is a wonderful way to discover Hawaii's unique and fascinating culture — and it's absolutely free. Call ☎ **808-839-5334** for the exact date and other details.

✔ **Late July:** Koloa, the historic town just inland from Poipu Beach on Kauai's southern coast, celebrates its plantation past with **Koloa Plantation Days,** a week of events that includes a rodeo, a craft fair and block party, a traditional luau, historic walks, cooking demonstrations, and much more. Not necessarily worth planning your trip around, this down-home community event offers local-style fun if you happen to be in town. Call ☎ **808-822-0734** or visit www.koloa plantationdays.com for this year's schedule of events.

✔ **Late July and early August:** The annual **Hawaii International Jazz Festival** presents a weekend of first-class jazz at the Hawaii Theater Center in Honolulu, followed the next weekend by an equally stellar lineup at the Maui Arts & Cultural Center. The festival features evening concerts and daily jam sessions by jazz and blues artists of local, national, and international renown. An absolutely wonderful event! Call ☎ **808-528-0506** to purchase tickets in Honolulu or ☎ 808-242-7469 to buy tickets to Maui performances. The complete schedule is available at www.hawaiijazz.com.

✔ **Mid-August:** Hawaii's most prestigious fishing tournament, the **Annual Hawaiian International Billfish Tournament,** takes place in the sportfishing capital of the Pacific: Kailua-Kona, on the Big Island. Watching teams from around the globe show off their monster catches is thrilling. Call ☎ **808-329-6155** or visit www.kona billfish.com for this year's schedule.

✔ **Third Friday in August:** Hawaii became the 50th state on August 21, 1959, which is now celebrated as **Admissions Day** on the third Friday in August; all state-related facilities are closed.

✔ **Mid-September:** Running exactly 26.2 miles from Kahului to Kaanapali, the **Maui Marathon** is regularly named one of the ten most scenic marathons in North America. Call ☎ **808-871-6441** or visit www.mauimarathon.com for this year's date and entry information.

✔ **Mid-September through October:** 'Tis the season in Hawaii for statewide **Aloha Festivals.** Each week from mid-September through October is Aloha Week on a different island, with events running the gamut from parades and royal balls to ethnic days and street festivals. This is serious celebration time. My favorite is always Waikiki's street party, usually the first on the annual calendar. Most events are free with the purchase of a yellow "Aloha Festivals" ribbon (usually around $10); call ☎ **800-852-7690** or 808-589-1771 or go online to www.alohafestivals.com for details and a complete schedule of events.

✔ **Mid-September: Taste of Lahaina and the Best of Island Music** is Maui's biggest foodie event. Some 30,000 people flock to the Lahaiana Special Events Area to sample the signature dishes of Maui's top restaurantsthroughout this weekend festival, which also includes cooking demonstrations, wine tastings, and nonstop live entertainment. The weekend before the main event features Maui Chefs Present, an elegant $100-a-plate dinner and cocktail party featuring about a dozen of the island's best chefs. Call ☎ **888-310-1117** or visit www.visitlahaina.com for details.

✔ **Mid-September:** The **Sam Choy Poke Festival,** a three-day event held at the Big Island's Hapuna Beach Prince Hotel, is my favorite of Hawaii's culinary events, hands down. Top chefs from across Hawaii and the U.S. mainland as well as local amateurs compete in making Hawaiian *poke* (po-KAY), chopped raw fish mixed with seaweed and spices. Yum-yum!! Here's your chance to sample *poke* at its best. An invitational golf tourney is also part of the fun. Call ☎ **808-880-3424** or visit www.pokecontest.com for details.

✔ **Early October:** The **Maui County Fair** is Hawaii's oldest and largest county fair. Expect a parade, rides, games, exhibits, and live entertainment — all with an island twist, of course. The fair takes place at the Wailuku War Memorial Complex. Call ☎ **800-525-MAUI** or 808-242-2721 or visit www.calendarmaui.com for this year's details.

✔ **Mid-October:** The world's finest athletes converge on the Big Island's Kona-Kohala Coast every October to run (26.2 miles), swim (2.4 miles), and bike (112 miles) in one of the most prestigious events in all of sports, the punishing **Ironman Triathlon World Championship.** I'm not necessarily suggesting that you join in; participate instead by cheering on the contestants along the route. The best place to see the 7 a.m. start is along the seawall on Alii Drive in Kailua-Kona; get there before 5:30 a.m. for a prime spot. Alii Drive is also the best vantage for watching the bike and run portions; park on a side street and walk down to Alii because it's closed to traffic. To watch the finishers come in, line up along Alii Drive from Holualoa Street to the finish at Palani Road and Alii Drive; the winner can come as early as 2:30 p.m., and the course closes at midnight. The Ironman is usually held on the Saturday nearest the full moon; call ☎ **808-329-0063** or visit www.ironmanlive.com for this year's date and details. If you're not interested, you may want to avoid the Kona-Kohala Coast while Ironman is in swing.

✔ **Late October through early November:** The **Aloha Classic World Windsurfing Championships,** the final event in the Pro Boardsailing World Tour, is held at Maui's Hookipa Beach, universally considered to be the best windsurfing beach on the planet. These daredevils and their colorful sails are quite a sight to see as they pirouette over the wild winter waves; spectating is absolutely free. Call ☎ **808-573-6586** or check www.calendarmaui.com for this year's dates.

✔ **October 31:** Some 30,000 people show up to celebrate **Halloween** in Lahaina, Maui, an event so festive and popular that some call it the "Mardi Gras of the Pacific." Front Street is closed off from 4 p.m. to 2 a.m. for the costumed revelers and accompanying festivities; a children's parade launches the day. The Great Halloween Costume Contest takes place in Banyan Tree Park at 7 p.m. Lahaina is so gung ho on Halloween, in fact, that the party starts the week prior to October 31 with haunted houses and myriad events about town. Call ☎ **888-310-1117** or 808-667-9193, or visit www.visitlahaina. com, for this year's program of events.

✔ **Early November:** Hawaii's finest coffee-growing country celebrates the mighty bean with the **Kona Coffee Cultural Festival,** Hawaii's oldest food festival, held in Kailua-Kona on the Big Island. The weeklong series of fully caffeinated events includes a bean-picking contest, farm tours, lei contests, art and craft exhibits, live music, a parade, the Miss Kona Coffee pageant, and more. Call ☎ **808-326-7820** or visit www.konacoffeefest.com for this year's schedule.

✔ **First two weeks in November:** The only statewide film festival in the United States, the **Hawaii International Film Festival** specializes in films from Asia, the Pacific Islands, and North America. Most screenings and related events take place on Oahu, but the final weekend finds events on all the islands. Call ☎ **808-528-4433** or point your browser to www.hiff.org for more information.

✔ **November through December:** The **Vans Triple Crown of Surfing Series** is the World Series of professional big-wave surfing, the final stop on the ASP (Association of Surfing Professionals) World Tour. These daredevils put on a world-class thrill show, guaranteed, so don't miss the opportunity to watch. Events are held on the North Shore beaches of Oahu; the wave action determines the schedules. Call ☎ **808-638-7700** or visit www.triplecrownofsurfing.com, for the latest information; the Web site can also fill you in on additional surfing events throughout the islands.

✔ **Early December:** The winners of the PGA's biggest championship tournaments meet up at Kauai's Poipu Bay Resort Golf Course to lock horns at the **PGA Grand Slam of Golf.** Needless to say, you'll probably spot Tiger here. Call ☎ **800-PGA-TCKT** or 808-742-8711 or visit www.pgatour.com for all the details.

✔ **Mid-December:** More than 25,000 runners converge annually on Oahu for the **Honolulu Marathon,** one of the largest marathons in the world — and definitely one of its most scenic. Whether you're a potential participant or merely a spectator, call ☎ **808-734-7200** or go online to www.honolulumarathon.com for all the details. If you're not coming to Honolulu specifically to run in or watch the marathon, you may want to avoid Oahu entirely while it's on — hotels get booked up to capacity, and the island is overrun with out-of-towners.

✔ **Throughout December:** It's a holly, jolly **Christmas,** island style. The mayor of Honolulu says "Mele Kalikimaka" by throwing the switch to light up the 40-foot-tall Norfolk pine and other trees in front of Honolulu Hale, followed by the Electric Light Parade. On Maui, Santa arrives for the annual lighting of Lahaina's historic banyan tree, followed by Christmas caroling in Hawaiian. Schedules vary, so call ☎ **808-527-6060** for Oahu events, 888-310-1117 for Maui events. Every island is bedecked in holiday finery throughout the month.

Part II
Planning Your Trip to Hawaii

© RICHTENNANT

HAWAIIAN RESORT ACTIVITY TO AVOID

SWIM WITH THE GIANT SQUID

SWIM WITH THE MORAY EELS

SWIM WITH THE JELLYFISH

SWIM WITH OCTOPUS

" SINCE WE LOST THE DOLPHINS, BUSINESS HASN'T BEEN QUITE THE SAME."

In this part . . .

The information in the following chapters make the nitty-gritty details of planning your trip to Hawaii as painless as possible. I show you how to get a handle on your expenses, help you weigh the pros and cons of buying a package deal, and walk you through booking your hotel and rental car. One chapter evens offers savvy advice for travelers with special needs, whether you have a disability, you're traveling with little ones, or you're trying to plan a memorable Hawaiian wedding. Before this part ends, I also help you gather all the loose ends together into one organized bunch.

Chapter 5

Managing Your Money

In This Chapter

▶ Thinking about your major expenses
▶ Using AAA and American Express memberships to your advantage
▶ Zeroing in on cost-cutting tips

"So, how much is this trip to Hawaii going to cost me, anyway?"

It's a reasonable question, no matter where you fall on the income ladder. A vacation is always a considerable endeavor, with costs that can add up before you know it — and, as destinations go, Hawaii is a relatively pricey one. So you'll want to plan ahead to keep your budget on track. In this chapter, I tell you what to expect and offer you tips that can help you save big bucks on major expenses.

Planning Your Budget

The good news is that you can easily structure a Hawaii trip to suit any budget. Airfare and hotels will probably end up being your largest cash outlays. Other things, like rental cars, are relatively cheap in Hawaii.

Your choice of activities also determines how much you spend: Relaxing on the beach or taking in Hawaii's natural beauty generally doesn't cost a dime. But guided tours and organized activities — like snorkel trips and helicopter rides during the day, luaus and dinner cruises after dark — can carry surprisingly hefty price tags (see Table 5-1).

Transportation

The cost of your flight to Hawaii will be one of your top two expenses (right up there with hotels). Airfares are almost impossible to predict and can change at the drop of a hat. Still, to give you an idea of what to expect, here's a sampling of potential fares from season to season: If you're going to Hawaii in the off-season — say, May or maybe October — you may be able to snag a round-trip ticket for as little as $400 or $500 from San Francisco or Los Angeles or $800 to $900 from the East Coast. If you're traveling in the high season (late December to April, or in summer), you'll pay more — probably in the $500 to $800 range from the West Coast and between $700 and $1,400 from back east.

Expect to pay more if you're departing from a city that's not a major airline hub. You may also pay a premium if you fly into a neighbor island airport — into Maui or Kona on the Big Island, for example — rather than Honolulu, but not always. If you're traveling to Hawaii over the Christmas holidays, expect to pay full fare.

You can score any number of money-saving deals, especially if you consider an all-inclusive package. (See Chapter 6 for more details on travel packages.) I also tell you how to save on airfares in that chapter.

Interisland flights

If you plan to visit more than one island at any time during your stay, you'll need to take an interisland flight. Fares for one-way trips between the islands, which are run through Aloha Airlines and Hawaiian Airlines, average about $106 in the high season. However, you rarely need to pay full fare. Numerous sales and special Internet-only fares are frequently available; one-way fares were available for around $70 at press time. See Chapter 7 for details.

Car rentals

Rental cars are relatively cheap in the islands. You can often get a compact for as little as $28 to $38 a day, sometimes even less if you hit on a bargain. If you need a family-size car, expect to pay more on the order of $35 to $50 per day, depending on where you're staying and the time of year you're booking. Of course, everybody wants a convertible in the islands, so expect to pay upward of $75 a day in season for one. (You can sometimes wheel and deal for one at the rental counter in the low season, when business is slower.) Weekly rates almost always save you a bundle.

Do yourself a favor and book a rental car with unlimited mileage. You'll be doing plenty of driving no matter which island you're on, and you don't want to end up paying for your rental on a per-mile basis. Trust me — you'll end up on the short end of this stick. Luckily, most of the major car-rental companies rent on an unlimited-miles basis. Be sure to confirm this policy when you book.

And because you'll probably cover a good deal of ground, don't forget to factor in gas, which is typically more expensive in Hawaii than on the mainland. (It's even higher on the neighbor islands than it is on Oahu.) Also remember to account for any additional insurance costs, which generally run an extra $10 to $15 a day, depending on the coverage you select. Parking, thankfully, is generally free (although most Waikiki hotels and many luxury resort hotels throughout the islands charge a daily fee for parking; check when you book).

You'll seldom save by waiting to rent your car; generally, prices only go up as your pick-up date approaches — especially in the busy travel seasons. Book as far in advance as possible for the best rate. Also see "Cutting Costs — But Not the Fun," later in this chapter, for additional money-saving tips.

You may not have to worry about shopping around or wrangling a lower rate on a car rental. Often, rental cars and interisland flights are part-and-parcel of a package deal. In many hotel and airline packages, they're thrown in for a nominal fee or for free. See Chapter 7 for more details.

Lodging

Hawaii has a wealth of luxury hotels and resorts, but it also offers plenty of affordable choices — especially on the condo market. Still, although you can find decent hotel rooms for $100 or so a night, you really shouldn't expect to pay much less than that. After you start adding on amenities — kitchenettes, room service, ocean views — expect room rates to climb from there.

The good news is that you can score very reasonable rates on a per-person basis if you're traveling in a group or with your family. Hawaii boasts lots of apartment-style condos that sleep four or more at very reasonable prices — between $100 and $150 per night on the bottom end, and $200 or more for quite luxurious digs. Of course, if you stay at a condo, you'll likely miss out on resort-style amenities and services — concierge, room service, kids' programs, and the like — but it may be worth it to you if you want to have more room to spread out, keep costs down, and enjoy the convenience of having a kitchen.

I've taken care to recommend a range of lodging choices in each of the destinations covered in this book to give you plenty to choose from, no matter what your needs or budget. The good news is that you rarely have to pay full rack rate for any hotel — you can find numerous ways to save. For one thing, booking a package deal can be a huge money saver when it comes to hotels; for more information on packages, see Chapter 6. For additional cost-cutting measures, see "Cutting Costs — But Not the Fun," later in this chapter.

So that you don't encounter any unwanted surprises at payment time, be sure to account for the 11.41 percent in taxes that will be added to your final hotel bill when planning your budget.

Dining

Hawaii has become something of a culinary mecca in the last few years, with each island boasting its own slate of top-quality restaurants — often charging top-dollar prices. So think about your bottom line. Many of you, no doubt, look forward to indulging in the island's bounty and won't mind paying for the privilege. But if you'd rather spend your vacation dollars on other activities and attractions, the islands offer plenty of opportunities to dine on the cheap: You can spend as little as $5 to $7 for breakfast (a continental breakfast may even be included in your hotel deal), grab a quick-and-easy lunch for around $10, and enjoy a casual dinner for $15 to $20. (Of course, extra niceties like wine or cocktails will drive up dinner costs quickly.)

Restaurant bills can add up fast, so if you want to save in this category, I strongly suggest booking a room or condo with kitchen facilities. By preparing a few daytime meals yourself (breakfast, in particular, can be a big money saver, and it's often convenient to pack sandwiches to take to the beach), you'll be in a better position to splurge on a great dinner. Kitchen facilities are a virtual must if you're traveling with kids.

Sightseeing and activities

Here's where the bills can really start to pile up, especially if you're traveling with the family — but it ultimately depends on what you want to do. If you're coming to Hawaii to simply kick back at the beach and leave your mainland worries behind, you won't have to budget much in this category because going to the beach is free. Even snorkel gear rentals are cheap.

But if you're planning to schedule some organized activities and tours — which I strongly suggest you do — plan ahead to see what your budget can handle because they can get pricey. Expect to pay $60 to $80 per person for your average snorkel cruise, and even more for your average luau. Helicopter rides can easily run more than $100 a head. Budget-minded golfers may want to think twice before they tee up — tee times at Hawaii's top courses don't come cheap.

This book lists exact prices for activities, entertainment, tee times, admission fees, and the like in the following chapters so that you can budget your money realistically. If there's a way to snag a bargain, I include that information, too.

Shopping and nightlife

These two areas are the most flexible parts of your budget. Shopping is a huge temptation in Hawaii. But if money is an issue, do yourself a favor and bypass the souvenirs.

The islands aren't overloaded with nightlife options; Oahu and Maui are the liveliest in terms of after-dark diversions. You can easily avoid racking up the bills in these categories if shopping and/or evening entertainment isn't a high priority for you.

Table 5-1	What Things Cost in Hawaii
Item/Activity	*Price*
An average cup of coffee	$1.25
Compact rental car on Oahu (per day)	$28
Convertible rental car on Maui (per day)	$62
All-day ticket aboard the Waikiki Trolley	$25
Admission to the Bishop Museum (Oahu)	$25
Helicopter tour	$125 to $280
Fair Wind snorkel cruise to Kealakekua Bay (Big Island)	$59 to $89
A day at the beach	Free!
Luxury room for two at Princeville Resort Kauai	$450 to $675
Moderate room for two at the Kaanapali Beach Hotel (Maui)	$169 to $300
Rainforest cottage for two or four at Carson's Volcano Cottages, breakfast included (Big Island)	$105 to $155
Budget oceanfront condo for two or four at Wailua Bay View (Kauai)	$110 to $120
Gourmet dinner for two at Alan Wong's (Oahu)	$150
Oceanfront dinner for two at Hula Grill (Maui)	$150
Casual dinner for two at Cafe Pesto (Big Island)	$40
Burgers for two at Duane's Ono Char Burger (Kauai)	$10

Cutting Costs — But Not the Fun

I don't care how much money you have — nobody wants to spend more than they have to. In this section, I give you some tips on how to avoid spending more of your hard-earned cash than is necessary.

Getting the best airfares

Getting the best fares on both trans-Pacific and interisland air travel is such a huge topic that I dedicate the better part of a chapter to it. Before you even start scanning for fares, see Chapter 6. That chapter also discusses how to find money-saving package deals.

Avoiding paying full price for your hotel room

There's often a huge gap between hotels' official "published" (full-price, or rack) rates and what you actually pay, so don't be scared off at first glance. What's more, savvy travelers can find ways to further widen the margin.

More often than not, the best way to score a cheap hotel room is to buy an all-inclusive travel package that includes airfare, hotel, and car, and sometimes other extras, in one low price; for details on scoring a good-value package, see Chapter 6.

The second-best way to avoid paying the full rack rate when booking your hotel is stunningly simple: Just ask the reservation agent for a cheaper or discounted rate. You may be pleasantly surprised — I've been, many times. But you have to take the initiative and ask because no one is going to *volunteer* to save you money.

Here are a few more potentially money-saving tips:

✔ **Rates are generally lowest in spring and fall.** The time of year you decide to visit may affect your bargaining power more than anything else. During the peak seasons — basically mid-December through mid-April and summer — when a hotel is booked up, management is less likely to extend heavily discounted rates or package deals. In the slower seasons — generally mid-April through mid-June and September through mid-December — when capacity is down, they're often willing to negotiate; in fact, many places drop rates by 10 to 30 percent automatically in the less busy times of year. If you haven't decided when you want to visit Hawaii yet, see Chapter 4.

✔ **Membership in AAA, AARP, or frequent flier/traveler programs often qualifies you for discounted rates.** (For details on joining AAA, see "The AAA advantage" sidebar, later in this chapter.) You may also qualify for corporate or student discounts. Attention, seniors: You may even qualify for discounts even if you're not an AARP member (although I highly recommend joining; see Chapter 9 for details). Members of the military or those with government jobs may also qualify for price breaks.

✔ **Inquire about the hotel's own package deals.** Even if you're not traveling on an all-inclusive package (see Chapter 6), you may be able to take advantage of packages offered by hotels, resorts, and condos directly. They often include such value-added extras as a free rental car, champagne and in-room breakfast for honeymooners, free dinners, discounted tee times or spa treatments, a room upgrade, an extra night thrown in for free (sometimes the fifth, sometimes the seventh), or some other freebie. I note what kinds of discounts are typically available in my hotel reviews. Properties usually list these deals on their Web sites, but not always, so it never hurts to ask additional questions about available specials.

- ✔ **If you're booking a hotel that belongs to a chain, call the hotel directly in addition to going through central reservations.** See which one gives you the better deal. Sometimes, the local reservationist knows about packages or special rates, but the hotel may neglect to tell the central booking line.

- ✔ **Surf the Web to save.** A surprising number of hotels advertise great packages via their Web sites, and some even offer Internet-only special rates.

  In addition to surfing the hotel's own sites, you may want to try using a general travel booking site like **Expedia.com, Travelocity.com, Hotels.com,** or **Orbitz.com** to book your hotel or a pay-one-price package that also includes airfare. Acting much like airline consolidators, these sites can sometimes offer big discounts on rooms as well. See Chapter 8 for a more complete discussion of how to use the Web to find a great hotel bargain.

- ✔ **Ask innkeepers for a break.** Bed-and-breakfasts are generally non-negotiable on price. Sometimes, however, you can negotiate a discount for longer stays, such as a week or more. You may also be able to score a price break if you're visiting off-season. And some do offer AAA and senior discounts. Remember that it never hurts to ask, politely.

- ✔ **Look for price breaks and value-added extras when booking condos.** Condos are usually pretty flexible on rates. They tend to offer discounts on multinight stays, and many throw in a free rental car to sweeten the deal. Some condo properties have units handled by multiple management companies; if that's the case, call both companies and see which one offers you the better deal. You may also want to check with **Hawaii Condo Exchange** (☎ **800-442-0404** or 323-436-0300; www.hawaiicondoexchange.com), which acts as a consolidator for condo properties throughout the islands.

Cutting other costs

Here are a few more useful money-saving tips:

- ✔ **Consult a reliable travel agent.** A travel agent can often negotiate a better price with certain hotels and assemble a better valued travel package than you can get on your own. In fact, in a recent *Condé Nast Traveler* investigation, travel agents could always price out Hawaii resort vacations more cheaply than any other outlet (including airline packagers). Even if you book your own airfare, you may want to contact a travel agent to price out your hotel.

  On the other hand, hotels, condos, and even B&Bs are sometimes willing to discount your rate as much as 30 percent — the amount they'd otherwise pay an agent in commissions — if you book direct. It may make sense to base your decision about using a travel agent on time rather than money — think of a travel agent as a convenience. If you do use a travel agent, it makes sense to be an informed consumer, going into the process with a general idea of what things cost so you'll know whether you're getting a bargain. A good first step is consulting this book so that you know which hotels appeal to you and their approximate costs. And don't let an agent steer you to a hotel that's not right for you just because he or she may be getting a better commission. If you sense that your agent isn't working hard to line up a trip that really suits your desires, move on and find someone else.

✔ **Surf the Web to save on your rental car, too.** In addition to surfing rental car agencies' own sites, you might try comparing rates through a general travel booking site like **Expedia.com, Travelocity.com, Orbitz.com,** or **Sidestep.com.** This one-stop-shopping method can save you more than money — it can save you time, too.

✔ **Don't rent a gas guzzler.** Renting a smaller car is cheaper, and you save on gas to boot (an especially important point, because gas prices are always higher in Hawaii than on the mainland). Unless you're traveling with a large group, don't go beyond the economy size.

See Chapter 7 for more money-saving tips to keep in mind while booking your island wheels.

✔ **Reserve a hotel room with a kitchenette, or a condo with a full kitchen, and do your own cooking.** You may miss the pampering that room service provides, but you can save lots of money. Even if you prepare only breakfast and an occasional picnic lunch in the kitchen, you'll save significantly in the long run. Plus, if the beach is right outside your door, you won't ever have to leave it to go on restaurant runs.

✔ **Skip the ocean views or stay away from the ocean altogether.** Being steps away from the surf is wonderful, but you'll pay through the nose for the privilege: Oceanview rooms are the most expensive rooms in any hotel, especially those on the upper floors. Mountain or garden views are usually much cheaper — and they make sense if you don't plan on hanging out in your room much, anyway. A stay in a hotel that's located a few blocks from the beach, especially in Waikiki, can be even cheaper. For more on this subject, see Chapter 8.

✔ **Ask whether the kids can stay in your room.** Or, better yet, book a condo with a sleeper sofa in the living room or a separate bedroom. A room with two double beds usually doesn't cost any more than one with a king-size bed, and most hotels don't charge an extra-person rate if the additional person is a kid. If that's a bit too much togetherness for you, book one of the many one-, two-, or three-bedroom condos that are available throughout the islands. These full apartments are often no more expensive than your standard hotel room — and they're always cheaper than having to book two or more hotel rooms. What's more, they solve the expensive eating-out-at-every-meal problem, too.

The AAA advantage

If you aren't already a member, consider taking a few minutes to join the American Automobile Association (AAA) before you launch your Hawaii vacation. In addition to providing you with a wealth of trip-planning services, membership can save you big bucks on hotel rates, car rentals, interisland airfares, and even admission to attractions in Hawaii.

The AAA Travel Agency can help you book air, hotel, and car arrangements as well as all-inclusive tour packages to Hawaii. Membership in AAA can also give you a full 25 percent savings on interisland flights with Aloha Airlines and let you qualify for hotel discounts of 10 percent or more. Discounts and benefits at 3,000 attractions and restaurants and 44,000 retail locations nationwide are available through AAA's Show Your Card and Save program. And don't forget the free maps — they're comprehensive, indispensable, and absolutely free to members.

I hate to sound like a shill, but you really can't go wrong with AAA. Whether it's a discount at an Outrigger hotel or a stress-relieving flat-tire fix, membership will pay itself back before you know it. Annual membership fees vary slightly depending on your home region, but you can expect to spend around $55 per individual (primary member) and $25 to $30 for each additional family member.

To find the AAA office nearest you, look in the phone book under "AAA" or log on to www.aaa.com, where you can link up to your regional club's home page after you enter your home zip code. You can even get instant membership by calling the national 24-hour emergency roadside service number (☎ 800-AAA-HELP), which can connect you to any regional membership department during expanded business hours (only roadside assistance operates 24 hours a day). If you're a resident of Canada, similar services (plus reciprocal benefits with AAA) are offered by the Canadian Automobile Association (www.caa.com).

After you arrive in Hawaii, the local office is in Honolulu at 1270 Ala Moana Blvd., between Piikoi Street and Ward Centre (☎ 800-736-2886 or 808-593-2221; www.aaa-hawaii.com). The office is open Monday through Friday from 9 a.m. to 5 p.m., and Saturday from 9 a.m. to 2 p.m. Roadside assistance is available on Oahu, Maui, the Big Island, and Kauai.

✔ **Remember that it doesn't take much luxury to make Hawaii feel like paradise.** To find true Hawaii happiness, the rule is always this: The simpler, the better. You don't need a 27-inch TV, 24-hour butler service, or a telephone in the bathroom to be happy here. So when reserving your accommodations, don't overdo it by booking a place that taxes your budget too much. Save that extra dough for having fun!

✔ **Skip the souvenirs.** I've heard it more than once: "That whale print that looked so right in the art gallery was all wrong back in my living room in Cincinnati." Spend your money on memories, not tchotchkes.

> ✔ **Look out for the Bargain Alert icon as you read this book.** This icon alerts you to money-saving opportunities and especially good values as you travel throughout Hawaii.

Handling Money

You're the best judge of how much cash you feel comfortable carrying or what alternative form of currency is your favorite. That's not going to change much on your vacation. True, you'll probably be moving around more and incurring more expenses than you generally do, and you may let your mind slip into vacation gear and not be as vigilant about your safety as when you're in work mode. But, those factors aside, the only type of payment that won't be quite as available to you away from home is your personal checkbook.

Using ATMs and carrying cash

The easiest and best way to get cash away from home is from an ATM (automated teller machine). The **Cirrus** (☎ **800-424-4787;** www.master card.com) and **PLUS** (☎ **800-843-7587;** www.visa.com) networks span the globe; look at the back of your bank card to see which network you're on and then call or check online for ATM locations at your destination. Make sure that you know your personal identification number (PIN) before you leave home and find out your daily withdrawal limit before you depart.

Also keep in mind that many banks impose a fee every time your card is used at a different bank's ATM. On top of this, the bank from which you withdraw cash may charge its own fee. (To compare banks' ATM fees within the U.S., use www.bankrate.com.) To beat these fees (and to avoid wasting precious vacation time running errands), it makes sense to withdraw larger sums rather than relying on lots of smaller withdrawals.

Charging ahead with credit cards

Credit cards are a safe way to carry money: They also provide a convenient record of all your expenses, and for foreign visitors, they generally offer relatively good exchange rates.

You can also withdraw cash advances from your credit cards at banks or ATMs, provided you know your PIN. If you've forgotten yours, or didn't even know you had one, call the number on the back of your credit card and ask the bank to send it to you. It usually takes five to seven business days, though some banks will provide the number over the phone if you tell them your mother's maiden name or some other personal information. But keep in mind that cash advances are a bad idea, only to be used in case of emergency. Your issuing bank will start charging interest from the day you make the withdrawal, usually at significantly higher rates than you're charged on regular purchases.

Some credit-card companies recommend that you notify them of any impending trip so that they don't become suspicious when the card is used numerous times in a new destination and block your charges. Even if you don't call your credit-card company in advance, you can always call the card's toll-free emergency number if a charge is refused — another good reason to carry the phone number with you.

It's a good idea to carry more than one card with you on your trip; a card might not work for any number of reasons, so having a backup is the smart way to go.

Toting traveler's checks

These days, it's so easy to find a 24-hour ATM that traveler's checks are becoming obsolete. Still, if you like the security of traveler's checks, and you don't mind showing identification every time you want to cash one, you may prefer to stick with the tried-and-true.

You can get traveler's checks at almost any bank. **American Express** offers denominations of $20, $50, $100, $500, and (for cardholders only) $1,000. You pay a service charge ranging from 1 to 4 percent (which negates any money you might have saved by avoiding fees for using other banks' ATMs while you're on the road). You can also get American Express traveler's checks over the phone by calling ☎ **800-221-7282;** Amex gold and platinum cardholders who use this number are exempt from the 1 percent fee.

Visa offers traveler's checks at Citibank locations nationwide, as well as at several other banks. The service charge ranges between 1.5 and 2 percent; checks come in denominations of $20, $50, $100, $500, and $1,000. Call ☎ **800-732-1322** for information. **AAA** members can obtain Visa checks without a fee at most AAA offices or by calling ☎ **866-339-3378.** **MasterCard** also offers traveler's checks. Call ☎ **800-223-9920** for a location near you.

If you choose to carry traveler's checks, keep a record of their serial numbers separate from your checks in the event that they're stolen or lost. You'll get a refund faster if you know the numbers.

Dealing with a lost or stolen wallet

Be sure to contact all of your credit-card companies the minute you discover your wallet has been lost or stolen and file a report at the nearest police precinct. Your credit-card company or insurer may require a police report number or record of the loss. Most credit-card companies have an emergency toll-free number to call if your card is lost or stolen; they may be able to wire you a cash advance immediately or deliver an emergency credit card in a day or two. Call the following emergency numbers in the United States:

  ✔ **American Express:** ☎ **800-221-7282** (for cardholders and traveler's check holders)

  ✔ **MasterCard:** ☎ **800-307-7309** or 636-722-7111

  ✔ **Visa:** ☎ **800-847-2911** or 410-581-9994

For other credit cards, call the toll-free number directory at ☎ **800-555-1212.**

If you need emergency cash over the weekend when all banks and American Express offices are closed, you can have money wired to you via **Western Union** (☎ **800-325-6000;** www.westernunion.com).

Identity theft or fraud are potential complications of losing your wallet, especially if you've lost your driver's license along with your cash and credit cards. Notify the major credit-reporting bureaus immediately; placing a fraud alert on your records may protect you against liability for criminal activity. The three major U.S. credit-reporting agencies are **Equifax** (☎ **800-766-0008;** www.equifax.com), **Experian** (☎ **888-397-3742;** www.experian.com), and **TransUnion** (☎ **800-680-7289;** www.transunion.com).

Finally, if you've lost all forms of photo ID, call your airline and explain the situation; it may allow you to board the plane if you have a copy of your passport or birth certificate and a copy of the police report you've filed.

Chapter 6

Getting to Hawaii

● ●

In This Chapter
▶ Finding the best airfares
▶ Considering a tour
▶ Taking advantage of package deals

● ●

*G*etting there may not *really* be half the fun, but it's a necessary
step — and a big part of the planning process. How can you beat
the high cost of transpacific airfares? Should you reserve a package
deal or book the elements of your vacation separately?

In this chapter, I give you all the information you need to make the
decision that's right for you.

Flying to Hawaii

The majority of transpacific flights arrive at Oahu's Honolulu International Airport, but an increasing number land directly on the bigger
neighbor islands — Maui, the Big Island, and Kauai.

The following major airlines fly between mainland North America and
one or more of Hawaii's major airports:

✔ **Air Canada** (☎ **888-247-2262;** www.aircanada.ca) flies from
Toronto and Vancouver to Oahu's Honolulu International Airport
and Maui's Kahului Airport.

✔ **Aloha Airlines** (☎ **800-367-5250;** www.alohaair.com), one
of Hawaii's two major interisland carriers, flies from Oakland,
Sacramento, Burbank (CA), Orange County (CA), Phoenix, Las
Vegas, Reno, and Vancouver to Honolulu, Maui, and the Big
Island's Kona International Airport. You can also make a connec-
tion to any neighbor island on Aloha.

✔ **American Airlines** (☎ **800-433-7300;** www.americanair.com)
flies from Chicago, St. Louis, Dallas, San Francisco, San Jose, and
Los Angeles to Honolulu, Maui, Kauai, and Kona on the Big Island.

- ✔ **American Trans Air (ATA; ☎ 800-225-2995;** www.ata.com) flies from Phoenix, Seattle, Los Angeles, and San Francisco to Honolulu and Maui.

- ✔ **Continental Airlines (☎ 800-525-0280;** www.continental.com) is the only airline to fly nonstop from New York (actually Newark) to Honolulu. The company also has service from Houston, Seattle, and Los Angeles to Honolulu. Continental has a code-sharing relationship with Hawaiian Airlines.

- ✔ **Delta Airlines (☎ 800-221-1212;** www.delta.com) flies direct from Atlanta, Houston, Cincinnati, San Francisco, and Los Angeles to Honolulu and Maui.

- ✔ **Hawaiian Airlines (☎ 800-367-5320;** www.hawaiianair.com) flies from Seattle, Portland, Sacramento, Las Vegas, Phoenix, Los Angeles, Ontario (east of L.A.), and San Diego to Honolulu and Maui, where you can make a Hawaiian Airlines connection to any neighbor island.

- ✔ **Northwest Airlines (☎ 800-225-2525;** www.nwa.com) flies from Minneapolis, Detroit, Los Angeles, and Seattle to Honolulu.

- ✔ **United Airlines (☎ 800-241-6522;** www.ual.com) flies direct from Chicago's O'Hare, Los Angeles, and San Francisco to Honolulu, Maui, Kona on the Big Island, and Kauai's Lihue Airport.

Getting the best airfare

Competition among the major U.S. airlines is unlike that of any other industry. Every airline offers virtually the same product (basically, a coach seat is a coach seat is a . . .), yet prices can vary by hundreds of dollars.

Business travelers who need to purchase their tickets at the last minute, change their itinerary at a moment's notice, or want to get home before the weekend pay the premium rate, known as the *full fare*. Passengers whose travel agenda is more flexible — who can book their tickets far in advance, who don't mind staying Saturday night, or who are willing to travel on a Tuesday, Wednesday, or Thursday — pay the least, usually a fraction of the full fare. On most flights to Hawaii, even the shortest hops, the full fare is more than $1,000, but a 7-day or 14-day advance-purchase ticket from the West Coast is often closer to $500 or $600. Obviously, I can't guarantee what fares will be when you book, but you can almost always save big by planning ahead.

Keep your eye out in the newspaper, on the Internet, and on TV for airfare sales. Sale fares carry advance-purchase requirements and date-of-travel restrictions, but the price is usually worth the restrictions: sometimes no more than $400 for a transpacific flight from the West Coast to Hawaii. The sales tend to take place in seasons of low travel volume (usually spring and fall). You'll almost never see a sale around the peak summer vacation months or in the winter high season.

Here are a few tips that can help you save on airfares:

✔ **Travel on off days of the week.** Airfares vary depending on the day of the week. Everybody wants to travel on the weekend; if you can travel on a Tuesday, Wednesday, or Thursday, you may find cheaper flights to Hawaii. When you inquire about airfares, ask whether you can get a cheaper rate by flying on a different day. Remember, too, that staying over on a Saturday night can cut your airfare.

✔ **Reserve your flight well in advance.** Take advantage of advance-purchase fares — or watch the last-minute "e-fares" online for bargains. (See the section "Booking your flight online," later in this chapter, for a discussion of online strategies.)

✔ **Fly direct to the island of your choice to save on interisland airfares.** The Big Island, Maui, and Kauai all receive direct flights from the mainland. (See the list of carriers in the section "Flying to Hawaii," earlier in this chapter.) It's not always possible to fly to or from the neighbor island of your choice; it all depends on the transpacific carrier you choose and your origination point. But look into it if your island-hopping itinerary dictates — because doing so can save you a few hours, not to mention the additional cost of an interisland flight (see Chapter 7).

Booking your flight online

The "big three" online travel agencies — **Expedia** (www.expedia.com), **Travelocity** (www.travelocity.com), and **Orbitz** (www.orbitz.com) — sell most of the air tickets bought on the Internet. (Canadian travelers should try www.expedia.ca and www.travelocity.ca; U.K. residents can go for expedia.co.uk and opodo.co.uk.) Each has different business deals with the airlines and may offer different fares on the same flights, so shopping around is wise. Expedia and Travelocity also send you an **e-mail notification** when a cheap fare becomes available to your favorite destination. All of these online travel agencies also purport to save you money with pay-one-price packaging — which is really becoming their key business, particularly at Expedia — although I suggest comparing the prices of each piece before you assume that you're saving.

Of the smaller travel agency Web sites, **SideStep** (www.sidestep.com) receives good reviews from users. It's a browser add-on that purports to "search 140 sites at once," but in reality only beats competitors' fares as often as other sites do.

If you're willing to give up some control over your flight details, use an *opaque fare service* like **Priceline** (www.priceline.com) or Expedia's own **Hotwire** (www.hotwire.com). Both offer rock-bottom prices in exchange for travel on a "mystery airline" at a mysterious time of day, often with a mysterious change of planes en route. The mystery airlines are all major, well-known carriers — and the possibility of being sent from Phoenix to Honolulu via Tampa is remote, but your chances of getting a 6 a.m. or 11 p.m. flight are pretty high. Hotwire tells you flight prices before you buy; Priceline usually has better deals than Hotwire, but you have to play their "name our price" game. *Note:* In 2004, Priceline added non-opaque service to its roster. You now have the option to pick exact flights, times, and airlines from a list of offers — or you can bid on opaque fares as before.

Great last-minute deals are also available directly from the airlines themselves through a free e-mail service called *E-savers.* Each week, the airline sends you a list of discounted flights, usually leaving the upcoming Friday or Saturday and returning the following Monday or Tuesday. You can sign up for all the major airlines at one time by logging on to **Smarter Living** (www.smarterliving.com), or you can go to each individual airline's Web site. Airline sites also offer schedules, flight booking, and information on late-breaking bargains.

Using a consolidator

Consolidators, also known as bucket shops, are a good place to find low fares, often below even the airlines' discounted rates. Basically, these companies are just big travel agents that get discounts for buying in bulk and pass some of the savings on to you.

Bucket shop tickets are usually nonrefundable or rigged with stiff cancellation penalties, often as high as 50 to 75 percent of the ticket price, and some put you on charter airlines with questionable safety records.

Some of the most reliable consolidators include the following:

- ✔ **AirSaver** (☎ 888-346-5795; www.airsaver.com) is an online consolidator that currently specializes in international fares, but it was offering some very good deals on transpacific round-trips at this writing.

- ✔ **Cheap Tickets** (☎ 888-922-8849; www.cheaptickets.com) was originally founded in Honolulu (though it has since closed its Hawaii offices since being acquired by Cendant). I almost always do better by calling than I do by pricing out fares on its Web site.

- ✔ **1-800-FLY-CHEAP** (www.1800flycheap.com) is owned by package-holiday megalith MyTravel and is known for good fares to sunny destinations, so it's worth checking, but I've yet to find an unbeatable fare to Hawaii here.

- ✔ **STA Travel** (☎ 800-226-8624 or 800-781-4040; www.statravel.com), the world's leader in student travel, offers good fares for travelers of all ages.

- ✔ **TFI Tours International** (☎ 800-745-8000 or 212-736-1140; www.lowestairprice.com) serves as a clearinghouse for unused seats on most of the world's major airlines.

- ✔ **Travel Avenue** (☎ 800-333-3335; www.travelavenue.com) is an online travel agency willing to rebate part of its commissions to you; this rebate can sometimes save you as much as 7 percent over what you'd pay through another agent.

✔ **The TravelHub** (www.travelhub.com) represents nearly 1,000 travel agencies, many of whom offer consolidator and discount fares.

Some of these consolidators can also save you money on hotels and car rentals as well.

Joining an Escorted Tour

Pay-one-price discount package tours are one thing, but escorted tours are a different animal altogether. Hawaii is such a foolproof place to visit — and its magic is so dependent on relaxing leisure time — that I strongly recommend traveling on your own rather than signing on to an escorted tour.

If you really prefer to be led around, however, or if you're not able to drive yourself, you may want to consider an escorted tour.

 If you decide to go with an escorted tour, buying travel insurance is a good idea, especially if the tour operator asks to you pay up front. But don't buy your coverage from the tour operator! If the tour operator doesn't fulfill its obligation to provide you with the vacation you paid for, there's no reason to think that it'll fulfill its insurance obligations either. Get travel insurance through an independent agency. (See Chapter 10 for the ins and outs of travel insurance.)

When choosing an escorted tour, be sure to find out whether you're required to put down a deposit and when final payment is due. Also ask a few more simple questions before you buy:

✔ **What is the cancellation policy?** Can the tour operator cancel the trip if it doesn't get enough people? How late can you cancel if you're unable to go? Do you get a refund if you cancel? If the operator cancels?

✔ **How jam-packed is the schedule?** Does the tour schedule try to fit 25 hours into a 24-hour day, or does it give you ample time to relax by the pool or shop? If getting up at 7 a.m. every day and not returning to your hotel until 6 or 7 p.m. sounds like a grind, certain escorted tours may not be for you.

✔ **How large is the group?** The smaller the group, the less time you spend waiting for people to get on and off the bus. Tour operators may be evasive about this information, because they may not know the exact size of the group until everybody has made reservations, but they should be able to give you a rough estimate.

✔ **What exactly is included?** Don't assume anything. You may have to pay to get yourself to and from the airport. A box lunch may be included in an excursion, but drinks may be extra.

> ✔ **How much flexibility do you have?** Can you opt out of certain activities, or does the bus leave once a day, with no exceptions? Are all your meals planned in advance?

The escorted trips offered by **Tauck Tours** (☎ 800-788-7885; www.tauck.com) are far more luxurious and less structured than your average escorted tour; they're pricey, but worth it if you'd rather put someone else in charge of the itinerary. If you're looking for more affordable options, try sister companies **Globus** (☎ 866-755-8581; www.globusjourneys.com) and **Cosmos** (☎ 800-276-1241; www.cosmosvacations.com); Globus offers more luxurious vacations, while Cosmos is more price-savvy. Both are excellent companies. **Perillo Tours** (☎ 800-431-1515; www.perillotours.com) also offers midpriced multi-island tours.

Choosing a Pay-One-Price Package

Comprehensive, pay-one-price travel packages are often the smart way to go when booking your Hawaii vacation. Besides the convenience of having all your travel needs taken care of at once, a package can often save you lots of money. In many cases, a package tour that includes airfare, hotel, and transportation to and from the airport costs less than the hotel alone if you book it yourself.

One reason for this savings is that packages are sold in bulk to tour operators, who resell them to the public. It's kind of like buying your vacation at a buy-in-bulk store — except the tour operator is the one who buys the 1,000-count box of garbage bags and resells them 10 at a time at a cost that undercuts the local supermarket.

Package trips can vary as much as those garbage bags, too. Some offer a better class of hotels than others; others provide the same hotels for lower prices. Some book flights on scheduled airlines; others sell charters. In some packages, your choice of accommodations and travel days may be limited. Some let you choose between escorted vacations and independent vacations; others allow you to add on just a few excursions or escorted daytrips (also at discounted prices) without booking an entirely escorted tour.

Every destination, including Hawaii, usually has a few packagers (tour operators) that are better than the rest because they buy in even bigger bulk. The time you spend shopping around is likely to be well rewarded.

Finding a package tour

To find package tours, check out the travel section of your local Sunday newspaper or the ads in the back of national travel magazines such as *Travel & Leisure, National Geographic Traveler, Arthur Frommer's Budget Travel,* and *Condé Nast Traveler.* Online, check out **Expedia** (www.expedia.com), **Travelocity** (www.travelocity.com), and **Orbitz** (www.orbitz.com), which are becoming more sophisticated "pay-one-price" packagers every day.

Liberty Travel (call ☎ **888-271-1584** to find the store nearest you; www.libertytravel.com) is one of the biggest packagers in the Northeast and usually boasts a full-page ad in Sunday papers. At press time, Liberty was offering excellent-value packages, with or without air, to all the Hawaiian Islands — and its agents are willing to help you construct a multi-island trip. Calling the toll-free number immediately connects you to the Liberty Travel store nearest your home.

Pleasant Hawaiian Holidays (☎ **800-7-HAWAII**; www.pleasantholidays.com), the biggest and most comprehensive packager to Hawaii, has more than 40 years of experience in the business and offers tons of package options: At press time, it was offering a high-quality collection of more than 100 condos and hotels to choose from, and booking air travel aboard multiple airlines (as well as on its own charters), which gives you lots of flexibility if you have an established frequent-flier account with an airline. Pleasant can arrange just about any kind of vacation you want, including fly/drive packages and land-only deals. And because it buys airfares and hotel-room blocks in such bulk, its deals are often excellent (although it offers better deals on some properties than others). Another plus is that Pleasant maintains service desks on all the major islands; its employees can help you book activities and answer any questions you might have. These guys can even finance your vacation for you — but that's a bad option, due to high interest rates.

SunTrips (☎ **800-SUNTRIPS** or 800-357-2400; www.suntrips.com) is committed to arranging affordable and comprehensive Hawaii vacations, and the majority of the 150 or so properties it can book you into are budget and moderately priced hotels and condos. If money is no object, head elsewhere — but if you're looking for a bargain, SunTrips may just be the packager for you.

If you want to work with a travel agency that specializes in booking packaged Hawaii vacations, offers a more personalized shopping experience, books at all price levels, and really knows its stuff, contact Melissa McCoy's Maui-based **Aloha Destinations Vacations** (☎ **800-256-4280** or 808-893-0388; www.alohadestinations.com).

 Be aware that some travel packagers — including Pleasant Hawaiian Holidays and SunTrips — are likely to book you on their own charter flights rather than on commercial flights on major airlines. It doesn't really make a difference, unless you have a particular allegiance to a specific airline (or to collecting miles in a frequent-flier program). Be sure that you know which airline you're flying when you book. And if you really do want to fly with a specific airline, that doesn't rule a packager out. In fact, Pleasant has established relationships with such major carriers as Delta, United, and Hawaiian — and just about any packager will be happy to book you a land-only vacation that lets you book your own airfare separately (even the airline packagers will do this; see the upcoming list).

Uncovering an airline package

Many major airlines also offer travel packages to Hawaii. I always recommend comparison shopping, but you may want to choose the airline that has frequent service to your hometown or the one on which you accumulate frequent-flier miles; you may even be able to pay for your package using accumulated miles. The following airlines offer travel packages to Hawaii as part of their services:

- ✔ **Air Canada Vacations** (☎ **800-662-3221**; www.aircanada vacations.com)

- ✔ **American Airlines Vacations** (☎ **800-321-2121**; www.aa vacations.com), one of the best, after United, in terms of value and range of accommodations

- ✔ **ATA Vacations** (☎ **800-573-3747**; www.atavacations.com)

- ✔ **Continental Airlines Vacations** (☎ **800-634-5555**; http:// continental.covacations.com)

- ✔ **Delta Vacations** (☎ **800-872-7786**; www.deltavacations.com)

- ✔ **Northwest WorldVacations** (☎ **800-800-1504**; www.nwaworld vacations.com)

- ✔ **United Vacations** (☎ **800-328-6877** or 888-854-3899; www.united vacations.com), which is the most comprehensive airline packager to Hawaii and offers the most direct flights to the neighbor islands

Choosing between a travel agent and a packager isn't an either/or proposition; in fact, your travel agent can be your best source in sorting through the various deals that are available. If you're an AmEx customer, you may consider going through **American Express Travel Service,** which can book travel packages through various vendors, including Continental Vacations and Delta Vacations. To locate the office (or official travel-agent representative) nearest you, call ☎ **800-297-3429** or go online to www.americanexpress.com and click "Find A Travel Service Location." You can also use the site's online locator to locate an agent who specializes in Hawaii travel.

Ditto for members of the American Automobile Association, who have access to the **AAA Travel Agency,** which can also book excellent value package deals. Visit www.aaa.com to find the regional office nearest you.

Weighing your options

With the multitude of packages on the market, you may need some help weighing the various merits of each one. Follow these tips as you sift your way through the options:

✔ **Read up on Hawaii.** Read through the hotel listings in this book and select the places that sound interesting. Compare the rates that I list with the packagers' prices to best gauge which packagers are really offering a good deal and which have simply gussied up the rack rates to make their full-fare offer sound like a smart buy. Remember that the amount you save depends on both the property and the packager; most packagers can offer bigger savings on some properties than on others. For example, Liberty Travel may give you a much better rate on Waikiki's Royal Hawaiian, say, than Pleasant Holidays can, but Pleasant may offer you a substantial savings on the Maui condo that you want.

✔ **Compare apples to apples.** When comparing packages, make sure that you know *exactly* what's included in the quoted price, and what's not. Don't assume anything: Some packagers include everything — including value-added extras like lei greetings, free continental breakfast, and dining discounts — and others don't even include airfare. Additionally, when considering package prices, be sure to factor in add-on costs if you're flying from somewhere other than Los Angeles or San Francisco — some packagers price packages directly from your hometown, and some require additional premiums for airfares from your hometown to their Los Angeles or San Francisco gateway.

✔ **Before you commit to a package, make sure that you know how much flexibility you have.** Some packagers require ironclad commitments, but others charge only minimal fees for changes or cancellations. Consider the possibility that your travel plans may change and select a packager with the degree of flexibility that suits your needs. And if you pay up front for a complete vacation package that carries stiff cancellation penalties, consider buying travel insurance that will reimburse you in case an unforeseen emergency prevents you from traveling. (See Chapter 10 for more on this topic.)

✔ **Don't believe in fairy tales.** Unfortunately, shady dealers and fly-by-night operations are out there. If a package appears too good to be true, it probably is. Any knowledgeable travel agent should be able to help you determine whether a specific packager is on the level or not.

If you're booking a last-minute getaway, you may be able to score a stellar deal through **Site 59** (www.site59.com). Site 59 books all-inclusive travel packages as much as 60 percent off what the major packages charge. The catch? You can only price and purchase your trip between 3 hours and 14 days before your departure, and all destinations are not available from all departure points. Still, if you're just dying to get away on the spur of the moment, it's worth checking out. You might also want to surf to **TravelHub** (www.travelhub.com) for last-minute package deals.

Chapter 7

Getting Around Hawaii

● ●

In This Chapter

▶ Traveling from island to island on interisland carriers
▶ Renting a car
▶ Considering a convertible

● ●

*O*nce you've made it all the way across the Pacific, things start to get easy. But you'll need to know how to travel between islands, as well as how to get around on each one.

The individual island chapters later in this book explain the specifics of navigating your way around, but in this chapter, I give you the general lowdown on how to book and save money on car rentals — and you'll almost certainly want to have a car during your trip. Only Oahu has a viable public transportation system, and even there, you'll appreciate the freedom that comes with having your own set of wheels.

Flying between the Hawaiian Islands

The only way to travel from island to island is by airplane. This flight used to be a relatively simple proposition, since island airports were casual affairs and shuttle-style flights left every 30 or 40 minutes. But since 9/11, there's been a dramatic reduction in the number of inter-island flights, making it important to book in advance. The airlines request that you show up at least 90 minutes before your flight to allow for security inspections, and I've found that to be good advice.

Two major interisland carriers serve the islands: Aloha Airlines and Hawaiian Airlines. Both offer similar schedules — flights between the major islands every hour or so — at competitive prices.

Aloha Airlines (☎ **800-367-5250** or 808-484-1111; www.aloha airlines.com) employs an all-jet fleet of Boeing 737 aircraft. Aloha's sibling company, **Island Air** (☎ **800-323-3345**, 800-652-6541, or 808-484-2222; www.islandair.com), operates deHavilland DASH-8 and DASH-6 aircraft and serves Hawaii's smaller interisland airports on **Maui (Kapalua Airport)**, **Molokai**, and **Lanai**, as well as Kona on the Big

Island. Try Aloha first; if you need to take an Island Air flight because there's no accommodating Aloha flight, Aloha can book it for you.

 Aloha Airlines is a mileage partner with United Airlines, so you can earn 500 miles in your United Mileage Plus account for every Aloha Airlines interisland segment you fly. Also, I strongly suggest checking Aloha's Web site, where you can join their AlohaPass frequent-flier program for free. Even if you don't plan on flying often enough to rack up miles for a free flight, you'll be entitled to bargain fares (and online booking wins you another 10 percent discount as of press time).

Hawaiian Airlines (☎ **800-367-5320**, 800-882-8811, or 808-838-1555; www.hawaiianair.com) offers interisland jet service aboard Boeing 717-200s; the entire fleet was replaced with brand-new aircraft in 2001, making this the youngest fleet in the Pacific.

 Hawaiian is mileage partners with Alaska, America West, Northwest, and Virgin Atlantic airlines, which gives you plenty of mileage-earning potential.

At press time, the full interisland fare was about $106 per one-way segment on both airlines, with fares dropping as low as $70 to $75, depending on the dates and routes you want to fly. Booking more than 14 days in advance gives you the best shot at a bargain fare.

If you're traveling on a package, you probably don't have to worry about any of this — your interisland flights are most likely included in your package deal, on whichever interisland carrier the packager is affiliated with. For more on all-inclusive travel packages, see Chapter 6.

Arranging for Rental Cars

Hawaii has so many fabulous things to see and do that it would be a real shame for you to miss out. The more you want to see, however, the more you'll be moving around. In order to maximize your time on each of the islands, you need to rent a car. The only island where you can go without a car is Oahu, but you'll be stuck in Waikiki and will be dependent on public transportation.

The following companies rent cars on all the major Hawaiian Islands:

- ✔ **Alamo:** ☎ **800-GO-ALAMO** (800-462-5266); www.alamo.com
- ✔ **Avis:** ☎ **800-230-4898;** www.avis.com
- ✔ **Budget:** ☎ **800-527-0700;** www.budget.com
- ✔ **Dollar:** ☎ **800-800-4000;** www.dollar.com
- ✔ **Enterprise:** ☎ **800-325-8007;** www.enterprise.com
- ✔ **Hertz:** ☎ **800-654-3131;** www.hertz.com

✔ **National:** ☎ **800-CAR-RENT** (800-227-7368); www.nationalcar.com

✔ **Thrifty:** ☎ **800-THRIFTY** (800-847-4389); www.thrifty.com

Be sure to book your rental cars well ahead. Rental cars are almost always at a premium on Kauai, Molokai, and Lanai and may be sold out on all the neighbor islands on holiday weekends.

For tips on renting hand-controlled cars or vans equipped with wheelchair lifts, see Chapter 9.

Getting the best deal

Rental cars are quite affordable in Hawaii, although they do vary from island to island and from season to season. Of course, I can't guarantee what you'll pay when you book, but you can often get a compact car for between $160 and $250 a week. If you want a family-size car — or a convertible — expect to pay anywhere from $225 to $400 a week, which is still reasonable.

Car-rental rates vary even more than airline fares. The price depends on the size of the car, the length of time you keep it, where and when you pick it up and drop it off, where you take it, and a host of other factors. Asking a few key questions may save you hundreds of dollars.

✔ **Book your rental car at weekly rates when possible.** Weekly rentals almost always save you money. Several major rental firms — most notably Hertz and Avis — offer multi-island contracts. For example, if you plan to visit both Oahu and Kauai, you can pick up a car in Oahu, keep it for four days, return it, fly to Kauai, and then pick up another car for your three days there, all under the same contract. You end up paying for one week at the weekly rate rather than four times the daily rate on Oahu and three times the daily rate on Maui — and that's always much cheaper. Ask when you book.

✔ **Mention membership in AAA, AARP, and frequent-flier programs when booking.** These memberships may qualify you for discounts ranging from 5 to 30 percent.

✔ **Ask the reservations agency that books your hotel or your interisland air travel if it books rental cars.** Many hotels, condo rental agents, and even B&B owners can book rental cars at seriously discounted rates; ditto for the interisland air carriers, Hawaiian and Aloha. (See the section "Flying between the Hawaiian Islands," earlier in this chapter.) Often, you can save as much as 30 percent off the standard rate. And many Hawaii hotels and condos offer excellent-value room-and-car packages that make your rental essentially free!

✔ **Shop online.** As with other aspects of planning your trip, using the Internet can make comparison shopping for a car rental much easier. You can check rates at most of the major agencies' Web sites. Plus, all the major travel sites — **Travelocity** (www.travelocity.com), **Expedia** (www.expedia.com), **Orbitz** (www.orbitz.com), and

Smarter Living (www.smarterliving.com), for example — have search engines that can dig up discounted car-rental rates. Just enter the car size you want, the pickup and return dates, and location, and the server returns a price. You can even make the reservation through any of these sites.

✔ **If you see an advertised special, ask for that specific rate when booking.** The car-rental company may not offer this information voluntarily. Make sure to remind them; otherwise, you may be charged the standard (higher) rate.

✔ **Consider booking your car as part of a complete travel package.** Package deals not only save you dollars on airfare and accommodations but also on your rental cars, too. This one-stop shopping can help streamline the trip-planning process. For more on package deals, see Chapter 6.

✔ **Don't forget to ask about frequent-flier mileage.** Most car rentals are worth at least 500 miles on your frequent-flier account. Be sure to find out which airlines the rental-car company is affiliated with, so that you can earn mileage. Bring your card with you, and make sure that your account is credited at pickup time.

✔ **Join the rental company's preferred customer program.** Most companies offer such promotions (such as National's Emerald Club). You may be able to snag a bargain rate or have a better shot at an upgrade if you're a member. Some companies make the process of picking up your car more hassle-free for members, too. And membership can work just like the airlines' frequent-flier plans: Renting from the same company several times can land you a free day or other perks.

✔ **Make sure that you're getting free unlimited mileage.** Thankfully, most of the major car-rental companies rent on an unlimited-miles basis, but you should confirm this policy when you book. Even on an island, the miles you drive can really add up.

✔ **Find out whether age is an issue.** Many car-rental companies add on a fee for drivers under 25, while some don't rent to them at all.

 Some companies assess a drop-off charge of around $50 if you don't return the car to the location where you rented it; others (notably National) don't. This fee may be an issue on the Big Island, where you might want to fly into Kona Airport, on one side of the island, and leave from Hilo, on the other side (or vice versa), so ask when you book.

In addition to the standard rental prices, other optional charges apply to most car rentals (and some not-so-optional charges, such as taxes). The *Collision Damage Waiver* (CDW), which requires you to pay for damage to the car in a collision, is automatically covered by many credit-card companies. Check with your credit-card company before you leave home so that you can avoid paying this hefty fee (as much as $20 a day).

But in any event, make sure that you're covered (see the upcoming section, "Following the rules of the road"; Hawaii is a no-fault state, which has important insurance implications).

The car-rental companies also offer additional *liability insurance* (if you harm others in an accident), *personal accident insurance* (if you harm yourself or your passengers), and *personal effects insurance* (if your luggage is stolen from your car). Your insurance policy on your car at home probably covers most of these unlikely occurrences. However, if your own insurance doesn't cover you for rentals or if you don't have auto insurance, definitely consider the additional coverage (ask your car-rental agent for more information). Unless you're toting around the Hope diamond — and you don't want to leave that in your car trunk anyway — you can probably skip the personal effects insurance, but driving around without liability coverage is never a good idea. Note that credit cards will not cover you for liability, even if they cover you for collision.

Some companies also offer *refueling packages,* in which you pay for your initial full tank of gas up front and can return the car with an empty gas tank. The prices can be competitive with local gas prices, but you don't get credit for any gas remaining in the tank. If you reject this option, you pay only for the gas you use, but you have to return the car with a full tank or face charges of $4 to $5 a gallon for any shortfall. If you usually run late and a fueling stop may make you miss your plane, you're a perfect candidate for the fuel-purchase option, but for most people, it's not much of a hardship to top off your tank on the way to the airport.

Hawaii how-to: Renting convertibles

Renting a convertible is a lot like booking an oceanview room. It's a great idea if you can afford it, but not worth it if it's going to put a strain on your budget. The cost of going topless can be double or more what you'd pay for a regular car. Expect to pay between $50 and $80 a day for a convertible, compared with $30 or $40 a day for a better equipped midsize car (with such extras as power windows and power locks that don't usually come with convertibles).

If you really want to rent a convertible for your island driving but you're worried about cost, consider the following:

- ✔ **Rent a convertible for just part of your trip.** If you're going to be visiting two or three islands, book a convertible on just one of them. Consider renting one on Maui — cruising the road to Hana with the top down really is the ultimate Hawaii vacation dream.

- ✔ **Ask about upgrades when you pick up your rental car.** This may prove especially beneficial if you're visiting in the off-season. Sometimes, if a rental-car branch has a few idle convertibles sitting around, it'll offer you an on-the-spot upgrade for just $10 or $15 more a day. If you negotiated a decent compact or midsize rate when you booked, the total should come out to substantially less than the convertible rate offered over the phone.

Following the rules of the road

Know these driving rules and common practices before you get behind the wheel in Hawaii:

- ✓ **Hawaii is a no-fault insurance state.** If you drive without collision-damage insurance, you're required to pay for all damages before you leave the state, regardless of who is at fault. Your personal auto policy may provide rental-car coverage; read your policy or check with your insurer before you leave home and be sure to bring your insurance ID card if you decline the rental-car company's optional insurance. Some credit-card companies also provide collision damage insurance; check with yours.

- ✓ **Seatbelts are mandatory for everyone in the car, all the time.** The law is strictly enforced, so be sure to buckle up. Hawaii's Child Passenger Restraint Law requires children under 4 years old to ride in a child safety seat.

- ✓ **You can turn right on red unless a posted sign specifies otherwise.** Make sure that you make a full stop first — no rolling.

- ✓ **Pedestrians always have the right of way.** This is true even if they're not on a crosswalk.

- ✓ **Use your horn judiciously.** Honking your horn to express your anger at another driver is considered the height of rudeness in Hawaii. Don't do it. Horns are used to greet friends in Hawaii.

Do *not* use your rental car as a safe in which to store valuables. Don't leave anything that you don't want to lose in the car or trunk, not even for a short time. Be especially careful when you park at beaches, where thieves know that you're going to leave your car for a while (and you're likely to leave goodies in the glove compartment).

The islands are very easy to negotiate, and all the rental-car companies hand out very good map booklets on each island. If all you have is what National or Hertz gives you, you'll do just fine.

Chapter 8

Booking Your Accommodations

- -

In This Chapter

▶ Figuring out what kind of accommodations are right for you
▶ Getting the best room at the best rate

- -

*H*awaii's resort hotels are notoriously expensive. Hotels won't hesitate to charge $300 a night for a partial-oceanview room with little more than a queen-size bed in it. So prepare yourself for the fact that accommodations may take up a larger portion of your total travel budget than you might expect.

That said, don't forsake Hawaii for the Jersey Shore just yet. The islands boast plenty of excellent values for every budget if you just know where to look — and I include the best of them in the chapters that follow. For general tips on how to save, check out Chapter 5.

Getting to Know Your Options

Before you book your accommodations, you need to figure out what kind of place you want. You find five types of accommodations in the islands: resorts, hotels, condos, bed-and-breakfasts, and vacation rentals. Table 8-1 gives you an idea of what you can expect to pay in each price category.

Table 8-1	Key to Hotel Dollar Signs*	
Dollar Sign(s)	**Price Range**	**What to Expect**
$	Less than $100 per night	Super-cheap — a very basic hotel room a distance from the beach
$$	$100 to $175	Still affordable — midpriced hotel room or condo, possibly on or near the beach

Dollar Sign(s)	Price Range	What to Expect
$$$	$175 to $250	Moderate — a good-quality hotel room or condo on or near the beach
$$$$	$250 to $375	Expensive but not ridiculous — a high-quality room in a full-service hotel, or a multibedroom condo, on or near the beach
$$$$$	more than $375 per night	Ultraluxurious — the ultimate in deluxe resort living, generally on the beach

Each range of dollar signs, from one ($) to five ($$$$$), represents the median rack-rate price range for a double room per night. This system applies to each resort, hotel, condo, or B&B.

Relaxing at a resort

Most resorts (or resort hotels) are multi-acre, multibuilding complexes located directly on the beach. Some are sophisticated (sometimes too sophisticated, for Hawaii), ultraluxury affairs geared to well-off adults; others are theme-park-like spreads that cater largely to families with kids. More than a few resorts fall somewhere in between the two extremes.

A resort (or resort hotel) offers everything that your average hotel offers — plus much more. Every resort hotel is different, of course, but you can expect such amenities as direct beach access, with beach cabanas and chairs, and often beach-toy rentals and ocean activities as well; pools (often more than one), often with poolside bar service; an activities desk; a fitness center and often a full-service spa; a variety of restaurants, bars, and lounges; a 24-hour front desk; concierge, valet, and bell services; twice-daily maid service (which can come in handy after you've dragged sand into your room and used all your towels by 4 p.m.); room service; tennis and golf (some of the world's best courses are at Hawaii's resorts); a business center; extensive children's programs; and more comforts.

Rooms may be in high-rise towers, but they're often scattered throughout the property in low-rise buildings or clustered cottages. They tend to be done in the same safe, mass-market style throughout the resort — generally, room 101 is going to look exactly like room 1901. As travelers' tastes increasingly demand more, however, many newer properties (and savvy new renovations) are reinventing the resort with smart, high-style concepts that are intended to heighten the resort's own unique setting, concept, or personality. Standards tend to be high, and rooms are usually outfitted with high-quality furnishings and linens. Many luxury resorts also boast an increasing slate of in-room extras, such as CD players and big TVs with Nintendo systems, on-screen Web access, and VCRs (and even DVD players).

Being the best outfitted, and usually the best located, of Hawaii's accommodations options, resorts are also the priciest choices on the market, although the islands do boast a few midrange resorts. That said, you can score attractive rates, even at some of the islands' most luxurious resorts, especially if you book through a packager (see Chapter 6), but sometimes by just hitting the reservations line or online booking engine at the right time and scoring a good deal; most resorts also offer special offers and package deals on their own Web sites.

Hanging at a hotel

Hotels tend to be smaller and have fewer facilities than resorts — you may get a swimming pool, but don't expect a golf course, more than one or two restaurants and/or bars, or the myriad amenities that come with a full-fledged resort. You'll find the greatest number of nonresort hotels in Waikiki, where the shoulder-to-shoulder urban setting simply hasn't allowed for much full-fledged resort development.

Hotels are often a short walk from the beach rather than beachfront (although some, like the Sheraton Moana Surfrider in Waikiki, are right on the sand). Generally, a hotel offers daily maid service and has a restaurant and/or coffee shop, a bar or lounge, on-site laundry facilities, a swimming pool, and a sundries or convenience-type shop (rather than the shopping arcades that many resorts have these days). Top hotels also have activities desks, concierge and valet services, limited room service, and a business center.

Boutique hotels are smaller — maybe 40 or 50 rooms rather than 200 or more — and more intimate than your average Doubletree or Hilton. The rooms are often more stylish and less cookie-cutter and usually have more amenities. They tend to cater to adults rather than families. Again, Hawaii's boutique-hotel boom is centered in Waikiki.

Hotels run the gamut from very expensive to downright cheap. But even the priciest ones (usually boutique hotels) tend to be less expensive than fully outfitted resorts.

Enjoying the comforts of a B&B

Staying in a bed-and-breakfast is a nice way to discover Hawaii's genuine aloha spirit. More often than not, B&Bs offer a more intimate, and often more romantic, setting than your average impersonal resort, as well as a host who's more than happy to help you get to know Hawaii as it really is. If you want to experience a real slice of island life, B&Bs are the way to go.

B&Bs vary widely in size, style, and services. Generally speaking, they're comprised of several bedrooms in a home or several cottages or suites scattered about a property, each of which may or may not have a private bathroom. (*Note:* All the B&Bs that I recommend in the accommodations chapters that follow have units with private baths.)

I recommend contacting one or more of the following agencies if you're considering a stay at a B&B:

- ✔ Tops in the state is **Hawaii's Best Bed & Breakfasts** (☎ **800-262-9912** or 808-985-7488; www.bestbnb.com). The owners and staff personally inspect (and regularly revisit) the B&Bs and inns that they represent, and they're not afraid to say "no" to any property that doesn't meet their exacting standards. You pay $20 on top of the regular nightly rate, and full payment is required well in advance, but it's well worth it to know that you're getting a great B&B. They represent only accommodations with private baths, and all are nonsmoking. Some of their units are free-standing cottages that resemble vacation homes more than B&Bs; they even represent a few really nice condos.

- ✔ **Bed & Breakfast Hawaii** (☎ **800-733-1632** or 808-822-7771; www.bandb-hawaii.com) can also book you into a range of vacation homes and B&Bs throughout the islands, with prices starting at $75 a night.

- ✔ You don't get the same personal service from the Web, but you can find lots of useful resources there. The **Hawaii Directory of Bed-and-Breakfasts, Country Inns, and Small Hotels** (www.virtualcities.com/ons/hi/hionsdex.htm) offers direct Web links to B&Bs and vacation rentals throughout the state. **InnSite** (www.innsite.com) features B&B listings in all 50 U.S. states, including Hawaii, and around the globe. Find an inn on the island of your choice, see pictures of the rooms, and check prices and availability; text is included only when the proprietor submits it. (It's free to have an inn listed.) The innkeepers write the descriptions, and many listings link to the inn's own Web sites. What's more, you may be able to score an additional discount by booking your reservation through InnSite. Another site that's well worth surfing for Hawaii B&Bs is **BedandBreakfast.com** (www.bedandbreakfast.com).

Rooming in a vacation rental

"Vacation rental" usually means that you have a full cottage or house all to yourself. You may never even see an owner, agent, or manager after you pick up the keys. This option is great for families or people who like their space, but if you prefer a full-service experience, a vacation rental may not be for you.

The rental may be a studio cottage in a residential neighborhood, a condo, or a huge beachfront multibedroom house — or anything in between. Vacation rentals usually have some sort of kitchen facilities (ask when booking), laundry facilities, at least one TV, and at least one phone. Because vacation rentals are often privately owned homes, they also may come with such extras as TV, VCR, and stereo (never assume; always ask if it matters to you). Like condos, many come outfitted with the basics, such as sheets or towels.

Vacation rentals vary greatly in price depending on their size, location, and amenities. They tend to be much better values than similarly priced resort or hotel accommodations, especially if you're trying to accommodate a group or plan a long stay (a week or more). Just make sure that you get a 24-hour contact person for those times when the toilet won't flush or you can't figure out how to turn on the air-conditioning.

Both **Hawaii's Best Bed & Breakfasts** and the **Hawaii Directory of Bed-and-Breakfasts, Country Inns, and Small Hotels** are useful sites for statewide vacation rentals. A statewide source that's also worth checking out is **Hawaii Beachfront Vacation Homes** (☎ 808-247-3637; www. hibeach.com).

Contact **Hawaii Condo Exchange** (☎ 800-442-0404 or 323-436-0300; www.hawaiicondoexchange.com), a Southern California-based agency that acts as a consolidator for condo properties throughout the islands. The agency works to match you up with the place that's right for you and tries to get you a good deal in the bargain.

You'll also find that most companies that offer all-inclusive travel packages to the islands can book you into any number of island condos, as can your travel agent.

Finding the Best Room Rate

The **rack rate** is the maximum rate a hotel charges for a room. It's the rate you get if you walk in off the street and ask for a room for the night. You sometimes see these rates printed on the fire/emergency exit diagrams posted on the back of your door.

Hotels are happy to charge you the rack rate, but you can almost always do better. Perhaps the best way to avoid paying the rack rate is surprisingly simple: Just ask for a cheaper or discounted rate. You may be pleasantly surprised. Great bargains can be unearthed if you politely ask the hotel's reservations agent to help you find a better rate. But you have to take the initiative and ask, because many hotels bank on the fact that they can get you to accept the first rate you're quoted. You should also chat with the reservations agent about which rooms are the best and which units match your needs. You never know what kind of insider advice or upgrade can be won by just asking a question and turning on the charm.

In all but the smallest accommodations, the rate you pay for a room depends on many factors — chief among them being how you make your reservation. A travel agent may be able to negotiate a better price with certain hotels than you can get by yourself. (That's because the hotel often gives the agent a discount in exchange for steering his or her business toward that hotel.)

Reserving a room through the hotel's toll-free number may also result in a lower rate than calling the hotel directly. On the other hand, the central reservations number may not know about discount rates at specific locations. For example, local franchises may offer a special group rate for a wedding or family reunion, but they may neglect to tell the central booking line. Your best bet is to call both the local number and the toll-free number and see which one gives you a better deal.

Room rates (even rack rates) change with the season, as occupancy rates rise and fall. But even within a given season, room prices are subject to change without notice, so the rates quoted in this book may be different from the actual rate you receive when you make your reservation.

Don't automatically shy away from a hotel if its rack rates seem out of your range at first glance. A hotel's official "published" (full-price, or rack) rates usually represent the upper end of what they charge when they're full to capacity, but most hotels routinely offer better prices. And special deals abound in Hawaii, so in each hotel listing throughout this book, I note what kind of bargains you can typically snag.

The best way to get a great deal on a hotel room is to book it as part of an all-inclusive travel package that includes airfare, hotel, and car, and sometimes other extras, in one low price; for details on how to find the best package deals, see Chapter 6.

There's a big list of money-saving strategies in Chapter 5. But here are a few reminders:

- ✔ **Rates are generally lowest in the slower seasons.** During peak season — basically winter and summer, and especially around Christmas — demand is high, and you're not going to have much luck fishing for a bargain rate. But in spring and fall, hotels aren't usually full. Not only will you find great deals, but if business is really slow, they'll be willing to negotiate; you might land a room upgrade by playing Let's Make a Deal.

- ✔ **Start by investigating the hotel's own special deals.** Hawaii's hotels regularly offer a dizzying array of special offers. You might get a free rental car, champagne and in-room breakfast for honeymooners, free dinners, discounted tee times or spa treatments, a room upgrade, an extra night thrown in for free (sometimes the fifth, sometimes the seventh), or some other freebie. Check out the Web site first, but even if you don't find anything on the Internet, ask about any specials when you call.

- ✔ **Membership in AAA, AARP, or frequent-flier programs often qualifies you for discounted rates.** Be sure to mention membership in these organizations and in any corporate rewards programs you can think of — or your Uncle Joe's Elks lodge in which you're an honorary inductee, for that matter — when you call to book. Even membership to a wholesale club, such as Costco, has been known to pay off. You never know when an affiliation may be worth a few dollars off your room rate.

✔ **Ask innkeepers for a break.** Bed-and-breakfasts are generally nonnegotiable on price. Sometimes, however, you can negotiate a discount for longer stays, such as a week or more. You may also be able to score a price break if you're visiting off-season. And some do offer AAA and senior discounts. It never hurts to ask.

✔ **Look for price breaks and value-added extras when booking condos.** Condo complexes often feature discounts on multinight stays, and many throw in a free rental car to sweeten the deal. Some condo properties have units handled by multiple management companies; if that's the case, price through both companies and see where you get the better deal. You may also want to check with **Hawaii Condo Exchange** (☎ **800-442-0404** or 323-436-0300; www.hawaiicondoexchange.com), which acts as a consolidator for condo properties throughout the islands.

Surfing the Web for Hotel Deals

Shopping online for hotels is generally done one of two ways: by booking through the hotel's own Web site or through an independent booking agency (or a fare-service agency like Priceline). Internet hotel agencies have multiplied in mind-boggling numbers of late, competing for the business of millions of consumers surfing for accommodations around the world. This competitiveness can be a boon to consumers who have the patience and time to shop and compare the online sites for good deals — but shop they must, for prices can vary considerably from site to site. And keep in mind that hotels at the top of a site's listing may be there for no other reason than that they paid money to get the placement.

Of the "big three" sites, **Expedia** offers a long list of special deals, as well as "virtual tours " or photos of available rooms so that you can see what you're paying for (a feature that helps counter the claims that the best rooms are often held back from bargain booking Web sites). **Travelocity** posts unvarnished customer reviews and ranks its properties according to the AAA rating system. Also reliable are **Hotels.com** and **Quikbook.com**.

You might also want to check out **TripAdvisor.com** when you're considering your options. TripAdvisor isn't a booking site, per se (although it does offer links to sites that allow you to make bookings), but it does offer untainted, straight-from-the-customer's-keyboard reviews of hotels. Now, I don't recommend putting too much stock in a single review — most of us have unrealistic expectations, or just plain-old bad-luck experiences, now and again — but trends in positive or negative experiences can become apparent.

An excellent free program, **TravelAxe** (www.travelaxe.net), can help you search multiple hotel sites at once, even ones you may never have heard of — and conveniently lists the total price of the room, including the taxes and service charges.

Another booking site, **Travelweb** (www.travelweb.com), is partly owned by the hotels it represents (including the Hilton, Hyatt, and Starwood chains), so it's worth checking for good deals.

 It's always a good idea to **get a confirmation number** and **make a print-out** of any online booking transaction to avoid any potential issues when you arrive at the hotel.

In the bidding-site Web site category, **Priceline** and **Hotwire** are even better for hotels than for airfares; with both, you're allowed to pick the neighborhood and quality level of your hotel before offering up your money. Priceline's hotel product even covers Europe and Asia, though it's much better at getting five-star lodging for three-star prices than at finding anything at the bottom of the scale. On the downside, many hotels stick Priceline guests in their least desirable rooms. Be sure to go to the **BiddingforTravel** Web site (www.biddingfortravel.com) before bidding on a hotel room on Priceline; it features a fairly up-to-date list of hotels that Priceline uses in major cities. For both Priceline and Hotwire, you pay upfront, and the fee is nonrefundable. *Note:* Some hotels don't provide loyalty program credits or points or other frequent-stay amenities when you book a room through opaque online services.

Reserving the Best Room

 After you make your reservation, asking one or two more pointed questions can go a long way toward making sure that you get the best room in the house. Most Hawaii hoteliers are very friendly and willing to take the time with you, so don't be shy — try to find out which units are the nicest. If the reservations agent doesn't have any specific recommendations, try asking for a corner room. In some (but not all) cases, they may be larger and quieter, with more windows and light than standard rooms, and they don't always cost more.

Also ask whether the hotel is renovating; if it is, request a room away from the renovation work. Inquire, too, about traffic and the location of the restaurants, bars, and discos in the hotel — all sources of annoying noise.

And if you aren't happy with your room when you arrive, talk to the front desk firmly but *nicely.* (Don't get emotional — your mom's old saying about attracting more flies with honey than with vinegar really was good advice.) If they have another room, they should be happy to accommodate you, within reason.

Chapter 9

Catering to Special Travel Needs or Interests

*T*ravelers don't come in a standard package, of course — they come in all ages, sizes, and configurations. You may want to know the answers to questions like How welcoming will Hawaii be to . . . (pick one or more) a) my kids? b) my senior status? c) my disability? d) my same-sex partner? If so, you're in the right chapter. I give you the details of traveling under any and all of these circumstances.

Plus, if you're looking to plan a dreamy tropical wedding, I tell you the ins and outs of tying the knot in the romantic islands of Hawaii.

Traveling with the Brood: Advice for Families

If you have enough trouble getting your kids out of the house in the morning, dragging them thousands of miles away may seem like an insurmountable challenge. But family travel can be immensely rewarding, giving you new ways of seeing the world through smaller pairs of eyes.

Hawaii is the perfect *ohana* (family) vacation destination. You and the *keiki* (kids) will love the beaches and the wealth of kid-friendly activities. Lots of families flock to the islands every summer and also at holiday time and during the spring break season.

Most hotels and condo complexes, from luxury to budget, welcome the entire family. Virtually all the larger hotels and resorts have great supervised programs for kids 12 and under — which means that you, Mom and Dad, can have plenty of relaxation time to yourselves as well as playtime with the kids. Most hotels can also refer you to reliable baby sitters if you want a night on the town sans the youngsters.

By Hawaii state law, hotels can only accept children between the ages of 5 and 12 into their supervised activity programs.

Condos are particularly suitable for families who want lots of living space in which to spread out. Parents also appreciate having a kitchen where they can prepare meals for fussy young eaters — and save significantly on dining costs. One drawback of condo complexes is that they typically don't have the extensive facilities (like kids' activities programs) you'd get in a big resort.

If you don't want to cart your own kid stuff across the ocean, **Baby's Away** (www.babysaway.com) rents car seats, cribs, strollers (including jogging strollers), high chairs, playpens, room monitors, and even toys. It serves Honolulu (☎ **800-496-6386** or 808-222-6041), Maui (☎ **800-942-9030** or 808-875-9030), and the Big Island (☎ **800-996-9030** or 808-987-9236). Give the company a call, and it'll deliver whatever you need to wherever you're staying and pick it up when you're done. I suggest arranging your rentals before you leave home to ensure availability. Unfortunately, there are no locations on Kauai.

You can find good family-oriented vacation advice on the Internet from sites like the **Family Travel Forum** (www.familytravelforum.com), a comprehensive site that offers customized trip planning; **Family Travel Network** (www.familytravelnetwork.com), an award-winning site that offers travel features, deals, and tips; **Traveling Internationally with Your Kids** (www.travelwithyourkids.com), a comprehensive site that offers customized trip planning; and **Family Travel Files** (www.thefamily travelfiles.com), which offers an online magazine and a directory of off-the-beaten-path tours and tour operators for families. **BabyCenter** (www.babycenter.com/travel) has terrific recommendations for planning baby's first trip, and even tips on traveling while pregnant.

Here are a few tips for family travel-planning:

✔ **Don't try to do too much.** I can't say this admonition too strongly. You'll all consider it the trip from you-know-where if you spend too much time in the car or on interisland flights.

✔ **Take it slow at the start.** Give the entire family time to adjust to a new time zone, unfamiliar surroundings, and just being on the road. The best way to make this adjustment is to budget a few days in your initial destination without strict itineraries or lots of moving around.

✔ **Look for the Kid Friendly icon as you flip through this book.** I use it to highlight hotels, restaurants, and attractions that are particularly welcoming to families traveling with kids. Zeroing in on these listings can help you plan your trip more efficiently.

✔ **Book some private time for Mom and Dad.** Most, if not all, hotels are prepared to hook you up with a reliable baby sitter who can entertain your kids while you enjoy a romantic dinner for two or another adults-only activity. To avoid disappointment, ask about baby sitting when you reserve. Local visitor centers can also usually recommend licensed and bonded baby-sitting services in their areas; see the Quick Concierge in the appendix for contact info.

Making Age Work for You: Tips for Seniors

One of the many benefits of getting older is that travel often costs less. Although all of the major U.S. airlines except America West have cancelled their senior discount and coupon book programs, many hotels and package-tour operators still offer discounts for seniors. Discounts for seniors are also available at almost all of Hawaii's major attractions, and occasionally at restaurants and luaus. So when you're making reservations or buying tickets, it's always worthwhile to ask about senior discounts. Keep in mind, though, that the minimum age requirement can vary between 50 and 65 (it's usually between 55 and 65). Always carry an ID card with you, especially if you've kept your youthful glow.

The statewide **Outrigger** (☎ **800-OUTRIGGER** or 800-688-7444; www.outrigger.com) and **Ohana** (☎ **800-462-6262;** www.ohanahotels.com) hotel chains offer all travelers over age 50 substantial discounts as well as seriously discounted rental cars through **Dollar Rent a Car** (☎ **800-800-3665;** www.dollar.com).

Members of **AARP** (formerly known as the American Association of Retired Persons), 601 E St. NW, Washington, DC 20049 (☎ **888-687-2277** or 202-434-2277; www.aarp.org), get discounts on hotels, airfares, and car rentals. AARP offers members a wide range of benefits, including *AARP: The Magazine* and a monthly newsletter. Anyone over 50 can join.

YMT Vacations (☎ **800-922-9000;** www.ymtvacations.com) and **White Star Tours** (☎ **800-437-2323** or 610-775-5000; www.whitestartours.com) are just two of the hundreds of travel agencies that specialize in vacations for seniors, including trips to Hawaii. But beware: Many of these outfits are of the tour-bus variety, with free trips thrown in for those who organize groups of 20 or more. If you're the independent type, a regular travel agent may be better for you.

Elderhostel (☎ **877-426-8056** or 978-323-4141; www.elderhostel.org), a nonprofit group that offers travel and study programs around the world, offers excellent low-cost trips to Hawaii for travelers ages 55 and older (plus a spouse or companion of any age). Trips usually include moderately priced accommodations and meals in one low-cost package.

Seniors 62 or older who want to visit Hawaii's national parks — including Hawaii Volcanoes National Park and Puuhonua o Honaunau National Historical Park on the Big Island, and Haleakala National Park on Maui — can save sightseeing dollars by picking up a **Golden Age Passport** from any national park, recreation area, or monument. This lifetime pass has a one-time fee of $10 and provides free admission to all the parks in the National Parks system, plus 50 percent savings on camping and recreation fees. You can get one at any park entrance as long as you have a proof-of-age ID on hand.

Recommended publications offering travel resources and discounts for seniors include the quarterly magazine *Travel 50 & Beyond* (www. travel50andbeyond.com); *Travel Unlimited: Uncommon Adventures for the Mature Traveler* (Avalon); *101 Tips for Mature Travelers,* available from Grand Circle Travel (☎ **800-221-2610** or 617-350-7500; www.gct.com); *The 50+ Traveler's Guidebook* (St. Martin's Press); and *Unbelievably Good Deals and Great Adventures That You Absolutely Can't Get Unless You're Over 50* (McGraw-Hill), by Joann Rattner Heilman.

Accessing Hawaii: Advice for Travelers with Disabilities

A disability shouldn't stop anyone from traveling. The Americans with Disabilities Act requires that all public buildings be wheelchair accessible and have accessible restrooms. Hawaii is very friendly to disabled travelers. The city of Honolulu alone has more than 2,000 ramped curbs, and most hotels throughout the islands are on the newer side and boast wheelchair ramps, extra-wide doorways and halls, and dedicated disabled-accessible rooms with extra-large bathrooms, low-set fixtures, and/or fire alarm systems adapted for deaf travelers.

Your best bet is to contact the local visitor center for the island you're interested in visiting. Its staff can provide you with all the specifics on accessibility in their locale; see the Quick Concierge at the back of this book for contact info.

The following are excellent resources for information on accessible travel:

✔ An excellent source for trip-planning assistance is **Access Aloha Travel** (☎ **800-480-1143** or 808-545-1143; www.accessaloha travel.com). This Hawaii-based travel agency has been planning accessible trips for disabled travelers for decades — and it donates half its profits to the disabled community.

✔ Both **Moss Rehab ResourceNet** (☎ 215-456-9900; www.moss resourcenet.org) and **Access-Able Travel Source** (☎ 303-232-2979; www.access-able.com) are comprehensive resources for disabled travelers. Both sites feature links to travel agents who specialize in planning accessible trips to Hawaii. Access-Able's user-friendly site also features relay and voice numbers for hotels, airlines, and car-rental companies, plus links to accessible accommodations, attractions, transportation, tours, and local medical resources and equipment repairers throughout Hawaii, making this an invaluable resource. **SeniorCitizens.com** also operates a page (www.seniorcitizens.com/accessible/travel.shtml) dedicated to accessible travel, with links to tour organizations that can meet assistive technology needs.

✔ You can join the **Society for the Advancement of Travelers with Handicaps (SATH; ☎ 212-447-7284;** www.sath.org) for $45 a year ($30 for seniors and students), to gain access to their vast network of travel connections. The group provides information sheets on destinations and referrals to tour operators that specialize in accessible travel. Its quarterly magazine, *Open World,* is full of good information and resources.

✔ The **Hawaii Services on Deafness** (☎ 808-946-7300 voice and TTY; www.hsod.org) can provide aid and advice to hearing-impaired travelers, including sign-language interpreters in emergency situations.

✔ Vision-impaired travelers who use a Seeing Eye dog can usually bypass Hawaii's animal quarantine rules (which were dramatically loosened in 2004). You can arrange for your guide or service dog to be inspected in the terminal at Honolulu International Airport (saving the owners a trip to the Airport Animal Quarantine Holding Facility) if you notify **Animal Quarantine** (☎ 808-483-7151) at least seven days in advance. Call or visit www.hawaiiag.org/hdoa for specifics on rules and fees. Contact the **American Foundation for the Blind** (☎ 800-232-5463; www.afb.org) for more travel information.

I highly recommend procuring a copy of the *Aloha Guide to Accessibility.* You can order a copy by phone from the **Disability and Communication Access Board** (☎ 808-586-2121 or 808-984-8219) or the **Hawaii Center for Independent Living** (☎ 808-522-5400).

Before you book any hotel room, always ask lots of questions based on your needs. After you arrive, call restaurants, attractions, and theaters to make sure that they're fully accessible.

Consider the following sources for getting around, either on your own or with assistance:

✔ **Avis Rent a Car** has an "Avis Access" program that offers such services as a dedicated 24-hour toll-free number (☎ 888-879-4273; www.avis.com) for customers with special travel needs; special car features such as swivel seats, spinner knobs, and hand controls; and accessible bus service. Many of the big car-rental companies — including Avis, **Hertz** (☎ **800-654-3131;** www.hertz.com), and **National** (☎ **800-227-7368;** www.nationalcar.com) — rent hand-controlled cars for disabled drivers at Hawaii's major airports. At least 48 to 72 hours advance notice is a must, but do yourself a favor and book further in advance to guarantee availability.

✔ **Handicabs of the Pacific** (☎ **808-524-3866**) offers taxi services and tours around Honolulu and the rest of Oahu for wheelchair-bound travelers. Its air-conditioned vehicles are specially equipped with ramps and wheelchair lock-downs.

✔ **Accessible Vans of Hawaii** (☎ **800-303-3750** or 808-871-7785; www.accessiblevanshawaii.com) has wheelchair-accessible vans for rent on Oahu, Maui, Kauai, and in Kona on the Big Island. Its staff can also help arrange accessible accommodations and recommend accessible activities, sightseeing, restaurants, medical equipment rentals, and personal care attendants at no additional charge to you.

Following the Rainbow: Resources for Gay and Lesbian Travelers

Hawaii is extremely popular with same-sex couples due to its long-standing reputation for welcoming all groups.

If you want help planning your trip, **IGLTA,** the **International Gay & Lesbian Travel Association** (☎ **800-448-8550** or 954-776-2626; www.iglta.org), is your best source. IGLTA can link you up with the appropriate gay-friendly service organization or tour specialist; the organization also offers quarterly newsletters and a membership directory that's updated quarterly. Members are kept informed of gay and gay-friendly hoteliers, tour operators, and airline and cruise-line representatives. The IGLTA site will link you to other useful Web sites that can help you plan your Hawaii vacation.

If you want assistance in planning a gay-friendly Hawaiian holiday, **Pacific Ocean Holidays** (☎ **800-735-6600** or 808-923-2400; www.gayhawaii.com) is your best resource. The staff can help you arrange a good-value trip that features either gay-friendly hotels serving the general public or those that serve a predominately gay clientele (your choice); you can even book your entire vacation online. Even if you don't want help planning your trip, the Web site is an invaluable resource. Its online island-by-island guide is a terrific community resource directory and guide to gay-owned and gay-friendly businesses throughout Hawaii.

Rainbow Handbook Hawaii, by Big Island resident Matthew Link, is an excellent source for gay and lesbian travelers. To order a copy, call ☎ **800-260-5528** or visit www.rainbowhandbook.com.

Out and About (www.outandabout.com) has been hailed for its "straight" reporting about gay travel. It offers a monthly newsletter packed with good information on the global gay and lesbian scene. Out and About's guidebooks are available at most major bookstores, but the Web site alone is a first-rate resource.

The **Gay and Lesbian Community Center,** 2424 S. Beretania Ave., in Honolulu (☎ 808-951-7000), offers referrals for nearly every kind of service that you might need. Another great helpline and referral resource for gay-friendly businesses is the Gay and Lesbian Education and Advocacy Foundation's **Gay Community Resource Directory,** which you can find online at www.hawaiigaymarriage.com.

Planning a Hawaiian Wedding

No question about it: Hawaii is the perfect place to get married — which is why so many couples from around the country, and the world, tie the knot here every year. What better way to start your life together? And the members of your wedding party will most likely be delighted because you've given them the perfect excuse for their own island vacation.

For a rundown of the legalities, visit www.hawaii.gov/doh and click "Vital Records," where you'll find all the details, including a downloadable license form.

A marriage license costs $60 and is good for 30 days from the date of issue. Both parties must be at least 18 years of age (16- and 17-year-olds must have written consent of both parents, legal guardian, or family court) and can't be more closely related than first cousins. You'll need a photo ID, such as a driver's license; a birth certificate is only necessary if you're 18 or under. No blood tests, citizenship, or residency minimum is required.

Using a wedding planner or coordinator

Wedding planning is a thriving industry in Hawaii. Whether you've got your heart set on a huge formal affair at a luxury resort or an informal beachside ceremony, you won't have any trouble finding assistance.

Many wedding planners are also marriage license agents. They can take care of the legalities for you with only minimal effort on your part and then arrange everything else, too — from providing an officiant to ordering flowers. A wedding planner can cost $500 or more, depending on how involved you want him or her to be and what kind of wedding you want.

Your best bet for finding a reputable wedding planner is to choose one endorsed by the **Hawaii Visitors and Convention Bureau,** whose Web site features a complete list of wedding planners to suit any budget; go to www.gohawaii.com and click "Weddings & Honeymoons." You can also call its staff for recommendations at ☎ **800-GO-HAWAII,** or — even better — contact the individual island bureaus for local recommendations; see the Quick Concierge at the back of this book for contact information. On Kauai, an even better wedding resource than the visitor center is the Kauai Chamber of Commerce (☎ **808-245-7363;** www.kauaichamber.org), which sells an extensive wedding guide for $15.

In addition, virtually all the big resorts employ full-time wedding coordinators. Arranging your nuptials directly through a resort may be pricey, but it's a relatively worry-free option. The hotel coordinators are experts, they'll take all the pesky little details off your hands, and they'll usually offer the whole event to you as a pay-one-price wedding package, including accommodations. What's more, the hotels generally offer prime locations for both the ceremony and reception, whether they're for 2 or 200 guests.

Great choices include

- ✔ The Halekulani, the Royal Hawaiian, the Sheraton Moana Surfrider, and the Kahala Mandarin Oriental on Oahu (see Chapter 11)

- ✔ The Four Seasons Maui, the Grand Wailea, the Kea Lani, and the Ritz-Carlton on Maui (see Chapter 13)

- ✔ The Four Seasons Hualalai, Kona Village, the Mauna Lani, and the Orchid at Mauna Lani on the Big Island (see Chapter 15)

- ✔ The Hyatt Regency Kauai and the Princeville Hotel on Kauai (see Chapter 17)

Keep in mind that more affordable hotels and condos, even some B&Bs, can often recommend wedding coordinators that have a proven track record with them. Maui's Kaanapali Beach Hotel, for example, makes a great affordable option (see Chapter 13). The setting is magical, the hotel works with a very reliable local planner, and the on-site food-and-beverage director can arrange a pleasing reception. Don't hesitate to contact any property that strikes your fancy; most have wedding experience or can offer recommendations.

Do-it-yourself planning

After you get to Hawaii, you and your intended must go together to the marriage license agent to get the license (bring cash). You can either go to the nearest Department of Health office (see www.hawaii.gov/doh/about/dho-info.html for locations), or the **Honolulu Marriage License Office,** State Department of Health Building, 1250 Punchbowl St., Honolulu, HI 96813 (☎ **808-586-4545** or 808-586-4544), can direct you to a marriage license agent (basically, a local official who helps you wrap up the legalities) closest to where you'll be staying in the islands.

Local marriage license agents that the office will refer you to are usually friendly, helpful people who can steer you to someone who's licensed by the state of Hawaii to perform the ceremony, whether you're looking for an officiant of a certain denomination or a plain ol' justice of the peace. These marriage performers are great sources of information; they usually know picturesque places to have the ceremony for free or a nominal fee.

Some marriage licensing agents are state employees, and, under law, they cannot recommend anyone with a religious affiliation; they can only give you phone numbers for local judges to perform the ceremony. Ask first what their limitations are if it matters to you. If you're interested in arranging a church ceremony, inquire with the visitor center to locate an appropriate venue.

You can have a ceremony at any state or county beach or park for free, but keep in mind that you'll be sharing the site with the general public. Here are some romantic spots you may want to consider:

- ✔ **Oahu:** Waikiki's **Kapiolani Park,** on Kalakaua Avenue, is ideal at sunset. You can take gorgeous wedding photos with Waikiki Beach in the background and then turn around and take another photo with Diamond Head as your backdrop. I also adore **Lanikai Beach,** on the lush and gorgeous windward side. Tucked away in a residential neighborhood, it's usually quiet and crowd-free. (Weekdays are best if you want the sand to yourself.)

- ✔ **Maui:** For a genuine Hawaiian experience, get married at **Keawali Congregational Church** (☎ 808-879-5557), a vintage 1831 oceanfront coral-block church in picturesque Makena. The gorgeous grounds — with palm trees, ti leaves, and exotic tropical flowers — make a perfect backdrop for your wedding photo. Another great site is **D.T. Fleming Beach Park,** just north of Kapalua in West Maui. This crescent-shaped beach is generally empty on weekdays, so you can enjoy a quiet wedding on the beautiful beach as sailboats skim along offshore.

- ✔ **Big Island:** If you picture yourself getting married on a long, white-sand beach with gorgeous, emerald-green waves rolling in, **Hapuna Beach State Park** is the spot for you. On the mistier side of the island, along bayfront Banyan Drive in romantic Hilo, is **Liluokalani Gardens,** the largest formal Japanese garden this side of Tokyo. This postcard-pretty park has a dozen different areas that are ideal for a tropical ceremony, and the half-moon bridge is a great spot for wedding photos.

- ✔ **Kauai:** One of the most dramatic spots in all Hawaii is the North Shore's **Hanalei Beach,** with gorgeous, green Bali Hai-like cliffs in the background. (Remember South Pacific? Filmed here!) If you're set on a church wedding, consider **Waioli Hui'ia** ("Singing Waters") **Church** (☎ 808-826-6253), built in 1912 as a mission hall and the oldest surviving church building on Kauai. The green-shingled, American Gothic-style church sits in an open field in the heart of the charming Hanalei town under the spectacular Bali Hai cliffs for an ultraromantic setting. For those who don't mind spending a little money for a bit more privacy, the extraordinary **Allerton Gardens** (☎ **808-742-2623;** www.ntbg.org), on the South Shore, is home to some prime examples of formal landscape gardening that would have made William Randolph Hearst turn green with envy. It's perfect for a wedding of any scope.

Chapter 10

Taking Care of the Remaining Details

*T*his chapter helps you shore up the final details — from getting travel insurance to planning for activities to packing the appropriate gear.

Playing It Safe with Travel and Medical Insurance

Three kinds of travel insurance are available: trip-cancellation insurance, medical insurance, and lost-luggage insurance. The cost of travel insurance varies widely, depending on the cost and length of your trip, your age and health, and the type of trip you're taking, but expect to pay between 5 and 8 percent of the cost of the vacation itself. Here is my advice on all three:

✔ **Trip-cancellation insurance** may make sense if you're paying for your vacation up front, say, by purchasing a cruise, package deal, or escorted tour. Coverage will help you get your money back if you have to back out of a trip, if you have to go home early, or if your travel supplier goes bankrupt. Allowed reasons for cancellation can range from sickness to natural disasters to the State Department declaring your destination unsafe for travel. (Insurers usually won't cover vague fears, though, as many travelers discovered when they tried to cancel their trips in October 2001 because they were wary of flying.)

A good resource is **"Travel Guard Alerts,"** a list of companies considered high-risk by Travel Guard International (www.travel insured.com). Protect yourself further by paying for the insurance with a credit card — by law, consumers can get their money back on goods and services not received if they report the loss within 60 days after the charge is listed on their credit card statement.

Note: Many tour operators include insurance in the cost of the trip or can arrange insurance policies through a partnering provider, a convenient and often cost-effective way for travelers to obtain insurance. Make sure that the tour company is a reputable one, however: Some experts suggest that you avoid buying insurance from the tour or cruise company you're traveling with, saying that it's safer to buy from a third-party insurer than to put all your money in one place.

✔ For domestic travel, buying **medical insurance** for your trip doesn't make sense for most travelers. Most existing health policies cover you if you get sick away from home — but check before you go, particularly if you're insured by an HMO.

✔ **Lost-luggage insurance** is also not necessary for most travelers. On domestic flights, checked baggage is covered up to $2,500 per ticketed passenger. On international flights (including U.S. portions of international trips), baggage coverage is limited to approximately $9.07 per pound, up to approximately $635 per checked bag. If you plan to check items more valuable than the standard liability, see whether your valuables are covered by your homeowner's policy, get baggage insurance as part of your comprehensive travel-insurance package, or buy Travel Guard's "BagTrak" product. Don't buy insurance at the airport, as it's usually overpriced. Be sure to take any valuables or irreplaceable items with you in your carry-on luggage, as many valuables (including books, money, and electronics) aren't covered by airline policies.

If your luggage is lost, immediately file a lost-luggage claim at the airport, detailing the contents. For most airlines, you must report delayed, damaged, or lost baggage within four hours of arrival. The airlines are required to deliver luggage, once found, directly to your house or destination free of charge.

For more information, contact one of the following recommended insurers: **Access America** (☎ 866-807-3982; www.accessamerica.com); **Travel Guard International** (☎ 800-826-4919; www.travelguard.com); **Travel Insured International** (☎ 800-243-3174; www.travelinsured.com); and **Travelex Insurance Services** (☎ 888-457-4602; www.travelex-insurance.com).

Staying Healthy When You Travel

Getting sick will ruin your vacation, so I *strongly* advise against it. (Of course, last time I checked, the bugs weren't listening to me any more than they probably listen to you.)

Talk to your doctor before leaving on a trip if you have a serious and/ or chronic illness. For conditions such as epilepsy, diabetes, or heart problems, wear a **MedicAlert identification tag** (☎ **888-633-4298**; www. medicalert.org), which immediately alerts doctors to your condition and gives them access to your records through MedicAlert's 24-hour hotline.

In the unlikely event that you do get sick in Hawaii, keep the following in mind:

✔ By law, all employers in Hawaii must provide health insurance for their employees, and almost all islanders have insurance. As a result, some doctors simply won't see patients who aren't insured. If you don't have insurance (or you don't have insurance that travels with you) and you need to see a doctor while you're in Hawaii, be sure to inform him or her when you call to make an appointment. Check the "Fast Facts" sections in Chapter 11 (Oahu), Chapter 13 (Maui), Chapter 15 (the Big Island), and Chapter 17 (Kauai) to find a doctor or medical-care clinic that regularly caters to visitors.

✔ Long's Drugs, which has branches throughout the islands, accepts most national prescription cards, such as PCS — so if you have a card, bring it with you. If you get sick and need to fill a prescription during your trip, chances are good that you'll only have to pay a copayment, just like back home, instead of the full price for pre-scribed medicines.

Avoiding "economy-class syndrome"

Deep vein thrombosis, or as it's know in the world of flying, "economy-class syndrome," is a blood clot that develops in a deep vein. It's a potentially deadly condition that can be caused by sitting in cramped conditions — such as an airplane cabin — for too long. During a flight (especially a long-haul flight), get up, walk around, and stretch your legs every 60 to 90 minutes to keep your blood flowing. Other preventative measures include frequent flexing of the legs while sitting, drinking lots of water, and avoiding alcohol and sleeping pills. If you have a history of deep vein thrombosis, heart disease, or any other condition that puts you at high risk, some experts recommend wearing compression stockings or taking anticoagulants when you fly; always ask your physician about the best course for you. Symptoms of deep vein thrombosis include leg pain or swelling, or even shortness of breath.

Staying Connected by Cellphone or E-mail

Just because your **cellphone** works at home doesn't mean it'll work elsewhere in the country (thanks to our nation's fragmented cellphone system). Take a look at your wireless company's coverage map on its Web site before heading out — T-Mobile, Sprint, and Nextel are particularly weak in rural areas. You should also check your particular cellphone contract, because coverage varies depending on the particular package you've purchased. If you need to stay in touch at a destination where you know your phone won't work, **rent** a phone that does from **InTouch USA** (☎ 800-872-7626; www.intouchglobal.com) or a rental-car location, but beware that you'll pay $1 a minute or more for airtime.

If you're not from the United States, you'll be appalled at the poor reach of our **GSM (Global System for Mobiles) wireless network,** which is used by much of the rest of the world. Your phone will probably work in most major U.S. cities; it definitely won't work in many rural areas. (To see where GSM phones work in the United States, check out www.t-mobile.com/coverage/national_popup.asp). You may or may not be able to send SMS (text messaging) home — something Americans tend not to do anyway. Assume nothing — call your wireless provider and get the full scoop. In a worst-case scenario, you can always rent a phone; InTouch USA delivers to hotels.

Travelers **accessing the Internet** away from home have any number of ways to check their e-mail and access the Internet on the road. Of course, using your own laptop — or even a PDA (personal digital assistant) or electronic organizer with a modem — gives you the most flexibility. But even if you don't have a computer, you can still access your e-mail and even your office computer from cybercafes.

It's hard nowadays to find a destination that *doesn't* have a few cybercafes. Although there's no definitive directory for cybercafes — these are independent businesses, after all — two places to start looking are at www.cybercaptive.com and www.cybercafe.com. Avoid **hotel business centers** unless you're willing to pay exorbitant rates.

Most major airports now have **Internet kiosks** scattered throughout their gates. These kiosks, which you'll also see in shopping malls, hotel lobbies, and tourist information offices around the world, give you basic Web access for a per-minute fee that's usually higher than cybercafe prices. The kiosks' clunkiness and high price mean that you should avoid them whenever possible.

To retrieve your e-mail, ask your **Internet service provider (ISP)** whether it has a Web-based interface tied to your existing e-mail account. If your ISP doesn't have such an interface, you can use the free **mail2web** service (www.mail2web.com) to view and reply to your home e-mail. For more flexibility, you may want to open a free, Web-based e-mail account with **Yahoo! Mail** (http://mail.yahoo.com). (Microsoft's Hotmail is another popular option, but Hotmail has severe spam problems.) Your home ISP may be able to forward your e-mail to the Web-based account automatically.

If you need to access files on your office computer, look into a service called **GoToMyPC** (www.gotomypc.com). The service provides a Web-based interface for you to access and manipulate a distant PC from anywhere — even a cybercafe — provided your "target" PC is on and has an always-on connection to the Internet (such as with Road Runner cable). The service offers top-quality security, but if you're worried about hackers, use your own laptop rather than a cybercafe computer to access the GoToMyPC system.

If you're bringing your own computer, the new buzzword in computer access is **wi-fi** (wireless fidelity). More and more hotels, cafes, and retailers are signing on as wireless "hotspots" from where you can get high-speed connection without cable wires, networking hardware, or a phone line. You can get a wi-fi connection one of several ways. Many laptops sold in the last year have built-in wi-fi capability (an 802.11b wireless Ethernet connection). Mac owners have their own networking technology, Apple AirPort. For those with older computers, an 802.11b/**Wi-fi card** (around $50) can be plugged into your laptop.

You sign up for wireless access service much as you do cellphone service, through a plan offered by one of several commercial companies that have made wireless service available in airports, hotel lobbies, and coffee shops, primarily in the U.S. (followed by the U.K. and Japan). **T-Mobile Hotspot** (www.t-mobile.com/hotspot) serves up wireless connections at more than 1,000 Starbucks coffee shops nationwide. **Boingo** (www.boingo.com) and **Wayport** (www.wayport.com) have set up networks in airports and high-class hotel lobbies. IPass providers also give you access to a few hundred wireless hotel lobby setups. Best of all, you don't need to be staying at the Four Seasons to use the hotel's network; just set yourself up on a nice couch in the lobby. The companies' pricing policies can be byzantine, with a variety of monthly, per-connection, and per-minute plans, but in general you pay around $30 a month for limited access — and as more and more companies jump on the wireless bandwagon, prices are likely to get even more competitive.

 Some places provide **free wireless networks** in cities around the world. To locate these free hotspots, go to www.personaltelco.net/index. cgi/WirelessCommunities.

If wi-fi is not available at your destination, never fear. Almost every hotel offers dataports for laptop modems at the very least, and high-speed Internet access using an Ethernet network cable is becoming ever more common. You can bring your own cables, but most hotels rent them for around $10. **Call your hotel in advance** to see what your options are.

In addition, major Internet service providers (ISPs) have **local access numbers** around the world, allowing you to go online by simply placing a local call. Check your ISP's Web site or call its toll-free number and ask how you can use your current account away from home, and how much it will cost. If you're traveling outside the reach of your ISP, the **iPass** network has dial-up numbers in most of the world's countries. You'll have to sign up with an iPass provider, who will then tell you how to set up your computer for your destination(s). For a list of iPass providers, go to www.ipass.com and click "Individual Purchase". One solid provider is **i2roam** (www.i2roam.com; ☎ **866-811-6209** or 920-235-0475).

Wherever you go, bring a **connection kit** of the right power and phone adapters, a spare phone cord, and a spare Ethernet network cable — or find out whether your hotel supplies them to guests.

Keeping Up with Airline Security Measures

Even after the federalization of airport security, security procedures at U.S. airports tend to be uneven. But generally you'll be fine if you arrive at the airport **one hour** before a domestic flight and **two hours** before an international flight. If you show up late, tell an airline employee, and she'll probably whisk you to the front of the line. Be sure to allow extra time if you're traveling on a high-volume holiday getaway day, or if the terrorism alert level has been raised.

 It used to be a snap to fly between the Hawaiian Islands; it was a casual procedure to catch shuttle-style flights that left every 30 or 40 minutes. But since 9/11, the number of interisland flights has been dramatically reduced, making advance booking important. The airlines request that you show up at least 90 minutes before your flight to allow for security inspections, and I've found that to be good advice.

Bring a **current, government-issued photo ID** such as a driver's license or passport. Keep your ID at the ready to show at check-in, the security checkpoint, and sometimes even the gate. (Children under 18 don't need government-issued photo IDs for domestic flights, but they do for international flights to most countries.)

The TSA phased out **gate check-in** at all U.S. airports. And **E-tickets** have made paper tickets nearly obsolete. Passengers with E-tickets can beat the ticket-counter lines by using airport **electronic kiosks** or even **online check-in** from their home computer. Online check-in involves logging on to your airline's Web site, accessing your reservation, and printing your boarding pass — and the airline may even offer you bonus miles to do so! If you're using a kiosk at the airport, bring the credit card you used to book the ticket or your frequent-flier card. Print your boarding pass from the kiosk and simply proceed to the security checkpoint with your pass and a photo ID. If you're checking bags or looking to snag an exit-row seat, you'll be able to do so using most airline kiosks. Even the smaller airlines are employing the kiosk system, but always call your airline to make sure these alternatives are available. **Curbside check-in** is also a good way to avoid lines, although a few airlines still ban curbside check-in; call before you go.

Security checkpoint lines are getting shorter than they were during 2001 and 2002, but some doozies remain. If you have trouble standing for long periods of time, tell an airline employee; the airline will provide a wheel-chair. Speed up security by **not wearing metal objects** such as big belt buckles. If you've got metallic body parts, a note from your doctor can prevent a long chat with the security screeners. Keep in mind that only **ticketed passengers** are allowed past security, except for folks escorting disabled passengers or children.

Federalization has stabilized **what you can carry on** and **what you can't.** The general rule is that sharp things are out, nail clippers are okay, and food and beverages must be passed through the X-ray machine — but that security screeners can't make you drink from your coffee cup. Bring food in your carryon rather than checking it, as explo-sive-detection machines used on checked luggage have been known to mistake food (especially chocolate, for some reason) for bombs. Travelers in the United States are allowed one carry-on bag, plus a "per-sonal item" such as a purse, briefcase, or laptop bag. Carry-on hoarders can stuff all sorts of things into a laptop bag; as long as it has a laptop in it, it's still considered a personal item. The Transportation Security Administration (TSA) has issued a list of restricted items; check its Web site (www.tsa.gov/public/index.jsp) for details.

Airport screeners may decide that your checked luggage needs to be searched by hand. You can now purchase luggage locks that allow screeners to open and relock a checked bag if hand-searching is neces-sary. Look for Travel Sentry–certified locks at luggage or travel shops and Brookstone stores (you can buy them online at www.brookstone. com). These locks, approved by the TSA, can be opened by luggage inspectors with a special code or key. For more information on the locks, visit www.travelsentry.org. If you use something other than TSA-approved locks, your lock will be cut off your suitcase if a TSA agent needs to hand-search your luggage.

Making Reservations before You Leave Home

In addition to buying your airfare, booking your accommodations, and reserving a rental car, you may want to make a few plans before you leave home.

In general, you don't have to call ahead to reserve most activities until you arrive in Hawaii. Most snorkel cruises, guided tours, and the like can be reserved a day or two in advance. Even high-profile restaurants can usually get you in within a few days of the day you call.

Still, planning is never a bad idea. And it's an absolute necessity for certain special events and activities, including the following:

✔ **Luaus:** Maui's **Old Lahaina Luau** is the best luau in the islands — and it always sells out at least a week in advance, often more, as does its sister luau, **The Feast at Lele.** It's never too early to reserve your seats; see Chapter 13 for contact information. Second-best is the Big Island's **Kona Village Luau,** which is only offered on Friday nights; see Chapter 15. Oahu's best luau, the romantic **Royal Hawaiian Luau,** lights up Waikiki Beach on Monday nights (and summer Thursdays) only, so plan accordingly; see Chapter 11.

✔ **Snorkel cruises:** Maui's finest snorkel-cruise operator is **Trilogy Excursions.** They're hugely popular, so you may want to book before you leave home (see Chapter 14). Ditto for the Big Island's **Fair Wind Cruises,** the only catamaran operator with rights to take you to the finest snorkel spot in all the Hawaiian Islands, Kealakekua Bay (see Chapter 16). And if you don't want to miss the spectacular dolphin-watching tours off Oahu's leeward coast by **Dolphin Excursions** — I wouldn't! — be sure to secure your spots before you leave home. See Chapter 12.

✔ **Special guided tours:** I especially recommend making advance bookings with **Hawaii Forest & Trail** on the Big Island (see Chapter 16) if you don't want to miss out on its special offerings. The same goes for the terrific garden tour at the **National Tropical Botanical Garden** on Kauai (see Chapter 18), which often sells out a week or two in advance.

✔ **Special events:** Certain special events require planning or arrangements, such as the **Merrie Monarch Hula Festival,** the **Hawaii International Jazz Festival,** the Brothers Cazimero **Lei Day Concert** at the Waikiki Band Shell, and the **Kapalua Wine & Food Festival.** Check Chapter 4 to see what will be on while you're in town, and whether it requires planning. You may also want to check with the individual island visitor centers; see the Quick Concierge at the back of the book for contact information.

✔ **Special-occasion or holiday meals:** You should always make reservations to avoid disappointment. I indicate reservations policies in all restaurant reviews. This is especially true on holidays, when the nicer restaurants are overrun with locals and visitors alike. Take it from me on this one — I couldn't get a same-day table at a decent restaurant in Honolulu on Mother's Day to save my life.

✔ **Scuba classes:** First-time scuba divers may want to look into the various resort courses that are available, because they differ from outfitter to outfitter. See Chapters 12, 14, 16, and 18 for reputable local dive instructors on each of the main islands.

Consider taking scuba certification classes before you leave home; that way, you don't waste time learning in some resort swimming pool and can dive right in as soon as you get to Hawaii. A great way to find a local scuba instructor is via the Professional Association of Diving Instructors (PADI) Web site; go online to www.padi.com and click on "Dive Centers and Resorts."

Planning your activities before you leave home is often the best way to guarantee that you won't miss out on an event or a restaurant that you've been counting on — that way, if there's a sudden rush on tour spots, if a group suddenly decides that it's going to take over a snorkel boat for a full day, or a restaurant is planning to close down for a week to install a new stove in the kitchen, you have the opportunity to amend your plans accordingly. Planning also gives useful form to your itinerary, so that you'll begin to have an idea of where your busy days and your free days fall. Besides, you don't want to spend your valuable Hawaii time on the phone in your hotel room, do you?

Part III
Honolulu and the Rest of Oahu

The 5th Wave   By Rich Tennant

In this part . . .

Busier and more developed than the other islands, Oahu is often called "the Great Gathering Place." It's home to Hawaii's leading gateway, Honolulu International Airport, so even if you plan to concentrate on the other islands, you'll probably come to Oahu first. The two chapters in this part help you plan your trip to this beautiful island and offer a preview of the island's best selection of accommodations, dining, adventures, and attractions.

Chapter 11

Settling into Oahu

. . . .

In This Chapter

▶ Getting from Honolulu Airport to your hotel
▶ Finding your way around Waikiki, Honolulu, and the rest of Oahu
▶ Choosing among the island's top accommodations
▶ Discovering Honolulu and Waikiki's best restaurants
▶ Arranging for a luau
▶ Using an easy reference list of important local contacts

. . . .

*O*ahu is the busiest and most complex island in the Hawaiian chain, but it's still relatively easy to learn your way around. It's the one island where it's possible to get by without a rental car because it has a reliable public transportation system. Still, you may want to book your own wheels for freedom of movement.

Whether you're traveling from the mainland or a neighboring island, you'll arrive at Honolulu International Airport. That's where this chapter picks up. I tell you everything you need to know to get situated in this beautiful spot.

Arriving at Honolulu International Airport

Some transpacific flights fly directly to the neighbor islands. However, most visitors arrive at Oahu first, even if you plan to visit other islands during your stay. **Honolulu International Airport** (☎ 888-697-7813, 808-836-6411, or 808-836-6413; www.state.hi.us/dot/airports/oahu/hnl) is located on the South Shore of Oahu near Pearl Harbor, west of downtown Honolulu and Waikiki. It's 9 miles, or about a 20- to 30-minute drive, away from Waikiki. Honolulu International is a large but easily navigable airport. All mainland flights arrive in the **Main Overseas Terminal;** the Baggage Claim area is on the ground level. After collecting your bags, exit to the palm-lined street, where you can pick up taxis, Waikiki shuttles, and rental-car vans. For more information on transportation options, see "Getting from the Airport to Your Hotel," later in this chapter.

If you're catching a neighbor-island flight, walk to the large **Interisland Terminal** serving Aloha and Hawaiian airlines, which takes 10 to 15 minutes, or hop on the **Wiki-Wiki Bus,** a free airport shuttle that links the

Oahu Orientation

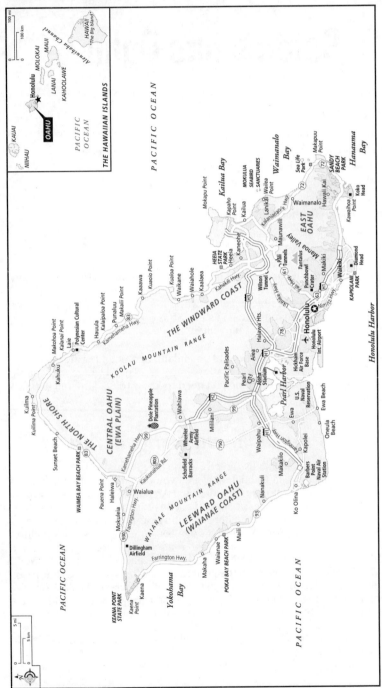

terminals ("wiki wiki" means "quick" in Hawaiian). I usually prefer the walk after being parked in an airline seat for hours.

Getting from the Airport to Your Hotel

Even though a rental car isn't a necessity on Oahu, it's my preferred method for getting around. Even if you leave your car parked and take other methods of transportation around Waikiki, you'll probably want a car for venturing farther afield. Luckily, rental cars are usually rather inexpensive on Oahu, and all the big companies have cars available at the airport. You'll get the best rate if you book before you arrive; see Chapter 7 for more on this subject.

Driving yourself

A van from your car-rental agency will take you to the lot where you can pick up your car. From baggage claim, head out to the well-marked curbside waiting area. The appropriate rental van should swing by within a few minutes.

You'll need a good map to get your bearings and find your way around during the course of your stay. All the rental-car agencies offer map booklets, which are invaluable for getting around the island. Some car-rental agents can even give you computer-generated, detailed directions from the airport to your hotel.

To get to Waikiki, simply turn right out of the airport (signs are clear) onto Nimitz Highway (Highway 92), which runs directly under the H-1 (one of Oahu's three freeways) for a few minutes. In about 10 minutes, Nimitz Highway deposits you onto Ala Moana Boulevard, which takes you past the huge Ala Moana Shopping Center (on your left) and grassy Ala Moana Beach Park (on your right). Moments later, you reach Kalakaua (ka-la-COW-ah) Avenue, Waikiki's main thoroughfare.

Taking a taxi

The taxi stand is located just outside the automated doors in the Baggage Claim area. You should have no trouble getting a taxi, but if you need help, an attendant is on hand to assist you. **SIDA Taxi** (☎ **808-836-0011**) is the sole company authorized to offer taxi-stand service at the airport. Taxi fare to Waikiki is about $25 to $30, plus tip.

Star Taxi (☎ **800-671-2999** or 808-942-7827) can offer pre-arranged airport pickups to Waikiki for $20 (plus tip); use the toll-free number to arrange your pickup before you leave home. Be sure to have your airline, flight number, and arrival time on hand when you call.

Catching a shuttle ride

The **Airport Waikiki Express Shuttle** (☎ **808-566-7333**; www.state. hi.us/dot/airports/oahu/hnl/hnl_ground_trans.htm) operates

Honolulu & Waikiki Orientation

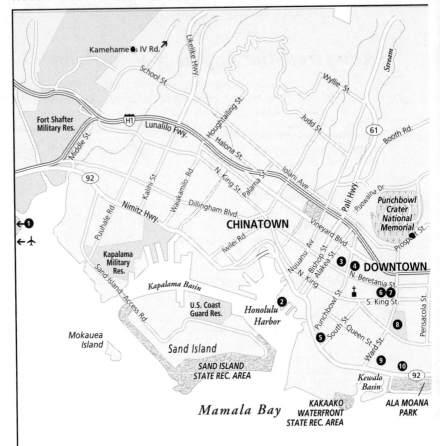

Kamehameha IV Rd.
Likelike Hwy.
School St.
Stream
Wyllie St.
Fort Shafter Military Res.
Lunalilo Fwy.
Houghtailing St.
Judd St.
Middle St.
Halona St.
61
Booth Rd.
92
Waikamilo Rd.
Kalihi St.
N. King St.
Palama St.
Iolani Ave
Dillingham Blvd.
Puuhale Rd.
Nimitz Hwy.
CHINATOWN
Vineyard Blvd.
Punchbowl Crater National Memorial
Prospect St.
Puowaina Dr.
Kapalama Military Res.
Iwilei Rd.
Nuuanu Av.
Bishop St.
N. King
Alakea St.
N. Beretania St.
DOWNTOWN
Sand Island Access Rd.
Kapalama Basin
U.S. Coast Guard Res.
Honolulu Harbor
Punchbowl St.
S. King St.
Pensacola St.
Mokauea Island
Sand Island
South St.
Queen St.
Ward Ave.
Kewalo Basin
92
Mamala Bay
SAND ISLAND STATE REC. AREA
KAKAAKO WATERFRONT STATE REC. AREA
ALA MOANA PARK

Ala Moana Center **11**
Aloha Stadium **1**
Aloha Tower Marketplace **2**
Battleship Row, Pearl Harbor **1**
Diamond Head Crater **15**
Honolulu International Airport **1**
Honolulu Police Department
   Main Station **6**
Neal Blaisdell Center **8**
Queen's Medical Center **4**
Restaurant Row **5**
Royal Hawaiian Shopping Center **13**
State Capitol **3**
State Convention Center **12**
Straub Clinic & Hospital **7**
Waikiki Band Shell **14**
Ward Centre **10**
Ward Warehouse **9**

0   5 mi
0   5 km
H1
ALA MOANA
area of detail
HONOLULU
DOWN-TOWN
Sand Island
WAIKIKI

Airport
Church
Information

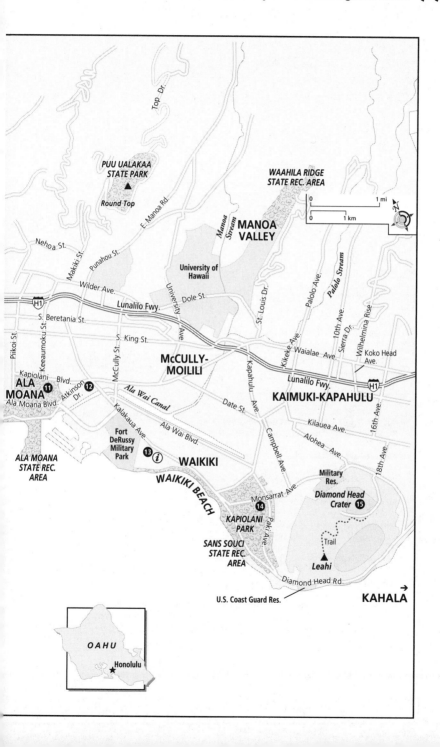

TheBus

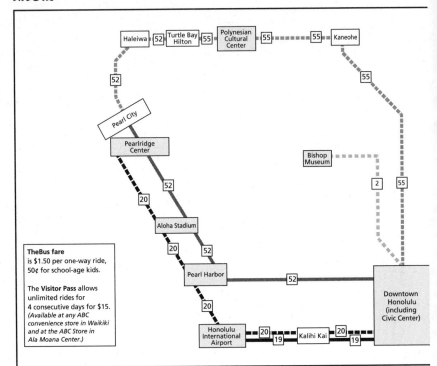

TheBus fare is $1.50 per one-way ride, 50¢ for school-age kids.

The **Visitor Pass** allows unlimited rides for 4 consecutive days for $15. *(Available at any ABC convenience store in Waikiki and at the ABC Store in Ala Moana Center.)*

BUS ROUTES TO MAJOR ATTRACTIONS FROM WAIKIKI

Ala Moana Center: Bus no. 8, 19, 20, 42, or 58 toward downtown Honolulu.

Aloha Tower Marketplace: Bus no. 19 or 20 toward downtown Honolulu.

Battleship Row, Pearl Harbor: Take no. 20 or 42 in the downtown Honolulu direction past the airport and get off across the street from the Arizona Memorial. Or take any bus to Ala Moana Center, and transfer to the no. 40, 40A, or 62 to Pearl Harbor.

Bishop Museum: Bus no. 2 to downtown Honolulu; get off at Kapalama Street, walk one block inland to Bernice Street and museum.

Chinatown: Bus no. 2, 13, 19, or 20 to downtown Honolulu.

Circle Island tour: Bus no. 52 or 55 from the Ala Moana Center.

The Contemporary Museum & Punchbowl Crater (National Cemetery of the Pacific): Bus no. 2 or 13 to downtown Honolulu to corner of Beretania and Alapai streets (across from police station); walk toward ocean on Alapai Street to Hotel Street and pick up bus no. 15.

Diamond Head Crater: Bus no. 22 or 58.

Hanauma Bay: Bus no. 22 in the Diamond Head direction to East Oahu.

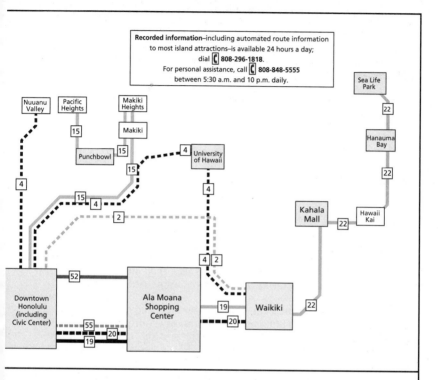

Recorded information–including automated route information to most island attractions–is available 24 hours a day; dial [C] **808-296-1818**. For personal assistance, call [C] **808-848-5555** between 5:30 a.m. and 10 p.m. daily.

Honolulu Academy of Arts: Bus no. 2 or 13 to downtown Honolulu to the corner of Beretania Street and Ward Avenue.

Honolulu Zoo: Bus no. 8, 19, 20, 42, or 58 toward Diamond Head.

Iolani Palace & Mission Houses Museum: Bus no. 2 or 13 to downtown Honolulu; get off at the corner of Punchbowl and Beretania streets toward the ocean to King Street.

Kapiolani Park & Waikiki Band Shell: Bus no. 2, 4, 8, 19, or 20 toward Diamond Head to Kapiolani Park.

Polynesian Cultural Center: Any bus toward downtown Honolulu to Ala Moana Center; transfer to bus no. 55.

Restaurant Row: Bus no. 19 or 20 toward downtown Honolulu.

Sea Life Park: Bus no. 22 or 58 in the Diamond Head direction to East Oahu.

Waikiki Aquarium: Bus no. 2, 4, 8, 19, 20, 22, 42, or 58 toward Diamond Head.

Waimea Valley Falls: Any bus to Ala Moana Center and transfer to no. 55.

Victoria Ward Centers: Bus no. 19, 20, or 42 toward downtown Honolulu.

shuttles between the airport and Waikiki hotels around the clock, with passenger vans departing every 20 to 30 minutes, depending on the time of day. The fare is $8 per person to Waikiki, $13 round-trip (2 bags per person allowed; you'll pay a few dollars extra for additional or oversized baggage). No reservation is necessary. You can buy your tickets at the Roberts Hawaii desk near Baggage Claim turnstile H.

No reservation is necessary for your trip to the airport, but be sure to book a hotel pickup for your departing flight at least 48 hours in advance by calling ☎ **808-566-7333.**

The island's descriptively named bus system, **TheBus,** does travel between the airport and Waikiki, and the one-way fare is just $2 ($1 for kids under age 19, or free for a child under age 6 who sits on your lap). Bus nos. 19 and 20 (Waikiki Beach and Hotels) run to downtown Honolulu and Waikiki. The hitch is that TheBus is a viable airport-transfer option only for the most freewheeling travelers, simply because you're not allowed to board with any substantive luggage. You can bring on a carryon or small suitcase as long as it fits under the seat and doesn't disrupt other passengers; otherwise, you have to take a shuttle or taxi. What's more, the ride to Waikiki will take more than an hour, as opposed to 20 minutes or a half-hour if you take a taxi or shuttle.

If you're not going to rent a car, I suggest taking a taxi or shuttle from the airport and then using TheBus to get around town after you've settled in. For more information on TheBus, see the section "Letting somebody else do the driving," later in this chapter.

Choosing Your Location

Waikiki is hardly Las Vegas — not by a long shot. Waikiki's version of raucous fun is pretty darn easygoing — more like a laid-back, high-rise beach party than anything else. Still, different areas of Waikiki have varying degrees of action.

Mid-Waikiki

Mid-Waikiki is prime Waikiki territory — the life of the party. This is Waikiki at its most densely built, but also Waikiki at its most convenient. Restaurants, shopping, and — most important — the city's most popular and celebrated stretch of sand are all within walking distance.

Although it retains some vestiges of cheese, mid-Waikiki has become more sophisticated of late, with respectable restaurants and both midrange and couture boutiques replacing former T-shirt shops and tacky souvenir posts. The midsection of the beach has been gloriously transformed into a public playground extraordinaire, with winding flagstone paths, blooming tropical foliage, and grassy knolls for sunbathers who nix the sand. Still, plenty of affordable hotels remain; the neighborhood has simply improved around them.

Ewa Waikiki

Ewa (EE-va) Waikiki is the western end of the neighborhood, on the way to downtown Honolulu. (Oahuans say "ewa" to indicate a westerly direction, meaning toward the town called Ewa on the west side of Oahu.) This western end of Waikiki, beyond Saratoga Road (on the other side of Fort DeRussy Park from mid-Waikiki), is a tad removed but plenty convenient. The beach is quieter at this more residential (mostly high-rise apartments), less dense end, but you may find yourself getting in the car (or hopping the Waikiki Trolley) to mid-Waikiki destinations.

The Outrigger hotel group has developed a mixed-use master plan for the western end of Waikiki along Beach Walk and Lewers Street, between Kalakaua Avenue and the beach. Among the developments will be 100,000 square feet of new retail dining, shopping, and entertainment facilities, plus new hotel rooms and timeshare units. The results should be spectacular, but may mean some serious noise and confusion into 2006. I have tried to avoid recommending hotels that fall in the heart of the construction, but a start date is indefinite and the construction zone could change at any time. If your hotel of choice is located in Ewa Waikiki (indicated in the listings below), inquire as to the state of the construction when you book and, if the hotel is near the construction, ask for a room away from the noise.

Diamond Head Waikiki

For those who want both quiet and convenience, this easternmost section of Waikiki is the place to stay. Many call Diamond Head Waikiki their favorite section of town, thanks to its pretty setting, easygoing vibe, great beach, and prime panoramic views of the rest of Waikiki. A handful of small hotels and condo buildings sit at the foot of Diamond Head crater, separated from the rest of the neighborhood by well-manicured **Kapiolani Park** (Honolulu's answer to Central Park). The beach here, called Sans Souci Beach, is the locals' favorite stretch, thanks to its attractive disposition (Diamond Head makes a gorgeous backdrop) and intimate, low-key vibe.

Beyond Waikiki: Kahala

This exclusive residential neighborhood on the other side of Diamond Head, just a 10-minute drive east of prime Waikiki, is the perfect compromise for those who want an away-from-it-all vibe and a freeway-convenient location. Expect to dig deep, though — the only hotel in these parts is the **Kahala Mandarin,** Honolulu's finest full-fledged resort.

Farther afield: The Ko Olina Resort

Past Pearl Harbor, about 40 minutes west of Waikiki via the H-1 freeway, is the carefully manicured **Ko Olina Resort,** the only full-fledged resort development on the arid leeward coast of Oahu. The **JW Marriott Ihilani Resort and Spa** is a refuge for golfers and spa-goers who want to see

Oahu's attractions without staying in an urban setting. The downside? Expect to spend a good portion of your island visit in the car and a good deal of money on resort dining because all the island's sights and restaurants are at least a half-hour's drive away.

Getting Around Oahu

Getting around Waikiki and Honolulu is a tad complicated, simply because so many streets are one-way. Still, this is no Los Angeles, by any means, and drivers are much more easygoing. With a good map in hand, you won't have a problem. After you get past the city, basically one road circles the island, so you'd have to work hard to lose your bearings.

Navigating your way around Honolulu

A big, bustling city, Honolulu is approximately 12 miles wide and 26 miles long, running east-west roughly between Diamond Head crater and Pearl Harbor. It folds over seven hills laced by seven streams and runs down to the sea.

Honolulu's most famous neighborhood, **Waikiki,** runs along Honolulu's central stretch of coast all the way to grassy Kapiolani Park and Diamond Head crater, Hawaii's most recognizable landmark, to the east. This well-developed strip of land is about 3 miles long, but it extends from the coast inland only a few blocks to the man-made Ala Wai Canal.

Waikiki's primary thoroughfares run east to west. Kalakaua Avenue runs one block away from and parallel to the coast in an easterly direction, toward Diamond Head. Ala Wai Boulevard runs along Waikiki's inland (northern) edge one way toward downtown. Sandwiched in between — one block north of Kalakaua, one block south of Ala Wai — is Kuhio Avenue, which handles two-way traffic.

The Outrigger hotel group has developed a mixed-use master plan for the western end of Waikiki along Beach Walk and Lewers Street, between Kalakaua Avenue and the beach. The results should be spectacular, but may mean some serious confusion into 2006. The good news: It's a small area, and easy to avoid. You may want avoid it once the construction begins sometime in late 2004 or early 2005. For the latest update, contact the **Oahu Visitors Bureau** (☎ **877-525-OAHU** or 808-524-0722).

West of Waikiki is the Ala Moana section of Honolulu, so named for the **Ala Moana Center,** Honolulu's retail and transportation hub. (You can pick up almost every major bus route here; see the section "Boarding TheBus," later in this chapter.) Drive west on Ala Moana, and you pass more shopping stops — Ward Centre, the Ward Warehouse, a mall of dining options called Restaurant Row, and the historic harborfront Aloha Tower Marketplace shopping and restaurant complex — before reaching downtown Honolulu.

Situated in the blocks inland from the Aloha Tower Marketplace —
basically between Nuuanu Avenue and Punchbowl Street — downtown
Honolulu is comprised of a tiny cluster of high-rises that serves as the
financial, business, and government center of Hawaii. Also here are the
Chinatown Historic District, the oldest Chinatown in America, and
some of Hawaii's most important historic landmarks, most notably
Iolani (ee-oh-LAN-ee) **Palace,** the only royal palace on American soil.

Inland from here, and north of the Ala Wai Canal above Waikiki, residential neighborhoods make their way up the hills, creating an urban backdrop unlike any other in a major American city. Running through these
neighborhoods is the freeway known as H-1, which leads to the east end
of Oahu.

To avoid frustration when driving around Waikiki and downtown
Honolulu, always have a map nearby that features directional arrows on
the city's many one-way streets. The map on the color tear-out Cheat
Sheet at the front of this book — which features Waikiki on one side and
the downtown and Ala Moana areas of Honolulu on the other — should
do the trick. Just think of the Waikiki side as the easterly portion and the
Honolulu side as the westerly portion; if you were to photocopy them
and put them side by side, they'd (roughly) align to cover, in large part,
the area where you'll be spending most of your time in the city.

If you stop a local and ask for directions, you're likely to hear a few
unfamiliar terms. That's because islanders tend to give directions a bit
differently than what mainlanders are used to, particularly in Honolulu:

- ✔ Seldom will anyone direct you north or south; instead, they'll send
  you either *makai* (ma-KAI), meaning toward the sea, or *mauka*
  (MOW-kah), toward the mountains.

- ✔ Instead of east and west, locals will tell you to go *Diamond Head*
  when they mean east (in the direction of the world-famous Diamond
  Head crater), and *Ewa* (EE-va) when they mean west (in the direction
  of the town called Ewa, beyond Pearl Harbor).

Keep these terms in mind, because if you ask a local for directions, this
is what you're likely to hear: "Drive two blocks *makai* (toward the sea)
and then turn Diamond Head (east) at the stop light. Go one block and
turn *mauka* (toward the mountains). It's on the *Ewa* (western) side of
the street."

Exploring the rest of Oahu

After you move beyond the city, Oahu is simple to navigate. That's
because just a few roads work in concert to form a rough circle.

The "Circle Island" route starts in Honolulu, travels up the middle of the
island to the North Shore, curves around the island's top knob, proceeds
down the eastern, or windward, coast, and around the island's eastern

knob back to Waikiki and Honolulu. (Thanks to a few highway tunnels drilled through the Koolau Mountains, you can also drive directly between Honolulu and the Windward Coast without having to go all the way around the east end of the island.)

Driving to the North Shore

The North Shore is the epicenter of Hawaii's surf culture. Small communities and collections of simple houses serve as scant interruption for the string of fabulous beaches that line this rural coast, where the schizophrenic surf is flat as a pancake in summer and kicks up to monster proportions in winter. The charming little surf town of Haleiwa (ha-lay-EE-vah) is the North Shore's main community and the heart of the culture.

I highly recommend coming here to explore, either to watch the world's most outrageous daredevil surfers in action in winter, or just to experience the laid-back vibe and play in the baby waves in summer. I discuss the beaches and other North Shore highlights in Chapter 12. But getting there is half the fun.

Haleiwa sits about an hour's drive north of Waikiki, at the junction of highways 99 and 83, both called Kamehameha Highway. The easiest way to get there is to cruise north through Oahu's broad and fertile central valley, past Pearl Harbor, Schofield Barracks of *From Here to Eternity* fame, and pineapple and sugar cane fields until the sea reappears.

From Waikiki, pick up the H-1 freeway heading west. Your best bet is probably to take Ala Wai Boulevard to McCully Street north to H-1, but it all depends on where your hotel is; ask at the front desk for the most direct route.

After you're on H-1, stay to the right because the freeway divides abruptly. Follow the signs for H-1 and then H-1/H-2. When the two roads divide, follow the H-2 up the middle of the island, heading north toward the town of Wahiawa (wa-hee-AH-va). That's what the sign will say — not North Shore or Haleiwa, but Wahiawa.

The H-2 runs out and becomes a two-lane road about 18 miles out of downtown Honolulu, near Schofield Barracks. It then turns into Kamehameha Highway (first Highway 99, then Highway 83) at Wahiawa. Kam Highway, as the islanders call it, is your road for the rest of the trip to Haleiwa.

You can also meander your way to the North Shore by driving along the lush Windward Coast and around Oahu's peak. In fact, I highly recommend driving the full circle and making a day of it. If you're in a hurry to get to the North Shore, take the central route and follow the Windward Coast back south. If you'd rather enjoy one or two of the windward side's magnificent beaches on the way north (see Chapter 12), do that in the morning and come back to Waikiki via the less scenic central route. For windward driving directions, see "Cruising along the scenic Windward Coast," later in this chapter.

Heading to East Oahu

At some point, you're likely to find yourself heading beyond Diamond Head, either bound for Hanauma Bay, one of Hawaii's finest snorkel spots (the best for first-timers), or Sea Life Park, or just to take in some extremely groovy desert-meets-the-sea scenery. You can reach East Oahu simply by heading east on the H-1, which dumps you onto the Kalanianaole (ka-lan-ee-an-OW-lay) Highway (Highway 72), the main thoroughfare that takes you around the elbow of Oahu.

Cruising along the scenic Windward Coast

Stand in the heart of Waikiki with your back to the ocean. To your right, you'll see a mountain range called the Koolaus (koo-OO-laus); on the other side of them is the east coast of Oahu. This windward-facing coast is the island's wettest side and, therefore, its most lush and gorgeous. Lined with suburban beach communities and some breathtakingly beautiful beaches, it's well worth seeing.

Three highways will get you from the city to the Windward Coast in about 20 minutes or so: the Pali Highway (Highway 61), the Likelike (lee-kay-LEE-kay) Highway (Highway 63), and the H-3 freeway, all of which cut right through the mountains. Your best bet from Waikiki is to take the H-1 to the Pali Highway. After you go through the tunnel, turn left on Kamehameha Highway (Highway 83); this coastal highway will be your roadway for the rest of the trip, whether you choose to follow it all the way to Haleiwa (about 1½ hours without stops), whether you're heading to the Polynesian Cultural Center (the South Pacific cultural theme park about an hour from Waikiki), or whether you're simply enjoying the ultralush scenery and some of best beaches in the islands. (See Chapter 12 for specific suggestions.)

 Dominating the west side of Oahu is the island's second mountain range, the Waianae (wah-ee-AN-eh) mountains. Beyond this ridge is the hot, dry leeward side of the island. You're by no means prohibited from heading there, but there's not much to see, and locals prefer to keep this one area of heavily touristed Oahu to themselves. Unless you're heading to the area's one master-planned resort community, Ko Olina, up to Waianae to meet a scheduled cruise with **Dolphin Excursions** (see Chapter 12), or for some other prearranged reason, I suggest honoring their wishes and concentrating your efforts on exploring the other parts of this wonderfully multifaceted island instead.

Letting somebody else do the driving

Oahu is the one island that's easy to visit if you can't — or won't — drive yourself. Oahu's islandwide public transportation system — **TheBus** (www.thebus.org) — has been named America's Best Transit System by the American Public Transit Association, so you can count on it being extremely user-friendly. The **Waikiki Trolley** is also available for getting around town.

Although TheBus can take you anywhere you want to go on Oahu, I don't recommend using it to reach areas beyond the city. Not only will you spend a total of 3½ to 4½ hours on the bus getting there and back, but the waits can be extremely long at lonely North Shore bus stops. If you don't want to rent a car for the duration of your stay, I strongly encourage you to rent one for your day of North Shore and Windward Coast exploring. If, for some reason, you can't rent a car but still want to explore, use one of the tour companies I mention in Chapter 12 to take you around the island.

Boarding TheBus

TheBus is an excellent transit deal. The service is good, the buses are clean, and the cost is low. The one-way fare to ride TheBus is $2 per one-way ride for adults and $1 for school-age children, seniors, or riders with disabilities. That low price can get you anywhere you want to go on the island. Service begins daily at 3:30 a.m. and runs until 1:30 a.m. Buses run about every 5 to 15 minutes during the day and every 30 minutes in the evening.

If you're going to be in town for a longer stay, you can buy a **Monthly Pass** for $40 ($20 for kids, seniors, and the disabled). Passes are sold at most 7-Eleven stores, as well as at Foodland, Star, and Times supermarkets. Or you can go directly to TheBus Pass Office at Kalihi Traffic Center, 811 Middle St. (between King Street and Kamehaha Highway) in downtown Honolulu (☎ **808-848-4444**); to get there, take the 1, 2, A, or B lines.

TheBus operates dozens of bus lines, but you'll only need to concern yourself with the handful that pass through Waikiki. Two-way Kuhio Avenue is the main thoroughfare for bus routes through Waikiki.

Virtually all the city's major bus routes converge at the Ala Moana Shopping Center, just west of Waikiki. TheBus makes three stops at the mammoth mall: two on the ocean side of the mall on Ala Moana Boulevard, and one on the mountain side, on Kona Street. Read the posted sign at the stop to make sure that the line you want is going where you want to go. Or, if you prefer to iron things out beforehand, call TheBus at ☎ **808-848-5555** to determine which stop is the right one for your destination.

Recorded information is also available around the clock; dial ☎ **808-296-1818.** In addition to providing a summary of general information — including the major Waikiki bus lines — this information line offers automated route information to major island attractions.

If you want help planning a specific route, or if you have other questions pertaining to TheBus system, call ☎ **808-848-5555,** where a real live information specialist can help you out daily between 5:30 a.m. and 10 p.m. Have your departure and destination points handy when you call, as well as the time of day you want to travel.

If you're planning on relying on TheBus to get around, I highly recommend visiting TheBus's excellent Web site at www.thebus.org to familiarize yourself with the system before you leave home. It offers timetables and maps for all routes, plus directions to many local attractions and a list of upcoming events. (Taking TheBus is sometimes easier than parking.)

Also, don't hesitate to ask the front desk or concierge at your hotel for assistance in navigating TheBus system. Chances are very good that they know the system well, and they'll be glad to help. And don't be shy about asking the bus drivers for help. In general, they're very friendly and helpful, and they'll be glad to point you in the right direction.

If you plan on using TheBus system a lot and want to get to know it well, pick up one of the handy system reference guides available at any convenience store for just a few dollars.

A few etiquette tips for using TheBus:

✔ When the bus you want approaches, wave to the driver to indicate that you want to board the bus. Back away from the stop if you don't want that particular bus.

✔ You must have the exact fare when you board the bus because the drivers don't make change. You can use either dollar bills or change.

✔ To transfer to another line, ask the driver of the first bus you board for a free transfer when you board. You can't use a transfer to pick up the same line going in the same direction, nor can you use a transfer to go back to where you came from.

✔ To open the rear door of the bus, push on the door or step on the first step when the green light is lit. Be sure to hold the door open as you get off the bus so that your fellow riders don't get hit by the slamming door.

Taking the Waikiki Trolley

The **Waikiki Trolley** (☎ **800-824-8804** or 808-593-2822; www.waikiki trolley.com) is an open-air, motorized trolley similar to a San Francisco cable car. I like using the trolley; it's a fun way to do some open-air sight-seeing. It may be the most fun you can have on public transportation. The trolley runs along three lines:

✔ The **Honolulu City (Red) Line** runs daily from 8:45 a.m. to 6:30 p.m. It makes a loop around Waikiki and downtown Honolulu every 30 minutes, stopping at key attractions such as the Royal Hawaiian Shopping Center, the Waikiki Aquarium, Aloha Tower Marketplace, the Bishop Museum, Iolani Palace, the Honolulu Academy of Arts, Ward Centre, Ala Moana Center, and other prime stops.

✔ The **Shopping and Dining (Yellow) Line** runs daily from 9 a.m. to 11 p.m. (7:30 p.m. on Sundays), following a similar loop but making different stops. (Don't be misled by the name of this line; you have to take the Red Line if you want to visit Hilo Hattie's or the Aloha Tower Marketplace.) This line also has an express version.

✔ The **Ocean Coast (Blue) Line** makes its rounds daily from 8:30 a.m. to 7:20 p.m., connecting Waikiki with East Oahu sites, including Hanauma Bay and Sea Life Park.

Due to some arcane state rule, trolley passengers are only allowed to disembark at Hanauma Bay for a quick photo-op; you aren't allowed to use this option to get to and from the marine preserve for a day of snorkeling. If you want to use the trolley to reach Hanauma Bay, disembark at Koko Marina Center, where you can either walk the mile to the park or catch a taxi.

A **one-day jump-on, jump-off pass** costs $25 for adults, $18 for seniors over age 62, $15 for military personnel, and $12 for kids ages 4 to 11. This pass allows you to hop on and off all three lines all day long, as much as you want.

A **four-day jump-on, jump-off pass** gives you unlimited trolley privileges for four consecutive days for $45 for adults, $27 for seniors, $25 for military personnel, and $18 for kids 4 to 11. The four-day pass is a good deal, relatively speaking; still, you're probably better off using TheBus to get around for that many days because the trolley routes are simply too limited.

The Waikiki Trolley also offers two sightseeing tours: the **First Adventures (Purple) Line** and the **Hidden Treasures (Orange) Line.** Both offer 2½-hour guided sightseeing tours without hop-on, hop-off privileges. For shoppers, there's also a Waikele Shuttle to suburban Oahu's premium outlet mall. Tickets for each are $22 for adults, $8 for kids ages 4 to 11.

You have to purchase your trolley tickets before you board the trolley. The main customer service kiosk is at the **Royal Hawaiian Shopping Center,** in the heart of Waikiki at Kalakaua and Seaside avenues. If this location isn't convenient, call one of the numbers listed in this section and ask the friendly operator for the one nearest you. You can also pre-book your tickets online or through the toll-free number listed earlier in this section.

Staying in Style

There's only one place to stay when you come to Oahu: Honolulu's most famous district, Waikiki. Frankly, if you're planning a trip to the liveliest island in the Pacific, you may as well revel in the energy of it. If staying in the heart of the action doesn't sound appealing to you, you may want to consider skipping Oahu entirely and heading to a neighbor island.

That said, if you do want peace and quiet, you can find it on Oahu, too. A number of the hotels listed in this chapter are located on the quieter fringe of Waikiki, in less densely developed or residential neighborhoods. And if you'd really prefer to stay beyond the city and get away from it all, I can point you to a luxury resort well beyond the reach of Waikiki and also show you how to book the B&B or vacation rental of your dreams on the gorgeous residential Windward Coast or the island's funky North Shore.

Oahu's best accommodations

As you peruse the options, keep in mind that Waikiki is a densely developed area, so it contains more hotels and fewer full-fledged resort spreads and condos than what you find on the neighbor islands.

In the following listings, each resort, hotel, or condo name is followed by a number of dollar signs, ranging from one ($) to five ($$$$$). Each represents the median rack-rate price range for a double room per night, as follows:

$	Super-cheap — less than $100 per night
$$	Still affordable — $100 to $175
$$$	Moderate — $175 to $250
$$$$	Expensive but not ridiculous — $250 to $375
$$$$$	Ultraluxurious — more than $375 per night

You almost never need to pay the asking price for a hotel room. Check out Chapter 8 for details on how to avoid paying full price. Also see Chapter 6 for advice on how to score an all-inclusive package that can save you big bucks on both accommodations and airfare, and sometimes, car rentals and activities, too.

Also, don't forget that the state adds 11.42 percent in taxes to your hotel bill.

A number of Waikiki's inexpensive and midpriced hotels feature rooms whose bathrooms have showers only, no tubs. If you need a full tub, be sure to check that one will be available when booking to avoid disappointment.

Aqua Bamboo
$$ Mid-Waikiki

This newish 90-room boutique hotel is a welcome antidote to the midpriced Waikiki standard. The look is hip, attractive, and Zen serene. The location is good, too; this central but relatively quiet corner of Waikiki, overlooking the pretty Ala Wai Canal, more than makes up for the three-block walk to the beach. The guestrooms are stylish and functional and wear a serene neutral palette in keeping with the Asian-modern style. All boast clean-lined, contemporary furniture, pleasant marble bathrooms, and private lanais. Most rooms have fully equipped kitchenettes or

Waikiki Accommodations

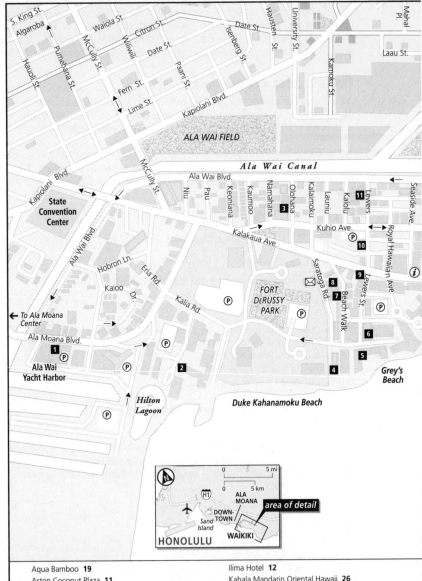

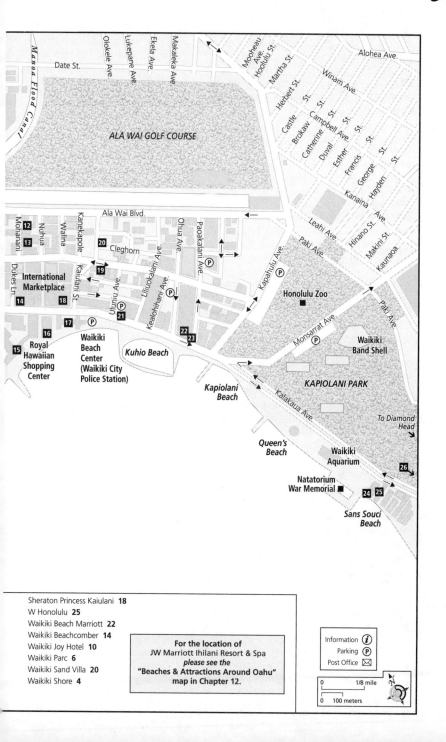

Manoa Flood Canal

Date St.

Olokele Ave.
Lukepane Ave.
Ekela Ave.
Makaleka Ave.

Mooheau Ave.
Hoolulu St.
Alohea Ave.

Martha St.
Winam Ave.

Herbert St.

Castle St.
Brokaw St.
Campbell Ave.
Catherine St.
Duval St.
Esther St.
Francis St.
George St.

Kanaina Ave.
Hayden St.

ALA WAI GOLF COURSE

Ala Wai Blvd.

Leahi Ave.
Hinano St.
Makini St.
Kaunaoa St.

Paki Ave.

Mohanani
Nuhua
Walina
Kanekapole
Kaiulani St.
Uluniu Ave.
Liliuokalani Ave.
Kealohilani Ave.
Ohua Ave.
Paoakalani Ave.
Kapahulu Ave.

Cleghorn

International
Marketplace

Dukes Ln.

Honolulu Zoo

Paki Ave.

12
13
20
19
14 **18**
17
16
15
21
22
23

Royal
Hawaiian
Shopping
Center

Waikiki
Beach
Center
(Waikiki City
Police Station)

Kuhio Beach

Monsarrat Ave.

Waikiki
Band Shell

KAPIOLANI PARK

Kapiolani
Beach

Kalakaua Ave.

To Diamond
Head

Queen's
Beach

Waikiki
Aquarium

26

Natatorium
War Memorial

24 **25**

Sans Souci
Beach

For the location of
JW Marriott Ihilani Resort & Spa
please see the
"Beaches & Attractions Around Oahu"
map in Chapter 12.

Information ⓘ
Parking Ⓟ
Post Office ✉

0   1/8 mile
0   100 meters

kitchens for extra convenience. The friendly staff excels at personalized attention. On-site is a petite but appealing pool in a lovely garden setting, plus a barbecue grill for guest use; you can also access the hot tub and sauna at the neighboring Hyatt Regency for a fee. And all of the perks of Waikiki — including copious restaurants and shopping — are an easy walk away. All in all, this hotel is a terrific choice for travelers who want sophisticated style with an affordable price tag.

If you're renting a car, be sure to reserve a parking space when you book, as the lot has a limited number of spaces.

See map p. 130. 2425 Kuhio Ave (at Kaiulani Avenue), Honolulu, HI 96815. ☎ 866-406-2782 or 808-922-7777. Fax: 808-922-9473. www.aquabamboo.com. *Parking: $5. Rack rates: $145–$195 double, $185–$265 1-bedroom suite. Deals: Check for Internet specials; as low as $109 at press time. Seniors can save even more; as low as $94 at press time. AE, DISC, MC, V.*

Aston Coconut Plaza
$$ Mid-Waikiki

This small hotel offers excellent value for those on a budget — and pretty good views, too, considering that it's blocks from the beach. The light and airy hotel establishes a tropical plantation vibe (quite an achievement in the heart of Waikiki) with lots of greenery, island-style rattan, and aloha-spirited service. Rooms have cool terra-cotta floors, fridge and coffee-maker, and lanais. (Ask for a room overlooking the pretty canal for maximum advantage, and on a higher floor for maximum quiet.) Studios and junior suites both have full kitchenettes with microwave; junior suites also add a sleeper sofa and a second lanai to the mix. Nice on-site amenities include a tiny but nice pool with a sun deck, plus a coin-op laundry. The free continental breakfast makes a good deal even better. The only downside is a four-block walk to the beach — but you can count the extra money in your pocket on the way.

See map p. 130. 450 Lewers St. (at Ala Wai Boulevard). ☎ 800-922-7866, 877-997-6667, or 808-923-8828. Fax: 808-923-3473. www.aston-hotels.com. *Valet parking: $9. Rack rates: $100 double, $115–$135 studio, $185 junior suite. Rates include continental breakfast. Deals: Excellent opportunities for discounts. Internet-only ePriceBreaker rates as low as $67 at press time. Ask for AAA, senior (50-plus), kids, and corporate discounts, and other special rate programs. AE, DC, DISC, MC, V.*

Aston Waikiki Beach Hotel
$$–$$$ Mid-Waikiki

All it took was a $30-million renovation for this freshly hip hotel to win kudos from *Travel + Leisure* magazine as one of its 50 favorite affordable beach resorts in the world (and the only Hawaii selection). It's a monster, with 717 rooms, but 85 percent of them offer ocean views, and the location can hardly be better — my favorite stretch of Waikiki Beach is just across the street. The renovation concept is Hawaiian nostalgia with a modern flair; the result is fun and funky, but the day-glo colors may be a bit much for some. Also, rooms are small — just 225 square feet, with junior suites running 300 square feet. But you didn't come to Waikiki to hang out in your room anyway, right? The furnishings are tropical and fun, if a little less practical than I would like. For example, the closets have a beaded hula dancer curtain that dances when the trade winds blow through your room; however, the beads can be a hassle when you're trying to get to your clothes. Still, the hotel's appealing energy and prime location make up for a lot. And on-site dining options are terrific: Tiki's Bar & Grill (see review later in this chapter) is one of my new Waikiki favorites for cocktails, pupus, and live music; Wolfgang Puck Express gives you instant affordable access to the master's creative California fare, while Cold Stone Creamery is the ice-cream star of the Waikiki strip. Practical perks include an on-site coin-operated laundry and a small but very appealing pool.

See map p. 130. 2570 Kalakaua Ave. (at Paoakalani Avenue). ☎ 800-922-7866, 877-997-6667, 800-877-7666 (property direct), or 808-822-2511. Fax: 808-923-3656. www.astonwaikiki.com. Valet or self-parking: $12.50. Rack rates: $153–$406 double, $440 suite. Most rates include breakfast. Deals: Excellent opportunities for discounts. Internet-only ePriceBreaker rates as low as $107 at press time. Ask for AAA, senior (50-plus), kids, and corporate discounts, and other special rate programs. AE, DC, DISC, MC, V.

Aston Waikiki Beachside Hotel
$$$ Mid-Waikiki

Situated directly across the street from a prime stretch of beach — with no buildings to interrupt ocean views or access — this boutique hotel is an oasis of unruffled elegance on Waikiki's main drag. It's intimate and attractive, with a gracious, attentive staff (and full-service concierge); lovely rooms with lots of extras, including VCRs; twice-daily maid service (a blessing after a day on the sand); and a location that can't be beat. The rooms are tastefully furnished and accented with Asian art, but they're miniscule — a tradeoff you may be willing to make in order to gain a stellar location and a level of style and service that usually comes with a much higher price tag. But if more than two are intending to share a room, or you just need your space, book elsewhere.

See map p. 130. 2452 Kalakaua Ave. (between Uluniu and Liliuokalani avenues). ☎ 800-922-7866, 877-997-6667, or 808-931-2100. Fax: 808-931-2129. www.astonhotels.com. Valet or self-parking: $9.50. Rack rates: $195–$285 double, $290–$350 oceanfront double with lanai. Rates include continental breakfast. Deals: Excellent opportunities for discounts. Internet-only ePriceBreaker rates as low as $98 at press time. Ask for AAA, senior (50-plus), kids, and corporate discounts, and other special rate programs. AE, DC, DISC, MC, V.

The Breakers
$ Mid-Waikiki

This low-rise charmer in the midst of high-rise Waikiki is a great option for budget-minded travelers who don't want to succumb to chain-hotel conformity simply to save a buck or two. This two-story '50s-style garden motel boasts a friendly staff, a loyal following, a fab location just a two-minute walk from the beach, and a warmly nostalgic Old Waikiki vibe. Units are set around an attractive pool and tropical garden blooming with brilliant hibiscus; wooden jalousies and Japanese-style shoji doors add to the ambience. The spacious rooms are older but very nicely maintained, and they boast electric-range kitchenettes and lanais overlooking the pool. The poolside cafe serves up killer burgers and great mai tais, and the hotel offers a formal Japanese tea ceremony twice a week. The Breakers is very popular with the local gay crowd, but the hotel caters to visitors from all walks of life, including families. A coin-op laundry is on-site.

The Breakers may be vulnerable to construction noise and access issues once Outrigger begins its Beach Walk redevelopment sometime in early 2005. Be sure to inquire about noise and accessibility when you book, especially if you have a rental car.

See map p. 130. 250 Beach Walk (between Kalakaua Avenue and Helumoa Road). ☎ *800-426-0494 or 808-923-3181. Fax: 808-923-7174.* www.breakers-hawaii.com. *Limited free parking; $8 a day across the street. Rack rates: $94–$100 studio, $135 garden suite. AE, DC, MC, V.*

Halekulani
$$$$$ Mid-Waikiki

For vacationers who only want the best, the Halekulani is as good as it gets. The finest hotel in Waikiki is the epitome of gracious and elegant aloha. This open, low-rise beachfront hotel exudes understated luxury (although some may consider it a tad formal for a beach hotel). The rooms are uniformly oversized and done in a classy but supremely comfortable natural-on-white style. Each one features a sitting area, a large furnished lanai, a sumptuous bath with a deep soaking tub and separate oversized shower, and all the extras you'd expect from a hotel of this caliber, including in-room check-in, twice-daily maid service, a DVD player, a bedside control panel, and wireless Internet access. About 90 percent of the rooms have some sort of ocean view.

Halekulani service is among the best I've ever experienced; the concierge can arrange everything from flowers and leis to limosine service. The hotel also supplies free tickets for the Bishop Museum, the Contemporary Museum, the Honolulu Academy of Arts, the Honolulu Symphony, and Iolani Palace. The two elegant oceanfront restaurants are first-rate, the alfresco lounge is Oahu's most romantic spot for sunset cocktails and hula, and the pool is magnificent. The tranquil, sumptuous SpaHalekulani offers a full range of pampering treatments drawn from Asian, Hawaiian, and South Pacific healing traditions. Only one niggling complaint: The beach is small, and the hotel offers only pool service. So if you want to sit in a chair rather than on a towel, you're stuck behind a hedge — and if you want to recline, forget about an ocean view.

The Halekulani may be vulnerable to construction noise and access issues once Outrigger begins its Beach Walk redevelopment sometime in late 2004 or early 2005. Be sure to inquire when you book.

See map p. 130. 2199 Kalia Rd. (at the beach end of Lewers Street). ☎ **800-367-2343** *or 808-923-2311. Fax: 808-926-8004.* www.halekulani.com. *Valet parking: $10. Rack rates: $325–$540 double, $775–$4,500 suite (most $775–$1,725). Deals: Packages usually available, sometimes including breakfast (from $295 at press time) or other extras. AE, DC, MC, V.*

Hawaiiana Hotel
$ Mid-Waikiki

Much like the neighboring Breakers (mentioned earlier in this section), this low-rise garden motel is affordable, comfortable, well-located — less than a block from the beach — and full of old-time aloha spirit. I always get good reports from guests about this place, and I was once again very impressed on my latest inspection. Every spacious room features a full kitchenette with microwave and coffeemaker; the concrete-block walls can be a bit of a downer, but the rooms are light and bright, most appliances are on the newer side, and maintenance is very impressive. The pricier Alii rooms boast better quality furnishings, prime positions in the complex, bathtub-shower combos, and such extras as hair dryers and bathrobes, but the standard rooms are just fine for tight budgets; ask for one with a private balcony overlooking the lush and pretty tropical courtyard. Free coffee and juice are served mornings in the courtyard, and the lush grounds feature two nice pools, barbecues, and a coin-op laundry. Hawaiian entertainment every Sunday evening — usually live music and hula — adds to the genuine local flavor.

The Hawaiiana Hotel may be vulnerable to construction noise and access issues once Outrigger begins its Beach Walk redevelopment sometime in early 2005. Be sure to inquire about noise and accessibility when you book, especially if you have a rental car.

See map p. 130. 260 Beach Walk (between Kalakaua Avenue and Helumoa Road). ☎ **800-367-5122** *or 808-923-3811. Fax: 808-926-5728.* www.hawaiianahotelat waikiki.com. *Parking: $10. Rack rates: $95–$105 standard double, $135 1-bedroom suite, $165–$195 Alii (deluxe) room or suite. Deals: Discounts for weekly stays and online booking. AE, DC, DISC, MC, V.*

Hawaii Prince Hotel Waikiki & Golf Club
$$$$–$$$$$ Ewa Waikiki

Here's a beautifully located hotel for vacationers with three things on their minds: shopping, golf, and ocean views. Sheathed in rose-colored glass, the hotel's 33-story tower twinset makes quite a statement at the gateway to Waikiki, across the street from the Ala Wai Yacht Harbor and a stone's throw from Ala Moana Center, the biggest and most elegant shopping mall in the Pacific. The Prince was built with business travelers in mind, but grown-up vacationers who want to avoid the bustle of central Waikiki enjoy its seamless combination of elegant contemporary style, flawless service (the Japanese owners demand nothing less), and zen-like serenity. Rates are high, but deals are abundant. And everybody gets an ocean view thanks to the clever architectural design; even the high-speed glass elevators boast views. Rooms are nondescript but very comfortably appointed (no balconies, though). Services include a complimentary shuttle to Waikiki Beach (a 5-minute walk away) and the resort's own Arnold Palmer/Ed Sea-designed 27-hole golf course, a 40-minute ride away. The east-meets-west Hawaii Regional Cuisine served in the Prince Court garners rave reviews.

See map p. 130. 100 Holomoana St. (just off Ala Moana Boulevard). ☎ *800-321-6248 or 808-956-1111. Fax 808-946-0811.* www.hawaiiprincehotel.com. *Parking: $14 valet, $10 self-parking. Rack rates: $310–$450 double, $550–$2,500 suite. Deals: Many value-added packages are usually available, including unlimited golf, romance, spa, room/car/breakfast, and two-rooms-for-the-price-of-one family packages; discounted rates from $169 at press time. Also inquire about AAA discounts. AE, DC, MC, V.*

Hilton Hawaiian Village Beach Resort & Spa
$$$–$$$$ Ewa Waikiki

Spread out over 22 tropical acres featuring exotic wildlife — including flamingoes, peacocks, and even tropical penguins! — and fronting a gorgeous stretch of beach that feels private even though it's not, Waikiki's biggest resort is my favorite choice for families. It feels like a tropical theme park, with its own lagoon (with Atlantis submarine rides), five pools, a wealth of restaurants (including the very good Golden Dragon for Chinese, the ultraromantic Bali by the Sea, and Benihana for fun slice-and-dice *teppanyaki* dining), enough shopping to stock a midsize mall, a full slate of bars and lounges, and more — even its own post office. Still, this Hilton isn't so big that it's overwhelming. On the contrary, it's a blast to stay here. Rooms are housed in multiple towers and range from comfortable to first-class depending on what you want to spend, but all are large, well-outfitted, and laden with amenities.

I do have two complaints, however: Rooms in the new Kalia Tower are overrated, and the casual dining throughout the hotel (operated by Round Table Pizza) is too mediocre for a resort charging such high rack rates. The plush Mandara Spa and the high-tech Holistica Hawaii Health Center (which is dedicated to such wellness programs as state-of-the-art cancer screening), on the other hand, are excellent additions. Ditto for the Bishop Museum at Kalia, a mini outpost of the prestigious museum of Hawaii and Pacific cultures (see Chapter 12) and a 24-hour full-service business center. Among the other pleasing extras is a wonderful program for kids, so your little ones will be entertained.

See map p. 130. 2005 Kalia Rd. (at Ala Moana Boulevard). ☎ *800-HILTONS or 808-949-4321. Fax: 808-947-7898.* www.hawaiianvillage.hilton.com. *Valet parking: $17; self-parking: $12. Rack rates: $195–$520 double, suites from $279. Deals: Several packages and special offers are almost always available, including romance packages, discounts on multinight stays, free giveaways for kids, and much more. Packages from $189 available at press time. Also ask for AAA, AARP, corporate, and other discounts. AE, DISC, MC, V.*

Ilima Hotel
$$ Mid-Waikiki

This local-style condo hotel is a bargain for families or anybody who wants accommodations that go above and beyond what an average hotel can offer. The roomy studios and one-, two-, and three-bedroom apartments are recently renovated and boast full modern kitchens with microwave and coffeemaker, nice new baths, sofabeds in the living room, and a lanai; one-bedrooms have Jacuzzi tubs, too. Extras include daily maid service (not a given in condo units), free local calls (a nice plus), a small heated pool with adjacent dry sauna, a rooftop sun deck, an exercise room, and laundry facilities. The service is friendly, and the heart-of-Waikiki location is central to shopping and dining. The beach is a ten-minute walk away, but at these prices, you'll happily put on your walkin' shoes.

See map p. 130. 445 Nohonani St. (between Kuhio Avenue and Ala Wai Boulevard). ☎ *800-801-9366 or 808-923-1877. Fax: 888-864-5462.* www.ilima.com. *Limited free parking; $8 self-parking across the street. Rack rates: $129–$175 studio, $159–$209 1-bedroom, $230–$270 2-bedroom, $355–$375 3-bedroom penthouse. Deals: Heavily discounted senior (50 and older) and corporate rates, plus Internet specials and discounts for AAA members, government, and military. AE, DC, DISC, MC, V.*

JW Marriott Ihilani Resort & Spa
$$$$$ Leeward Oahu

It's got a lot going for it, but I'm not a huge fan of this resort. It's a beautifully designed property nestled in a lovely manicured resort with a quartet of white-sand coves that are forever calm for even your littlest ones. Rooms are extra-large, averaging 660 square feet; each has a large lanai and a massive marble bath with double vanities, a huge soaking tub, and a separate shower; and some 85 percent boast ocean views. The excellent 35,000-square-foot Ihilani Spa (with rooftop tennis courts) has been voted one of the best spas in the world by readers of *Condè Nast Traveler*. The Mediterranean-accented Azul is one of Hawaii's best resort restaurants, and food service is terrific throughout the hotel. For the kids, the Keiki Beachcomber Club offers numerous activities (including outdoor adventures and a computer center), and for the adults, the Ko Olina Golf Club boasts 18 challenging holes of Ted Robinson–designed golf.

That said, Marriott doesn't seem capable of offering a high-quality luxury resort experience — not here, anyway. Although you do have an ocean view, you may also have an industrial plant in your line of vision. And I'm still annoyed that I was assigned a room with dirty carpet and then told I couldn't be moved because no more rooms were available in my rate class (pricier accommodations were available) — not exactly what I'd call top-notch service. Whether you'll like the way-out-of-town location is up to you, but be prepared for a half-hour drive to get anywhere — even to a nonresort restaurant. (The hotel does supply transportation to Waikiki and Ala Moana Shopping Center.)

See p. 172 in Chapter 12. At the Ko Olina Resort, Kapolei (off Highway 93, 17 miles west of Honolulu International Airport). ☎ 800-626-4446 or 808-679-0079. Fax: 808-679-0080. www.ihilani.com. Valet or self-parking: $10. Rack rates: $354–$600 double, suites from $800. Deals: Inquire about value-added package rates (from $269, including car or breakfast, at press time). AE, DC, MC, V.

Kahala Mandarin Oriental Hawaii
$$$$$ **Kahala**

If you want easy access to Honolulu's sights but Waikiki sounds like a big fat drag, the Kahala Mandarin is the perfect compromise. It's just a ten-minute drive east of Waikiki, staked out on its own perfect crescent beach in one of Honolulu's most upscale neighborhoods. (The hotel provides shuttle service to Waikiki and major shopping centers.) In fact, the tranquil Mandarin is ideal for anybody who likes first-rate service, an ambience that blends T-shirts-and-flip-flops comfort with gracious elegance, and big, beautiful rooms with CD players and high-quality amenities — including the best bathrooms in the business, with a soaking tub, separate shower, and his-and-her sinks and dressing areas. Hoku's, one of Honolulu's most celebrated restaurants, is named for the most charming of the bottlenosed dolphins that live on the premises; ask for a room with a lanai that overlooks the dolphin lagoon and sea, and the world is yours. Even if you end up in a mountain-view room, take heart: The vistas are almost as fine. Romance-seeking couples will love the candlelit Veranda at the music-and-cocktails hour. The dolphin-encounter program and year-round kids' club make the Kahala great for families, too.

See map p. 130. 5000 Kahala Ave. (east of Diamond Head, next to the Waialae Country Club). ☎ 800-367-2525 or 808-739-8888. Fax: 808-739-8800. www.mandarinoriental.com. Valet parking: $15. Rack rates: $295–$700 double, $900–$4,325 suite. Deals: Numerous package deals (including honeymoon, golf, and room-and-car packages) are almost always on offer, so ask. Also inquire about AAA discounts and check for Internet specials. AE, DC, DISC, MC, V.

New Otani Kaimana Beach Hotel
$$–$$$ **Diamond Head Waikiki**

Located at the quietest, prettiest end of Waikiki, this boutique hotel is the neighborhood's best beachfront bargain. It sits right on the locals' favorite stretch of Waikiki Beach, Sans Souci, with leafy Kapiolani Park and Diamond Head at its back door, which means that the views are pleasing in almost any direction. An inviting open-air lobby leads to contemporary rooms that are more Holiday Inn than stylish, but are perfectly comfortable. The most basic rooms are tiny, so spring for a superior one if you can. The junior suites are large enough for families, and corner rooms boast Waikiki's finest views. The airy lobby opens onto the Hau Tree Lanai, a wonderfully romantic restaurant that sits right on the sand; great breakfasts make it the right place to start the day even if you're not staying here. Amenities include VCRs, minifridges, and a coin-op laundry. Many regular visitors who can afford it camp out in the well-priced suites, almost all of which are sizable and offer lovely views. Units in the Diamond Head wing are ideal for longer stays because they add a microwave and coffeemaker to the mix. This is one of my favorite midpriced hotels — an excellent value on all fronts.

See map p. 130. 2863 Kalakaua Ave. (across the street from Kapiolani Park). ☎ *800-356-8264 or 808-923-1555. Fax: 808-922-9404.* www.kaimana.com. *Valet parking: $12. Rack rates: $145–$355 double, $215–$1,125 suite. Deals: Ask about package rates (including wedding packages, room-and-car deals, and free nights for families). AE, DC, DISC, MC, V.*

Ohana Islander Waikiki
$$$ Mid-Waikiki

This newish hotel is attractive and well located, across the street from the Royal Hawaiian and just 2½ blocks from the beach. A pleasant tropical-style lobby leads to guest rooms that are more sophisticated than most in the Outrigger chain, with such pleasant touches as Italian tile entryways and soft Berber carpets underfoot; a minifridge, coffeemaker, hair dryer, and Nintendo in every room; and a small furnished lanai. The furniture was bulk-purchased from the no-personality catalog, but everything is pleasant and fresh. Affordable connecting rooms are great for families who don't want too much togetherness. Amenities include a nice pool, a coin-op laundry, shops, casual restaurants (including an on-site Starbucks, perfect for the morning joe), and a 24-hour self-serve business center, in case you have to connect back to the mainland. Attention, Mom and Dad: Kids ages 5 to 13 even have access to the supervised activities at the Outrigger Reef's Cowabunga Kids Club, so the grown-ups can enjoy some quality time.

The Ohana Islander is adjacent to parent company Outrigger's Beach Walk redevelopment and may be vulnerable to construction noise and access issues once construction begins sometime in early 2005. Be sure to inquire about noise and accessibility when you book.

In addition to Ohana Islander, the **Ohana Hotels & Resorts** family features value-minded hotels throughout Honolulu, all highly recommendable and within walking distance of Waikiki Beach. If you're looking for cheap sleeps, it's hard to go wrong with Ohana; at most of their properties, rack rates start at just $129, and discounted SimpleSaver rates can go as low as an astoundingly wallet-friendly $69 a night. For more information, call ☎ **800-462-6262** or surf your way to www.ohanahotels.com.

See map p. 130. 283 Lewers St. (at Kalakaua Avenue). ☎ *800-462-6262 or 808-923-7711. Fax: 808-924-5755.* www.ohanahotels.com. *Parking: $10. Rack rates: $189–$219 double, $229 studio, $450 suite. Deals: Better-than-average discounts for AAA and AARP members and seniors (50-plus), plus corporate, government, and military discounts. First night free, bed-and-breakfast, room-and-car, and other packages regularly on offer; also ask about heavily discounted SimpleSaver rates. AE, DC, DISC, MC, V.*

Outrigger Waikiki on the Beach
$$$$ **Mid-Waikiki**

I'll make no bones about it — the rack rates here are just too high. Still, I like this 16-story oceanfront hotel, the flagship of the Outrigger chain, I really do, because you can usually score a discounted rate or value-added package deal quite easily. The Outrigger's flagship hotel sits in the center square, right in the heart of the party on Waikiki's absolute best stretch of beach. In 2003, Outrigger completed a $15 million renovation of the guest rooms, upgrading with new furniture and lovely new bathrooms. (Fifteen special oceanfront rooms now have oceanfront bathtubs for the ultimate relaxing soak!) Even the standard units are large and comfortable, with big closets, good amenities (fridge, hair dryer, and coffeemaker), and spacious lanais. A $3 million facelift of the lobby and public areas honors Hawaiian history while bestowing a fresh tropical look. Facilities include a fitness center, an oceanfront pool and Jacuzzi, a round-the-clock self-serve business center, and plenty of shops and restaurants — including one of my Waikiki faves, Duke's Canoe Club, plus a Seattle's Best Coffee for rise-and-shine java and a new oceanfront restaurant that made its debut in July 2003. Still, if they're not in the bargaining mood on the day you call, I suggest staying elsewhere.

Here, as at other Outrigger and sister Ohana hotels, guests ages 5 to 13 have access to the supervised activities at the Cowabunga Kids Club at the nearby Outrigger Reef, so the grown-ups can enjoy some quality time. (Even though the Outrigger Reef has the kids' club and the Serenity Spa, I'm not a huge fan of that beachfront hotel; I'd choose to stay here instead.)

See map p. 130. 2335 Kalakaua Ave. (on the ocean, between the Royal Hawaiian Shopping Center and the Sheraton Moana Surfrider). ☎ *800-688-7444 or 808-923-0711. Fax: 808-921-9749.* www.outrigger.com. *Valet parking: $13. Rack rates: $290–$450 double, $650–$1,050 suite. Deals: Better-than-average discounts for AAA and AARP members and seniors (50-plus), plus corporate, government, and military discounts. First night free, bed-and-breakfast, room-and-car, and other packages regularly on offer. AE, DC, DISC, MC, V.*

Patrick Winston's Waikiki Condos
$–$$ **Mid-Waikiki**

Pat Winston deals in budget apartments, so don't show up expecting the condo equivalent of the Ritz, but you will find great value for your dollars here. This friendly man manages two-dozen clean, comfortable suites in a well-kept, five-story, garden-apartment building with a cute pool and attractive landscaping located on a quiet, central-to-everything street 2 blocks from the beach. Each of the individually decorated units has a sofa bed, a furnished lanai overlooking the tropical courtyard and pool, air-conditioning and ceiling fans, a full kitchen with microwave, and a private bath (with shower only); most have washer/dryers (coin-op facilities are also on-site). Pat does all the renovation, maintenance, and cleaning himself, and he does a great job; still, the budget doubles are beginning to show some wear. Bursting with aloha spirit, Pat goes the extra mile to do what he can — book activities, make restaurant recommendations, and so on — to make sure that you go home happy.

See map p. 130. In the Hawaiian King, 417 Nohonani St. (between Kuhio Avenue and Ala Wai Boulevard). ☎ *800-545-1948, 808-924-3332, or 808-922-3894 (front desk). Fax: 808-924-3332.* www.winstonswaikikicondos.com. *Parking: $7. Rack rates: $79–$109 budget double or moderate family suite, $99–$119 deluxe 1-bedroom suite, $125–$145 2-bedroom suite. 4-night minimum; extra person beyond two $10 each. Deals: Internet discounts and monthly rates (as low as $65 nightly) available. AE, DC, DISC, MC, V.*

Royal Garden at Waikiki Hotel
$$–$$$ **Ewa Waikiki**

This rather elegant little hotel is tucked away on a tree-lined side street, in the quieter section of Waikiki, about a ten-minute walk to the beach. A lobby dressed in European marble and chandeliers leads to spacious and very nicely outfitted guest rooms. Each unit contains a minifridge and wet bar, an Italian marble-clad bathroom with a hair dryer, and a private lanai; the city views are impressive even if you don't have a clear line of sight to the ocean. On-site amenities include two freshwater swimming pools, including a divine one with a waterfall; a pair of Jacuzzis, and a matched set of saunas; a fitness room; two very nice restaurants (one Continental, one Japanese); a petite business center; coin-op washers and dryers as well as laundry and dry-cleaning service; and complimentary shuttle service around Waikiki.

See map p. 130. 440 Olohana St. (between Kuhio Avenue and Ala Wai Boulevard). ☎ *800-367-5666 or 808-943-0202. Fax: 808-946-8777.* www.royalgardens.com. *Valet parking: $8. Rack rates: $105–$185 double, $285–$320 1-bedroom suite, $800 2-bedroom suite. Deals: Always inquire about price breaks and packages. AE, DC, DISC, MC, V.*

Royal Hawaiian
$$$$$ **Mid-Waikiki**

This shocking-pink oasis hidden among blooming gardens in the heart of Waikiki has been the symbol of Hawaiian luxury since 1927. Now managed by Sheraton, it still exudes glamor and elegance, recalling a time when travelers arrived by Matson Line ships rather than jumbo jet, with steamer trunks instead of nylon totes in tow. The hotel sits right in the heart of the action on Waikiki's most exciting stretch of sand. You couldn't dream up a better location. Every guest room is lovely, and I have a real soft spot for the Historic wing; still, that Pepto Bismol pink gets old after awhile. You'll likely end up in a modern room if you want an ocean view, but the period vibe persists (as does the pink). Perks abound, including lei greetings, concierge service, an oceanfront patio restaurant that's an ideal place to start your day, poolside bar service, a romantic Monday-night luau (Waikiki's best), and one of Waikiki's best spas, the intimate and utterly modern Abhasa Spa (www.abhasa.com). Guests can also use the facilities at the neighborhing Sheraton Moana Surfrider and charge items directly to their rooms. The hotel has two fancy dining rooms, but I love the casual oceanfront patio restaurant. Overall, I prefer the Moana (see the following listing), but the Royal is second in terms of nostalgic appeal.

See map p. 130. 2259 Kalakaua Ave. (at the end of Royal Hawaiian Avenue). ☎ 800-782-9488 or 808-923-7311. Fax: 808-924-7098. www.royal-hawaiian.com *or* www.sheraton-hawaii.com. *Valet parking: $15; self-parking $10. Rack rates: $380–$440 double, $475 junior suite, $565–$655 luxury oceanfront room or suite. Deals: Numerous package deals are almost always available, so be sure to ask. Romance, wedding, and honeymoon packages are legendary — and, if you're lucky, may include airport transfers in the Royal's signature pink limousine. Also ask for AAA-member and senior discounts as well as Sheraton SureSaver rates. AE, DC, DISC, MC, V.*

Sheraton Moana Surfrider
$$$$–$$$$$ Mid-Waikiki

The Moana isn't quite as luxurious as the neighboring Royal Hawaiian, but I still prefer it on all counts. Even with a '60s extension and a modern tower, this elegant white-clapboard Victorian — Waikiki's first hotel, built in 1901 — overflows with beachy nostalgia. It's more understated and intimate (and generally less expensive) than the Royal, and the location is equally ideal.

The original U-shaped building embraces a 100-year-old banyan tree and the ocean beyond; it exudes a magical back-in-time vibe that all guests share in, even if your room has a stucco ceiling. I recommend the Banyan rooms, which are small but have high ceilings and loads of historic charm; for the ultimate in old Hawaii vibe, book one with a grand lanai overlooking the Banyan Courtyard and the turquoise surf beyond. If space or ocean views win out over retro ambience for you, book in one of the newer wings, where you'll get more modern fixtures and a lanai. (In fact, the tower wing is currently undergoing a major renovation that should be completed by the time you visit. Guest rooms in this section will receive all-new furniture and spacious new bathrooms.) Both the service and the facilities are great (though guests must walk a couple of minutes down the beach to the Sheraton Waikiki to use a fitness room). The Banyan Courtyard is the best place to lounge poolside in Waikiki, period, and I love any excuse — breakfast, high tea, Sunday brunch — to snag a seat on the oceanfront veranda, where live music and mai tais set the right island mood every evening. Other winning features include a full children's program, ongoing Hawaiian arts and craft demonstrations, and a guests-only beach area with full cocktail service on one of Waikiki's finest stretches of sand. You simply can't go wrong here!

See map p. 130. 2365 Kalakaua Ave. (on the beach, across from Kaiulani Street). ☎ 800-782-9488 or 808-922-3111. Fax: 808-923-0308. www.moana-surfrider.com *or* www.sheraton-hawaii.com. *Valet parking: $15; $10 self-parking. Rack rates: $270–$390 standard or city-view double, $450–$600 oceanview room, $975–$1,125 suite. Deals: Promotional rates and/or package deals are almost always available, so ask for these as well as AAA-member and senior discounts, plus Sheraton SureSaver rates (from $210 at press time). AE, DC, DISC, MC, V.*

Sheraton Princess Kaiulani
$$$ Mid-Waikiki

The way to score Sheraton-level amenities and service for a fraction of what you'd pay across the street is to stay at this hidden gem of a hotel, just a block from the beach in the high-class heart of the new Waikiki. It doesn't have the charm of the Sheraton Moana Surfrider or its steps-from-the-sand location — but it doesn't have the high rates, either. Rooms are outfitted in a bright and pleasant (if nondescript) island style, with a coffeemaker and a cute lanai; everything is comfortable and very nicely maintained. There's a lovely pool deck with a freshwater swimming pool and nightly poolside entertainment; good food service at two restaurants, the Japanese Momoyama and the all-American Pikake Terrace for all-you-can-eat buffets; authentic arts and crafts on display in the lobby daily; and access to Sheraton's excellent Keiki Aloha program for kids ages 5 to 12. Guests can also use the facilities at any neighboring Sheraton and charge items back to their own room. Also on-site is *Creation — A Polynesian Journey,* Waikiki's best Polynesian revue, complete with Samoan fire-knife dancer. The beach is just a five-minute walk away.

See map p. 130. 120 Kaiulani Ave. (just off Kalakaua Avenue). ☎ *800-782-9488 or 808-922-5811. Fax: 808-931-4577.* www.princess-kaiulani.com *or* www.sheraton-hawaii.com. *Rack rates: $165–$280 standard or city-view double, $305–$360 oceanview room, $670–$1,450 suite. Self-parking: $10. Deals: Multiple money-saving promotions and/or package deals are almost always on offer, including Internet-only rates. Also check for AAA-member and senior discounts. AE, DC, DISC, MC, V.*

W Honolulu
$$$$$ Diamond Head Waikiki

This super-stylish, midrise boutique hotel boasts just 48 impeccable rooms, a tranquil location at the foot of Diamond Head, and an impressively attentive staff that could easily fit in at the standard-bearing Halekulani. The large, gorgeous Balinese-style rooms boast rich white-on-white textiles, elegantly rustic teak furnishings, simply celestial beds, marble bathrooms with plush bathrobes, huge furnished lanais, and high-tech extras — cordless phones, CD players, 27-inch TVs with VCR, wireless Web TV, and video games. Luxury-level services include leis and juice upon arrival, twice-daily maid service, terry *and* cotton pique robes, the best minibars in the islands, excellent concierge service, 24-hour room service, and valet service. The highly regarded Diamond Head Grill serves top-flight Hawaii Regional Cuisine and super-sexy cocktails. Unfortunately, the building is saddled with a couple of permanent physical faults: a perpendicular orientation to the coastline, giving all rooms only mediocre views, and another building between it and the sand, requiring you to walk across a parking lot to reach the beach. Still, it's the ultimate outpost of 21st-century Polynesian chic; I'd move in if they'd let me.

See map p. 130. 2885 Kalakaua Ave. (across the street from Kapiolani Park). ☎ *877-W-HOTELS or 808-922-1700. Fax: 800-923-2249.* www.starwood.com/whotels. *Valet parking: $15. Rack rates: $410–$800 double or suite. Deals: Several packages* *usually available, including spa and birthday deals. Look for Internet-only specials, and unusually good AAA discounts (50 percent at press time!). AE, DC, DISC, MC, V.*

Waikiki Beach Marriott

$$$–$$$$ **Mid-Waikiki**

I really like this hotel; kudos to Marriott for transforming a formerly dour hotel into a delightful place to stay. It's spectacularly located, directly across the street from the newly renovated stretch of Waikiki Beach, with no buildings blocking views or access, and steps from Kapiolani Park. The 1,300-room hotel is massive, but a tropically furnished open-air lobby adds a sense of cohesion, not to mention an inviting place to lounge with your morning coffee (a Seattle Coffee Roasters is on-site). The hotel is also home to one of Hawaii's most spectacular spas, the **Spa Olakino & Salon,** where you'll feel that you've just stepped into a gorgeous rainforest retreat overlooking the sands.

All the guest rooms were given the royal treatment in the last couple of years, with all-new furnishings and top-quality textiles in eye-catching tropicals; the feather beds are more comfy than most available at any price. The 600-square-foot family room sleeps up to six comfortably and features two queen beds, two twin beds, and a sitting area; a few even have a second bathroom. More family-friendly perks: Not only can kids stay in their parent's room, but a rollaway or crib is provided free of charge. The staffed Kids Salon playroom offers Mom and Dad both day and evening respite from the little ones. Each of the two towers boasts its own pleasant and popular pool deck; there's also a 24-hour fitness center. The Kuhio Beach Grille is a pleasing and affordably priced place to dine, and one of Hawaii's most beloved entertainers, Auntie Genoa Keawe, entertains Thursday evenings (call for times) in the lovely lobby lounge.

See map p. 130. 2552 Kalakaua Ave. (at Papakalani Avenue just west of Kapiolani Park). ☎ *800-367-5370 or 808-922-6611. Fax: 808-921-5255.* www.marriottwaikiki. com. *Valet parking: $14; self-parking: $10. Rack rates: $159–$369 double, $329–$409 family room, from $1,500 suite. Deals: Package deals (including spa packages) abound; "Paradise Plus" room-and-car or room-and-breakfast deals from $199 at press time. Also inquire about AAA, senior, corporate, government, and other special rates. AE, DC, DISC, MC, V.*

Waikiki Beachcomber

$$$–$$$$ **Mid-Waikiki**

First-rate package deals and online discounts make this attractive, sparklingly maintained, and well-located hotel — just 297 steps from the beach — an excellent value. It lies in the heart of Waikiki's gentrified main drag, across the street from the Royal Hawaiian; the lovely, open Hawaii-style lobby is located on the second floor, which keeps it blissfully free of main-drag bustle; tropical floral arrangements add a splash of elegance. Rooms boast Berber carpets, aqua and soft pink colors with wood detailing, nice firm beds, minifridges, coffeemakers, handheld showers, hair dryers, private lanais, and a nice island-style feeling. Housekeeping is impeccable. The Moana side of the building scores you gorgeous partial ocean views. Also on-site are a nice pool and Jacuzzi, a cafe, and a coin-op laundry. Hawaiian cultural activities (hula, lei-making, and ukulele lessons) contribute to the genuine island flair, and a summer kids' program adds to the family fun. A top-notch midrange choice. Another selling point? The Beachcomber is home to the legendary Don "Tiny Bubbles" Ho show (see Chapter 12).

See map p. 130. 2300 Kalakaua Ave. (at Duke's Lane). ☎ ***800-622-4646*** *or 808-922-4646. Fax: 808-923-4889.* www.waikikibeachcomber.com. *Parking: $9. Rack rates: $230–$280 double, $395–$935 suite. Deals: Bargains abound. Room-and-car and room-and-breakfast packages from $129; seniors over 55 save 50 percent off rack; and terrific Internet specials are on regular offer, as low as $99 at press time. AE, DC, MC, V.*

Waikiki Joy Hotel
$$–$$$ Mid-Waikiki

This stylishly contemporary hotel features a Jacuzzi tub and a Bose entertainment system in every room — otherwise unheard of for these prices. The lovely open-air lobby sets the scene for bright, clean-lined, comfortable guest rooms, each with a marble entryway, a fridge, a coffeemaker, a nice bathroom with that groovy tub, and a lanai that's wide enough for you to sit and enjoy the views while you listen to your stereo; some suites have wet bars, and others have full kitchens. A cafe, laundry, and a furnished deck with heated pool and sauna are on-site, plus a karaoke studio if you're in the mood for a little warbling. In the negative column, the beach is a good 4 blocks away — but cheer up, the free breakfast makes a good deal even better.

See map p. 130. 320 Lewers St. (between Kalakaua and Kuhio avenues). ☎ ***877-997-6667*** *or 808-923-2300. Fax: 808-924-4010.* www.aston-hotels.com. *Valet parking: $10. Rack rates: $150–$185 double, $205–$295 suite. Rates include continental breakfast. Deals: Excellent opportunities for discounts; "e-PriceBreaker" rates $105–$154 double at press time. Also ask for AAA, senior (50-plus), and corporate discounts, and other special rate programs. Business travelers can often score free parking, so it never hurts to ask. AE, DC, DISC, MC, V.*

Waikiki Parc
$$$–$$$$ Mid-Waikiki

This sister hotel to the ultradeluxe Halekulani is the ideal choice for travelers looking for impeccable service and little luxuries at bargain rates, plus a terrific at-the-beach location. What's more, a phenomenal slate of packages improves an already good value. Boasting an Asian-tinged island vibe, the stylish rooms feature chic rattan, tile floors, plush carpeting, sitting areas, lanais with louvered shutters (go for an ocean view if you can — they're fabulous), minifridges, and generous bathrooms. Amenities include a first-rate Japanese restaurant; the Parc Cafe, which will win over even avowed buffet phobes with its high-quality, bounteous spread; concierge and room service; a coin-op laundry as well as valet service; and a gracious staff that doesn't skimp on signature Halekulani service. There's an eighth-floor pool, but why bother? The sand is 100 yards away, via a beach-access walkway.

The Waikiki Parc may be vulnerable to construction noise and access issues once Outrigger begins its Beach Walk redevelopment sometime in late 2004 or early 2005. Be sure to inquire when you book — and splurge on an oceanview room to avoid any unsightly views.

See map p. 130. 2233 Helumoa Rd. (at Lewers Street, east of the Halekulani). ☎ *800-422-0450 or 808-921-7272. Fax: 808-931-6638 (reservations) or 808-923-1336 (front desk). Internet:* www.waikikiparc.com. *Valet parking: $12. Rack rates: $225–$320 double. Rates include full buffet breakfast. Deals: A bevy of excellent money-saving packages are always on offer, including the Parc Sunrise ($182–$220 double, including parking and breakfast), the Free Car package (from $199 double), plus family plans (offering 50–60 percent off a second room), and additional options. AE, DC, MC, V.*

Waikiki Sand Villa
$–$$ Mid-Waikiki

Here's a terrific choice for wallet watchers who don't want to sacrifice any of the three Cs: comfort, convenience, or cleanliness. This well-priced hotel is located on the quieter side of Waikiki, across the street from the lovely Ala Wai Canal, which is popular with practicing outrigger teams. It's small, quiet, and decidedly unsexy, but it does the trick. The ten-story tower features medium-sized rooms, most outfitted with a double bed plus a twin (great for small families or shares; you can also opt for two double beds or three twin beds), a bathroom with full tub (uncommon in this price range), Nintendo on the TV, and a lanai with lovely canal and mountain views. The adjacent three-story building features ten studio apartments with two double beds, a kitchenette (fridge, cooktop, and microwave) fully outfitted with dishware and utensils, a full bath with tub, and sitting and dining areas. Outdoors is a cool kidney-shaped 70-foot outdoor pool with adjacent Jacuzzi; there's also a coin-op laundry and a friendly bar and lounge where you can e-mail your friends back home with greetings from paradise.

See map p. 130. 2375 Ala Wai Blvd. (near Kaiulani Avenue; entrance on Kanekapolei Avenue). ☎ *800-247-1903, 800-342-1557 (interisland), or 808-922-4744. Fax: 808-923-2541.* www.waikikisandvillahotel.com. *Parking: $7.30. Rack rates: $99–$143 double, $162–$173 studio with kitchenette, $303–$315 Alii suite. Rates include continental breakfast. Deals: Substantial discounts for AAA members, seniors over 55, military, or groups. Check for special Internet rates (as low as $66 at press time). AE, DC, DISC, MC, V.*

Waikiki Shore
$$$–$$$$ Mid-Waikiki

Operated by Outrigger, Hawaii's homegrown hotel chain, Waikiki's only beachfront condo option is a wonderful choice for families looking for at-home comforts in an on-the-sand location. The individually decorated one- and two-bedroom condos feature full kitchens with microwaves and dishwashers (studios have kitchenettes), air-conditioning and ceiling fans, washer/dryers, and big lanais. Two-bedrooms come with either one or two bathrooms, depending on your needs. Daily maid service makes it feel like a real vacation. Because full-time residents live here, the complex tends to be quiet, and security is tight. Outrigger guests have access to the concierge, pool, 24-hour self-serve business center, fitness room, and full-service Serenity Spa (www.serenityhawaii.com) at the adjacent Outrigger Reef, as well as the Cowabunga Kids Club, a supervised activities program for tykes between the ages of 5 and 13. Reservations are hard to get — book way in advance.

See map p. 130. 2161 Kalia Rd. (on the ocean at Saratoga Road). ☎ *800-688-7444 or 808-971-4500. Fax: 808-971-4580.* www.outrigger.com. *Valet parking: $13. Rack rates: $250 studio double, $265–$365 1-bedroom (sleeps up to 4), $460–$650 2-bedroom (sleeps up to 6). Deals: Better-than-average discounts for AAA and AARP members and seniors (50-plus), plus corporate, government, and military discounts are available. First night free, bed-and-breakfast, room-and-car, and other packages regularly on offer. AE, DC, DISC, MC, V.*

Arranging for a rental

Ingrid Carvahlo's **Pacific Islands Reservations** (☎ 808-262-8133; www.oahu-hawaii-vacation.com) is my favorite rental agency on Oahu. This lovely lady can also hook you up with a gorgeous Windward Coast vacation rental, as well as a handful of North Shore estates and a number of condos right in the heart of Waikiki.

If you really want to stay in the heart of the North Shore's Surf City action, you can also call **Team Real Estate** (☎ 800-982-8602 or 808-637-3507; www.teamrealestate.com). This friendly Haliewa-based agency manages a fleet of fully furnished vacation homes on the North Shore, from affordable cottages to multibedroom beachfront homes, at rates ranging from $110 to $300 per night. Most rates are based on a minimum stay of one week, but shorter stays are available, and you may be able to arrange a discount on longer stays.

Naish Hawaii (☎ 808-262-6068; www.naish.com/lodging.html), which also happens to be Hawaii's premier windsurfing school, can help arrange for accommodations in and around Kailua, Oahu's premier windward coast community. Double rooms, cottages, and apartments for two run $50 to $125 nightly, and larger homes range from $150 to $300 nightly, depending on size and location.

Also contact **Hawaii's Best Bed & Breakfasts** (☎ 800-262-9912 or 808-985-7488; www.bestbnb.com) and **Bed & Breakfast Honolulu** (☎ 800-288-4666 or 808-595-7533; www.hawaiibnb.com) for additional Windward Coast and North Shore options. You may also want to check with **Hawaii Beachfront Vacation Homes** (☎ 808-247-3637; www.hibeach.com).

Dining Out

Once the land of overcooked fish and frozen peas, Hawaii has become a culinary mecca in recent years, attracting worldwide attention for its growing constellation of star chefs and its unique brand of Pacific Rim cooking — known as Hawaii Regional Cuisine, Hawaiian Island, or just Island cuisine. Honolulu, as you may expect, is the epicenter of this fabulous foodie revolution, so expect to eat well while you're here. Of course, the good stuff doesn't come cheap, but even if you're looking for affordable options, great choices abound.

If you're a foodie who's looking to splurge on one *really* fabulous meal while you're in Hawaii, you need to know only two names: **Chef Mavro** and **Alan Wong's.** These are the two finest restaurants in the entire Pacific, hands down — and the unassuming masters behind them deserve megastar status on the world culinary map.

In the restaurant listings that follow, the emphasis is on Waikiki and Honolulu, because a) that's where you're likely to spend most of your time; and b) that's where most of Oahu's restaurants are located. You can also find some excellent options for North Shore and Windward Coast dining for those days you spend touring the rest of this glorious island.

Each restaurant review is followed by a number of dollar signs, ranging from one ($) to five ($$$$$). The dollar signs give you an idea of what a complete dinner for one person — including appetizer, main course, dessert, one drink, tax, and tip —is likely to set you back. The price categories go like this:

$	Cheap eats — less than $15 per person
$$	Still inexpensive — $15 to $25
$$$	Moderate — $25 to $40
$$$$	Pricey — $40 to $70
$$$$$	Ultraexpensive — more than $70 per person

Of course, cost all depends on how you order, so stay away from the surf and turf or the north end of the wine list if you're watching your budget.

To give you a further idea of how much you can expect to spend, I also include the price range of main courses in the listings. (Keep in mind that prices can change at the whim of the management, so call before you go to confirm the price range.)

The state adds 4 percent in sales tax to every restaurant bill. A 15 to 20 percent tip is standard in Hawaii, just like the rest of the States.

Ahi's Restaurant
$–$$ Windward Coast Seafood/Local

This legendary Windward Coast spot is a wonderful place to break for a casual bite during your Circle Island drive. Housed in a simple rural bungalow tucked among the trees, Ahi's is the embodiment of true island spirit and harks back to a time before prepackaged, prefab Hawaii set the tone. The highlight of the basic fish-and-steak menu is the shrimp, prepared any of four ways: cocktail, scampi, tempura, or deep-fried (a combo plate is available if you can't decide). A few naysayers complain that it's not as good as the original locale (which succumbed to fire a few years back), but I find that this newer place captures the funky old vibe beautifully.

See p. 178 in Chapter 12. 53-146 Kamehameha Hwy. (Highway 83), Punaluu (south of the Polynesian Cultural Center). ☎ *808-293-5650. Reservations not taken. Main courses: $6.50–$15; complete meals $2.50–$4 extra. No credit cards. Open: Lunch and dinner Mon–Sat.*

Alan Wong's Restaurant
$$$$–$$$$$ Honolulu Hawaii Regional

If there is one master of true Hawaii Regional cuisine, it is Alan Wong — and his restaurant offers a world-class experience that's not to be missed. Koa, rattan, and other tropical touches create a real Hawaiian ambience in the warmly contemporary, gently bustling dining room, which serves as an ideal showcase for Wong's masterful elevation of the local culinary tradition. Expect perfectly prepared island fish bursting with clean, fresh flavors; Asian accents galore (the seaweed-wrapped tempura bigeye ahi with soy mustard is magnificent); and modernist takes on island favorites: Ahi tartare is adorned with truffled ponzu and grated chili daikon, while luau pork accompanies baby romaine, poi, and anchovy dressing in a delightful twist on a classic Caesar. Cap off your meal with a beautifully crafted dessert like the decadent chocolate crunch bars (layers of milk chocolate macadamia crunch and bittersweet chocolate mousse) and a fine selection of island coffees. Service is appropriately sophisticated yet completely unpretentious, rounding out the best-of-show dining experience.

See map p. 150. 1857 S. King St. (1½ blocks west of McCully Street), 3rd Floor, Honolulu. ☎ *808-949-2526.* www.alanwongs.com. *Reservations highly recommended (online reservations accepted). To get there: Take Kalakaua west from Waikiki and turn right on S. King Street. Main courses: $25–$37. 5-course tasting menu: $65 ($85 for 7 courses). AE, DC, MC, V. Open: Dinner nightly.*

Arancino
$–$$ Mid-Waikiki Northern Italian

If Arancino can draw island residents into the heart of Waikiki, you know that it has to be good. This intimate and affordable trattoria-style Italian restaurant is hugely popular with Japanese visitors, mainlanders, and locals alike, all of whom bond over their love of good Italian food. Creative pizzas and pastas, homemade risottos, and fresh island seafood comprise

Restaurants In & Around Waikiki

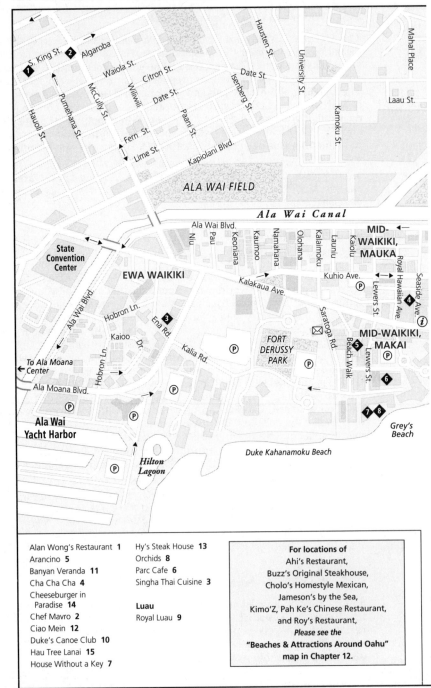

Alan Wong's Restaurant **1**
Arancino **5**
Banyan Veranda **11**
Cha Cha Cha **4**
Cheeseburger in
  Paradise **14**
Chef Mavro **2**
Ciao Mein **12**
Duke's Canoe Club **10**
Hau Tree Lanai **15**
House Without a Key **7**

Hy's Steak House **13**
Orchids **8**
Parc Cafe **6**
Singha Thai Cuisine **3**

Luau
Royal Luau **9**

For locations of
Ahi's Restaurant,
Buzz's Original Steakhouse,
Cholo's Homestyle Mexican,
Jameson's by the Sea,
Kimo'Z, Pah Ke's Chinese Restaurant,
and Roy's Restaurant,
Please see the
"Beaches & Attractions Around Oahu"
map in Chapter 12.

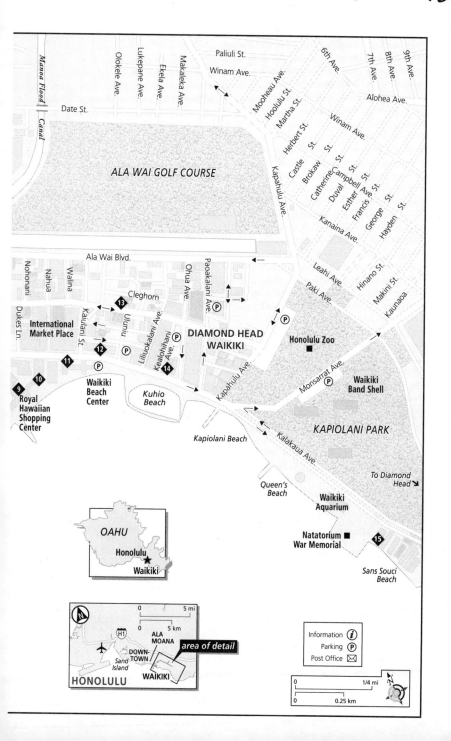

a simple but very appealing menu that delivers on all counts. With burnished terra-cotta walls, tile floors, and red-checked cloths on the tables, the charming room is inviting, and friendly service caps the good news. Don't be surprised if you find a patient line when you arrive — but the excellent value is worth the wait.

See map p. 150. 255 Beach Walk (just south of Kalakaua Avenue), Waikiki. ☎ *808-923-5557. Reservations not taken. Main courses: $8.50–$16. AE, DC, DISC, MC, V. Open: Lunch and dinner daily.*

Banyan Veranda
$$$ Mid-Waikiki   Breakfast/Afternoon Tea/Island-Continental

This glorious oceanfront Victorian-era terrace is my favorite spot for daytime alfresco dining. Hau Tree Lanai (listed later in this chapter) runs a close second for breakfast, but I love the historic charm here. Settled into an oversized rattan chair, tucking into a fluffy omelet as you watch the waves roll in — there's no better way to start the day. The multistation Sunday brunch buffet is spectacular enough to befit royalty. An ideal blending of old-world custom and casual island style, afternoon tea on the wide veranda offers a delightful midday respite. The meal follows the traditional pattern — finger sandwiches, scones with Devonshire cream and fruit preserves, sweet pastries — but each course is kept on the lighter side, which suits the tropical setting (and won't spoil your appetite for dinner). The wide selection and careful presentation of teas is delightful and includes a number of fragrant floral and aromatic Asian blends. Evening brings a short menu of continental classics prepared with island flair, accompanied by nightly live music (usually piano standards or Hawaiian slack key guitar) and glorious sunset views.

See map p. 150. At the Sheraton Moana Surfrider, 2365 Kalakaua Ave. (on the beach, across from Kaiulani Street), Waikiki. ☎ *808-922-3111.* www.moana-surfrider. com. *Reservations recommended. Main courses: $25–$29 at dinner; $13–$18 at breakfast; set menu $22; Sun brunch $35 adults, $18 kids 5–12; 3-course afternoon tea $21 ($27 with champagne). AE, DC, DISC, MC, V. Open: Breakfast Mon–Sat, Sun brunch, afternoon tea and dinner daily.*

Brew Moon
$$ Ala Moana   Eclectic

A comfortable-chic setting, satisfying contemporary pub food, and even better microbrews have made Brew Moon into a comfortable favorite among locals and visitors alike. This trendy spot won't exactly wow the gourmands among you, but the casual eats are nicely prepared and boast a winning island flair. Brew Moon's celebrated hand-crafted beers (like the Orion red ale, an amber brew with a robust caramel flavor) wash down offerings like coconut shrimp, fire-roasted ribs, sesame-seared ahi, veggie stir-fry, and thick-crust Luau pizza (topped with smoke-roasted pulled pork, roasted garlic, and Maui onion) perfectly. A full selection of salads, sandwiches, burgers, and creative pizzas complements the array of globe-trotting small plates, making this a good place to come with a group and share. Tiki torches flicker on the pleasant lanai after the sun goes down, and live jazz and R&B set a festive mood every night. Brew Moon went high-tech in 2003, when it became a wireless Internet hotspot.

See map p. 154. In Ward Centre, 1200 Ala Moana Blvd. (between Kamakee and Queen streets), Honolulu. ☎ *808-593-0088.* www.brewmoon.com. *Reservations accepted. Sharing plates, sandwiches, and pizzas $8–$14 (most less than $12), main courses: $11–$25 (most less than $18). AE, DC, MC, V. Open: Lunch and dinner daily (bar open late).*

Buzz's Original Steak House
$$–$$$ Windward Coast   American

This Windward Coast fixture exudes casual local style — and the food is really good, too, making Buzz's a perennial favorite among visitors and locals alike. The restaurant is housed in a little grass shack across from Kailua's gorgeous beach park; a small covered deck with (limited) beach views, a varnished koa bar, rattan furniture, and wood-paneled walls adorned with surf photos set the ideal tropical tone. Lunch is well-prepared, straightforward fare: steak sandwiches, fresh fish (always a beautifully prepared local catch), and teriyaki burgers. Dinner is pricier but worth it; expect traditional steakhouse fare — including well-grilled sirloins, rack of lamb, and teriyaki chicken — plus a top-notch soup and salad bar. Service is always welcoming, and the tropical cocktails are everything they should be. Don't pass on starting with the yummy artichoke "surprise" — you won't be disappointed. ***Note:*** Despite the at-the-beach location, shoes and shirts are required.

See p. 172 in Chapter 12. 413 Kawailoa Rd. (across from Kailua Beach Park, just past the bridge that leads to Lanikai Beach), Kailua. ☎ *808-261-4661. Reservations highly recommended for dinner. Main courses: $7–$15 at lunch, $12–$30 at dinner. No credit cards. Open: Lunch and dinner daily.*

Cha Cha Cha
$ Mid-Waikiki   Caribbean-Mexican

Finding a great meal in Waikiki without overspending isn't easy, but this tropical charmer comes through every time. This small indoor-outdoor restaurant is set back from the street, but establishes a colorful tropical presence on the patio with vibrant red and yellow umbrellas. The kitchen takes Mexican staples and globetrots them across the tropics — witness such dishes as lava-grilled chicken fajitas, a Jamaican jerk chicken quesadilla, blackened mahi burritos, and the delectable Pacifico quesadilla (grilled mahi in a spinach tortilla, topped with papaya-pineapple salsa). Dishes are always boldy flavored, authentically spiced, and artistically presented, with drizzled sauces on colorful plates. Here you can also find a help-yourself wall of hot sauces for zesty palates, well-blended margaritas, not one but two Happy Hours (from 4 to 6 p.m. and again from 9 to 11 p.m.), and a kids' menu for smaller appetites.

Downtown & Ala Moana Restaurants

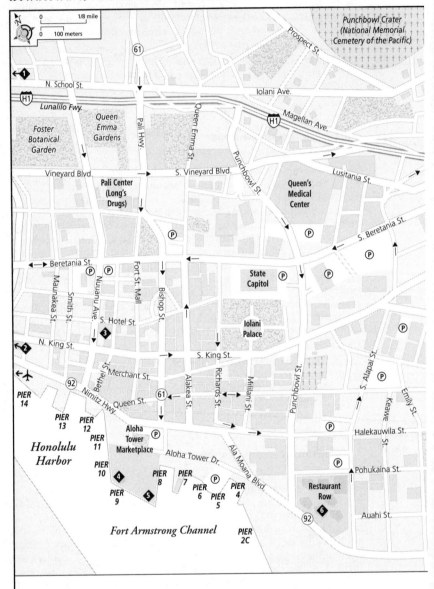

Brew Moon **8**
Don Ho's Island Grill **4**
Gordon Biersch Brewery Restaurant **5**
Helena's Hawaiian Food **1**
Indigo **3**

Kakaako Kitchen **7**
Kua Aina Sandwich **6**
L'Uraku **10**
Pineapple Room **11**

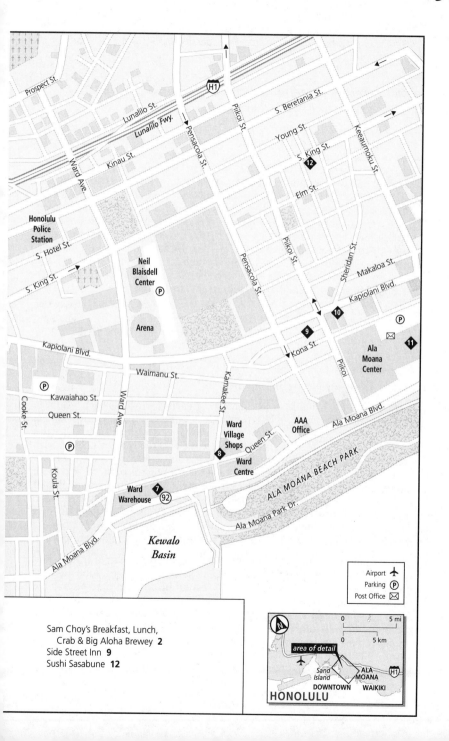

Airport ✈

Parking Ⓟ

Post Office ✉

Sam Choy's Breakfast, Lunch,
  Crab & Big Aloha Brewey **2**
Side Street Inn **9**
Sushi Sasabune **12**

See map p. 150. 342 Seaside Ave. (between Kalakaua and Kuhio avenues). ☎ **808-923-7797.** *Reservations not accepted. Main courses: $6.50–$13. MC, V. Open: Lunch and dinner daily.*

Cheeseburger in Paradise
$ Diamond Head Waikiki   American

Located just across the street from a prime stretch of Waikiki Beach, this fun 'n' funky outpost of the wildly successful Maui burger joint is the perfect spot for a casual sit-down meal. The tropical-style gourmet burgers are big, juicy, and served on fresh-baked buns, the bar mixes first-rate tropical cocktails — including one of the best piña coladas in the islands — and the attractive retro-Hawaii decor makes for an enjoyable kitschfest. Chili dogs, a tender and healthy chicken breast sandwich, crispy onion rings, coconut shrimp, and spiced fries broaden the menu, and vegetarians can opt for the terrific garden burger, a tofu burger, or a meal-sized salad. You can even launch your beach day here with hearty omelets, French toast, eggs Benedict, and other morning favorites. The food is universally satisfying. There's live music — usually classic rock tunes performed with a tropical flair by a local duo — daily from 4 to 11 p.m.

See map p. 150. 2500 Kalakaua Ave. (at Kealohilani Avenue, 3 blocks west of Kapahulu Avenue), Waikiki. ☎ **808-923-3731.** www.cheeseburgerwaikiki.com. *AE, DISC, MC, V. Main courses: $6–$13. Open: Breakfast, lunch, and dinner daily.*

Chef Mavro
$$$$$ Honolulu   Hawaii Regional

Marseilles transplant and James Beard award-winner George Mavrothalassitis has long been considered one of Hawaii's finest chefs, and he brings a one-of-a-kind Provençal-Mediterranean accent to the Hawaii Regional table. Chef Mavro prepares ethereally light cuisine with an unfailing sense of culinary balance; with only a few worthwhile exceptions, he uses no butter or cream, generally opting for olive oil and fresh herbs instead. The *onaga* (longtailed snapper) baked in a Hawaiian salt pastry crust and served with a ratatouille-herb sauce is a signature delight. One of Mavro's latest inventions is a remarkable Keahole lobster brochette with Hawaiian vanilla bubble sauce and coconut-Molokai sweet potato. I haven't found a dish yet that doesn't surpass its tempting description.

The dazzling menu even goes a delightful step further, matching each and every dish with the perfect glass of wine selected not by a lone authoritarian wine snob but by a vote of the restaurant's entire staff after blind tastings; it's a uniquely democratic system that prevails with every pairing. The clean-lined, candlelit setting is simple, elegant, and romantic, and the sociable, well-informed waitstaff couldn't be more spot-on. A faultless dining experience from start to finish — just ask *Gourmet* magazine, which raved that Mavro's is "where we would dine if we had only one night in Hawaii." Haute Hawaii dining hardly gets better than this — although Alan

Wong's may be a better choice for maximum local style. Really, you can't go wrong in either room.

See map p. 150. 1969 S. King St. (at McCully Street), Honolulu. ☎ **808-944-4714.** www. chefmavro.com. *Reservations highly recommended. To get there: Take McCully Street north to King Street. Main courses: $32–$42. 3- to 6-course tasting menus: $56–$93 ($79–$135 with wine). Open: Dinner Tues–Sun.*

Cholo's Homestyle Mexican
$ North Shore   Island-Style Mexican

Yummy fresh island fish tacos, burritos, and fajitas make this laid-back restaurant one of my favorite Hawaii dives. It's cheap, ultracasual, and super friendly — everything you want in a North Shore noshing spot. The cheery hole-in-the-wall dining room is a tad cramped, but service is just as attentive at the outdoor tables. The combo plates are a bargain-basement deal, and veggie and beef *asada* (cooked on a charcoal grill) options are available for avowed fish-o-phobes.

See p. 172 in Chapter 12. At the North Shore Marketplace (in back), 66-250 Kamehameha Hwy., Haleiwa. ☎ **808-637-3059.** *A la carte items: $4–$8. Combo plates: $6–$14. No credit cards. Open: Breakfast, lunch, and dinner daily.*

Ciao Mein
$$$–$$$$ Mid-Waikiki   Italian/Chinese

Chinese tonight? Maybe Italian instead? No need to decide! Just head to this cross-cultural hybrid of a restaurant, which may seem gimmicky but is actually a big-time culinary success. Surprisingly good Chinese and pasta standards are served up side by side in the unexpectedly stylish multiroom restaurant, which is rich with Asian-style furnishings and lots of red and black lacquer. The noodles are particularly heavenly; I especially love the cake noodle, crisp fried noodles topped with stir-fried chicken, lobster, and veggies. The spicy wok-fried Szechuan eggplant appetizer is a Taste of Honolulu award winner, and deservedly so. The "collision cuisine" dishes (such as Chinese roast duck canneloni and seafood lasagna made with chow fun noodles) are quite successful, too, and the mix-and-match pasta/sauce combos are a big hit with kids. Don't miss the tiramisu if you're a fan.

See map p. 150 In the Hyatt Regency Waikiki, 2424 Kalakaua Avenue (between Kaiulani Street and Uluniu Avenue), Waikiki. ☎ **808-923-2426** *or 808-923-1234.* www. ciaomein.com. *Reservations recommended. Main courses: $17–$35 (most less than $24); complete dinners (served family style) $30–$42. AE, DC, DISC, MC, V. Open: Dinner daily.*

Don Ho's Island Grill
$$–$$$ Downtown/Aloha Tower Marketplace   Contemporary Hawaiian

Sure, it's kinda touristy, but I really like this nostalgic-minded harborfront restaurant. The little-grass-shack décor is accented with photos of Don and his celebrity friends dotting the koa-paneled walls. Eating inexpensively or moderately is easy to do here. The menu features contemporary versions of classic local dishes — ahi *poke,* luau pork, kalbi short ribs, fried rice topped with fried eggs — that have been tweaked a bit to suit mainland palates. You'll also find well-stuffed sandwiches, entree-sized salads, Hawaii-style "surfboard" pizzas, and a few dressed-up entrees like macadamia-crusted lamb chops (a surprisingly good cut and very nicely prepared). Everything is hearty and satisfying; I dreamed about that yummy fried rice for days after I cleaned my plate. Silly-named tropical drinks wash the casual fare down nicely.

The aloha-shirted staff is friendly but not in a particular hurry, so you shouldn't be, either. Don't expect to find Don himself chowing down on a Pacific blue crab melt; he's over at the Waikiki Beachcomber, where he still sings "Tiny Bubbles" most nights (see Chapter 12). However, the place does transform into quite a hip spot for live party music and hip-shakin' disco on weekends; during the dinner hour, local talent sets a more relaxed tone, serenading diners with island songs.

See map p. 154. Aloha Tower Marketplace, 1 Aloha Tower Dr., just south of downtown Honolulu. ☎ *808-528-0807.* www.donho.com/grill/grill.htm. *Reservations recommended. To get there: Take Ala Moana Boulevard west from Waikiki. Main courses $9–$23 (most less than $13). AE, DC, DISC, MC, V. Open: Lunch and dinner daily.*

Duke's Canoe Club
$–$$$ Mid-Waikiki   Steaks/Seafood

Duke's is everything that Waikiki dining should be, complete with sarong-wearing cocktail waitresses, open-air beachfront dining, and tiki torches in the sand. This inviting restaurant manages to be all things to all people: a kid-friendly choice for families, a romantic lair for lovers, a magnet for Hawaiian music fans, and a hot spot for party hoppers. The menu deserves high marks, too, from the fresh-caught local fish (with a half-dozen preparations to choose from) to the succulent prime rib. I particularly love the *"poke"* rolls, made with sushi-grade ruby-red ahi, to start. Duke's is also well-loved for its Barefoot Bar, with a mile-long drink menu, budget-friendly food, and top-notch island music nightly. It's a great place to watch the sunset.

At the Outrigger Waikiki on the Beach, 2335 Kalakaua Ave. (between the Royal Hawaiian Shopping Center and the Sheraton Moana Surfrider), Waikiki. ☎ *808-922-2268.* www.hulapie.com. *Reservations recommended for dinner. Main courses: $18–$25 at dinner (salad bar included). Barefoot Bar menu (served all day): $6–$11. Breakfast and lunch buffets $11. AE, DC, DISC, MC, V. Open: Breakfast, lunch, and dinner daily.*

Gordon Biersch Brewery Restaurant
$$–$$$ Downtown/Aloha Tower Marketplace   New American

"Never mind the perfect beaches. This is why they call it Paradise." A bold claim, but not too far of a stretch — especially for beer lovers. The German-style microbrews fermented on-site at this lively hangout would be enough of a draw, but the harborfront setting is unparalleled, and the grown-up pub food is terrific, too, making this the best all-around spot in the restaurant-rich Aloha Tower Marketplace. Stop by the bar to nosh on veggie potstickers, honey-glazed spare ribs, chicken wings, individual pizzas, and other well-prepared casual fare. Or make it a meal: The huge menu boasts choices ranging from a three-napkin cheeseburger to seared ahi and sake-braised lamb shank, all prepared with a deft hand and accented with cross-cultural touches. Live music ignites a party atmosphere Thursday through Saturday (and some Sundays — call ahead to confirm).

See map p. 154. Aloha Tower Marketplace, 1 Aloha Tower Dr., just south of downtown Honolulu. ☎ *808-599-4877.* www.gordonbiersch.com. *Reservations recommended. To get there: Take Ala Moana Boulevard west from Waikiki. Main courses: $8–$13 at lunch, $9–$21 at dinner. AE, DC, DISC, MC, V. Open: Lunch and dinner daily.*

Hau Tree Lanai
$$$ Diamond Head Waikiki   Eurasian/Continental

Shaded by an ancient hau tree that twinkles with tiny lights at dinnertime, this informal outdoor terrace on the sand is one of the most romantic beachfront restaurants in all Hawaii. The A-1 location surpasses the food at any time of day — but, frankly, it would be hard for any chef to live up to this magical setting. Breakfast is best: Throw caution to the wind and start the day with the sausage sampler — three kinds of local sausage and a side of fluffy poi pancakes — or the eggs Benedict, which wears a perfect hollandaise. Lunchtime features burgers, sandwiches, and salads, while the fresh island fish preparations are the standouts at dinner. Live music enhances the romantic mood on weekends and during the Friday lunch hour.

See map p. 150. In the New Otani Kaimana Beach Hotel, 2863 Kalakaua Ave. (across the street from Kapiolani Park), Waikiki. ☎ *808-921-7066.* www.kaimana.com. *Reservations recommended. Main courses: $8–$17 at breakfast and lunch, $19–$32 at dinner. AE, DC, DISC, MC, V. Open: Breakfast, lunch, and dinner daily.*

Helena's Hawaiian Food
$ Downtown   Local Hawaiian

This six-decade-old diner may have relocated to new digs in 2002, but the old-time ambience and all the hallmarks of Helena's remain, making this the best place in town to experience genuine island-style eats. Helena's is so renowned for its local fare that the James Beard Foundation has lauded it as a regional classic. Grandson Craig Katsuyoshi now mans the stove while lively 80-something Helena handles the cash register, but all her classic dishes are served, including *pipikaula,* strips of seasoned beef hung to dry over the stove, as well as moist and tender pulled kalua pork, pork laulau (wrapped and steamed in ti leaves), short ribs, squid luau, fried butterfish collars, and other ethnic island staples. Don't be afraid to ask these friendly folks for dish descriptions or recommendations. Helena's is a great place to experience Hawaii at its most down-to-earth authentic.

See map p. 154. 1240 N. School St. (near Pohaku Street, north of the H-1 freeway). ☎ *808-845-8044. Reservations recommended for dinner. Main courses: Most less than $12. No credit cards. Open: Lunch and early dinner (to 7 p.m.) Tues–Sat.*

House Without a Key
$$$ Waikiki   Eclectic

Sure, it's worth pulling out the platinum card for an evening of fine ocean-side dining and top-notch Hawaiian entertainment — but you don't have to. Everybody in the islands knows that this alfresco beachside lounge is Waikiki's best spot for sunset cocktails, but few realize how good the food is, too. The dinner menu fuses casual dining and elegance without a hitch. Consider starting with premium-grade ahi sashimi or a beautifully realized spinach salad — with crumbled bacon, Roquefort, and a light *lilikoi* (passion fruit) mustard dressing — followed by a perfectly grilled Angus beef burger. Or start with casual finger foods (maybe delicately fried calamari or steamed Peking duck buns) and follow with lump crab-crusted mahimahi or a thick-cut New York steak. The mai tais are Hawaii's best, but the bar even excels at nonalcoholic creations; try the lime-tart Calamansi soda or a frozen lemonade for a refreshing thirst quencher. A masterful trio entertains with traditional Hawaiian music nightly, accompanied by an elegant hula dancer of the highest regard (Kanoelehua Miller, a former Miss Hawaii, most nights). Romantic, nostalgic, and breathtaking; one of my Waikiki favorites.

See map p. 150. In the Halekulani, 2199 Kalia Rd. (at the beach end of Lewers Street), Waikiki. ☎ *808-923-2311.* www.halekulani.com. *Reservations highly recommended for sunset dining. Main courses: $12–$28; breakfast buffet $21 adults, $11 kids ages 5–12. AE, DC, MC, V. Open: Breakfast, lunch, and dinner daily.*

Hy's Steak House
$$$$–$$$$$ Waikiki   Steaks/Seafood

I just love Hy's — it's the only place in town that still serves a great steak and flaming bananas Foster in true old-world style. This dark and clubby steakhouse is the perfect setting for classics like oysters Rockefeller, beef Wellington, rich and garlicky steak Diane, lamb chops à la Hy's (perfectly broiled and served with tropical fruit chutney), and chateaubriand for two. A number of surf-and-turf combos are available to choose from, plus a good selection of seafood options (including calamari, ahi, and *kiawe* [mesquite]-charred scallops). I suggest starting with the Caesar salad show (prepared tableside with all of the classic flourishes) and crowning the meal with a flambéed dessert, such as cherries jubilee or the aforementioned bananas Foster.

See map p. 150. In the Waikiki Park Heights, 2440 Kuhio Ave. (near Uluniu Avenue). ☎ *808-922-5555.* www.hyssteakhousehawaii.com. *Reservations highly recommended. Main courses: $18–$50. AE, DC, DISC, MC, V. Open: Dinner nightly.*

Indigo
$$$ **Downtown Eurasian**

This intimate downtown restaurant is a wonderful choice for a romantic midpriced meal. Boasting a casual-chic tropical look, the contemporary main room sets an appealing scene. But call ahead for a table on the magical lanai, which overlooks a charming pocket park; dark woods and rattan, oversize palm fronds, a trickling water fountain, and conspiratorially dim candlelight make this outdoor dining room feel as if it had been transplanted from exotic Thailand or deepest Malaysia. Chef/owner Glenn Chu's east-meets-west menu is best described as pan-Asian — Chinese and Thai traditions are most apparent — with serious French twists: Witness such taste treats as goat cheese wontons in a four-fruit sauce, and Mongolian lamb chops sauced with minted tangerines. Light eaters or the chronically indecisive can choose to make a meal of dim sum-style plates (lobster potstickers, anyone?). Come early for a relaxed martini, or stay late for some rollicking live music, in the adjacent Green Room lounge.

See map p. 154. 1121 Nuuanu Ave. (between S. King and S. Hotel streets), downtown Honolulu. ☎ *808-521-2900.* www.indigo-hawaii.com. *Reservations recommended. To get there: Take Ala Moana Boulevard from Waikiki to Bethel Street; turn right, then left on Pauahi Street, then left on Nuuanu Avenue. Main courses: $8–$18 at lunch, $17–$26 at dinner. Lunch buffet with trio of dim sum $14. DC, DISC, MC, V. Open: Lunch and dinner Tues–Fri, dinner only Sat.*

Jameson's by the Sea
$$–$$$$ **North Shore Steaks-Seafood-American**

Don't come to this North Shore institution for the food — come for the tropical cocktails and breathtaking oceanfront setting surrounding the casual, lively patio. The food isn't bad, by any stretch — it's just not very memorable, especially compared to those spectacular sunset views. Expect capably prepared surf-and-turf choices in the evening, plus sandwiches (crab and shrimp on sourdough bread is a winner), salads, and other casual eats throughout the day. Everything goes better with a celebratory fruity drink or ice-cold beer at cocktail (and sunset-viewing) hour.

See p. 172 in Chapter 12. 62-540 Kamehameha Hwy., Haleiwa (just north of town). ☎ *808-637-4336. Reservations recommended for the pricier upstairs dining room (also taken for downstairs Mon–Tues, when upstairs is closed). Main courses: $10–$15 downstairs lunch and pub menu, $14–$32 in dining room. AE, DC, DISC, MC, V. Open: Lunch and dinner daily.*

Kakaako Kitchen
$ **Ala Moana Hawaii Local/American**

This contemporary dine-and-dash elevates takeout to gourmet status. The huge menu can please even the most finicky eaters with choices ranging from Chinese *char siu* (barbeque) chicken salad with crispy wontons to an all-American oven-roasted turkey sandwich with sage dressing and mashies. The island-style chicken linguine in chile-hoisin cream is a standout, but you can also come by for a juicy beef or homemade veggie burger, home-style pot roast, sandwiches ranging from seared ahi to grilled pastrami, and daily vegetarian specials. Breakfast stars include omelets, corned-beef hash, and fresh-baked scones. You order at the counter, pay, pick up your utensils, and then choose a table in the simple but bright indoor space or on the lanai; a server delivers your freshly made, affordable, and tasty meal in short order. Beware the workday lunch hour, which can be maddening.

See map p. 154. At Ward Centre, 1200 Ala Moana Blvd. (entrance 1 block north, on Auahi Street at Kamakee Street), Honolulu. ☎ *808-596-7488. Main courses: $5–$8 at breakfast, $6.50–$13 at lunch and dinner. AE, DC, MC, V. Open: Breakfast and lunch daily, dinner Mon–Sat.*

Kimo'Z

$ East Oahu   Local Hawaiian

This local favorite makes an ideal meal stop on your Circle Island drive, or after a morning spent at nearby Sea Life Park or Hanauma Bay. A simple but pleasant room filled with picnic tables and a long bar, this friendly family restaurant boasts an extensive menu with something for everyone, from morning egg-and-Hormel meat combos to good all-American burgers to classic Hawaiian plate lunches to sizzling stir-frys. But the reason to come is the huli huli chicken, generously seasoned with rosemary and Hawaiian salt, baked slowly, and then rotisserie grilled. It's moist, tender, and succulent — chicken worth writing home about. Another winner is the king *kal-bi,* pulled short-rib meat marinated in zesty Korean sauce and slow-grilled to perfection. There's a karaoke machine if you're in the mood to croon on your way back from a day at the beach, plus live music on weekend evenings.

See p. 172 in Chapter 12. 41-1537 Kalanianaole Hwy., Waimanalo. ☎ *808-259-8800. Reservations not taken. Main courses: $6–$14. AE, DC, DISC, MC, V. Open: Breakfast, lunch, and dinner daily.*

Kua Aina Sandwich

$ Ala Moana/North Shore   Island Style/American

This North Shore legend has pleased many Honolulu residents — who used to have to drive an hour for the ultimate burger — by opening a second Ala Moana–area location. Cheeseburger in Paradise (see earlier in this chapter) wins on both burger and atmosphere, but Kua Aina (KOO-ah EYE-na) runs a close second on the burger and makes for a better quickie meal. The gourmet sandwiches are equally good, especially the mahimahi with a green-chile sauce and cheese. Whatever you order, don't forget a side of the spindly fries, which elevate the fried spud to new levels. Take-out is a good idea at the perpetually packed North Shore location; the larger Honolulu branch offers more indoor and outdoor seating.

See map p. 154. In Honolulu: At Ward Village Shops, 1116 Auahi St. (at Kamakee Street, 1 block inland from Ala Moana Boulevard, directly behind Ward Centre).

☎ *808-591-9133. Sandwiches and burgers: $4.50–$6. No credit cards. Open: Lunch and dinner (to 9 p.m.) daily. On the North Shore: 66- 214 Kamehameha Hwy., Haleiwa.* ☎ *808-637-6067. Sandwiches and burgers: $4.50–$6. No credit cards. Open: Lunch and early dinner (to 8 p.m.) daily.*

L'Uraku
$$$–$$$$ Ala Moana   Euro-Japanese

As soon as you enter L'Uraku, you see that you're in for something different: The room is clean, and corporate lines are interrupted by a welcoming touch of whimsy: a collection of umbrellas festively painted with impulsive brush strokes and suspended from the ceiling, creating the impression of an upside-down garden in bloom. The dishes are light, fresh, and bursting with spirited flavor. Lighter tastes will love the creative, contemporary sushi; the vegetarian's dream, a medley of grilled tomatoes, eggplant, portobello mushrooms, and seasonal vegetables; or the seared sea scallop, infused with a divine smoky flavor. The setting is bustling and lively, perfect for a special meal for two or a family affair; service is impeccable; and plates are beautifully presented in the Japanese tradition. A real gem — I can't wait to return yet again!

See map p. 154. At Uraku Tower, 1341 Kapiolani Blvd. (near Piikoi Street), Honolulu. ☎ *808-955-0552.* www.luraku.com. *Reservations highly recommended. To get there: Take Ala Moana Boulevard east from Waikiki; turn right onto Piikoi Street, just beyond the Ala Moana Center, then right on Kapiolani Boulevard and pull into free lower-level lot. Main courses: $9–$20 at lunch, $16–$28 at dinner. 4-course weekender lunch $16; 4-course dinner tasting menu $34, $47 with wine. AE, DC, MC, V. Open: Lunch and dinner daily.*

Orchids
$$$$–$$$$$ Waikiki   International Seafood

There's no arguing with the fabulousness of the Halekulani's classic French restaurant, La Mer — but oceanside Orchids is equally fabulous, less expensive, and better suits the Hawaii mood. Everything about Orchids is sigh-inducing: the gorgeous alfresco setting; the spectacular ocean and Diamond Head views; the seamless service; and an impressive surf-and-turf menu that offers time-tested classics to traditionalists and globe-hopping innovations for adventurous spirits. It's very pricey — the wine list alone will cause you to do a double-take — but if you have something to celebrate, this is a wonderful place to do it. Live music adds to the romantic vibe nightly and during the legendary Sunday brunch.

See map p. 150. In the Halekulani, 2199 Kalia Rd. (at the beach end of Lewers Street), Waikiki. ☎ *808-923-2311.* www.halekulani.com. *Reservations highly recommended. Main courses: $7–$20 at breakfast, $22–$39 at dinner (chef's tasting menu $53); Sun brunch $25. AE, DC, MC, V. Open: Breakfast and dinner Mon–Sat; brunch and dinner Sun.*

Pah Ke's Chinese Restaurant
$–$$ Windward Coast   Chinese/Island

This top-flight Chinese restaurant from brothers Raymond and Barry Siu is well worth the 20-minute trip from Waikiki. Pah Ke's serves Hong Kong–style Chinese food with a local flair thanks to the use of healthy cooking techniques and island-grown ingredients. Specialties of the house include Ka'u orange spinach salad and a steamed fresh local catch, but you can't go wrong with any of the dishes here. Delightful versions of all your Chinese favorites are on the menu, but the staff will be happy to order for you if you'd like to dine creatively with some direction. The brightly lit room bustles with positive energy and happy diners, where seating is both family-style and at private tables for two and four. BYOB if you'd like beer or wine with your meal.

See p. 172 in Chapter 12. 46- 018 Kamehameha Hwy., Kaneohe. ☎ *808-235-4505. Reservations recommended for dinner. To get there: Take the Likelike Highway (Highway 63) from Waikiki, turn left on Kamehameha Highway (Highway 83), just over 1 mile; Pah Ke's will be on your right. Main courses: $4.50–$16 (most less than $9). Fixed-price meals $5 at lunch, $6–$7 at dinner. AE, MC, V. Open: Lunch and dinner daily.*

Parc Cafe
$$–$$$ Mid-Waikiki   Island American

Sure, the Parc Cafe offers standard order-off-the-menu dining, but everybody — locals and in-the-know visitors alike — comes to this smart little hotel restaurant for the high-quality buffet spreads at value-minded prices. Don't let the buffet concept scare you away — this is winning gourmet cuisine. The theme changes by day and meal; my favorite is the fabulous Hawaiian buffet (available at Wednesday and Friday lunch and Wednesday dinner), which offers a well-prepared introduction to the local dining tradition. The nightly (except Wednesday) prime-rib buffets boast succulent beef and rotisserie chicken along with a wide array of accompaniments; on Friday, Saturday, and Sunday, fresh seafood (including excellent sushi) and a wok station broaden the appeal.

See map p. 150. In the Waikiki Parc, 2233 Helumoa Rd. (at Lewers Street, east of the Halekulani). ☎ **808-921-7272.** www.waikikiparc.com. *Reservations recommended. Main courses: $7.50–$14 at lunch, $14–$18 at dinner. All-you-can-eat buffets: $15 at breakfast, $17–$18 at lunch, $20–$29 at dinner. Parents pay $5–$12 for kids 5–12, based on $1-per-year ratio. AE, DC, MC, V. Open: Breakfast, lunch, and dinner Mon–Sat; brunch and dinner Sun.*

Pineapple Room
$$$ Ala Moana   Hawaii Regional

Culinary star Alan Wong (see Alan Wong's, earlier in this section) has made a surprising addition to his stable of successes: a genuine, all-day department-store restaurant — and it's a winner. Dining at the warm, comfortable Pineapple Room offers a wonderful opportunity to sample the master chef's impressive cuisine in more casual preparations and in a more laid-back atmosphere than what you find at his namesake restaurant — and at a lower price tag to boot. Sure, you can blow a wad of cash on dinner here, but you don't have to. Opt for a round of affordable family-style appetizers instead (all under $13), such as luau pork nachos, crispy fried salt-and-pepper shrimp, vine-ripened Waimea tomato salad, and one of the day's wood-fired pizzas. The breakfasts are the best in town, there's an array of delectable patisserie sweets (including gift items to go), and lunch offers a gourmet take on the shopping break.

See map p. 154. On the third floor of Macy's, Ala Moana Center, 1450 Ala Moana Blvd. (at Atkinson Drive, just west of Waikiki). ☎ *808-945-8881.* www.alanwongs.com. *Reservations recommended for dinner. Main courses: $9.75–$27 at breakfast and lunch (most less than $17), $14–$30 at dinner. Fixed-price lunch $20; 5-course dinner sampling menu: $49 ($64 with wines). AE, DC, MC, V. Open: Breakfast Sat–Sun, lunch daily, dinner Mon–Sat.*

Roy's Restaurant — Honolulu
$$$ Hawaii Kai   Hawaii Regional

Roy Yamaguchi isn't the sole mastermind behind the Hawaii Regional Cuisine concept, but he is responsible for bringing it an international audience. The flagship restaurant of his worldwide chain is a full 20 minutes east of Waikiki; still, the original Roy's is worth visiting if you want to see what the fuss was all about. Indeed, Roy's hasn't lost its sheen — readers of *Honolulu* magazine once again named Roy's Restaurant of the Year in 2004. You can go whole hog or keep costs down by ordering from the wide selection of appetizers and creative wood-oven pizzas, virtually all less than $10. The menu changes nightly, but count on such signatures as Szechuan-spiced baby-back ribs, crispy crab cakes in spicy sesame butter, and several inventively prepared fresh catches. Roy offers his own private-label ultrapremium sake, which perfectly complements his menu. Tables are big and comfortable, and service is friendly and impressively attentive. Kids are welcome, and Roy's is particularly well-suited to groups, making it an ideal choice for a multigenerational family meal. There's also live music Friday, Saturday, and Sunday evenings.

See p. 172 in Chapter 12. In Hawaii Kai Corporate Plaza, 6600 Kalanianaole Hwy. (Highway 72 at Keahole Street), east of Honolulu in Hawaii Kai. ☎ ***808-396-7697.*** www.roysrestaurant.com. *Reservations recommended. Appetizers and pizzas: $6–$12. Main courses: $14–$29. AE, DC, DISC, MC, V. Open: Dinner nightly.*

Sam Choy's Breakfast, Lunch, Crab & Big Aloha Brewery
$$$ Honolulu   Hawaii Regional/Seafood

This informal island-style restaurant and crab house is a favorite for its gargantuan portions and fun, energetic atmosphere. I love Sam for his mammoth morning meals and lunches; with appetite ragin' full on, I usually head here straight off my transpacific flight for a piled-high fried *poke* (ahi) lunch or a monster Lava burger (topped with crabmeat and Swiss cheese). Thoughts invariably turn to crab at dinner: The variety changes with the season, but you can expect a national atlas of choices, from Kona to Alaskan to Maryland crabmeat, in preparations that range from steamed legs to rich chowder to delectable cakes. The food is great, but come for the whole festive experience; you're welcome — nay, expected — to roll up your sleeves and get messy with the shellfish. Sam's own Big Aloha beer is brewed on-site. Beware: Service can be slack at times, although it's always friendly.

See map p. 154. 580 Nimitz Hwy. (on the way to the airport), Honolulu. ☎ *808-545-7979.* www.samchoy.com. *Reservations recommended. Main courses: $7.50–$13 at breakfast, $8–$38 at lunch (most less than $13), $18–$40 at dinner (most less than $26). AE, DC, DISC, MC, V. Open: Breakfast, lunch, and dinner daily.*

Side Street Inn
$–$$ Ala Moana Local

The popularity of this unassuming sports-and-karaoke bar exploded when locals realized that this is where Honolulu's best chefs gather to nosh after their own kitchens close. This is as casual as it gets: neon beer signs in the plate-glass windows, long picnic-style tables, TVs turned to the current game, no-nonsense service, and chatting, happy crowds digging in family style to plates of tangy buffalo wings, hoisin-glazed baby-back ribs, *kal bi* (charbroiled Korean-style short ribs), and other diet-defying delights. Many consider the pan-fried pork chops to be the world's best, and they just may be; the fried rice is equally delectable. For such low-brow fare, the ingredients are of surprisingly high quality; you can even order a fresh veggie-packed salad here. Genuine family-style fun — and a great choice for late-night dining, since the Side Street is open until 12:30 a.m. daily. *Note:* Parking is limited to street parking and nearby lots, but it's not hard to find.

See map p. 154. 1225 Hopaka St. (just west of Piikoi St., one block south of Kapiolani Blvd.), Honolulu. ☎ *808-591-0253. Reservations recommended for large parties. Main courses: $4–$7 at lunch, $6–$19 at dinner. AE, DC, DISC, MC, V. Open: Lunch Mon–Fri, dinner daily.*

Singha Thai Cuisine
$$$ Ewa Waikiki Thai

This spiffy restaurant serves up imaginative Thai-Hawaiian hybrid cuisine that wins fans among Asian-food addicts and novices alike. Thai-born chef Chai Chaowasaree's complete dinners for two to five are family-style feasts — perfect for introducing first-timers to this rich, flavorful cuisine, as well as elements of Hawaii Regional Cuisine that the chef has incorporated into his cooking. Highlights of the varied menu include yummy blackened ahi rolls; fresh island fish in a light black-bean sauce; a kaleidoscope of curries; and excellent seafood dishes. Dishes are presented prettily, and service is first-rate. The graceful Royal Thai Dancers perform nightly, adding to the one-of-a-kind experience.

See map p. 150. 1910 Ala Moana Blvd. (at Kalia Road, below California Pizza Kitchen), Waikiki. ☎ *808-941-2898.* www.singhathai.com. *Reservations recommended.*

Main courses: $13–$34; 3-course dinner with appetizer sampler $38. AE, DC, DISC, MC, V. Open: Dinner nightly.

Sushi Sasabune
$$$–$$$$ Honolulu   Japanese

In a town that swims with top-notch fresh fish, this unassuming restaurant — the Honolulu outpost of the famous but equally unassuming L.A. joint — is the king of quality sushi. You have two choices here: You can grab a table and order for yourself or pony up to the sushi bar, where chef Seiji Kamagawa always knows best. Everyone who dines at the sushi bar eats *omakase* — a multicourse meal of the day's freshest morsels, chosen by the chef. Because you won't have any say in the ordering, this is not an option for fussy eaters. But if you're willing to put yourself in the hands of the master behind the counter, you'll be rewarded with exotic treats flown in that day from ports around the world. Depending on the day, your meal might globetrot from Nova Scotia salmon to Louisiana blue crab to Pacific yellowtail to Hawaiian sea urchin to Japanese abalone — you get the idea. The sushi is prepared with warm rice, so you're expected to eat it with chopsticks. You'll also be presented with dipping sauce and are not expected to use soy unless instructed to do so. Listen — you won't be steered wrong. Excellent through and through, but not for hesitant sushi eaters (no California rolls made here). Table diners can easily keep the bill moderate, but those who opt for omakase should be prepared to spend in the $$$$ range.

See map p. 154. 1419 S. King St. (between Kalakaua Avenue and Piikoi Street). ☎ *808-947-3800.* www.members.aol.com/nobib. *Reservations recommended. Per-piece sushi and sashimi $3.50–$15 (most $4–$7). AE, DC, DISC, MC, V. Open: Lunch and dinner Mon–Fri, dinner only Sat.*

Luau!

None of Oahu's luaus are on par with those offered on the neighbor islands, especially Maui's Old Lahaina Luau, so I recommend skipping the experience on this island. But if you're wedded to the idea, or you're not visiting any of the neighboring islands on this trip, try the **Royal Luau at the Royal Hawaiian** (See map p. 150. 2259 Kalakaua Ave. [at the end of Royal Hawaiian Avenue], Waikiki; ☎ **808-931-8383;** www.royal-hawaiian.com/de_luau.htm; admission: $81 adults, $48 kids 5–12; discounts for Royal Hawaiian guests; online discounts up to 20 percent sometimes available. Price includes unlimited cocktails; reservations highly recommended. Open: Monday and summer Thursdays at 6 p.m. May be cancelled or moved to an indoor venue in inclement weather.). This is Waikiki's only luau and while it's not the most authentic luau in the islands, it is intimate and romantic. Also consider the nightly (except Sunday) luau at the **Polynesian Cultural Center;** see Chapter 12 for more information. See map p. 172.

Fast Facts: Oahu

American Automobile Association (AAA)

Hawaii's only AAA office is at 1130 Nimitz Highway, Honolulu (☎ 800-736-2886 or 808-593-2221; www.aaa-hawaii.com). The office is open Monday through Friday from 9 a.m. to 5 p.m., and Saturday from 9 a.m. to 2 p.m.

American Express

At 677 Ala Moana Blvd., Honolulu (☎ 808-585-3200); two offices at Hilton Hawaiian Village, 2005 Kalia Rd., at Ala Moana Boulevard, Waikiki (☎ 808-947-2607 or 808-951-0644); and at the Hyatt Regency Waikiki, 2424 Kalakaua Ave. (☎ 808-926-5441).

Doctors

Straub Doctors on Call (☎ 808-522-4777 for the 24-hour appointment line; www.straubhealth.org/clinics/docsoncall.htm) offers around-the-clock care at its 24-hour health clinic on the ground floor of the Sheraton Princess Kaiulani Hotel, 120 Kaiulani Ave., just north of Kalakaua Avenue in the heart of Waikiki (☎ 808-971-6000). It also has additional walk-in clinics at the Hyatt Regency Waikiki, 2424 Kalakaua Ave., Diamond Head Tower, 4th floor (☎ 808-971-8001; open Mon–Fri 8 a.m.–4 p.m.), the Hawaiian Regent Hotel, 2552 Kalakaua Ave., Kuhio Tower (☎ 808-923-3666; open Mon–Fri 8:00 a.m.–4:30 p.m.), and the Kahala Mandarin Oriental, 5000 Kahala Ave. (☎ 808-739-8909; open Mon–Fri 9 a.m.–1 p.m.). It accepts more than 150 health plans, so pack your insurance card. They can send a van to bring you to their main clinic, or house calls can be arranged.

Walk-in health care is also available at the **Urgent Care Clinic Waikiki,** 2155 Kalakaua Ave., between Beach Walk and Lewers Street, Suite 308 (☎ 808-432-2700; open daily 8 a.m.–8 p.m.). You can call ahead for free taxi pickup from your Waikiki hotel.

Emergencies

Dial **911** from any phone, just like back home on the mainland.

Hospitals

Nearest to Waikiki is **Straub Clinic and Hospital,** 888 S. King St., at Ward Avenue (☎ 808-522-4000; www.straubhealth.org); the Emergency Room entrance is on Hotel Street. Also offering 24-hour emergency care is **Queens Medical Center,** 1301 Punchbowl St., between Beretania Street and Vineyard Boulevard (☎ 808-538-9011, or 808-547-4311 for the ER; www.queens.org).

Information

The **Hawaii Visitors and Convention Bureau** operates an office on the seventh floor of 2270 Kalakaua Ave. in the heart of Waikiki (☎ 800-464-2924 or 808-923-1811; www.gohawaii.com). Tons of info is available on the Web site. The **Oahu Visitors Bureau,** 733 Bishop St., Makai Tower, Suite 1872, downtown Honolulu (☎ 877-525-OAHU or 808-524-0722; www.visit-oahu.com), offers good island-specific information on its Web site, and you can order a good vacation planner by calling the 877 number.

You can stop into either of these offices while you're in town to pick up information, but chances are you won't have to; plenty of information is available right at the airport. Just stop at the information desk near Baggage Claim and pick up a copy of *This Week Oahu, 101 Things to Do on Oahu,* and other free tourist publications; they're packed with good maps. All Waikiki's hotels, from budget to deluxe, also overflow with printed info, and the staffs are generally well-informed and helpful.

Newspapers/Magazines

The *Honolulu Advertiser* (www.honoluluadvertiser.com) and *Honolulu Star-Bulletin* (www.starbulletin.com) are Oahu's daily papers. The *Honolulu Weekly* (www.honoluluweekly.com) is the best source for entertainment listings and information on what's happening around town; it's available free at restaurants, clubs, shops, and newspaper racks around Oahu. *Honolulu* magazine is a popular glossy monthly.

Pharmacies

Long's Drugs (www.longs.com), Hawaii's biggest drugstore chain, has convenient locations at Ala Moana Center, 1450 Ala Moana Blvd., next to Sears (☎ 808-941-4433), and at other locations around the island. The city's only 24-hour store is at 1330 Pali Hwy., at Vineyard Boulevard, downtown Honolulu (☎ 808-536-7302).

Police

The **Waikiki City Police Station** is in the Duke Paoa Kahanamoku Building at 2405 Kalakaua Ave., between Kaiulani and Uluniu streets on the ocean side of the street (☎ 808-529-3801). **Honolulu Police Department Main Station** is at 801 S. Beretania St., west of Ward Avenue (☎ 808-529-3111; www.honolulupd.org). Of course, if you have an emergency, dial **911** from any phone.

Post Offices

The **Waikiki Post Office** is at 330 Saratoga Rd., just south of Kalakaua Avenue, adjacent to Fort DeRussy Park. Another convenient location is in the Ala Moana Shopping Center. To find the location nearest you, call ☎ 800-275-8777 or visit www.usps.com.

Taxes

Hawaii's sales tax is 4 percent. Expect taxes of about 11.42 percent to be added to your hotel bill.

Taxis

Oahu's major cab companies offer island-wide, 24-hour radio-dispatched service. Call **Star Taxi** (☎ 800-671-2999 or 808-942-7827); **SIDA Taxi** (☎ 808-836-0011); **Aloha State Cab** (☎ 808-847-3566); **City Taxi** (☎ 808-524-2121); or **TheCab** (☎ 808-422-2222). **Coast Taxi** (☎ 808-261-3755) serves Windward Oahu, while **Hawaii Kai Hui/Koko Head Taxi** (☎ 808-396-6633) serves east Honolulu/southeast Oahu.

See Chapter 9 for wheelchair-accessible transportation.

Transit Info

For information on routes and schedules, call TheBus at ☎ 808-848-5555, or 808-296-1818 for recorded route information. Point your browser to www.thebus.org for online info.

Weather and Surf Reports

For **National Weather Service** reports, call ☎ 808-973-4380 or 808-973-5286. For **marine conditions** and sunrise/sunset times, call ☎ 808-973-4382. For **surf reports,** call ☎ 808-973-4383 or the **Surfline** at ☎ 808-596-7873.

Chapter 12

Exploring Oahu

. . . .

In This Chapter

▶ Heading to Oahu's best beaches

▶ Playing in the waves

▶ Exploring Oahu's top attractions

▶ Scoping out the shopping scene

▶ Enjoying Oahu's island nightlife

. . . .

*O*ahu is the place to rev up and have some fun. This island boasts more than you can see or do in the span of five vacations, much less one — so save the kicking-back portion of your vacation for the next island.

Then again, there are those wonderful white sands and warm turquoise waters. . . .

Enjoying the Sand and Surf

Oahu's warm and wonderful diversity also extends to its wealth of beautiful beaches and ocean activities. Whether you want to kick back under the sun or find an ocean thrill, Oahu has the answer for you.

Combing the Beaches

When you're at the beach, maintain a healthy respect for the ocean. Big waves can come seemingly out of nowhere and travel far upshore in a matter of minutes. Never turn your back on the ocean and always remember to get out of the water when the swells come. Take extra care to heed this advice in winter, when the surf is at its least predictable.

Also, never leave valuables in your rental car while you're at the beach. Thieves prey on tourists, and they'll have no trouble getting into your car to take whatever you've left there.

The Waikiki Coast and East Oahu

Ala Moana Beach Park

Gold-sand Ala Moana ("by the sea") is the city's most popular beach playground for local families, and it's easy to see why. Stretching for more than a mile along Honolulu's coast between downtown and Waikiki, the long, man-made beach is one of the best-sheltered beaches on Oahu, so the water's calm and safe year-round for even little ones. The area called Magic Island, the peninsula that extends from Ala Moana Park, is especially well-protected thanks to a man-made breakwater that cuts the surf down to zero and offers great views of the Waikiki skyline. The park boasts concessions, lifeguards, bathhouses, tennis courts, a nice paved path for joggers, picnic tables, and wide-open grassy lawns. It's the only beach along this coast that's not lined with high-rise hotels, which gives it a nice, open feeling, and the sands are set far enough back from Ala Moana Boulevard that traffic doesn't interfere. The ambience is laid-back on weekdays, while a fun, festive party mood prevails on weekends. Plenty of free parking is at hand, but it fills up on weekends, so come early or catch TheBus to Ala Moana Center and walk across the street.

See map p. 174. Along Ala Moana Boulevard, between Atkinson Drive and Ward Avenue (directly across the street from Ala Moana Center).

Waikiki Beach

Probably the most famous beach on the planet — or in the United States, at least — Waikiki is center stage for Hawaii's biggest and best beach party. Five million global visitors a year descend onto this 1½-mile-long sunny crescent of sand. Sure, it gets crowded, but that's a big part of what makes Waikiki such a blast.

Waikiki is actually a long, narrow continuous string of beaches that extends between Ala Wai Harbor to the west and Diamond Head to the east. Each one is wonderful for surfing, swimming, and just frolicking in the mini swells — and the tight chain of high-rise hotels abutting the beaches actually helps to block street noise and traffic sounds. Every imaginable type of beach toy is available for rent at concessions that line the beach. I like to think of Waikiki as the giant "Jacuzzi of Hawaii" because the sparkling turquoise water is always calm, warm, crystal-clear, and great for floating the real-life stress away. Waves can kick up a bit in the spring, when the south swells come — and the local surfers show up — but it's never so severe that you need to stay out of the water; wave jumping just becomes part of the fun! You can't go wrong along any of the easily accessible Waikiki beaches described in the following paragraphs.

Duke Kahanamoku (ka-ha-na-MOW-koo) **Beach** is the west end of the beach, the section fronting the Hilton Hawaiian Village hotel. Access is off Kalia Road via Paoa Place — or just walk through the hotel grounds. **Waikiki Beach Prime Time Sports** operates two excellent beach chair-and gear-rental stands just east of the Hilton and west of the Outrigger

Beaches & Attractions Around Oahu

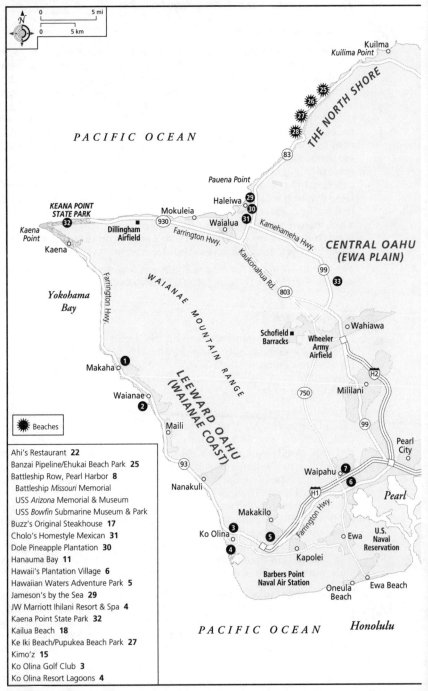

N

0   5 mi

0   5 km

Kuilma

Kuilima Point

THE NORTH SHORE

PACIFIC OCEAN

25
26
27
28

83

Pauena Point

KEANA POINT STATE PARK

32

Kaena Point

Kaena

Mokuleia

Haleiwa 29
30
Waialua 31

930

Dillingham Airfield

Farrington Hwy.

Kamehameha Hwy.

CENTRAL OAHU (EWA PLAIN)

Kaukonahua Rd.

99

33

803

Yokohama Bay

WAIANAE MOUNTAIN RANGE

Farrington Hwy.

Schofield Barracks

Wheeler Army Airfield

Wahiawa

Makaha 1

Waianae 2

LEEWARD OAHU (WAIANAE COAST)

Maili

750

Mililani

H2

99

☀ Beaches

Pearl City

Waipahu 7
6

93

Nanakuli

Makakilo

Ko Olina 3
4

5

H1

Farrington Hwy.

Pearl

Ewa

U.S. Naval Reservation

Kapolei

Pearl

Ahi's Restaurant 22
Banzai Pipeline/Ehukai Beach Park 25
Battleship Row, Pearl Harbor 8
  Battleship *Missouri* Memorial
  USS *Arizona* Memorial & Museum
  USS *Bowfin* Submarine Museum & Park
Buzz's Original Steakhouse 17
Cholo's Homestyle Mexican 31
Dole Pineapple Plantation 30
Hanauma Bay 11
Hawaii's Plantation Village 6
Hawaiian Waters Adventure Park 5
Jameson's by the Sea 29
JW Marriott Ihilani Resort & Spa 4
Kaena Point State Park 32
Kailua Beach 18
Ke Iki Beach/Pupukea Beach Park 27
Kimo'z 15
Ko Olina Golf Club 3
Ko Olina Resort Lagoons 4

Barbers Point Naval Air Station

Oneula Beach

Ewa Beach

PACIFIC OCEAN   Honolulu

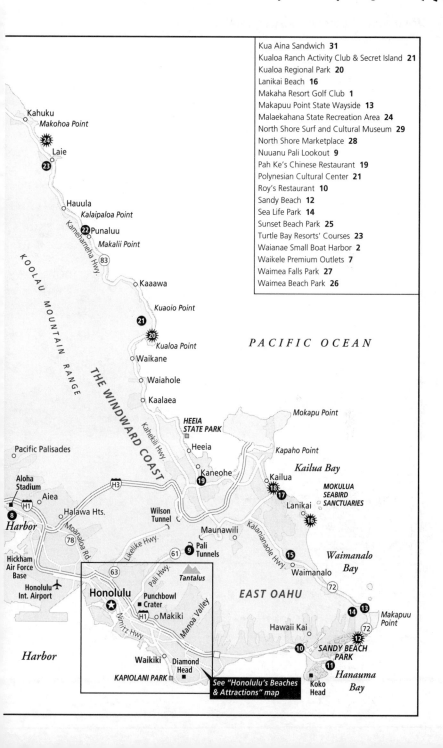

Kua Aina Sandwich **31**
Kualoa Ranch Activity Club & Secret Island **21**
Kualoa Regional Park **20**
Lanikai Beach **16**
Makaha Resort Golf Club **1**
Makapuu Point State Wayside **13**
Malaekahana State Recreation Area **24**
North Shore Surf and Cultural Museum **29**
North Shore Marketplace **28**
Nuuanu Pali Lookout **9**
Pah Ke's Chinese Restaurant **19**
Polynesian Cultural Center **21**
Roy's Restaurant **10**
Sandy Beach **12**
Sea Life Park **14**
Sunset Beach Park **25**
Turtle Bay Resorts' Courses **23**
Waianae Small Boat Harbor **2**
Waikele Premium Outlets **7**
Waimea Falls Park **27**
Waimea Beach Park **26**

Honolulu's Beaches & Attractions

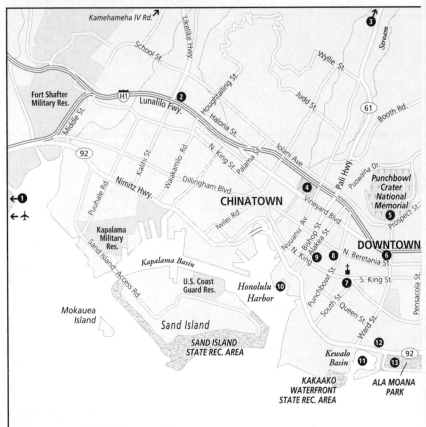

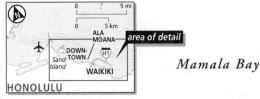

Ala Moana Beach Park **13**
Ala Moana Center **14**
Aloha Tower Marketplace **6**
Bishop Museum **2**
The Contemporary Museum **24**
Diamond Head Crater **22**
DFS Galleria **17**
Foster Botanical Garden **4**
Hanauma Bay **23**
Hawaii Maritime Center **10**
Hawaii State Art Museum **8**
Hawaii's Plantation Village **1**

Hawaiian Waters Adventure Park **1**
Hilo Hattie's **1**
Hilton Hawaiian Village Pier **15**
  (departure point for Atlantis Submarines)
Honolulu Academy of Arts **6**
Honolulu Zoo **21**
Iolani Palace **9**
Kewalo Basin **11**
Ko Olina Golf Club **1**
Mission Houses Museum **7**
National Cemetery of the Pacific
  at Punchbowl Crater **5**

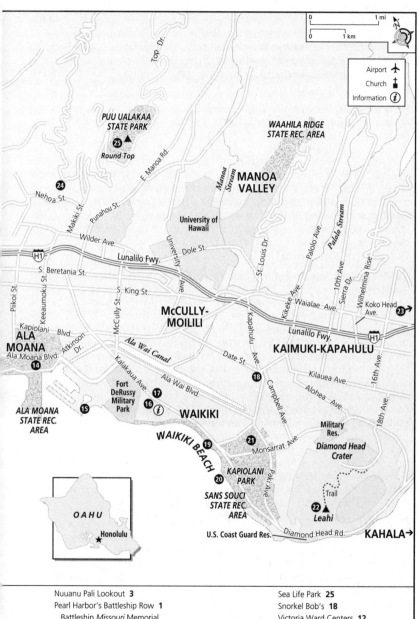

Nuuanu Pali Lookout **3**
Pearl Harbor's Battleship Row **1**
  Battleship *Missouri* Memorial
  USS *Arizona* Memorial & Museum
  USS *Bowfin* Submarine Museum & Park
Puu Ualakaa State Park **25**
Royal Hawaiian Shopping Center **16**
Sandy Beach **23**

Sea Life Park **25**
Snorkel Bob's **18**
Victoria Ward Centers **12**
  Ward Centre
  Ward Village Shops
  Ward Warehouse
Waikiki Aquarium **20**
Waikiki Beach **19**

Reef. You pay just $10 a day for a cushioned lounge chair (it's $12 in front of the Hilton, sans cushion), which the beach boy will even carry out to the sand for you (and haul back in when you're done). Prime Time Sports also rents umbrellas, oversized two-person rafts with anchors, fun aquacycles for paddling on the waves, and more. Friendly and hospitable service is the cherry on the cake, making these my favorite rental shacks on Waikiki Beach!

Gray's Beach, the arc of sand between the Halekulani and the Sheraton Moana Surfrider hotels, is my favorite stretch of Waikiki Beach. It's everybody else's, too — particularly the area in front of the historic Royal Hawaiian and Moana hotels — so bring your beach chair and stake a claim because this beach is where the party begins. (If you're lucky enough to be staying at the Royal or the Moana, the hotel will provide you with a beach chair.) Waikiki's waters are at their calmest and shallowest here. The beach has a number of access points, including a beach access pathway off Kalia Road, just to the left of the Halekulani and to the right of the Waikiki Parc hotel (as you face the coast); walk to the left to get to the wider sands. (Or, better yet, just parade through one of the hotels, such as the Royal, the Outrigger, or the Moana.)

Kuhio Beach, which begins just to the east of the Sheraton Moana Surfrider at the end of Kaiulani Avenue, continues the festive party atmosphere. Because fewer hotels separate Kalakaua Avenue from the beach, this one affords the quickest access to the Waikiki shoreline. This is where the majority of concessionaires are set up if you want to rent a boogie board, catch an outrigger canoe ride, or take a surfing lesson. (For more on what's available, see the section "Playing in the Surf," later in this chapter.) The swimming is good here, but some deep pools exist (heed the "Watch out for Holes" signs because you can suddenly find yourself in very deep water), and the surf kicks up a bit a few hundred yards offshore (where the line of surfers are). To the east of the Moana between Kaiulani and Uluniu avenues is Waikiki's newest renovation project, a wonderful parklike area of grassy knolls, winding paths, and tiki torches that makes an excellent place to watch the sunset; this spot has become such a popular stretch of beach that the city regularly hosts sunset entertainment here and occasionally sets up a big outdoor movie screen to show classic films; ask the concierge at your hotel or condo for the current schedule. At the end of Kapahulu Avenue, a seawall marks a favorite boogie-boarding spot that draws local daredevils when the swells kick up.

Queen's Beach, directly across from Kapiolani Park (between the zoo and the aquarium), is the easiest place to park along Waikiki. This is also the quietest stretch of beach because no hotels line the road, and a grassy, palm-dotted lawn backs the sand. Head here if you want to get away from the crowds because Queen's Beach tends to be much less crowded than its sister sands to the west. The facilities include showers, restrooms, barbecue grills, picnic tables, volleyball courts, and a pavilion with a food concession. The middle section of the beach (in front of the pavilion) is a popular gay hangout, but everybody's welcome.

Sans Souci Beach is the easternmost section of Waikiki, the bit that fronts the New Otani Kaimana Beach Hotel and the other small hotels and condos at the foot of Diamond Head. This is the locals' favorite stretch of Waikiki thanks to its beautiful setting (Diamond Head makes a gorgeous backdrop) and intimate, low-key vibe. It's also on the quiet side, with easy-access parking along Kalakaua Avenue and beach showers. The swimming here is excellent — a shallow reef close to shore.

See map p. 174. Lifeguards patrol all Waikiki, and all the hotels have public restrooms and casual beachfront restaurants. For more information, contact the Hawaiian Lifeguard Association (3823 Leahi Ave., Honolulu. ☎ *808-922-3888.* www.aloha. com/~lifeguards/).

Hanauma Bay

Everybody should visit Hanauma (ha-now-ma) Bay, which offers the best snorkeling in Hawaii, especially for novices. The curved, gold-sand beach is packed blanket-to-blanket with people year-round, and, sometimes, it seems there are more people than fish in the water — but put on a mask and gaze down into the clear, warm water, and a whole new world opens up to you. Cradled in an old volcanic crater, this marine life conservation district is home to an underwater metropolis of friendly reef fish, most of which are so used to people that they'll swim right up to your face mask. (But be sure not to touch or feed the exotic critters here.) The inner reef is calm, clear, and shallow — so much so, in fact, that even nonswimmers can wade and look down. Serious divers come to shoot "the slot" through the reef to Witch's Brew, a turbulent, 70-foot-deep cove featuring coral gardens, turtles, and sharks, but I suggest you stick to the safe, shallow, well-protected inner reef, which can keep even veteran seen-it-all snorkelers entertained.

A new $13-million Marine Education Center opened in 2002, as extensive improvements were made to the grounds and facilities at Hanauma Bay. The facility features a theater (you will be required to watch a seven-minute video about Hanauma Bay and ocean safety before you enter the park), an education alcove, a gift shop, and food concession at the upper level of the bay; a motorized tram (50¢ to go down the hill, $1 to go up) can take you down the steep road to the beach. Restrooms, outdoor showers, a snorkeling concession, and a new information center are located in the lower bay area. Pack a picnic, as the only food concession is at the top of the hill.

Admission is $5 per person, free for kids 12 and younger. Parking at Hanauma Bay costs $1 per car and is severely limited, so go bright and early to snare a spot (8 a.m. isn't too early); arrive after 10 a.m., and you may find yourself shut out until another car leaves. You can also take TheBus No. 22 (marked Hawaii Kai – Sea Life Park), which runs down Kuhio Avenue and takes about 45 minutes to reach Hanauma Bay. Or call **Tommy's Tours** (☎ **808-373-5060**), which offers round-trip shuttle service from most Waikiki hotels for $15 per person, $12.50 for kids 5 to 11; the price includes gear and an instructional briefing for first-time snorkelers. Call a day in advance to schedule your pickup.

Even though snorkel gear is available at Hanauma Bay, I much prefer to stop by Snorkel Bob's on the way to Hanauma Bay to pick up higher quality gear, which is well worth the extra $2 or $3; see the section "Playing in the Surf," later in this chapter, for details.

See map p. 172. In Koko Head Regional Park, off Kalanianaole Highway (the exit is well marked). ☎ *808-396-4229. Admission: $3; free for kids under 12. Open: Wed–Mon 6 a.m.–7 p.m.; closed Tues.*

Sandy Beach

The most famous bodysurfing beach in Hawaii is this beautiful gold-sand beach, which is all the more beautiful for the dramatic desert landscape behind it. This local favorite has starred in countless TV shows, from *Hawaii Five-O* to *Magnum P.I.,* and is well worth a visit just to take in its great natural beauty. In summer, the ocean is fine for swimming and boogie-boarding, but come just to watch in winter. Makapuu's big, pounding winter waves draw expert bodysurfers in droves, but they're simply too dangerous for regular swimmers. The wave riders can be thrilling to watch in action, though. If you come to play in the summer waves, boogie boards are fine, but leave any boards with *skegs* (bottom fins) at home. Whenever you get in the water, be sure to heed the lifeguard warnings and get out of the water if the swells or undertow kicks up. Facilities include restrooms, beach showers, lifeguard, and plenty of parking; a hot food truck usually shows up at lunchtime.

See map p. 172. On Kalanianole Highway. To get there: Drive east on H-1, which becomes Kalanianaole Highway; go past Hawaii Kai, up the hill to Hanauma Bay, past the Halona Blow Hole, and along the coast. The next big, gold, sandy beach you see ahead on the right is Sandy Beach.

Along the Windward Coast

If you have the time, I highly recommend spending a day at the beach along this stunning, uncrowded, residential coast. Come midweek, and you find these beaches almost deserted, which offers a nice change of pace from Waikiki. They're even a pleasant relief on weekends, when local families set the tone.

Plan on arriving for your day of east shore beachgoing early because the windward Koolau mountains block the afternoon sun, and you don't want to end up sitting in the shade on a beautiful day!

Kailua Beach

The Windward Coast's premier beach park is a 2-mile-long gently sloping golden strand with dunes, palm trees, panoramic views, gentle waves, and a gorgeous green-mountain backdrop. With excellent swimming, water that's about 78°F year-round, and good facilities, it's ideal for families — and your kids will love the bodysurfing and boogie-boarding here. Set up your toddlers in the freshwater shallows in the middle of the park, near the mouth of the stream, and they'll be happy as clams all day. Facilities

---

Picnicking at Lanikai or Kailua

Both Lanikai and Kailua beaches are ideal places to bring a picnic lunch and camp out for the day. And the perfect place to pack it? **Kalapawai Market,** 306 S. Kalaheo Ave. (☎ **808-262-4359**), just down the street from Kailua Beach and Buzz's Original Steak House (Chapter 11). Established in 1932, this charming market housed in a green plantation-style storefront has evolved into an easygoing gourmet market complete with home-style deli sanwiches and an excellent collection of snacks, soft drinks, wine, and beer. See map p. 172.

---

include picnic tables, barbecues, restrooms, a volleyball court, a bike path, an open-air cafe (which may be closed on weekdays), and plenty of free parking; lifeguards are usually on hand. Kayak and windsurf rentals are often available, too, because this is also Oahu's premier windsurfing beach.

See map p. 172. At the end of Kailua Road, Kailua. To get there: Take the Pali Highway (Highway 61) to Kailua, where it becomes Kailua Road as it proceeds through town; at Kalaheo Avenue, turn right and follow the coast to the park.

Lanikai Beach

This is one of the most tranquil and beautiful beaches in the entire state and my favorite place to spend a beach day on the entire island. It's almost always excellent for swimming, snorkeling, and kayaking, plus a little easy wave-jumping on occasion. The beach is long and narrow, with gold sand as soft as talcum powder and lightly rippled turquoise water. Two tiny off-shore islets provide the perfect panoramic finish. Unfortunately, the trade-off for all this unspoiled beauty is an utter lack of facilities, so bring your own water, snacks, and beach toys.

See map p. 172. Off Mokulua Drive, Kailua. To get there: Follow the directions to Kailua Beach Park (see preceding entry); just past Kailua Beach Park, turn left at the T inter-section and drive uphill on Aalapapa Drive, a one-way street that loops back as Mokulua Drive; park on Mokulua Drive and walk down any of the eight public access lanes to the shore.

Kualoa Regional Park

Farther north on the Windward Coast is one of Hawaii's most scenic beach parks, a 150-acre coco palm-fringed peninsula on Kaneohe Bay's north shore, at the foot of spiky green mountains. The biggest beach park on the windward side, it has a broad, grassy lawn that's great for picnicking. The long, narrow white-sand beach is ideal for swimming, beachcombing, kite-flying, or just enjoying the natural beauty of this once-sacred Hawaiian shore (it's listed on the National Register of Historic Places), but keep in mind that it can get pretty windy out here. The waters are shallow and safe for swimming year-round. It doesn't offer much in the way of facili-ties, but lifeguards are on duty. Offshore is Mokolii (mow-ko-LEE-ee), the picturesque mini-isle more commonly known as Chinaman's Hat (because it looks like one). At low tide, people like to wade out to the island, which has a small sandy beach; it's just a bad idea to walk on the reef, however, so if you're going to go, swim it instead. Chinaman's Hat is a bird preserve, so tread gently to avoid spooking the red-footed boobies.

See map p. 172. On Kamehameha Highway (Highway 83), Kualoa (about halfway up the coast, north of Waikane). Parking: The beach has a free lot.

Malaekahana State Recreation Area

Big, brawny Malaekahana (ma-lie-ka-HA-na) Beach is a nearly mile-long white-sand crescent with sheltered waters that are excellent for swimming year-round and waves that are great for beginning bodysurfers in summer. On any weekday, you may be the only one here; should someone intrude on your privacy, however, you can take an easy swim out to Goat Island, a bird sanctuary (you can wade it, but don't — it's bad for the reef). Stands of trees offer daytime shade, and restrooms, barbecue grills, picnic tables, outdoor showers, and tons of free parking are at hand.

See map p. 172. On Kamehameha Highway (Highway 83), 2 miles north of the Polynesian Cultural Center, Laie. The beach is hidden from the road, so look carefully for the main gate; as soon as you enter you'll come upon the wooded beach park. Parking: There's a free lot.

On the North Shore

This is surf country, where daredevils gather from around the world to ride monster waves in surf season, basically from late September through April. Don't even think about going into the water in winter, as the rip currents along this shore are killers. The North Shore coast is seasonally schizophrenic: The monstrous surf recedes entirely in summer, leaving glassy ponds and idle surfboards.

The waves may kick up even in the fairest months, so don't go near the water in any season if the lifeguards have put out the red warning flags, or if you just suspect that conditions might be too rough for all but easy swimming.

Sunset Beach Park

This surprisingly small beach is one of those legendary surf spots, the kind that draws fearless wave riders from around the world in winter, when the waves grow to huge, thundering peaks — sometimes as high as 15 to 20 feet. Come to watch the board-riding daredevils, who put on a jaw-dropping show. This is a great place to people-watch: It's a blast to eye the local surfers, the sunbathing beauties, and even your fellow vacationers catching a glimpse of the action. Weekends are best for prime spectating. The summer surf is fun for frolicking, and the beach is virtually empty midweek. No facilities are available, save for a small parking lot; join the other cars on the shoulder if it's full.

See map p. 172. On Kamehameha Highway (Highway 83), Pupukea.

Banzai Pipeline/Ehukai Beach Park

The Japanese word *banzai* means "10,000 years"; it's used as a toast or battle cry, meaning "go for it." (As you may remember from high-school history class, the Japanese liked to invoke it during WWII suicide missions.) In the late 1950s, filmmaker Bruce Brown was shooting one of the first surf movies ever made, *Surf Safari,* at Ekuhai Beach Park when he saw a bodysurfer ride a huge wave. Brown yelled "Banzai!", and the name stuck. The Banzai Pipeline section of the beach is about 100 yards to the left of the Ehukai Beach Park sign as you face the ocean, but you won't need to look hard to find it in surf season. When the winter surf rolls in and hits the shallow coral shelf offshore, the waves that form are so steep that the crest of the wave falls forward, forming a near-perfect tube, or "pipeline," just like in the opening credits of *Hawaii Five-O.* Hang-ten fanatics flock here from around the globe all winter long to master this holy grail of surf challenges, but the wild, wild Pipeline is one tough cookie. If you want to watch top-flight, pro-level wave-riding action, a winter weekend visit to the Pipeline is well worth the long drive from Waikiki — heck, the crowd alone is enough to keep you entertained for hours. Needless to say, head elsewhere to swim.

See map p. 172. Off Kamehameha Highway on Ke Nui Road (which parallels the highway 1 mile north of Pupukea), just south of Sunset Beach. A small lot is available for parking.

Ke Iki Beach/Pupukea Beach Park

This secret beach is my other Oahu favorite, along with Lanikai (see the "Along the Windward Coast" section, earlier in this chapter). Unlike most North Shore beaches, Ke Iki is hidden from the road by private homes, so most visitors don't know about it, but this white-sand beach of sloping dunes is well worth seeking out. It's big, wide, open, and virtually empty year-round. Ke Iki is a wonderful place for swimming and wave jumping in summer; stay out of the water entirely in winter, however, when the big swells come. At the lava-dotted east end of the sand is a collection of warm tidepools where you can lie back and take in the natural glory of it all. Sorry, no facilities.

See map p. 172. On Kamehameha Highway (Highway 83), Haleiwa. To get there: From Haleiwa town, take the second left after the Foodland at Pupukea Road and then turn left again; park along the shoulder and walk down the graded public access path (marked with the "No Parking Beyond This Point" sign).

Waimea Beach Park

This legendary beach is yet another world-famous surfing mecca, a gorgeous one-of-a-kind sandy bowl whose placid fair-weather waves are excellent for swimming, snorkeling, and bodysurfing in summer. But what a difference a season makes: Winter waves pound the narrow bay, sometimes rising a phenomenal 50 feet to the sky — wow! Yes, no-fear bravehearts (or certifiable nutcases, depending on your point of view) do come to take on these record-breakers, and it's well worth the drive to see them in action. Waimea turns into a rollicking beach party when the surf is up and the crowds come to watch. Visit on weekdays to avoid the crowds, weekends to join in. Facilities include lifeguards, restrooms, and showers. The small lot fills up when the crowds come, so just pull over to the shoulder with everybody else.

See map p. 172. On Kahehameha Highway (Highway 83), just outside the entrance to Waimea Valley Adventure Park, about 3 miles north of Haleiwa. TheBus: no. 52 or 55. A safety tip: Don't get too distracted by the waves and forget to pay attention when parking or crossing the road.

On the remote leeward coast

No matter what time of year you visit remote Kaena Point, check with the lifeguard near the park entrance before you venture into the water. There are also restrooms and parking near the lifeguard stand. This is a remote area that is generally populated by locals, so please respect them and give them their space — and leave *nothing* in your car.

Kaena Point State Park

Tired of the Waikiki crowds? Here's the place for you. Where Farrington Highway ends, the wilderness of Kaena Point State Park begins. Kaena Point is a remote 853-acre coastline park of wide white sands, sand dunes, and desert cliffs overlooking the deep-blue water of Yokohama Bay. When the surf's calm in summer, the beach is pleasant for swimming and snorkeling. When the surf kicks up, stick to the shore, as conditions can be very rough. However, there's good reason to come at any time of year: You can't find a better place onshore to watch spinner dolphins play. The bay is their favorite spot on the island, so it's common to see hundreds on any given day.

If you want to pick up a bite to eat on your way to Kaena Point State Park, stop into **Aloha 'Aina Café,** 85-773 Farrington Hwy., in Waianae, on the ocean side of the highway across from McDonald's, about halfway up the leeward coast (☎ 808-697-8808). This charming healthy foods cafe offers excellent breakfasts and lunches for takeout or to eat in. Specialties include Hawaiian sweet bread French toast, taro burgers, zesty chili with a side of sweet bread, kalua pig quesadilla, and Portuguese bean soup, a staple of the local diet. Everything is delicious, and service is as friendly as can be.

See map p. 172. On Farrington Hwy. (Highway 93), at the end of the road. To get there: Take H-1 west to Farrington Highway and drive up the leeward coast. The drive will take an hour (or slightly more, depending on traffic) from Waikiki.

Playing in the Surf

If you want to rent boogie boards, surfboards, snorkel gear, kayaks, and other beach toys, you won't have a problem doing so on Oahu. In fact, you won't even need to leave Waikiki Beach because beach boys have rental huts set up right on the sand; they'll even take you out on outrig-ger canoe rides that anybody can join in. For details, see "Catching a wave," later in this section. You can also rent beach chairs, life vests, and boogie boards from **Snorkel Bob's,** which you can read about in the following section.

If you want to learn how to kayak while you're on Oahu, the best place to do it is at Waimea Valley Adventure Park, which offers both river and bay paddles. See "Exploring the rest of the island," later in this chapter, for details.

Snorkeling offshore

Hanauma Bay (see the section "The Waikiki Coast and East Oahu," ear-lier in this chapter) is not only Oahu's best snorkel spot, but one of the finest snorkel spots in all Hawaii.

Although you can rent gear right at Hanauma Bay — or on Waikiki Beach if you want to do some fish-finding there — I suggest renting instead from **Snorkel Bob's,** on the way to Hanauma Bay at 700 Kapahulu Ave., at Date Street (across from the Ala Wai Golf Course), Honolulu (☎ **808-735-7944;** www.snorkelbob.com). Snorkel Bob's can rent you much better quality gear than you'll get elsewhere — and it's well worth spending the few extra bucks for a mask that doesn't leak and a snorkel that doesn't fill with water. The best-quality gear — the "Ultimate Truth" — rents for $7.50 a day, or $30 a week ($22 per week for kids) for the mask/snorkel/fins set. For an additional $10, prescription masks (including snorkel and fins set) are available to those near-sighted snorkelers who'd actually like to see the little fishes without getting their glasses wet. Snorkel Bob's is open every day from 8 a.m. to 5 p.m. There's no need to reserve in advance, but you can book your gear online if you want to. When you stop by to pick up your gear, the staff can also recommend other local snorkel spots that are currently offering calm conditions and good underwater sightseeing.

One of the best things about renting gear from Bob is that you can rent a set of snorkel gear at the start of your trip, carry it with you as you travel throughout the islands, and then return it to another Snorkel Bob's loca-tion on Maui, the Big Island, or Kauai. (All shops offer 24-hour gear return service.) I highly recommend doing this, even if you intend to go on snorkel cruises or kayak trips that provide gear.

Safety is key when snorkeling. Always snorkel with a buddy and keep an eye on each other at all times. Come up every few minutes to check your bearings in relation to the shoreline and make sure that no boat traffic is coming your way. Don't touch anything underwater: Undersea coral is delicate and easily damaged and can also leave you with nasty cuts. And always, always check surf conditions before you set out (a local surf-and-snorkel shop can usually help you here). You should also inquire about the specific currents and tides of the area you plan to snorkel, as well as any potentially dangerous spots to avoid.

All hands on deck: Ocean-cruising adventures

All Oahu's cruise-boat operators combine whale-watching with their regular activities in season (humpback whales migrate to Hawaii's warm waters each winter, roughly December through March or early April). If you're on Oahu during these months, be sure to set out on a cruise — there's nothing like seeing these mammoth creatures up close and personal. Even if you miss out on the whales, keep your eyes peeled for dolphins, flying fish, and sea turtles.

Making reservations is always a good idea for the following cruises and outings.

Captain Bob's Sailing Adventure

Hop aboard the *Barefoot I,* which shows you Oahu's breathtaking Windward Coast the way it should be seen — from the water. Captain Bob takes you exploring on serene Kaneohe Bay aboard his 42-foot catamaran, which skims across the usually tranquil water — it's just the right mood for this gorgeous turquoise, almost violet-hued surf. You cruise past picture-perfect offshore islands and snorkel a spectacular shallow reef where you can spot a kaleidoscope of tropical fish and, sometimes, turtles. The color of the water alone is worth the price of admission. Plan to spend the whole day with Bob, from roughly 9 a.m. to 4 p.m., but it's a day well spent.

Cruises depart from Kaneohe Bay, Kaneohe. ☎ *808-942-5077 or 888-222-3601.* www. barefoothawaii.com. *All-day cruise: $69 adults, $59 children 13–17, $49 for kids 12 and under. Prices include all-you-can-eat barbecue lunch and shuttle from Waikiki. Online discounts available.*

Dolphin Excursions

Cruise the Oahu's little-explored leeward coast in a Zodiac, a motorized inflatable rubber raft, with friendly and extremely knowledgable owner/guide Victor Lozano, or one of his equally knowledgable captains, in search of friendly pods of spinner dolphins. These low-slung, intimate boats are great for getting close to the water and the dolphins. The pods of spinner dolphins that live off Oahu's arid west coast are so large that Victor can pretty much guarantee copious sightings every day of the year. Victor always has the best interests of you and the dolphins in mind; if conditions are safe and doing so won't interfere with their actions or behavior, he'll allow the bravest among you to do water "drops" wearing snorkels and masks so that you can watch the dolphins below you in their underwater habitat; decisions are made at the moment based on conditions, but the trip is magic even if you don't get to do this. Book at least a week ahead, more if you don't want to miss out.

Boats depart from Waianae Small Boat Harbor, Farrington Highway (Highway 93), Leeward Oahu. ☎ *808-239-5579.* www.dolphinexcursions.com. *Half-day adventure: $70 adults, $45 kids 4–12. Earlybird morning cruises (slightly longer and more likelihood of seeing dolphins at their most active) $95 adults, $55 kids 4–12. Prices include shuttle from Waikiki and lunch.*

Dream Cruises

This company offers a variety of cruises aboard the fast, modern *American Dream* yacht, as well as the ketch-rigged sailing catamaran the *Rainbow I*. Wave adventures departing from convenient Ala Moana include whale-watching in season; kid-friendly snorkel-sails off Waikiki, a day of water play that includes an off-the-boat water slide for creative entrances; dinner-and-dancing cruises with sunset cocktails and great views of the Waikiki skyline; and a combo cruise that pairs dolphin-watching with a visit to Hawaiian Waters Adventure Park. Additionally, Dream Cruises offers dolphin tours out of leeward Oahu's Ko Olina Marina aboard the *Rainbow I*, which includes a narrated bus tour from Waikiki.

Most cruises depart from Kewalo Basin, off Ala Moana Boulevard just west of Ala Moana Beach Park. Dolphin-watching cruises depart Ko Olina Resort and Marina, Kapolei (off Highway 93, 17 miles west of Honolulu International Airport). ☎ *800-400-7300 or 808-592-5200.* www.dream-cruises.com. *Prices: $28–$99 adults, $19–$61 kids 4–12. Rates include Waikiki hotel transfers and breakfast, lunch, brunch, or dinner, depending on the cruise.*

Honolulu Sailing Co.

This very reliable company offers half- and full-day sailing and snorkeling cruises off the Waikiki shoreline aboard its 54-foot sailing yacht *Escapade*. You can also set up an exclusive sail trip or multiday charter aboard a range of sailing ships and yachts that comprise one of Hawaii's finest fleets. Honolulu Sailing Co. can even teach you to sail or arrange your nautical dream wedding.

Cruises depart from Pier 2, Honolulu Harbor, off Ala Moana Boulevard. ☎ *800-829-0114 or 808-239-3900.* www.honsail.com. *Half-day sail with snorkeling, whale-watching, or sightseeing $60–$75 adults; 6-hour sail with snorkeling or surfing $125 adults; half-price for kids. Beginning sailing lessons $445 for one, $495 for two.*

Ko Olina Ocean Adventures

If you want to take a dolphin-watching cruise but Dolphin Excursions' Zodiac (described earlier in this section) sits a little too close to the action for you, catch a ride aboard Ocean Adventures' more substantial cruiser, the *Lanikila*, which also cruises the western shore in search of playful spinner dolphins. Snorkel and Snuba trips are also available. (Snuba is a cross between snorkeling and Scuba diving that allows you to go as much as 20 feet below the surface of the water without getting scuba-certified or carrying cumbersome oxygen tanks. The Snuba outing begins with instruction in the resort's pool before you set out.)

Cruises depart from Ko Olina Resort and Marina, Kapolei (off Highway 93, 17 miles west of Honolulu International Airport, a 45-minute drive from Waikiki). ☎ *808-396-2068.* www.ocean-adventures.com. *Prices: $48–$99 per person. Only the half-day adventure and picnic includes Waikiki hotel pickup.*

MaiTai Catamaran

This sleek new 44-foot twin-hulled catamaran prides itself on being the party boat of Waikiki. The *MaiTai* offers 90-minute daytime "Tradewind" and late-afternoon sunset sails right off Waikiki beach. With a built-in bar and 45 of your closest friends aboard, you're bound to have a good time and enjoy some spectacular views while you're at it.

Cruises depart from Waikiki Beach between the Sheraton Waikiki and Halekulani hotel. ☎ *800-462-7975 or 808-922-5665.* www.leahi.com. *90-minute afternoon sails $23 adults, $12 kids ages 4–12; sunset sail $34 adults, $17 kids ages 4–12. Sunset sail includes beverages; drinks are available for purchase on afternoon sails.*

Navatek Cruises

For the smoothest ride in the Pacific, hop aboard the *Navatek I,* a high-tech 140-foot SWATH (Small Waterplane Area Twin Hull) vessel that promises even the most perpetually queasy passengers a seasick-free ride. The *Navatek* offers a number of different cruises, from lunchtime whale watches to the finest dinner cruises on the Waikiki coast (complete with a romantic candlelit setting, a multicourse sit-down dinner, top local entertainers, and an exclusive route along Kahala, Oahu's "Gold Coast," east of Diamond Head). The *Navatek* is operated by Atlantis Adventures Oahu, a company known for submarine dives that feature close-up views of sunken ships and tropical fish; combo packages offer a substantial discount if you want to book both activities.

Cruises depart from Pier 6, Honolulu Harbor, Aloha Tower Drive (just off Ala Moana Boulevard/Nimitz Highway intersection, next to the Aloha Tower Marketplace), Honolulu. ☎ *808-973-1311.* www.atlantisadventures.com *(click on "Oahu," then click on "Atlantis Cruises Coastal Adventures.") Prices: Lunch cruise $52 adults, $33 kids ages 2–11; sunset cruise with entertainment and dinner buffet $60 adults, $40 kids 2–11; Royal Sunset cruise with entertainment and sit-down steak-and-lobster dinner $100–$159 adults, $73–$135 kids 2–11; combo package of Royal Sunset dinner cruise plus submarine dive $140 adults, $100 kids 2–11.*

"Chumming" around with sharks

You're 4 miles out from land, which is just a speck on the horizon, with hundreds of feet of open ocean. Suddenly from out of the blue depths, a shape emerges: the sleek, pale shadow of a 6-foot-long gray reef shark, followed quickly by a couple of 10-foot-long Galapagos sharks. Within a couple of heartbeats, you are surrounded by sharks on all sides. Do you panic? Did you just drop into a scene from *Open Water*? No, you paid $120 to be in the midst of these jaws of the deep. Of course, there is a 6-by-6-by-10-foot aluminum shark cage separating you from all those teeth.

Looking for an unparalleled adventure, snorkelers? **North Shore Shark Adventures** (☎ **808-228-5900,** www.hawaiisharkadventures.com) has what you're looking for. Captain Joe Pavsek offers up-close-and-personal encounters with Jaws from the safety of an aluminum cage. He takes you out from Haliewa Small Boat Harbor 3 miles offshore in his 26-foot boat, *Kailolo,* where he drops his cage into the cobalt-blue water. To make sure that the predators of the deep appear, Captain Pavsek heaves "chum" — a not very appetizing concoction of fish trimmings and entrails — over the side. It's much like ringing the dinner bell; after a few minutes, the sharks arrive, ready to nosh. Depending on the sea conditions and the weather, snorkelers can stay in the safety of the cage as long as they want, with the maneaters just inches away. You can expect to see sharks ranging in size from 5 to 15 feet, generally of the gray reef, Galapagos, and sandbar variety. Visibility is so clear — often up to 200 feet — that you can see them swimming in from the deep. The cage can hold two to four snorkelers, who pay $120 per person for the two-hour adventure. You're also welcome to view the sharks from a more respectable distance — the boat deck — for just $60.

Delving into the deep: Submarine rides

You can dip into Hawaii's spectacular underwater world even if you don't swim by taking a submarine ride with **Atlantis Adventures Oahu** (☎ **800-548-6262** or 808-973-9811; www.goatlantis.com). Atlantis's state-of-the-art subs deliver you a mile offshore and deep beneath the surface to see not only clouds of tropical fish and sea critters, but also sunken ships, the remains of two airliners, and ongoing work on the University of Hawaii's reef enhancement project. Shuttle boats to the sub leave from Hilton Hawaiian Village Pier, on the beach at 2005 Kalia Rd. (at Ala Moana Boulevard). The 90-minute tours cost between $70 and $100 for adults, $40 for kids (children must be at least 36 inches tall), depending on the tour you choose. *A word of warning:* The ride is perfectly safe, but skip it if you suffer from serious claustrophobia. *On the other side of the coin:* If you're a swimmer — even if you just have basic paddle skills — skip this expensive adventure, don a mask, and hit the waves yourself instead for a primo underwater experience.

Catching a wave

Book your surfing lesson, or your windsurfing lesson (see the following section), for early in your stay. That way, if conditions aren't right on your scheduled day, you'll have plenty of time to reschedule.

Learning to surf

If you've always dreamed of learning to surf, Waikiki is the perfect place to do it. The Waikiki beach boys swear that they can teach anybody to stand up on a surfboard and catch a wave, as long as they have basic swimming skills. If you want to learn, go early to the section of Waikiki Beach called Kuhio Beach, next to the Sheraton Moana Surfrider. (See the section "The Waikiki Coast and East Oahu," earlier in this chapter.) Both **Aloha Beach Service** and **Hawaii Beach Boys Services** offer surfing lessons for about $35 an hour, plus surfboard rentals to experienced wave riders for $10 for one hour, $5 for each hour after that (for use on Waikiki Beach only). The small waves are also great for bodysurfing and boogie-boarding, and both surf shacks are happy to rent you the appropriate gear. Regular catamaran and outrigger canoe rides are offered from this stretch of sand as well, usually for about ten bucks a head; the beach boys will call out for participants when they're ready to go out. (FYI: If you're expecting Waikiki's beach boys to be strapping young lads on break between semesters, think again. Most of these perma-tanned fellows haven't been "boys" since the Nixon administration.)

If you're more serious-minded about learning to surf, book a lesson at least a day in advance with the **Hans Hedemann Surf School** (☎ **808-924-7778**; www.hhsurf.com), whose pro instructors teach private and group lessons in surfing and body boarding off the Diamond Head end of Waikiki. (He also has a newer North Shore location in the Turtle Bay Resort.) Prices start at $50 for an hour-long group lesson (five people max), $95 for private surf instruction ($80 for body boarding).

For experienced surfers only

If you're already a skilled surfer, stop at any surf shop to check the latest wave conditions. A good surfing spot for advanced surfers is the Cliffs, at the base of Diamond Head. The 4- to 6-foot waves churn here, allowing for high-performance surfing — and the views of Diamond Head are great. Call or stop at the **Hans Hedemann Surf School** in the Diamond Head Beach Hotel, 2947 Kalakaua Ave. (☎ **808-924-7778;** www.hhsurf.com), to rent a board and check conditions. Surfboards are available for rent at **Local Motion,** 1958 Kalakaua Ave., near McCully Street at the west end of Waikiki (☎ **808-979-7873;** www.localmotionhawaii.com) — yes, this was the Local Motion store in MTV's *Real World Hawaii* — as well as on the beach at Waikiki. (See Aloha Beach Service and Hawaii Beach Boys Services in the preceding section.)

Of course, if it's winter and you really know what you're doing — or you simply want to watch those who do — visit one of the North Shore beaches. (See "On the North Shore," earlier in this chapter.) Head to **Surf 'n' Sea,** 62-595 Kamehameha Hwy., Haleiwa (☎ **808-637-9887**), which also can arrange lessons for you. Do not — I repeat, do not — get in the water on the North Shore in winter unless you are appropriately skilled to handle the big waves.

 Check conditions by calling ☎ **808-973-4383** or the **Surfline** at ☎ **808-596-7873.** You can also check the latest surf report online at www.hawaii.edu/news/localweather/surf.

Windsurfing and kiteboarding

Kailua Beach, on the Windward Coast, is the best place to learn to windsurf — and the folks to learn from are **Naish Hawaii,** 155A Hamakua Dr., Kailua (☎ **800-767-6068** or 808-262-6068; www.naish.com), the domain of champion and pioneer windsurfer Robbie Naish. Beginning, intermediate, and advanced lessons are available, with prices starting at $55 for one, $75 for two for private 1½-hour lessons (includes use of equipment for 1½ hours following the lesson), $35 per person for a three-hour group clinic (includes use of equipment for a half-hour following the lesson). There's no minimum age requirement, but you must weigh at least 75 pounds. (Naish has taught kids as young as 8 or 9.) You can expect to be up and sailing (in one direction, anyway) in three to four hours; it takes 12 to 20 hours to become actually good at it. They'll also teach you how to kiteboard if you're up to the challenge. Equipment rentals are available for experienced windsurfers and kiteboarders.

Scuba diving

Oahu is a wonderful place for wreck diving. One of the more famous wrecks in Hawaii is the *Mahi,* a 185-foot former minesweeper with an abundant marine population that looks like it came straight out of *Finding Nemo.* Schools of lemon butterfly fish, eagle rays, green sea turtles, manta rays, and white-tipped sharks cruise by, and eels slither from the wreck.

For nonwreck diving, **Kahuna Canyon,** a massive underwater amphitheater, is among the island's best offshore summer dive spots. But your smartest bet may be to discuss with your outfitter the best places to go. Whether you're a first-timer in search of a resort course or a veteran diver just looking for a ride, the outfitter to contact is **Aaron's Dive Shop,** 307 Hahani St., Kailua (☎ **888-84-SCUBA** or 808-262-2333; www. hawaii-scuba.com), Hawaii's oldest and largest dive shop, in business for more than three decades. Aaron's offers boat and beach dive excursions at all of Oahu's top dive spots, plus night dives, cave dives, photography dives, and more. Prices for two-tank dives start at $100, with equipment. Aaron's can also offer uncertified introductory dives, or PADI (Professional Association of Diving Instructors) certify you in three days if you're ready to commit. If you don't want to leave Waikiki, **South Seas Aquatics,** 2155 Kalakaua Ave. (near Beach Walk), Suite 112 (☎ **808-922-0852;** www.ssahawaii.com), can meet all your Scuba needs, from daily dive trips ($85–$95, including gear) to full PADI open-water certification ($340, including four dives, or $220 if you do your book and pool work at home, before you arrive on Oahu).

Keep these **snorkel tips** in mind as you don your fins and head into the water:

✔ Make mornings your offshore snorkel time, because the winds often start to kick up around noon, making surf conditions rougher and less conducive to fish-spying.

✔ Always snorkel with a friend and keep an eye on each other.

✔ Look up every few minutes to get your bearings. Check your position in relation to the shoreline and whether there's any boat traffic.

✔ Don't touch anything. Not only can your fingers and feet damage coral, but it can give you nasty cuts. Moreover, camouflaged fish and spiny shells may surprise you.

✔ Before you set out, check surf conditions by calling one of the local dive or snorkel shops, which can give you the latest on local conditions and recommend alternative spots if the prime ones are too rough for snorkeling.

Sportfishing

Oahu-based **Sportfish Hawaii** (☎ 877-388-1376 or 808-396-2607; www.sportfishhawaii.com) can book a first-class charter for you out of Kewalo Basin, the main charter-boat marina on Oahu. From Waikiki, take Kalakaua west beyond Ala Moana Center; Kewalo Basin is on the left, across from Ward Centre. On lucky days, the captains display the day's catch after they tuck back into their slips in the afternoon. Prices range from $700 to $825 for a full-day charter just for you and five friends; $500 to $625 for a half-day exclusive; or from $150 for a full-day share charter (you share the boat with five other people).

You can also hit the surf in search of marlin, ahi, mahimahi, and wahoo off the island's arid leeward coast aboard a 31-foot Cabo Express with **Legend Sport Fishing,** which operates out of the lovely Ko Olina Resort and Marina, about a 45-minute drive west of Waikiki (☎ **808-987-7312;** www.konaweb.com/legend).

Exploring on Dry Land

You may be able to save money on a few of your big-ticket Oahu activities by booking them through Maui-based **Tom Barefoot's Cashback Tours** (☎ **888-222-3601;** www.barefoothawaii.com), which also books activities on Oahu. Tom Barefoot is a very reliable activities center that's willing to split its commissions with you so that everybody comes out ahead. You'll save 7 percent on select activities and outfitters if you pay with a credit card, 10 percent if you send a check — which may add up to substantial savings, especially if you're bringing the entire family along. At press time, you can save on a number of water adventures I recommend earlier in this chapter, including Dream Cruises and Navatek I adventures, plus admission fees to such attractions as Hawaiian Waters Adventure Park and the Don Ho Show, golf greens fees, and more; check the Web site or call for current offerings.

Taking a guided tour

If your mobility is limited, or if you have limited time and want an introductory look at the big picture, you may want to hook up with a guided tour. If you've rented a car and can get around easily, though, I'd recommend going out on your own. Most tour operators do little more than whiz by the major sights in tour buses — including some places where you may actually want to spend some time — or charge you an arm and a leg to take you to places like the *Arizona* Memorial, which is absolutely free to tour if you show up on your own.

If you intend to visit the **National Cemetery of the Pacific at Punchbowl Crater** (see the section "Visiting Honolulu's top attractions," later in this chapter), don't go with a tour if you want to look around and pay your respects. Tour buses are not allowed to disembark passengers in the Punchbowl; they can merely drive through.

Polynesian Adventure Tours (☎ 800-622-3011 or 808-833-3000; www.
polyad.com) offers a range of guided tours in minivans, big-windowed
minicoaches (good for small groups and big views), and full-size buses.
First launched to take visitors along Maui's Heavenly Road to Hana,
Polynesian Adventure's tours tend to be a little more action-oriented than
those offered by competing companies. They also tend to offer multiple
variations on each theme. Offerings range from city sightseeing and
outlet-shopping tours to circle island tours that include a beach picnic
(recommended if you don't have a car and your other alternative is to
skip visiting the rest of this multifaceted island altogether) to full-day
excursions to the Polynesian Cultural Center. (See the section "Exploring
the rest of the island," later in this chapter.) Check the Web site to peruse
the full range of options and snag a 10-percent online booking discount.

Roberts Hawaii (☎ 800-831-5541 or 808-539-9400; www.roberts
hawaii.com) is Hawaii's biggest name in narrated bus tours. Roberts
offers a similar slate of tours as Polynesian Adventure, plus add-ons
such as sightseeing cruises, luaus, and dinner shows.

Roberts also offers day excursions to the neighbor islands, but the itineraries are so intense that sites tend to whiz by in a blur. If you can't
sleep there, don't bother.

E Noa Tours (☎ 800-824-8804 or 808-591-2561; www.enoa.com) offers a
range of guided minibus tours around the city and around the island.
E Noa's tours tend to be smaller than those offered by its competitors,
and they're usually cheaper because the tours are intimate enough to
allow the driver to serve as your tour guide. Ask about online-booking,
AARP, and AAA discounts.

The **Waikiki Trolley** (☎ 800-824-8804 or 808-593-2822; www.waikiki
trolley.com), an open-air motorized trolley similar to a San Francisco
cable car (operated in affiliation with E Noa), offers narrated hop-on,
hop-off tours throughout Honolulu and select farther-flung destinations;
for more complete details, see Chapter 11.

Guided city walks

The **Native Hawaiian Hospitality Association** (☎ 808-737-6442; www.
nahha.com) offers beautifully narrated two-hour guided walking tours
along the **Waikiki Historic Trail.** The **Queen's Tour** tells the story of
Hawaii's royal past as you explore the portion of the trail along Prince
Kuhio Beach, ending at the Honolulu Zoo. Tours depart daily at 9 a.m.
from the Royal Hawaiian Shopping Center stage near the fountain, on
Kalakaua at Seaside. You must purchase tickets by calling the association; the cost is $15 per person. You can also download text and a
map that you can follow on your own self-guided tour at www.waikiki
historictrail.com.

The **Mission Houses Museum,** 553 S. King St., at Kawaiahao Street in
downtown Honolulu (☎ 808-531-0481; www.lava.net/~mhm), offers a

terrific 2½-hour walking tour of Honolulu's historic downtown on Thursdays at 10 a.m. A guide takes you first through the Mission Houses site (where American missionaries set up house to convert the natives in the 1820s) and then through the surrounding historic capitol district, taking in such sights as Iolani Palace, the statue of King Kamehameha the Great (the Big Island boy who grew up to unite the independent Hawaiian isles into a single kingdom), the Royal Tomb of King William Lunalilo, and other intriguing sites. Tickets are $15, including admission to the museum. The tour is well worth booking if you're a history buff; reservations are required at least 24 hours in advance.

You're welcome to stop in to tour the museum, which tells the story of the arrival of Protestant missionaries in the 19th century and the subsequent cultural sea change in the islands, on your own, or on a guided tour that's limited to the museum itself. Three restored mission buildings are open for exploring Tuesday through Saturday between 9 a.m. and 4 p.m.; tours are included in the price and offered daily at 10 a.m., 11:15 a.m., 1 p.m., and 2:45 p.m. Admission is $10 for adults, $8 for seniors and military, $6 for students age 6 and older.

Guided ecowalks

Mauka Makai Excursions (☎ 808-593-3525) offers half- and full-day tours revealing a hidden side of Oahu that even most island residents haven't seen. The emphasis is on archaeology and ancient history, but Mauka Makai's tours are also a great choice for nature walkers. On the half-day "Legends and Myths" tour, guide Dominic Aki can show you hidden petroglyphs, the ruins of a royal palace tucked away in a bamboo forest, an ancient temple presiding over modern suburbia, and other cultural treasures, complete with fascinating narrative. Full-day tours go farther afield and also include shore fishing, snorkeling, or other beach activities. Prices range from $47 to $78 for adults, $32 to $63 for kids 6 to 17, including hotel pickup. Discounts are available if you book through **Tom Barefoot's Cashback Tours** (☎ 888-222-3601; www.barefoot hawaii.com).

Visiting Honolulu's top attractions

Put on your walking shoes because Oahu boasts the finest collection of sights and attractions in the islands, bar none.

Bishop Museum

If you come inside to visit just one museum while you're in Hawaii, make it this one. The state museum of cultural history houses the world's greatest collection of natural and cultural artifacts from Hawaii and the Pacific. If your time is limited, head straight to the Hawaiian Hall, which provides a wonderful introduction to island life and culture. You'll see the great feathered capes of kings, the last grass shack in Hawaii, preindustrial Polynesian art, and even the skeleton of a 50-foot sperm whale. Hawaiian Hall gallery tours are offered Monday through Friday at noon (weekends at 10 a.m. and 1:30 p.m.); catch one for the most informed overview of the gallery. A terrific traditional hula show is also offered every day at 11 a.m. and 2 p.m., and garden tours are offered daily at 12:30 p.m. Watch for frequent demonstrations of Hawaiian crafts like lei making, feather working, and quilting. Call or check the Web site for the current schedule of exhibitions and planetarium shows.

 If you liked the Bishop Museum and want to see more — or if you're intrigued by the idea of the museum but have limited museum-going time — visit the **Bishop Museum at the Hilton Hawaiian Village,** in the Kalia Tower at Hilton Hawaiian Village, 2005 Kalia Rd., Waikiki, 2nd floor (☎ **808-947-2458**). This mini-museum offers an insider's view of life in Waikiki from ancient times to today in just about 1½ hours. As you move from ancient times to the arrival of the missionaires to the monarchy period and arrive in the groovy surf culture of 20th-century Waikiki, you'll be amazed at how time flies. You can also try your hand at such ancient island arts as lei making, weaving cordage from coconut fibers, pounding kapa into cloth, or playing a shark-skin drum or nose flute — a real delight! Admission is $7 for adults, free for kids 4 to 12 years; open daily from 10 a.m. to 5 p.m.

See map p. 174. 1525 Bernice St., just off the Lunililo Freeway (H-1), Honolulu. ☎ *808-847-3511; 808-848-4136 for planetarium info.* www.bishopmuseum.org. *To get there: From the H-1, take the Houghtailing exit; turn right (toward the mountains); at the first light, turn left onto Bernice Street; the museum will be a half-block past Kapalama Street on your left. Admission: $14.95 adults, $11.95 seniors and kids 4–12. Open: Daily 9 a.m.–5 p.m.*

The Contemporary Museum

Housed in a beautiful 1925 estate in one of Honolulu's most exclusive residential communities, TCM is best for fans of modern art; if you want to see Hawaiian art, use your time more wisely by visiting the Honolulu Academy of Arts (listed later in the chapter) instead. Temporary exhibits predominate, filling the main gallery space and changing six to eight times a year, so it's catch as catch can — sometimes terrific, sometimes not so much. (It's best to check the online calendar before you go.) The museum currently doesn't have space to display its entire permanent collection, so exhibitions rotate a selection of highlights, including works from such artists as Jasper Johns, Jim Dine, and William Wegman. David Hockney's post-modern stage sets for Ravel's opera *L'Enfant et Les Sortilèges* are always on display, but they're something of a disappointment; better are the lovely Japanese gardens for strolling, the impressive sculpture garden, and the Contemporary Cafe, one of Honolulu's best-kept secrets for lunch.

See map p. 174. 2411 Makiki Heights Dr., Honolulu. ☎ *808-526-0232.* www.tcmhi.org. *To get there: Take Kalakaua Avenue to Beretania Street and make a left; turn right on Keeamoku, turn right on Wilder to Makaki Street, turn left, and follow it up the hill; turn left on Makiki Heights Drive and proceed to the museum (which will be on your right). Admission: $5 adults, $3 seniors and students, free for kids 12 and under. Open: Tues–Sat 10 a.m.–4 p.m., Sun noon to 4 p.m.*

Diamond Head Crater

Called Mt. Leahi (lee-AH-hi) by the Hawaiians, Waikiki's most famous landmark is a mountain that just about anyone with a little stamina can climb. The easy but steep 1¼-mile, 1½-hour round-trip climb is a lot of fun — and the 360° views from the top are spectacular. To prepare for your hike to the top, wear a reasonable pair of walking shoes (sneakers or Tevas are fine) and get your hands on a flashlight (you'll walk through several dark tunnels), a bottle of water, and a camera. If you don't have a flashlight or your hotel can't lend you one (most can, precisely for this purpose), you can buy one at just about any ABC store. (You can hardly walk a block in Waikiki without tripping over an ABC store.) If you have binoculars, bring them along. Go early in the day, before the afternoon sun starts beating down. The trailhead begins in the parking lot on the crater's inland side and proceeds along a paved walkway (with handrails) that turns rocky as it ascends the slope. You'll pass old World War I and II pillboxes, gun emplacements, and tunnels built as part of the Pacific defense network. Yes, you'll be climbing lots of steps, but it's well worth the effort — after you reach the observation post up top, the views are indescribable.

See map p. 174. Access road at Monsarrat (also called Diamond Head Avenue) and 18th avenues. To get there: Follow Kalakaua Avenue to Kapiolani Park; turn north on Monserrat Avenue and follow it around to the back of Diamond Head. Just past Kapiolani Community College, turn right and go ⁹⁄₁₀ mile to the parking lot. Admission: $1. Parking $5. Open: Daily 6 a.m.–6 p.m.

Foster Botanical Garden

This intimate, leafy oasis amid the high-rises of downtown Honolulu is a living museum of plants — some rare and endangered — collected from the tropical regions of the world. Of special interest are 26 "Exceptional Trees" protected by state law, a large palm collection, a primitive cycad garden, and a hybrid orchid collection. It's easy to tour the garden in a half-hour or so, but bring insect repellent because this is a buggy place. Guided tours are offered weekdays at 1 p.m.; call for reservations.

See map p. 174. 50 N. Vineyard Blvd. (at Nuuanu Avenue, across the street from Zippy's), downtown Honolulu. ☎ *808-522-7066 or 808-552-7060.* www.co. honolulu.hi.us/parks/hbg. *Admission: $5 adults, $1 kids 6–12. Open: Daily 9 a.m.–4 p.m.*

Hawaii Maritime Center

If you're interested in Hawaii's rich maritime heritage, or you're just nostalgic for the long-gone cruise-ship days, stop at this harborfront museum — the maritime branch of the Bishop Museum (listed earlier in this chapter) — for an hour-long visit. The museum tells the islands' complete maritime story, from the ancient journey of Polynesian voyagers to Hawaii's whaling era to the high-style Matson Line days of the 1940s and '50s. Outside, the famous *Hokulea,* a reconstruction of the double-hulled sailing canoe that the ancients used to reach Hawaii, is moored next to the *Falls of Clyde,* a four-masted, fully rigged 1878 schooner.

See map p. 174. Pier 7, Honolulu Harbor, Aloha Tower Drive (off Nimitz Highway, next to Aloha Tower Marketplace), Honolulu. ☎ **808-536-6373.** www.bishopmuseum. org/hmc. *Admission: $7.50 adults, $4.50 kids 6–17. Open: Daily 8:30 a.m.–5 p.m.*

Hawaii State Art Museum

This new-in-2002 museum houses the largest collection of art by Hawaii-based artists. All 360 works currently on display were created by 284 artists who live in the islands. The museum is well worth visiting if you want to understand the creative heart that beats within these beautiful islands.

See map p. 174. No. 1 Capitol District Building, 250 S. Hotel St. (at Richards St.), 2nd Floor, downtown Honolulu. ☎ *808-586-0900.* www.state.hi.us/sfca *or* www.hawaiimuseums.org/mc/isoahu_hisam.htm. *Admission: Free! Open: Tues–Sat 10 a.m.–4 p.m.*

Honolulu Academy of Arts

This first-class museum houses one of the finest collections of Asian art in the country, a top-notch collection of American and European masters, and terrific ancient and Pacific art, all in a stunning open-plan, Hawaiian-style building that first opened its doors in 1927. See what's on when you're in town — the temporary exhibits can range from treasures from ancient Egypt to the world's greatest collection of aloha shirts — or just stop by to explore a few rooms of the excellent permanent collection. Highlights include the John Dominis and Patches Damon Holt Gallery of Hawaiian Arts; the Textile Gallery; and the James A. and Mari Michener Gallery, boasting a fantastic collection of Japanese woodblock prints tagged with insightful, delightful observances by the author himself. It's easy to spend an hour here, or four — it all depends on your interest level. No matter how long you stay, be sure to spend a few minutes contemplating one of the courtyard Zen gardens — and a few extra perusing the excellent Academy Shop. The museum is a real delight for any art lover! Guided one-hour tours are offered Tuesday through Saturday at 11 a.m. and Sunday at 1:15 p.m.

See map p. 174. 900 S. Beretania St. (between Victoria Street and Ward Avenue), downtown Honolulu. ☎ *808-532-8701 or 808-532-8700.* www.honoluluacademy. org. *Admission: $7 adults; $4 seniors and students; free for kids 12 and under. Open: Tues–Sat 10 a.m.–4:30 p.m., Sun 1–5 p.m.*

Honolulu Zoo

Located in the heart of Waikiki's lovely Kapiolani Park, this 43-acre zoo is a real charmer. Globe-trotting highlights include the Karibuni Reserve, an African savanna habitat with exotic African mammals roaming around in the open, separated from visitors by hidden rails and moats; a wonderful South American aviary filled with colorful toucans and other eye-catching birds; and the Tropical Forest exhibit, a draw for horticultural buffs as well as animal lovers. The Children's Zoo features friendly critters that love to be petted, including a llama, a monitor lizard, and a pot-bellied pig.

See map p. 174. In Kapiolani Park, 151 Kapahulu Ave. (at Kalakaua Avenue), Waikiki. ☎ *808-971-7171.* www.honoluluzoo.org. *Admission: $6 adults, $1 kids 6–12, free for kids 5 and under; Family Pass $25. Open: Daily 9 a.m.–4:30 p.m.*

Iolani Palace

I highly recommend visiting this royal palace, the official residence of the last monarchs of Hawaii: King David Kalakaua (ka-la-COW-ah) and his sister, Queen Liliuokalani (li-lee-uh-ka-LA-nee). You can see the Italian Renaissance structure only on a docent-led 90-minute tour, which tells the fascinating story of the coming of Western ways to the islands, the rebirth of Hawaiian culture in the last years of royal rule, and the story of the monarchy's final defeat in a bloodless coup.

Very Important: The Iolani Palace Grand Tour sells out regularly, so you must call ahead and reserve your tour spots. Call at least a day ahead, or a few days in advance if you don't want to be disappointed. (It took me three tries before I was able to make my first visit.) Leave the little ones behind, however, as they'll be less than enthralled.

You can also take the 30-minute self-guided Galleries Tour, which takes you through the lower galleries, which house the Hawaiian crown jewels plus royal gowns, the re-created chamberlain's office, and other period goodies; a real highlight is an ancient feather cloak that was the symbolic trophy won in the battle that united the Hawaiian Islands in the first place. If you opt for the Grand Tour, the galleries will automatically be part of your Iolani experience, but the shorter self-guided tour is an ideal alternative for those with limited time, limited budgets, or limited attention spans, or those with small children in tow.

See map p. 174. 364 S. King St. (at Richards Street), downtown. ☎ *808-522-0832, 808-522-0823, or 808-538-1471 for recorded info.* www.iolanipalace.org. *Grand Tour tickets: $20 adults, $5 kids 5–17; kids under 5 not admitted. Grand Tour times: Every 30 minutes Tues–Sat 9 a.m.–2 p.m. Tickets should be picked up 15 minutes before your tour. Grand Tours include a screening of the 16-minute video on the Hawaiian monarchy and the palace. Tickets to Galleries only: $6 adults, $3 for kids 5–17; free for kids under 5. Gallery hours: Tues–Sat 9 a.m.–2 p.m.*

Makapuu Point State Wayside

I just love this one-mile uphill hike, an enjoyable walk through the island's southeastern desert landscape that leads to one of the most spectacular vistas on the island. The trail isn't marked, but it's quite obvious; just follow the directions below until you see the black gate on the ocean side of the highway. It's okay to come through; the gate is just meant to prevent cars. Follow the one-mile paved road up the hill to the lighthouse and lookout; even though it leads uphill, the slope is gradual as it curves around the point, so anyone wearing good-soled shoes and in reasonably good shape can handle it. The contrast between the cactus-dotted landscape and the deep-blue waves below is reason enough to come; however, the lookout also offers a good place to watch whales between January and

March, so bring binoculars. Bring drinking water and wear sunscreen at any time of year. You might also want to pack a picnic lunch, as there are plenty of flat spots for you to enjoy it and the view.

See map p. 172. Take Kalanianaole Highway (Hwy. 72) past Hanauma Bay and Sandy Beach to Makapuu Head, Oahu's southeastern tip; look for a black gate bearing a sign that says "NO VEHICLES ALLOWED" on a gate to the right. Park on the side of the highway with the other cars.

The National Cemetery of the Pacific at Punchbowl Crater

This collapsed volcanic cone in the middle of Honolulu offers some of the most spectacular views in the city. But most people don't come for the views (although you shouldn't miss them; the observation platform is on the ocean side of the crater); they come to honor the 33,230 victims, buried over 116 verdant acres, of three American wars whose theaters were Asia and the Pacific: World War II and the Korean and Vietnam wars. Among the graves are many unmarked ones bearing only the date December 7, 1941, the day Pearl Harbor was bombed and the United States entered the Last Great War. Some of the honorees are destined to be unknown forever; others are world-famous, like war correspondent Ernie Pyle. The Courts of the Missing's white stone tablets bear the names of 28,788 Americans missing in action in WWII. You can search for any specific grave locations on the computer in the office, near the entrance, where you'll also find a small tribute to some servicemen buried in this hallowed ground.

See map p. 174. 2177 Puowaina Dr. (at the end of the road), Honolulu. ☎ *808-532-3720 or 808-566-1430.* www.interment.net/data/us/hi/oahu/natmem. *To get there: Take Ward Avenue north; turn left on Prospect Street; turn right onto Puowaina Drive. Admission: Free. Open: Daily 8 a.m.–6:30 p.m. Mar–Sept, to 5:30 p.m. Oct–Feb.*

Nuuanu Pali Lookout

Sometimes, gale-force winds howl through this misty mountain pass, so hold on to your hat. But if you walk up from the parking lot to the precipice, you'll be rewarded with a stunning view of the luxuriant Windward Coast. Bring a jacket or sweater with you because the weather's windy and cool up here year-round, even when it's 85°F and sunny at the beach.

See map p. 174. Near the summit of Pali Highway (Highway 61); take the Nuuanu Pali Lookout turnoff.

Puu Ualakaa State Park

The summit of this 1,048-foot-high hill offers majestic panoramic views over the whole of Honolulu and Waikiki, all the way from Diamond Head to the east to Punchbowl, Pearl Harbor, and beyond to the west. Daytime offers clear viewing, while sunset, with the bright lights of the city below, is pure magic.

See map p. 174. On Round Top Drive. To get there: From Waikiki, take Ala Wai Boulevard to McCully Street, turn right; cross over the H-1 freeway and turn left onto Wilder Street; turn right onto Makiki Street and go onward and upward about 3 miles. Park in the second lot and walk to the viewing platform. Admission: Free! Open: Daily 7 a.m. to sunset.

Waikiki Aquarium

The small but first-class Waikiki Aquarium is a must for anybody who wants to know what they're actually seeing when they're snorkeling. It features tanks full of an amazing variety of marine life found in the offshore waters; a fascinating jellyfish tank; a Hawaiian reef habitat with sharks and eels; a kid-friendly touch tank with urchins and sea cucumbers; and habitats for the endangered Hawaiian monk seal and green sea turtle. Newer exhibits focus on biodiversity and the world's fragile coral reefs. You can watch the monk seals being trained and fed most days; call for the daily schedule.

See map p. 174. 2777 Kalakaua Ave. (across from Kapiolani Park on the ocean side of the road), Waikiki. ☎ **808-923-9741.** www.waquarium.org. *Admission: $7 adults; $5 seniors and students; $3.50 kids 13–17; free for kids under 12. Open: Daily 9 a.m.–5 p.m. (last entry at 4:30 p.m.).*

In Pearl Harbor

If you want to see all of Pearl Harbor's sights, arrive early and plan on spending the better part of a day here. To reach Pearl Harbor, drive west on the H-1 freeway or Nimitz Highway (reachable via Ala Moana Boulevard) past the Honolulu International Airport; take the USS *Arizona* Memorial exit (no. 15-A). Follow the green-and-white highway signs to the free parking lots.

Shuttle service is available from Waikiki daily from 6:50 a.m. to 1 p.m. for $7 per person round-trip; to schedule pickup at your hotel, call **VIP Trans** at ☎ **866-836-0317** or 808-839-0911 24 hours in advance. If you'd rather take TheBus, hop on no. 20 (see Chapter 11 for complete information on TheBus system). Either way, expect the ride to take about an hour from Waikiki. (It's about a half-hour if you drive yourself.)

Security for visitors is tight at Pearl Harbor. At press time, the following items were not permitted *at all:* baby strollers, backpacks, diaper bags, fanny packs, camera bags, purses (yes, purses), luggage, shopping bags, and any other items that allow concealment. A storage container is available for visitors to check their prohibited items for a $2 fee; size restrictions apply (no bigger than 30 inches by 30 inches by 18 inches), and large luggage cannot be accepted. The concierge at your hotel or condo should have the latest information; you can also call ☎ **808-422-0561** or check the National Parks Web site at www.nps.gov/usar for the latest restrictions.

It's never a smart idea to leave valuables in your rental car, and Pearl Harbor is a high-crime area — so that piece of good advice goes double here.

Please see the "Beaches & Attractions Around Oahu" map on page 172.

USS Arizona Memorial and Museum

On December 7, 1941, while moored in Pearl Harbor, this 608-foot battleship was bombed in a Japanese air raid. The USS *Arizona* sank in nine minutes without firing a shot, taking 1,177 sailors and Marines to a fiery death and plunging the United States into World War II. Today, boat launches take you out to the stark white 184-foot memorial that spans the sunken hull of the *Arizona,* which lies 6 feet below the surface of the sea. The memorial contains the ship's bell, recovered from the wreckage, and a shrine room with the names of the dead carved in stone. Try to arrive early at the visitor center (which is operated jointly by the National Parks Service and the U.S. Navy) to avoid the huge crowds because advance reservations are not taken and waits of an hour or two are common. While you're waiting for the shuttle to take you out to the ship — you'll be issued a number and time of departure, which you must pick up yourself — you can explore the small but arresting museum, which features personal mementoes, photos, and historic documents. An informative and moving 20-minute film precedes your trip to the ship. Allow about three hours for your visit and be sure to remain respectfully silent when you're on the actual memorial.

See map p. 172. On Battleship Row, Pearl Harbor. ☎ *808-422-0561.* www.nps.gov/usar. *Admission: Free! Shirts and shoes required. Open: Daily 7:30 a.m.–5 p.m. (boat shuttles and programs run 8 a.m.–3 p.m.).*

USS Bowfin Submarine Museum and Park

The USS *Bowfin* is one of only 15 World War II submarines still in existence today. You can go below deck of this famous submarine — nicknamed the "Pearl Harbor Avenger" for its successful retaliatory attacks on the Japanese — and see how the 80-man crew lived during wartime. The museum holds an impressive collection of submarine-related artifacts, the Waterfront Memorial honors submariners lost during World War II, and the minitheater shows a constant run of sub-related videos.

See map p. 172. 11 Arizona Memorial Dr. (next to the USS Arizona Memorial Visitor Center), Pearl Harbor. ☎ *808-423-1341.* www.bowfin.org. *Admission to sub and museum: $8 adults, $6 seniors and military, $3 kids 4–12 (kids under 4 are not allowed on the submarine, but can visit the museum and mini-theater). Admission to museum only: $4 adults, $2 kids. Open: Daily 8 a.m.–5 p.m. (last tour at 4:30 p.m.).*

Battleship Missouri Memorial

The newest addition to Pearl Harbor's Battleship Row memorial fleet is this 58,000-ton, 887-foot battleship — the last one the U.S. Navy built — which served in three wars, but is most famous for being the site of Japanese surrender to Douglas MacArthur and the Allied forces in 1945.

Decommissioned in 1955, the *Missouri* went back into action to the Gulf War before its final retirement to Hawaii in 1998. After you check in at the visitor center at the USS *Bowfin* (see the listing later in this section), you'll be shuttled by trolley to Ford Island for ship boarding. You're free to explore the mammoth battleship from bow to stern after you watch a short informational film, which is a blast: You can see the biggest guns the Navy ever built, climb up the flying bridge, visit the officer's quarters, and experience how sailors lived at sea. I highly recommend hooking up with one of the hour-long guided tours (no reservations necessary), which offer the best insights; you can pair this with a two-hour AcousticGuide tour for the complete experience, or choose to take the AcousticGuide tour only. Allow about three hours total for your visit if you plan on working in a tour.

See map p. 172. On Battleship Row, Pearl Harbor; check in at the Visitor's Center of the USS Bowfin, where a trolley will take you for the 7-minute ride to the battleship. ☎ **877-MIGHTY-MO** *or 808-423-2263.* www.ussmissouri.com. *Admission: $16 adults, $7 kids 4–12. Hour-long guided tours or 2-hour-long AcousticGuide tour $22 adults, $14 kids. Premium tours including otherwise restricted areas $49 adults, $39 kids. Open: Daily 9 a.m.–5 p.m. (ticket window closes at 4 p.m.).*

In nearby East Oahu

Visitors without wheels can hitch a ride to and from Sea Life Park aboard the E Noa company's Sea Life Shuttle from Waikiki. See the park's Web site for pickup points and a schedule; no reservations are necessary.

Sea Life Park

This marine-themed park is Hawaii's very own version of SeaWorld, and it's lots of fun. Highlights include a sea lion feeding pool; the quarter-million-gallon Hawaiian Reef Tank, brimming with tropical fish plus a few sharks and stingrays; performing seals, dolphins, and penguins strutting their smarts and skill in choreographed shows, which run every 45 minutes (it takes about two hours to see all four shows); and a pirate-themed play area for the little ones. The chief curiosity, though, is the world's only "wholphin," a genuine genetic cross between a false killer whale and an Atlantic bottle-nosed dolphin. On-site marine biologists operate a recovery center for endangered marine life that allows you to visit with rehabilitated Hawaiian monk seals and seabirds.

Sea Life Park offers add-on programs that allow you to get up-close and personal with the park's residents. **Sea Trek** gives you the opportunity to actually dive into the Hawaiian Reef Tank with a guide for 15 minutes, no previous diving experience necessary; the cost is $90 per person, and you must be 12 or older to participate. **Splash U** allows you to interact with dolphins in a shallow-water environment (read: no swimming); you'll learn communication and training techniques and even be allowed to feed your new friends. The cost for Splash U is $80 for adults, $67 for kids ages 4 to 12. A more in-depth dolphin encounter that allows you to try swimming with the dolphins is $130 (no kids under age 13). For details on these and a half-dozen other cool special programs, visit the Web site or call ☎ **808-259-2500.**

See map p. 172. 41-202 Kalanianaole Hwy. (Highway 72), Waimanalo. ☎ *808-259-7933.* www.sealifeparkhawaii.com. *To get there: Take H-1 east to Highway 72; after the road has narrowed to two lanes, it's just past Sandy Beach on the left. Parking: $3. Admission: $25 adults, $12.50 kids 4–12. Open: Daily 9:30 a.m.–5 p.m.*

Exploring the rest of the island

Oahu has so much to offer you'll not be lacking in things to do. The following are some of Oahu's standouts that you won't want to miss.

Hawaii's Plantation Village

This impeccably restored 50-acre outdoor museum offers a genuine look back to the days when sugar planters from America — and field workers from Japan, China, Portugal, the Philippines, Puerto Rico, and Korea — shaped the land, economy, and culture of territorial Hawaii. You can only explore the village on an hour-long guided tour, which takes you through more than two dozen faithfully restored camp houses, a Buddhist temple and a Shinto shrine, a plantation store, and even a sumo-wrestling ring.

See map p. 172. In the Waipahu Cultural Garden Park, 94-695 Waipahu St. (at Waipahu Depot Road), Waipahu. ☎ *808-677-0110.* www.hawaiiplantation village.org. *To get there: Take H-1 west to the no. 7 (Waikele) exit; turn south onto Paiwa Street, pass 4 traffic signals, turn right onto Waipahu Street, and go ¾ mile. Admission: $10 adults, $7 seniors and military, $4 kids 5–12. Open: Mon–Fri 9 a.m.–4:30 p.m., Sat 10 a.m.–4:30 p.m.; escorted tours offered hourly on the hour; last tour at 3 p.m.*

Hawaiian Waters Adventure Park

This 25-acre water-theme amusement park is the place to play if the beach just isn't enough for you. Highlights include an inner-tube cruise along an 800-foot "river"; two phenomenal seven-story water slides; a multilevel playpool that's fun for the whole family; mind- and body-bending tube slides and rides; a wave pool that's as big as a football field (and better for bodysurfing, I might add); and more waterlogged fun. Adults have their own "spa" area for relaxing and hot-tubbing. There's something for even the littlest ones here, but you have to be at least 48 inches tall to enjoy everything. Locker rooms, changing rooms, showers, and a well-endowed food court are on hand.

You can order a package ticket that includes round-trip bus transportation to Hawaiian Waters from Waikiki by calling ☎ **808-674-9283,** ext. 107.

See map p. 172. 400 Farrington Hwy. (Highway 90), Kapolei. ☎ *808-674-9283.* www. hawaiianwaters.com. *To get there: Take H-1 west to exit no. 1 (Campbell Industrial Park/Barbers Point Harbor). Admission: $34 adults, $15 seniors 60 and over, $23 kids 3–11; free for kids under 3. Open: Daily from 10:30 a.m.; closing times vary between 4 and 6 p.m., depending on day and season.*

Kualoa Ranch Activity Club & Secret Island

This 4,000-acre formerly working cattle ranch is now a gorgeous outdoor playground (parts of *Jurassic Park* were filmed here). Five separate full-day adventure packages are on offer, including such activities as helicopter rides, horseback riding, mountain biking, rifle shooting, jet skiing, kayaking, windsurfing, snorkeling, scuba diving, freshwater fishing, and more. The beach activities, in particular, are terrific: You'll be shuttled out to a private area that's decked out like a country club with hammocks on the beach, volleyball courts, ping-pong tables, horseshoe pits, and beach pavilions; if you don't want to kick back here, you can catch a catamaran ride out to Kaneohe Bay for snorkeling. Reservations are required, and you'll need to talk to an agent in advance to sort out the package that's right for you.

See map p. 172. 49-560 Kamehameha Hwy. (Highway 93), Kaaawa. ☎ *800-231-7321 or 808-237-7321.* www.kualoa.com. *To get there: Take H-1 to the Likelike Highway (Highway 63); turn left at Kahekili Highway (Highway 83) and continue on to Kaaawa. Activity packages: $50–$139 adults, $35–$89 kids 3–11. Open: Daily 9 a.m.–3 p.m.*

Polynesian Cultural Center

This remarkable cultural theme park allows you to tour the vast Pacific in just a single day. Seven Pacific island villages (representing Fiji, New Zealand, Marquesas, Samoa, Tahiti, Tonga, and Hawaii) let you experience first-hand each island or island group's lifestyle, traditions, songs, dance, costumes, and architecture as you tour the 42-acre park.

You can "travel" through this living-history museum/theme park either on foot or in a pole boat navigated along a man-made freshwater lagoon system. Each village is "inhabited" by native students from Polynesia who attend Hawaii's Bright Young University. Operated by the Mormon Church, the park also features a variety of stage shows celebrating the music, dance, history, and culture of Polynesia. An IMAX theater offers two gorgeous movies telling the story of Polynesian migration. An all-you-can-eat luau is served every evening (sorry, no alcohol) capped by a two-hour Polynesian entertainment extravaganza.

The whole thing may sound hokey, and it is — to a degree. But it's extremely well done and teaches a fascinating cultural lesson about the peoples of Polynesia and their cultural distinctions. Still, it's a lot to take in, and many people will find that the regular daytime activities are satisfactory. My recommendation is that you come for just the day and save your luauing for a neighbor island, especially if you're going to Maui, where the Old Lahaina Luau feast is of better quality, and you won't be required to maintain your theme-park stamina from noon 'til night. If you do want to stay for the entire affair, you'll have to choose between the different price packages, whose options include quality of food, quality of seating, and souvenirs. Because a visit is an all-day affair even if you don't stay for the evening show (straight-admission guests are kicked out at 6:30 p.m.), plan to arrive before 2 p.m.

Even if you have a rental car, you may want to take an alternate method of transportation to the Polynesian Cultural Center if you're planning to spend the day and evening; the drive back to Waikiki at 10 p.m. can be a real drag after an exhausting day at the park. You can book bus, minibus, and limo transportation starting at $15 per person through the PCC by calling ☎ **800-367-7060**.

See map p. 172. 55-370 Kamehameha Hwy. (Highway 83), Laie. ☎ *800-367-7060, 877-722-1411, or 808-293-3333.* www.polynesia.com. *To get there: Take the Pali Highway (Highway 61) or the Likelike Highway (Highway 63) to the Windward Coast and turn left on Kamehameha Highway (Highway 83). Basic admission: $35 adults, $24 kids 5–11. Buffet, IMAX, evening show, and luau packages: $79–$175 adults, $55–$115 kids, depending on which package you choose. Open: Mon–Sat 12:30– 9:30 p.m. (box office opens at noon); regular exhibits close at 6:30 p.m.*

Waimea Falls Park

This scenic 1,800-acre river valley is a botanical extravaganza, with gorgeous gardens and groves blooming with flora from all over the world. A small collection of native birds and animals is on hand, including the endangered Hawaiian nene geese, the state bird. The park is also a great cultural discovery ground, with remnants of old Hawaiian settlements. For decades, it was run as a minitheme park, with hula shows, cliff divers, and ATV rides, but in 2003, those activities were discontinued as the Audubon Society took over the park's management and dramatically lowered admission prices. The emphasis now is on hiking and quiet appreciation of the beauty of this extraordinary ecosystem.

See map p. 172. 59-864 Kamehameha Hwy., Haleiwa. ☎ *808-638-9199.* www.audubon. org *(click "States, Centers & Chapters," then click "States & Chapters," and then search for Hawaii). Admission: $8 adults, $5 kids and seniors. Open: Daily 10 a.m.– 5:30 p.m.*

Hitting the links

Oahu has a handful of championship courses, but hard-to-get tee times and inaccessibility from Waikiki make this my least favorite island for teeing off. Still, if you're on Oahu and in the mood, these courses are your best bets.

For last-minute and discounted tee times, try calling **Stand-By Golf** (☎ **888-645-BOOK;** www.stand-bygolf.com), a reservation agency that can offer as much as 50 percent off tee times when courses are anxious to fill tee times.

Another great information resource on Oahu's golf courses is **808Golf. com** (☎ **808-949-6079;** www.808golf.com), whose extensive Web site offers comprehensive course descriptions and the opportunity to book advance tee times at some courses online. 808Golf.com can even grant you discounts at select courses.

Haleiwa

Little more than a collection of faded clapboard storefronts with a picturesque harbor, the North Shore town of Haleiwa (ha-lay-EE-va) is the unofficial capital of Hawaii's surf culture and a major roadside attraction filled with art galleries, restaurants, surf shops, and boutiques. This beach town really comes alive in winter, when the timid summer waves swell to monster proportions and draw big-wave surfers — and the people who love to watch them risk their necks — from around the world.

Haleiwa is definitely worth a stop to soak in some surf-style atmosphere. Shoppers will find an hour or two worth of good browsing to be had, and your kids will love the wild and wacky surf shops. For directions on getting here, see Chapter 11. Here are a few of the best places to visit:

✔ **Dole Pineapple Plantation:** If you're heading up to the North Shore via the Central Oahu route, you may want to make a pit stop here, 64-1550 Kamehameha Hwy. (Highway 99), Wahiawa (☎ 808-621-8408; www.doleplantation.com). The two draws of this ticky-tacky tourist attraction have long been a) the world's largest maze (pineapple shaped, no less), which you can take a shot at navigating for $5 adults, $3 kids; and b) three words: pineapple ice cream. The shop is open daily from 9 a.m. to 6 p.m. (maze until 5 p.m.). Newly added features include a 20-minute train ride through the grounds ($7.50 adults, $5.50 for kids) and a Plantation Garden tour ($3.50 adults, $2.50 kids).

✔ **North Shore Surf and Cultural Museum:** Tucked into the North Shore Marketplace at 66-250 Kamehameha Hwy. (across from Twelve Tribes) in Haleiwa (☎ 808-637-8888), Oahu's only surf museum is a fun place to spend 20 minutes. The collection of memorabilia includes everything from vintage surfboards to old beach movie posters to trophies won by surfing's biggest legends. Admission is free, but donations are gladly accepted. The museum is open Tuesday to Sunday from about noon to 5:00 p.m., but call ahead, because "once in awhile somebody doesn't make it" to open up. Surf's up, anyone?

✔ **Strong Current Surf Design:** This is the place for surf memorabilia and gear. You can't miss Strong Current — just look for the vintage Woody station wagon parked in front of the store. Strong Current has two locations in Haleiwa, in the North Shore Marketplace at 66-214 Kamehameha Hwy. (☎ 808-637-3406; www.strongcurrenthawaii.com), and at 66-208 Kamehameha Hwy. (just down the block past Kua Aina Sandwich; ☎ 808-637-3410).

✔ **Matsumoto's:** To really get into Haleiwa's surf city groove, stop into this simple general store at 66-087 Kamehameha Hwy. in Haleiwa for a taste of Hawaii's favorite sweet treat: shave ice (never "shaved ice"), the island version of a snow cone. Shave ice comes in a generous cup (don't get the cone — you'll be sorry!) sweetened with your choice of syrup: strawberry, root beer, banana, passion fruit — it really doesn't matter, because they all come out rainbow-colored and tasting vaguely the same. I highly recommend doing as the locals do and ordering yours with a scoop of ice cream and sweet red azuki beans nestled in the middle — yum! I never pass up an opportunity to visit Matsumoto's, and you shouldn't, either. Don't be daunted by the long line, as it moves fast.

If you're coming up to the north shore in winter to catch the surfers in action — and you should, if you're on the island — you'll want to head to Waimea Beach Park, the Banzai Pipeline, and Sunset Beach; see "Combing the Beaches," at the start of this chapter, for details.

For recommendations on where to head for food and sunset cocktails while you're in the Haleiwa area, see Chapter 11.

Ko Olina Golf Club

Located on Oahu's arid west side, this 6,324-yard, par-72 Ted Robinson–designed course is a standout with rolling fairways, multitiered greens, and no fewer than 16 water features. The signature hole is the picturesque 12th, a par-3 with an elevated tee sitting on a rock garden, plus its very own cascading waterfall. Wait until you get to the 18th hole; you'll see and hear water all around you. You'll have no choice but to play to the left and approach the green over the water. This course isn't overly difficult, but you'd better be on your game as soon as the wind picks up. Facilities include a driving range, locker rooms, Jacuzzi/steam rooms, and a restaurant and bar. Book in advance because the course is always crowded. Men are asked to wear collared shirts.

See map p. 172. 92-1220 Aliinui Dr., Ewa Beach. ☎ **808-676-5300.** www.koolina golf.com _or_ www.resortatkoolina.com. _To get there: Take H-1 west until it becomes Farrington Highway (Highway 93); exit at Ko Olina and turn left onto Aliinui Drive. Greens fees: $150 ($125 for Ihilani resort guests), $80 after 1 p.m. in winter or 2:30 p.m. in summer._

Makaha Resort Golf Club

Ask any local duffer, and he's bound to name this course as one of his favorites on the island — everybody does. In fact, _Honolulu_ magazine recently celebrated this course as Oahu's best. Designed by William Bell, the challenging par-72, 7,077-yard course is one of Oahu's longest, most difficult, most beautiful, and best maintained. But don't let the rugged beauty of wrinkled cliffs or the luxuriant valley setting distract your attention from the challenges: eight water hazards, 107 bunkers, and frequent and brisk winds that you'll have to play into on three holes, minimum. Facilities include a pro shop, a driving range, bag storage, and a particularly fine clubhouse with food service.

See map p. 172. 84-626 Makaha Valley Rd., Waianae (45 miles west of Honolulu). ☎ **808-695-9544** _or_ 808-695-7111. www.makahavalleycc.com. _To get there: Take H-1 west until it turns into Highway 93, which will wind up the leeward coast; turn right on Makaha Valley Road and follow it to the fork, and the course will be on the left. Greens fees: $100._

Turtle Bay Resort Courses

Situated on the gorgeous North Shore, the Arnold Palmer and Ed Seay–designed **Palmer Course** is the most spectacular golf course on the island. With rolling terrain, only a few trees, and lots of wind, the front nine holes play like a Scottish course, while the back nine have narrower tree-lined fairways and lots of water (including wonderful ocean views from the 17th hole). Several holes skirt a wetlands preserve, giving the course a tranquil vibe and beautiful native flora and fauna. This course is a really fun place to play, and five sets of tees on every hole accommodate golfers of all abilities. No wonder senior PGAers like Chi Chi Rodriguez and Hale Irwin consider this place to be one of their favorite stops on the annual Senior PGA tour. Turtle Bay is also home to the **Fazio Course,** renowned course architect George Fazio's only course in the islands. This nine-holer can be played twice for a regulation par-71, 6,200-yard course. It's known for its generous fairways, deep bunkers, and immaculately shaped greens. Two sets of tees — one designed for men, one for women — let you enjoy a slightly different game the second time around. Facilities include a pro shop, driving range, putting and chipping green, and snack bar.

See map p. 172. 57-049 Kuilima Dr., Kahuku. ☎ *808-293-8811.* www.turtlebay resort.com/golf. *To get there: Follow directions to Haleiwa outlined in Chapter 11; proceed through town and follow Highway 83 to the Turtle Bay Country Club. Greens fees: $160 at the Palmer Course ($115 for resort guests); $155 at the Fazio Course ($110 for resort guests). Twilight fees $85 ($60 for resort guests).*

Shopping the Local Stores

Most of the city's shopping is conveniently concentrated in a few big malls and shopping centers. Additionally, browsers shouldn't neglect Waikiki's main drag, **Kalakaua Avenue,** as well as Kuhio Avenue one block to the north. Both avenues and the side streets that connect them are lined with an eclectic mix that ranges from haute couture boutiques to tacky souvenir stalls. Kalakaua is becoming the Rodeo Drive of Hawaii, lined as it is with shops like **Prada, Burberry, Versace, Bulgari, Celine,** and others. These runway names cater largely to the Japanese crowd, who apparently find this stuff affordable compared with what they pay in Tokyo. You'll find that many of the stores along Kalakaua are open until late into the evening.

Shopping malls

Honolulu is the crux of commerce in the Pacific — people fly in from as far away as Tahiti to do their Christmas shopping at the finest collection of malls in the Pacific.

Ala Moana Center

This monster-size mall (which is growing even bigger, thanks to an expansion that was still underway at press time) is the largest open-air shopping center in the United States. With a selection of stores that ranges from

Sears and **JC Penney** to **Fendi** and **Gucci,** there really is something for everybody here. Among the standouts are three department stores. The first is **Macy's.** In addition to surpassing the Macy standard in most departments, this flagship store boasts a wonderful Hawaiian crafts department (Kuu Home on the fourth floor) and a phenomenally good restaurant, the **Pineapple Room** (see Chapter 11). Also worth seeking out is the endlessly entertaining **Shirokiya,** a Japanese department store with a divine food department. **Neiman-Marcus** is a bastion of high-society elegance, and it boasts its own fabulous fine-dining restaurant, **Mariposa.** You can meet all your practical needs here because the mall is home to everything from **LensCrafters** to the U.S. Post Office to a massive food court. You can shop for aloha wear at **Reyn's** (one of my favorites for island prints), find footwear at a terrific branch of **Nordstrom Shoes,** and meet just about any other need you have. It's a must for mall lovers.

1450 Ala Moana Blvd. (between Piikoi Street and Atkinson Drive), Honolulu. ☎ *808-955-9517.* www.alamoana.com.

Aloha Tower Marketplace

This waterfront restaurant and dining complex is better for dining (**Chai's Island Bistro** is here, as is **Don Ho's Island Grill** and **Gordon Biersch Brewery;** see Chapter 11) and views than it is for actual shopping — most of the stores are ticky-tacky. The choices (lots of gift boutiques and T-shirt shops) are more tourist-oriented than those at neighbors Ala Moana Center, Ward Centre, and Ward Warehouse. It's a great place to stroll, but don't expect the find of a lifetime. The few standouts include **Martin & MacArthur** for handcrafted Hawaiian furniture and art objects; **Bungalow Bay** for top resort-wear lines for men and women ; and **Beyond the Beach** for a surprisingly good collection of surf apparel. If you're looking for a java fix, the **Bad Ass Coffee Company** will do the trick. They want you here so badly that the marketplace even offers free shuttle service from select Waikiki hotels; ask your concierge or call for pickup points and times (not a bad strategy, since parking is tough here).

At Honolulu Harbor between piers 8 and 11 (just past the point where Ala Moana Boulevard meets Nimitz Highway), Honolulu. ☎ *808-566-2337 or 808-528-5700.* www.alohatower.com.

DFS Galleria

This three-story shopping emporium in the heart of Waikiki is a symbol of Waikiki's tourism struggle: It was built to the tune of $65 million and outfitted with a host of top-dollar merchants designed to cater to Japanese tourists — from **Kipling** to **Guess** to **Kate Spade** to **Alfred Dunhill** — to be unveiled just as the yen withered and the tourism trail from Tokyo all but dried up. (The Japanese still come to Waikiki, but in smaller numbers and with less money to burn.) As a result, it's still struggling to find an audience, but it boasts some nice shopping outlets and gimmicks like a virtual golf course and The Tube, a walk-through aquarium complete with sting rays that's actually worth a look. The main level features some very nice Hawaiian food-product outlets where you can pick up Kona coffee and the like for the folks back home, plus a **Jamba Juice** and a **Starbucks** for your morning eye-opener. The brand names line the second and third floors, where you'll find everything from designer cosmetics and fragrances to fashion, luggage, and the like. **Beware:** Certain duty-free shopping areas are off-limits to mainland shoppers. There's free live entertainment every evening at 7 p.m., often featuring hula.

At Kalakaua and Royal Hawaiian avenues, Waikiki. ☎ *808-931-2655.* www.dfs galleria.com.

Royal Hawaiian Shopping Center

Located in central Waikiki, this mall is the heart of Honolulu's European designer shopping. It's where you'll find **Chanel, Cartier, Hermès, Versace, Van Cleef & Arpels,** and other big-ticket boutiques. You'll find the Waikiki Trolley service desk here as well (see Chapter 11).

2201 Kalakaua Ave. (at Seaside Avenue), Waikiki. ☎ *808-922-0588.*

Victoria Ward Centers

What used to be two simple two-story sister shopping centers has bloomed into a six-center mini-empire of quality midpriced shopping. Of the two original malls, Ward Centre is largely dedicated to dining, but has a few standouts, most notably **Borders Books & Music**, which boasts an excellent Hawaiian music department; **The Gallery at Ward Centre**, which carries a notable collection of works by Hawaii artists (Doug Young's city landscapes are particularly noteworthy, and relatively affordable); and the **Honolulu Chocolate Company**, makers of fine island-made chocolates from island-grown cocoa beans. **Ward Warehouse's** good choices include the **Nohea Gallery**, a constant favorite for its terrific collection of high-quality Hawaii-made crafts; and **Mamo Howell,** for both traditional and contemporary muumuus in Mamo's wonderful signature fabrics. There's much, much more, even a tropical Farmer's Market, a state-of-the-art 16-screen movie multiplex, and a bunch of good restaurants, including **Brew Moon, Kakaako Kitchen,** and **Kua Aina Sandwich** (all reviewed in Chapter 11).

 Attention, diners: Stop by the concierge desk on the mezzanine level in front of the movie theater, where the concierge can show you menus, make dinner reservations for you, and even present you with two-fers and other discount dining coupons.

Ala Moana Boulevard and Auahi Street (1 block inland from Ala Moana Boulevard) between Ward Avenue and Queen Street, just west of the Ala Moana Center. ☎ *808-591-8411.* www.victoriaward.com.

Waikele Premium Outlets

 This top-flight outlet mall in west Oahu offers one of the island's best rainy day activities. Options run from the ultrachic (Barneys New York, Brooks Brothers, Calvin Klein, Kenneth Cole, Coach, Max Mara) to the comfort-casual (Banana Republic, Jockey, Easy Spirit, Samsonite). The out-lets are well worth the 20-minute drive if you're a discount shopping fan. *94–790 Lumiaina St., Waipahu (about 20 miles west of Waikiki).* ☎ *808-676-5656.* www.premiumoutlets.com. *To get there: Take H-1 west toward Waianae and turn off at exit 7.*

Other shopping of note

Hilo Hattie's has been Hawaii's first name in aloha wear for decades, and I'm happy to report that both the quality and selection are better than ever. The flagship store is out toward the airport at 700 N. Nimitz Hwy., at Pacific Street (☎ 808-536-6500; www.hilohattie.com). You'll find a big children's department, as well as macadamia nuts, Hawaii-grown coffees, contemporary Hawaiian music, and lots of other souvenirs to choose from. One of their best recent inventions are Hawaiian print car seat covers, which are selling like hotcakes — be the first on your block to have 'em! A more manageable location is at Ala Moana Center, where the selection tends toward the high end (☎ 808-973-3266).

For the best selection of vintage aloha shirts, visit **Bailey's Antiques and Aloha Shirts,** 517 Kapahulu Ave. (across from the Ala Wai Golf Course), north of Kapiolani Park in the Kapahulu section of Honolulu (☎ 808-734-7628). A '50s-era cotton or silkie in A-1 condition can cost upwards of $600, but some cheapies are on hand, too; prices begin around $20. Besides, browsing is a big part of the fun. You'll also find hula-girl lamps, vintage costume jewelry, and other bits of kitsch, all priced at top dollar — but a joy to discover, anyway.

Contemporary aloha wear is everywhere, but my favorite prints and styles are made by **Reyn's** (www.reyns.com). Reyn's has a number of boutiques throughout Hawaii, including one at the Ala Moana Center, plus a charming shop on the lobby level of the Sheraton Waikiki hotel.

In addition to the **Nohea Gallery** at Victoria Ward Centers (see the list-ing earlier in this section), some of the finest stops for Hawaiian-made gifts are museum shops: The **Academy Shop** at the Honolulu Academy of Arts, 900 S. Beretania St., between Victoria and Ward avenues in down-town Honolulu (☎ 808-523-8703), and both **Native Books and Beautiful Things** and **Shop Pacifica** at the Bishop Museum, 1525 Bernice St. at Kalihi Street, also downtown (☎ 808-847-3511). The Academy Shop, Native Books, and Shop Pacifica are great choices for traditional Hawaiiana, crafts, and books. Native Books and Beautiful Things also has a larger gallery-style location at Ward Warehouse, 1050 Ala Moana Blvd. (☎ 808-596-8885). Another first-class showcase for island crafts and gifts in the Ward Warehouse is the **Nohea Gallery** (☎ 808-596-0074).

Nothing says "aloha" like a lei. If you'd like to skip the overpriced, less-than-interesting selections available in most tourist 'hoods, head to Chinatown in downtown Honolulu, where the aroma of flowers being woven into beautiful treasures fills the air. The stretch of Maunakea Street between Beretania and King streets and the adjacent block of Beretania Street are lined with lei shops on both sides of the street. The designs of the leis made here are almost always exceptional, and the prices are the best on the island. Wander through all the shops before you decide which lei you want and feel free to ask questions about any unfamiliar tropical flowers and styles. Worth seeking out, for both selection and friendliness, are **Cindy's Lei and Flower Shoppe,** 1034 Maunakea St. (☎ **808-536-6538**); **Lin's Lei Shop,** 1017A Maunakea St. (☎ **808-537-4112**); and **Lita's Leis,** 59 N. Beretania St. (☎ **808-521-9065**).

Living It Up after Dark

Your best bet for finding out what's going on around town is to pick up a copy of *Honolulu Weekly* (www.honoluluweekly.com), available free at restaurants, clubs, shops, and newspaper racks around Oahu; the "Happenings" section can tell you what's on tap for the week, from live music to dancing to performing arts. Also check the daily papers, particularly *Honolulu Advertiser* (www.honoluluadvertiser.com). But most important, don't forget to make use of that most valuable of resources: your hotel concierge. He or she is always up on what's happening around town, whether you're looking for a hot Polynesian revue or a cool nightclub.

If the Brothers Cazimero are putting on a show while you're in town, don't miss it. This legendary musical duo is one of Hawaii's most beloved and gifted acts; their contemporary Hawaiian music exudes aloha. Check the papers or ask your concierge if they're playing anywhere in town. At press time, they were appearing every Wednesday at **Chai's Island Bistro** (☎ **808-585-0011**) in the Aloha Tower Marketplace.

If you're in the party mood and ready to luau, see the listing for the Polynesian Cultural Center, earlier in this chapter, or check out Chapter 11.

The really big shows

The shows listed in this section are Waikiki staples. Still, performers move around from time to time, and schedules, prices, and other parameters do change, so always call ahead.

Don Ho

Perennial favorite Don "Mr. Mellow" Ho still packs in the crowds, just like he's been doing for four decades now. (He has a Dick Clark thing going on, though, so you wouldn't know his age by looking at him — he's 71.) Hawaii's best-known singer is engaging to the core, singing nostalgic numbers like "Tiny Bubbles" and "I'll Remember You" and telling cheeky off-the-cuff jokes in an intimate nightclub setting. It's an extremely interactive show; audience members will be called upon to dance the hula, tell jokes, and more (I somehow ended up dueting with him on "New York, New York" — don't ask). If Don's youngest daughter, the burgeoning pop star Hoku, is in town, she'll join him onstage, which is a real treat. It's a rather touristy show, but can be a good bit of fun for genuine fans, nostalgia buffs, and lovers of kitsch.

You can often get tickets on the day of the show, but you're better off planning ahead. (It's often sold out by showtime.) Do yourself a favor and skip the dinner option; stick with drinks only. Come early because Don takes a photo with every fan who's interested (you're welcome to bring your own camera, if you want); he also signs post-show autographs.

At press time, ticket-buyers who made their reservations online at www. donho.com qualify for heavily discounted rates: $42 for the dinner show and $27 for the cocktail and show, plus a special show-only rate of $20.

At the Hoku Hale Theater, Waikiki Beachcomber hotel, 2300 Kalakaua Ave. (at Duke's Lane), Waikiki. ☎ 877-693-6646 or 808-923-3981. www.donho.com. Showtimes: Sun–Tues and Thurs at 8:15 p.m. Tickets: Dinner and show $52, cocktail and show $32.

Magic of Polynesia

This extravaganza is downright Vegas-worthy. Master illusionist John Horikawa performs mind-boggling feats of magic on an elaborate stage set, aided by a large costumed cast and state-of-the-art lighting and sound. This production is first-class, and the audience usually eats it up (although I've run into showgoers who've walked away less than dazzled). This show sells out regularly, so reserve seats a day or two in advance. As with the Don Ho show, I'd vote to skip the dinner option.

At the Waikiki Beachcomber hotel, 2300 Kalakaua Ave. (at Duke's Lane), Waikiki. ☎ 877-971-4321 or 808-971-4321. www.waikikibeachcomber.com. Showtimes: Most nights 6:30 p.m. and 8:45 p.m. (call for exact schedule). Tickets: $41 per person for the cocktail show, $69 for dinner show.

Society of Seven

Waikiki's longest-running nightclub act (inching up on three decades now) still puts on one of the best shows in Waikiki. Expect a lively blend of skits, impersonations, show tunes, '50s and '60s pop hits, and more.

Stop by any Outrigger or Ohana hotel in Waikiki and ask the activities agent to arrange your Society of Seven tickets; if there's a special running, he or she may be able to save you anywhere from $6 to $14 per ticket.

In the Outrigger Main Showroom, Outrigger Waikiki on the Beach, 2335 Kalakaua Ave. (between the Royal Hawaiian Shopping Center and the Sheraton Moana Surfrider), Waikiki. ☎ 808-922-6408 or 808-923-7469. www.outriggerentertainment. com. Showtimes: Tues–Sat at 8:30 p.m. Tickets: $37 for cocktail show, $53 for dinner show.

Cocktails, music, and dancing

Hands down, my favorite spot for sunset cocktails is the **House Without a Key** at the Halekulani hotel, 2199 Kalia Rd. (at the beach end of Lewers Street), Waikiki (☎ 808-923-2311; www.halekulani.com). On an ocean-front patio shaded by a big kiawe tree, you can sip the best mai tais on the island, listen to masterful steel guitar music, and watch a traditional hula dancer (often former Miss Hawaii Kanoe Miller) sway with the palms. It's romantic, nostalgic, and simply breathtaking. (Also consider the House Without a Key for a casually sophisticated alfresco dinner; see Chapter 11.) Afterward, move indoors to the Lewers Lounge, where light jazz continues the romantic tone.

Another top spot for Hawaiian music and orchid-adorned cocktails is the oh-so-romantic **Banyan Veranda** at the Sheraton Moana Surfrider, 2365 Kalakaua Ave. (on the beach, across from Kaiulani Street), in the heart of Waikiki (☎ 800-325-3535). I just love this Victorian-style beach-front hotel, situated around a 100-year-old banyan tree — the perfect setting for some soft island sounds.

Nothing separates you from the sand at the **Royal Hawaiian's Mai Tai Bar**, 2259 Kalakaua Ave., at the end of Royal Hawaiian Avenue (☎ 808-923-7311), giving this one of the most lovely views of Waikiki Beach. The Mai Tai Bar maintains an all-Hawaiian music program, which adds to the magical mood.

There's always something cooking at **Duke's Canoe Club,** at the Outrigger Waikiki on the Beach, 2335 Kalakaua Ave. (between the Royal Hawaiian Shopping Center and the Sheraton Moana Surfrider), Waikiki (☎ 808-922-2268). This lively spot is the quintessential beachfront bar and restaurant, with tiki torches in the sand, a tropical party vibe, and a mammoth drink menu to suit the scene. It's crowded in the evening, but that's part of the fun. The Hawaiian entertainment is always top-notch — and best of all, it usually starts around 4 p.m.

The Sheraton Waikiki, 2255 Kalakaua Ave. (at Royal Hawaiian Avenue, west of the Royal Hawaiian), Waikiki (☎ 808-922-4422), is home to **Esprit,** Waikiki's only dance club. You'll find an oceanfront setting, live rock, and a lively scene every night of the week; the cover charge is $5.

If you're at the Diamond Head end of Waikiki, head to the Sunset Lanai at the New Otani Kaimana Beach Hotel, 2863 Kalakaua Ave., across the street from Kapiolani Park (☎ 808-923-1555). Shaded by a giant light-festooned hau tree and practically on the sand, it's no wonder that this magical spot is a favorite Waikiki watering hole. Live Hawaiian music heightens the ambience at sunset hour Monday, Tuesday, Friday, and Saturday.

Hawaii's queen of falsetto, **Auntie Genoa Keawe,** fills the Lobby Bar of the Waikiki Beach Marriott (☎ 808-922-6611) with her larger-than-life voice. You'll find her here every Thursday (call for hours) — her traditional island sounds are definitely worth seeking out. Call to confirm the schedule.

Hawaii's finest musicians operate at two top Aloha Tower Marketplace venues: **Chai's Island Bistro,** Aloha Tower Marketplace, 1 Aloha Tower Dr., just south of downtown Honolulu (☎ **808-585-0011**), where the pricey dinners are more than worth the price of admission to see some of the finest names in Hawaiian entertainment (including Robert Cazimero, half of the justifiably legendary Brothers Cazimero duo). The calendar here is always jam-packed with top-quality talent, so don't miss it. Another terrific stop in the Marketplace for contemporary talent is **Don Ho's Island Grill** (☎ **808-528-0807**), which also transforms into a hip-shakin' dance club as the weekend evenings wear on.

The locals' best-loved venue for live music is **Anna Bannanas,** 2440 S. Beretania St. (☎ **808-946-5190**), which has been rocking Honolulu for more than three decades now. Music can run the gamut from reggae to blues to rock at the easygoing bar and club, so call to see what's on.

Rumours Nightclub, at the Ala Moana Hotel, 410 Atkinson Dr. (☎ **808-955-4811**), is a great place to hit the dance floor Tuesday through Sunday, especially if you're into Top 40 and the pop sounds of the 1960s, '70s, and '80s. Rumours has also grown into a center for Honolulu's sizzling salsa scene on Thursdays.

After years of partying, stylish **Ocean Club,** at Restaurant Row, 500 Ala Moana Blvd. (☎ **808-531-8444;** www.oceanclubonline.com), is still going strong as one of Honolulu's hottest and hippest nightspots with locals and visitors alike. Expect attractive happy-hour prices, a very good seafood-heavy small-plates menu, and DJs spinning a smart mix until 4 a.m., Tuesday through Saturday. The minimum age is 23 nightly except Thursday (when it's 21), and you're expected to dress smartly (no beach wear, T-shirts, ripped jeans — you get the picture).

Sailing into the sunset

Nothing closes a perfect day in paradise like a sunset cruise. If you're looking for a place to cruise into the sunset, do it on Oahu, where the Waikiki skyline and Diamond Head come together in an unforgettable backdrop. **Dream Cruises, Navatek I,** and the **MaiTai Catamaran** offer sunset and dinner options to choose from; see the section "All hands on deck: Ocean-cruising adventures," earlier in this chapter, for complete details.

Part IV
Maui

The 5th Wave
By Rich Tennant

"Did you want to take the Schwinn bicycle dive, the Weber gas grill dive, or the Craftsman riding lawn mower dive?"

In this part . . .

*M*aui is such a wildly popular destination that it's doubly important to do some smart trip-planning before you leave home. The chapters in this part help you map out everything you need for an unforgettable Maui vacation — whether you're after heart-pounding adventure or simply a week of lounging blissfully on the soft white sands.

Chapter 13

Settling into Maui

● ●

In This Chapter

▶ Getting from the airport to your hotel without a hassle

▶ Finding your way around Maui and its major resort areas

▶ Choosing among the island's top accommodations

▶ Discovering Maui's best restaurants

▶ Arranging for a luau

▶ Using an easy-reference list of important local contacts

● ●

*M*aui is slightly more difficult to navigate than the other islands —
instead of uniting to circle the island, all the major roads meet
and crisscross on the flat land between the island's two volcanoes. Still,
getting around isn't overly complicated; with a good map in hand, you're
golden.

You'll most likely arrive at the island's centrally located main gateway,
Kahului (ka-hoo-LOO-ee) Airport, in Central Maui.

Arriving at Kahului Airport

Kahului Airport (☎ **808-872-3893;** www.state.hi.us/dot/airports/
maui/ogg) is conveniently located 3 miles from the town of Kahului,
Maui's main community, at the end of Keolani Place (just west of the
intersection of Dairy Road and the Haleakala Highway).

Flying directly between the mainland and Maui is quite easy these days.
Aloha Airlines and **Hawaiian Airlines** provide both interisland and
direct mainland services to Kahului. **American, Air Canada, Delta,
United,** and **ATA** all serve Kahului directly from the mainland as well.
Nearly all the island's highways are accessible just outside the airport,
ready to whisk you to wherever you'll be staying.

Open-air Kahului Airport is easy to negotiate. The airport is relatively
small, and the route from your gate to Baggage Claim is clearly marked.

Maui Orientation

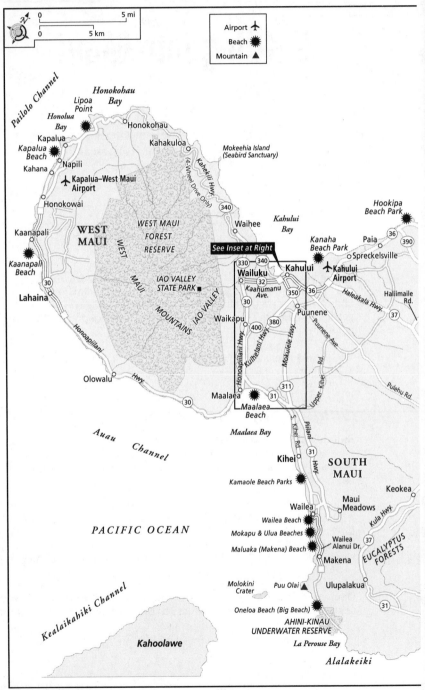

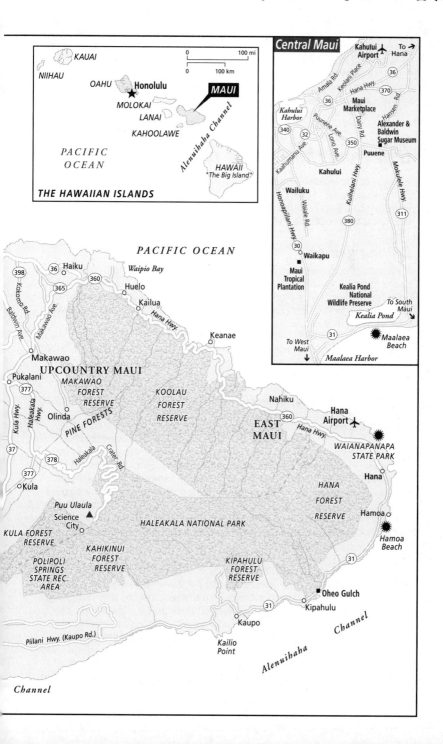

THE HAWAIIAN ISLANDS

KAUAI

NIIHAU

OAHU Honolulu

MOLOKAI

LANAI

KAHOOLAWE

MAUI

PACIFIC OCEAN

HAWAII "The Big Island"

Alenuihaha Channel

0 — 100 mi
0 — 100 km

Central Maui

Kahului Airport · To Hana

Amala Rd.

Keolani Place

Hana Hwy. 36

Kahului Harbor 340

36

Maui Marketplace

Puunene Ave.

Dairy Rd.

370

Hansen Rd.

Alexander & Baldwin Sugar Museum

350

Puuene

Mokulele Hwy.

Kaahumanu Ave.

32

Lono Ave.

Kuihelani Hwy.

Kahului

Wailuku

Waiale Rd.

Honoapiilani Hwy.

380

311

30

Waikapu

Maui Tropical Plantation

Kealia Pond National Wildlife Preserve

To South Maui

Kealia Pond

31

Maalaea Beach

To West Maui

Maalaea Harbor

PACIFIC OCEAN

398

36 Haiku

365

360

Huelo

Waipio Bay

Kailua

Hana Hwy.

Keanae

Kokomo Rd.

Makawao Ave.

Baldwin Ave.

Makawao

UPCOUNTRY MAUI

Pukalani

377

MAKAWAO FOREST RESERVE

Olinda

PINE FORESTS

Kula Hwy.

Haleakala Hwy.

37

378

377

Kula

Haleakala Crater Rd.

Puu Ulaula

Science City ▲

KULA FOREST RESERVE

POLIPOLI SPRINGS STATE REC. AREA

KAHIKINUI FOREST RESERVE

KOOLAU FOREST RESERVE

Nahiku

EAST MAUI

360

Hana Airport

Hana Hwy.

WAIANAPANAPA STATE PARK

Hana

HANA FOREST RESERVE

Hamoa

Hamoa Beach

HALEAKALA NATIONAL PARK

KIPAHULU FOREST RESERVE

31

Oheo Gulch

Kipahulu

31

Kaupo

Piilani Hwy. (Kaupo Rd.)

Kailio Point

Alenuihaha

Channel

Channel

Although almost everyone arrives at Kahului Airport, Maui does have two single-strip airports served by commercial propeller carriers — one in Kapalua (West Maui), and another one in Hana. If you're interested in avoiding busy Kahului altogether, contact **Island Air** (☎ **800-323-3345,** 800-652-6541, or 808-484-2222; www.islandair.com), a division of inter-island carrier Aloha, or **Pacific Wings** (☎ **888-575-4546** or 808-873-0877; www.pacificwings.com).

Getting from the Airport to Your Hotel

All the big car-rental names have cars available at Kahului, and I suggest that you arrange for one in advance. (For more on this subject, see Chapter 7.) If you'd rather not drive yourself, I give you some alternative transportation options in this section.

Driving yourself

Step outside to the curbside rental-car pickup area at the ocean end of the terminal (to your right as you exit the building). Either go over to the counter, if your rental company is represented, or wait for the appropriate shuttle van — they circle the airport at regular intervals — to take you a half-mile away to your rental-car check-out desk.

All the rental-car agencies offer map booklets that are invaluable for getting around the island.

Getting from the airport to your hotel can be a bit of a trial because Kahului is Maui's main business district, and all of Maui's main highways intersect just outside the airport.

If you're heading to **West Maui,** take the Kuihelani (koo-ee-hay-LA-nee) Highway (Highway 380) to the Honoapiilani (ho-no-ah-pee-ee-LA-nee) Highway (Highway 30). The Honoapiilani Highway curves around the knob that is West Maui, leading to Lahaina, Kaanapali, Kahana, Napili, and finally Kapalua. To pick up the Kuihelani Highway, exit the airport at Keolani Place and turn left onto Dairy Road, which turns into the highway you want. Expect it to take 30 minutes to reach Lahaina, 40 minutes to reach Kaanapali, and 50 to 60 minutes to reach Kapalua, maybe a little longer if the traffic's heavy.

If you're heading to **South Maui,** exit the airport at Keolani Place, turn left onto Dairy Road, and then left onto Puunene (poo-oo-NAY-nay) Avenue (Highway 350), which takes you immediately to the Mokulele (mow-koo-LAY-lay) Highway (Highway 311), which leads directly south. Just north of Kihei, the Mokulele ends; you can choose to continue on the highway — now called Piilani (pee-ee-LA-nee) Highway (Highway 31) — which takes you through Kihei and to Wailea along the speediest route, with frequent exits along the way. If you're staying at the north end of Kihei, though, exit the Mokulele Highway onto South Kihei Road, Kihei's main drag.

Taking a taxi

As long as you arrive before 10 p.m., you won't need to arrange for a taxi to pick you up at the airport before you leave home; you can just go out to the well-marked curbside area and hop into the next available cab.

If you want to arrange for pickup ahead of time, call **Maui Airport Taxi** (☎ **808-877-0907**), **Maui Central Cab** (☎ 877-244-7279 or 808-244-7278; www.mauicab.com), **Kihei Taxi** (☎ **808-879-3000**), or **Wailea Taxi** (☎ **808-874-5000**). Expect to pay $45 to $70 depending on your West Maui destination, and about $22 to $38 to the Kihei/Wailea area. Don't forget to tack on a 10- to 15-percent tip, of course. For limousine service, contact **Star Limousine** (☎ **808-875-6900** or 808-669-6900; www.limo hawaii.com).

Catching a shuttle ride

If you're not renting a car, the cheapest way to get to your hotel is via airport shuttle. **SpeediShuttle** (☎ **800-977-2605** or 808-875-8070; www.speedishuttle.com) can take you between Kahului Airport and any of the Maui resort areas between 6 a.m. and 11 p.m. daily. Rates vary depending on your destination, but figure on $30 to Wailea (one-way) and $41 one-way to Kaanapali. (Rates also change based on the number of people traveling together.) You can either set up your airport pickup in advance (which allows you to snag a 10-percent online booking discount on your return trip) or use the courtesy phone in Baggage Claim to summon a van (dial 65). Call at least 24 hours before your departure flight to arrange pickup.

Choosing Your Location

The commercial hub of Maui is **Kahului** (ka-hoo-LOO-ee); just east of Kahului is **Wailuku,** Maui's appealingly funky county seat (and a burgeoning antiques center). These two Central Maui communities are Maui's largest, but despite their central-to-everything convenience, they aren't really vacation destinations. Visitors almost never stay there, although Maui's finest B&B, the impeccable **Old Wailuku Inn,** is located here; see the section "Staying in Style," later in this chapter.

Instead, most visitors stay on one of Maui's two major resort coasts: West Maui and South Maui. Both are comprised of smaller beach resorts and communities, each with its own distinct personality.

West Maui

Look at a map of Maui; the island faintly resembles the head and shoulders of a person in left profile. The West Maui coastline serves as the island's forehead (and Kahului is on Maui's "neck"). In winter, this coast is a little greener — and a little wetter — than the South Maui coast. Some of the best beaches on the island fringe West Maui; eastward, the beautifully jagged mountain peaks of the West Maui mountains rise in the distance.

Of the communities along this resort coast, only Lahaina is a real town. The others are really just a collection of condos or hotels, each targeted to a different audience and anchored by a few fancy resorts or a high-end minimall. The communities described in the rest of this section start at the southern end of West Maui and move northward along the Honoapiilani (ho-no-ah-pee-ee-LA-nee) Highway (Highway 30).

The historic port town of **Lahaina** (la-HA-nah) isn't really all that historic anymore; in fact, it has superceded Waikiki as the tacky tourist center of Hawaii. The blocks are lined with bustling waterfront restaurants, tourist-targeted galleries and shops, and aggressive activity centers that catcall onto the street, begging to book your activities for you (or, if they can, talk you into sitting through a timeshare presentation). The predominant vibe is that of one big, surf-oriented street party. Some people love the freewheeling ambience, lively energy, and oceanfront setting. Lahaina also has two more things going for it: some of Maui's best accommodations values and an extremely convenient location. Lahaina has a couple of beaches that will do in a pinch, but you should expect to drive to enjoy the best ones.

Three miles north of Lahaina is **Kaanapali** (kah-na-PA-lee), Hawaii's first master-planned family resort, and a real favorite of mine. Kaanapali's chain of resort hotels and condos fronts a gorgeous golden beach and exudes a nice sense of continuity. All are linked by a landscaped parkway and a walking path along the sand, with a very nice shopping and dining complex sitting at its midpoint. Kaanapali is pricey, but not quite as expensive as Kapalua or Wailea; in fact, it's home to my favorite mid-priced resort, the **Kaanapali Beach Hotel,** and some of Maui's best midrange condos.

Two condo communities, **Kahana** and **Napili,** sit off the highway a few minutes north of Kaanapali, offering great deals for those who want an affordable place to stay and a nice oceanfront setting. Apartment-style units offer good value for families or anyone who wants homelike amenities that give you the freedom to cook a meal for yourself or wash your own socks. Restaurants and supermarkets are right at hand. The only down side is a lack of personality — expect homogeneous, rather generic condo complexes.

North of Kahana is Hawaii's most beautiful master-planned community, **Kapalua,** the exclusive domain of two gracious luxury hotels, fabulous gold-sand beaches, and world-class golf. Kapalua is a marvelous place to settle in and unwind, if you have the bucks to do it. But keep in mind that, situated as it is at the north end of the Honoapiilani Highway, Kapalua isn't the most convenient base. Even Lahaina is a 20-minute drive to the south. Still, the glorious setting can be well worth the trade-off. Kapalua also tends to get more rain than other Maui resorts, even those a few minutes south on the West Maui coast.

South Maui

South Maui is the island's hottest, driest, and sunniest coast. Actually western-facing, but well-protected from the elements by peninsula-like West Maui, South Maui receives only about 15 inches of annual rainfall, and temperatures stay around 80°F year-round.

If you drive south along Piilani Highway (Highway 31) or Kihei Road (Highway 310), you first reach Kihei and then Wailea. Which one you choose depends entirely on your budget.

Centrally located **Kihei** (KEY-hay) is Maui's bargain coast. Its main drag is South Kihei Road, which is bordered by a continuous string of condos and minimalls on one side and a series of sandy beaches on the other. Kihei isn't charming or quaint — it feels more like southern California than Hawaii at times, especially when the traffic is bumper to bumper along Kihei Road — but ongoing renovation is improving its appeal somewhat. And what Kihei lacks in physical charm it more than makes up for in sunshine, affordability, and convenience. Just a few minutes south of Kihei, **Wailea** (why-LAY-ah) sits at the opposite end of the budget-deluxe continuum. This ritzy, well-manicured neighborhood is home to Maui's best luxury resort spreads, enough championship golf courses to keep you busy for a week (in fact, Wailea was named the world's top golf resort by *Travel & Leisure* in 2003), five outstanding beaches, the elegant new Shops at Wailea for dining and credit card-flexing, and the Wailea Tennis Center (known as Wimbledon West). The strip is well-developed and tightly packed, but my favorite Wailea resorts remain worlds unto themselves. Even though Kapalua is more beautiful, Wailea is no slouch — and I prefer its more accessible location and wider range of hotel choices. You'll even find some midrange and upscale condos in this appealing neighborhood.

Hana

A few visitors like to stay way out in Hana, in easternmost Maui, for the ultimate escape. In Hana, you can relax in a lush, green, rural setting with access to wonderful beaches. Hana tends to receive more rain than on the dry South Maui coast, but as compensation, the vegetation is green like a luxuriant rainforest — think giant ferns, vibrant tropical flowers, and swaying palms. Hana is a sleepy area, where the accommodations tend to be intimate and exquisite, but not laden with facilities.

You can see this beautiful area on a day's drive from the major resort coasts (see Chapter 14), but that tends to be a rushed experience. If you have the leisure — and the wallet — I recommend doing the drive at a leisurely pace and staying overnight at the gloriously renovated **Hotel Hana-Maui** (reviewed later in this chapter) if you can. It's a wonderful departure from the bustle of South and West Maui — a step back into Hawaii's simpler days before tourism spawned such intense development.

Getting Around Maui

To really see the Valley Island, you have to drive it yourself. Maui has only a handful of major roads, but they all meet in a complicated web in the center of the island, and untangling them can take some effort. Be sure to study a good island map and know exactly where you're going before you set out.

Maui is growing by leaps and bounds, with new housing developments going up in almost every direction. As a result, traffic can be challenging at times. Try to allow yourself extra time to get where you're going during rush hours, especially in the Central and South Maui areas.

Navigating your rental car around the Valley Isle

If you get in trouble on Maui's highways and you don't have your cell-phone with you, look for the flashing blue strobe lights on 12-foot poles; at the base are emergency call boxes (programmed to dial 911 as soon as you pick up the handset).

Starting out in Central Maui

Kahului, in Central Maui, is where the major airport is, and where you'll arrive. Kahului isn't a vacation destination, but a real town with Wal-Marts, car lots, malls, and so on. Still, you will occasionally find yourself in Kahului as you head to other areas of the island because this area is where Maui's highways intersect.

Kahului's main drag is **Kaahumanu** (ka-ah-hoo-MA-noo) **Avenue** (Highway 32). If you're heading to the town of Wailuku, either for some antiquing or to visit scenic Iao Valley, just follow Kaahumanu Avenue west for about ten minutes and — *voilà* — you're there.

Reaching the West and South Maui resorts

If you're heading to any of Maui's beach resort areas, either in West Maui or South Maui, you first have to head south through the Central Maui corridor (often referred to as Maui's "neck").

To reach West Maui, you take the **Kuihelani Highway** (Highway 380) south from Kahului to the **Honoapiilani Highway** (Highway 30). The Honapiilani Highway actually starts in Wailuku (it meets up with the end of Kaahumanu Avenue to make a neat inverted "L" there) and runs directly south to Maalaea (mah-LAY-ah), a windy harborfront village at the south end of Central Maui — where you may be picking up a snorkel cruise to Molokini or visiting the state-of-the-art Maui Ocean Center aquarium. Past Maalaea, the southbound Honoapiilani Highway begins to follow the curve of the land, turning abruptly west and north along the coast toward Lahaina.

All West Maui's resort communities lie directly off the Honoapiilani Highway on the ocean side of the road. As you go from south to north, you'll first reach the old whaling town of Lahaina; then Kaanapali, Hawaii's first master-planned beach resort; then two quiet beachfront condo communities, Kahana and Napili; and, at the end of the road, the Kapalua resort, a stunning manicured beauty. It's about a half-hour of easy highway driving from Lahaina to Kapalua.

Be extra alert as you drive the Honoapiilani Highway (Highway 30) because the road is rather winding, and drivers who spot whales in the channel between Maui and Lanai sometimes slam on the brakes in awe, precipitating tie-ups and accidents.

From Kahului, South Maui (the island's hottest, driest, and sunniest resort coast) is basically a straight shot. The **Mokulele Highway** (Highway 311) heads straight south across the Central Maui corridor from Kahului to the north end of Kihei, west of the Kuihelani Highway, Highway 380.

At the end of the Mokulele Highway, you have two choices: You can either pick up South Kihei Road, Kihei's main drag, which is what you should do if you're heading to a destination in the north portion of Kihei or if you're looking for a supermarket or gas station; or, if you're on your way to the southern portion of Kihei — to Wailea for a round of golf, or to Makena, farther south, to hang out on a quiet beach or go snorkeling — stick to the right as the Mokulele ends and pick up the **Piilani Highway** (Highway 31), which continues south to Wailea. Near the end of the Piilani Highway, you'll veer right onto the coastal road to reach the Wailea resorts or Makena.

The Mokulele Highway (Highway 311) is often the scene of crashes involving intoxicated and speeding drivers, so be extra careful.

If you're traveling from South Maui to West Maui, or vice versa, you don't need to travel all the way back to Kahului to pick up the appropriate road. **Highway 310** (North Kihei Road) connects the Mokulele Highway (Highway 311, the road to South Maui) to the Honoapiilani Highway (Highway 30, the road to West Maui), running east-west at the south end of Maui's "neck."

Going Upcountry and to East Maui

The giant volcanic crater that dominates the main body of the island is Haleakala (ha-lay-ah-KA-la), officially preserved as **Haleakala National Park.** The distance from Kahului to the summit of Haleakala is only about 38 miles, but the drive takes about 1½ hours because of its curving nature and steep ascent (to about 10,000 feet). The drive is called the **Haleakala Highway,** which is Highway 37 as it passes through open flatlands, past turnoffs for groovy rural towns like Haliimaile (home to **Haliimaile General Store**, a great restaurant; see later in this chapter) and Makawao (a charming shopping stop). Then, just past Makawao Avenue, the Haleakala Highway becomes Highway 377 — so be sure to take the turn for it. After you pass through the little town of Kula, turn onto **Haleakala Crater Road** (Highway 378), which delivers you to the summit.

From Kahului to Haleakala

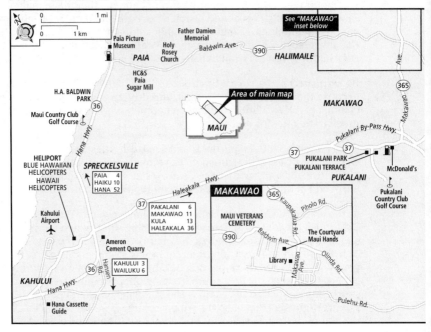

If you don't take the Haleakala Crater Road turnoff, you'll continue south on Highway 377, which soon connects up with Highway 37 again, here called the **Kula Highway.** If you stay on this road, it will eventually take you all the way to Hana, the small, isolated town at the east end of the island.

If you're trying to get to Hana, the more popular route is the **Hana Highway** (Highway 360), which hugs the north cliffs of Maui for about 52 miles east of Kahului. **The Heavenly Road to Hana,** as it's often called, is a winding drive that borders on treacherous in each direction, crossing more than 50 one-lane bridges in the process. Still, it's one of the most spectacular scenic drives you'll ever take in your life. I guide you through it, mile by mile, in Chapter 14. Even if you don't head all the way to Hana, consider making a visit to charming Paia (pa-EE-ah), a hip little surf town about ten minutes east of Kahului that has two main draws: some hip and artsy boutiquing and the best windsurfing beach in the world, Hookipa Beach Park, which I discuss in Chapter 14.

I discuss the south route to Hana — which is officially Highway 31, but most folks call it the **Kaupo** (COW-po) **Road** — in further detail in Chapter 14, but some warnings about it bear mention here, too. Although the road has been considerably improved in recent years, it's still a risky route. Before you set out on it, check with your hotel regarding current road conditions. It's usually fine if the weather has been clear, but stay away if it's

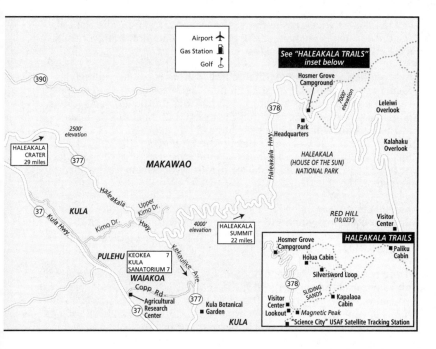

been raining because unpaved sections of the road can wash out. And check with your rental-car company before you set out; many rental contracts actually *forbid* customers from driving their cars on Kaupo Road, so if you get stuck, the cost for the tow will be your responsibility.

Getting around without wheels

Your options are limited if you're not going to rent a car because the island has no islandwide public transportation system.

Holo Ka'a Public Transit is a public/private partnership that recently began to offer economical and air-conditioned shuttle-bus service in Central, West, and South Maui. The costs range from $1 for routes in Kaanapali-Lahaina or along South Kihei Road, $2 for routes in Kapalua-Kaanapali, up to $5 for stops from Wailea to Maalaea. For more information, call ☎ **808-879-2828** or visit www.akinatours.com. Maui does have islandwide taxi service. The meter can run up fast, but a taxi will get you where you need to go if you don't have your own wheels. Call **Alii Cab** (☎ **808-661-3688** or 808-667-2605), **Maui Central Cab** (☎ **877-244-7279** or 808-244-7278; www.mauicab.com), **Kihei Taxi** (☎ **808-879-3000**), or **Wailea Taxi** (☎ **808-874-5000**). If you want to be shuttled around in style, call **Star Limousine** (☎ **808-875-6900** or 808-669-6900; www.limohawaii.com).

If you're going to skip renting a car on Maui, a good bet is to base your-self in Lahaina where restaurants, shops, and attractions are right at hand. Your beach enjoyment will be limited, though; Lahaina does have a beach, but it's not the greatest.

An even better alternative for auto-free visitors is basing yourself in Kaanapali — the beach is excellent here, and restaurants and shops are right at hand in Whaler's Village. A free resort shuttle connects hotels, golf, and other attractions within the resort, but most of Kaanapali's attractions are within walking distance of one another. What's more, Kaanapali is an easy place to pick up the $1 or $2 shuttle van services mentioned earlier to destinations all along the coast. Ask the concierge or front desk staff at your hotel for details; everyone in Kaanapali is well-versed on the shuttle.

Kapalua and Wailea also have local resort shuttles that you can rely upon to transport you between destinations within the resort: to the golf course, to local restaurants, and to resort shops. This is, however, another very limited option.

If you're coming to Maui and not renting a car, ultimately, your best bet may be to call the concierge at the hotel at which you'll be staying before you leave home. He or she will be able to give you a clear heads-up on how convenient the hotel or resort is to nearby restaurants, shopping, and the beach, as well as what kinds of transport are readily available for you to get to other destinations on the island. Also see Chapter 14 for info on bus tours that can pick you up and drop you off at your hotel.

Staying in Style

Ever-popular Maui boasts a terrific crop of resorts. But high demand means that both resort hotels and condos can — and do — garner ridiculously high rack rates. Take heart, however: Some good bargains are available, especially in the condo market. I list some of the best values in the section "Maui's best accommodations," later in this chapter, but those of you looking for budget accommodations can choose from an even wider array of options by also contacting one of the condo-rental agencies listed at the end of this chapter.

You may be able to save more money on Maui than anywhere else in Hawaii by purchasing an all-inclusive package deal, especially if you're looking for an upscale vacation. In the package market, Maui's popular-ity may work in your favor: Packagers scoop up huge numbers of Maui hotel rooms, and because they're buying rooms in bulk, they can negoti-ate substantial price breaks and pass the savings on to you. Of course, I can't guarantee what the prices will be when you book, but checking out what's available is worth the extra effort, even if you're booking the rest of your vacation on your own. (Some packagers can arrange land-only vacations if you already have your plane tickets covered.) See Chapter 8 for tips on where to look for the package deal that's right for you.

Maui's best accommodations

In the following listings, each property is followed by a number of dollar signs, ranging from one ($) to five ($$$$$). Each represents the median rack-rate price range for a double room per night, as follows:

$	Super-cheap — less than $100 per night
$$	Still affordable — $100 to $175
$$$	Moderate — $175 to $250
$$$$	Expensive but not ridiculous — $250 to $375
$$$$$	Ultraluxurious — more than $375 per night

 You almost never *need* to pay the asking price for a hotel room. See Chapter 8 for tips on how to avoid paying the full price for hotel rooms. Also see Chapter 6 for advice on how to score an all-inclusive package that can save you big bucks on both accommodations and airfare and, sometimes, car rentals and activities, too.

Also, don't forget that the state adds 11.42 percent in taxes to your hotel bill.

 ### Aston at the Maui Banyan
$$–$$$ South Maui (Kihei)

Skip the standard hotel rooms, if you can, and go straight for a condo unit — which offers much more value for your dollar — at this very nice apartment-like complex situated across Kihei Road from Kamaole (kam-a-OH-lay) Beach Park II. The roomy, open-plan one- and two-bedroom units are all nicely outfitted and well maintained; a few three-bedroom units are also available. They've all been recently renovated and feature comfy, contemporary island-style furniture, full kitchens with microwave, washer/dryers, and furnished lanais. Light daily maid service is included, and two pools, tennis courts, and a Jacuzzi are on-site. The building sits perpendicular to the coast, so partial ocean views are the best you can do; most upper units overlook the parking structure or the building next door. Still, this complex is a great value, especially if you can score one of the many price breaks.

See map p. 236. 2575 S. Kihei Rd., Kihei. ☎ ***800-822-4409**, 800-922-7866, or 808-875-0004. Fax: 808-874-4035.* www.aston-hotels.com. *Parking: Free! Rack rates: $150–$200 double, $190–$280 1-bedroom, $250–$375 2-bedroom, $395–$510 3-bedroom. Deals: Excellent opportunities for discounts. Internet-only ePriceBreaker rates as low as $104 double, $129 1-bedroom, $169 2-bedroom at press time. Ask for AAA, senior (50-plus), and corporate discounts; packages that include airfare; and other special rate programs. AE, DC, DISC, MC, V.*

Maui's Accommodations

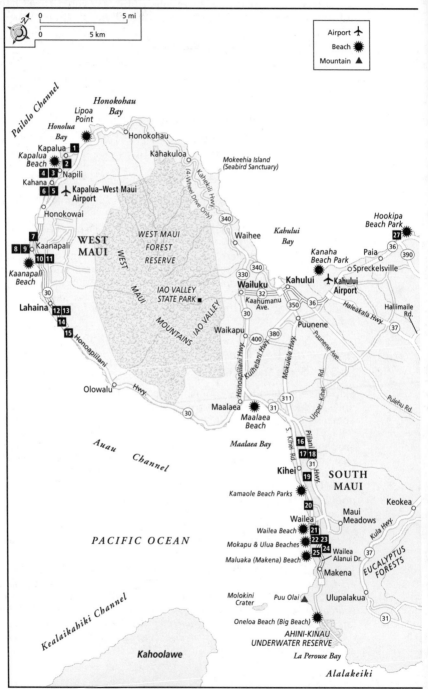

0 ____ 5 mi
0 ____ 5 km

Airport ✈
Beach ✹
Mountain ▲

Pailolo Channel

Honokohau Bay

Lipoa Point

Honolua Bay

Kapalua 1

Kapalua Beach 2

4 3 Napili

Kahana 6 5 ✈ Kapalua–West Maui Airport

Honokowai

Honokohau

Kahakuloa

Mokeehia Island (Seabird Sanctuary)

Kahekili Hwy. (4-Wheel Drive Only)

340

Waihee

Kahului Bay

Hookipa Beach Park 27

Kanaha Beach Park

Paia 36

Spreckelsville 390

WEST MAUI

WEST MAUI FOREST RESERVE

7

8 9 Kaanapali

10 11

Kaanapali Beach

Lahaina

12 13

14

15 Honoapiilani

IAO VALLEY STATE PARK

340

330

Wailuku

32

Kaahumanu Ave.

30

Kahului ✈ Kahului Airport

350 36

Haleakala Hwy.

Haliimaile Rd.

37

WEST MAUI MOUNTAINS

IAO VALLEY

Waikapu

Puunene

Puunene Ave.

Pulehu Rd.

Olowalu Hwy.

30

Maalaea

Maalaea Beach

400 380

31 311

Honoapiilani Hwy.

Kuihelani Hwy.

Mokulele Hwy.

Upper Kihei Rd.

Kula Hwy.

Auau Channel

Maalaea Bay

16

17 18

Kihei

19

Kamaole Beach Parks

20

Wailea

Wailea Beach 21

Mokapu & Ulua Beaches 22 23

25 24 Wailea Alanui Dr.

Makena

S. Kihei Rd.

Pilani Hwy.

31

SOUTH MAUI

Keokea

Maui Meadows

EUCALYPTUS FORESTS

37

PACIFIC OCEAN

Maluaka (Makena) Beach

Molokini Crater

Puu Olai ▲

Ulupalakua

31

Oneloa Beach (Big Beach)

AHINI-KINAU UNDERWATER RESERVE

La Perouse Bay

Kealaikahiki Channel

Kahoolawe

Alalakeiki

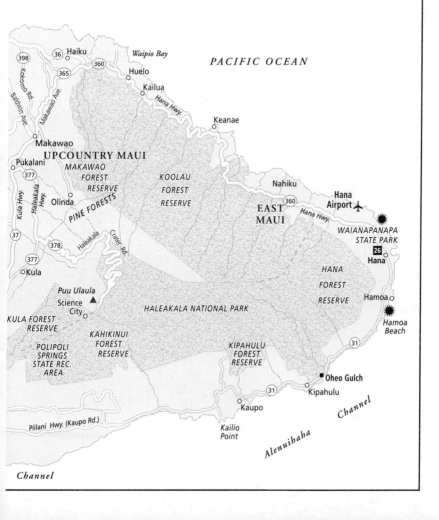

Lahaina & Kaanapali Accommodations

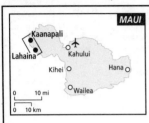

Best Western Pioneer Inn **7**

Kaanapali Alii **5**

Kaanapali Beach Hotel **2**

Lahaina Shores Beach Resort **9**

Ohana Maui Islander **8**

Plantation Inn **6**

Sheraton Maui **1**

Westin Maui **4**

The Whaler on Kaanapali Beach **3**

MAUI

Kaanapali

Lahaina

Kahului

Kihei

Hana

Wailea

0   10 mi

0   10 km

0   1/2 mi

0   0.5 km

To Kahana,
Napili & Kapalua

Kahekili
Beach Park

Honoapiilani Hwy.

Puukolii Rd.

Kekaa Dr.

LK & P Sugar Cane Train

30

1

Black Rock

2

3

Whalers Village

Kaanapali
Beach

4

Kaanapali Parkway

Nohea Kai Dr.

5

KAANAPALI

Kaanapali North
Golf Course

Kaanapaii
Golf Courses
Club House

Kaanapali South
Golf Course

Hanakaoo
Beach Park

Wahikuli
Beach Park

Police

Lahaina
Civic Center

Fleming Rd.

Lahaina Cannery
Mall

Kapunakea St.

Mala Wharf

Kenui St.

Honoapiilani Hwy.

Kahoma Stream

Lahainaluna
School
(1837)

Train Depot

Hilo Hattie

Lahaina
Square

Lahaina Center

Papalaua St.

Pioneer
Sugar Mill

Lahainaluna Rd.

Lahaina
Shopping Center

6

Front St.

LAHAINA

Dickenson St.

Wainee St.

Luakini St.

30

Lahaina
Small Boat Harbor

7

Banyan
Tree

Prison St.

8

505 Front St.
(Shops
& Restaurants)

9

Shaw St.

Airport ✈

Beach ✳

Golf ⛳

Parking Ⓟ

Post Office ✉

Best Western Pioneer Inn
$$ **West Maui (Lahaina)**

This delightfully restored 1901 whaler's inn overlooking Lahaina Harbor blends a genuine old-time ambience with proven Best Western comforts, and it's a winning combination. Rooms are small and on the dark side, but they're cool, pretty, and comfortable, with new curtains and carpets, modern tiled baths, and coffeemakers; deluxe rooms also have wet bars with minifridge, and suites add an additional Murphy bed. The quietest rooms face the garden courtyard pool or the massive banyan tree next door; a few have harbor views that heighten the maritime experience. Front Street-facing rooms are noisy, but shaded and furnished lanais give you a ringside seat for the sidewalk party. The hotel has an appealing indoor-outdoor restaurant and bar on-site; the beach is a drive away, but the town couldn't be more convenient. All in all, it's not Maui's roomiest or quietest place to stay, but it's nonetheless a real charmer.

See map p. 232. At Lahaina Pier, 658 Wharf St. (at Front Street), Lahaina. ☎ *800-457-5457 or 808-661-3636. Fax: 808-667-5708.* www.pioneerinnmaui.com *or* www.bestwestern.com. *Parking: $4 in lot 2 blocks away. Rack rates: $115–$135 standard double, $150–$185 deluxe double, $165–$200 suite. Deals: Discounts for AAA and AARP members as well as seniors (55-plus); inquire about family rates and other special packages. AE, DC, DISC, MC, V.*

Fairmont Kea Lani Maui
$$$$–$$$$$ **South Maui (Wailea)**

Now under the guiding hand of the fabulous Fairmont hotel chain, this fanciful Moorish palace is just as pricey as Maui's other luxury resorts, but it gives you so much more room for your money. Spread out and enjoy a giant one-bedroom suite, complete with a gorgeous living room with a full entertainment center (VCRs and CD and DVD players, plus a second TV in the bedroom); a wet bar with coffeemaker and microwave; a mammoth marble bath with a soaking tub big enough for two, double sinks, separate shower, and terrific toiletries; and a furnished lanai that's ideal for an alfresco breakfast. The villas are even more luxurious, each boasting a gourmet kitchen, a gas barbecue and plunge pool on the private patio, and a prime on-the-sand location. Amenities include three swimming pools and two Jacuzzis, an excellent spa (second only to the neighboring Grand Wailea's), a fitness center, a full beach activities center, a wealth of daily activities and kids' programs, and excellent dining, including one of my favorite Maui restaurants, Nick's Fishmarket (see review later in his chapter). It's a first-rate choice on every level.

See map p. 236. 4100 Wailea Alanui Dr., Wailea. ☎ *800-441-1414, 800-882-4100, or 808-875-4100. Fax: 808-875-1200.* www.kealani.com. *Parking: Free! Rack rates: $345–$785 suite; $1,400–$2,200 2- or 3-bedroom villa. Deals: Many available specials, including golf and spa packages, and deals that throw in a rental car or a fifth night free. Be sure to check the Web site or ask. AE, DC, DISC, MC, V.*

Four Seasons Resort Maui at Wailea
$$$$$ South Maui (Wailea)

Averaging an extra-large 640 square feet (although the Kea Lani's suites are even more spacious), the guest rooms here are done in soft, warm yellows and feature cushy furnishings, grand and gorgeous bathrooms (among the best in Hawaii), and big lanais. About 80 percent have ocean views, but beware those that overlook the driveway — it's a real mood killer. You're better off with a gardenview room overlooking the lovely sculpture gardens and waterfalls (and most of these have a bit of an ocean view anyway). At just $345, the mountainview rooms are a good value for pricey Maui, considering the cream-of-the-crop quality of the accommodations and service. The gorgeous grounds overflow with first-rate facilities — including the only Hawaii branch of Wolfgang Puck's legendary Spago restaurant and a sublime spa offering yoga, Pilates, and a wide variety of pampering treatments — and the beach is one of Maui's finest. If you prefer to lounge poolside, you can recline in comfort under a shaded cabana or on a grassy lawn; a pool attendant will even bring you chilled towels and spritz you with Evian if you break a sweat. Don't be surprised if you see Britney, Cameron, or another big star lounging poolside — this resort is a big-time Hollywood favorite. The kids will be duly pampered in an excellent activities program.

See map p. 236. 3900 Wailea Alanui Dr., Wailea. ☎ *800-334-6284 or 808-874-8000. Fax: 808-874-6449.* www.fourseasons.com/maui. *Rack rates: $345–$775 double, $800–$6,500 suite. Parking: Free! Deals: Multiple package deals almost always on offer, including room-and-car, bed-and-breakfast, golf, spa, and others. Also ask about fifth-night-free deals and special family rates. AE, DC, DISC, MC, V.*

Grand Wailea Resort & Spa
$$$$$ South Maui (Wailea)

I didn't want to love this outrageous resort, but it's just too glorious to deny. This monument to monied excess won me over with its lush, art-filled grounds (boasting works by such masters as Botero, Legér, Picasso, and Warhol) and its exclusive tropical-theme-park vibe; the fantastic 50,000-square-foot Spa Grande, the island's ultimate temple to the pampered life; and Hawaii's best water playground, a fantasy of falls, rapids, slides, grottos, hidden hot tubs, and swim-up bars. The world's only water-powered elevator merely puts the finishing touch on the ultimate pool complex. Rooms are huge and elegantly appointed, with luxurious marble baths. If you can afford it, stay in the Napua Tower; this exclusive 100-room hotel-within-a-hotel offers personalized concierge service plus free continental breakfast. Restaurants, shops, and lounges abound, and the high-tech Tsunami night club is the place to hit the dance floor in South Maui. What's more, both food and service are first rate, making this resort the place to stay if you can afford to live large. And bring the kids — they'll think that they've died and gone to heaven, especially after they see the whopping 20,000-square-foot kids' camp. This elegant fantasyland is an ideal place to tie the knot, too, because it's home to a picture-perfect seaside wedding chapel. Minimalists, on the other hand, should book elsewhere.

Kapalua, Napili & Kahana Accommodations & Dining

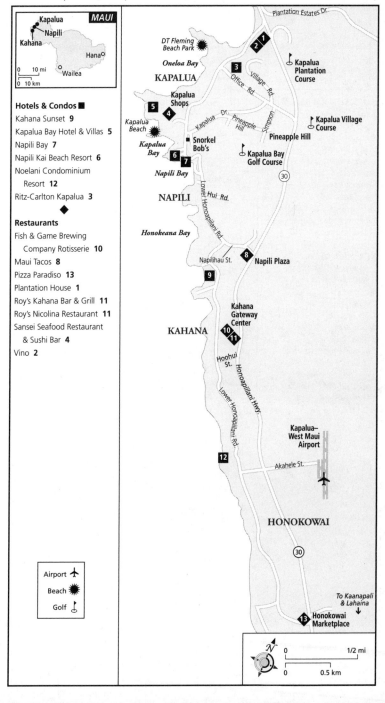

Hotels & Condos ■

Kahana Sunset **9**
Kapalua Bay Hotel & Villas **5**
Napili Bay **7**
Napili Kai Beach Resort **6**
Noelani Condominium
　Resort **12**
Ritz-Carlton Kapalua **3**

◆

Restaurants

Fish & Game Brewing
　Company Rotisserie **10**
Maui Tacos **8**
Pizza Paradiso **13**
Plantation House **1**
Roy's Kahana Bar & Grill **11**
Roy's Nicolina Restaurant **11**
Sansei Seafood Restaurant
　& Sushi Bar **4**
Vino **2**

South Maui Accommodations & Dining

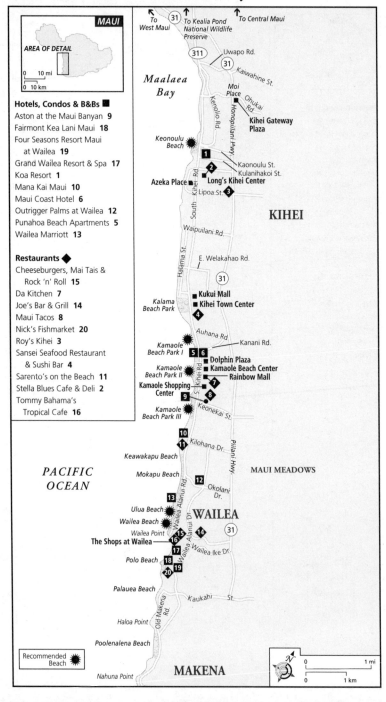

Hotels, Condos & B&Bs ■
Aston at the Maui Banyan **9**
Fairmont Kea Lani Maui **18**
Four Seasons Resort Maui
   at Wailea **19**
Grand Wailea Resort & Spa **17**
Koa Resort **1**
Mana Kai Maui **10**
Maui Coast Hotel **6**
Outrigger Palms at Wailea **12**
Punahoa Beach Apartments **5**
Wailea Marriott **13**

Restaurants ◆
Cheeseburgers, Mai Tais &
   Rock 'n' Roll **15**
Da Kitchen **7**
Joe's Bar & Grill **14**
Maui Tacos **8**
Nick's Fishmarket **20**
Roy's Kihei **3**
Sansei Seafood Restaurant
   & Sushi Bar **4**
Sarento's on the Beach **11**
Stella Blues Cafe & Deli **2**
Tommy Bahama's
   Tropical Cafe **16**

MAUI

AREA OF DETAIL

0   10 mi
0   10 km

To
West Maui
To Kealia Pond
National Wildlife
Preserve
To Central Maui

Uwapo Rd.

Kaiwahine St.

*Maalaea
Bay*

Moi
Place
Ohukai
Rd.
Kihei Gateway
Plaza

Kenolio Rd.

Homapiliani Hwy.

Keonoulu
Beach

Kaonoulu St.
Kulanihakoi St.
Long's Kihei Center

Azeka Place

South Kihei Rd.

Lipoa St.

KIHEI

Waipuilani Rd.

Halama St.

E. Welakahao Rd.

Kukui Mall
Kalama
Beach Park
Kihei Town Center

Auhana Rd.

Kanani Rd.

Kamaole
Beach Park I

Dolphin Plaza
Kamaole Beach Center
Kamaole
Beach Park II
Rainbow Mall

Kamaole Shopping
Center

S. Kihei Rd.

Keonekai St.

Kamaole
Beach Park III

Kilohana Dr.

Keawakapu Beach

Pillani Hwy.

**PACIFIC
OCEAN**

Mokapu Beach

MAUI MEADOWS

Okolani
Dr.

Ulua Beach

Wailea Alanui Dr.

WAILEA

Wailea Beach
Wailea Point
The Shops at Wailea

Wailea Alanui Dr.
Wailea Ike Dr.

Polo Beach

Palauea Beach

Kaukahi   St.

Old Makena Rd.

Haloa Point

Poolenalena Beach

Recommended
Beach

N

0   1 mi
0   1 km

MAKENA

Nahuna Point

See map p. 236. 3850 Wailea Alanui Dr., Wailea. ☎ *800-888-6100 or 808-875-1236. Fax: 808-874-2442.* www.grandwailea.com. *Valet parking: $12. Rack rates: $465–$825 double, $1,650–$10,850 suite. Mandatory $15-per-night "resort fee" for "free" self-parking, "free" local and 800 calls, in-room coffee, daily fitness classes, and other resort extras. Deals: Numerous packages are usually available, including room-and-car, bed-and-breakfast, spa, golf, kids, and more. AE, DC, DISC, MC, V.*

Hotel Hana-Maui
$$$$$ Hana

The best news to come out of Maui — and maybe all of Hawaii — in years is the rebirth of the Hotel Hana-Maui, a breathtaking oceanfront property with great bones that languished in disrepair for too many years. It's now under management by the same folks behind Big Sur's breathtaking Post Ranch Inn and Fiji's Jean-Michel Cousteau Fiji Islands Resort — and the Hotel Hana-Maui has been transformed into one of Maui's most magical resorts. It's reason enough alone to cruise to the end of the road to Maui's remote eastern shore.

It's a small hotel, with just 66 rooms and suites nestled in one-story Hawaiian-style cottages on meticulously landscaped grounds that slope gently to glorious Hana Bay. The expansive grounds allow for plenty of privacy and quiet relaxation, and both the setting and warmhearted staff exude an old-Hawaii feeling. Accommodations, on the other hand, boast only the most luxe comforts: Warm and welcoming interiors featuring indigenous island materials, textiles, and patterns; all of the generously apportioned units are at once designer-stylish and sigh-inducingly comfortable. The duplex Sea Ranch cottages are the most luxurious, with cathedral ceilings, gorgeous oversized bathrooms, and private lanais; about half have patio Jacuzzis. But you can't go wrong with the low-rise Bay View suites a little farther up the slope if your wallet is tighter. A lack of TVs, radios, and air-conditioning (you don't need it out here) suits the mood perfectly; no one travels to the end of the road in Hana to watch *The Sopranos* or CNN. (The common Club Room has a giant screen TV, VCR, and Internet access if you really need a fix.) A wealth of marvelous outdoor activities keep you content — from cultural walks and horseback riding to sunbathing at Hamoa Beach, which James Michener once called the most beautiful beach in the world — as does the utterly pampering and peaceful spa.

See map p. 303. At Hana Ranch, Hana Hwy., Hana. ☎ *800-321-HANA or 808-248-8211. Fax: 808-248-7202.* www.hotelhanamaui.com. *Valet parking: Free! Rack rates: $375–$425 Bay cottage for two, $495–$845 Sea Ranch cottage for two, $1,195–$2,000 2-bedroom suite or Plantation guesthouse. Deals: Numerous value-added packages available; call or check Web site for current offers. AE, DC, DISC, MC, V.*

The Inn at Mama's Fish House
$$$ East Maui: On the Road to Hana

These tropical cottages on one of Maui's most gorgeous oceanfront lots are ideal for those who want a quiet but still central location. Nestled in a coconut grove on secluded Kuau Cove — just a ten-minute drive from the airport — six beautifully furnished vacation rentals feature setting-appropriate rattan furnishings, lovely local artwork, terra-cotta floors, and complete kitchens (even dishwashers). Extras like big TVs with VCR, CD players, Weber gas barbecues, laundry facilities, and tons of beach toys make this a great place to stay with friends or family. The one-bedrooms can sleep up to four — Mom and Dad on the queen bed in the bedroom, two kids on the sleeper sofa. The two-bedrooms can sleep up to six: one bedroom has a queen bed, and the second has a full or two twin beds, plus a sleeper sofa in the bedroom. Two-bedrooms also benefit from a prime beachfront location, while the one-bedrooms are just steps from the beach nestled in colorful tropical foliage. The divine Mama's Fish House — my favorite Maui restaurant (see review later in this chapter) — is next door, and inn guests benefit from discounts at lunch and dinner. Just down the road is hip-as-can-be Paia, the fun 'n' funky surf town that serves as the gateway to the road to Hana.

See map p. 298. 799 Poho Place (off the Hana Hwy. in Kuau), Paia. ☎ *800-860-HULA or 808-579-9764. Fax: 808-579-8594.* www.mamasfishhouse.com. *Parking: Free! Rack rates: $175 1-bedroom unit; $475 2-bedroom unit. Three-night minimum stay. AE, DISC, MC, V.*

Kaanapali Alii
$$$$$ West Maui (Kaanapali)

If you want luxury living and condo conveniences, this high-rise beach-front complex is the place for you. These are Maui's finest (and priciest) condos, but they're worth it. Each condo is privately owned, so décor varies, but owners are held to a high standard. The one- and two-bedroom apartments are universally large (between 1,500 and 1,900 square feet) and come with a fully equipped gourmet kitchen, huge living room and dining room, two TVs and VCR, two full baths (even in the one-bedrooms), washer/dryer, and private lanais. The luxuriant grounds feature a fitness room, tennis, a heated pool with hot tub and poolside snack service plus a separate kids' pool, a beach activities center, and poolside gas grills for fun family meals. Among the resortlike amenities are daily maid service; concierge, bell, valet, and room service; complimentary kids' club activities in summer; and even grocery delivery and a resident tennis pro.

See map p. 232. 50 Nohea Kai Dr., Kaanapali. ☎ *800-642-6284 or 808-661-3339. Fax: 808-667-1145.* www.classicresorts.com. *Parking: Free! Rack rates: $350–$525 1-bedroom, $475–$740 2-bedroom. Three-night minimum. Deals: Numerous deals are usually on offer, including fifth-night free, seventh-night free, room-and-car, and romance packages. AE, DC, MC, V.*

Kaanapali Beach Hotel
$$$ West Maui (Kaanapali)

The Kaanapali Beach is the last hotel left in Hawaii that gives you a real resort experience in this price range. It's older and it's not luxurious, but it boasts a genuine spirit of aloha that's absent in so many other hotels. Set beachfront around a wide, grassy lawn with a whale-shaped pool, three low-rise wings house spacious, well-maintained rooms; still rather motel-like, they're nevertheless perfectly comfortable and feature all the conveniences, plus lanais overlooking the pretty yard or beach. Tiki torches, hula, and music create an irresistible Hawaiian ambience every evening, and the service is some of the friendliest around. An extensive Hawaiiana program goes beyond the standard hula lessons to include lauhala weaving, lei-making, and cultural tours. A kids' program, three good restaurants, and a coin-op laundry are also on-site. This hotel is one of my all-time favorites, and one of *Travel & Leisure*'s, too: The magazine has dubbed the Kaanapali Beach Hotel as Hawaii's top hotel for value, and second-best hotel in the world for less than $200 a night.

See map p. 232. 2525 Kaanapali Pkwy., Kaanapali. ☎ *800-262-8450 or 808-661-0011. Fax: 808-667-5978.* www.kaanapalibeachhotel.com. *Self-parking: $5. Valet parking: $7. Rack rates: $169–$300 double, $255–$610 suite. Deals: Free-breakfast, free-car, free-night, golf, and romance packages are almost always available, as well as senior (50-plus) and corporate discounts and Internet specials. AE, DC, DISC, MC, V.*

Kahana Sunset
$$–$$$ West Maui (Kahana/Napili)

These oceanfront condos are an excellent value, one of Maui's best. The attractive wooden complex stair-steps down pretty terraced grounds to a petite but perfect white-sand-fringed swimming cove. The apartments are roomy enough to accommodate families, especially the two-bedrooms, which boast two full bathrooms. Every unit has nice island-style furniture; a complete kitchen with dishwasher, microwave, and even an icemaker in the fridge; washer/dryer; VCR and sleeper sofa in the living room; and big lanais with terrific views. Nestled between the coastline and the road above, the complex is much more private than many on this condo coast. On-site are a lovely heated pool and Jacuzzi, a separate kids' pool, barbecues, and beach showers. What's more, daily maid service (not a given in condos) makes it actually feel like vacation.

See map p. 235. 4909 Lower Honoapiilani Hwy., at the northern end of Kahana (8 miles north of Lahaina). ☎ *800-669-1488, 800-367-7052, or 808-669-8011. Fax: 808-669-9170.* www.kahanasunset.com *or* www.premier-hawaii.com. *Parking: Free! Rack rates: $130–$240 1-bedroom, $195–$375 2-bedroom. Three-night minimum. Deals: Car-and-condo packages, special rates, and Internet offers often available, so always mine for discounts. AE, MC, V.*

Kapalua Bay Hotel & Ocean Villas
$$$$$ West Maui (Kapalua)

The standard rooms are just a step above dowdy here, but a downright phenomenal setting and an open, airy island feeling brings loyal guests coming back for more. Sprawling over 18 oceanfront acres, the lush grounds command gorgeous views in every direction. The beach cove is virtually private and excellent for swimming, and golf and tennis facilities don't get any better. Additional facilities include two pools, a fitness center, a full-service beach activities desk, a great kids' program, and easy access to classes at the Kapalua Golf Academy and Kapalua Art School. The amenity-laden one- and two-bedroom Bay Villas — freestanding luxury homes with full kitchen, washer/dryer, and multiple lanais — are a great choice for families who have the necessary cash. Bay Villa guests also enjoy three private pools. For the ultimate in Kapalua luxury, score a stay in one of the new Coconut Grove Villas, where a mere $4,500 a night scores you a three-bedroom luxury oceanfront condo (at this price, it had better be luxurious) with round-the-clock butler service.

See map p. 235. 1 Bay Dr., Kapalua. ☎ *800-782-9488 or 808-669-5656. Fax: 808-669-4694.* www.kapaluabayhotel.com *or* www.luxurycollection.com. *Valet parking: $15. Rack rates: $390–$630 double; suites and villas $540–$4,500. Mandatory "resort fee" of $13 per day for welcome lei, local and toll-free phone calls, use of fitness center, lobby coffee and tea, in-room safe, incoming faxes, resort shuttles, self parking, and daily newspaper. Deals: Excellent package deals often include unlimited golf, activity, and romance options, so be sure to inquire. AE, DC, MC, V.*

Koa Resort
$–$$ South Maui (Kihei)

These nice condos sit right across the street from the ocean, and they make a good choice for active families on tight budgets: On-site are two tennis courts, a very nice swimming pool, a hot tub, and an 18-hole putting green. The spacious, privately owned one-, two-, and three-bedroom units are fully equipped and have plenty of room for even a large clan. Each comes with a full kitchen (complete with dishwasher, microwave, and cof-feemaker), a large lanai, ceiling fans, and a washer/dryer. The majority of two- and three-bedroom units have multiple bathrooms. The smaller units have showers only, so ask for one with a tub if it matters to you. Also, for maximum peace and quiet, ask for a unit removed from Kihei Road.

See map p. 236. 811 S. Kihei Rd. (between Kulanihakoi Street and Namauu Place), Kihei. Reservations c/o Bello Realty (Maui Beach Homes). ☎ *800-541-3060 or 808-879-3328. Fax: 808-875-1483.* www.bellomaui.com. *Parking: Free! Rack rates: $85–$110 1-bedroom, $100–$130 2-bedroom, $135–$180 3-bedroom. No credit cards.*

Lahaina Shores Beach Resort
$$$ West Maui (Lahaina)

This pleasant plantation-style complex of studios and one-bedroom suites sits right on the sand at the quiet end of Lahaina, within easy walking dis-tance of restaurants, shopping, and entertainment, but nicely out of the noisy fray. The hotel isn't exactly what you'd call stylish, but the pastel-hued units are comfortable and well-outfitted, and the price is right, espe-cially considering the on-the-beach location. Even the smallest unit is a spacious 550 square feet. Every one comes with a fully equipped, like-new kitchen with a microwave, sitting and dining areas, and a furnished lanai. Obviously, those units overlooking the waves and the island of Lanai across the channel are best, but the mountain views aren't shabby here, either. Outside is a lovely grassy lawn with a small pool, hot tub, and lounge chairs; just beyond it is a narrow stretch of swimming beach. (First-time surfers often learn on the low-riding waves here.) Other pleasantries include on-site laundry facilities, and tennis courts just across the street. *See map p. 232. 475 Front St. (near Shaw Street), Lahaina.* ☎ *800-642-6284 or 808-661-3339. Fax: 808-667-1145.* www.lahainashores.com *or* www.classic resorts.com. *Parking: $3. Rack rates: $180–$215 studio, $250–$280 1-bedroom, $290–$310 penthouse. Deals: Fifth-night-free specials offered at press time. Also ask about room-and-car packages, romance packages, and other available discounts. AE, MC, V.*

Mana Kai Maui
$–$$$ South Maui (Kihei)

Situated on a beautiful white-sand beach with excellent snorkeling, this eight-story hotel-condo hybrid is one of my favorite affordable choices. About half the units are hotel rooms, which are smallish but offer great value. The larger apartments feature full like-new kitchens, nice island-style furnishings, well-maintained baths, and open living rooms that lead to small lanais with ocean views. These units are older, but they're clean and comfortable, thanks to daily maid service. A coin-op laundry is located on each floor, a restaurant and lounge are downstairs, and a nice pool and a grassy lawn with beach chairs complement that fabulous beach. Management is friendly and conscientious. But the Mana Kai's real ace in the hole is its location: It lies on Wailea's doorstep, on the prettiest, most quiet end of Kihei, away from the strip-mall fray.

See map p. 236. 2960 S. Kihei Rd., Kihei (just before Wailea). ☎ *800-367-5242 (800-663-2101 from Canada) or 808-879-2778. Fax: 808-879-7825.* www.crhmaui.com. *Parking: Free! Rack rates: $95–$135 double hotel room, $175–$245 1-bedroom, $220–$300 2-bedroom. $25 reservation fee added to every booking. Deals: Excellent car-and-condo packages usually on offer; also ask about other available specials. Discounts available on monthly stays. AE, MC, V.*

Maui Coast Hotel
$$–$$$ South Maui (Kihei)

After a $2.5-million renovation a couple of years back, this affordable hotel is recommended for its fresh feel, great package deals, and its central (if rather unpretty) location, about a block from the beach and a short walk away from restaurants, shopping, and nightlife. This isn't the Four Seasons, so don't expect luxury — but the nicely designed rooms feature good-value extras, including sitting areas, coffeemakers, minifridges, Nintendo game systems, and furnished lanais. Add a pretty good restaurant, room service, free use of laundry facilities, two pools (one for the kids) with pool-side service, two Jacuzzis, a restaurant, and tennis courts (with lights for night play), and you end up with a full-service hotel at a bargain price. The suites offer families excellent value, especially if you can find a package to suit you.

See map p. 236. 2259 S. Kihei Rd. (at Ke Alii Alanui Drive), Kihei. ☎ 800-895-6284, 800-663-1144, or 808-874-6284. Fax: 808-875-4731. www.mauicoasthotel.com *or* www.westcoasthotels.com. *Parking: Free! Rack rates: $165–$185 double, $215 alcove suite, $255 1-bedroom suite. Deals: Inquire about golf and romance packages; room-and-car and fifth-night-free packages from $185 at press time. AE, DC, DISC, MC, V.*

Napili Bay

$$ **West Maui (Kahana/Napili)**

You can find this excellent bargain right on Napili's beautiful half-mile white-sand beach. This small, two-story complex is perfect for an afford-able romantic getaway; the sound of the waves creates a comfortable and relaxing atmosphere. The studio apartments are definitely small, but still, you have a full kitchen (with fridge and coffeemaker), a comfortable queen bed, a queen sleeper sofa that lets you sleep two more (if you don't mind lots of togetherness), TV with VCR, and a spacious lanai where you can sit and watch the sun set. Louvered windows and ceiling fans keep the units cool during the day. You have plenty of restaurants and a convenience store within walking distance, and you're about 10 to 15 minutes away from Lahaina and some great golf courses. Coin-op washer/dryers and a barbecue are nice features. The beach right out front is one of the best on the coast, with great swimming and snorkeling right out your door. Book early because this place fills up fast. Attention, Internet addicts: A few units have high-speed Internet access, so ask for one if you want it.

If Napili Bay is booked — or you need a larger unit — inquire with **Maui Beachfront Rentals** (☎ **888-661-7200** or 808-661-3500; www.mauibeach front.com), which offers good-value condo rentals throughout West Maui and in Maalaea, the appealing harbor town situated on the "neck" of Maui, on the way to Kihei.

See map p. 235. 33 Hui Dr. (off Lower Honoapiilani Highway, in Napili). Bookings han-dled by Maui Beachfront Rentals, 256 Papalaua St., Lahaina. ☎ 888-661-7200 or 808-661-3500. Fax: 808-661-5210. www.mauibeachfront.com. *Parking: Free! Rack rates: $125–$140 studio. Five-night minimum stay. Deal: 10-percent discount for stays of 21 days or more (lucky you!). MC, V.*

Napili Kai Beach Resort

$$$–$$$$ **West Maui (Kahana/Napili)**

Make yourselves right at home at this terrific complex of bright one- and two-story units embracing its own, wonderful white-sand snorkeling beach. All but a handful of basic hotel rooms have lovely tropical-modern décor, a large lanai, and top-notch kitchenettes (all with microwave, some with dishwasher); the hotel rooms have minifridges and coffeemakers. The one-bedrooms have sleeping accommodations in both rooms — usually a king bed in one room, two twin beds in the other — making this a great configuration for families; some even have a second bathroom. The two bedrooms can sleep as many as six or seven, and all have a second bath. The Kehaka suites unite two or three adjoining hotel rooms or studios in one value-priced package for families or shares. Most, but not all, units offer air-conditioning, so ask if you want it (you'll only need it in summer); otherwise, ceiling fans do the trick. The complex has a nice restaurant and bar, a beach pagoda serving daytime snacks and drinks and doling out snorkel gear for your free use, daily maid service, four pools and a hot tub, barbecues, a fitness room, dry cleaning as well as self-serve laundry, two putting greens, and the new Makai Massage and Bodywork Center. During family seasons (Easter, summer, and Christmas), kids 6 to 12 can enjoy the supervised Keiki Club, with two to three hours of activities daily (except Sunday). Help yourself to free coffee every morning, and tea every afternoon. This place has a very loyal following, so book way in advance.

See map p. 235. 5900 Honoapiilani Rd., Napili (at the extreme north end of Napili, next to Kapalua). ☎ *800-367-5030 or 808-669-6271. Fax: 808-669-0086.* www.napilikai. com. *Parking: Free! Rack rates: $190–$245 double, $220–$325 studio, $360–$515 1-bedroom or 2-room Keaka suite, $525–$735 2-bedroom or 3-room Keaka suite. Deals: Ask about room/car, fifth-night-free, bed-and-breakfast, and spa packages. AE, MC, V.*

Noelani Condominium Resort
$$ West Maui (Kahana/Napili)

I stand by all my recommendations, but that doesn't mean I don't get a teensy bit nervous when my boss says that she's going to take me up on one. So I was thrilled when she came home from Maui confirming my own observations — that this top-notch oceanfront condo is a stellar value and a great place to stay. All the well-maintained apartments sport kitchens, VCRs, ceiling fans (no air-conditioning), and spectacular ocean views; all but the studios have dishwashers and washer/dryers, too (laundry is available for studio dwellers). Best is the Antherium building, where apartments have ocean-facing lanais just 20 feet from the surf. Concierge and midweek maid service, two freshwater pools (one heated for night swimming), and an oceanfront Jacuzzi round out the good value. You're invited to a continental breakfast orientation on the first day of your stay, and mai tai parties in the evenings, while oceanfront barbecues are ideal for family outings. Next door is a sandy cove that's popular with snorkelers, but you may find yourself driving to a prettier beach; at these prices, you won't mind.

See map p. 235. 4095 Lower Honoapiilani Rd., Kahana. ☎ *800-367-6030 or 808-669-8374. Fax: 808-669-7904.* www.noelani-condo-resort.com. *Rack rates: $107–$142 studio, $157–$165 1-bedroom, $237 2-bedroom, $297 3-bedroom. Three-night minimum. Parking: Free! Deals: Check for 5-percent Internet booking discount, 10-percent discount on monthly stays, weekly discounts for seniors and AAA members, and honeymoon specials. AE, MC, V.*

Ohana Maui Islander
$$ **West Maui (Lahaina)**

Run by Outrigger, the value-minded, Hawaii-based hotel chain, this well-managed plantation-style complex offers one of Maui's best deals. The complex has a few hotel rooms (with coffeemaker and minifridge), but most of the spacious units are apartment-style studios and one- and two-bedrooms (some of which can be linked to form a three-bedroom), all with fully outfitted kitchens (some with microwaves). In the last couple of years, all the rooms have been renovated and brightened. The grounds are tropically lush and feature a coin-op laundry, tennis courts, barbecues, and a pool. The larger units are perfect for families; your kids will love the heart-of-Lahaina location, and you'll appreciate the tranquil ambience that results from a peaceful side-street location (a rarity in Lahaina). The complex is very quiet in general, but ask for a unit away from the highway for minimum intrusion. Rack rates are high, but discounts and stellar package deals abound.

See map p. 232. 660 Wainee St. (between Dickenson Street and Prison Street), Lahaina. ☎ 800-462-6262 or 808-667-9766. Fax: 808-661-3733. www.ohanahotels. com. *Parking: $5. Rack rates: $149 double, $179 studio, $209 1-bedroom, $299 2-bedroom. Deals: Better-than-average discounts for AAA and AARP members and seniors (50-plus), plus corporate, government, and military discounts. Ask about heavily discounted SimpleSaver rates and first-night-free, bed-and-breakfast, room-and-car, and other package deals. AE, DC, DISC, MC, V.*

Outrigger Palms at Wailea
$$$ **South Maui (Wailea)**

This freshly renovated villa-style apartment complex is an excellent choice if a sunny Wailea location appeals to you, but you just don't want to shell out for one of those ridiculously expensive resorts. The smart, upscale complex boasts contemporary Southwestern-style buildings spread over tidy greens. The modern apartments are quality-furnished and feature all the expected amenities, including a fully outfitted kitchen, fully furnished lanai, VCR, and washer/dryer. On-site is a very nice pool and hot tub, and championship Wailea golf and tennis facilities are right at hand. Daily maid service and concierge-style desk service are part of the package. Guests have easy access to excellent Ulua Beach, located just across the street.

See map p. 236. 3200 Wailea Alanui Dr., Wailea. ☎ 800-688-7444 or 808-879-5800. Fax: 808-874-3723. www.outrigger.com. *Parking: Free! Rack rates: $235–$265 1-bedroom, $279–$305 2-bedroom. Deals: Better-than-average discounts for AAA and AARP members and seniors (50-plus), plus corporate, government, and military discounts. Fifth-night-free, bed-and-breakfast, and room-and-car packages regularly on offer. AE, DC, DISC, MC, V.*

Plantation Inn
$$–$$$ **West Maui (Lahaina)**

This charming Victorian-style hotel in the heart of Lahaina offers both in-town convenience and old-fashioned romance. It's actually of 1990s vintage, but modern extras like soundproofing (a plus in downtown Lahaina), VCRs, fridges, and private bathrooms (some with shower only) don't detract from the period appeal. Deluxe rooms have lanais, and a few have kitchenettes. No. 17 is a standout for romantics, with a writing desk and a canopy bed, and light and spacious no. 20 features a terrific kitchen and makes an excellent family suite. The inn wraps around a nice large tiled pool and deck with a hot tub. On-site are coin-op laundry facilities and Gerard's, a top-notch French restaurant. The staff is excellent. You'll have to drive to a good beach, but Lahaina Harbor is a walk away (great for early-morning snorkel cruises).

See map p. 232. 174 Lahainaluna Rd. (between Wainee and Luakini streets), Lahaina. ☎ *800-433-6815 or 808-667-9225. Fax: 808-667-9293.* www.theplantationinn. com. *Parking: Free! (A rarity in Lahaina.) Rack rates: $157–$215 double, $220–$255 suite. Rates include continental breakfast. Deals: 10-percent discounts for long stays (7 nights or more). $10 discounts for AAA members, military personnel, and seniors over 50. Ask about gourmet, honeymoon, rental-car, and other packages, and check for great Internet specials. AE, DC, DISC, MC, V.*

Punahoa Beach Apartments
$–$$ South Maui (Kihei)

With the best location in Kihei, this friendly little complex is a bonafide beachfront bargain. The setting — off noisy, traffic-congested Kihei Road, on a quiet side street that faces the ocean — is fabulous: A grassy lawn extends down to the sand, where great offshore snorkeling awaits, and a popular surfing spot sits just next door. A coin-op laundry is on site, and markets and restaurants are but a stroll away. The apartments aren't fancy, but they're nicer than you'd expect for the money; each has a fully equipped kitchen and a lanai with great ocean views. Only one unit has air-conditioning, but ceiling fans draw in the trade winds. Guests keep coming back, so reserve your bargain unit as far in advance as possible.

See map p. 236. 2142 Iliili Rd. (off S. Kihei Road, near Kamaole Beach Park I), Kihei. ☎ *800-564-4380 or 808-879-2720. Fax: 808-875-9147.* www.punahoabeach.com. *Parking: Free! Rack rates: $94–$130 studio, $130–$200 1-bedroom, $160–$220 2-bedroom. 5-night minimum. Deals: 10-percent discount on stays of 10 nights or more Apr–Nov; 15-percent discount on stays of 21 nights or more year-round. AE, DC, DISC, MC, V.*

Ritz-Carlton Kapalua
$$$$–$$$$$ West Maui (Kapalua)

Situated at the end of the road in glorious Kapalua, Maui's most gorgeous planned resort, the Ritz is a destination resort by default alone. But you won't need to hop in the car every day in search of fun, because everything is right at hand. There's a small but fabulous beach and activities galore, including Kapalua's 54 holes of world-class, tournament-quality golf, as well as its justifiably renowned art school for vacationers who want to feed a creative appetite. The natural setting — on 50 terraced oceanfront acres, surrounded by century-old Norfolk pines and ironwood trees — is breathtaking. The spacious and tropically gorgeous rooms surpass the chain's usual high standard with heavenly featherbeds and extra-large marble baths. The dining is excellent (especially the superb sushi bar), the amenities are extensive (including a full-service spa and the outstanding Ritz Kids program, so bring 'em along), and the service is unsurpassed. Designed to look like a grand plantation house, the hotel is airy and graceful, with a gracious pool area, two hot tubs, and a professional croquet lawn. You get what you pay for at this spectacular resort — and, frankly, it's less overpriced than so many of Maui's resorts are these days. You may find it worthwhile to spend a few extra dollars for a club-level room; club guests enjoy individualized concierge service and five — yes, five — complimentary food presentations throughout the day, including a generous morning continental spread.

See map p. 235. 1 Ritz-Carlton Dr., Kapalua. ☎ 800-241-4333 or 808-669-6200. Fax: 808-665-0026. www.ritzcarlton.com. *Self-parking: Free! Valet parking: $10. Rack rates: $340–$500 double, suites from $610. Mandatory $15-per-night "resort fee" covers such amenities as shuttle service, use of fitness center, kids' program, and other extras. Deals: Romance, golf, room-and-car, and other packages often available. AE, DC, DISC, MC, V.*

Sheraton Maui
$$$$–$$$$$ West Maui (Kaanapali)

This expansive resort hotel boasts the best location on Kaanapali Beach: on a spectacular stretch of sand at the foot of Black Rock, one of Maui's best offshore snorkel spots. Much like its Kauai sister, this Sheraton is ideal for those who don't care for the forced formality or over-the-top excesses that often go hand-in-hand with resort vacations. The Sheraton Maui has an easygoing, open style, and great facilities for families and active types, including a nice fitness center and an open-air spa. After a recent renovation, the resort is looking great, with a new lagoonlike pool that features lava-rock waterways, wooden bridges, and an open-air whirlpool. You're greeted with a lei upon arrival, and then the valet takes you and your luggage straight to your room so you don't need to stand in line. The big rooms are simple yet comfortable and feature nice extras like minifridges and coffeemakers. A class of oversize two-room suites is dedicated to families. Restaurants and bars, a nightly torch-lighting and cliff-diving show, a terrific year-round kids' program, tennis courts, and lots of other extras further the appeal.

See map p. 232. 2605 Kaanapali Pkwy., Kaanapali. ☎ 800-782-9488 or 808-661-0031. Fax: 808-661-0458. www.sheraton-maui.com. *Valet parking: $5. Rack rates: $350–$630 double, family suite $750, luxury suites from $850. Mandatory "resort fee" of $14 per day for "free" self-parking, newspaper delivery, local and toll-free phone calls, in-room coffee, and fitness center access. Deals: Special rates and/or package deals are almost always available, including family, romance, and rental-car deals. Also ask for AAA-member and senior discounts, and look for Internet specials. AE, DC, DISC, MC, V.*

Wailea Marriott, an Outrigger Resort
$$$$–$$$$$ **South Maui (Wailea)**

This is the oldest and least glamorous of Wailea's resorts, but it's the most authentically Hawaiian of the bunch. The open-air 1970s-style hotel is airy, comfortable, and roomier than its younger neighbors, and a $25-million upgrade in 2000 added a dash of contemporary tropical luxury to an already-appealing property. Eight buildings, all low-rise except for an eight-story tower, are thoughtfully spread over 22 gracious acres, with lots of open parklike space and a half-mile of prime oceanfront. Minifridges, hair dryers, and lanais come standard in the spacious rooms. There's a comprehensive kids' program for *keiki* ages 5 to 13, plus three pools — including a kid-friendly water activities playground complete with a pair of water slides — and a terrific beach out front. A good indoor/outdoor restaurant and nightly Hawaiian entertainment, a coin-op laundry, a newly renovated fitness center, and the full-service Mandara Spa and salon make life easier for the grown-ups in your group, too.

See map p. 236. 3700 Wailea Alanui Dr., Wailea. ☎ *800-688-7444 or 808-879-1922. Fax: 808-874-8331.* www.outriggerwailea.com. *Parking: Free! Rack rates: $340–$525 double, $650–$3,000 suite. Deals: Better-than-average discounts for AAA and AARP members and seniors (50-plus), plus corporate, government, and military discounts. Fifth-night-free, bed-and-breakfast, room-and-car, and spa packages regularly on offer. AE, DC, DISC, MC, V.*

Westin Maui
$$$$$ **West Maui (Kaanapali)**

This hotel isn't quite as fabulous as the Grand Wailea (reviewed earlier in this chapter), but it's considerably cheaper, and your kids will be in water-hog heaven here, too, thanks to an 87,000-square-foot "Aquatic Playground" complete with swim-through grottos, waterfalls, and a 128-foot water slide. Rooms are on the smallish side, but they're stylishly contemporary in the W Hotels mode, and each and every one boasts a celestial Heavenly Bed, which will keep me coming back to Westin every time. The Heavenly Shower adds to the luxury in the bathroom, and your youngest ones can enjoy Westin's own plush-as-can-be Heavenly Cribs. A prime stretch of Kaanapali Beach and a wealth of facilities are on hand, including a well-outfitted fitness center, a brand-new 13,000-square-foot spa, and a full children's program. The stylish new Tropica restaurant isn't the best on Maui, but the innovative fare is just fine, and the oceanfront setting is both designer-sleek and romantic at the same time. Beware the timeshare salesperson in the lobby; if you get suckered in, don't say I didn't warn you.

See map p. 232. 2365 Kaanapali Pkwy., Kaanapali. ☎ *866-500-8313 or 808-667-2525. Fax: 808-661-5764.* www.westinmaui.com. *Valet parking: $10. Rack rates: $370–$680 double, $900–$3,000 suite. Mandatory "resort fee" of $15 per day for "free" self-parking, newspaper delivery, local and toll-free phone calls, in-room coffee, and fitness center access. Deals: Inquire about family, golf, wedding and honeymoon,* *and other packages, as well as special promotions that may include a sixth night free and/or resort credits. Promotional rates from $279 at press time. AE, DC, DISC, MC, V.*

The Whaler on Kaanapali Beach
$$$–$$$$$ West Maui (Kaanapali)

Not only would I stay at this beachfront midrise condo complex again, but I'd move in here if I could. The Whaler was built in the '70s and still sports a few "Me Decade" hallmarks, but in a good way — it feels like the kind of place where Jack Lord would keep his neighbor island bachelor pad. The relaxing atmosphere starts in the clean-lined, open-air lobby and continues in the impeccably kept apartments. They're privately owned and individually decorated, but all have fully equipped kitchens, VCRs, marble baths, and big, blue-tiled lanais. Many one-bedrooms have two full bathrooms, making them great for small families or shares. Most units have some kind of ocean view, but the garden views are also pleasant. Luxuries include daily maid service, plus bell and concierge services. The grounds are private and well-manicured, and on-site extras include an oceanfront pool and spa, an exercise room, and great dining and shopping at neighboring Whalers Village. Both property managing agents are reliable, so go with the best rate.

*See map p. 232. 2481 Kaanapali Pkwy., Kaanapali. ☎ 808-661-4861. Fax: 808-661-8315. Parking: Free! Rack rates: $235–$255 studio, $330–$485 1-bedroom, $600–$700 2-bedroom. Deals: Car-and-condo packages and other bargains often available through both booking agents, so always mine for specials and off-season discounts. Internet-only ePriceBreaker rates from $180 at press time. Ask for AAA, senior (50-plus), and corporate discounts, and other special rate programs. AE, DC, MC, V. Reserve through either one of the following companies: **Premier Resorts:** ☎ 888-211-7710.* www.the-whaler.com. ***Aston Resorts:*** *☎ 877-997-6667.* www.aston-hotels.com.

Home sweet vacation condo

Well-developed Maui abounds with condo developments, above and beyond my favorites listed in this chapter. Many complexes aren't handled by a single management company; instead, real-estate agencies tend to manage individual rentals throughout a variety of complexes in a given area. So if you want more choices, your best bet is to contact one of the following agencies, which can match you up with the unit that meets your needs and budget.

For a complete selection of upscale condos throughout sunny, luxury-minded Wailea, reach out to **Destination Resorts Hawaii** (☎ 877-347-0347 or 808-891-6200; www.destinationresortshi.com). Prices start as low as $175 or so for a studio and go as high as $1,200 per night for a spacious oceanfront four-bedroom.

If you like the sound of the tranquil Kapalua resort but the luxury hotel rates are out of your league, consider renting an elegant condo or vacation home through **Kapalua Villas** (☎ 800-545-0018 or 808-669-8088;

Staying off the beaten path

Situated at the far east end of the winding Hana Highway (Highway 36/360), isolated from the rest of the island by a three-hour drive, **Hana** makes a dreamy place to kick back and stay awhile, surrounded by little but lush natural beauty. One of Maui's most popular attractions is the drive along the winding 50-plus-mile route, one of the most beautiful scenic drives in the world. (I cover it in detail in Chapter 14.)

Most people drive to Hana and back again in a day, an entirely doable trip. It makes for one long day, however, as the curving highway has only one lane in each direction and 50 or so one-lane bridges. What's more, since the drive itself boasts so many wonderful stops, simply getting there can turn into an all-day event. So consider booking a place to stay at the end of the road in lush and lovely Hana for a couple of nights. It's a good idea, except for a few down sides: Many of the area's B&Bs and rentals require a two-night stay at least (sometimes longer); and, in general, Hana accommodations aren't cheap.

If you would like to stay in Hana but you can't afford the gloriously reinvented Hotel Hana-Maui (reviewed earlier in this chapter), I recommend contacting **Hawaii's Best Bed & Breakfasts** (☎ 800-262-9912 or 808-885-4550; www.bestbnb.com), which has a wonderful selection of B&Bs, inns, and vacation rentals the company has personally inspected and approved in Hana as well as other off-the-beaten-path areas of the island. Hawaii's Best holds all of the property owners it represents to a very high standard, so you can be assured of quality lodgings if you book with the company. Two of my absolute favorites are the **Heavenly Hana Inn** and **Hana Oceanfront Cottages**, both available through Hawaii's Best.

Bed & Breakfast Honolulu (☎ 800-288-4666 or 808-595-7533; www.hawaiibnb.com) also offers vacation rentals in Hana, in Kula on the slopes of Haleakala, and around the island. **Bed & Breakfast Hawaii** (☎ 800-733-1632 or 808-822-7771; www.bandb-hawaii.com) can also book you into a range of vacation homes and B&Bs throughout the islands, with prices starting at $65 a night.

www.kapaluavillas.com). Nightly rates range from $199 for a one-bedroom apartment with a fairway view to $469 for an oceanfront two-bedroom. Golf, tennis, rental-car, and romance packages are available.

 Bello Realty (☎ 800-541-3060 or 808-879-3328; www.bellomaui.com) represents affordable condos throughout the Kihei/Wailea area, with prices starting as low as $75 in the low season, $95 in the high season. Be sure to check out **Koa Resort,** one of Maui's best under-$125 bargains (reviewed earlier in this chapter).

Maui Beachfront Rentals (☎ 888-661-7200 or 808-661-3500; www.maui beachfront.com) offers good-value condo rentals throughout West Maui and in Maalaea, on the way to Kihei.

Condominium Rentals Hawaii (☎ 800-367-5242, 800-663-2101 from Canada, or 808-879-2778; www.crhmaui.com) has moderately priced condos throughout Kihei and handles the **Mana Kai** (reviewed earlier in this chapter). The car-and-condo packages and other regular specials can really up the value-to-dollar ratio on their units.

You can choose from a range of good apartments along West Maui's condo coast through **Maui Beachfront Rentals** (☎ 888-661-7200 or 808-661-3500; www.mauibeachfront.com). One of their best values for budget-minded couples are the studios at the **Napili Bay,** which start out as low as $125. They may even be able to save you a few dollars at two of my favorite Kaanapali Beach condo complexes, **The Whaler** and **Kaanapali Alii** (reviewed earlier in this chapter). Ask about packages that include a free night or a rental car.

A southern California-based agency, **Hawaii Condo Exchange** (☎ 800-442-0404 or 323-436-0300; www.hawaiicondoexchange.com), acts as a consolidator for condo properties throughout the islands. They represent a number of excellent properties on Maui.

Dining Out

Maui's dining scene is excellent — maybe even better than Oahu's in overall scope and innovation. The lovely and charismatic Valley Isle has attracted so many top chefs from around the globe that choosing among their outposts can be a trying business.

But be prepared to pay for the privilege of dining on Maui. Generally speaking, you can expect to spend more for dinner here than you will on the other islands. Maui is overflowing with restaurants, so choice isn't a problem, but you'll have to navigate a minefield of overpriced, mediocre-quality restaurants in order to get value for your dollar. The listings in this chapter offer a recommendable course of action, whether you're looking for a splurge-worthy special-occasion restaurant or a satisfying casual meal that relieves the pressure on your wallet.

Lahaina, on Maui's west shore, is the heart of the island's dining scene. Luckily, it's quite convenient — no more than a half-hour's drive or so from any of the beach resorts (45 minutes from Wailea). Many of its restaurants — even the affordable ones — boast front-row, on-the-water seats for spectacular sunset-watching. But nowhere else is the minefield of mediocrity more explosive, so choose carefully.

In the restaurant listings that follow, each restaurant name is followed by a number of dollar signs, ranging from one ($) to five ($$$$$). The dollar signs are meant to give you an idea of what a complete dinner for one person — with appetizer, main course, dessert, a drink, tax, and tip — is likely to cost. The price categories go like this:

$	Cheap eats — less than $15 per person
$$	Still inexpensive — $15 to $25
$$$	Moderate — $25 to $40
$$$$	Pricey — $40 to $70
$$$$$	Ultraexpensive — more than $70 per person

If you're on a budget, don't order the most expensive entree and bottle of wine so that you can still enjoy yourself at the more expensive restaurants. To give you a further idea of how much you can expect to spend, I also include the price range of main courses in the listings. (Prices can change at any time, of course, but restaurants usually don't raise their prices by more than a dollar or two at any given time.)

The state adds 4 percent in sales tax to every restaurant bill. A 15- to 20-percent tip for the server is standard, just like on the mainland.

Aloha Mixed Plate
$ West Maui (Lahaina)   Local Hawaiian

This charming, cheap patio restaurant specializes in traditional foods of Hawaii: great _saimin_ (ramen noodle soup), teriyaki chicken, finger-lickin' Korean-style barbecue ribs, coconut shrimp, mahimahi sandwiches, stir-frys, and other local staples, plus burgers (both garden and beef). Most dishes are served as complete meals (a style called "plate lunch"), accompanied by "two scoop" rice and a scoop of macaroni salad for a sumo-sized starchfest, making them a real bargain in the process. Brought to you by the people behind the Old Lahaina Luau (the top luau in the islands, described later in this chapter), this colorful place serves up the best local food around. Don't expect gourmet — this is Hawaii's version of paper-plate eats. Still, Aloha Mixed Plate offers real value — and in an oceanfront setting to boot! The restaurant even has a bar, so you can celebrate the sunset with a tropical cocktail or wash down your hearty meal with an ice-cold beer.

See map p. 255. 1285 Front St. (across from Lahaina Cannery Mall), Lahaina. ☎ **808-661-3322.** www.alohamixedplate.com. _Reservations not necessary. Pupus, burgers, salads, and noodles: $3.25–$8; plate lunches $7–$14. MC, V. Open: Lunch and dinner daily._

Charley's Restaurant & Saloon
$$ Central Maui (Paia)   American/International

Before I set out on any drive to Hana, I always make time for breakfast at Charley's. This is my favorite breakfast place on Maui, thanks to over-stuffed breakfast burritos, fluffy omelets, mac-nut pancakes, and eggs Benedict with perfectly puckery hollandaise. Lunch and dinner bring burgers, kiawe-smoked ribs and marlin, calzones baked fresh to order, and a

Maui's Restaurants

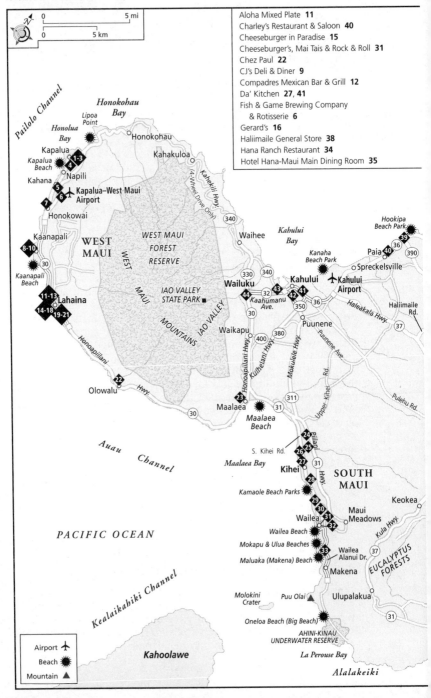

Aloha Mixed Plate **11**
Charley's Restaurant & Saloon **40**
Cheeseburger in Paradise **15**
Cheeseburger's, Mai Tais & Rock & Roll **31**
Chez Paul **22**
CJ's Deli & Diner **9**
Compadres Mexican Bar & Grill **12**
Da' Kitchen **27, 41**
Fish & Game Brewing Company
   & Rotisserie **6**
Gerard's **16**
Haliimaile General Store **38**
Hana Ranch Restaurant **34**
Hotel Hana-Maui Main Dining Room **35**

Hula Grill **10**
I'o **19**
Joe's Bar & Grill **30**
Kimo's **17**
Kula Lodge & Restaurant **37**
Kula Sandalwoods Restaurant **36**
Lahaina Coolers **18**
The Maalaea Waterfront Restaurant **23**
Mama's Fish House **39**
Mañana Garage **42**
Maui Tacos **4, 14, 28, 43**
Nick's Fishmarket **33**
Pacific'o **20**
Pizza Paradiso **7, 8**

The Plantation House **1**
Roy's Kahana Bar & Grill/Roy's Nicolina Restaurant **5**
Roy's Kihei **25**
A Saigon Cafe **44**
Sansei Seafood Restaurant & Sushi Bar **3, 26**
Sarento's on the Beach **29**
Stella Blues Cafe & Deli **24**
Tommy Bahamas's Tropical Café **32**
Vino **2**

Luaus
The Feast at Lele **21**
Old Lahaina Luau **13**

> **For detailed locations, see the following maps
> in this chapter:**
> *"Kapalua, Napili & Kahana Accommodations & Dining"*
> *"Lahaina Restaurants"*
> *"South Maui Accommodations & Dining"*

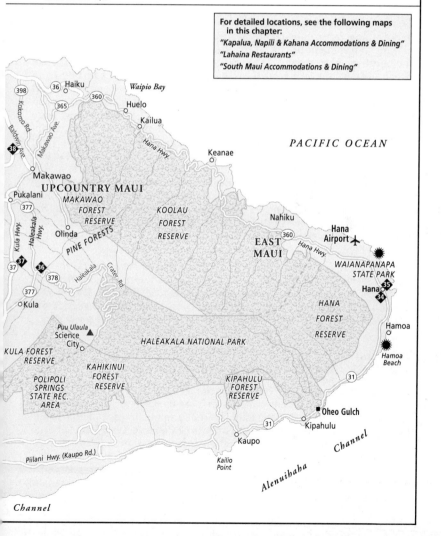

variety of vegetarian delights, from veggie lasagna to bounteous salads and stir-frys. Expect nothing in the way of ambience, but service is friendly, and prices are low, making Charley's worth the half-hour drive from Kihei for an affordable and unpretentious meal, even if you're not heading to Hana. The adjacent roadhouse-style bar serves up a good selection of microbrews.

See map p. 252. 142 Hana Hwy. (at Baldwin Avenue), Paia. ☎ *808-579-9453. Reservations not taken. Main courses: $6–$12 at breakfast and lunch, $12–$25 at dinner. AE, DC, DISC, MC, V. Open: Breakfast, lunch, and dinner daily.*

Cheeseburger in Paradise/Cheeseburgers, Mai Tais & Rock 'n' Roll
$–$$ West Maui (Lahaina)/South Maui (Wailea) American

This oceanfront burger joint is a perennial favorite thanks to an always-lively atmosphere, consistently terrific food, and million-dollar views, all at bargain-basement prices. At the original Lahaina location — the first in the burgeoning minichain — the second-level open-air room offers a prime ocean view from every seat; the Wailea location is set back farther from the surf, but an upstairs location gives it its own terrific ocean vistas, and the retro-hip décor sets just the right mood. No matter which location you choose, the tropical-style burgers are first class all the way — big, juicy mounds of natural Angus beef, served on fresh-baked buns, and guaranteed to satisfy even the most committed connoisseur. Chili dogs, fish and chips, crispy onion rings, and spiced fries broaden the menu. Dieters and vegetarians can opt for the excellent garden and tofu burgers, a lean chicken breast sandwich, or a meal-size salad. Two full bars boast a festive, first-rate menu of tropical drinks (including one of the best piña coladas in the islands). There's lively music every night to round out the party-hearty appeal at both locations. You can even launch your day oceanside with hearty omelets, French toast, eggs Benedict, and other morning faves.

See map p. 236. In Lahaina: 811 Front St. (oceanside near the end of Lahainaluna Road), Lahaina. ☎ *808-661-4855.* www.cheeseburgermaui.com. *In Wailea: At the Shops at Wailea, 3750 Wailea Alanui Dr., second floor.* ☎ *808-874-8990.* www.cheeseburgerwailea.com. *Reservations not taken. Main courses: $8–$17 (burgers less than $10). AE, DISC, MC, V. Open: Breakfast, lunch, and dinner daily.*

Chez Paul
$$$$–$$$$$ West Maui (Lahaina) Provençal French

Boasting cozy country-style décor, luscious French cuisine that could hold its own in Paris, and career waiters who care more about your needs than tomorrow's surf report, Chez Paul is a real original in a sea of chic island hot spots. Under the guiding hand of Patrick Callarec, Chez Paul is better than ever. Locally grown veggies and the freshest catches of the day make copious appearances, but preparations are single-mindedly rich and classic: Witness such winning dishes as out-of-the-shell Kona lobster served in a delicate saffron-basil cream sauce; crispy duck roasted with exotic island fruits and bathed in sweet-tart pineapple juice; and a brilliant filet mignon

Lahaina Restaurants

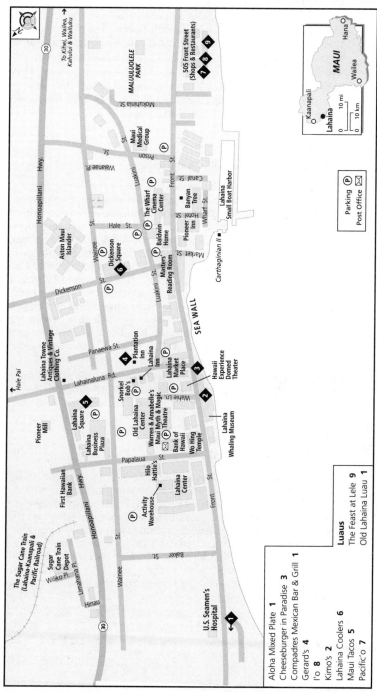

Aloha Mixed Plate **1**
Cheeseburger in Paradise **3**
Compadres Mexican Bar & Grill **1**
Gerard's **4**
I'o **8**
Kimo's **2**
Lahaina Coolers **6**
Maui Tacos **5**
Pacific'o **7**

Luaus
The Feast at Lele **9**
Old Lahaina Luau **1**

in tricolor peppercorn sauce. Save room for dessert, because the deliciously sweet treats (such as a classic vanilla crème brulee served in a Maui pineapple shell) are beautifully presented. Be prepared for a tab that's heftier than it needs to be, but if you're willing to pay for quality, you won't be disappointed.

See map p. 252. 1 Olowalu Village, Honoapiilani Highway, Olowalu (4 miles south of Lahaina, on the mountain side of the highway). ☎ *808-661-3843.* www.chezpaul. net. *Reservations highly recommended. Main courses: $29–$39. AE, MC, V. Open: Dinner nightly.*

CJ's Deli & Diner

$ West Maui (Kaanapali)   American

"Comfort food at comfort prices" — that's the motto at CJ's, and this cheap-chic diner does a great job delivering. An extensive chalkboard menu hangs from the brightly colored wall above the open-air kitchen; the friendly staff stands behind the counter, just waiting to cook up your order. Food runs the gamut from hearty farmer-style breakfasts to hearty veggie-packed salads to half-pound burgers and classic reubens to roasted chicken and fresh-grilled fish. There's a pleasing local flair to the offerings. Don't miss the hot malasadas, a light and flaky sweet pastry, sort of like a powdered-sugar-covered donut hole, which is one of the islands' favorite sweet treats; CJ's can be downright addictive. Food can be prepared for takeout or plated to enjoy in the casual, colorful dining room; there's even an Internet-connected computer on hand so you can check your e-mail while you wait. Stop by for a box lunch if you're heading to Hana, Haleakala, or the beach. There's also a kids' menu on hand.

See map p. 252. At the Kaanapali Fairway Shops, 2580 Keka'a Dr. (facing Honoapiilani Highway, on the access road), Kaanapali. ☎ *808-667-0968. Reservations not accepted. Main courses: $6-$13. MC, V. Breakfast, lunch, and early dinner daily.*

Compadres Mexican Bar & Grill

$$ West Maui (Lahaina)   Mexican

This big, airy, comfortable, and lively restaurant serves up high-quality South-of-the-Border fare and the best margaritas on the island. The monster menu features all your Mexican favorites, including eight kinds of enchiladas, a half-dozen quesadillas, and four variations on the chile relleno. The fish tacos are always first rate (you can even get them to go at a new takeout window), and you can't go wrong with the huevos rancheros at any time of day. The chips are light and greaseless, the guacamole is fresh and chunky, and the combos are big enough to satisfy even Hungryman appetites, making Compadres an excellent value in an over-priced restaurant town.

See map p. 255. In the Lahaina Cannery Mall, 1221 Honoapiilani Hwy. (on the Front Street side of the mall, facing Aloha Mixed Plate), Lahaina. ☎ *808-661-7189. Reservations accepted. Main courses: $10–$20 (most less than $15). AE, DC, DISC, MC, V. Open: Breakfast, lunch, and dinner daily.*

Da' Kitchen
$ **South Maui (Kihei)/Central Maui (Kahului)** **Local Hawaiian**

Just ask any local: Da' Kitchen is the place to come for the most authentic local grinds on the island. The simple but comfortable Kihei closet is the original; come for the food, not the mood. Place your order at the counter and then grab one of the handful of tables to chow down on the extra-hearty eats. All the classic Hawaiian plate lunches come with two scoops of rice, plus potato *and* macarani salad (you can request a green salad instead) — trust me, you won't leave here hungry. Top-notch choices include pulled kalua pork, slow-cooked until tender and seasoned with Hawaiian salt; chicken katsu, breaded in panko crumbs and served with Japanese barbecue sauce; and loco moco, a hamburger patty grilled, topped with two fried eggs, and smothered in gravy (a dieter's delight!). There's also a yummy lemon chicken and a couple of teriyaki dishes for more mainstream tastes, plus big Asian-style noodle bowls, hamburgers, and a better-than-you'd-expect Chinese chicken salad. The newer Kahului location is more cafe-style, with full table service.

See map p. 252. **In Kihei:** *In Rainbow Mall, 2439 S. Kihei Rd. (at the south end of town).* ☎ *808-875-7782. Reservations not taken. Open: Late breakfast (from 9 a.m.), lunch, and dinner daily.* **In Kahului:** *In Triangle Square, 425 Koloa St. (off Dairy Road).* ☎ *808-871-7782. Reservations not taken. Open: Lunch and dinner Mon–Fri, lunch only Sat, closed Sun. At both locations, most items $6–$12, plate lunches $7–$13. No credit cards.*

Fish & Game Brewing Company & Rotisserie
$$$ **West Maui (Kahana)** **Seafood/Steaks**

This restaurant has all the style of a bad toupee, but I really like it anyway. It's part brewpub, part sports bar (with live nightly music), part fish market, and part clubby restaurant — but despite the schizophrenic ambience and straight-outta-the-'80s décor, the kitchen's got it going on. The fare is straight-ahead seafood and grill fare. Start with a half-dozen oysters on the half-shell, or maybe the kiawe (mesquite)-grilled brewer's sausage, and then move on to a first-rate fresh catch or something meatier, if you've eaten your fill of seafood in Hawaii. Fishes are prepared to your taste, one of four ways: blackened Cajun style, habañero cornmeal crusted, seven spiced with soy mirin glaze, and "just plain" grilled. (Beware the seven spiced — five of them are peppers. I like the "just plain" best, because it lets the quality of the fish shine.) The 10-oz. kiawe-smoked prime rib is a steal at $19.95, especially considering the high quality of the cut. The rotisserie also produces a lovely herb-rubbed chicken with a golden crust. All the housemade beers are terrific — especially the amber-hued Plantation Pale Ale and the dark, robust Wild Hog Stout — and I found the service to be an ideal combination of easygoing and attentive. A kids' menu is on hand for family meals, plus a late-night menu of casual bar fare in case the munchies strike between 10:30 p.m. and 1 a.m.

See map p. 235. In the Kahana Gateway Shopping Center, 4405 Honoapiilani Hwy. (Hwy. 30), Kahana. ☎ *808-669-3474.* www.fishandgamerestaurant.com. *Reservations recommended. Main courses: $7–$14 at lunch, $18 to $33 at dinner (most less than $25; steak-and-lobster combo $46). AE, DC, DISC, MC, V. Open: Lunch and dinner daily.*

Gerard's
$$$$–$$$$$ **West Maui (Lahaina)** **New French**

Chez Paul's has a slight edge cuisine-wise, but Gerard's boasts an even more romantic setting, especially for couples who prefer to swoon in an alfresco setting. A regular winner of the *Wine Spectator* Award of Excellence and named "Maui's little French jewel" by *Bon Appetit* magazine, Gerard's offers refined cuisine that never disappoints. Gerard Reversade excels at seeking out the freshest local ingredients and preparing them in traditional Gallic style. My favorite among the starters is the shiitake and oyster mushrooms in puff pastry, but the foie gras terrine is a must for those who indulge. A wealth of meat and poultry dishes are at hand (including a terrific rack of lamb in mint crust), plus divine daily fresh fish preparations that depend on what the boats bring in. Inventive desserts provide a memorable finale, unless you opt for a cheese plate, served with toasted country bread and poached pears. Service is appropriately attentive.

See map p. 255. In the Plantation Inn, 174 Lahainaluna Rd. (between Wainee and Luakini streets), Lahaina. ☎ *877-661-8939 or 808-661-8939.* www.gerardsmaui. com. *Reservations highly recommended. Main courses: $29.50–$39.50. AE, DC, DISC, MC, V. Open: Dinner nightly.*

Haliimaile General Store
$$$$ **Upcountry Maui** **Hawaii Regional**

This simple but attractive plantation-style restaurant is a nice choice for those who prefer to sample top-quality island-style cooking in a refreshingly casual and pretension-free setting. Star chef Bev Gannon presents a heartier-than-average Hawaii Regional menu full of American homestyle favorites prepared with an island spin. Look for such signature satisfiers as succulent barbecued pork ribs; long-simmering coconut fish and shrimp curry; pumpkinseed-crusted scallops accompanied by a roasted veggie enchilada in mole sauce; and New Zealand rack of lamb prepared Hunan style. The desserts — created by Bev's daughter Teresa Gannon, now a well-known chef in her own right — are better than Mom used to make; I never miss the light and tangy *lilikoi* (passion fruit) tart. Prices have crept higher than they should have, but it's still worth the 45-minute drive Upcountry (but if you're in South Maui, head to sibling restaurant Joe's Bar & Grill first; see review later in this chapter).

See map p. 252. 900 Haliimaile Rd., Haliimaile (ha-lee-ee-MY-lee). From the Hana Highway (Highway 36), take Highway 37 for 4½ miles to Haliimaile Road (Highway 371); turn left and drive 1½ miles to the restaurant. ☎ *808-572-2666.* www.haliimailegeneralstore.com. *Reservations recommended. Main courses: $10–$20 at lunch, $22–$32 at dinner. AE, DC, MC, V. Open: Lunch Mon–Fri, dinner nightly.*

Another dining option in Hana

Hana's other option is the more casual, affordable, and freshly renovated **Hana Ranch Restaurant** ($–$$$), in town on the mountain side of Hana Highway (☎ **808-248-8255**). At lunchtime, choose between the informal takeout window, serving up local fare like teriyaki chicken and hot dogs that you can enjoy at outdoor picnic tables, or the indoor all-you-can-eat lunch buffet ($11–$15). The restaurant is also open for pizza on Wednesday evenings and a sit-down dinner on Friday and Saturday for somewhat higher priced fare such as New York steaks and grilled fish (reservations required).

Hotel Hana-Maui Main Dining Room
$$$$ East Maui   Continental-Island Fusion

This formerly dowdy luxury resort has been reborn, and, thankfully, so has the dining room. Now under the guiding hand of executive chef (and Hawaii native) Larry Quirit, it's once again the best restaurant in Hana. Quirit has crafted a fresh new menu that matches island-style ingredients and regional island influences with contemporary techniques and flavors. Expect lots of local fresh fish, meats, and crisp Maui-grown greens in elegant and pleasing preparations. It's a perfect match for the freshly remade dining room, with its elegant island-style blend of traditional materials, ocean views, and original island-inspired art that includes the breathtaking *Red Sails* painting, with its imagery of the first Hawaiians voyaging to the islands. Come for dinner on Friday to enjoy live island-style music and dance.

If you're coming for dinner or cocktails in the adjacent Paniolo Lounge, please adhere to the restaurant's dress code: collared shirts and slacks or dress shorts for men, skirts or slacks for women.

See map p. 252. In the Hotel Hana-Maui, Hana Highway, Hana. ☎ *808-248-8211. Reservations recommended for dinner. Main courses: $10–$20 at breakfast and lunch, $18–$33 at dinner. AE, DC, MC, V. Open: Breakfast, lunch, and dinner daily.*

Hula Grill
$–$$$ West Maui (Kaanapali)   Steaks/Seafood

My favorite Kaanapali restaurant features a killer beachfront setting and a midpriced island-style steak-and-seafood menu brought to you from Big Island star chef Peter Merriman and the people behind Waikiki's renowned Duke's Canoe Club. Kissed by the trade winds, the patio is the ideal setting for sunset-watchers, and tiki torches make for after-dark magic. The wide-ranging menu has something for everyone, including superb wood-grilled or macadamia-crusted fresh island fish, yummy barbecued pork ribs in mango barbecue sauce, or steamed Alaskan king crab legs (with a side of top sirloin, if you like). Those on a budget can stick to the bar menu, which features Merriman's famous *poke* rolls (filled with seared fresh ahi), kiawe-fired (mesquite-fired) pizzas, and creative salads and sandwiches. Hawaiian music, hula dancing at sunset, and well-blended tropical drinks dressed up with umbrellas round out the carefree island vibe. If you want a patio table, you should request one when you book. The more casual Barefoot Bar invites you to sit with your toes in the sand while you enjoy burgers, fish, pizza, and salads.

See map p. 252. In Whaler's Village, 2435 Kaanapali Pkwy., Kaanapali Beach. ☎ *808-667-6636.* www.hulapie.com. *Reservations recommended for dinner. Main courses: $20–$29 at dinner (most less than $25). Barefoot Bar menu (served all day): $8–$16. AE, DISC, MC, V. Open: Lunch and dinner daily.*

I'o
$$$$ West Maui (Lahaina)   New Pacific

You can't get closer to the ocean than I'o's alfresco tables, some of which sit just feet from the surf (request one when you book). Overseen by award-winning chef James McDonald, I'o is a multifaceted joy, with winningly innovative fusion cuisine, first-rate service, and a top-notch wine list that has won the *Wine Spectator* Award of Excellence. The seafood-heavy menu features copious Pacific Rim accents, plus a few creative twists courtesy of the Western hemisphere: The tropical seafood cocktail gets a chipotle tomatillo sauce for zest; Maine lobster tails are stir-fried and served with sweet potatoes flamed in a dark rum and mango Thai curry sauce; the grilled lamb tenderloin lies on a bed of wasabe-spiced mashies; and the fresh catch gets a crust of foie gras for the ultimate decadence. Each dish is paired with a recommended wine for easy ordering. Skip the silken purse appetizer, though — it's an overrated signature. A full, friendly bar (including a tempting array of specialty martinis) makes this restaurant an all-around terrific choice.

You might also consider I'o's equally divine, equally pricey, and equally well-situated sister restaurant, **Pacific'o** ($$$$), also overseen by star chef James McDonald and located at 505 Front St. (☎ **808-667-4341;** www.pacificomaui.com), serving lunch daily as well as dinner.

See map p. 255. 505 Front St. (on the ocean at Shaw Street), Lahaina. ☎ *808-661-8422.* www.iomaui.com. *Reservations recommended. Main courses: $23–$34 ($59 for 4 lobster tails). AC, MC, V. Open: Dinner nightly.*

Joe's Bar & Grill
$$$$ South Maui (Wailea)   New American/Hawaii Regional

I prefer Joe's over its more widely lauded sister restaurant, the Haliimaile General Store (reviewed earlier in this chapter). It's a little slicker than its Upcountry sibling and serves a similarly pleasing menu of American home cooking with a island-regional twist, this time without the strong Asian influence. Top choices include the signature grilled applewood salmon, smoky and sublime; a creamy lobster and seafood pot pie with a light and flaky crust; and innovative preparations of such classics as meatloaf, rack of lamb, and center-cut pork chops. The wood-paneled room is casual and welcoming, rock 'n' roll memorabilia lines the walls (Joe Gannon managed Alice Cooper for years), and open-air views take in the tennis action below. At night, low lighting and well-spaced tables make for a surprisingly romantic ambience, but the room takes on a laid-back liveliness after it fills up. The service is top-notch.

See map p. 236. At the Wailea Tennis Center, 131 Wailea Ike Place (between Wailea Alanui Driveand Piilani Highway.), Wailea. ☎ *808-875-7767. Reservations recommended. Main courses: $18–$32. AE, DC, DISC, MC, V. Open: Dinner nightly.*

Kimo's
$$$ West Maui (Lahaina)   Steaks/Seafood

This casual waterfront restaurant boasts a winning combination of affordable prices, good food, and great ocean views. The menu isn't quite as innovative as that of sister restaurant Hula Grill, but it still offers a reliable and satisfying selection of fresh fish preparations (a good half-dozen are available to choose from), hefty sirloins served with garlic mashed potatoes, and island favorites like koloa pork ribs with plum barbecue sauce. With Caesar salads and sides included, dinners make for a very good deal, and there's nightly entertainment to boot. Dessert lovers should save room for Kimo's own Hula Pie, macadamia-nut ice cream in a chocolate-wafer crust with fudge and whipped cream — a decadent island delight.

See map p. 255. 845 Front St., Lahaina. ☎ *808-661-4811.* www.kimosmaui.com. *Reservations recommended for dinner. Main courses: $7–$12 at lunch; $17–$26 at dinner, including Kimo's Caesar salad. AE, MC, V. Open: Lunch and dinner daily.*

Lahaina Coolers
$$ West Maui (Lahaina)   American/Eclectic

Billing itself as "The *Cheers* of the Pacific," this lively, friendly spot serves up affordable eats at breakfast, lunch, and dinner that are a step above the standard. Despite its side-street location, this happy-hour favorite maintains an appealingly laid-back tropical vibe. Start the morning with an over-stuffed breakfast burrito with black beans and rice or fluffy Portuguese sweet-bread French toast. For lunch try one of the tropical pizzas (I love the Evil Jungle Pizza, with grilled chicken and spicy Thai peanut sauce), or perhaps a grilled portabello mushroom sandwich on focaccia bread. The famous fresh fish tacos and homemade pastas are excellent dinner choices, follow by $1.75 drafts and crispy calamari to munch on. The full dinner menu is served until midnight (tropical cocktails until 2 a.m.), making this a Hawaii late-night rarity. Live music — often blues, sometimes folk or rock — adds to the lively atmosphere on Saturdays and on the occasional weeknight.

See map p. 255. 180 Dickenson St. (between Front and Wainee streets), Lahaina. ☎ *808-661-7082.* www.lahainacoolers.com. *Reservations accepted. Main courses: $7.50–$11 at breakfast and lunch, $10–$22 at dinner (most less than $15). AE, DC, DISC, MC, V. Open: Breakfast, lunch, and dinner daily.*

The Maalaea Waterfront Restaurant
$$$$ South Maui   Continental/Seafood

Family-run for many years, this decidedly unhip seafooder is a tradition-alist's delight. The European-style waitstaff, which serves every dish with a professional flourish, regularly wins the annual "Best Service" and "Best Seafood" awards from the *Maui News*. A half-dozen fresh catches are usu-ally on hand, and you can choose the preparation you'd prefer. Your choices include à la meuniere; baked and stuffed with Alaskan king crab-meat; Provençal style (sauteed with olives, peppers, and tomatoes in garlic and olive oil); and Cajun spiced. But my absolute favorite is the *en Bastille,* in which the fish is "imprisoned" (get it?) in grated potato and sauteed and then crowned with scallions, mushrooms, tomatoes, and meuniere sauce — yum! Meat and poultry are on hand for nonseafood-eaters, includ-ing a well-prepared steak Diane. The bread comes with a delectable beer cheese spread (how retro is that?), and your server will prepare your Caesar salad tableside if you ask. Book a table on the lanai before sunset for pretty harbor views.

See map p. 252. In the Milowai Condominium, 50 Hauoli St., Maalaea (north of Kihei). ☎ *808-244-9028.* www.waterfrontrestaurant.net. *Reservations recom-mended. To get there: From Highway 30, take the second right into Maalaea Harbor and then turn left. Main courses: $18–$38. AE, DC, DISC, MC, V. Open: Dinner nightly.*

Mama's Fish House
$$$$$ Central Maui Seafood

Despite pay-through-the-nose prices and a touch of touristiness, Mama's is my favorite restaurant on Maui, and one of my all-time favorite Hawaii restaurants — and one of its most popular, too. The tiki-room setting is an archetype of timeless Hawaii cool, and fresh island fish simply doesn't get any better than this; it's all caught locally, with the provenance indicated on the menu. ("Opakapaka caught by Earle Kiawi bottom-fishing outside his homeport of Hana Bay.") The beachhouse dining room has ambience in excess, with lavish tropical floral arrangements, sea breezes ruffling the tapa tablecloths, soft lighting, and gorgeous views galore. The day's catches are the stars of the show, and you choose from four prepara-tions. My favorite is the Pua Me Hua Hana, two of the day's fresh catches steamed gently and served traditional luau style with purple Molokai sweet potato, baked banana, fresh island fruit, and a fresh young coconut — plates just don't get prettier than this. The service is sincere if a bit serious ("And what will the lady have?"), but, somehow, it suits the mood. A lengthy list of tropical drinks (dressed with umbrellas, of course) completes the tropical-romantic picture. A kids' menu is on hand for fam-ilies. It's a real island-style delight!

See map p. 252. 799 Poho Place, Paia (just off the Hana Highway, 1½ miles past Paia town). ☎ *808-579-8488.* www.mamasfishhouse.com. *Reservations recom-mended for lunch, required for dinner. Main courses: $22–$32 at lunch, $32–$49 at dinner. AE, DC, DISC, MC, V. Open: Lunch and dinner daily.*

Mañana Garage
$$ Central Maui (Kahului)   Latin American

This recent addition to the Maui dining scene draws locals and visitors alike from all corners with a winning indoor/outdoor setting and creative, nicely prepared Latin American cuisine that scores on all fronts. The boldly colored décor could be described as retro-industrial; it's cute and fun, but the groovy patio is the place to be. Having to pay for chips and salsa is kind of a drag ($5–$7.50 with guacamole!), but all is forgiven after the basket arrives with its trio of zesty "samba" salsas. Everything just gets better from there. At lunchtime, I like the adobo barbecued duck and sweet potato quesadilla, mildly spiced with delicate green chiles, and the classic pressed Cuban sandwich. At dinner, you might start with green tomatoes, fried just right with smoked mozzarella and slivered red onions, or the *arepas con queso* — cornmeal and cheese griddle cakes topped with smoked salmon "pastrami," caper tobiko relish, and wasabi sour cream that manage to meld pan-continental flavors and textures without a hitch. For your main course, consider the pumpkin-crusted shrimp, a black-pepper-rubbed New York strip steak grilled in roasted pepper butter, or the seafood-rich paella. You can't go wrong with anything on the menu; every pan-Latin dish sings with flavor. Live entertainment adds to the cha-cha ambience Tuesday through Saturday evenings. It's a real winner!

See map p. 252. 33 Lono Ave. (at Kaahumanu Avenue), Kahului. ☎ **808-873-0220.** *Reservations recommended, especially for Fri–Sat dinner. Main courses $7–$13 at lunch, $13–$26 at dinner. AE, DC, DISC, MC, V. Open: Lunch and dinner Mon–Sat, dinner only Sun.*

Maui Tacos
$ Central Maui/West Maui (Lahaina, Napili)/South Maui (Kihei) Island-Mexican

This growing Maui chain (which now has several mainland locations) serves up high-quality, island-accented Mexican food with a healthy bent in a fast-food format. All menu items are prepared using top-quality produce, lean steak, skinless chicken, light sour cream, and vegetable oil and stocks only (no lard). Chips, beans, and guacamoles are all made fresh on the premises, making Maui Tacos a terrific choice for a quickie meal that you won't regret later. A big bar offers a half-dozen or so homemade salsas at every location; the pineapple salsa's just silly, but the top-notch tomatillo salsa is perfectly zested with the just-right touch of lime and vinegar. Go with one of the generously stuffed big surf burritos for maximum satisfaction and take it to the beach for the ultimate setting.

See map p. 236. **Central Maui:** *In Kahukui Kaahumanu Center, 275 Kaahumanu Ave., Kahului.* ☎ **808-871-7726.** **West Maui:** *In Lahaina Square, 840 Wainee St. (at Lahainaluna Road), just off Honoapiilani Highway, Lahaina.* ☎ **808-661-8883.** *Also in Napili Plaza, 5095 Napilihau St. (at Honoapiilani Highway), Napili.* ☎ **808-665-0222.** **South Maui:** *In Kamaole Beach Center, 2411 S. Kihei Rd. (across from Kamaole Beach II), Kihei.* ☎ **808-879-5005.** www.mauitacos.com. *Main courses: $4–$8. AE, DISC, MC, V. Open: Lunch and dinner daily.*

Nick's Fishmarket
$$$$$ South Maui (Wailea)   Mediterranean Seafood

Wow! This expensive Mediterranean-accented seafooder gets everything just right: food, wine list, setting, and service. It's not on the beach, but the ambience is romantic to the max anyway; I prefer the vine-covered terrace, but the gorgeous, dimly-lit dining room doesn't disappoint, either. The straightforward preparations let the clean, fresh flavor of the top-quality seafood shine: Kona-raised lobster is perfectly steamed and shelled at your table; mahimahi is kiawe-grilled (mesquite-grilled) and dressed with a sweet corn relish and aged balsamic vinegar; and an elegant *opakapaka* (pink snapper) is sauteed with meaty rock shrimps and lightly dressed with lemon butter and capers. The young, elegantly dressed servers have been schooled as pros, and it shows; you'll want for nothing here. The wine list is pricey, but excellent. A nice kids' menu (with dinners priced at $13) is at hand if an upscale family dinner is in your plans.

See map p. 236. In the Fairmont Kea Lani Maui, 4100 Wailea Alanui Dr., Wailea. ☎ *808-879-7224.* www.tri-star-restaurants.com. *Reservations highly recommended. Main courses: $27–$46. AE, DC, DISC, MC, V. Open: Dinner nightly.*

Pizza Paradiso
$ West Maui (Honokowai, Kaanapali)   Italian

This sit-down pizzeria serves up top-quality pies that manage to wow even skeptical New Yorkers (really!). In addition to a long list of create-your-own traditional toppings, Pizza Paradiso also offers a variety of theme pies, from the Maui Wowie (with ham and pineapple) to the Clam Slam (with juicy clams and tons of garlic); pastas; fresh, bounteous salads; and surprisingly good desserts (including a lovely homemade tiramisu). This pizzaeria is a terrific choice for bargain-hunting families or anybody who needs a break from high-priced ahi for awhile. The Kaanapali location is an express takeout joint, but you can enjoy your pie at a table in the adjacent Whaler's Village food court. Both locations offer free delivery in the immediate area.

See map p. 235. **In Honokowai:** *In the Honokowai Marketplace (next to the Star Market), 3350 Honoapiilani Rd., Honokowai (south of Kahana).* ☎ **808-667-2929.** **In Kaanapali:** *At Whaler's Village, 2435 Kaanapali Pkwy., Kaanapali Beach.* ☎ **808-667-0333.** www.pizzaparadiso.com. *Full-size pizzas: $13–$26. Pastas and sandwiches: $6–$12. MC, V. Open: Lunch and dinner daily.*

The Plantation House
$$$$ West Maui (Kapalua)   Hawaii Regional/Mediterranean

Overlooking luxuriant golf greens and the stunning Kapalua coastline beyond, the absolutely wonderful Plantation House may have the most glorious setting on Maui. Chef Alex Stanislaw and his team have crafted a one-of-a-kind Asian-Mediterranean fusion menu that changes frequently to take advantage of fresh seasonal produce. Expect to find dishes like scallop skewers with apple-smoked bacon and honey glaze; macadamia nut and goat cheese salad with Kula greens, Kalamata olives, and passionfruit vinaigrette; or roasted Molokai pork tenderloin with caramelized Maui onions. Fresh-caught island fish is the star of the menu, with several preparations available, including the divine Rich Forest option (the fish is pressed with bread crumbs and porcini mushroom powder, sauteed, and nestled in garlic-braised spinach and mashed potatoes). Chef Alex even lends his descriptive thoughts to the impressive wine list, one of the finest on the island. Book a terrace table and come at sunset for maximum enjoyment.

See map p. 235. In the Plantation Course Clubhouse, 200 Plantation Club Dr., Kapalua. ☎ *808-669-6299.* www.theplantationhouse.com. *Reservations highly recommended for dinner. Main courses: $8.50–$16 at breakfast and lunch, $16–$390 at dinner ($54 for surf and turf). AE, DC, MC, V. Open: Breakfast, lunch, and dinner daily.*

Roy's Kahana Bar & Grill/Roy's Nicolina Restaurant/Roy's Kihei
$$$–$$$$ West Maui (Kahana)/South Maui (Kihei)   Hawaii Regional

Roy Yamaguchi is the most famous name in Hawaii Regional Cuisine. His island restaurants have always been terrific, and they continue to shine. There's hardly any difference between these two bustling side-by-side siblings, which share the same executive chef and the same basic menu; Roy's Kahana has an open kitchen and a livelier atmosphere, while Roy's Nicolina is quieter, a tad more sophisticated, and boasts outdoor dining on the lanai. Thanks to an oversized menu of dim sum, appetizers, and *imu*-baked pizzas (an imu is the underground oven traditionally used to roast the whole pig at a luau), you can easily eat affordably in either dining room. The daily menu revolves around a few standards, such as sublime Szechuan baby-back ribs and blackened ahi with a delectable soy mustard butter. The service is always attentive, and Roy's well-priced private-label wines are an excellent value (though you may be tempted to sample the outstanding private-label sakes instead). Roy's newest location, in Kiehi, makes a wonderful addition to the South Maui dining scene.

See map p. 235. In the Kahana Gateway Shopping Center, 4405 Honoapiilani Hwy. (Highway 30), Kahana. Roy's Kahana: ☎ *808-669-6999. Roy's Nicolina:* ☎ *808-669-5000. Roy's Kihei: In the Piilani Shopping Center, 303 Piikea Ave., Kihei.* ☎ *808-891-1120.* www.roysrestaurant.com. *Reservations highly recommended. Appetizers and pizzas: $8–$14. Main courses: $16–$33. AE, DC, DISC, MC, V. Open: Dinner nightly.*

A Saigon Cafe
$$ Central Maui (Wailuku)   Vietnamese

This family-run restaurant in decidedly untouristy Wailuku serves up outstanding Vietnamese cuisine that's worth seeking out, especially if you're looking for a high-quality culinary return on your dollar. The wide-ranging menu features a dozen different soups (including a terrific lemongrass version), a complete slate of hot and cold noodle dishes, and numerous wok-cooked Vietnamese specialties starring island-grown produce and fresh-caught fish. Expect a taste sensation no matter what you order; every authentic dish bursts with piquant flavor. Ambience is minimal, but the quality of the food, low prices, and caring service more than compensate.

See map p. 252. 1792 Main St. (between Kaniela and Nani streets), Wailuku. To get there: Take Kaahumanu Avenue (Highway 32) to Main Street; it's the white building under the bridge. ☎ 808-243-9560. Reservations recommended for 4 or more. Main courses: $7.50–$17. DC, MC, V. Open: Lunch and dinner daily.

Sansei Seafood Restaurant & Sushi Bar
$$$ West Maui (Kapalua)/South Maui (Kihei)   Japanese/ Pacific Rim Seafood

Both of sushi chef D.K. Kodama's Maui sushi palaces offer some of the best dining on the island, especially for sushi lovers. Composed primarily of pan-Asian seafood dishes with multicultural touches, Sansei's winningly innovative menu has won raves from fans around the globe. Entrees are available, but I recommend assembling a family-style meal from the adventurous sushi rolls and small plates: The rock shrimp cake in ginger-lime-chili butter, topped with crispy Chinese noodles, and Thai ahi carpaccio in a red pepper-lime sauce are both standouts, but it's hard to go wrong with anything here. I love the beautifully presented flower sushi; don't miss it if you're a fishhead. For premier sushi service, cozy up to the bar at the bustling Kihei location; you won't be disappointed. Even the desserts are divine at this low-key, Japanese-style place. Book in advance so that you don't miss out. There's late-night dining and live karaoke from 10 p.m. to 1 a.m. on Thursday and Friday evenings, and early-bird and late-night specials can take the sting out of the bill. It's a real winner!

*See map p. 235. **In Kapalua:** In the Shops at Kapalua, 115 Bay Dr. ☎ 808-669-6286. **In Kihei:** Kihei Town Center (near Foodland), 1881 S. Kihei Rd. ☎ 808-879-0004. www.sanseihawaii.com. Reservations highly recommended. Sushi and sashimi: $3–$17. Main courses: $19–$38. AE, DISC, MC, V. Open: Dinner nightly.*

Sarento's on the Beach
$$$$–$$$$$ South Maui (Kihei)   Italian-Mediterranean

The Maui outpost of a Honolulu special-occasion favorite has won over well-dressed couples in droves with its gorgeous setting — which fuses white-linen elegance and white-sand romance seamlessly — and first-class service. The sophisticated Italian-Mediterranean cuisine more than lives up to the rest of the package. The stellar Greek salad is a Sarento's signature dish, and an excellent way to begin any meal. Veal lovers rave without fail about the osso buco, served on a bed of saffron risotto. I love the swordfish "saltimbocca," dressed with prosciutto and porcinis, and the seafood fra diavolo, with Kona lobster, diver scallops, and Manila clams. If you don't want to splurge on dinner, pony up to the sexy bar to revel in a perfectly poured cocktail and stupendous sunset views.

See map p. 252. At the Maui Oceanfront Inn, 2980 S. Kihei Rd. (at the south end of Kihei, just north of Kilohana Street), Kihei. ☎ 808-875-7555. www.tri-star-restaurants.com. Reservations highly recommended. Main courses: $13–$18 at lunch, $26–$40 at dinner. AE, DC, DISC, MC, V. Open: Lunch and dinner daily.

Stella Blues Cafe

$$–$$$ South Maui (Kihei)   New American

Stella Blues has moved down the street and uptown in a big way. I'm very pleased with the great job that this former Deadhead-themed deli has done in reinventing itself as a stylish and sophisticated grown-up restaurant. The rock-and-roll memorabilia still dresses the walls, but now it adds a pleasingly funky touch to a open and airy dining room dressed in rich colors and warm woods, with an open stainless-steel kitchen and a big, backlit bar; tiki torches add romance to the outdoor patio after dark. But the great thing about Stella Blues is that it's still friendly, unpretentious, and affordable; in fact, you'd be hard-pressed to find another restaurant in the islands that offers this much panache and good cooking at such affordable prices. Start your day with a hearty create-your-own omelette and then move on to a French dip or another hefty sandwich at lunch. The place really comes alive at dinner: Start with the surprisingly good Caesar salad, the delectable homemade hummus served with hot pita, or the funky nachos, blue and yellow corn chips layered with mahimahi, ahi, jalapenos, jack cheese, and guacamole. Choose from a range of creative pizzas, pastas, and big plates for your main course; the New York steak (homegrown by the Maui Cattle Company) is as good as most that cost twice the price. Late-night dining (until midnight weekdays, to 1:30 a.m. Friday and Saturday nights) is another plus. Good job, Stella — you go, girl!

See map p. 252. In Azeka II Shopping Center, 1279 S. Kihei Rd. (at the north end of Kihei). ☎ *808-874-3779.* www.stellablues.com. *Reservations not necessary. Main courses: $6–$10 at breakfast, $7–$10 at lunch, $11–$22 at dinner. DISC, MC, V. Open: Breakfast, lunch, and dinner daily.*

Tommy Bahama's Tropical Cafe

$$$ South Maui (Wailea)   Caribbean

Housed in the Tommy Bahama's fashion emporium at the Shops at Wailea, this delightful restaurant perfectly embodies the tropical haberdasher's breezily sophisticated style. The open-air room is a mélange of bamboo, rattan, and tropical prints that come together in a postmodern tropical plantation style. The restaurant actually looks more expensive than it is — much like Tommy Bahama's delightful tropical-print wear. I love Tommy Bahama's for lunch, when the menu focuses on Caribbean-inspired sandwiches and bounteous entree-sized salads. Pleasing choices include the Habana Cabana pulled-pork sandwich, finished with the restaurant's own blackberry brandy barbecue sauce; and the South Seas spinach salad, tossed in a warm bacon-balsamic viniagrette and garnished with goat cheese, hardboiled egg, crispy fried onions, and shrimp or chicken (your choice). Dinner brings more substantial fare, like char-grilled baby-back ribs, and pan-seared sashimi-grade ahi crusted in cilantro and lemongrass. As good as the food is, Tommy Bahama's Tropical Cafe is really about soaking up the carefree mood along with a few fruity cocktails. Come early for dinner, because the second-level setting enjoys gorgeous sunset views.

See map p. 252. At the Shops at Wailea, 3750 Wailea Alanui Dr., second floor. ☎ *808-875-9983. Reservations recommended. Main courses: $8–$17 at lunch, $22–$35 at dinner (most less than $30). AE, MC, V. Open: Lunch and dinner daily.*

Vino

$$$ **West Maui (Kapalua)   Italian**

This first-class addition to the full-throttle Maui dining scene also happens to be a great value, too. Vino is the brainchild of chef D.K. Kodama of the celebrated Sansei restaurants (earlier in this chapter) and master sommelier Chuck Furuya, and the results of this impeccable breeding show. Kodama may be better known for his sushi, but it doesn't matter — this is world-class Italian fare (with the requisite island flair, of course). Highlights of the pasta-heavy menu (all are housemade) include delicately fried calamari dressed with a delicate lemon aioli and a side of spicy marinara; "silk handerchiefs," squares of egg pasta tossed with a light pesto (made with fresh-grown basil) and oven-roasted roma tomatoes, toasted almonds, and romano cheese; and a grilled half chicken "under a brick," stuffed with fennel and fresh herbs and grilled — well, you know where — for a delightful finish. I didn't find any dish that took a wrong turn here; everything was delightful. Furuya's wine list is equally captivating, with a good selection of well-priced choices by the glass accompanied by candid descriptions that let you pair easily. The high-ceilinged plantation-style room is outfitted with generous wood tables and open to the tropical breeze, setting the perfect stage for such an enjoyable and casually sophisticated dining experience. It's a real value, and a real find!

See map p. 252. In the Kapalua Village Course Golf Club House, 2000 Village Rd., Kapalua. ☎ *808-661-8466. Reservations recommended. Main courses: $13–$25. AE, DISC, MC, V. Open: Lunch and dinner daily.*

Luau!

Maui is Hawaii's hands-down winner in the luau department. If you're going to attend just one, do it on this island.

Reservations are required for both luaus listed in this section. Make reservations as far in advance as possible — preferably before you leave home — because all these first-rate beach parties are often fully booked a full week or more ahead of time, sometimes two. Don't give up if you're trying to make last-minute plans, though; it never hurts to call and ask whether a few spots have opened up due to cancellations. Also, if you're booking at the last minute or you want more island luaus to choose from, check with **Tom Barefoot's Cashback Tours** (☎ 888-222-3601; www.tombarefoot.com), a very reliable Maui-based activities center that can hook you up with a number of other luaus on Maui, and, sometimes, even save you a few bucks in the process.

The Feast at Lele

Here's a winning new concept in luaus, and it's ideal for those who don't mind paying more for a more intimate oceanfront setting and a private table. Here you'll enjoy an excellent five-course meal, prepared by a skilled chef and served at your own table (no standing in line at an all-you-can-eat buffet). You'll experience a lovely flower-lei greeting but no traditional *imu* (underground oven) ceremony or craft demonstrations, like at the Old Lahaina Luau, and the performance troupe is smaller, but it's held to the same exacting standards. This feast celebrates not only Hawaii but three more Polynesian islands: Tonga, Tahiti, and Samoa. The structure here diverges from your standard luau: Each course is dedicated to an island culture, comprised of gourmet versions of foods from the native cuisine, followed by a native song and dance performance. Although the Feast at Lele welcomes all visitors, it tends to cater to a more sophisticated, kid-free grown-up crowd than most luaus, making it an ideal choice for romance-seeking couples or anyone wanting a more refined experience. A full wine list and tropical cocktail menu are on hand in addition to the included well cocktails, and you can expect your two dedicated servers to be friendly, knowledgeable, and attentive.

See map p. 252. 505 Front St. (on the ocean at Shaw Street), Lahaina. ☎ *808-667-5353.* www.feastatlele.com. *Times: Nightly at 6 p.m. (at 5:30 p.m. Oct–Mar). Admission: $99 adults, $68 kids 2–12. Cocktails are included, but tips are not.*

Going for a post-Haleakala-sunrise breakfast

Rising at 3 a.m. to drive two hours upcountry to catch the glorious sunrise from atop Haleakala crater is one of Maui's greatest pastimes (see Chapter 14). But the real treat comes after, in the form of a hearty, country-style breakfast. Happily, two wonderful breakfast stops sit at the base of the mountain, in a tiny town called Kula that you can't help but drive through on your way back to the beach.

Kula Sandalwoods Restaurant, on Haleakala Highway ($; Hwy. 377; ☎ 808-878-3523), is a family-run restaurant that starts serving home-baked pastries, omelets prepared with fresh-from-the-chicken-coop eggs and garden-fresh veggies, and eggs Benedict topped with hollandaise sauce (made from scratch) every morning at 7 a.m. All of the homestyle breakfasts and lunches are hearty and delicious. You can choose to eat in the large diner-like room, or out on the lanai if it's not too chilly. See map p. 252.

For slightly more upscale dining, head down the road apiece to **Kula Lodge & Restaurant** ($$; ☎ 808-878-1535), whose cozy lodgelike dining room features a big stone fireplace; breakfast is served from 6:30 a.m. Picture windows with lush panoramic views on three sides let the outside in as you enjoy egg scrambles with bacon and sausage, French toast made with home-baked Portuguese sweetbread, and justifiably famous banana–macadamia nut pancakes. See map p. 252.

Old Lahaina Luau

Old Lahaina Luau is Hawaii's must authentic and acclaimed luau, and my absolute favorite. The oceanfront luau grounds provide a stunning setting, both the luau feast and riveting entertainment serve as a wonderful introduction to genuine island culture, and the staff exudes aloha. When you book, choose between Hawaiian-style seating, on mats and cushions set at low tables at the foot of the stage, or traditional seating, at generously proportioned common tables with comfortable wooden chairs; all tables have great views, but earlier bookings garner the best seats. You'll be welcomed with a fresh flower lei (the yellow plumeria is the fragrant one) and greeted with a tropical cocktail. Arrive early, so that you'll have plenty of time to stroll the grounds — watching craftspeople at work and taking in the gorgeous views — before the *imu* (underground oven) ceremony, in which the luau pig is unearthed from the underground oven. After dinner is the excellent show, which features authentic hula and traditional chants accompanied by an intelligent narrative charting the history of Hawaii from the first islanders to modern day. Don't mistake this show for a deadly dull history lesson; it's compelling entertainment, and both the male and female dancers are first-rate performers. (Don't expect fire dancers, though, because ancient Hawaiians didn't play with fire.) It's well worth the money, and a joy from start to finish — and an excellent choice for families, groups, and couples alike.

See map p. 252. 1251 Front St. (on the ocean side of the street, across from Lahaina Cannery Mall), Lahaina. ☎ *800-248-5828 or 808-667-1998.* www.oldlahaina luau.com. *Times: Nightly at 5:45 p.m. (at 5:15 p.m. Oct–Mar). Admission: $86 adults, $54 kids 2–12. Cocktails included.*

Fast Facts: Maui

American Automobile Association (AAA)

Roadside service is availalble to members by calling ☎ 800-AAA-HELP; however, the only Hawaii office is on Oahu (see Chapter 11).

American Express

There's one in Kaanapali at the Westin Maui, 2365 Kaanapali Pkwy. (☎ 808-661-7155).

Baby Sitters & Baby Stuff

Any hotel or condo should be able to refer you to a reliable baby sitter with a proven track record. If yours can't, contact **Happy Kids** (☎ 808-667-5437), **The Nanny**

Connection (☎ 808-875-4777 or 808-667-5777; www.thenannyconnection.com), or **Nana Enterprises** (☎ 888-584-6262). **Baby's Away** (☎ 800-942-9030 or 808-875-9030; www.babysaway.com) rents cribs, strollers, highchairs, playpens, infant seats, and the like; they'll deliver whatever you need to wherever you're staying and pick it up when you're done.

Doctors

West Maui Healthcare Center, Whaler's Village, 2435 Kaanapali Pkwy., second floor (behind Leilani's), Kaanapali (☎ 808-667-9721), takes walk-ins daily from 8 a.m.

to 9 p.m.; note that they charge an additional $30 for visits after 6 p.m. In Kihei, call **Urgent Care Maui**, 1325 S. Kihei Rd, Suite 103 (at Lipoa St., across from Star Market), Kihei (☎ **808-879-7781**), which is open daily from 6 a.m. to midnight. **Doctors on Call** (☎ 808-667-7676) takes appointments at the Hyatt Regency in Lahaina, at the Westin Maui in Kaanapali, and at the Ritz-Carlton in Kapalua. If you need medical attention while you're out in Hana, contact the **Hana Community Health Center**, 4590 Hana Hwy. (☎ 808-248-8294). The concierge or front-desk staff of your hotel should also be able to direct you to a reliable doctor in the immediate area, should you need one.

Emergencies

Dial **911** from any phone, just as you would in the rest of the United States.

Hospitals

Around the clock emergency care is available from **Maui Memorial Hospital**, 221 Mahalani St., Wailuku (☎ 808-244-9056), in Central Maui.

Information

The **Maui Visitors Bureau** is located in Central Maui at 1727 Wili Pa Loop, Wailuku, HI 96793 (☎ 800-525-6284 or 808-244-3530; www.visitmaui.com), but it's not really designed as a walk-in office. Call before you leave home to order your free Maui travel planner, or check the Web site for a wealth of good information. Some of Maui's resort areas have dedicated visitor associations that provide information, including the **Kaanapali Beach Resort Association** (☎ 800-245-9229 or 808-661-3271; www.kaanapaliresort.com), the **Kapalua Resort** (☎ 800-527-2482; www.kapaluamaui.com), and the **Wailea Resort** (☎ 800-332-1614; www.wailea-resort.com).

After you land at Kahului Airport, stop over at the state-operated **Visitor Information Center** while you're waiting for your baggage and pick up a copy of *This Week Maui, 101 Things to Do on Maui,* and other free tourist publications. If you forget, don't worry; you'll find them at malls and shopping centers around the island.

In addition, all the big resort hotels are overflowing with printed info. Even if your hotel or condo doesn't have a dedicated concierge, they should be happy to point you in the right direction, make recommendations, and give advice.

Newspapers/Magazines

The *Maui News* (www.mauinews.com) is the island's daily paper; the Web site can provide you with a great source of information before you leave home. Additionally, a number of free newspaper weeklies, such as *Maui Time* and the *Maui Weekly,* are available from racks around town.

Pharmacies

Long's Drugs (www.longs.com), Hawaii's biggest drugstore chain, has a branch in Central Maui at the Maui Mall, 70 Kaahumanu Ave. (between Puunene Avenue and the Hana Highway), Kahului (☎ 808-877-0041). If you're in West Maui, head to the branch at Lahaina Cannery Mall, 1221 Honoapiilani Hwy. (between Kapunkea and Kenui streets), Lahaina (☎ 808-667-4384). In South Maui, head to Long's Kihei Center, 1215 S. Kihei Rd. (just north of Lipoa Street), Kihei (☎ 808-879-2259).

Police

The main headquarters of the **Maui Police Department** are in Wailuku at 55 Mahalani St., near Maui Memorial Hospital (☎ 808-244-6400). District stations are located next to the Lahaina Civic Center, 1760 Honoapiilani Hwy., on the mountain side of the highway, just north of Lahaina (☎ 808-661-4441); and in Hana on the Hana Highway, near Ua Kea Road (☎ 808-248-8311). Of course, if you have an emergency, **dial 911** from any phone.

Post Offices

In West Maui, a big branch office is next to the Lahaina Civic Center at 1760 Honoapiilani Hwy. between Kaanapali and Lahaina (on the mountain side of the highway; it's easy to spot); and in downtown Lahaina adjacent to the Lahaina Shopping Center, 132 Papalaua St. (between Front and Wainee streets; ☎ 808-661-0904). In South Maui, you'll find a post office at 1254 S. Kihei Rd., across the street from Long's Kihei Center (☎ 808-879-1987). Satellite post offices are located around the island; to find the one nearest you, call ☎ 800-275-8777 or visit www.usps.com.

Taxes

Hawaii's sales tax is 4 percent. Expect taxes of about 11.42 percent to be added to your hotel bill.

Taxis

Call **Alii Cab** (☎ 808-661-3688 or 808-667-2605), **Maui Airport Taxi** (☎ 808-877-0907), **Maui Central Cab** (☎ 877-244-7279 or 808-244-7278; www.mauicab.com), **Kihei Taxi** (☎ 808-879-3000), or **Wailea Taxi** (☎ 808-874-5000).

Weather & Surf Reports

For Maui's current weather and forecasts, call ☎ 808-877-5111, which also supplies sunrise and sunset times, as well as forecasts for Molokai and Lanai. For marine conditions, dial ☎ 808-877-3477 or 808-877-3949; for wind and surf reports, call ☎ 808-877-3611.

Chapter 14

Exploring Maui

● ●

In This Chapter

▶ Locating Maui's best beaches

▶ Playing in the waves

▶ Exploring Maui's top attractions

▶ Scoping out the shopping scene

▶ Enjoying Maui's lively island nightlife

● ●

*M*aui is much like a smorgasbord: Even if you have no intention of sampling everything it has to offer, you'll be wowed by the bounty of choice — and your plate is bound to be full well before you satisfy all of your cravings.

This action-packed island has something for everyone — and then some — so staying active and happy will *not* be a problem on Maui. Your biggest dilemma will likely be just trying to fit everything you want to see and do into your vacation calendar.

Enjoying the Sand and Surf

Although some accessible beaches are on the east (Hilo-Volcano) coast, the west (Kona-Kohala) coast is the exclusive domain of water sports on the Big Island.

Combing the beaches

Maui wouldn't be the glamour girl that it is without a breathtaking set of beaches.

Never leave valuables in your rental car while you're at the beach. Knowledgeable thieves like to prey on tourists, and they know how to get into your interior, trunk, and glove box in no time flat. Be especially diligent about leaving your stuff behind at your condo or in your hotel safe when you're heading off to a remote beach. Also, if you see a red flag hoisted at any beach, don't venture into the water; the flag indicates that conditions are unsafe for swimmers. Even if the waves look placid, trust the warning.

Maui's Best Beaches & Attractions

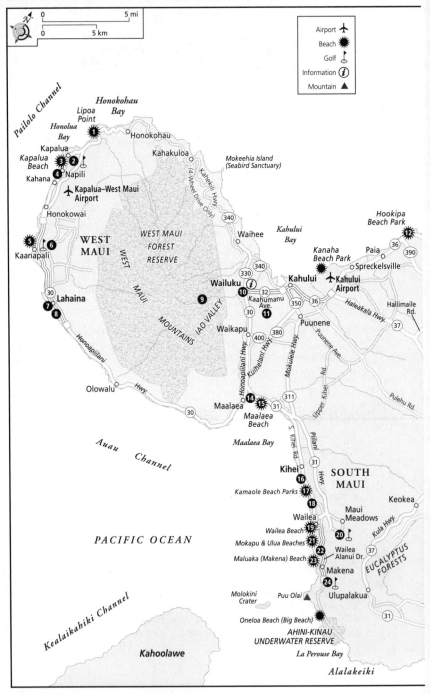

N

0 ————— 5 mi
0 ————— 5 km

Airport ✈
Beach ✴
Golf ⛳
Information ⓘ
Mountain ▲

Pailolo Channel

Honokohau Bay

Lipoa Point

1

Honolua Bay

Honokohau

Kapalua

Kapalua Beach

2 3

4 Napili

Kahana

Mokeehia Island (Seabird Sanctuary)

Kahakuloa

Kahekili Hwy.
(4-Wheel Drive Only)

✈ Kapalua–West Maui Airport

Honokowai

WEST MAUI

WEST MAUI FOREST RESERVE

340

Kahului Bay

Waihee

340

Hookipa Beach Park

12

Paia

36

390

Kanaha Beach Park

Spreckelsville

5

6

Kaanapali

330

Wailuku ⓘ

10

32

Kaahumanu Ave.

11

Kahului ✈ Kahului Airport

350   36

Haleakala Hwy.

Haliimaile Rd.

37

30

Lahaina

7

8

Honoapiilani Hwy.

WEST MAUI MOUNTAINS

9

IAO VALLEY

30

Waikapu

400

380

Puunene

Puunene Ave.

Pulehu Rd.

Olowalu

30

Maalaea

14

15

311

Kihei

Maalaea Beach

31

31

Auau Channel

Maalaea Bay

S. Kihei Rd.

Piilani Hwy.

SOUTH MAUI

Keokea

Kihei

16

Kamaole Beach Parks **17**

18

PACIFIC OCEAN

Wailea

Maui Meadows

Kula Hwy.

Wailea Beach **19**

20 ⛳

Mokapu & Ulua Beaches **21**

22

Wailea Alanui Dr.

37

Maluaka (Makena) Beach **23**

Makena

24 ⛳

EUCALYPTUS FORESTS

Ulupalakua

31

Puu Olai ▲

Oneloa Beach (Big Beach) ✴

AHINI-KINAU UNDERWATER RESERVE

Molokini Crater

La Perouse Bay

Kealaikahiki Channel

Kahoolawe

Alalakeiki

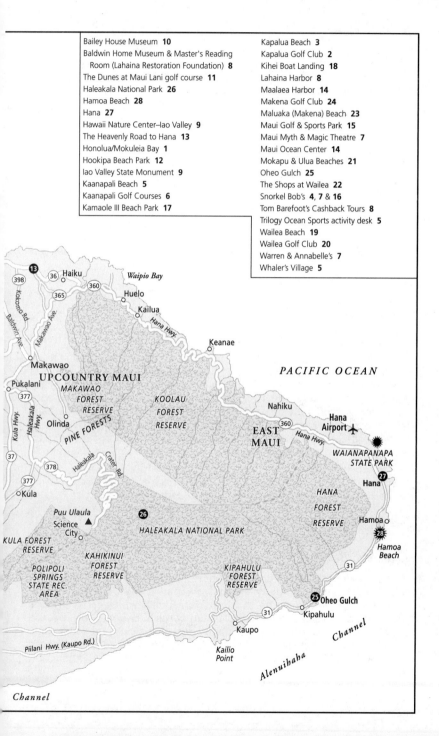

In West Maui

These fine beaches are easily accessible from the Honoapiilani Highway, which connects the island's commercial heart, Kahului, to Lahaina, Kaanapali, and Kapalua. Each one offers excellent opportunities for whale-watching in humpback season.

Honolua/Mokuleia Bay Marine Life Conservation District

Snorkelers love this gorgeous cove for its smooth surf, clear waters (which are protected as a marine-life conservation district), excellent coral formations, and abundance of tropical fish, especially on the west side of the bay. The beige-sand crescent is lovely, and never too crowded. In winter, stay out of the water; come instead to watch daredevil surfers ride some of the finest breaks in the islands. Sorry, this beach has no facilities.

See map p. 274. At the northernmost end of Honoapiilani Highway (Highway 30), about 2 miles past Office Road (the turnoff for Kapalua); park with the other cars in the available spaces or along the roadside and walk 200 yards down the stairs and to the beach.

Kapalua Beach

This gorgeous golden crescent bordered by two palm-studded points is justifiably popular for sunbathing, swimming, and snorkeling. The sandy bottom slopes gently to deep water that's so clear you can see where the gold sands turn to green, and then deep blue. Well-protected from strong winds and currents, Kapalua's calm waters are usually great for swimmers of all ages and abilities year-round, and waves come in just right for easy riding. The rocky points offer good fish-communing opportunities for both snorkelers and offshore divers. The beach is also great for offshore whale-watching in winter, too. The inland side of the beach is edged by a shady path and cool lawns. Facilities include indoor and outdoor showers, restrooms, and a rental shack. The small parking lot is limited to about 30 spaces, so arrive early.

See map p. 274. On Lower Honoapiilani Road at the south end of Kapalua, just before the Napili Kai Beach Club. To get there: From Honoapiilani Highway, turn left just past Mile Marker 30, go ⅒ of a mile to Lower Honoapiilani Road; turn left and go ⅗ of a mile to the access point.

Kaanapali Beach

It's no wonder that Maui's first resort developers chose this beach to start building on — it's absolutely fabulous. Swimming and wave jumping are excellent, but beware the rough winter shorebreak, which can really kick up. At the north end of the beach, in front of the Sheraton, is Black Rock, the best offshore snorkel spot on Maui: The water is clear, the reef is well-protected, and the clouds of tropical fish are used to finned folks. A paved beach walk links the hotels and the open-air Whaler's Village shopping and dining complex, a great place to cure the midday munchies or tuck into a tropical cocktail. Lifeguards and beachboys from the resorts man the beach, beach-gear rental shacks are set up right on the sand, and most hotels have outdoor showers (and sometimes restrooms) that you can use; restrooms are also available at Whaler's Village. The only downside is that you'll likely have to pay for parking if you're not staying here, but it'll be worth the few bucks for such prime beachgoing. (A few free spaces are available, but good luck snaring one — I've never been able to.)

See map p. 274. Kaanapali Parkway, off Honoapiilani Highway (Highway 30), Kaanapali.

Along the South Maui Coast

These fabulous beaches are located along Maui's sunny southwest-facing shore, where you find the resort areas of Kihei and Wailea.

Kamaole III Beach Park

Three popular beach parks — Kamaole I, II, and III — face the waves across from South Kihei Road in mid-Kihei. The biggest and best is Kamaole III (or Kam-3, as the locals call it), which boasts a playground and a grassy lawn that meets the finely textured golden sand. Swimming is generally safe, but parents should make sure that little ones don't venture too far out because the bottom slopes off quickly. Families may prefer the grassy end of the beach with shade trees, where the ocean bottom has a fairly gentle slope. Both the north and south ends have rocky fingers that are great for snorkelers, and the winter waves attract bodysurfers. This west-facing beach is also an ideal spot to watch the sun go down or look for whales offshore in winter. Facilities include restrooms, showers, picnic tables, barbecues, volleyball nets, and lifeguards. Food and beach-gear rentals are available at the malls across the street, but be careful crossing busy Kihei Road!

See map p. 274. On South Kihei Road just south of Keonekai Street (across from the Maui Parkshore and Kamaole Sands condos), Kihei.

Mokapu and Ulua Beaches

Situated at the north end of Wailea, these lovely side-by-side sister beaches boast pretty golden sand, good grassy areas for sandless picnicking, and nice facilities, including restrooms and a freshwater shower pole. The ocean bottom is shallow and gently slopes down to deeper waters, making swimming generally safe; snorkelers will find Wailea's best snorkeling at the rocky north end. When the surf kicks up, the waves are excellent for bodysurfers. Although these gems are popular with the nearby upscale condo crowd, the sand rarely gets too crowded; the parking lot is tiny, though, so come early.

See map p. 274. On Wailea Alanui Road at Hale Alii Place, just south of the Renaissance Wailea (across from the Palms at Wailea condos), Wailea.

Wailea Beach

The ultrafine gold-sand beach is big, wide, and protected on both sides by black lava points with a sandy and sloping bottom, making the clear waters excellent for swimming (and okay for snorkeling, too). The year-round waves are just right for easy board-riding or bodysurfing, but trade winds can kick up in the afternoon, so come early. The view out to sea is gorgeous, with the islands of Kahoolawe and Lanai framing the view; this beach is an ideal spot to watch for humpback whales in winter. This stretch of shoreline may feel like it belongs to the ultradeluxe resorts that line it, but it doesn't; just look for the blue "Shoreline Access" signs for easiest access. Restrooms and showers are available.

See map p. 274. Fronting the Grand Wailea and Four Seasons resorts, Wailea. To get there: The blue "Shoreline Access" sign is between the two resorts on Wailea Alanui Drive.

Maluaka (Makena) Beach

This wonderful beach park offers a pleasing off-the-beaten-path experience for those in search of a first-rate snorkel experience, or for anybody who wants a break from Maui's ever-present crowds. Short, wide, and palm-fringed, this unspoiled crescent of golden, grainy sand is set between two protective lava points and bounded by big, grassy sand dunes. Snorkelers will find surprisingly colorful coral and an impressive array of vibrantly hued reef fish at the rocky south end of the beach, past the lava point. Sunbathers and casual swimmers will want to stick to the beautiful strand closer to the hotel, which is virtually empty on weekdays. Facilities include restrooms and showers.

See map p. 274. Makena Alanui Drive, Makena (south of Wailea). To get there: Follow Wailea Alanui Drive south through Wailea to Makena and look for the "Shoreline Access" sign near the Maui Prince hotel; turn at the "Dead End" sign past the hotel for public access parking.

Central and East Maui

These glorious sands are accessible from the Hana Highway, which runs along the island's lush north shore.

Hookipa Beach Park

Possibly the most famous windsurfing beach in the world, this small, gold-sand beach at the foot of a grassy cliff attracts top windsurfers and wave-jumpers from around the globe with hard, constant winds and endless waves that result in near-perfect wave-riding conditions. Come on weekday afternoons to watch the local experts fly over the waves with their colorful sails; winter weekends host regular competitions. When the winter waves die down, snorkelers and divers explore the reef. Even then, you should be extremely careful because these waters are rough year-round; summer mornings are best. Facilities include some rustic restrooms and showers, plus pavilions, picnic tables, and barbecues. The lower parking lot is generally reserved for windsurfers and their equipment, so park in the upper lot (see the following directions), where the high, grassy bluff offers a better perch for watching the action, anyway.

See map p. 274. Off Hana Highway (Highway 36), 2 miles east of Paia, about 6 miles east of Haleakala Highway (Highway 37). To get there: Drive past the park and turn left at the entrance at the far side of the beach, at the Hookipa Lookout sign.

Hamoa Beach

This remote, half-moon-shaped beach near the end of the Hana Highway is one of the most breathtakingly lovely beaches in all Hawaii, celebrated in writing by no less than James Michener for its singular beauty. The Hotel Hana-Maui likes to maintain the beach as its own, but it has to share, so feel free to march right down the steps from the lava-rock lookout point and stake out a spot on the open sand. Even if you don't want to swim or sunbathe, come to peek at this stunner from above: You'll find surf that's the perfect color of turquoise, golden-gray sand, and luxuriant green hills serving as the postcard-perfect backdrop. The beach is generally good for swimming and wave-riding in the gentle seasons, but stick close to the shore because this is open, unprotected ocean; in winter, staying out of the water entirely is best. The hotel maintains minimal facilities for nonguests, including a restroom.

See map p. 274. Off the Hana Highway (Highway 36), about 2½ miles past Hana town. To get there: Turn at the small white sign that says "Hamoa Beach" and go about 1½ miles to the lava-rock lookout point; you can park on the roadside or in the dirt area across the street. The stairs are just beyond the lookout point (if you reach the steep service road to the beach, you've gone too far).

Playing in the surf

If your hotel or condo doesn't provide beach gear or beach toys, you won't have a problem finding a place to rent these items. In addition to top-quality snorkel gear, **Snorkel Bob** rents boogie boards and beach chairs at its three Maui stores (see the following section, "Snorkeling"), and rental shacks on popular beaches like Kaanapali and Kapalua can rent you whatever you need while you're there. You can also rent all manner of gear — from beach chairs and picnic coolers to boogie boards and surfboards to ocean kayaks — at very reasonable prices from **Duke's Surf Shop,** 578 Front St. (at Prison Street), Lahaina (☎ **808-661-1970**).

Snorkeling

Maui is justifiably famous for its snorkel cruises to Molokini and Lanai (see the following section), both of which offer first-class fish spotting — some of the best in the state. But anybody who's already perused the "Combing the Beaches" section, earlier in this chapter, knows that the island offers a wealth of terrific snorkel spots that are accessible from shore. Probably the best of these is Black Rock at the north end of **Kaanapali Beach.** Also excellent are **Honolua Bay,** north of Kapalua; **Mokapu and Ulua Beaches,** in Wailea; and one of my lesser known favorites, **Maluaka (Makena) Beach,** south of Wailea in Makena.

Additionally, many of the island's hotels and condo complexes sit on coves that are excellent for snorkeling — and not just the super-expensive ones. The affordable Mana Kai Maui in Kihei, for example, fronts a gem of a snorkeling area. Your hotel staff is sure to have nearby recommendations.

If you want to take advantage of Maui's offshore snorkeling opportunities, you'll likely need to rent some gear. My favorite rental-gear supplier in Hawaii is **Snorkel Bob's;** it rents the best-quality gear, with friendly service and a refreshing dose of snarky good humor thrown in for good measure. Snorkel Bob's maintains three Maui locations, with two in West Maui. One is at 1217 Front St. in Lahaina, at the north end of town near the Old Lahaina Luau (☎ **808-661-4421**); look for the landmark "Jesus Coming Soon" sign (it's hard to miss). There's another West Maui store almost to Kapalua in Napili Village, 5425 Lower Honapiilani Hwy. (☎ **808-669-9603**). In South Maui, you'll find Bob's at the Kamaole Beach Center at Kihei Marketplace, 2411 S. Kihei Rd., between Rainbow Mall and Dolphin Plaza, across from Kamaole I Beach Park (☎ **808-879-7449**). The best-quality gear — the "Ultimate Truth" — rents for $7.50 a day, or $30 a week ($22 per week for kids) for the mask/snorkel/fins set. For $10 more, near-sighted snorkelers can opt for prescription masks (including snorkel and fins set). You don't need to reserve gear in advance, but you're welcome to book your gear online at www.snorkelbob.com. The shops are open daily from 8 a.m. to 5 p.m.

Keep these **snorkel tips** in mind as you don your fins and head into the water:

- ✔ Make mornings your offshore snorkel time on Maui because the winds often start to kick up around noon, making surf conditions rougher and less conducive to fish-spying.

- ✔ Always snorkel with a friend and keep an eye on each other.

- ✔ Look up every few minutes to get your bearings, to check your position in relation to the shoreline, and to see whether there's any boat traffic.

- ✔ Don't touch anything. Not only can your fingers and feet damage coral, but it can give you nasty cuts. Moreover, camouflaged fish and spiny shells may surprise you.

- ✔ Before you set out, check surf conditions by calling one of the local dive or snorkel shops, such as Snorkel Bob's, which can give you the latest on local conditions and recommend alternative spots if the prime ones are too rough for snorkeling.

Ocean cruising to Molokini and Lanai and other on-deck adventures

Maui boasts two top day-cruising destinations: the sunken offshore crater **Molokini,** which is hugely popular among snorkelers and divers; and the island of **Lanai,** terrific for snorkelers and sunbathers alike.

(Do note, however, that only Trilogy and Paragon take their guests onshore at Lanai; other operators just anchor offshore for snorkeling in the surrounding waters.) If you're a snorkeler and you have to choose, I'd say head to Molokini first; then, if you have the time and money, follow up with a day of snorkeling around Lanai. (However, I have heard some recent complaints that the omnipresent crowds and worn-down reef at Molokini have made for a less-than-optimal experience.) In whale-watching season, though (from mid-December through April) go with a Lanai cruise first because the channel that separates Maui from Lanai is a favorite hangout for wintering humpback whales.

 Dramamine or nausea-prevention wristbands are an excellent idea if you're prone to seasickness. A very important tip: Be sure to take the Dramamine *before* the boat gears up for the return trip to Maui. After the return sail is under way, it's too late for the drug to do any good.

 The outfitters listed in this section hardly scratch the surface of the glut of cruise operators that sail from Maui. I consider these to be the best. If you want additional options, contact the island's most reliable activity center, **Tom Barefoot's Cashback Tours,** 834 Front St. (near Lahainaluna Road), Lahaina (☎ **888-222-3601** or 808-661-8889; www.tombarefoot.com), which can also save you a few bucks by booking you with some of the operators that I list.

 All the sail-snorkel cruises I recommend are family-friendly, but Trilogy boasts the kid-friendliest crew of them all.

Blue Water Rafting

Blue Water's cruises are distinct for four reasons. First, this outfit takes small groups of guests (no more than 24) out on fast-flying, rigid-hulled inflatable boats for an exciting ride. Second, its Molokini Express cruises arrive at Molokini in between the big boats' trips, so passengers have the perpetually overpopular crater largely to themselves. Third, the speed and extra-maneuverability of its boats allows Blue Water to take you to South Maui's otherwise untouristed Kanaio Coast beyond Makena, where you'll visit sea caves and snorkel in pristine areas favored by sea turtles and spinner dolphins on both Kanaio-only and Molokini-combination tours. And lastly, the low-to-the-water boats put you as close as possible to turtles and dolphins, as well as humpback whales in winter. This cruise is an excellent choice for adventure-seekers in search of something different.

Cruises depart from Kihei Boat Landing, on South Kihei Road just south of Kamaole III Beach Park (between Keonekai Street and Kilohana Drive), Kihei. ☎ **808-879-7238.** www.bluewaterrafting.com. *2- to 5½-hour raft cruises: $55–$110 adults, $45–$95 kids under 12. Prices include deli lunch, plus continental breakfast on the 5½-hour tour.*

Maui Classic Charters

This company can offer you Molokini snorkel-sail experiences on two great boats: The *Four Winds,* a modern 55-foot, 149-person-capacity catamaran featuring a glass-bottom hull for on-ship viewing, a water slide and three swim ladders, and barbecues; and the *Maui Magic,* a super-fast state-of-the-art 54-foot, 71-passenger power catamaran with similarly cool features in a more intimate environment. A naturalist accompanies the whale-watching trips in season.

Cruises depart from Maalaea Harbor (at the Highway 30/130 junction), Maalaea. ☎ *800-736-5740 or 808-879-8188.* www.mauicharters.com. *1½- to 6-hour cruises: $29–$99 adults, $24–$79 kids 12 and under. Prices include continental breakfast and BBQ lunch on longer cruises; beer, wine, and soda on all cruises. 15-percent online 7-day advance-booking discount available at press time.*

Pacific Whale Foundation Eco-Adventures

If you consider yourself to be ecologically minded, you can't do better than to give your snorkel-cruise dollars to the Pacific Whale Foundation. This nonprofit organization has been at the forefront of Maui-based whale research, education, and conservation since the 1970s, and it also happens to host very fine cruises. Its first-rate modern catamaran fleet offers some of the best tours of Molokini and offshore Lanai. Its 5½-hour Lanai snorkel-sail takes in the island's less visited bays and includes a search for wild dolphins in its regular itinerary. The five-hour Molokai trip is as fine as any and includes a visit to a second snorkel spot, Turtle Arches. Not only is at least one naturalist always onboard, but the entire crew is knowledgeable, ecoconscious, and friendly; the boats (each of which carries 100 people maximum) even burn ecofriendly fuel. What's more, the cruises are great for beginning snorkelers because guides lead fish talks and reef tours, and a wide variety of flotation devices are available. The winter whale-watching cruises are unparalleled, of course. You simply can't go wrong with these folks.

Departures from Maalaea Harbor (at the Highway 30/130 junction), Maalaea, and Lahaina Harbor, on Front Street, Lahaina, depending on cruise. ☎ *800-942-5311 or 808-879-8811.* www.pacificwhale.org. *Cruises: $20–$110 adults, $15–$55 kids 7–12. Prices include continental breakfast and/or deli lunch, depending on cruise. Online advance-booking discount available at press time.*

Paragon Sailing Charters

Paragon is most notable for its state-of-the-art, high-performance catamarans, intimate gatherings (only 24 to 38 passengers, depending on the trip), and landing rights at Manele Bay, which give its Lanai trip a special edge. (Trilogy is the only other outfitter that lands on Lanai, and the only one that will take you on a tour of the island.) This quality outfitter is a nice choice if you want to embark on a Molokini cruise or a champagne sunset sail, too.

Departures from Maalaea Harbor (at the Highway 30/130 junction), Maalaea, and Lahaina Harbor, on Front Street, Lahaina, depending on cruise. ☎ *800-441-2087 or 808-244-2087.* www.sailmaui.com. *Cruises (which include drinks and hors d'oeuvres or full meals, depending on the outing you choose): $51–$85 adults, $29–$43 kids ages 4–12. 15-percent online advance-booking discount available at press time.*

Trilogy Excursions

Book these trips in advance because Trilogy (the Mercedes of Maui snorkel-sail operators) offers the island's best and most popular snorkel-sail trips, hands down. They're the most expensive, too, but they're worth every penny. The trips feature first-rate catamarans, top-quality equipment, great food, and the best crew in the business. What's more, Trilogy is the only Lanai cruise operator that's allowed to land on the island's Hulopoe Beach, a terrific marine preserve that's one of the best snorkel and dolphin-watching spots in Hawaii, for a fun-filled day of sailing and snorkeling; it's also the only operator that can offer a ground tour of the island.

Departures from Maalaea Harbor (at the Highway 30/130 junction), Maalaea; Lahaina Harbor, on Front Street, Lahaina; or Kaanapali Beach, Kaanapali, depending on cruise. ☎ **888-225-6284** *or 808-661-4743.* www.sailtrilogy.com. *Full-day Lanai cruises: $169 adults, $85 kids 3–15, including BBQ lunch and island tour. (Deluxe "Ultimate Adventure" version with Jeep safari and champagne return sail $229 adults, $115 kids.) 5½- to 6½-hour Molokini or Kaanapali cruise: $95 adults, $48 kids. Shorter Kaanapali sunset cruise $59 adults, $30 kids; 2-hour Kaanapali whale-watching cruise $39 adults, $20 kids. Lanai Overnighters from $320 per person. 10-percent online advance-booking discounts available at press time.*

Delving into the deep: Submarine rides

There's a great way to see Maui's spectacular underwater world even if you don't swim: Take a submarine ride with **Atlantis Adventures Maui** (☎ 800-548-6262 or 808-667-6604; www.goatlantis.com). From Lahaina Harbor, you'll go 125 feet beneath the surface in one of Atlantis's state-of-the-art subs to see a whole new world of sea critters, including — if you're lucky — humpback whales in season. The 90-minute tours cost $80 for adults, $40 for kids. (Children must be at least 36 inches tall.) *A word of warning:* The ride is perfectly safe, but skip it if you suffer from serious claustrophobia. *On the other side of the coin:* If you are a swimmer — even if you just have basic paddle skills — skip this expensive adventure, don a mask and snorkel, and hit the waves yourself instead for a primo underwater experience.

Ocean kayaking

Maui's best kayaking outfitter for beginners and accomplished kayakers alike is **South Pacific Kayaks & Outfitters,** in the Rainbow Mall, 2439 S. Kihei Rd., Kihei (☎ 800-776-2326 or 808-875-4848; www.southpacifickayaks.com). It offers a range of kayak tours that launch from both South and West Maui and incorporate whale-watching in winter. The excellent guides are all very knowledgeable and ecology-minded; you get to meet at its office, where you can stow valuables (rather than leaving them in your car — always a no-no) and choose your equipment before it's loaded (another big plus). Tour prices run from $55 to $89 per person, with custom options available.

If you're an experienced kayaker capable of setting out on your own, South Pacific can rent you single or double kayaks for $30 or $40 a day, respectively and point you to good launching areas. Weekly rates and islandwide delivery (for an additional charge) are also available.

Winter whale-watching

More than any other Hawaiian island, Maui is your best perch for spotting Pacific humpback whales in winter. Virtually every boat that operates from Maui combines whale-watching with their regular adventures from December through April, and a good number offer dedicated whale-watching cruises in season, most notably the Pacific Whale Foundation. (See the section "Ocean cruising to Molokini and Lanai and other on-deck adventures," earlier in this chapter.) The channel separating Maui from Lanai and Molokai is a whale-watching hot spot, so Lanai cruises, in particular, are always an excellent bet.

You don't have to shell out the bucks for a pricey cruise to see whales. In season, you can spot them right from shore. Just look out to sea; just about any west-facing beach offers you a prime whale-watching opportunity. Follow these tips to increase your humpback-spotting chances:

- ✔ **Once you see a whale, keep watching in the same vicinity.** They often stay down for 20 minutes or so and then pop back up to take in some air and play a little. Be patient, and you're likely to be rewarded.

- ✔ **Bring your binoculars from home.** You'll see so much more with a little magnification.

- ✔ **Anywhere along the West Maui coast is a good bet for whale-watching.** A great place to park yourself is **MacGregor Point,** a scenic lookout at mile marker 9 on the Honoapiilani Highway (Highway 30), on the way to Lahaina from Maalaea. Another good West Maui whale-watching perch is the straight part of Honoapiilani Highway between MacGregor Point and Olowalu (where Chez Paul is). However, do yourself — and everybody else — a favor and pull over to the side of the road before you look out to sea, as whale-spotting along here has been known to cause more than a few accidents.

The nonprofit Pacific Whale Foundation (see the section "Ocean cruising to Molokini and Lanai and other on-deck adventures," earlier in this chapter) operates a **Whale Information Station** at MacGregor Point that's staffed by friendly and knowledgeable whale-expert naturalists, daily from 8:30 a.m. to 3:30 p.m. from December through April. Just stop by — they even have high-powered binoculars you can use and are happy to share whale-watching tips and facts galore — or call ☎ **800-WHALE-1-1** (800-942-5311) or 808-249-8811 for further details.

Catching a wave

Book your surfing or windsurfing lesson (the upcoming sections give you more information on how to do that) for early in your stay. That way, if conditions aren't right on your scheduled day, you'll have plenty of time to reschedule.

Learning to surf

If you've always wanted to learn to surf, Maui is a great place to fulfill the dream because it's known for having the easiest learning surf in Hawaii. The motto at the **Nancy C. Emerson School of Surfing** (☎ 808-244-7873; www.surfclinics.com) is, "If a dog can surf, so can you!" — a dubious challenge, but a surprisingly comforting one, too. A pro international surfing champ, an instructor since 1973, a stunt performer in movies like *Waterworld,* and a surf teacher to such celebs as Kiefer Sutherland and Beau Bridges, Nancy has pioneered the technique of teaching completely unskilled folks to surf in one two-hour lesson. You can, really — I've seen it happen firsthand. The instructors are professional and personable; you'll probably have your lesson on the beach behind 505 Front St. in Lahaina, where the surf breaks are big enough to learn on but not overwhelming. A beginning lesson starts at $100 per person for a one-hour private lesson, $70 per person for two hours with a group; I recommend going for the group option. Experienced surfers can take full- and multiday private lessons and group clinics with Nancy's skilled instructors (or Nancy herself, whose time is worth top dollar; check the Web site or call for rate schedules).

Action Sports Surf School (☎ 808-871-5857; www.actionsportsmaui. com) offers everything from kiddie lessons to extreme tow-in and strap surfing lessons for experienced board riders. **Hawaiian Island Surf and Sport,** 415 Dairy Rd., Kahului (☎ 800-231-6958 or 808-871-4981; www. maui.net/hisurf), also offers lessons for beginners and kids as well as intermediate and advanced surfers looking to take their skills and experience to the next level. The average lesson is $79 for both of these companies.

For experienced surfers only

Expert surfers visit Maui in winter when the surf's really up. The best surfing beaches include **Honolua Bay,** north of Kapalua; **Maalaea,** just outside the breakwall of the Maalaea Harbor; and **Hookipa Beach Park** in Paia, where surfers get the waves until noon, when the windsurfers take over. If you have a bit of experience but don't want a serious challenge, head to the **505 Front Street Beach,** next to Lahaina Harbor in Lahaina, where even long-surfing locals regularly catch the easy waves.

Second Wind Surf, Sail & Kite, 111 Hana Hwy. (between Dairy Road and Hobron Avenue), Kahului (☎ 800-936-7787 or 808-877-7467; www.second windmaui.com), has the best fleet of rental boards on the island ($18 per day, or $105 for a week), and friendly service to boot.

For daily reports on wind and surf conditions, call the **Wind and Surf Report** at ☎ 808-877-3611.

Windsurfing and kiteboarding

Expert windsurfers will want to head to Paia's world-famous **Hookipa Beach,** known all over the globe for its brisk winds and excellent waves, in the afternoons. When the winds turn northerly, **Kihei** is the spot to be; some days, you can see whales in the distance behind the windsurfers. The northern end of Kihei is best: At **Ohukai Park,** the first beach along South Kihei Road, the winds are good, the water is easy to access, and a long strip of grass is available to assemble your gear. If you have enough experience to head out on your own but you want manageable waves, head to **Kanaha Beach Park** near the airport in Kahului, which is where all the top schools take their students to learn.

Endorsed by Robbie Naish, Hawaii's most famous windsurfer (who has his own windsurfing school on Oahu; see Chapter 12), **Hawaiian Island Surf and Sport,** 415 Dairy Rd., Kahului (☎ **800-231-6958** or 808-871-4981; www.maui.net/hisurf), offers beginning 2½-hour windsurf lessons for $79 (plus equipment), as well as instruction in shortboard sailing for those ready to move to the next level. The island's best assortment of quality gear rentals are available as well.

Top-quality rental gear for windsurfing and kitesurfing can be had from **Second Wind Surf, Sail & Kite,** 111 Hana Hwy. (between Dairy Road and Hobron Avenue), Kahului (☎ **800-936-7787** or 808-877-7467; www.second windmaui.com or www.mauikitesurfing.com). They're also an excellent contact if you want to arrange for windsurfing lessons, for beginners and experienced windsurfers alike, as well as kiteboarding lessons for experienced waveriders. **Action Sports Maui** (☎ **808-871-5857;** www.actionsportsmaui.com) also offers lessons in both windsurfing and kiteboarding, as well as paragliding for high-soaring adventurers.

Scuba diving

Molokini is one of Hawaii's top dive spots thanks to calm, clear, protected waters and an abundance of marine life at every level, from clouds of yellow butterfly fish to white-tipped reef sharks to manta rays. This crescent-shaped crater has three tiers of diving: a 35-foot plateau inside the crater basin (used by beginning divers and snorkelers), a wall sloping to 70 feet just beyond the inside plateau, and a sheer wall on the outside and backside of the crater that plunges 350 feet below the surface.

Other top dive spots include the pristine waters off the island of **Lanai,** whose south and west coasts are a dream come true for divers looking for a one-of-a-kind setting.

You need to book a dive boat to get to Molokini or Lanai. **Lahaina Divers** (☎ **800-998-3483** or 808-667-7496; www.lahainadivers.com) is a five-star PADI (Professional Association of Diving Instructors) facility that has been lauded as one of Hawaii's top dive operators by publications like *Scuba Diving* magazine. Lahaina Divers can take certified divers to Molokini or Lanai aboard one of its big, comfortable dive boats for two- to four-tank dives ranging in price from $119 to $179; West Maui dives start at $99. Instruction is available for divers of all experience levels, and the "Discover Scuba" package for beginners starts at just $129 (check for Internet specials). Full open-water training packages are also available, as well as specialty training in deep diving, underwater photography, and more. Lahaina Divers is happy to take divers with disabilities out, too.

Or contact **Ed Robinson's Diving Adventures (☎ 800-635-1273** or 808-879-3584; www.mauiscuba.com/erd1.htm), which caters to certified divers from his South Maui base. A widely published underwater photographer, Ed is one of Maui's best; most of his business is repeat customers. Ed offers personalized two-tank dives, three-tank adventures, Lanai trips, and sunset and night dives; prices start at $120. Custom dives are also available, plus discounts for multiple-day dives.

Also recommendable for two-tank boat dives to Molokini and nearby Maui waters is **Mike Severns Diving (☎ 808-879-6596;** www.mike severnsdiving.com), which takes 12 divers at a time out from Kihei in two groups of six for a quiet and crowd-free experience. The price is $125, with discounts available if you have your own equipment or schedule multiday dives.

If you've never scuba dived before but want to learn, contact either Lahaina Divers or **Bobby Baker's Maui Sun Divers (☎ 877-879-3337;** www.mauisundivers.com). This outfit specializes in training beginners, and it offers a whole slate of introductory dives (for around $110) and multiple-day starter and certification programs.

Sportfishing

Ready to head out on the open waves in search of big-game fish like marlin, tuna, and wahoo? **Sportfish Hawaii (☎ 877-388-1376** or 808-396-2607; www.sportfishhawaii.com) can book a first-class charter for you out of Maalaea or Lahaina harbors on Maui. Half-day private charters start at $600.

Exploring on Dry Land

Maui is home to two of Hawaii's most renowned attractions: **Haleakala National Park,** a remarkable, crater at the heart of the island that offers some of the best sunrise-watching in the world, not to mention one-of-a-kind hiking and biking fun; and the **Heavenly Road to Hana,** one of the most well-known scenic drives in the United States.

If you need a little reliable personal assistance in making sense of Maui's wealth of activity options (or glut, depending on your perspective), you can get it. The best and most reliable activity booker on Maui is **Tom Barefoot's Cashback Tours,** in the heart of Lahaina at 834 Front St., near Lahainaluna Road (☎ **888-222-0350** or 808-661-8889; www.tombarefoot. com). Unlike most other so-called "activity centers" on Maui, this professional operation has nothing to do with timeshares — activities are its business, and I've found the salespeople's recommendations to be consistently good ones. Their office is filled with pictures and descriptive information on all the activities they represent. What's more, Tom Barefoot's offers 10- to 20-percent discounts on most activities. However, if you tell them that you want the top-of-the-line snorkel cruise or luau, they'll freely recommend and book you with Trilogy or Old Lahaina, even though they can't offer you a savings and won't make a dime — because they figure that a happy customer is a returning customer. You can book discounted activities before you leave home via their Web site or toll-free number.

 Do yourself a favor and avoid those activities bookers that are trying to sell you a timeshare. Believe me, spending a half-day of your precious vacation time warding off the hard-sell advances of a salesperson trying to force you to buy a timeshare you don't need in exchange for a "free" snorkel cruise on a cut-rate operator is simply not worth it.

Taking a guided van or bus tour

If you've rented a car and can get around easily on your own, driving yourself around the island is definitely the preferable way to go.

But you might want to hook up with a guided tour if your mobility is limited, if you're traveling solo and don't want to make the drive to Hana on your own, or if you just want to kick back and let somebody else take the wheel. The downside is that with a guided tour, you'll have little or no control over where you go and how long you stay, and your time communing with nature will be limited. Still, for some people, a guided tour is the best way to see Haleakala National Park and take in the glories of the Heavenly Road to Hana.

For small-scale, local-led van tours of the Heavenly Road to Hana and Haleakala National Park's sunrise extravaganza, book your guided trip with family-owned **Ekahi Tours** (☎ **888-292-2422** or 808-877-9775; www.ekahi.com). One of the great advantages of its Hana tour is that it's a circle island tour; you'll not only drive the road to Hana, but you'll experience the desert landscape of the little-traveled back road on the return trip, which takes you along the south coast and around the back side of the Haleakala Volcano (weather permitting). Ekahi can take you not only to Hana but also to hidden Kahakuloa, a half-day tour that offers an insightful look at Maui's ancient past and rural present. Ekahi tour prices range from $70 to $95 adults, $50 to $70 kids under 12, depending on the tour you choose; prices include a deli lunch. Discounts are available for seniors over age 60.

Now offering guided bus tours statewide, **Polynesian Adventure Tours** (☎ **800-622-3011** or 808-877-4242; www.polyad.com) offered the very first guided tours along the Heavenly Road to Hana, and it's still going strong in this department. In addition to the Hana option, it offers both Haleakala sunrise and Iao Valley tours in minivans, big-windowed mini-coaches, and full-size luxury buses. Prices run $60 to $79 for adults, $35 to $50 for kids 3 to 11.

Book your Polynesian Adventure Tour online to get a 10-percent price break.

If you choose to visit Haleakala National Park on a guided tour, remember to dress warmly, because it gets *cooooold* at 10,000 feet. For more on Haleakala's weather, see the complete section on the park later in this chapter.

Enjoying guided nature hikes

Maui's oldest and best-guided hiking company is Ken Schmitt's **Hike Maui** (☎ **808-879-5270**; www.hikemaui.com). Hike Maui has been universally lauded for the quality of its hikes; you can't go wrong with them. The expert guides are all trained naturalists who really know their stuff. Hike Maui is a fabulous way to see beautiful Maui at its natural best.

Hike Maui offers an array of hikes from easy to strenuous, but most fall in the moderate category. Two rainforest and waterfall hikes are available, plus two Haleakala Volcano hikes that offer an excellent way to see this splendid national park, which can be difficult to appreciate if you don't know what you're seeing. If you're an accomplished hiker and fit for it, don't miss the longer hike. It takes you all the way to the crater floor — which looks so much like the moon that the lunar astronauts trained here — for an otherworldly experience.

The shortest option is a three-hour waterfall hike for $60. The longer half- and full-day outings are spectacular off-the-beaten-path trips ranging from $95 to $140 per person. Prices include equipment and transportation from Central Maui (one of the company's air-conditioned vans will take you from the office to the trailhead), and a simple, healthy lunch of sandwiches and fruit. You can book as late as a couple of days in advance, but your best bet is to call before you arrive on the island. (At press time, you received a 10-percent discount for booking online a week in advance.)

If Hike Maui's schedules don't suit your needs, call **Maui Eco-Adventures** (☎ **877-661-7720** or 808-661-7720; www.ecomaui.com), which specializes in guided cultural and hiking adventures that explore untrammeled areas of the island, including the little-known Maunalei Arboretum; Nakele Point, the northernmost point on Maui; and more, including waterfall hikes and hike/kayak combos. Prices run $70 to $160 per person, including continental breakfast, lunch, a day's supply of water, and pickup from West Maui hotels.

Maui Hiking Safaris (☎ **888-445-3963** or 808-573-0168; www.maui.net/
~mhs), is another reputable company offering guided hikes for all levels,
including waterfall hikes and guided hikes of Haleakala. Prices run from
$59 to $109 per person (10 percent less for kids 13 and under).

Maui Hiking Safaris extends 10-percent discounts to hikers who book
more than two weeks in advance as well as for kids under 13 and groups
of six or more.

Getting a bird's-eye view

Flightseeing is an excellent way to explore Maui's stunning, untouched
natural areas that are simply unviewable by any other means. Maui-
based helicopter tours also offer you the opportunity to see a neighbor
island — Molokai, Lanai, or even the Big Island — from the air in addition to the Valley Isle itself. There are, however, some considerations.
Although the companies that I recommend all feature skilled pilots and
helicopters with excellent safety records, the truth of the matter is that
flightseeing can be risky business. Twenty-eight people have died in
commercial helicopter crashes in Hawaii over the last decade — six of
those in a 1998 Kauai accident, seven in a Maui crash in July 2000. Of
course, just as with airplane travel, you are more likely to have a car
accident than a helicopter crash. Still, you should make informed
decisions.

When reserving a helicopter tour with any company, check to make sure
that safety is its first concern. The company should be an FAA-certified
Part 135 operator, and the pilot should be Part 135 certified as well; the
135 license guarantees more stringent maintenance requirements and
pilot training programs than those who are only Part 91 certified. And
any time weather conditions look iffy, reschedule.

Blue Hawaiian Helicopters (tours depart from Kahului Airport; ☎ **800-
745-2583** or 808-871-8844; www.bluehawaiian.com; 30- to 90-minute
tours: $125–$280 per person [kids under age 2 fly free; others must pay
full fare]) is an excellent flightseeing company that's family run by David
and Patti Chevalier and a loyal long-employed staff. Blue Hawaiian flies a
fleet of superb American Eurocopter AStar 350 helicopters that carry six
passengers, providing each with a 180° view and a Bose noise-canceling
headset that lets you enjoy a surprisingly quiet ride. A world leader in
the flightseeing industry, Blue Hawaiian also features Hawaii's only EC-
130B4 Eco-Stars; these shiny new cutting-edge helicopters lower noise
pollution with a super-quiet design, and maximize comfort and views
with state-of-the-art design, technology, and materials. They offer one
phenomenal ride. A range of available flight options includes some
or all of the following spectacular sights: the misty, green West Maui
Mountains; impressive Haleakala Volcano; luxuriant, unspoiled East Maui
and Hana; and Molokai, where you'll fly by the highest sea cliffs in the
world.

If you book seven days or more in advance via e-mail or call and mention that you visited its Web site, Blue Hawaiian will award you a 15-percent price break.

Visiting Haleakala National Park

Haleakala (HA-lay-ah-KA-la) — the House of the Sun — is the massive 10,023-foot-high mountain that forms the core of the island of Maui. It's also Hawaii's second national park (after the Big Island's Hawaii Volcanoes National Park), and Maui's biggest natural attraction. About two million people drive to the summit of Haleakala to peer down into the crater of the world's largest dormant volcano. (Its official status is "active but not currently erupting," even though Haleakala has remained silent since 1790.) The crater is impressive: At 3,000 feet deep, 7½ miles long by 2½ miles wide, and encompassing 19 square miles, it's big enough to hold the entire island of Manhattan. More than anything else, it resembles a barren moonscape.

This stark, rugged place is actually breathtakingly beautiful in its own way. Just driving up the mountain is an experience in itself: The road climbs from sea level to 10,000 feet in just 37 miles, and the views are magnificent along the entire route. At first glance, the landscape looks like nothing more than a dry and barren wasteland. But soon, a fascinating, multihued geologic world emerges — a surprisingly fragile one that supports a number of the world's rarest examples of flora and fauna. Among the rare endangered species that call Haleakala home are the nene (NAY-nay), a gray-brown Hawaiian goose that doesn't migrate, prefers rock-hard lava beds to lakes, and is now protected as the state bird. There's also the silvery-green, porcupiney silversword plant, which grows only in Hawaii, lives for about 50 years, blooms once in a beautiful purple bouquet, and dies.

Haleakala is best known for its mystical sunrise vistas. Crowds of visitors drive here in the dark predawn hours to watch the spectacle of dawn breaking over the crater. If you decide to join the early-morning crowds, stick around after sunrise for some excellent hiking opportunities. Or do what a lot of people do: Hop on a bike and coast down the switchbacked, view-endowed road to the base of the mountain.

The park actually contains two separate and distinct destinations: Haleakala Summit and the Kipahulu coast. Lush, green, and tropical, Kipahulu is a world apart from the summit — and accessible only from the east side of the island, near Hana. No road links the summit and the coast, so Hana is a completely separate outing. For a discussion of Kipahulu and its biggest attraction, Oheo Gulch, see the section "Driving the Heavenly Road to Hana," later in this chapter.

See the "Haleakala National Park" map on p. 292 for listings in this section.

Haleakala National Park

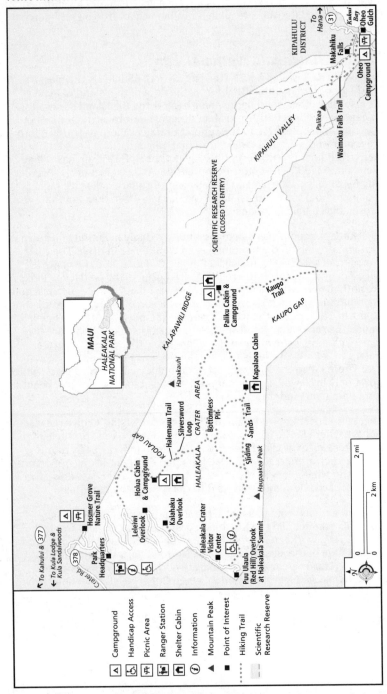

MAUI

HALEAKALA NATIONAL PARK

To Kahului & ← (377)

← To Kula Lodge & Kula Sandalwoods

(378)

Crater Rd.

Park Headquarters

Hosmer Grove Nature Trail

Leleiwi Overlook

Holua Cabin & Campground

Kalahaku Overlook

KOOLAU GAP

Halemauu Trail

Silversword Loop

Hanakauhi

KALAPAWILI RIDGE

HALEAKALA CRATER AREA

Bottomless Pit

Sliding Sands Trail

Haupaakea Peak

Haleakala Crater Visitor Center

Puu Ulaula (Red Hill) Overlook at Haleakala Summit

Kapalaoa Cabin

Paliku Cabin & Campground

Kaupo Trail

KAUPO GAP

SCIENTIFIC RESEARCH RESERVE (CLOSED TO ENTRY)

KIPAHULU VALLEY

Palikea

Waimoku Falls Trail

KIPAHULU DISTRICT

To Hana →

(31)

Kukui Bay

Makahiku Falls

Oheo Gulch

Oheo Campground

N

0 2 mi

0 2 km

Legend

- △ Campground
- ♿ Handicap Access
- ⛱ Picnic Area
- 🏕 Ranger Station
- ⛺ Shelter Cabin
- ⓘ Information
- ▲ Mountain Peak
- ■ Point of Interest
- ⋯ Hiking Trail
- Scientific Research Reserve

The legend behind the House of the Sun

The name *Haleakala* actually means "House of the Sun." The story of how this wild-looking volcano got such a magnificent name goes like this: One day, a mom complained that the sun sped across the sky so quickly that her tapa cloth didn't have enough time to dry. So in the predawn hours of the next morning, her thoughtful son, the demi-god Maui, climbed to the top of the volcano. When the sun rose above the horizon, Maui lassoed it, bringing it to a halt in the sky.

The sun begged Maui to let go. Maui said he would, on one condition: That the sun slow its trip across the sky to give the island more sunlight. The sun agreed. In honor of the agreement, islanders dubbed the mountain "House of the Sun."

Getting ready for your visit

For information before you go, contact **Haleakala National Park** at ☎ **808-572-4400** for information on the Haleakala summit (main) area of the park (dial ☎ **808-248-7375** for information and the ranger station at the park's Kipahulu district, near Hana, which is a separate outing I discuss later in this chapter). Or visit the park's official Web site at www.nps.gov/hale. You can also find lots of useful information at an unofficial but excellent site, www.haleakala.national-park.com.

The summit of Haleakala is 38 miles, or about a 1½-hour drive, from Kahului in Central Maui. To get there, take the Haleakala Highway (Highway 37 and then Highway 377) to wiggly Haleakala Crater Road (Highway 378), the heavily switchbacked road that leads you to the 10,000-foot summit. Allow two hours to reach the summit if you're driving from Lahaina or Kihei, 2½ hours if you're arriving from Wailea or Kaanapali, 15 minutes more if you're coming from Kapalua.

For the sunrise time and viewing conditions at Haleakala summit, call ☎ **808-877-5111.**

Admission to the park is $10 per car, which allows you to come and go as you please for seven days.

Keep these tips in mind as you plan your visit to Haleakala National Park:

✔ **If Maui is the first Hawaiian island you're visiting, schedule your sunrise visit for the first full day of your trip.** Your body clock won't be on Hawaii time yet, so it shouldn't be too hard to get up at 3 a.m. since it will feel like anywhere from 5 to 9 a.m. if you're from the mainland. If Maui is the last island on your itinerary, schedule your sunrise visit for the final day of your trip, because it's time to reacclimate yourself to the at-home hour anyway.

- ✔ **Dress warmly, in layers, no matter what time of year you visit.** Temperatures at the summit usually range between 40 and 65°F but can drop below freezing any time of year once you factor in the wind chill, especially in the predawn hours. Wear a hat and sturdy shoes and bring a blanket if you don't have a warm jacket. The weather is unpredictable at the summit, so be prepared for wind and rain in winter no matter what the time of day; don't be fooled by the coastline conditions. Call ☎ 808-877-5111 for the summit forecast.

- ✔ **Bring drinking water.** You'll need plenty of water on hand, especially if you plan on hiking.

- ✔ **Remember that this is a high-altitude wilderness area.** The thinness of the air makes some people dizzy; you may also experience lightheadedness, shortness of breath, nausea, headaches, and dehydration. The park recommends that pregnant women and those with heart or respiratory problems consult a doctor before ascending to high elevations.

- ✔ **Fill up your gas tank before you head to Haleakala.** The last gas station is 27 miles below the summit at Pukalani. Fill up the night before if you're going for sunrise, because it will be near impossible to find an open gas station at 4 a.m.

Arriving at the park and making the drive to the summit

About a mile from the entrance is **Park Headquarters,** open daily from 7:30 a.m. to 4 p.m. It's a great place to pick up park information, including the latest schedule of guided walks and ranger talks. If, however, you arrive before dawn, all you can do here is use the around-the-clock restrooms; the ones here are much nicer than the ones at the summit, so I highly recommend making a pit stop on the way up. Drinking water is also available.

You'll pass two scenic overlooks on the way to the summit. Stop at the one just beyond mile marker 17, **Leleiwi Overlook,** if only to get out, stretch, and get accustomed to the heights. From the parking area, a short trail leads to a panoramic view of the lunarlike crater. (The other overlook, Kalahaku, is most easily accessible on the descent.)

Continue on, and you'll soon reach **Haleakala Visitor Center,** 11 miles from the park entrance (open daily from sunrise to 3 p.m.), which offers spectacular views and some bare-bones restrooms. Park rangers also offer excellent, informative, and free naturalist talks daily at 9:30, 10:30, and 11:30 a.m. from the center. (Call ahead to confirm the next day's schedule to avoid disappointment.)

The actual summit — and the ideal sunrise-viewing perch — is beyond the turnoff for the visitor center, at **Puu Ulaula Overlook** (Red Hill). At Puu Ulaula, a triangular glass building serves as a windbreak and the best sunrise viewing spot. After the spectacle of sunrise, you can often see all the way to the snowcapped summit of Mauna Kea on the Big Island if it's clear. Haleakala Observatories (nicknamed Science City), which isn't open to the public, is also located here.

Hiking the park

If you want to hike the park, I strongly suggest going with a guide. This is an outlandishly huge, empty place that is best seen with someone who can lead you in the right direction and help you understand what you're seeing. Park rangers offer a range of free guided hikes; call for the latest schedule (☎ 808-572-4400) and to find out what to wear and bring (sturdy shoes and drinking water are musts). Also consider taking one of the guided Haleakala Crater hikes offered by Hike Maui and Maui Hiking Safaris; see the section "Enjoying guided nature hikes," earlier in this chapter.

If you don't want to bother with a serious hike but just want a glimpse of the park's peculiar brand of natural beauty, take a half-hour walk down the half-mile **Hosmer Grove Nature Trail,** which anybody can do. The trail is well-marked, with placards that point out what you're seeing along the way. Ask the ranger at the visitor center to direct you to the trailhead.

If you'd like to strike out on your own along the park's more serious trails, preview your options online at www.haleakala.national-park. com (click "Hiking Guide") or call ahead; the rangers will be happy to send you complete trail information.

Driving back down the mountain

As you start to head down the volcano, put your rental car in low gear on the way down so that you don't ride your brakes.

Around mile marker 24 is **Kalahaku Overlook,** the best place to spot the spiky, alienlike silversword plant and to take in some fabulous panoramic views.

At the base of the mountain, where you'll turn onto Haleakala Crater Road from the Haleakala Highway, is **Kula,** the closest thing to a gateway town that Haleakala has. Kula is most notable for its two restaurants, Kula Sandalwoods and the Kula Lodge, both of which serve great post-sunrise breakfast and lunch.

Biking down the volcano

Another great way to experience Haleakala is to cruise down it, from summit to base, on a bicycle. The guided ride is quite an experience, with stunning views the entire way. And you don't need to be an expert cyclist to do it; you just have to be able to ride a bike. In fact, you barely have to pedal — you'll coast down at a nice, leisurely pace. (The constant switchbacks keep you from picking up too much speed.)

A number of companies offer these trips with minor variations — some offer midday tours, others have go-at-your-own-pace options — but they generally work like this: A van picks you up at your hotel or condo anywhere between 2 and 3:30 a.m. and transports you to headquarters, where they'll outfit you with a custom-fitted bike (with a comfy seat and good brakes), a helmet, rain gear, and any other equipment you'll need for the downhill cruise. You and your fellow bikers then get back in the van, which takes you (and the bikes on an attached trailer) up to Haleakala's summit.

Just after the miracle of sunrise, you mount your bike and start down Haleakala Crater Road, usually riding single file behind a guide on the right shoulder of the road so that you don't interfere with traffic. The group generally stops for photo ops along the way. By about 10 a.m., you've come 22 miles to the end of Haleakala Crater Road. Some tours end with breakfast in Kula, while others break for breakfast and then proceed the rest of the way down the hill, to sea level.

Maui's oldest downhill company is **Maui Downhill** (☎ **800-535-2453** or 808-871-2155; www.mauidownhill.com). Maui Downhill offers a variety of guided Haleakala bike "safaris" at both sunrise and midday that run $150 per person. Other reliable companies include **Maui Mountain Cruisers** (☎ **800-232-6284** or 808-871-6014; www.mauimountain cruisers.com), and **Mountain Riders** (☎ **800-706-7700** or 808-242-9739; www.mountainriders.com). Prices usually include hotel pickup, transport to the top, all equipment, meals, and dropoff. Generally, riders have to be at least 12 and at least 4'10" tall. Younger kids and pregnant women can usually ride along in the van.

At press time, you can save a bundle on most of these tours by booking in advance via the companies' own Web sites (for example, Maui Downhill was offering $48 per person discounts!). But if you're already on the island and don't have access to a computer, Maui's most reliable activity booker, **Tom Barefoot's Cashback Tours,** 834 Front St., near Lahainaluna Road in Lahaina (☎ **888-222-3601** or 808-661-8889; www.tombarefoot.com), might also be able to save you a few bucks.

If you'd prefer a more independent — and more affordable — downhill ride, contact **Haleakala Bike Company** (☎ **888-922-2453** or 808-575-9575; www.bikemaui.com). Haleakala Bike Company outfits you with all the gear and takes you up to the top, but, after a little initial guidance, leaves you to proceed down the mountain at your own pace. Tours are $65 to $85 per person, with no hotel pickup or meal included (you'll meet at their Upcountry bike shop), and gear is available for kids as young as 8. The company also offers straight bike rentals of newer model Gary Fisher mountain bikes for $45 a day, including gear.

Coasting down Haleakala can be an incredible ride, and thousands of people come home from Maui every year claiming that it was the highlight of their trip. Still, you should know a few things before you book one of these trips. I'm not trying to discourage you, by any means; I just want you to know exactly what to expect:

✔ Virtually all the outfitters advertise these trips as safe, no-strain bicycle rides that anyone can do, even Grandma. However, these downhill bike tours do require some stamina, particularly in winter. Conditions can be harsh, you have to stay in line and keep up the pace with the other riders as cars go by (drivers are usually quite respectful, so you don't have to worry about dodging traffic), and the entire trip makes for a very long day.

✔ Summer and fall — when drive conditions and relatively mild temperatures usually prevail — are the best seasons for Haleakala downhill rides. Even though the better outfitters provide you with slick jumpsuits and headgear to protect you from the rain you'll almost inevitably encounter at some point, count on getting cold and wet in winter and spring.

Driving the Heavenly Road to Hana

No road in Hawaii is more celebrated than the Hana Highway (Highway 36), the super-curvaceous two-lane highway that winds along Maui's northeastern shore, offering some of the most scenic natural sightseeing in the entire state.

The Hana Highway winds for some 52 miles east from Kahului, in Central Maui, crossing more than 50 one-lane bridges, passing greener-than-green taro patches, magnificent seascapes, gorgeous waterfalls, botanical gardens, and rainforests before passing through the little town of Hana and ultimately ending up in one of Hawaii's most beautiful tropical places: the Kipahulu section of Haleakala National Park. Kipahulu is home to Oheo (oh-HAY-oh) Gulch, a stunning series of waterfall pools that tumble down to the sea.

Despite the draws at the end of the road, this drive is about the journey — *not* the destination. The drive from end to end takes at least three hours, but you should allow all day for it. If you race along just to arrive in Hana as quickly as you can, you'll wonder what all the fuss was about. Start out early, take it slow and easy, stop at the scenic points along the way, and let the ride along Hana work its magic. It will, I promise.

Take these points into consideration as you plan your Hana road trip:

✔ **Leave early.** Get up just after dawn, have an early breakfast (Charley's Restaurant & Saloon in Paia opens at 7 a.m.; see Chapter 13), and hit the road by 8 a.m. If you wait until midmorning to leave, you'll get stuck in bumper-to-bumper Hana Road traffic, you won't have enough time to enjoy the sights along the way, and you'll arrive at Oheo Gulch too late in the day to take a hike or a dip. It's especially important to make the most of the daylight hours in winter, when days are shortest.

The Heavenly Road to Hana

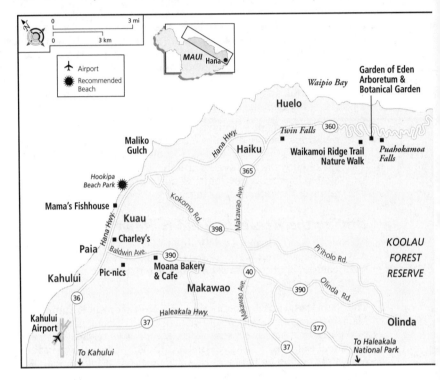

✔ **Consider booking a place to stay in Hana if you'd really like to take your time.** That way, you can head out to Hana against the traffic in the afternoon, stay for a couple of nights so that you have a full day to enjoy East Maui's attractions (including an abundance of peace and quiet), and meander back at your own pace (once again avoiding the traffic) on the morning of the third day. See Chapter 13 for accommodations in Hana.

✔ **Fill up on gas before you set out.** If all else fails, make sure that you stop in Paia, just east of Kahului, as the next gas is in Hana — 44 miles, 50-some bridges, and 200-plus hairpin turns down the road.

✔ **Don't bother if it's been raining heavily.** The Hana Highway is well paved and well maintained but can nevertheless be extremely dangerous when wet — and it's easy to get stuck in muddy shoulders and pull-offs.

✔ **Bring your bathing suit and a towel in warm weather.** You'll find a number of waterfall pools along the way that are ideal for a refreshing dip, and folks love to swim in Oheo Gulch's placid summer pools. (However, don't enter the pools unless the park rangers say conditions are safe. Please take their warnings seriously; visitors

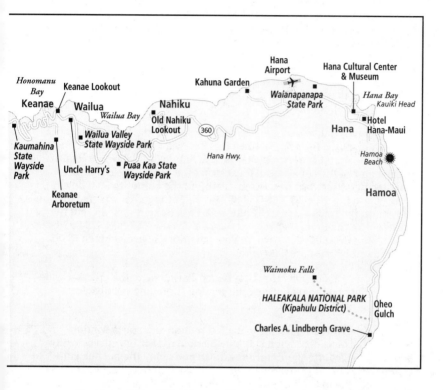

Honomanu
Bay
Keanae Lookout
Keanae
Wailua
Wailua Bay
Kaumahina
State
Wayside
Park
Uncle Harry's
Wailua Valley
State Wayside Park
Keanae
Arboretum
Puaa Kaa State
Wayside Park
Nahiku
Old Nahiku
Lookout
360
Hana Hwy.
Kahuna Garden
Hana
Airport
Waianapanapa
State Park
Hana Cultural Center
& Museum
Hana Bay
Kauiki Head
Hana
Hotel
Hana-Maui
Hamoa
Beach
Hamoa
Waimoku Falls
HALEAKALA NATIONAL PARK
(Kipahulu District)
Oheo
Gulch
Charles A. Lindbergh Grave

have been killed here.) Also bring mosquito repellent, because lush
East Maui is a buggy place.

✔ **Leave your mainland road rage on the mainland.** Practice aloha
as you drive the Hana Road: Give way at the one-lane bridges. Wave
at passing motorists. Let the locals who drive this road with jaw-
dropping speed and who pass on blind curves have the right-of-
way; if the guy behind you blinks his lights, let him pass. And don't
honk your horn — it's considered rude in Hawaii.

There's one exception to the no-horn-honking rule: If you reach a blind
curve, *do* honk your horn to indicate that you're coming around the
bend — and proceed slowly.

See the "The Heavenly Road to Hana" map on p. 298 and the "Hana" map
on p. 303 for listings in this section.

Highlights worth seeking out along the way

If you'd like some narration to accompany what you're seeing along the
Road to Hana, pick up a **Hana Cassette Guide** on your way out of town.

The 90-minute tape or CD is $20 at the Hana Cassette Guide shop in Kahului on Dairy Road (Highway 380), next to the Shell Service Station just before the Hana Highway (☎ 808-572-0550). I highly recommend using it in tandem with the following text, as it covers many more sights and includes much more background than I have the space for here.

If you want to see the Hana Road but you just don't want to drive it yourself, consider taking a guided van or bus tour. See the section called "Taking a guided van or bus tour," earlier in this chapter, for recommended tour operators.

Setting Out: A half-dozen miles east of Kahului on the Hana Highway is Paia (pa-EE-ah), a former mill town that's now a neo-hippie, boutique-dotted surf spot. **Charley's Restaurant & Saloon,** at Baldwin Avenue in the heart of town, makes an ideal stop for a hearty breakfast (see Chapter 13); afterward, you can bop around the corner to 30 Baldwin Ave., where **Pic-nics** (☎ 808-579-8021) can put together a picnic for you to take on the road. I also like **Cakewalk Paia Bakery,** just around the corner from the Hana Highway on Baldwin Avenue (☎ 808-579-8870; www.cakewalkmaui.com), where you can grab a gourmet lunch to go, and the sandwiches are *very* yummy.

Just beyond Paia town is **Hookipa Beach Park,** one of the greatest windsurfing spots on the planet; see the section "Combing the Beaches," earlier in this chapter, for details.

The road narrows to one lane in each direction and starts winding around Mile Marker 3. But it's at Mile Marker 16 that the curves really begin, one right after another. Slow down and enjoy the bucolic surroundings. After Mile Marker 16, the highway number changes from 36 to 360, and the mile markers start again at 0. (I have no idea why.)

At Mile Marker 2: The first great place to stop is **Twin Falls,** on the inland side of the road; the Twin Falls Fruit Stand marks the spot. Hop over the short ladder on the right side of the red gate and walk about 3 to 5 minutes to the waterfall off to your left, or continue on another 10 to 15 minutes to the second, larger waterfall. The gate has a "No Trespassing" sign, but you'll see from the crowds that it doesn't bother most folks. If it bothers you, skip Twin Falls altogether; there's plenty more to see farther down the road.

After Mile Marker 4: The vegetation grows more lush as you head east. This area is the edge of the **Koolau Forest Reserve,** where the branches of 20- to 30-foot-tall guava trees are laden with green (not ripe) and yellow (ripe) fruit, and introduced eucalyptus trees grow as tall as 200 feet.

The upland forest gets 200 to 300 inches of rainfall annually, so you'll begin to see waterfalls around just about every turn as you head east from here. The one-lane bridges start, too, so drive slowly and be prepared to yield to oncoming cars.

After Mile Marker 6: Just before Mile Marker 7 is a forest of waving bamboo. The sight is so spectacular that drivers are often tempted to take their eyes off the road, so be very cautious. Just after Mile Marker 7, you can pull over at the **Kaaiea Bridge,** which offers a terrific view of the bamboo grove.

At Mile Marker 9: The sign says Koolau State Forest Reserve, but the real attraction is the **Waikamoi Ridge Trail,** an easy and well-marked ¾-mile loop. This trail makes a great place to stretch your legs; look for the turnout on the right.

Between Mile Markers 10 and 11: At the halfway point, on the inland side of the road, is the **Garden of Eden Arboretum and Botanical Garden** (☎ **808-572-9899;** www.mauigardenofeden.com), featuring more than 500 exotic plants, flowers, and trees from around the Pacific (including lots of wild ginger and an impressive palm collection) on 26 acres. You can drive through the garden in about 5 minutes, walk its main loop in about 20 minutes, or stay a bit longer and follow any number of nature trails. The garden is open daily from 8 a.m. to 3 p.m., and admission is $7.50 per person. A fruit and smoothie stand offers refreshment at the gate.

At Mile Marker 11: Park at the bridge and take the short walk up the stone wall-lined trail to 30-foot **Puohokamoa Falls,** tucked away in a fern-filled amphitheater surrounded by banana trees, colorful heliconias, and sweet-smelling ginger. The gorgeous pool is a great place to take a plunge.

Just Beyond Mile Marker 12: Kaumahina State Wayside Park has portable toilets and picnic tables at the large parking area, plus a gorgeous view of the rugged coastline across the road.

Just Beyond Mile Marker 14: One of my favorite stops on the entire drive is **Honomanu Bay,** a stark rocky beach popular with net fishermen that faces a beautiful bay. Tear your eyes away from the water, and you'll find incredible golden-green cliffs forming an intense backdrop as you look inland and up. The turnoff is on the left, at the stop sign just after the mile marker; don't attempt the rutted and rocky road if it has been raining recently.

Just Beyond Mile Marker 17: Keanae Lookout is a wide spot on the ocean side of the road where you can see the entire Keanae Peninsula jutting out into the sea, with its checkerboard pattern of green taro fields and its ocean boundary etched in black lava. If time is precious, though, wait to stop after Mile Marker 19, where the view from the **Wailea Valley** viewpoint is even better.

At Mile Marker 18: The road widens, and fruit and flower stands begin to line the road. Many of these stands operate on the honor system: You select your purchase and leave your money in the basket. I recommend stopping at **Uncle Harry's,** just beyond Keanae School on the ocean side of the road. Harry Kunihi Mitchell was a legend in his time, an expert in native plants who devoted his life to the Hawaiian-rights and nuclear-free movements.

A Quarter-Mile After Marker 19: For the best view of the **Wailua Peninsula,** stop at the lookout and parking area on the ocean side of the road, where sun-dappled picnic tables serve up great views.

A bit farther down the road, just before the bridge on the inland side, is a pretty waterfall view.

Between Mile Markers 22 and 23: At **Puaa Kaa** (poo-AH-ah KA-ah) **State Wayside Park,** the splash of waterfalls provides the soundtrack for a small park area with restrooms and a picnic area. On the opposite side of the road from the toilets is a well-marked and paved path that leads through a patch of sweet-smelling ginger to the falls and a swimming hole.

After Mile Marker 25: After the mile marker, turn toward the ocean at the steep turnoff just before the one-lane bridge and follow the well-paved but winding road 2½ miles down to the **Old Nahiku Lookout,** one of the very few points along the entire route that lets you get close to the ocean, and the finest picnic spot on the entire route. A small grassy lawn faces rocky lava points and crashing turquoise surf for a breathtaking, up-close view. You can walk down to the rocky beach at the backside of the parking lot.

At Mile Marker 31: Turn toward the ocean on Ulaino Road and go a half-mile to **Kahanu Garden,** one of four National Tropical Botanical Gardens in Hawaii (☎ 808-248-8912; www.ntbg.org). Surrounded by a native pandanus forest (the leaf that *Lauhala* products are woven from), the garden features a remarkable collection of ethno-botanical plants from the Pacific islands (with a particular concentration on plants of value to the people of Polynesia and Micronesia), plus the foundation of Poolanihale Heiau, the largest Hawaiian temple in Hawaii. The self-guided walking tour is $10 and takes 30 to 40 minutes to complete; open Monday through Friday from 10 a.m. to 2 p.m. The road that leads to the garden entrance is rough and unpaved, but not bad; still, don't bother if it's been raining.

At Mile Marker 32: The turnoff for 122-acre **Waianapanapa** (wa-ee-na-pa-NA-pa) **State Park** leads to shiny black-sand **Waianapanapa Beach,** whose bright-green jungle backdrop and sparkling cobalt water make for quite a stunning view. On hand are picnic pavilions, restrooms, trails, and fruit stands lining the road, so come down to take a peek. The beach here is not for swimming, though. A blowhole appears when the winter surf kicks up. This natural hole in the rocks is configured so that when harsh surf kicks up, water shoots through the hole like a spout — quite a neat sight.

Arriving in Hana

Postage stamp–sized Hana is a lush and charming little hamlet, but frankly, there's just not much to see in the town itself.

The few attractions include the **Hana Coast Gallery,** on the Hana Highway adjacent to the Hotel Hana-Maui (☎ 808-248-8636), an excellent showcase for island-made products hewn by master craftspeople,

Hana

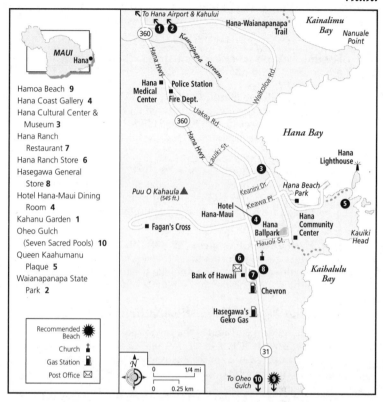

MAUI
Hana

Hamoa Beach **9**
Hana Coast Gallery **4**
Hana Cultural Center &
Museum **3**
Hana Ranch
Restaurant **7**
Hana Ranch Store **6**
Hasegawa General
Store **8**
Hotel Hana-Maui Dining
Room **4**
Kahanu Garden **1**
Oheo Gulch
(Seven Sacred Pools) **10**
Queen Kaahumanu
Plaque **5**
Waianapanapa State
Park **2**

Recommended Beach
Church
Gas Station
Post Office

To Hana Airport & Kahului
Hana-Waianapanapa
Trail
Kainalimu
Bay
Nanuale
Point
Kawuipapa Stream
Hana Hwy
Waikoloa Rd.
Hana
Medical
Center
Police Station
Fire Dept.
Uakea Rd.
Hana Hwy
Kauiki St.
Hana Bay
Hana
Lighthouse
Puu O Kahaula
(545 ft.)
Keanini Dr.
Keawa Pl.
Hana Beach
Park
Hotel
Hana-Maui
Fagan's Cross
Hana
Ballpark
Hauoli St.
Hana
Community
Center
Kauiki
Head
Bank of Hawaii
Chevron
Kaihalulu
Bay
Hasegawa's
Geko Gas
To Oheo
Gulch
N
0   1/4 mi
0   0.25 km

including gorgeous woodworks. The quirky **Hasegawa General Store**
(☎ **808-248-8231**) is worth stopping in for kicks (look for the Spam
sushi vending machine near the entrance) or to use the ATM, but the
prices on practicals and munchies are better across the road and up the
hill at the **Hana Ranch Store** (☎ **808-248-8261**). If you want a meal, you
have two choices: the casual **Hana Ranch Restaurant,** or the **Hotel
Hana-Maui Dining Room;** for details, see Chapter 13.

History buffs may want to head toward Hana Bay; overlooking the bay is
the **Hana Cultural Center and Museum,** 4974 Uakea Rd. (☎ **808-248-
8622;** www.hookele.com/hccm), open daily from 10 a.m. to 4 p.m. (most
of the time). This charming museum is dedicated to preserving the history of Hana, with exhibits showcasing traditional Hawaiian quilts and
such implements of life as poi boards and fish hooks carved out of the
tusks of wild pigs. Also on-site is the Old Hana Courthouse and Jailhouse,
plus Kauhala O Hana, four *hale* (living structures) where you can see what
it was like to live in the style of Hana's earliest settlers.

If you want to see more of what's available in town, pick up a copy of the **Hana Visitors Guide,** a fold-out map and pamphlet that's available free around town. If you don't run across one, stop into Hasegawa's to pick one up.

For those of you spending some time in these parts, a number of active adventures are at hand:

- ✔ **Hang Gliding Maui** (☎ **808-572-6557;** www.hanggliding maui. com) offers tandem instructional flights aboard its engine-powered ultralight aircraft. Prices are $115 for a 30-minute lesson, $190 for an hour-long lesson.

- ✔ If you want to explore the lush Kipahulu District on horseback, reach out to **Maui Stables** (☎ **808-248-7799;** www.mauistables. com), which offers a taste of real island culture as you explore the gorgeous scenery. Choose a morning or afternoon half-day tour; prices are $150 per person, including a deli lunch. Advance reservations are a must.

- ✔ **Maui Cave Adventures** (☎ **808-248-7308;** www.mauicave.com) offers cave-exploring hikes for every age and ability, including kids as young as 7, through Kaeleku Caverns; prices run $29 to $69 per person, depending on the length and difficulty of your tour.

Exploring beyond Hana: Hamoa Beach and Oheo Gulch

About 2½ miles past Hana is the turnoff for Hamoa Beach, one of the most gorgeous beaches in all Hawaii — and great for swimming to boot (in summer, anyway). For details, see the section "Combing the Beaches," earlier in this chapter.

About 10 luxuriant miles past Hana along the highway is **Oheo** (oh-HAY-oh) **Gulch,** a dazzling series of waterfall pools cascading into the sea that some folks call Seven Sacred Pools, even though there are more like two dozen. This area is the Kipahulu district of Haleakala National Park, and a **ranger station** located at the back of the unpaved parking lot (☎ **808-248-7375**) is staffed daily from 9 a.m. to 4:30 p.m. Restrooms are available, but no drinking water, so be sure to pick some up in Hana if you're out. Visiting this area of the park is free.

The easy, half-mile **Kuloa Point Loop Trail** leads to the lower pools, where you can take a dip when the weather is warm and the water is placid. This well-marked 20-minute walk is a must for everyone.

Stay out of the Oheo Gulch pools in winter or after a heavy rain, when the otherwise placid falls can wash you out to sea in an instant, to the waiting sharks below. (No kidding — they actually do hang out in the brackish water at the foot of the falls.) No matter what the season, if you do take a dip, always be extra-vigilant — keep an eye on the water in the streams. Even when the sky is sunny near the coast, upland rain can cause flood waters to rise in minutes, so if the water seems to be running between the pools at all, stay out. A mainland visitor was washed away to sea during a seemingly innocuous Oheo Gulch photo op in May 2002. Don't let this terrible tragedy be repeated; always check with the rangers before you go in the pools.

The 2-mile (each way), moderate **Pipiwai Trail** leads upstream to additional pools and 400-foot Waimoku Falls. The often-muddy but rewarding uphill trail leads through taro patches and bamboo, guava, and mango stands to the magnificent falls. The trail is unmarked but relatively easy to follow. Wear sturdy shoes, bring water, and don't attempt the trek in the rain.

Heading back to the resorts

Most visitors head back the way they came, along the Hana Highway.

But if the weather is good, you have an alternative. The Hana Highway continues past Kipahulu around Maui's southern coast, becoming the Piilani Highway (Highway 31) as it traverses the empty desert that meets the southern sea along a route that's informally but universally known as the **Kaupo** (COW-po) **Road.** The Kaupo Road ultimately meets up with Highway 37 (the Kula/Haleakala Highway), which will take you back to Central Maui and the resorts. The route is no shorter or less time-consuming than the Hana Road — just different.

You should know a few things about the Kaupo Road — and consider them very carefully — before you set out on it. For one thing, you'll find nothing at all out here, except for a few lone cows, some desert scrub, and amazing ocean views. There are no structures at all, let alone any modern conveniences. Those who appreciate desert beauty will find the landscape striking, but anyone else will feel like they've arrived in Mad Max territory.

Seven miles of road remain unpaved, but the entire stretch between Mile Markers 39 and 23 (the markers run west to east) is dreadful. In fact, the unpaved portion is an improvement over the other pitted 9 miles, whose pavement is so lumpy that it doesn't deserve to be called pavement.

Although the Kaupo Road is fine for average cars in dry weather, the road washes out with a little rain, so don't go near it if the weather has been poor. Ask around, both at your hotel and in Hana; news on the current conditions gets out. And check with your rental-car company before you set out, because many rental contracts forbid you from taking their cars on this road. If you get stuck, you'll pay a hefty tow charge, but that will be the least of your problems, because you'll be stuck in the real middle of nowhere, where other cars may not pass by for hours.

All that said, I love the Kaupo Road and the little-seen side of Maui it shows. Still, before you consider it, be sure to take all my warnings and recommendations extremely seriously. And if one person tells you that conditions are less than optimum and advises you against it, skip it — go back the way you came.

Before departing Hana, don't forget to check your gas gauge no matter which road west you're traveling. There's nowhere to fill up along either route back to civilization. If you need gas, stop at one of the town's two service stations, Chevron and Hasegawa's Hana Geko Gas, which sit nearly side by side on the right side of the Hana Highway as you leave town.

More attractions worth seeking out

Here are some more attractions that you may not want to miss.

Central Maui

These attractions are located in and around the commercial heart of the island, Kahului, and nearby Wailuku, the charming county seat.

Bailey House Museum

This 19th-century missionary and sugar planter's home — built in 1833 on a royal Hawaiian site — is a treasure trove of Hawaiiana that includes a notable collection of precontact Hawaiian artifacts as well as items from post-missionary times. Excellently curated island-themed temporary exhibits are also part of the mix. This little museum is well worth a half-hour stop for history buffs. It boasts lovely gardens and a wonderful gift shop, too, neither of which require admission.

See p. 274. 2375-A Main St., just west of the Kaahumanu Ave./Honoapiilani Hwy. (Hwy. 32/30) intersection, Wailuku. ☎ *808-244-3326.* www.mauimuseum.org. *Admission: $5 adults, $4 seniors, $1 kids 7–12. Open: Mon–Sat 10 a.m.–4 p.m.*

Hawaii Nature Center — Iao Valley

Before you head into Iao Valley to explore (directly following), families will want to stop into this small, kid-centered interactive science center, which features great hands-on exhibits for kids and displays relating to the park's natural history. There's also a nice gift shop if you're in the market for nature-themed toys.

Call ahead to reserve a spot on Hawaii Nature Center's daily Rainforest Walk through Iao Valley, offered at 11:30 a.m. and 1:30 p.m.; your guide can offer historical, cultural, and natural insight that you just can't gain on a self-guided tour. The price is $24.95 for adults, $22.95 for kids ages 8 to 12.

At the gateway to Iao Valley State Monument, 875 Iao Valley Rd. ☎ *808-244-6500.* www.hawaiinaturecenter.org. *Admission: $6 adults, $4 kids under 12. Open: Daily 10 a.m.–4 p.m.*

Iao Valley State Monument

As you head west to Iao Valley, the transition between town and wild is so abrupt that most people who drive up into the valley don't realize they're suddenly in a rainforest. The walls of the canyon rise, and a 2,250-foot needle pricks gray clouds scudding across the blue sky. This is Iao

(EE-ow) Valley, a place of great natural beauty and a haven for Mauians and visitors alike. You could easily spend a day here, but you can see everything in an hour or two. Two paved walkways loop the just-over-6-acre park; a leisurely ⅓-mile loop takes you past lush vegetation and lovely views of the Iao Needle, a fabulously impressive spire jutting 2,250 feet above sea level. An architectural park of Hawaiian heritage houses — including a Japanese teahouse with a lovely koi pond, a Chinese pagoda, a New England–style mission house, a Hawaiian *hale,* and a Portuguese garden — stands in harmony by Iao Stream at Kepaniwai Heritage Garden, near the entrance to the park; it makes an excellent picnic area, as tables are at hand. You'll see ferns, banana trees, and other native and exotic plants in the streamside botanic garden.

See map p. 274. On Iao Valley Rd. (at the end of Main St.), Wailuku. To get there: From Kahului, follow Kaahumanu Ave. east directly to Main St. and the park entrance. Admission: Free! Open: Daily 7 a.m.–7 p.m.

West Maui: Historic Lahaina Town

It may be hard to believe these days, overrun as Lahaina is with contemporary tourist schlock. But any of you who've read James Michener's *Hawaii* know that back in the whaling and missionary days, Lahaina was the capital of Hawaii and the Pacific's wildest port. Now it's a party town of a different kind and has lost much of its historic vibe, but history buffs with an interest can unearth a half-day's worth of historic sites.

Your best bet is to start at the **Baldwin Home Museum,** a beautifully restored 1838 missionary home at the corner of Front and Dickenson streets, where the **Lahaina Restoration Foundation** (☎ 808-661-3262; www.lahainarestoration.org) is headquartered here. Stop in any day between 10 a.m. and 4:30 p.m. to pick up the free self-guided walking tour brochure and map of Lahaina's most historic sites.

South Maui

These terrific attractions are located in Maalaea Harbor Village, at the northernmost end of South Maui.

Maui Ocean Center

This state-of-the-art aquarium is too pricey for its own good — it's no Monterey Bay Aquarium after all — but it's still one cool place. All exhibits feature the creatures that populate Hawaii's waters, which makes this a great place to visit before you set out on a snorkel cruise. Start at the surge pool, where you'll see shallow-water marine life like spiny urchins and cauliflower coral; then move on to the reef tanks, a turtle lagoon (where you'll meet some wonderful green sea turtles), a "touch" pool featuring tidepool critters, a stingray pool populated by the graceful bottom dwellers, and a disappointing whale discovery exhibit (no live creatures) before you get to the star of the show: the 600,000-gallon main tank, which features tiger, gray, and white-tip sharks, as well as tuna, surgeon fish, triggerfish, and other large-scale tropicals. The neatest thing about the tank is that it's punctured by a clear acrylic tunnel that lets you walk right through it, giving you a real idea of what it might be like to stand at the bottom of the deep blue sea. Allow about two hours for your visit.

See map p. 274. In Maalaea Harbor Village, 192 Maalaea Rd. (at the triangle between Honoapiilani Highway (Hwy. 31) and Maalaea Road), Maalaea. ☎ ***808-270-7000.*** www.mauioceancenter.com. *Admission: $20 adults, $17 seniors, $13 kids 3–12. Open: Daily 9 a.m.–5 p.m. (July–Aug, daily 9 a.m.–6 p.m.).*

Maui Golf & Sports Park

Maui's coolest new attraction may be this first-class miniature golf playland, whose two courses have been designed with both fun and duffing precision in mind. The park also offers bumper boats with water cannons (great on a hot day), a rock climbing wall, and an "xtreme" trampoline. All activities carry separate charges, or you can bundle them into a package deal. Tiki torches set the mood after dark, and the staff is very friendly. It's ideal for both family fun and an after-dinner date.

See map p. 274. In Maalaea Harbor Village, (at the triangle between Honoapiilani Highway (Hwy. 31) and Maalaea Road; the entrance is on Maalaea Road), Maalaea. ☎ ***808-242-7818.*** *Activity prices: $13 for adults, $10 kids for 18 holes of golf (add $5 for a second round); other activities $8 adults, $6 kids. Package rates available. Open: Daily 10 a.m.–10 p.m.*

Hitting the links

Always book your tee times well in advance on popular Maui, especially in high season. Weekdays are best for avoiding the crowds and securing the tee times that you want. The **Maui Golf Shop,** 357 Huku Lii Place, Kihei (☎ **800-981-5512** or 808-875-4653; www.golf-maui.com), can book discounted tee times for you at many of Maui's finest courses (including, at press time, the Dunes, Kaanapali, and Makena, all listed later in this section). If you want to schedule your tee times before you leave home, you can even submit your discount requests online (where you'll also find information and insider tips on playing a wealth of Maui links). After you arrive, the Maui Golf Shop is the best place on the island to rent clubs and stock up on gear; it's located just off the Piilani Highway (Highway 31) at Ohukai Road (behind Tesoro Gas Express).

The Dunes at Maui Lani

This dramatic British links-style course — new to Maui in 1997 — plays like an old pro. Inspired by the old-growth links of Ireland, Honolulu-based course architect Robin Nelson built this public course on the former home of a sand-mining operation, which has allowed the fairways to mature in record time. Several blind and semi-blind shots give this all-around enjoyable course an edge. Considering the quality of the course, the rates are a veritable bargain. Private lessons and half-day schools at the PGA pro-taught golf school even make improving your swing a comparatively affordable endeavor.

See map p. 274. 1333 Mauilani Pkwy., Kahului. ☎ 808-873-0422. www.dunesat mauilani.com. *Greens fees: $98, $60 after 2 p.m.*

Kaanapali Golf Courses

Both of these popular, rolling resort courses pose a challenge to all golfers, from high handicappers to near-pros. The par-71, 6,136-yard Tournament North Course is home to the Senior PGA Tour, and a true Robert Trent Jones, Jr., design, with an abundance of wide bunkers, several long, stretched-out tees, the largest, most contoured greens on Maui, and one of Hawaii's toughest finishing holes. The par-71, 6,067-yard Resort South Course is an Arthur Jack Snyder design that, although shorter than the North Course, requires more accuracy on the narrow, hilly fairways. The 18th has a tricky water hazard, so don't tally up your scorecard until the final putt is sunk. Facilities include a driving range, putting green, clubhouse, and comprehensive golf academy.

See map p. 274. 2290 Kaanapali Pkwy. (off Highway 30), Kaanapali. ☎ **808-661-3691.** www.kaanapali-golf.com. *Greens fees: $142–$160 ($117–$130 for Kaanapali resort guests); $85 at noon, $74–$77 after 2 p.m.*

Kapalua Golf Club

These three spectacularly sited championship courses are worth the sky-high greens fees for the views alone. Resort golf hardly gets finer; *Hawaii* magazine regularly names the Bay and the Plantation courses two of the top nine courses in Hawaii. An Arnold Palmer/Francis Duane design, the par-72, 6,600-yard Bay Course is a bit forgiving thanks to generous and gently undulating fairways, but even the pros have trouble with the 5th, which requires a tee shot over an ocean cove. The breathtaking — and breathtakingly difficult — Ben Crenshaw/Bill Coore–designed Plantation Course is prime for developing your low shots and precise chipping; this 7,263-yard, par-73 showstopper is home to the PGA's annual Mercedes Championships. The par-71, 6,632-yard Village Course, a Palmer/Ed Seay design and the most scenic of the three courses, suits beginners and pros alike, but winds can make for a challenging day among the Cook and Norfolk pines. Facilities include locker rooms, driving range, and restaurant. The first-rate **Kapalua Golf Academy** (☎ **808-669-6500**) just may be Hawaii's best place to improve the swing of beginners and almost-pros alike.

Check for money-saving seasonal specials and golf packages at Kapalua's Web site.

See map p. 274. Off Honoapiilani Highway (Highway 30), Kapalua. ☎ **877-527-2582** or 808-669-8044. www.kapaluamaui.com. *Greens fees: $180–$225 ($125–$140 for Kapalua resort guests); $80–$90 after 1:30 p.m.*

Makena Golf Club

Robert Trent Jones, Jr., was in top form when he designed these 36 holes. The par-72, 7,017-yard oceanside South Course is considered the more forgiving of the two, but has a couple of holes that you'll never forget: Running parallel to the ocean, the par-4 16th has a two-tiered green that slopes away from the player, while the par-5, 502-yard 10th is one of Hawaii's best driving holes. With tight fairways and narrow doglegs, the par-72, 6,914-yard North Course is both more difficult and more spectacular because it sits higher up the slope of Haleakala. Facilities include a clubhouse, driving range, two putting greens, pro shop, lockers, and lessons. Additional bonuses include a gorgeous rural setting and spectacular views.

See map p. 274. 5415 Makena Alanui Dr., Makena (south of Wailea). ☎ *808-879-8530.* www.makenagolf.com. *Greens fees: $165–$175 ($95–$105 for Makena resort guests), $95–$105 after 2 p.m.*

Wailea Golf Club

Most difficult among Wailea's courses is the par-72, 7,070-yard Gold Course, home to the Champions Skins Game, which features senior golf legends in competition. This classic Robert Trent Jones, Jr., design boasts a rugged layout, narrow fairways, several tricky dogleg holes, daunting natural hazards, and only-in-Hawaii features like lava outcroppings and native grasses. Both the Blue and the Emerald are easy for most golfers to enjoy, but the par-72, 6,407-yard Emerald Course — another Trent Jones, Jr., design — is both the prettiest and easiest for high-handicappers to enjoy. The par-72, 6,700-yard Blue Course, an open course designed by Arthur Jack Snyder, has wide fairways that also appeal to beginners, but bunkers, water hazards, and undulating terrain make it a course that all can enjoy. Facilities include two clubhouses, two pro shops, restaurants, lockers, club rentals, and a complete training facility.

Call to inquire about discounted afternoon rates, money-saving triple- and unlimited-play passes, and other specials, including junior golf rates.

See map p. 274. Off Wailea Alanui Drive, Wailea. ☎ *888-328-MAUI, 800-322-1614, or 808-875-7450.* www.waileagolf.com. *Greens fees: $175–$185 ($135–$145 for Wailea Resort guests); twilight rates $90–$100.*

Shopping the Local Stores

When it comes to shopping opportunities, the Valley Isle is the reigning king among the neighbor islands in terms of quantity. Its status is a bit more dubious when it comes to quality, but you will find some real gems in the eclectic mix.

Central Maui: Wailuku

Although Kahului is the island's hub and the place to go for practical items, the historic town of Wailuku immediately to the west offers reasonably good hunting grounds for antiques hounds. It's still a mixed bag, but a few quality shops featuring both new and used treasures can be found on North Market Street; to get there, simply go west from Kahului on Kaahumanu Avenue and turn right when you reach Market, in the heart of Wailuku.

Highlights include **Brown-Kobayashi,** 38 N. Market St. (☎ **808-242-0804** or 808-242-0805), a treasure trove of graceful Asian antiques (mostly large pieces, but affordable prices make the shipping worth it for committed collectors); and **Bird of Paradise Unique Antiques,** 54 N. Market St. (☎ **808-242-7699**), a jumble of collectible glassware, pottery, and Hawaiiana.

Wailuku's top stop is **Sig Zane,** 53 N. Market St. (☎ **808-249-8997;** www. sigzane.com), the Maui outpost of this famed Big Island designer. Sig's distinctive, two-color all-cotton aloha wear is the height of simple style and good taste. The stunningly beautiful fabrics are sold in a variety of clean-lined, easy-to-wear styles as well as off the bolt if you want to take some home. If you buy one article of aloha wear to bring home, buy it here. And if you've already visited the Big Island boutique, stop in anyway because you'll find unique patterns and colors here.

West Maui: Lahaina and Kaanapali

Lahaina's main drag, Front Street, overflows with surf-wear shops, contemporary art galleries, trendy boutiques, cheesy T-shirt shops, and much, much more — you'll tire of browsing well before you run out of places to flex your credit card.

Your best bet is to just start at one end and browse. Highlights include **Serendipity,** 752 Front St. (☎ **808-667-7070**), for casual, island-style women's wear in comfortable, loose-fitting styles. Next door is **Tropical Blues,** 754 Front St. (☎ **808-667-4008**), specializing in high-quality tropical wear for women, plus a small men's collection; you'll also find fun tropical-themed accessories, bags, and sandals. **Honolua Surf Co.,** 845 Front St. (☎ **808-661-8848;** www.honoluasurf.com), carries its own fabulous line of surf wear and gear. **Kamehameha Garment Company,** in the Pioneer Inn, 109 Hotel St. (just off Front Street; ☎ **808-667-2269**), sells the company's own line of gorgeous new aloha wear in vintage patterns; all the telltale signs of quality aloha wear are here, including patterns that match on the seams and coconut-shell buttons.

Célébrités, 764 Front St. (☎ **800-428-3338** or 808-667-0727; www. celebrityfineart.com), features art by and about celebrities. It's the height of over-the-top conspicuous consumption, but it's a compelling browse nonetheless. **Vintage European Posters,** 744 Front St. (☎ **808-662-8688**), boasts a fantastic array of original poster art from 1890 to 1950, mostly European and all in mint condition; prices are excellent considering the quality of the stock. For a hand-painted original, visit the **Curtis Wilson Cost Gallery,** 710 Front St. (☎ **808-661-4140;** www.costgallery.com). The Maui-based painter is a landscape traditionalist; his islandscapes are luminescent and alive with detail.

If you want to stock up on contemporary island tunes, stop by the **Hawaiian Music Store,** in an open-air kiosk at the north end of Front Street next to Longhi's, across from the Bubba Gump Shrimp Co. (☎ **808-661-9225;** www.hawaiianmusicstore.com).

An island of artistic integrity in the sea of Lahaina kitsch is **Na Mea Hawaii Store,** in the Baldwin Home, 120 Dickenson St., at Front Street (☎ **808-661-5707**), which sells only fine-quality island-made crafts and gifts. That doesn't mean expensive, though; you'll find a surprising number of affordable prizes among the bounty.

For marine-themed goods and educational gifts for kids, you can't do better than the surprisingly nice nonprofit **Pacific Whale Foundation** store, 143 Dickenson St., a block up from Front Street (☎ **808-667-7447**; www.pacificwhale.org). Members save 15 percent off all whale- and ecothemed goodies as well as whale-watching cruises and snorkel tours that can be booked right at the shop (see the section "Ocean cruising to Molokini and Lanai and other on-deck adventures," earlier in this chapter), so consider joining up for a good cause.

You'll find a second Pacific Whale Foundation shop in South Maui at Maalaea Harbor Village, 300 Maalaea Rd. (in the same complex as the Maui Ocean Center), on the north end of Kihei (☎ **808-249-8977**).

At the far south end of Front Street, in the 505 Front St. complex, is **Lei Spa Maui** (☎ **808-661-1178**; www.leispa.com), which carries a wonderful line of fragrant and rejuvenating Hawaii-made bath and body products, while therapists offer massages, body wraps, and facials. Tucked away in the south end of the mall is **Old Lahaina Book Emporium** (☎ **808-661-1399**), for used and new fiction, nonfiction, music, and videos.

At the opposite, north end of Front Street are a couple of shopping centers, including **Lahaina Cannery Mall,** 1221 Honoapiilani Hwy. (☎ **808-667-0592**; www.lahainacannerymall.com), for practicals and a few special names like **Lahaina Printsellers** and the **Totally Hawaiian Gift Gallery.** The **Lahaina Center,** 900 Front St. (☎ **808-667-9216**; www.lahainacenter.com), is a pleasant open-air mall that boasts **Local Motion** for surf wear and gear; **Hilo Hattie,** Hawaii's biggest name in affordable aloha wear; and mall standards like **Banana Republic.**

On the beach in Kaanapali, **Whaler's Village,** 2435 Kaanapali Pkwy. (☎ **808-661-4567**), has blossomed into quite an upscale shopping and dining complex, offering a surprisingly appealing open-air shopping experience (once you get past the ordeal of parking). Although it has become the Rodeo Drive of Maui in recent years — with **Gucci, Dior, Chanel, Prada, Louis Vuitton,** and **Versace** all represented — it also has some surprisingly excellent midrange boutiques, including two branches of **Honolua Surf Co.,** whose stylish surf gear and wear I just love; **Sandal Tree,** for an excellent collection of women's footwear, sunhats, and handbags; **Clio Blue** for whimsically elegant silver jewelry, much of it shaped like fish (despite the fish theme, it's a Parisian import); a branch of **Reyn's,** the Hawaii-based company that makes my second-favorite contemporary aloha wear (after Sig Zane; see "Central Maui: Wailuku," earlier in this section); **Martin & MacArthur** for island crafts; and **The Body Shop,** in case you need to stock up on ecofriendly sunscreen.

South Maui: Wailea

The lovely open-air **Shops at Wailea,** 3750 Wailea Alanui Dr. (☎ 808-891-6770; www.shopsatwailea.com), has been an excellent addition to the Wailea Resort, bringing in both much-needed practical retailers and elegant gift outlets. Stores run the gamut from familiar names ranging from **Tiffany & Co.** to **The Gap.** Specialty stores worth seeking out include **Footprints** for an excellent selection of sandals for men, women, and children; **Martin & MacArthur** for hand-crafted koa and other Hawaii crafts; **Blue Ginger,** which has brought batik into the 21st century with its bold prints and flowing modern cuts; the new **Wailea Body & Bath;** and **Tommy Bahama's,** whose tropically sophisticated clothing emporium also boasts a winning oceanview cafe and bar (see Chapter 13); and much more.

Off the beaten path: Paia and Makawao

The hip little surf town of Paia (pa-EE-ah), just 15 minutes east of Kahului on the Hana Highway (Highway 36), makes an eclectic but appealing stop for shoppers looking for funkier goods. The boutiques sprawl in a T-shape from the intersection of the Hana Highway and Baldwin Avenue, and the choices range from the sublime to the ridiculous. On the sublime end is **Maui Crafts Guild,** on the ocean side of Hana Highway at no. 43 (☎ 808-579-9697; www.mauicraftsguild.com), an artist-owned cooperative that represents some of the finest fine artists and craftspeople on Maui; you'll find artworks and gifts in all price ranges here. At the opposite end of the spectrum is **Big Bugga Sportswear,** 18 Baldwin Ave. (☎ 808-579-6216; www.bigbugga.com), which carries the largest men's casual wear you've ever seen in your life — from XL to a sumo-sized 10X. In between, you'll find **Moonbow Tropics** at 20 and 36 Baldwin Ave. (☎ 808-579-8775 or 808-579-8592; www.moonbowtropicsmaui.com), which offers the finest contemporary aloha-wear lines available. **Necessories Boutique,** 21 Baldwin Ave. (☎ 808-579-9805), bills itself as "Hawaiian Bohemian funk," but the collection of home décor and wearables is surprisingly well chosen and creatively displayed, making this one of my favorite stops in a shopping-rich town. There's plenty more good stuff; just park and browse.

From Paia, drive toward the mountain on Baldwin Avenue (Highway 390), and in 7 miles you'll reach Makawao (ma-KA-wow), a cowboy town turned New Age village that's another petite shopper's paradise.

The shopping is so good in Makawao that the whole *town* is a highlight. Serious shoppers should definitely save an afternoon to explore. Seek out **Hurricane,** 3639 Baldwin Ave. (☎ 808-572-5076), a wonderful split-level boutique that carries a well-displayed selection of fine casuals for women; and **Tropo,** next door (☎ 808-573-0356), Hurricane's boutique for men. **The Courtyard,** at 3620 Baldwin Ave., houses a number of interesting crafts shops of varying quality, including **Maui Hands** (☎ 808-352-4278; www.mauihands.com) — plus a fascinating glassblower's studio that's worth a peek: **Hot Island Glass Studio & Gallery** (☎ 808-572-4527; www.hotislandglass.com).

The highlight of Makawao is the **Hui Noeau Visual Arts Center,** a mile outside of town at 2841 Baldwin Ave. (☎ **808-572-6560;** www.huinoeau. com). A tree-lined driveway leads to the 1917 estate (designed by noted Hawaii architect C.W. Dickey) that houses the island's most renowned artists' collective and features rotating exhibits by both established and up-and-coming island artists, plus an excellent shop featuring original works. There's a $2 suggested donation for the exhibit gallery. The artistically active among you might also want to inquire about workshops, demonstrations, visiting-artist events, and other short-term opportunities for study.

Living It Up after Dark

After Oahu, Maui boasts Hawaii's second-biggest after-dark scene. Many of the island's restaurants — particularly the oceanfront ones — do double-duty as post-dinner hot spots, often hosting lively bar scenes, live music, and dancing. The epicenter of island nightlife is lively Lahaina.

For the most complete calendar of what's happening while you're on Maui, pick up a copy of the weekly *MauiTime Weekly* newspaper, available for free at kiosks all over the island.

If you're interested in the more refined performing arts, look for a copy of *Centerpiece,* the free bimonthly magazine published by the **Maui Arts and Cultural Center,** the finest cultural venue in the neighbor islands; hotel concierges usually have copies. You can also call the center, located in Kahului, at ☎ **808-242-7469** or visit the Web site at www.maui arts.org for a current schedule. The diverse calendar might feature big names like Melissa Etheridge, Natalie Cole, or George Winston; Maui Film Festival screenings; or performances by Hawaii's most renowned musicians (don't miss Amy Hanaialii Gilliom if she's on the calendar).

The island's best sunset cruises are offered by **Paragon Sailing Charters** (☎ **808-441-2087;** www.sailmaui.com). For further details, see the section "Ocean cruising to Molokini and Lanai and other on-deck adventures," earlier in this chapter.

And, of course, don't forget that Maui is home to the finest examples of the ultimate island form of after-dark entertainment: the luau! I highly recommend planning to participate in one while you're on the Valley Isle. For details, see Chapter 13.

West Maui

All Lahaina takes on a festive atmosphere as sunset nears. The restaurants along oceanfront Front Street boast stellar views and energetic bar scenes, some with live music; just stroll the street and join whatever party suits your fancy. Among the best are **Cheeseburger in Paradise,** 811 Front St. (☎ **808-661-4855**), a regular forum for live-and-lively music;

Hard Rock Cafe, 900 Front St. (☎ **808-667-7400**); **Kimo's,** 845 Front St. (☎ **808-661-4811**); and **Maui Brews,** in Lahaina Center at 900 Front St., next to the Front Street Theaters (☎ **808-667-7794**), which offers Lahaina's largest on-tap selection and an eclectic calendar of DJ dance parties and live music; call to see what's on.

Lahaina is also home to two nightly shows that are well worth seeking out. If you love the performing arts — and even if you don't think that you do — don't pass up an opportunity to see *'Ulalena,* at the **Maui Myth & Magic Theatre,** in Old Lahaina Center, 878 Front St. (☎ **877-688-4800** or 808-661-9913; www.ulalena.com). This incredible, Broadway-quality 75-minute live show interweaves the natural, historical, and mythological tales of the birth of Hawaii, using a near-perfect mix of original contemporary music and dance, ancient chant and hula, and creative lighting, gorgeous costumes, visual artistry (including some mind-blowing puppets), and live musicianship. This universally lauded production is bold, mesmerizing, and like nothing Hawaii has ever seen before — sort of like Laurie Anderson hooks up with Cirque du Soleil in Hawaii. Lest you think it all sounds too artsy for you, *'Ulalena* has been so popular among tourists and visitors alike that two shows are performed nightly (except on Tuesdays) at 6 p.m. Tickets are $48 to $75 for adults, $28 to $45 for kids ages 3 to 10 — yes, they'll love *'Ulalena,* too. Don't miss it!

On my last visit to *'Ulalena,* I was able to save about 10 percent on my tickets by purchasing them at the **Hawaiian Music Store,** which also serves as an official ticket outlet for the show. It's just around the corner from Old Lahaina Center on Front Street (next to Longhi's, across from the Bubba Gump Shrimp Co.; ☎ **808-661-9225;** www.hawaiianmusic store.com).

For something completely different, spend an evening at **Warren & Annabelle's,** 900 Front St. in Lahaina (☎ **808-667-6244;** www.hawaii magic.com). This genuinely fun and surprisingly uncheesy mystery-and-magic cocktail show stars illusionist Warren Gibson and "Annabelle," a ghost from the *previous* turn of the century who plays a grand piano — and even takes your requests. Expect the requisite audience participation, of course. Tickets are $45 per person, with dinner packages ranging from $73 to $80 per person; you must be 21 or older to enter. Food and drinks are available for an additional charge. The show is very popular, so book at least a few days in advance to avoid disappointment; no shows occur on Sundays. An early-evening family-friendly show is sometimes added to the Warren & Annabelle's schedule; call for details.

Kaanapali has its own family-friendly entertainment as well. **Kupanaha** is the terrific magic show at the Kaanapali Beach Hotel (☎ **808-667-0128;** www.kbhmaui.com), starring husband-and-wife illusionists Jody and Kathleen Baran and their daughters, child prodigy magicians Katrina and Crystal. The dazzling show interweaves illusions, Hawaiian hula and chant, and the stories and myths of ancient Hawaii into a show that the whole family will love. No kidding — the show has been a huge hit. Shows are offered Tuesday through Saturday at the family-friendly hour of 5 p.m.; dinner is included, and you'll be out by 8 p.m. Tickets are $69 to $79 for adults, $49 for teens, $29 for kids 6 to 12, including a three-course dinner; a kids' menu is available.

For live music in Kaanapali, head to **Whaler's Village,** on Kaanapali Beach at 2435 Kaanapali Pkwy., where you can take an open-air seat facing the ocean at the bar at **Hula Grill** (☎ 808-667-6636), which features Hawaiian music and hula. Or head next door to **Leilani's on the Beach** (☎ 808-661-4495) where the party starts every afternoon with live music at 2:30 p.m. or so. With tiki torches flickering and the waves rolling in, you can't go wrong at either spot.

South Maui

South Maui is a tad quieter overall, but boasts a couple of hopping joints, including **Hapa's Nightclub,** in the Lipoa Shopping Center, 41 E. Lipoa St. (between South Kihei Road and Piilani Highway), Kihei (☎ 808-879-9001; www.hapasmaui.com). Hapa's serves up live music and microbrews nightly from 9 p.m. to 1:30 a.m. This large, popular place is simple and lively, boasting good sound and a big dance floor. Call to see what's on: It could be jazz, blues, rock, reggae, funk, or Hawaiian.

A DJ spins Top-40 hits at chic **Tsunami,** the neighbor islands' biggest and best dance club, at the Grand Wailea Resort, 3850 Wailea Alanui Dr., Wailea (☎ 808-875-1234), where a well-heeled crowd shakes its collective booty Friday and Saturday nights from 9:30 p.m. to 2:00 a.m. **Bocalino,** at 1279 S. Kihei Rd. (☎ 808-874-9299), is a great place to boogie down to live music from 10 p.m. to 1 a.m. nightly except Thursday; the tempo varies from Hawaiian contemporary to Latin to rock, depending on the night, so call for the schedule.

Upcountry Maui

Somewhat unexpectedly, one of the hottest party spots on the island is upcountry, in the cowboy town of Makawao. The party never ends at the Italian restaurant **Casanova,** 1188 Makawao Ave. (☎ 808-572-0220; www.casanovamaui.com) (see Chapter 13). The bar area has large booths, all the better for socializing around the stage and dance floor. Wednesday nights usually feature the venue's famous ladies' night disco, while Friday and Saturday nights feature live music. Expect good blues, rock, reggae, jazz, Hawaiian, and the top names in local and visiting entertainment, which generally starts at 9:45 p.m. and continues to 1:30 a.m.

Part V

Hawaii, the Big Island

The 5th Wave   By Rich Tennant

FEW MOMENTS IN SAILING COMPARE IN MAJESTY TO THE SHRINERS SUNSET REGATTA.

In this part . . .

The island of Hawaii is not called the Big Island for nothing. Measuring 4,028 square miles, the island is more than twice the size of all the other islands combined. You'll do plenty of driving here if you plan to explore the island's many attractions, and I hope that you do — this is the land of salt-and-pepper beaches, active lava flows, and tropical rain forests. The chapters in this part help you make the most of your time in this enchanting place.

Chapter 15

Settling into the Big Island

In This Chapter

▶ Getting from the airport to your hotel

▶ Finding your way around the Big Island and its major resort areas

▶ Choosing among the island's top accommodations

▶ Discovering the Big Island's best restaurants

▶ Arranging for a luau

▶ Using an easy-reference list of important local contacts

At 4,038 square miles, the Big Island really is *big*. Not only that, but a handful of volcanic mountains dominates the interior, making crossing from coast to coast a challenge, to say the least. If you want to visit all the Big Island's major attractions, I strongly suggest that you choose not one but two places to stay while you're here: one on the hot, arid Kona Coast, and the other on the lush, rainforested volcano coast.

You *can* stay just on the Kona side of the island and visit Hawaii Volcanoes National Park on a daytrip. Expect a long day, however: It takes at least three hours to reach the park from anywhere on the western coast. And because the best time to see the flowing lava in the park is after dark, you won't get back to Kona anytime before midnight.

If you're planning to visit both sides of the island, here's a way to cut down on driving time and maximize sightseeing (or relaxation) time. I suggest scheduling your Big Island visit so that you fly in to one side of the island and fly out on the other. Either land at Kona airport and fly out of Hilo, or vice versa — it really doesn't matter. Doing so will likely cost you about 50 bucks in car-rental drop-off charges, but can save an extra 3- to 3½-hour drive to return to the coast you started from for your outbound flight.

Visit www.hawaiispecials.com, operated by the Big Island Visitors Bureau, for easy-as-pie one-stop shopping. Here you'll find the best accommodations bargains and value-added vacation packages currently available on the Volcano Isle.

Arriving on the West Side at Kona Airport

Kona International Airport at Keahole (☎ 808-329-3423; www.state. hi.us/dot/airports/hawaii/koa) is located 7 miles north of Kailua-Kona, just off Queen Kaahumanu Highway (Highway 19). Kona is served direct from the mainland by three airlines: **American Airlines, United Airlines,** and **Aloha Airlines.** Otherwise, you can take an interisland flight from another Hawaiian island, via Aloha or **Hawaiian Airlines.** This small, open-air airport is a breeze to navigate. The major rental-car companies have counters directly across the street (in the wooden hut), but because of increased airport security, you must now take a shuttle van to a nearby offsite lot to pick up your car.

While you're at the rental counter, be sure to pick up a map booklet from the agent; all the car-rental agencies offer them, and they're invaluable for getting around the island. They often include money-saving coupons for attractions as well.

If you're heading to **Kailua-Kona,** turn right out of the airport onto Queen Kaahumanu (ka-a-hoo-MA-noo) Highway (Highway 19). Clearly marked turnoffs take you down to the town's main drag, Alii (ah-LEE-ee) Drive, about 7 miles to the south. If you're continuing on to **South Kona** or **Keauhou** (kay-A-ho), stay on Highway 19 for another 7 or so miles; for Keauhou, turn toward the coast on Kamehameha III Road.

If you're heading to a **Kohala Coast** resort, turn left out of the airport onto Queen Kaahumanu Highway (Highway 19) and proceed to one of the following locations:

- ✔ **Kaupulehu** (cow-poo-LAY-hoo), home to the Four Seasons Hualalai and Kona Village, is 7 miles north of the airport, or a ten-minute drive.

- ✔ **Waikoloa** (why-ko-LO-ah), home to the Waikoloa Beach Marriott and Hilton Waikoloa Village, is 18 miles north, or a 20- to 25-minute drive.

- ✔ **Mauna Lani,** home to the Orchid and the Mauna Lani Bay Hotel and Bungalows, is about 23 miles north, or a half-hour drive.

- ✔ **Mauna Kea** has its entrance 28 miles north of the airport, or a 40-minute drive.

Look for the gateway to your resort on the ocean side of the road; the only one that's on the right side of the road is the turnoff for the Westin Hapuna Prince Beach Hotel, just before Mauna Kea's entrance. The resort entrances tend to be marked in a rather understated way, so look carefully.

If you're staying at one of the Kohala Coast resorts and don't need a rental car for your entire stay, you can usually arrange for the resort shuttle to pick you up at the airport. Then you can arrange to have a rental car delivered to your hotel only on the day(s) you need it. Call the concierge at your hotel for details before you arrive.

Taxis are also readily available at the airport, so you don't need to arrange for one in advance. Expect the cost to be about $21 to Kailua-Kona, more if you're heading to one of the Kohala Coast resorts. You can also prearrange airport transfers with **SpeediShuttle** (☎ **800-977-2605** or 808-329-5433; www.speedishuttle.com). If you forgot to call SpeediShuttle before you left home, dial "65" from one of the courtesy phones in baggage blaim.

If you prefer to have a private car service transport you to your Kohala Coast resort in style, contact **Luana Limousine** (☎ **800-999-4001** or 808-326-5466). Vehicles run the gamut from Lincoln Town Cars to stretch limos to 14-passenger vans, and prices are actually quite reasonable; about $35 will get you to Mauna Lani. Be sure to call a couple of days before you leave home to arrange pickup.

Arriving on the East Side at Hilo Airport

Hilo (HEE-low) **International Airport** (☎ **808-934-5840** or 808-934-5838; www.state.hi.us/dot/airports/hawaii/ito) is 2 miles east of downtown Hilo, at the junction of Kamehameha Avenue and Kanoelehua Avenue (Highway 11). **Aloha Airlines** and **Hawaiian Airlines** serve Hilo International from Honolulu; tiny **Pacific Wings Airlines** also offers flights to Hilo from other islands.

Step outside and proceed straight to the rental car desk. Be sure to pick up a map booklet at the rental counter — they're invaluable for getting around the island.

If you're staying in **Hilo,** turn right out of the airport onto Kanoelehua Avenue (Highway 11), which will lead you right to Banyan Drive and the Hilo Hawaiian and Hawaii Naniloa hotels. To reach downtown and the waterfront, turn left onto Kamehameha Avenue just before Banyan Drive.

If you're heading to **Volcano Village,** turn left out of the airport onto Kanoelehua Avenue (Highway 11). Highway 11 will take you the 27 miles (a 45-minute or so drive), to Volcano Village, at the entrance of Hawaii Volcanoes National Park.

Taxis line up at the airport's curb, so you don't have to worry about arranging for one in advance. Expect to pay $8 to $10 to a Hilo destination, plus tip.

Choosing Your Location

The west, or Kona, side of the Big Island is the hot, arid, beachy side, where all the island resorts and condos are located. The misty,

Big Island Orientation

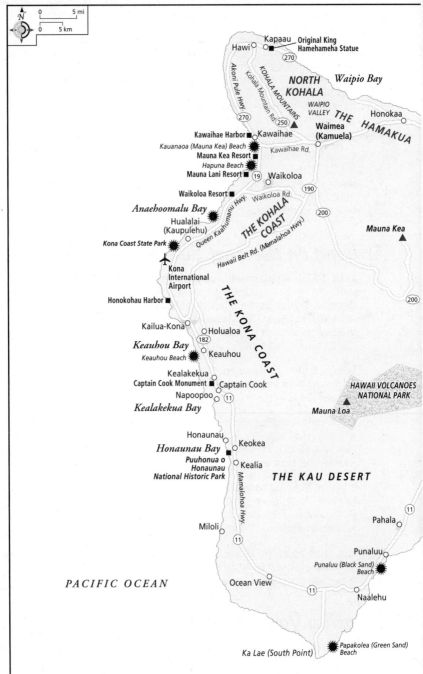

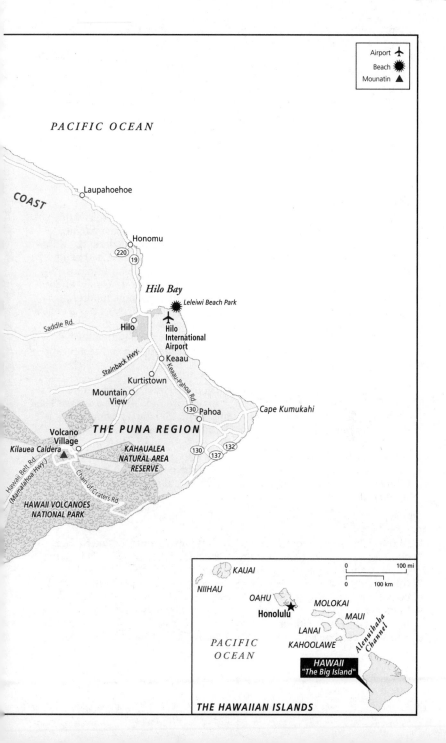

Airport ✈
Beach ✸
Mounatin ▲

PACIFIC OCEAN

COAST

Laupahoehoe

Honomu

(220) (19)

Hilo Bay

✸ Leleiwi Beach Park

Saddle Rd.

✈
Hilo ○
Hilo International Airport

○ Keaau

Stainback Hwy.

Kurtistown

Mountain View ○

Keaau-Pahoa Rd.

(130) Pahoa

Cape Kumukahi

Volcano Village ○

THE PUNA REGION

Kilauea Caldera ▲

Hawaii Belt Rd. (Mamalahoa Hwy.)

KAHAUALEA NATURAL AREA RESERVE

(130) (137) (132)

Chain of Craters Rd

HAWAII VOLCANOES NATIONAL PARK

KAUAI

NIIHAU

OAHU
Honolulu ★

MOLOKAI

MAUI

LANAI

KAHOOLAWE

Alenuihaha Channel

PACIFIC OCEAN

HAWAII "The Big Island"

0   100 mi
0   100 km

THE HAWAIIAN ISLANDS

luxuriantly green east side is home to the pretty, petite city of Hilo and spectacular Hawaii Volcanoes National Park.

On the west (Kona) side

This hot, dry, almost-always-sunny side of the island is where you go when you want to hit the beach. West Hawaii may come as a shock to some — this is parched, black-lava-covered land fringed by swaying palms, salt-and-pepper sand, and gorgeous Pacific waves. Still, it's a landscape of dramatic, otherworldly beauty. This side is where you'll find some of Hawaii's most gorgeous beaches (and some of the state's most expensive real estate).

The Kohala Coast

This ritzy resort coast stretches for about 30 miles north from Kona International Airport. No other resort coast in Hawaii boasts luxury spreads this sprawling or fabulously grand. Every hotel along the Kona-Kohala coast is part of a "resort" — Kaupulehu (cow-poo-LAY-hoo), Waikoloa, Mauna Lani, and Mauna Kea, in order, from south to north — each of which functions something like a neighborhood, usually encompassing two resort hotels, upscale residential developments (condos, freestanding homes, or both), and golf courses. Each resort has a clearly marked gateway off Queen Kaahumanu Highway (Highway 19, the coast's main drag) and its own network of roads, plus public beach access. Waikoloa even boasts its own sizable shopping and restaurant complex.

 When you're making your resort decision, take distance into consideration if you're planning to do lots of running around. Mauna Kea is at least a 30-minute drive from the airport and 40 or 45 minutes from Kailua-Kona town, which can make popping into town for dinner more work than you'd like. Kaupulehu (where the Four Seasons and Kona Village resort hotels are), on the other hand, is only about 10 or 15 minutes from Kailua-Kona and practically around the corner from the airport (7 miles to be exact, which qualifies as "around the corner" on this island).

Kailua-Kona

About 7 miles south of the Kona International Airport, Kailua-Kona is the commercial hub of the island's west side. It's similar to Maui's Lahaina, down to the tacky-touristy shopping and open-air restaurants along Alii (ah-LEE-ee) Drive that open to spectacular ocean views. Kailua-Kona is a convenient and affordable place to stay, with lots of hotel and condo bargains. Keep in mind, however, that you'll usually have to drive to get to a decent beach. Go for one of the condo complexes south of town if you want easy beach access and a respite from crowds and noise.

Upcountry Kona

Drive 15 minutes inland and upland from Kailua-Kona, and you'll enter a whole different world. Lush, green, cool, and quiet, this is the world-famous Kona coffee country. Charming Holualoa village serves as a great alternative to the beach resorts if you're looking to get away from it all. Views are spectacular, the streets are lined with art galleries, and you won't hear much but birdsong and the sound of the tropical fruit growing on the trees. It's an excellent choice for off-the-beaten-path types.

South Kona

A 10-minute drive south of Kailua-Kona town is South Kona, a quieter and more lush territory than Kona central. It's still convenient to everything, but much more sedate, with a handful of nice hotels and condo complexes, plus an excellent B&B on the slope above the coast, **Horizon Guest House** (see listing later in this chapter). You'll have wonderful ocean views no matter where you stay in South Kona, but expect a short drive to reach a swimmable beach (although some of the best snorkel spots on the island are within easy reach).

The east (volcano) side

The east side of the Big Island seems like the polar opposite of the Kona side — it's cool, wet, rainforested, fragrant with tropical flowers (the Big Island is also known as the Orchid Isle), and decidedly *not* the place for a day at the beach. Stay on this side of the island if you want to dedicate some time to exploring **Hawaii Volcanoes National Park,** but expect a whole different kind of island experience here.

Volcano Village

The gateway to Hawaii Volcanoes National Park is **Volcano Village,** a network of charming B&Bs and vacation rentals tucked into the rainforest just outside the national park's gate. Needless to say, Volcano Village makes the best base for exploring the park. No matter where you stay, you'll be just minutes from the park entrance.

Hilo

Hawaii's largest city after Honolulu embodies Hawaii the way it used to be: It's a quaint, misty, flower-filled city with a gorgeous half-moon bay, a charmingly historic false-fronted downtown, some beautifully restored Victorian houses, and a real penchant for rain — 128 inches a year makes it one of America's wettest cities. Not everybody loves Hilo, but those of us with a passion for anything retro do. If you can't find a place to stay in Volcano Village, try Hilo; it's just 45 minutes from the national park and offers many more dining options.

Driving Around the Big Island

You *will* need a rental car on the Big Island. Not having one will leave you dependent on what your resort has to offer — or worse, relegate you to the confines of touristy Kailua-Kona. Distances on this island are just too long to rely on taxis. An island-wide bus system, the **Hele-On Bus** (☎ 808-961-8744), is available, but all it really does is transport passengers (mostly locals) between the Kona-Kohala coast and Hilo.

All the major car-rental firms have cars available at both island airports: Kona International Airport, on the arid, beachy west side of the island; and Hilo International Airport, on the east, or volcano, side of the island. Arrange for one before you arrive; otherwise, you may find yourself paying top dollar at the airport counter (or run the risk of not getting a car at all if their inventory is depleted). If you visit more than one island, ask about interisland rentals, which can allow you to benefit from lower weekly rates even if you island-hop.

If your heart's set on some heavy-duty exploring along the Saddle Road, up to the summit of Mauna Kea, or to the southernmost tip of the island (which is also the southernmost point in the United States), you'll need a four-wheel-drive vehicle. Keep in mind that most standard rental contracts for garden-variety front-wheel-drive cars restrict access to each of these rough-and-ready destinations. For more information, see the upcoming information on Saddle and South Point roads.

If you're not going to rent a car, contact your hotel concierge or condo front desk and ask about local shuttle services. A few shuttles cover the Kailua-Kona area and the South Kona coast. In addition, most of the Kona-Kohala coast resorts offer free resort shuttles that transport guests within the resort, to golf courses, neighboring hotels, and any other nearby facilities. If you plan on relying on a resort shuttle, though, expect to be confined largely to your resort.

For transportation around Kailua-Kona and down to Keauhou, in South Kona, catch a ride on the **Alii Shuttle** (☎ 808-938-1112), which travels up and down Alii Drive between Kailua-Kona's Lanihau Shopping Center to Keauhou, every 1½ hours Monday through Saturday from 8:30 a.m. to 7 p.m. The fare is $2 per person, per ride. Just flag the bus down on Alii Drive in the direction that you want to go, and the kindly driver will stop. Be sure to call ahead first to confirm hours because they're subject to change at any time.

It's pretty hard to get lost on the Big Island. It has only a handful of main roads, all of which basically stick to the perimeter of the island because of the five volcanic mountains that dominate the interior.

The most important thing to keep in mind is the island's sheer size — they don't call it the Big Island for nothing. Driving from coast to coast — from Kailua-Kona to Hilo, say, or from Volcano to the Kohala Coast — takes 3 to 3½ hours; circling the entire island takes between six and seven hours. Distances are often longer than they seem, much like they are in the southwest United States, so be sure that you have a realistic idea of how far you need to travel before you set out. If you're not sure, check with the concierge or the front-desk staff of your hotel or condo before you leave.

Here are some estimated island drive times:

- ✔ **From Kailua-Kona to the Waikoloa Resort:** 35 minutes
- ✔ **From Waikoloa Resort to Waimea:** 25 minutes
- ✔ **From Waimea to Hilo:** 1 hour
- ✔ **From Hilo to Volcano Village (gateway to Hawaii Volcanoes National Park):** 45 minutes
- ✔ **From Hawaii Volcanoes National Park to Kailua-Kona via South Point:** 2¾ to 3 hours

If you're a driver who sticks to the conservative side of the speed limit or you're setting out on a rainy day, expect drive times to be slightly longer. And don't forget to factor in pit stops.

If you arrive at Kona Airport, the first of the Big Island's main highways that you'll encounter is **Queen Kaahumanu Highway** (Highway 19), which runs along the Kona-Kohala coast for 33 miles, from Kailua-Kona at the south to the industrial port of Kawaihae at the north. All the major Kohala Coast resorts and beaches are accessible from this main coastal highway.

The Big Island has one main highway that circles the island: the **Hawaii Belt Road,** also known as the **Mamalahoa Highway,** which is labeled **Highway 11** as it runs south from the sunny, arid resort town of Kailua-Kona around the island's southern tip (a 60-mile drive); another 36 miles through Volcano (gateway to Hawaii Volcanoes National Park); and then about 27 miles north to Hilo, a misty, funky-cool bayfront town that's the second-largest city in the state (after Honolulu). Go north from Hilo, and the road becomes **Highway 19** as it travels north along the misty and ruggedly beautiful Hamakua Coast, then west to the upland cowboy town of Waimea, the heart of the Big Island's ranchland, for a total of 54 miles.

In Waimea, Highway 19 continues directly west, connecting up with the north end of the coastal Queen Kaahumanu Highway, which runs down the Kohala Coast. This roughly 10-mile stretch of east-west road connecting Waimea and the industrial port of Kawaihae (ka-WHY-high) is called **Kawaihae Road.**

An interior road offers a more direct route between Waimea and Kailua-Kona: The continuation of the Hawaii Belt Road (Mamalahoa Highway) is **Highway 190,** a scenic "upper" road that cuts along the western slope of

Mauna Kea back to the coast, meeting up with the Queen Kaahumanu Highway (Highway 19) right in Kailua-Kona — thus completing the loop.

One more road links east to west: **The Saddle Road** (Highway 200) is so named because it crosses the "saddle" between Mauna Kea and Mauna Loa volcanoes as it runs from Highway 190 south of Waimea direct to Hilo; from this road, you can take the access road to the 14,000-odd-foot summit of Mauna Kea. Your rental-car agreement will most likely demand that you avoid the Saddle Road because it's rough and narrow, and the ever-changing weather conditions can be tough to handle (not to mention the locals, who drive like bats out of hell between Hilo and the Kona Coast along this road). So don't take it; stick to the main highways instead. You're also supposed to stay away from **South Point Road,** the road that runs from the Mamalahoa Road at the south end of the island directly south, to the southernmost point in the United States. Although this road is less treacherous, you're best off avoiding it in order to honor the built-in restrictions on your rental-car contract.

If you plan to take on the Saddle Road or the South Point Road, or both, I suggest renting a four-wheel-drive SUV — and check your rental contract first before setting out. If you disregard any disclaimer or restriction in your contract and get stuck on a forbidden road, and your rental-car company then sticks you with a wallet-busting tow bill, don't say I didn't warn you.

Also stay off of the steeply graded **Waipio Valley Road,** at the north end of the Hamakua Coast, which isn't meant for cars — you *will* get stuck here.

For a more complete discussion of the major resort areas as well as Hilo and Volcano, check out the section "Choosing Your Location," earlier in this chapter. If you drive north from the intersection of the Kohala Coast's Queen Kaahumanu Highway and the Kawaihae Road, you'll enter North Kohala, the peninsula that extends off the northern end of the island. The drive north along the **Akoni Pule** (ah-KO-nee POO-lay) **Highway** (Highway 270) offers a peek at a different side of the Big Island, one where lava cedes to gorgeous rolling ranchlands. It's a beautiful hour-long drive that leads to some wonderful wilderness activities that I discuss in detail in Chapter 16. You can circle back from the town of Hawi (HA-vee) at North Kohala's tip along the **Kohala Mountain Road** (Highway 250), ending up back on the Kawaihae Road just west of Waimea.

Staying in Style

In the following listings, each property is followed by a number of dollar signs, ranging from one ($) to five ($$$$$). Each represents the median rack-rate price range for a double room per night, as follows:

$	Super-cheap — less than $100 per night
$$	Still affordable — $100 to $175
$$$	Moderate — $175 to $250
$$$$	Expensive but not ridiculous — $250 to $375
$$$$$	Ultraluxurious — more than $375 per night

Remember that you almost never need to pay the asking price for a hotel room. Check out Chapter 8 for tips on how to avoid paying for a full-price hotel room. Also see Chapter 6 for advice on how to score an all-inclusive package that can save you big bucks on both accommodations and airfare, and, sometimes, car rentals and activities, too.

Also, don't forget that the state adds 11.42 percent in taxes to your hotel bill.

In addition to the following choices, you might also want to consider the **Sheraton Keauhou Bay Resort & Spa** (☎ **888-488-3535,** www.sheraton keauhou.com), set to debut on a spectacular 22-acre oceanfront lava point on the sunny south Kona Coast in late 2004. The former Kona Surf hotel was in the process of being gloriously reborn as a deluxe Sheraton at editorial time. Among the perks of the $45-million makeover are 530 brand-new guest rooms, featuring tropical-modern décor and cloudlike Sheraton SweetSleeper beds; the full-service, open-air Keauhou Spa; two restaurants, plus luau grounds; a wedding chapel; an eye-popping fantasy pool with a 200-foot lava-tube water slide; and much more. The jury is still out at this writing, but all signs point to a winner.

Carson's Volcano Cottages
$$ Volcano

Hands down, Carson's Volcano Cottages is my favorite place to stay in Volcano Village. Warm and wonderful innkeepers Tom and Brenda Carson offer an accommodation for everyone just outside Hawaii Volcanoes National Park: a half-dozen charming guest rooms with private baths in the main house (including two that can be combined into a nice family suite for four), for travelers looking for good value; three ultraromantic tin-roofed cottages, each with full kitchen; and two dedicated family cottages with full kitchen and TV. All units brim with island-style charm and feature cozy beds with goose-down comforters, plush terry robes, and daily maid service. (The family cottages are serviced every second or third day.) Some cottages feature wood-burning stoves (a wonderful extra on cold nights) and/or private hot tubs; my favorite is the magical Koa Cabin, which boasts both, plus wonderful Jadite dinnerware and other midcentury collectibles. The property also features a hot tub tucked under the ferns for everybody's use. A few of the units are located a few blocks off-property, so you'll have to drive or walk to breakfast. Ask if it matters to you (we actually enjoyed the rainforesty seclusion). The bountiful breakfast buffet is a hearty, delicious feast — good carb-loading for your day at the park.

The Big Island's Accommodations

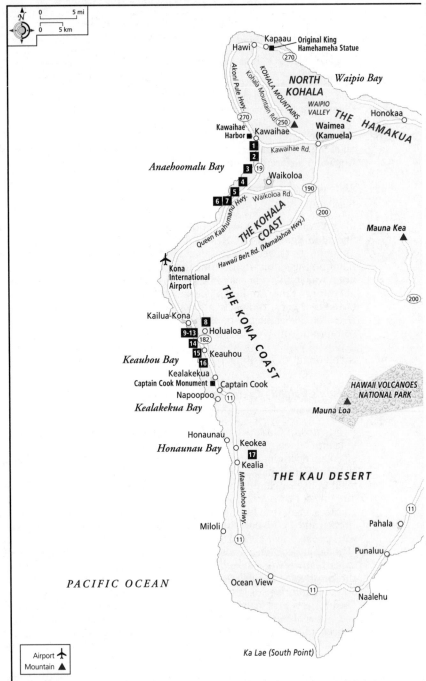

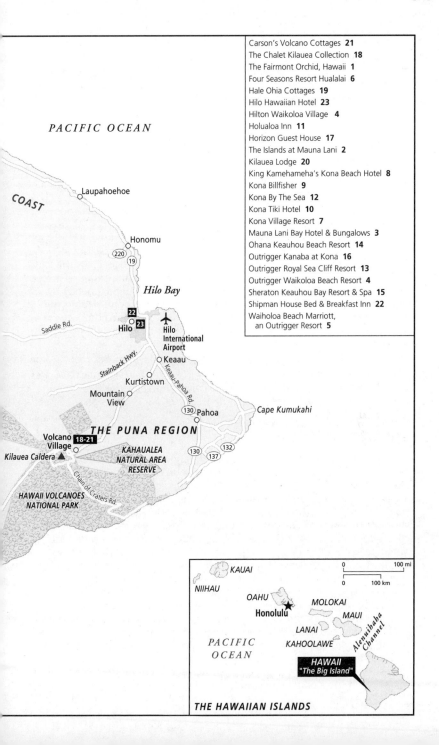

PACIFIC OCEAN

COAST

Laupahoehoe

Honomu

(220) (19)

Hilo Bay

Saddle Rd.

22
23 Hilo

Hilo International Airport

Stainback Hwy.

Keaau

Kurtistown

Keaau-Pahoa Rd.

Mountain View

(130) Pahoa

Cape Kumukahi

THE PUNA REGION

Volcano Village **18-21**

Kilauea Caldera ▲

KAHAUALEA NATURAL AREA RESERVE

(130) (137) (132)

Chain of Craters Rd.

HAWAII VOLCANOES NATIONAL PARK

Carson's Volcano Cottages **21**
The Chalet Kilauea Collection **18**
The Fairmont Orchid, Hawaii **1**
Four Seasons Resort Hualalai **6**
Hale Ohia Cottages **19**
Hilo Hawaiian Hotel **23**
Hilton Waikoloa Village **4**
Holualoa Inn **11**
Horizon Guest House **17**
The Islands at Mauna Lani **2**
Kilauea Lodge **20**
King Kamehameha's Kona Beach Hotel **8**
Kona Billfisher **9**
Kona By The Sea **12**
Kona Tiki Hotel **10**
Kona Village Resort **7**
Mauna Lani Bay Hotel & Bungalows **3**
Ohana Keauhou Beach Resort **14**
Outrigger Kanaba at Kona **16**
Outrigger Royal Sea Cliff Resort **13**
Outrigger Waikoloa Beach Resort **4**
Sheraton Keauhou Bay Resort & Spa **15**
Shipman House Bed & Breakfast Inn **22**
Waiholoa Beach Marriott,
  an Outrigger Resort **5**

KAUAI

NIIHAU

OAHU
Honolulu ★

MOLOKAI
MAUI
LANAI
KAHOOLAWE

Alenuihaha Channel

PACIFIC OCEAN

HAWAII "The Big Island"

0   100 mi
0   100 km

THE HAWAIIAN ISLANDS

If you're looking for a secluded, off-the-beaten-path hideaway, ask Tom and Brenda about their two oceanview rental cottages in sunny Kapoho, in the remote Puna District, on the Big Island's southeast coast.

See map p. 330. 501 Sixth St. (near Pearl Street), Volcano. ☎ *800-845-5282 or 808-967-7683. Fax: 808-967-8094.* www.carsonsvolcanocottage.com. *Parking: Free! Rack rates: $105–$125 double, $155 suite, $125–$165 cottage. Full breakfast buffet included. Deals: Ask about weekly, monthly, and off-season rates. AE, DISC, MC, V.*

The Chalet Kilauea Collection
$–$$$$$ **Volcano**

Brian and Lisha Crawford have built a mini-empire outside the gates of Hawaii Volcanoes National Park. They own a B&B for every budget, as well as a selection of vacation rentals, ranging from a cozy one-bedroom cottage to a fully equipped three-bedroom home that sleeps six. All are well furnished, well maintained, and well priced. I think their luxury suites are overpriced and too heavy-handed in the decoration department to be called elegant, but the rest of their accommodations — especially the vacation rentals — offer reasonably good value for your dollar. (I prefer Carson's Volcano Cottages and Hale Ohia in the B&B department.) All are conveniently located, nicely outfitted, and feature comfortable public spaces for lounging. Your best bet is either to peruse the comprehensive Web site or call and speak to an attendant who will pair you up with an accommodation that's right for you.

See map p. 330. 988 Wright Rd., Volcano. ☎ *800-937-7786 or 808-967-7786. Fax: 800-577-1849 or 808-967-8660.* www.volcano-hawaii.com. *Parking: Free! Rack rates: $49–$399 double or suite. Rates include breakfast. AE, DC, DISC, MC, V.*

The Fairmont Orchid, Hawaii
$$$$–$$$$$ **Kohala Coast**

This elegant, attractive, and thoroughly appealing beach resort boasts gorgeous views and some of the best extras on the coast. The sports facilities are extensive (championship golf, tennis, catamaran rides, and outrigger canoe trips), the oceanside "Spa Without Walls" is as stress-relieving as they come, and the heated oceanfront pool (a whopping 10,000 sq. ft.) and hot tubs are tiki-torchlit for maximum romance at night. The resort also offers an excellent Hawaiian program for culture and crafts buffs; on the flip side, reality-TV fans might be interested to know that this was the setting for *Celebrity Mole Hawaii.* Brown's Beach House is the coast's most romantic restaurant (see the section "Dining Out," later in this chapter); and eight other bars and restaurants are on the property, including a sushi restaurant and a New York-style deli. The spacious rooms are more boldly colorful than most, with an eye-catching teal palette, comfy furnishings, and large marble baths. The beach is small but pretty and perfect for snorkeling and kids at play. All in all, the Orchid is a tad less opulent and a bit more intimately sized and accessible than many other Big Island resorts. The service is top-notch, and even employees at competing resorts admit that the Orchid's concierge staff is the island's best. The only downside is

Kona Coast Accommodations

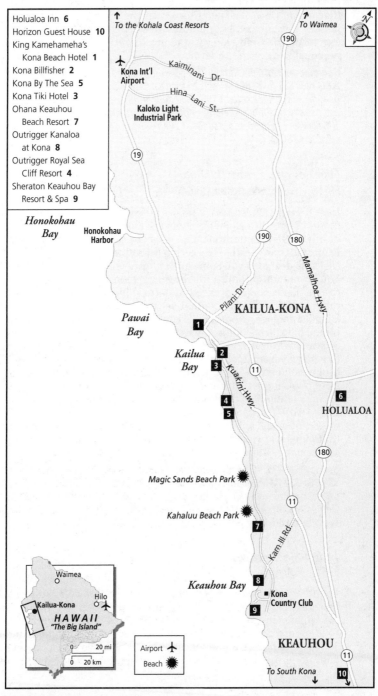

Holualoa Inn **6**
Horizon Guest House **10**
King Kamehameha's
  Kona Beach Hotel **1**
Kona Billfisher **2**
Kona By The Sea **5**
Kona Tiki Hotel **3**
Ohana Keauhou
  Beach Resort **7**
Outrigger Kanaloa
  at Kona **8**
Outrigger Royal Sea
  Cliff Resort **4**
Sheraton Keauhou Bay
  Resort & Spa **9**

To the Kohala Coast Resorts

To Waimea

(190)

Kona Int'l
Airport

Kaiminani Dr.

Hina Lani St.

Kaloko Light
Industrial Park

(19)

*Honokohau
Bay*

Honokohau
Harbor

(190) (180)

Pilani Dr.

Mamalhoa Hwy.

KAILUA-KONA

*Pawai
Bay*

1

*Kailua
Bay*

2
3

Kuakini Hwy.

(11)

4
5

6
HOLUALOA

(180)

Magic Sands Beach Park

Kahaluu Beach Park

(11)

7

Kam III Rd.

Keauhou Bay

8

Kona
Country Club

9

KEAUHOU

(11)

To South Kona

10

Waimea

Hilo

Kailua-Kona

HAWAII
"The Big Island"

0   20 mi
0   20 km

Airport ✈
Beach ✺

the building's U shape, which gives most of the rooms courtyard rather than ocean views. Fairmont took over the property in January 2003, eliminating the sneaky $12-per-day "resort fee" and lowering room rates, except on the Gold Floor, where guests receive upgraded amenities and personalized concierge service.

See map p. 335. 1 N. Kaniku Dr., Mauna Lani resort. ☎ *800-845-9905 or 808-885-2000. Fax: 808-885-1064.* www.fairmont.com/orchid *or Valet parking: $11. Self-parking: Free! Rack rates: $299–$900 double, $999–$2,000 suite. Deals: Package deals are usually available (including fifth-night-free offers), so be sure to ask (bargains were as low as $299 at press time). Also ask for AAA-member and senior discounts. AE, DC, DISC, MC, V.*

Four Seasons Resort Hualalai
$$$$$ **West Side (Kona Coast)**

Here it is: the finest luxury resort hotel in the islands, and the Hope diamond of the glittering Four Seasons chain. Island-style elegance simply doesn't get any better than this one. Low-rise clusters of clean-lined ocean-facing villas are nestled between a lovely sandy beach and a fabulous Jack Nicklaus-designed golf course (for guests only — so start dialing, duffers!). You'll want for nothing in the huge, gorgeous, and supremely comfortable rooms. Each comes dressed in natural hues and materials — including raffia, rattan, and slate — that set the perfect kick-off-your-shoes Pacific island ambience; ground-level rooms even have private outdoor showers off the big marble bathrooms, so you can shower *au naturel* under the sun or stars. Wireless high-speed Internet access is ideal for guests who want to get away from it all without forsaking complete connectivity. The beautiful beach can be too rough for swimming, but no matter — three ocean-front pools more than compensate, including a stocked snorkel pond (with friendly stingrays!) that's ideal for beginners. An exclusive spa (named by *Condé Nast Traveler* as the world's best resort spa), a state-of-the-art fitness center, and sublime beachfront dining round out the experience. Now that superstar Honolulu chef Alan Wong is the lead chef in the delightful clubhouse restaurant, who could ask for anything more?

See map p. 335. 100 Kaupulehu Dr., Kaupulehu-Kona (7 miles north of the airport). ☎ *800-332-3442, 888-340-5662, or 808-325-8000. Fax: 808-325-8200.* www.four seasons.com. *Parking: Free! Rack rates: $540–$725 double, $850–$6,500 suite. Deals: Ask about romance, golf, spa, fifth-night-free, room-and-car, bed-and-breakfast, and other packages. AE, DC, DISC, MC, V.*

Hale Ohia Cottages
$–$$ **Volcano**

Condé Nast Traveler named Hale Ohia the top place to stay in Volcano in its February 2004 issue, and the honor is well-deserved. This charming and tranquil assemblage of suites and cottages offers a wonderful opportunity to step into the past and get back to nature. The gorgeous red-shingled 1931 estate boasts an impeccable blend of 1930s Hawaii plantation style and modern-day sophistication. The stunning botanical grounds are the

The Kohala Coast

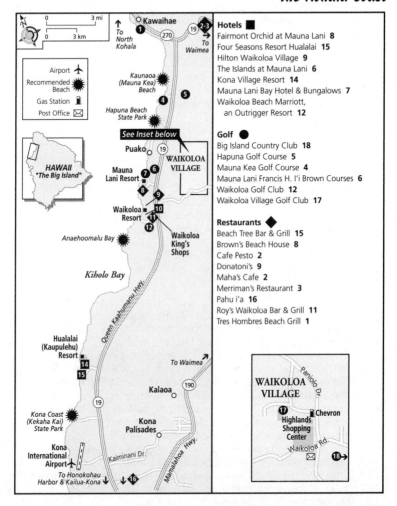

Hotels ■
Fairmont Orchid at Mauna Lani **8**
Four Seasons Resort Hualalai **15**
Hilton Waikoloa Village **9**
The Islands at Mauna Lani **6**
Kona Village Resort **14**
Mauna Lani Bay Hotel & Bungalows **7**
Waikoloa Beach Marriott,
    an Outrigger Resort **12**

Golf ●
Big Island Country Club **18**
Hapuna Golf Course **5**
Mauna Kea Golf Course **4**
Mauna Lani Francis H. I'i Brown Courses **6**
Waikoloa Golf Club **12**
Waikoloa Village Golf Club **17**

Restaurants ◆
Beach Tree Bar & Grill **15**
Brown's Beach House **8**
Cafe Pesto **2**
Donatoni's **9**
Maha's Cafe **2**
Merriman's Restaurant **3**
Pahu i'a **16**
Roy's Waikoloa Bar & Grill **11**
Tres Hombres Beach Grill **1**

result of more than 30 years' work by a master Japanese gardener. All the accommodations are lovely and comfortable. The Ihilani Cottage is a honeymooner's dream, with its own enclosed lanai with a bubbling fountain, and the three-bedroom Hale Ohia Cottage, with its own full kitchen, is a great deal for families. The recent transformation of the property's original redwood water tank into Cottage #44, a beautiful and fully outfitted suite (complete with kitchenette and Jacuzzi tub), adds yet another offbeat delight to the retro-romantic collection. The massive Master Suite (where the owner stays when he's on the island) is a steal if you can snare it. The in-room continental breakfast makes this spot an excellent choice for privacy seekers.

See map p. 330. On Hale Ohia Road (off Highway 11), Volcano. ☎ 800-455-3803 or 808-967-7986. Fax: 808-967-8610. www.haleohia.com. *Parking: Free! Rack rates: $95–$150 double. Rates include continental breakfast. MC, V.*

Hilo Hawaiian Hotel
$$ Hilo

This eight-story waterfront hotel on picturesque Hilo Bay features nice rooms that do the job at a fair price. It's generic but is set on a gracious setting on leafy Banyan Drive. There aren't many facilities, but you'll still find a pool and sun deck, a gift shop, a laundromat, and a restaurant and lounge here. Pay the few extra bucks for a bay view if you can swing it; you won't be disappointed. Check online for frequent money-saving Internet specials; at press time, rooms could be had for as little as $80.

See map p. 330. 71 Banyan Dr., Hilo. ☎ 800-367-5004 or 808-545-3510. Fax: 808-545-2163. www.castleresorts.com/HHH. *Parking: Free! Rack rates: $125–$180 double, $190–$385 suite. Deals: Check for deeply discounted Internet rates (as low as $80 at press time). Also ask about free-car, free-night, and other special packages. AE, DC, DISC, MC, V.*

Hilton Waikoloa Village
$$$–$$$$ Kohala Coast

With 1,240 rooms spread over 62 acres, this massive hotel is too big for its own good. Just getting from your room to the lobby is a 15- to 20-minute production, so check in, park yourself, and don't be in any hurry to leave. This is a destination resort of the highest order, Hawaii's very own version of Disneyland. Its high-rise towers, water slide-riddled megapools, dolphin lagoons, and gaggle of restaurants (including the divine Donatoni's; see the section "Dining Out," later in this chapter), bars, and shops are connected by trams, boats, and art-lined walkways. Thanks to so many eye-popping diversions, your kids will think that they've died and gone to heaven. Mom and Dad are bound to be entertained, too, thanks to a tremendous spa and championship golf course — if you don't run screaming from sensory overload first. The rooms are well-appointed, comfortable, and relatively affordable considering the level of luxury and the full slate of amenities that you'll find here. You won't find any sandy beach, though; you have to go next door for that.

See map p. 335. 425 Waikoloa Beach Dr., Waikoloa. ☎ 800-HILTONS or 808-886-1234. Fax: 808-886-2900. www.hiltonwaikoloavillage.com *or* www.hilton.com. *Valet parking: $11. Rack rates: $199–$689 double, suites from $1,030. Mandatory daily $18 "resort fee" covers "free" local phone calls, in-room coffee, use of safe, use of spa for two, and $25 credit towards beach rental and tennis. Deals: A range of packages and special offers is usually available, including romance, golf, and family packages, and more. Also ask for AAA, AARP, corporate, and other discounts. AE, DC, DISC, MC, V.*

Holualoa Inn
$$$ Upcountry Kona

Set on 40 pastoral acres on the slopes above Kailua-Kona, in the charmingly artsy town of Holualoa, this impeccable inn offers the ultimate tranquil escape, yet it's also conveniently located just 15 minutes from great beaches and all the other conveniences. Built entirely of golden woods and outfitted in a simple Balinese style — all clean lines, rattan, and subtle colors — this gorgeous contemporary Hawaiian home boasts six spacious guest rooms, window-walls that slide away to reveal stunning panoramic ocean views, and an easygoing island vibe. The lovely pool and Jacuzzi overlook a backyard coffee farm and fruit trees (which supply the morning brew and breakfast papayas) and offer spectacular views of the coastline below. Nice extras include a gas grill with all the supplies you need to barbecue a romantic dinner, wonderful common spaces for dining and lounging, and a pool table to entertain yourself on quiet evenings. Even B&B-phobes will feel right at home.

See map p. 333. 76-5932 Mamalahoa Hwy., Holualoa (a 15-minute drive uphill from Highway 19, along Hualalai Road). ☎ ***800-392-1812*** *or 808-324-1121. Fax: 808-322-2472.* www.holualoainn.com. *Parking: Free! Rack rates: $175–$225 double. Rates include substantial continental breakfast and sunset pupu. Children under 13 not accepted. Two-night minimum stay. Deals: 15-percent discount on stays of 7 nights or more. AE, MC, V.*

Horizon Guest House
$$$$ South Kona

This impeccable B&B offers the ultimate in luxurious relaxation. The house is located on 40 acres of lush pastureland at 1,100 feet elevation, offering unparalleled coastline views. The four carefully designed one-room suites are cantilevered off the end of the house for maximum privacy. Each has its own private entry and furnished lanai and is filled with gorgeous island antiques, hand-quilted Hawaiian bedspreads, a minifridge, coffeemaker, and cushy robes. A dramatic 20-x-40-foot infinity pool (the pool appears to have no edge) and a romantic hot tub are situated to take full advantage of the breathtaking views. Guests have free use of laundry facilities and beach toys galore. Innkeeper Clem Classen serves a gourmet buffet breakfast in the artifact-filled main house, which also features a multimedia room with an extensive book and video library and a TV with VCR and DVD. Impeccable personalized (but completely unobtrusive) service is the elegant finish that justifies the high price tag.

See map p. 333. 86-3992 Highway 11 (between mile markers 100 and 101), Honaunau. ☎ ***888-328-8301*** *or 808-328-2540. Fax: 808-328-8707.* www.horizonguesthouse. com. *Parking: Free! Rack rates: $250 double. Rate includes full gourmet breakfast. Children under 14 not accepted. Deals: 15 percent off bookings of 7 nights or more. Inquire about other discounts (rates can sometimes fall as low as $175). MC, V.*

The Islands at Mauna Lani
$$$$$ Kohala Coast

If you're in the market for a two- or three-bedroom condo — be it for a family, sharing couples, or plenty of spreading-out for yourself — you can't do better than the Islands. Light, bright, airy, and gorgeous, these contemporary Mediterranean-style townhomes boast a massive 2,100 square feet of living space. On the first floor, you find a gourmet kitchen, full dining and living rooms (both with furnished lanais), and a laundry room with full-size washer and dryer. Upstairs are two (or three) master-size bedrooms, each with a firm, well-dressed king bed, a furnished lanai, and a monster bathroom with an oversized Jacuzzi tub and yards of counter space. Every luxury is at hand, from a cordless phone to a gas grill to daily maid service to your own garage with automatic door opener. The views of the lushly manicured grounds and surrounding fairways more than make up for the lack of ocean vistas. The perks don't end there. On-site is a very nice heated pool and hot tub; what's more, Islands guests can hop the free on-call shuttle to an exclusive beach club, which boasts its own perfect white-sand cove, excellent snorkel reef, gear-rental shack, and restaurant. The shuttle also takes you to and from the Mauna Lani Spa, the island's best. Service is excellent but completely non-intrusive.

See map p. 335. 68-1050 Mauna Lani Point Dr., Mauna Lani resort. ☎ 800-642-6284 or 808-661-3339. Fax: 808-667-1145. www.classicresorts.com. *Parking: Free! Rack rates: $540 2-bedroom, $695 3-bedroom. 3-night minimum. Deals: Fifth night free at press time. Also ask about room-and-car packages, return guest packages, and other available discounts. AE, MC, V.*

Kilauea Lodge
$$ Volcano

Built in 1938 as a YMCA camp, this popular roadside lodge sits on 10 wooded acres just a stone's throw from the main gate of the national park. The lodge is a real woodsy charmer, with stone pillars and beamed ceilings. Twelve comfortably outfitted rooms offer private baths, attractive artwork by local artists, lovely garden views, and individual heat controls and towel warmers (nice plusses on chilly Volcano nights). A phone, lending library, games, and a TV set for shared viewing are found in the common room. Two charming cottages are also available, one with two bedrooms and a full kitchen that's great for families, plus a pleasant, newly renovated house on the fairway at the Volcano Golf Course. A complete, satisfying breakfast is served in the restaurant, which is my Volcano favorite for dinner (see the section "Dining Out," later in this chapter). All in all, this is an excellent choice, especially for those who prefer hotel-style anonymity over the intimacy of many of Volcano's B&B-style stays.

See map p. 330. 19-4055 Volcano Rd. (just off Highway 11 at Wright Road), Volcano. ☎ 808-967-7366. Fax: 808-967-7367. www.kilauealodge.com. *Parking: Free! Rack rates: $135–$155 double, $165–$175 1- or 2-bedroom cottage. Rates include full breakfast. AE, MC, V.*

King Kamehameha's Kona Beach Hotel
$$ Kailua-Kona

Located in the heart of Kailua-Kona town, just a stroll away from everything, this hotel can't be beat for convenience. The King Kam is Holiday Inn simple, but it's clean, ocean-facing, and an ideal choice for those who don't want to have to go far for shopping and dining. Every room features a private lanai; ask for one overlooking sparkling Kailua Bay for only-in-Hawaii views. (Note that bathrooms have showers only.) The small, gold-sand beach isn't exactly your dream strand, but it will satisfy in a pinch. Other on-site extras include shops, a pool and Jacuzzi, tennis, sauna, a massage center, restaurants and a poolside bar, a luau, and a coin-op laundry plus valet service. Nicer beaches are just a short drive away. The numerous, always-available package deals are a steal, so be sure to inquire.

See map p. 333. 75-5660 Palani Rd. (at Alii Drive), Kailua-Kona. ☎ *800-367-6060 or 808-329-2911. Fax: 808-922-84602.* www.konabeachhotel.com. *Parking: $5. Rack rates: $155–$225 double, $500–$900 1- to 3-bedroom suite. Deals: Very good packages are usually on offer; at press time, from $155 with breakfast and free parking, $165 with car added; family package gets you a second room at half price. Also ask about corporate and senior rates, and check for Internet rates (as low as $95 at press time). AE, DC, DISC, MC, V.*

Kona Billfisher
$ Kailua-Kona

This place is my favorite under-$100 bargain. The units aren't fancy, but you can't do better for the money — and discounts on longer stays make the rooms practically free. The management company invests in constant renovations, and the resident manager keeps everything neat and fresh. Each apartment has a full kitchen with all-electric appliances, a large lanai, decent newish furniture, and king-size beds. The one-bedrooms have sliding doors that allow you to close off the living room into another bedroom, which makes them a real deal for penny-saving families. On-site extras include a pool, barbecues, and a coin-op laundry, and the town is just a walk away. You'll have to drive to a swimmable beach, but at these prices, you won't mind. Book well in advance because this place fills up fast, usually with repeat guests.

See map p. 333. On Alii Drive (on the mountain side of the street, across from the Royal Kona Resort), Kailua-Kona, c/o Hawaii Resort Management. ☎ *800-622-5348 or 808-329-9393. Fax: 808-326-4137.* www.konahawaii.com. *Parking: Free! Rack rates: $80–$95 1-bedroom, $105–$125 2-bedroom/1-bath. 3-night minimum, plus $50 nonrefundable cleaning fee (higher rates available for shorter stays). Deals: Big discounts available on weekly and monthly stays; also ask about Internet specials (from $70 at press time). DISC, MC, V.*

Kona By The Sea
$$$$ **Kailua-Kona**

The units and grounds at this deluxe oceanfront condo complex are a tad more inviting than those at the nearby Outrigger Royal Sea Cliff (see later in this chapter), but not dramatically so. The bright, spacious, nicely decorated apartments boast complete kitchens with microwave, washer/dryers, daily maid service, and large lanais (most with ocean views). On-site you find a nice oceanfront freshwater pool, Jacuzzi, barbecues, and an activities desk that can book your island fun. One of the nice plusses exclusive to this property is the personal grocery-shopping service — just leave a shopping list with the manager, and your staples are delivered right to your door. The white-sand beach here is lovely but unswimmable, so plan on heading 4 miles south to Kahaluu Beach for first-rate snorkeling.

See map p. 333. 75-6106 Alii Dr., Kailua-Kona (2 miles south of town). ☎ 877-997-6667 or 808-327-2300. Fax: 808-327-2333. www.aston-hotels.com. *Parking: Free! Rack rates: $196–$330 1-bedroom, $245–$405 2-bedroom. Deals: Excellent discounts. Ask for AAA, senior (50-plus), and corporate discounts, and other special rate programs such as the kids stay, play, and eat for free package. AE, DC, DISC, MC, V.*

Kona Tiki Hotel
$ **Kailua-Kona**

This friendly family-run motel is one of the best cheap sleeps in the state. Staying here is like stepping into a time warp — one where you can have a reasonable room for two, right on the ocean, for as little as $61. The rooms are budget-basic on every level, but the beds are firm and comfy, ceiling fans and minifridges are on hand (a few have kitchenettes for just a bit more moolah), and every room has a lanai with front-row ocean views. New paint and carpets were in the works at press time. A basic continental breakfast is served poolside every morning, making this incredible value that much more astounding. The location is pleasant, away from the hustle and bustle of downtown. The ocean here isn't swimmable, and you'll find no TVs, phones, or coin-op laundry (a local laundry will pick up and deliver), but those are the sacrifices you make for such a bargain. Book way in advance, because people *loooove* this place.

See map p. 333. 75-5968 Alii Dr. Kailua-Kona (a mile south of town). ☎ 808-329-1425. Fax: 808-327-9402. www.konatiki.com. *Parking: Free! Rack rates: $61–$75 double, $84 double with kitchenette. Rates include continental breakfast and tax. 3-night minimum. No credit cards.*

Kona Village Resort
$$$$$ **Kohala Coast**

Hawaii may have fancier and more amenity-laden resorts, but the state's only all-inclusive is truly something special: a super-deluxe version of *Gilligan's Island,* where it feels perfectly natural to tuck a flower behind your ear and sip cocktails out of coconuts. This South Seas paradise of swaying palms and lagoons offers blissful escape, Robinson Crusoe style: no TVs, phones, or fax machines around to interrupt your tropical reverie for even a minute. You'll stay in your own thatch-roofed *hale,* which is much like a comfortably furnished tropical cottage. The dark-sand beach offers first-rate snorkeling with green sea turtles, who climb up on shore nearly every afternoon for a nap; manta rays hang out in the flood-lit bay after dark, proving that all species love Kona Village. A tenderly attentive staff — one of the best in the islands — is on hand to meet your needs and desires even before you know you have them, and the food is abundant and absolutely terrific at every meal. There's something going on most nights, whether it's dancing to a Hawaiian trio or the terrific Friday-night luau (see the section "Luau!," later in this chapter), and the kids' program is excellent. Utterly restful, and simply divine, this resort is Hawaii vacationing as it was really meant to be.

See map p. 335. At the Kaupulehu resort, 7 miles north of the airport. ☎ *800-367-5290 or 808-325-5555. Fax: 808-325-5124.* www.konavillage.com. *Parking: Free! Rack rates: $515–$910 double. Rates include all meals, in-room refreshments, most activities, children's program, airport transfers, and more. All rates are based on double occupancy; $38–$193 per person extra. No kids' rates or programs in May and Sept. Deals: Ask about honeymoon, family, car, and other packages. AE, DC, MC, V.*

Mauna Lani Bay Hotel & Bungalows
$$$$$ Kohala Coast

Hawaiian elders named this section of the sunny lava coast Mauna Lani, or "Mountain reaching Heaven," and it's an apt name for so heavenly a resort. Mauna Lani has a finer swimming and snorkeling beach than any other Big Island resort hotel. The hotel is designed in the shape of an arrow on the sands to take advantage of its prime coastal location, providing most rooms with substantial ocean views. A vast open-air lobby spilling over with tropical greenery leads to serene and simple rooms that exude island style — teak floors, lauhala headboards, ceiling fans, natural-hued textiles, and lanais. VCRs, opposing vanities, seersucker robes, and twice-daily maid service add a luxury touch. Families can stay in the homelike villas, but those with bottomless bank accounts should opt for one of the incredible bungalows, each of which has its own private pool and a butler who doesn't know the word "no." The historically and culturally sensitive resort features the finest, most Hawaiian spa in the islands, an extensive calendar of daily activities, a first-rate tennis center, and easy access to some of Hawaii's best golf. One sour note: Dinner in the celebrated CanoeHouse just isn't what it used to be.

See map p. 335. 68-1400 Mauna Lani Dr., Mauna Lani resort. ☎ *800-367-2323 or 808-885-6622. Fax: 808-885-1484.* www.maunalani.com. *Parking: Free! Rack rates: $385–$750 double, $1,200 suite, $550–$1,050 1- to 3-bedroom villa, $4,900–$5,600 bungalow. Deals: Many packages usually available, including 2-room deals as low as $575, and a 4-night deal with airfare from L.A. for $1,078. Discounted weekly rates available on villas. AE, DC, DISC, MC, V.*

Ohana Keauhou Beach Resort
$$$–$$$$ South Kona

Unveiled in 2000 after a $15-million-plus overhaul and managed by Ohana (the value-minded arm of the reliable Hawaii-based Outrigger chain), this hotel has been restored to like-new condition and is a great choice for culture buffs, active vacationers, or anybody in search of affordable oceanfront accommodations. Situated on a tranquil and lovely stretch of coast, the midrise structure boasts a central location, lovely views, and a genuine Hawaiian ambience. The island's best snorkeling is right next door at Kahaluu Beach Park, while the hotel's own 10 acres of tropical grounds feature an oceanside pool, a fitness center, and tennis courts lit for night play. A grassy oceanfront area is dedicated to the easy life, with hammocks strung between coconut palms. There's a surprisingly good restaurant and an open-air lounge with live Hawaiian music and glorious golden sunsets. The rooms themselves are less distinctive, but perfectly comfortable. They're fresh and pleasant, with good bedside reading lights, generous counter space and cushy towels in the bathrooms (some of which have showers only), coffeemakers, and lanais — most with some kind of ocean view. Adjoining rooms make this resort a good family choice, too.

See map p. 333. 78-6740 Alii Dr., Keauhou (3 miles south of Kailua-Kona). ☎ *800-462-6262 or 808-322-3441. Fax: 808-322-3117.* www.ohanahotels.com. *Parking: $5. Rack rates: $189–$309 double, $559–$599 suite. Deals: Better-than-average discounts for AAA and AARP members and seniors (50-plus), plus corporate, government, and military discounts. Ask about heavily discounted SimpleSaver rates and first-night-free, bed-and-breakfast, room-and-car, and other package deals. AE, DC, DISC, MC, V.*

Outrigger Kanaloa at Kona
$$$–$$$$ South Kona

Tucked away in a quiet, attractive neighborhood, these big, well-managed oceanfront condos (by the reliable, value-oriented Hawaii-based Outrigger hotel chain) are a cut above the average and ideal for families. Comfortably furnished in quality island style with Hawaiian wood accents, the apartments have all the comforts of home and then some, including dressing rooms, big kitchens loaded with appliances, huge bathrooms (with whirlpools in oceanview suites!), and washer/dryers. Two tennis courts lit for night play, three swimming pools with hot tubs, and playgrounds dot the pleasant, attractively manicured ocean-facing grounds. The coast is lava rock here, however, so you'll have to drive a half-mile to Kahaluu Beach (one of Hawaii's best for snorkeling). An excellent restaurant, Edward's at Kanaloa (see the section "Dining Out," later in this chapter), is on-site; a big, modern, well-stocked supermarket is just up the hill; and Kailua-Kona's restaurants and shops are a ten-minute drive away. Guests receive discounted rates on 36 holes of championship golf at the neighboring country club.

See map p. 333. 78-261 Manukai St., Keauhou. ☎ *800-688-7444 or 808-322-9625. Fax: 808-322-3818.* www.outrigger.com. *Parking: Free! Rack rates: $205–$290 1-bedroom, $220–$330 2-bedroom. Deals: Better-than-average discounts for AAA* and AARP members and seniors (50-plus), plus corporate, government, and military discounts. Fifth-night-free, bed-and-breakfast, and room-and-car packages regularly on offer. AE, DC, DISC, MC, V.

Outrigger Royal Sea Cliff Resort
$$$ **Kailua-Kona**

Parents with kids in tow will love these apartments. They're not fancy, but they're large, well outfitted, and older but well cared for by the reliable Outrigger hotel chain. The big five-story complex steps down a terraced cliff to a black-sand beach. The water's too rough for swimming, but the views are spectacular, and the privacy is unsurpassed. Gardens and hanging bougainvillea give the whole place a pleasant, tropical ambience. The spacious, air-conditioned apartments carry on the vibe, with lots of rattan, sunny lanais, full kitchens with microwave, washer/dryer, TV with VCR in the living rooms, and daily maid service, making for easy vacation living. Two pools (one freshwater, one saltwater), a Jacuzzi, sauna, tennis, and barbecues are all on-site. The nearest swimming beach is about a mile away, but it's a winner for snorkelers.

See map p. 333. 75-6040 Alii Dr., Kailua-Kona (2 miles south of town). ☎ *800-688-7444 or 808-329-8021. Fax: 808-326-1887.* www.outrigger.com. *Parking: Free! Rack rates: $183–$233 studio, $215–$318 1-bedroom apartment, $250–$803 2-bedroom apartment or villa. Deals: Many discounts and packages available (some as low as $151 at press time), including reduced rates for AAA and AARP members and seniors (50-plus), as well as members of the government or the military. AE, DC, DISC, MC, V.*

Shipman House Bed & Breakfast Inn
$$–$$$ **Hilo**

Misty, flower-filled Hilo wows nostalgics with its Victorian homes and charming downtown overlooking a romantic half-moon bay. One of those century-old Victorians is this dreamy B&B, my favorite place to stay in town. Impeccably renovated and on the National Register of Historic Places, it's right in step with Hilo's old Hawaii vibe. Barbara Ann and Gary Andersen have kept the inn true to its original form, but they haven't lost sight of its present-day purpose. It's full of modern conveniences, including full baths, ceiling fans, minifridges, and kimono robes (but no TVs) in each of the five spacious, impeccably done rooms. Most romantic is Auntie Clara's, a corner room with windows on two walls overlooking a lush rainforest and bay, with a clawfoot tub in the bathroom. (The bathroom for this room is private, but is detached from the bedroom.) Breakfast is served on the wide veranda. This B&B is perfect for romance-seeking couples, history buffs, and national park–goers alike. Hawaii Volcanoes is a half-hour's drive south. Smoking and shoes are forbidden inside the house, and children are discouraged.

See map p. 330. 131 Kaiulani St. (off Waianuenue Avenue), Hilo. ☎ *800-627-8447 or 808-934-8002. Fax: 808-934-8002.* www.hilo-hawaii.com. *Parking: Free! Rack rates: $169–$189 double. Rates include generous continental buffet breakfast. Rates $25 higher for single-night stays. AE, MC, V.*

Waikoloa Beach Marriott, an Outrigger Resort
$$$–$$$$ Kohala Coast

This used to be the Kohala Coast's best value back when it was the Royal Waikoloan. Today, after a $23-million renovation, it's the product of a new partnership between Marriott and the Hawaii-based Outrigger chain. The upgrade has really lightened and upscaled the place and removed much of the budget feel from the smallish rooms, giving them a genuinely lovely island vibe as well as conveniences like coffeemakers and minifridges. Still, the biggest plus remains the location: The resort is situated on palm-lined A-Bay, one of the island's prettiest white-sand beaches and best bays for watersports. An excellent beach-activities desk provides easy access to snorkeling, diving, kayaking, and windsurfing; championship golf and salon and spa services are also on hand. All in all, the resort looks great. The food, service, and trappings aren't on par with its more luxury-minded neighbors, but neither are the rates. They're higher than they should be, but Outrigger excels in handing out packages and discounts, so this hotel usually wins the race as the bargain of the Kohala Coast (although it's worth price-comparing against Hilton Waikoloa Village, reviewed earlier in this chapter).

See map p. 335. 69-275 Waikoloa Beach Rd., Waikoloa. ☎ ***800-688-7444** or 808-886-6789. Fax: 808-886-1554.* www.outrigger.com. *Valet parking: $5. Rack rates: $215–$335 double, $965–$3,100 suite. Deals: Better-than-average discounts for AAA and AARP members and seniors (50-plus), plus corporate, government, and military discounts. Fifth-night-free, bed-and-breakfast, and room-and-car packages regularly on offer. AE, DC, DISC, MC, V.*

Home, sweet vacation home

Local real-estate agencies offer a wealth of additional condo choices in and around Kailua-Kona and South Kona. One of the more trusted names is **Knutson & Associates** (☎ **800-800-6202** or 808-329-6311; www.kona hawaiirentals.com), a vacation-rental broker representing everything from affordable condos to multibedroom oceanfront houses.

Hawaii Resort Management (☎ **800-622-5348** or 808-329-9393; www.konahawaii.com) represents a dozen or more condo properties in the Kailua-Kona area (including the Kona Billfisher, listed above) and is a good source for budget-watching travelers. Also inquire with these folks about discounted car rates through Avis.

If you prefer a luxury rental on the sunny, golf course-riddled Kohala Coast, reach out to **South Kohala Management** (☎ **800-822-4252** or 808-883-8500; www.southkohala.com), which offers first-rate condos and townhomes plus a couple of upscale oceanfront houses.

If you'd like a full-scale vacation home outside the gates of Hawaii Volcanoes National Park, contact the folks behind the **Chalet Kilauea Collection** (see earlier in this chapter), who offer five nice vacation homes in the Volcano area, ranging from a cozy one-bedroom cottage to a fully equipped three-bedroom home that sleeps six. Call ☎ **800-937-7786** or 808-987-7786 or visit www.volcano-hawaii.com for details.

Hawaii's Best Bed & Breakfasts (☎ **800-262-9912** or 808-885-4550; www.bestbnb.com) also represents some excellent vacation homes on the Big Island, as well as delightful B&Bs. The staff can book a room for you in a cozy cottage or a larger home that they have personally inspected and approved, and service is always friendly.

Dining Out

The Big Island is home to some wonderful restaurants, including a handful of special-occasion oceanfront spots that are just right for some grand island-style wooing. But you don't have to spend a fortune to eat well; in fact, the Big Island is home to some of my favorite affordable restaurants in the state.

On the downside, things are a little spread out on this oversized rural island, so choose your dining spots carefully; you don't want to make a reservation for dinner only to realize that the restaurant is an hour's drive from where you're staying. I've worked to include the best restaurants in and around all the major resort and visitor areas in which you may be staying. Still, you may find that your choices are limited; the area around Hawaii Volcanoes National Park, for example, has only a small handful of restaurants, period. If you want additional choices, your concierge, front-desk staff, or innkeeper are usually happy to make recommendations.

If you're staying at a Kohala Coast resort, you'll find that the resort restaurants are almost universally overpriced. I've included a few worthy local favorites near the resorts, for those of you who are weary of paying a minimum of 30 bucks for an entree or $16 for a room-service burger that little Johnny isn't going to finish anyway.

In the restaurant listings in this chapter, each review is followed by a number of dollar signs, ranging from one ($) to five ($$$$$). The dollar signs are meant to give you an idea of what a complete dinner for one person — including appetizer, main course, dessert, one drink, tax, and tip — is likely to set you back. The price categories go like this:

$	Cheap eats — less than $15 per person
$$	Still inexpensive — $15 to $25
$$$	Moderate — $25 to $40
$$$$	Pricey — $40 to $70
$$$$$	Ultraexpensive — more than $70 per person

The Big Island's Restaurants

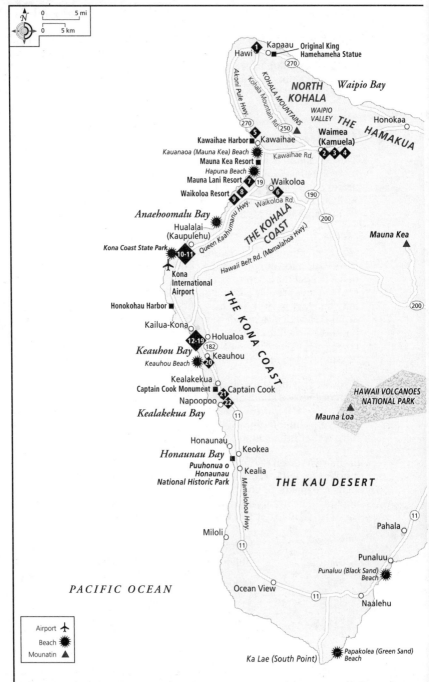

PACIFIC OCEAN

COAST

Laupahoehoe

Honomu

(220)
(19)

Hilo Bay

Leleiwi Beach Park

26-31 32
Hilo

Saddle Rd.

Hilo
International
Airport

Stainback Hwy.

Keaau

Kurtistown

Keaau-Pahoa Rd.

Mountain
View

(130) Pahoa

*Cape
Kumukahi*

Volcano
Village

Kilauea Caldera

THE PUNA REGION

23-25

KAHAUALEA
NATURAL AREA
RESERVE

(130) (132)
(137)

Hawaii Belt Rd.
(Mamalahoa Hwy.)

Chain of Craters Rd.

*HAWAII VOLCANOES
NATIONAL PARK*

Bamboo Restaurant & Gallery **1**
Beach Tree Bar & Grill **10**
Big Island Grill **12**
Brown's Beach House **7**
Cafe Pesto **2, 26**
The Coffee Shack **22**
Donatoni's **9**
Edward's at Kanaloa **19**
Fiascos **27**
Huggo's **14**
Kaikado **28**
Keei Cafe **21**
Ken's House of Pancakes **29**
Kenichi Pacific **20**
Kilauea Lodge & Restaurant **23**
Kona Brewing Co. **15**
Lava Rock Café **24**
Maha's Cafe **4**
Merriman's Market **6**
Merriman's Restaurant **3**
Ocean Sushi Deli **30**
Oodles of Noodles **13**
Pahu i'a **11**
Pescatore Italian Restaurant **31**
Roy's Waikoloa Bar & Grill **8**
Seaside Restaurant & Aqua Farm **32**
Sibu Cafe **16**
Thai Rin **17**
Thai Thai Restaurant **25**
Tres Hombres Beach Grill **5**
Tres Hombres Steak & Seafood
  Cantina **18**

Luaus
Kona Village Luau **10**

For detailed locations, see the following maps:
"The Kohala Coast Resorts" earlier in this chapter
"Kailua-Kona Town" in Chapter 16
"Waimea" in Chapter 16
"Hilo" in Chapter 16

Of course, it all depends on how you order, so stay away from the surf and turf or the north end of the wine list if you're watching your budget. To give you a further idea of how much you can expect to spend, I also include the price range of main courses in the listings. (Keep in mind that prices can change at the whim of the management, but restaurants usually don't raise their prices by more than a dollar or two at any given time.)

The state adds 4 percent in sales tax to every restaurant bill. A 15- to 20-percent tip is standard in Hawaii, just like on the mainland.

Just dying to take home a **Hard Rock Cafe Kona** T-shirt? The Big Island branch of the rock-and-burger chain is in the heart of Kailua-Kona at the Coconut Grove Marketplace, 75-5815 Alii Dr. (☎ **808-329-8866**).

Bamboo Restaurant & Gallery
$$–$$$ North Kohala   Hawaii Local/Pacific Rim

This wonderful restaurant provides the perfect excuse to venture up to pastoral North Kohala. Housed in a delightful plantation-era building and done up in well-worn rattan and retro-tropical prints, Bamboo bubbles over with old Hawaii appeal — like Trader Vic's without the kitsch. The pleasing menu features delicious island cuisine that, refreshingly, doesn't bother with "gourmet" or "culinary" pretensions. This is real food, well prepared with local pride. Almost everything is fresh-caught or locally grown by Kohala fishermen and farmers, and the owners grow their own herbs and flowers. The quality is excellent, portions are generous, and Pacific and Thai influences add zip. Chicken satay potstickers are hand-wrapped and pan-fried in chili oil for a spicy signature treat. Island fish is prepared four winning ways, and a moist and tender herb-marinated pork tenderloin is flame-broiled and paired with black tiger shrimp and green papaya salad. The lunch menu is simpler but equally satisfying, and eggs Bamboo (eggs Benedict with kalua pork and *lilikoi* hollandaise) is a winner at Sunday brunch. Passion-fruit margaritas and live slack key guitar music round out the island appeal. Plan on an early dinner so that you can enjoy the scenic drive in the daylight.

See map p. 346. On Akoni Pule Hwy. (at Highway 270/250 intersection), Hawi (a 30- to 45-minute drive from most Kohala Coast resorts). ☎ **808-889-5555.** http:// arcturus.org/bamboorestaurant. *Reservations recommended for dinner. Main courses: $5–$12 at lunch, $10–$24 at dinner. DC, MC, V. Open: Lunch and dinner Tues–Sat, Sun brunch.*

Beach Tree Bar & Grill
$$$–$$$$ Kohala Coast   Pacific Rim/International

Kudos to the Four Seasons for creating such an unpretentious, and relatively affordable, beachfront spot. This lovely, casual outdoor patio restaurant sits right on the sand, and every generously sized, comfortable table is angled to make the most of the surf and sunset views. Hawaiian music and hula make an already enchanting setting simply exquisite at sunset.

The regular menu focuses on fusion dishes like kiawe-smoked baby-back ribs with jalapeño corn bread; a fresh mozzarella and Waimea-grown tomato salad with Maui onion and herbed champagne viniagrette, with pesto-crusted chicken for an extra kick; and the day's catch, pan-seared and served with local greens, papaya pineapple salsa, and a mango-kaffir lime drizzle. I've eaten here numerous times, and the casual gourmet fare always shines. Don't miss out on the marvelous tropical cocktails. But the Beach Tree really sparkles on all-you-can-eat nights, when the staff mounts a bountiful, top-quality themed spread. Wednesday is Italian night, but the hands-down winner is Saturday's Surf, Sand, and Stars Barbecue, a traditional cookout featuring fresh island fish, steak, ribs, oysters, clams, and snow-crab claws grilled over an open flame. A staff astronomer is even on hand to help guests with their stargazing.

Book your table at the Beach Tree's Surf, Sand, and Stars Barbecue in advance because this festive Saturday-night beach party is a hugely popular weekly event.

See map p. 346. At the Four Seasons Resort Hualalai, 100 Kaupulehu Dr., Kaupulehu-Kona (7 miles north of Kona Airport). ☎ *808-325-8000.* www.fourseasons.com. *Reservations recommended for dinner (highly recommended on buffet nights). Main courses: $11–$18 at lunch, $22–$40 at dinner; all-you-can-eat buffets $48–$58 adults, $24–$29 kids 6–12. AE, DC, DISC, MC, V. Open: Lunch, afternoon pupus, and early dinner (to 8:30 p.m.) daily.*

Big Island Grill
$ Kailua-Kona   American/Local

This local favorite offers huge portions of homestyle cooking at retro prices, making it one of the island's most beloved restaurants. And the love shows: The grill is always hopping, from the first cup of coffee at breakfast to the last bite of dessert after dark. Expect American favorites with a local spin, including excellent fresh fish and generous salads and sandwiches; don't miss out on a side of the fabulous mashed potatoes. It's a excellent choice for families. In a hurry? No worries: Head to the drive-up window for coffee, cappuccino, smoothies, fresh baked pastries, lunch specials, and the like.

See map p. 346. 75-5702 Kuakini Hwy., Kailua-Kona. ☎ *808-326-1153. Reservations not accepted for breakfast or lunch; reservations only accepted for dinner a day or more in advance. Main courses: $6.25–$16. MC, V. Open: Breakfast Mon–Fri, lunch and dinner Mon–Sat.*

Brown's Beach House
$$$$$ Kohala Coast   Hawaii Regional

On-the-beach dining experiences don't come finer than Brown's, an excellent alfresco restaurant that consistently shines in all categories: food, service, and setting. Chef de Cuisine Etsuji Umezu has created an east-meets-west cuisine that fuses Japanese culinary arts and French cooking traditions to great effect (you can watch the staff in action in the exhibition kitchen). You might start with pan-seared Hudson Valley foie gras and bar-becued eel served over sushi rice and painted with a pineapple and bal-samic reduction, or miso-marinated butterfish with fresh *edamame* (soybeans) and vine-ripened tomatoes. Follow with wok-seared Kona lob-ster, with a wasabi butter sauce for dipping and crisp wonton ravioli; lin-guine with Kauai shrimp; and a gorgeous rib-eye, pan-seared in the style of Japanese Kobe beef. The food at Pahu i'a (see listing later in this chapter) has the slight edge, but the one-of-a-kind ambience here, with nightly enter-tainment under the stars, is pure magic. What's more, presentation and service are both faultless. Reserve a table close to the spotlit surf for the ultimate in romance (and bring a light jacket or wrap to ward off the ocean breeze, which can be nippy after dark).

See map p. 346. In the Fairmont Orchid, 1 N. Kaniku Dr., Mauna Lani resort. ☎ *808-885-2000.* www.fairmont.com. *Reservations highly recommended for dinner. Main courses: $12–$20 at lunch, $28–$55 at dinner. AE, DC, DISC, MC, V. Open: Lunch and dinner daily.*

Cafe Pesto
$$–$$$ Hilo/Kohala Coast   Pizza/Italian/Island

These casual favorites are a long-standing hit with locals and visitors alike. The well-prepared pastas and Pacific Regional specialties are pleasing, but the pizza is the real star — and the real value — of the menu. Both branches serve top-flight gourmet brick-oven-baked pies featuring fresh organic herbs, island-grown produce, and a thick, slightly sweet golden crust. My favorite is the pizza luau, with kalua-style pork, sweet onions, and fresh pineapple, but you can choose from a full slate of creative com-binations or build your own from a list of more than two dozen toppings. I find the food to be consistently better at the original Hilo branch (which also boasts a lovelier setting), but the branch at the northernmost end of the Kohala Coast provides a great escape for families tired of feeding on resort food.

*See map p. 346. **Hilo:** In the S. Hata Building, 308 Kamehameha Ave. (at Mamo Street).* ☎ *808-969-6640. **The Kohala Coast:** In the Kawaihae Shopping Center at Kawaihae Harbor, at Akoni Pule Highway and Kawaihae Road, Kawaihae (at the Highway 19/270 junction).* ☎ *808-882-1071.* www.cafepesto.com. *Reservations recommended for dinner. Main courses: $8–$18 at lunch, $8–$26 at dinner. AE, DC, DISC, MC, V. Open: Lunch and dinner daily.*

The Coffee Shack
$ South Kona   American

This bare-bones roadside charmer prepares some of South Kona's best eats. Take a seat on the pleasant terrace (which boasts ocean views beyond the banana trees) for table service or pony up to the friendly counter to order takeout. You can start the day with a first-class eggs Benedict or thick French toast or come by at lunch for the best sandwiches on the coast. Top-notch fillings range from smoked Alaskan salmon to fresh local veggies to warmed corned beef and Black Forest ham, and you have them applied to any one of six kinds of fresh-baked bread. The thick-crusted, generously topped pizzas are even better than Cafe Pesto's (see the preceding listing), and when it's time for dessert, lots of homemade pies and baked goods tempt you. The service can be slow, but what's your hurry? You're on vacation. Sit back, take it in stride, and consider it a blessing that you have more time to take in the million-dollar view.

See map p. 346. On Highway 11, between mile markers 108 and 109, a mile south of Captain Cook (about 10 minutes south of Keauhou). ☎ *808-328-9555.* www.coffee shack.com. *Breakfast and sandwiches: $6.50–$11. Pizzas: $10–$16. MC, V. Open: Breakfast and lunch daily.*

Donatoni's
$$$$ Kohala Coast Northern Italian

This wildly romantic restaurant replicates the feel of an Italian villa, with tables overlooking a tranquil lagoon and boasting unforgettable sunset views. Make sure to book a table on the twinkle-lit, European-elegant patio. Excellent choices include a delectable, fall-off-the-bone osso bucco alla Milanese, delicate and delicious veal scallopine alla Montovana, and any of the housemade pastas. But if something else entices you, go for it; I dined with a large party on my last visit, and every dish at the table was a star. Desserts are equally impressive. For something really special, opt for the Venetian Carnival Mask, made of white chocolate and resting atop a lightly bittersweet chocolate marquis with Franjelico sauce. The restaurant offers an excellent wine list, too. Come for sunset because the view is everything it should be.

 Be sure to arrive at the Hilton Waikoloa a full 15 to 20 minutes before your reservation time; it will take you that long to walk (or take one of the resort's silly shuttles) to the restaurant because the resort sprawls over a massive 62 acres.

See map p. 346. At Hilton Waikoloa Village, 69-425 Waikoloa Beach Dr., Waikoloa. ☎ *808-886-1234.* www.hiltonwaikoloavillage.com. *Reservations highly recommended. Main courses: $24–$37. AE, DISC, MC, V. Open: Dinner nightly.*

Edward's at Kanaloa
$$$$ South Kona Mediterranean

Not much more than a covered pier reaching out to sea, Edward's is one of the most romantic restaurants in Hawaii. The tables for two sit so close to the melodious surf that the outermost ones have to be pulled in when the waves kick up. Sunset is breathtaking, and tiki torches make magic after dark. The food wins high praise, too: Edward's broadly Mediterranean cuisine — a Provençal flair here, a taste of Verona there — is rich, flavorful, and delicious. I love to start with the escargot medley, deftly seasoned with fresh herbs and accompanied by mushrooms, asparagus spears, and artichoke hearts. In addition to the requisite fresh island fish preparations, ricotta-stuffed squid dressed in *herbes de provence* and tomato caper sauce is a standout. The food isn't cheap, but it's not overpriced, either, like so many other restaurants boasting a winning combination of cuisine, service, and views. The wine list is short but also reasonably priced.

See map p. 346. At Kanaloa at Kona, 78-261 Manukai St., Keauhou. ☎ 808-322-1003. Reservations required. To get there: From Highway 11, turn right on Kamehameha III Road (between mile markers 117 and 118), and then right on Manukai Street. Main courses: $6–$12 at breakfast, $8–$16 at lunch, $19–$36 at dinner (most less than $30). AE, DC, MC, V. Open: Breakfast, lunch, and dinner daily.

Fiascos
$$ Hilo   American/Eclectic

In the mood for some saucy enchiladas? How about Italian — maybe scampi, or spaghetti and meatballs? Down-home pork chops or fried chicken? Or just a good, juicy burger or a thick-cut prime rib? Fiascos tries to be all things to all people, and it doesn't come off half bad, really. Don't expect gourmet cuisine — just good all-American favorites, which happen to be made with Big Island–raised beef and locally grown produce. The menu is multicultural, but it doesn't venture far from the familiar. The fajitas, which come on a sizzling cast-iron platter with all the fixin's, are a real standout, as is the help-yourself soup-and-salad bar. This is a fun, jazzy place that particularly caters to kids; they'll even make kid-size portions of dishes off their regular menu.

See map p. 346. In Waiakea Square, 200 Kanoelehua Ave. (Highway 11, between Kuawa and Piilani streets), Hilo. ☎ 808-935-7666. Reservations recommended for parties of five or more. Main courses: $9–$22. AE, DISC, MC, V. Open: Lunch and dinner daily.

Huggo's
$$$$ Kailua-Kona   Seafood

Happy, hopping Huggo's serves reliably fine seafood to a jovial crowd drawn in by the festive vibe and remarkable Kailua Bay views. Fresh fish — grilled, blackened, sauteed, or steamed — is the specialty, as it should be. They could practically cast a line over the side of the deck. The kitchen isn't going to set the world on fire with its culinary creativity, but the simplicity can be refreshing when so many restaurants smother the freshness and flavor of top-quality local catches with heavy-handed preparations. Ginger orange chicken, New York steak, and wild mushroom pasta are on hand for the fish-o-phobic. There's casual all-day dining and live music nightly at the lively bar next door, the thatch-roofed Huggo's on the Rocks, which prepares an extensive tropical cocktail menu, making this the perfect place to watch the sunset. Come extra-early for your sunset perch because the secret's out. From 6:30 to 11 a.m., this same location turns into Java on the Rocks, a great place to greet the day.

See map p. 346. 75-5828 Kahakai Rd., off Alii Drive (behind Snorkel Bob's and next to the Royal Kona Resort), Kailua-Kona. ☎ 808-329-1493. www.huggos.com. *Reservations highly recommended. Main courses: $7–$14 at lunch, $20–$46 at dinner (most less than $30). AE, DC, DISC, MC, V. Open: Lunch and dinner daily.*

Kaikodo

$$–$$$ Hilo   East-West Fusion/Sushi

Kaikodo has swept into sleepy Hilo like a welcome tsunami, quickly establishing itself as the city's finest restaurant. Kaikodo is the cooperative brainchild of owners Howard and Mary Ann Rogers — art historians and collectors who have transformed the majestic, century-old Toyama Building into an exquisite restaurant filled with light and art — and James Beard star chef Michael Fennelly, who has also been feted by *Food & Wine* magazine and featured on PBS's "Great Chefs" series. Fennelly, formerly of Santa Fe's Santacafé, Mike's on the Avenue in New Orleans, and Mecca in San Francisco, wows with his inspired and innovative Japan-meets-Southwest cooking, which is prepared with the best local meats and fish, as well as veggies and herbs from the restaurant's own private garden. Stars of the menu include coconut- and lentil-crusted baked ono dressed with Hawaiian pumpkin puree; tapioca-crusted mahimahi married with zesty Thai eggplant and sweet chili sauce; and a tender-to-the-bone lamb shank braised in Mahana red ale. The lunch menu is equally appetizing, if a bit more casual: You'll find housemade pumpkin raviolis, a grilled steak sandwich glazed in sherry and oyster sauce, even a teriyaki-basted bacon cheeseburger. Next door to the main restaurant is the Zen-like Kaiko Sushi Bar, which boasts a stellar selection of sushi, both classic and visionary.

See map p. 346. 60 Keawe St. (at Waianuenue St.), Hilo. ☎ *808-961-2558.* www. restaurantkaikodo.com. *Reservations essential. Main courses: $8–$12 at lunch, $5–$15 at Sun brunch, $19–$28 at dinner. AE, MC, V. Open: Lunch Mon–Sat, brunch Sun, dinner daily.*

Keei Cafe

$$–$$$ South Kona   Island/Eclectic

Keei (KAY-ee) Cafe prepares some of the Big Island's finest food in a casual, low-key environment. After operating for eight years in a former fish market, Keei relocated a bit farther north to somewhat more upscale digs. The ambience remains as comfortable as ever, the service is friendly, and the island-style meals are excellent. Expect hearty Mediterranean- and Asian-slanted dishes in pleasantly light sauces accompanied by fresh, crisp vegetables, such as half-roasted chicken in red Thai curry, or marvelous fresh Kona catches in a puckery picatta sauce. Every dish is made from scratch, and virtually all ingredients are caught, grown, or harvested on the island. Keei Cafe offers one of the best dining values in the state; it's easy to pay a lot more for a lot less elsewhere in Hawaii. Save room for dessert, because both the bread pudding, made with bananas and pineapple, and coconut flan with *lilikoi* sauce (secret recipe of the owner's Portuguese mother-in-law) are homestyle tropical delights.

See map p. 346. On Highway 11 at mile marker 113, Kealakekua. ☎ *808-322-9992. Reservations highly recommended. Main courses: $12–$20. No credit cards. Open: Dinner Tues–Sat.*

Kenichi Pacific
$$$ South Kona   Pacific Rim Fusion/Sushi

Master sushi chef Kenichi Kamada, who has already made a splash in Austin and Aspen with his thrilling Pacific Rim fusion cuisine, has thankfully blessed the Big Island with his hip signature style, famous sushi bar, and a welcome blast of cool. The setting is Zen-modern, the service is efficient, and the food is fantastic, making Kenichi Pacific a winner on all fronts. You can enjoy some of the best sushi and sashimi in the islands, opt for more traditional appetizer/main-course ordering, or mix it up family style, if you prefer. Dishes that make grazing pure pleasure include ginger-marinated squid, Saikyo black cod — cured for 48 hours in miso blend and then broiled with a teriyaki glaze until it's melt-in-your-mouth perfection — and Dungeness crab cakes, fresh crab encased in crispy phyllo and dressed in a sambal-pickled ginger sauce. Kenichi's special roast duck with orange hoisin sauce, wrapped mu shu-style and served with tempura asparagus, is the stuff that culinary dreams are made of. Thank you, Kenichi!

See map p. 346. In the Keauhou Shopping Center, Keauhou. ☎ *808-322-6400. Reservations recommended for dinner. To get there: From Highway 11, turn right on Kamehameha III Road (between mile markers 117 and 118) and head downhill to the shopping center. Main courses: $17–$32. AE, MC, V. Open: Lunch Mon–Fri, dinner daily.*

Ken's House of Pancakes
$ Hilo   Coffee Shop

The classic coffee shop goes Hawaiian at Ken's, the only round-the-clock joint on the Big Island. This cheery place is your average all-American diner, where the food is familiar and pleasingly prepared, and the old-fashioned service comes with a dash of island-style aloha. Ken's is a three-meals-a-day-plus kind of place: Start your day bright and early with French toast or a macadamia-nut waffle (topped with passion-fruit or coconut syrup, if you want); come back at noon for a garden-fresh salad or a flame-broiled burger; stop in for a roast turkey, teriyaki chicken, or kalbi rib dinner; and drop by for a late-night piece of pie and a cup of Kona joe.

See map p. 346. 1730 Kamehameha Ave. (at Kanoelehua Avenue), Hilo. ☎ *808-935-8711. Reservations not taken. Main courses: $2–$11. AE, DC, DISC, MC, V. Open: Daily 24 hours.*

Kilauea Lodge & Restaurant
$$$$ Volcano   Continental

My favorite Volcano restaurant is dressed like a cozy old-world hunting lodge and is tucked away in the rainforest just outside the national park. The large, high-ceilinged room is appealingly attractive, with country-style furniture polished to a high sheen and a roaring stone fireplace. The knowledgeable and warmly welcoming servers are dressed in beautiful island prints by renowned Big Island designer Sig Zane (see Chapter 16 for info on where to get your own Sig Zane aloha wear). A skilled bartender mixing up perfect martinis rounds out the picture. Chef/owner Albert Jeyte specializes in hearty old-world cuisine. Sure, a well-prepared fresh catch is always on offer, but Jeyte's heart lies with such richly flavored dishes as venison medallions, which arrive pan-seared, brandy-flamed, and sporting a yummy Nicole sauce. Seafood Mauna Kea is sautéed and topped with crème fraîche, shiitake mushrooms, and fresh basil. Or try the *hasenpfeffer:* succulent braised rabbit in a red-wine sauce. Dinners come with soup, salad, and fresh-baked bread, which makes the excellent fare an excellent value, too.

See map p. 346. 19-4055 Volcano Rd., (just off Highway 11 at Wright Road), Volcano. ☎ *808-967-7366.* www.kilauealodge.com. *Reservations recommended. Main courses: $19–$39 (most less than $30). AE, MC, V. Open: Dinner nightly.*

Kona Brewing Co.
$–$$ Kailua-Kona   Island/Pizza

Kona Brewing Co. is Hawaii's finest microbrewery, specializing in flavorful hand-crafted brews with island-rooted names like Longboard Lager, Fire Rock Pale Ale, and Hula Hefewiezen. You can enjoy them fresh from the tap at this pleasingly casual pub, along with equally well-prepared island-style pub grub. The hand-tossed pizza crusts are topped with top-quality Parmesan and mozzarella, locally grown herbs, and a range of creative ingredients, from traditional pepperoni to *lilikoi* (passion fruit) barbecue chicken. Or you can opt for hearty salads with crisp island-grown veggies, and generously stuffed sandwiches on the brewery's own focaccia. A nice selection of pupu (appetizers) is on hand for those who merely want to pull up to the blond-wood bar for some munchies and a brewski. Inside service is available, but snare a table on the pretty tropical patio if you can. Friendly service rounds out the affordable, easygoing appeal.

See map p. 346. 75-5629 Kuakini Highway, in the North Kona Shopping Center, (1 block inland from Alii Drive) and Palani Road ☎ *808-334-2739.* www.konabrewing co.com. *Reservations taken only for parties of 10 or more. To get there: Heading toward the ocean on Palani Road, turn left on Kuakini Highway, and then right into the shopping center. Sandwiches and salads: $8–$11. Pizzas: $9–$23. DC, DISC, MC, V. Open: Lunch and dinner daily.*

Lava Rock Cafe
$$ Volcano Village   American/Hawaii Local

This easygoing local favorite is a very nice choice for a casual meal (especially because your choices are rather limited in Volcano Village). It's a cheerful spot furnished in knotty pine, with both indoor and covered open-air dining. The fare is American with a cross-cultural bent, from beefy burgers to teriyaki chicken to chow-fun noodles to hearty chili to T-bone-and-shrimp combos — you get the something-for-everybody idea. It's pretty straightforward island fare — simple, unfussy, and served with a smile. This is a great place to start the day if your accommodations don't include breakfast. (I love the pancakes, which come with yummy house-made *lilikoi* — passion fruit —

butter.) The kitchen will even pack its "seismic sandwiches" to go for hikers who want to bring a lunch along the trail. Ask 'em to throw in a macadamia nut cookie or two; they're divine. Live music adds to the local flavor on Thursday and Saturday evenings.

The Lava Rock also happens to be Volcano Village's only Internet cafe, so this is also the place to check your mail if you want to keep in e-touch with the folks back home.

See map p. 346. On Highway 11, behind Kilauea General Store, Volcano Village. ☎ *808-967-8526.* www.volcanovillage.com/LavaRock.htm. *Reservations not necessary. Main courses: $4.50–$7 at lunch, $6–$18 at dinner (most items under $12). MC, V. Open: Breakfast and lunch daily, dinner Tues–Sat.*

Maha's Cafe
$ Waimea   Island/Sandwiches

Maha's alone makes a trip to Waimea well worth the effort. This cozy country cottage (Waimea's first frame house, built in 1852) is one of the Big Island's best restaurants. Maha's magic touch raises simple homestyle cooking to new heights. I dream about Maha's oven-roasted turkey sandwich: Served on dark squaw bread with homemade mushroom stuffing and cranberry sauce (with added zest from Kau oranges), this open-faced symphony of a sandwich shouldn't be relegated to holiday time. Other choices are similarly ethereal: honey-smoked ahi with *lilikoi* (passion fruit) salsa; roasted lamb with spicy mango chutney; and fresh fish with local taro and sweet potato. Winning morning choices include yummy poi pancakes with coconut syrup and a homemade granola parfait with fresh island fruits, nuts, and yogurt. Don't skip dessert even if you don't usually indulge because each and every one of the fresh-baked sweets is divine. Maha's is a real island find!

See map p. 346. In front of Waimea Center, 65-1148 Mamalahoa Highway (Highway 19), near Highway 190 junction (next to McDonald's), Waimea. ☎ *808-885-0693.* www.hawaiinow.com/mahas. *Reservations not taken. Breakfast items: $2.50–$4. Lunch menu: $5.50–$11. Afternoon tea: $12. MC, V. Open: Breakfast, lunch, and afternoon tea (3–4:30 p.m.) daily except Tues.*

Merriman's Restaurant
$$$$ Waimea   Hawaii Regional

One of the original purveyors of Hawaii Regional cuisine, James Beard–nominated chef Peter Merriman reigns over this cozy cowboy-country enclave. Over the years, it has matured into a still-pleasing — and still hugely popular — culinary institution. Residents and visitors alike happily make the long drive Upcountry (20 minutes from the Kohala Coast, about an hour from Kona or Hilo) to feast on Merriman's winning cuisine, the long-lasting success of which lies in its simplicity. Waimea-raised beef and lamb, fish caught daily in Kona waters, and organically grown local veggies are used in uncomplicated yet innovative preparations that let the fresh natural flavors of the top-quality ingredients shine through. Wok-charred ahi,

Pahoa corn-and-shrimp fritters, and slow-roasted chicken are among the many standouts on the perpetually pleasing menu. Meals are more affordably priced than most of this caliber, and lunch is a downright bargain. The only downside is the big '80s-reminiscent pastel interior, which is nicely maintained but nevertheless sorely in need of an update.

 If you'd like to try Peter Merriman's winning fare but don't feel like driving all the way to Waimea — or if you're simply in the mood for something more casual — visit the new **Merriman's Market Café** in the Waikoloa Kings Shops at the Waikoloa Beach Resort, 250 Waikoloa Beach Dr. ($$; ☎ **808-886-1700**). This casually sophisticated market-style cafe features Italian- and Mediterranean-style fare prepared with fresh local produce, meats, and fish that give every dish a delightful local flair. Expect housemade sausages, artisan-style breads, a wide range of cheeses, hearty salads, individual pizzas, and the like, plus beautifully prepared dishes for takeout or enjoying on-site, either indoors or out. It's a wonderful place to prepare a picnic, relax at lunch, or enjoy a light dinner. The full-service bar includes a good wine selection.

See map p. 346. 65-1227 Opelo Road, in Opelo Plaza, Highway 19 (at Opelo Road, on the Kona side of town), Kamuela. ☎ *808-885-6822.* www.merrimanshawaii.com. *Reservations recommended. Main courses: $9–$14 at lunch, $18–$35 at dinner. AE, MC, V. Open: Lunch Mon–Fri, dinner nightly.*

Ocean Sushi Deli
$$ Hilo Japanese

Sushi lovers who visit Hilo shouldn't miss this plain and simple sushi restaurant, which makes the most of the bounty of the sea, both island-caught and flown in fresh from Japan. Always of A-1 quality, the fish is skillfully prepared by master sushi chefs and served with aloha by a young, friendly, and attentive waitstaff. Creative rolls are a forte, and combination plates are a bargain. The restaurant is very popular at dinnertime, so make reservations or be prepared for a wait. Across the street, at no. 250, is sister restaurant **Tsunami Grill and Tempura,** which excels at noodle bowls, bentos, tempura, katsu, and other Japanese comfort foods; the sushi-phobic members of your party can order nonfish items from the Tsunami menu at Ocean Sushi Deli.

See map p. 346 239 Keawe St. (near Haili Street, next to Pescatore), Hilo. ☎ *808-961-6625. Reservations recommended for dinner. 2-piece sushi and rolls: $2–$8. Complete meals: $4.50–$23. Family platters: $20–$50. DC, MC, V. Open: Lunch and dinner Mon–Sat.*

Oodles of Noodles
$$–$$$ Kailua-Kona Pan-Asian/International

Oodles isn't just any Formica-countered quickie noodle stand; rather, it's the domain of top Hawaii Regional chef Amy Ota, who has reinvented noodle dishes for discriminating diners with resounding success. Noodles are the unifying theme on a creative global-gourmet menu that runs the gamut from Vietnamese *pho* (beef noodle soup) to pasta primavera with grilled vegetables to wok-seared ahi noodle casserole to the world's best macaroni and cheese. Save room for the surprisingly scrumptious desserts, which are often the finest feature of an all-around pleasing meal; the ice cream coated with sweet Japanese *mochi* is my favorite dessert on the island. The hip, warm-hued restaurant has doubled in size in recent years, but its popularity among locals and visitors alike means that you may still encounter a wait for a table. BYOB or stick with the delightful juices and flavored teas. A kids' menu is available, and kids under 3 eat free.

See map p. 346. In the Crossroads Shopping Center (the Safeway Center), 75-1027 Henry St. (at Highway 11 and Palani Road), Kailua-Kona. ☎ 808-329-9222. Reservations accepted for parties of 6 or more. Main courses: $8–$14 at lunch, $12–$26 at dinner. AE, DC, DISC, MC, V. Open: Lunch and dinner daily.

Pahu i'a
$$$$$ Kohala Coast Euro-Pacific Fusion

Done in an elegant haute-plantation style and open to the trade winds and ocean views, this ultraromantic candlelit dining room is the Big Island's most beautiful restaurant — and the sublime food and faultless service live up to the setting in every respect. The regularly changing menu features only the finest regional ingredients, and both Pacific-born and continental preparations take inspired turns in the capable kitchen. For example, while a thick-cut ahi steak wears a Szechuan pepper crust, the threat of excessive spice is undone by a light and aromatic Kau orange citrus sauce. Crispy-skin *opakapaka* (snapper) meunière comes with both Maui onions and macadamia-nut brown butter. I'm clearly not alone in considering Pahu i'a phenomenal on all fronts; it has won stellar ratings from Zagat and four-diamond status from AAA and was recognized as one of America's top hotel restaurants by *Food & Wine*. Scoring a table can be rather difficult, but your efforts will be well-rewarded, so book well in advance (before you leave home, if possible) or opt for an early or late meal.

See map p. 346. At the Four Seasons Resort Hualalai, 100 Kaupulehu Dr., Kaupulehu-Kona (7 miles north of the airport). ☎ 808-325-8000. www.fourseasons.com/hualalai. Reservations essential. Main courses: $9–$24 at breakfast, $32–$48 at dinner. AE, DC, DISC, MC, V. Open: Breakfast and dinner daily.

Pescatore Italian Restaurant
$$$ Hilo Southern Italian

One of Hilo's top fine-dining spots is this old-world restaurant with wood-paneled walls, ornately cushioned chairs, and delicate lace curtains on the windows. The traditionally Southern Italian, seafood-heavy menu stars excellent scalloppines, primaveras, and puttanescas. Dishes are consistently well-prepared and pleasing: Ahi carpaccio is sliced paper-thin and dressed in fine extra-virgin olive oil to heighten the fresh flavor, the seafood Fra Diavolo is a spicy bounty of fresh seafood in zesty marinara, and the veal is always a tender triumph. Service is attentive, and the wine list is affordable. The lunch menu is simpler but no less satisfying.

See map p. 346. 235 Keawe St. (at Haili Street), Hilo. ☎ *808-969-9090. Reservations recommended for dinner. Main courses: $5–$12 at lunch, $16–$29 at dinner. AE, DC, DISC, MC, V. Open: Lunch and dinner daily, breakfast buffet Sat–Sun.*

Roy's Waikoloa Bar & Grill
$$$–$$$$ Kohala Coast   Hawaii Regional

The Waikoloa branch of Roy Yamaguchi's high-profile, high-end restaurant chain is not quite as winningly casual as the other Roy's throughout Hawaii (particularly my favorite, Roy's Poipu Grill on Kauai), but this brightly lit restaurant is a great place to sample the original Hawaii Regional cuisine nonetheless. Roy's food is more overtly Asian than what you'll find in many other Hawaii Regional restaurants (like Merriman's; see listing earlier in this chapter). The menu changes daily, but usually includes standards such as sublime Szechuan baby-back ribs, blackened ahi with a delectable soy mustard butter, or roasted macadamia-nut mahimahi in lobster cognac butter sauce. You can easily eat affordably here thanks to an oversized menu of dim sum, appetizers, and pizzas. The wines and sakes bottled under Roy's own label are affordable and surprisingly good. Service is a little too attentive, but it's a minor complaint — like complaining that the Moët's too cold, if you know what I mean.

See map p. 346. In the King's Shops, 250 Waikoloa Beach Dr., Waikoloa. ☎ *808-886-4321.* www.roysrestaurant.com. *Reservations highly recommended. Appetizers and pizzas: $5–$12. Main courses: $14–$28. AE, DC, DISC, MC, V. Open: Lunch and dinner daily.*

Seaside Restaurant & Aqua Farm
$$–$$$ Hilo   Seafood

Enterprising aquaculture farmers, the Nakagawa family has struck on a winning concept: a simple, satisfying restaurant overlooking well-stocked fish ponds, into which the chef himself drops a line to fulfill each night's dinner orders. Seaside is a refreshing alternative for fish lovers who want a break from the ahi and mahimahi — not to mention the high prices — so prevalent on Hawaii menus. Farm-raised mullet, catfish, and golden perch are steamed in a ti leaf with lemon and onion, a wonderfully unfussy preparation that lets the flavor of the state's freshest-caught fish star on the plate. *Aholehole* (Hawaiian flagtail bass), fried and served whole, is another house specialty, known to draw day-trippers from as far as Honolulu. Dinners come complete with salad, veggies, rice, apple pie, and tea or coffee for an excellent value. Chicken and steak are available for landlubbers, as are more familiar island fishes like ahi, mahi, and ono. It's a genuine island dining experience, complete with aloha-friendly service. Reserve ahead so that the angler knows how big to make the day's catch.

See map p. 346. 1790 Kalanianaole Ave. (at Lokoaka Street, 2.6 miles east of Banyan Drive), Hilo. ☎ *808-935-8825.* www.seasiderestaurant.com. *Reservations highly recommended. Complete dinners: $11–$26 (most $17–$24). MC, V. Open: Dinner Tues–Sun.*

Sibu Cafe

$$ Kailua-Kona Indonesian

Tucked away in a nondescript Alii Drive minimall, affordable Sibu offers flame-grilled satays (including a terrific all-veggie version), rich and flavorful curries, fresh stir-fries, and a creative list of daily specials that offer a welcome change of pace from Kona's ubiquitous and overpriced surf-and-turf fare. Both the Balinese chicken with peanut sauce and the garlic shrimp linguine with black pepper and green chili more than justify their long-standing popularity. The closet-size dining room is colorful but otherwise devoid of ambience, so I recommend grabbing a well-shaded courtyard table, where the table service is equally attentive.

See map p. 346. In Banyan Court, 75-5695 Alii Drive, Kailua-Kona. ☎ 808-329-1112. Reservations not taken. Main courses: $10–$14. No credit cards. Open: Lunch and dinner daily.

Thai Rin

$$ Kailua-Kona Thai

An oasis of good value in a town that falls short more often than not, this affordable and authentic spot features an expansive menu of well-prepared Thai favorites. The noodle dishes and multicolored curries are universally pleasing and include a pad Thai that borders on greatness. Thai Rin's version of chicken with cashew nuts — a dish that can often be pedestrian in lesser restaurants — is light, flavorful, and overflowing with a bounty of fresh veggies. The menu features lots of seafood choices, of course (to be expected in the deep-sea-fishing capital of the Pacific). The dining room is plain, high-ceilinged, and simple, but patio tables offer views of the bay across Alii Drive. Service is graciously attentive from start to finish.

See map p. 346. Alii Sunset Plaza, 75-5799 Alii Dr., in the heart of Kailua-Kona. ☎ 808-329-2929. Reservations accepted. Lunch specials: $6–$11. Main courses: $7–$18 (most less than $15). AE, DC, DISC, MC, V. Open: Lunch Mon–Sat, dinner nightly.

Thai Thai Restaurant

$$ Volcano Thai

I was thrilled to find this wonderful Thai restaurant in Volcano Village, which doesn't exactly brim with quality dining spots, especially not ethnic places. An attractive high-ceilinged room with Thai decorative touches, pretty table linens, and Thai pop music on the sound system sets the stage for simple, freshly prepared dishes. The menu is on the smallish side, but every dish I tasted was a winner. The tom yum soup was clear and well-spiced with lemongrass and kaffir lime leaves; the masaman curry was rich with coconut milk and potatoes; and a stir-fry starred crisp Asian veggies and jumbo shrimp. The green papaya salad makes an excellent way to start a wholly satisfying meal.

See map p. 346. 19-4084 Old Volcano Rd., Volcano. ☎ 808-967-7969. Reservations accepted. Main courses: $9–$15. MC, V. Open: Dinner nightly.

Tres Hombres Beach Grill/Tres Hombres Steak & Seafood Cantina
$$ **Kohala Coast/Kailua-Kona   Mexican**

Set on the second floor of a harborfront center at the very north end of
the Kohala Coast, this cheerful tropical Mexican restaurant is perfectly sit-
uated for watching outrigger canoe clubs paddle out to sea from the
nearby launch. The food is only a step above average-quality gringoized
Mexican grub, but I like Tres Hombres anyway. A welcome alternative to
the generally overpriced resort dining, this fun, easygoing, surf-themed
restaurant features a nice Trader Vic's–style bar with a big, creative tequila
and tropical drinks menu and a simply furnished outdoor patio. The afford-
able menu has an island flair: fresh mahimahi tacos, mammoth surf burri-
tos, sizzling fajitas, and more, all sizably portioned and satisfying. A
second, slightly more upscale branch is conveniently located in Kailua-
Kona, ideally suiting the resort town's party mood. The kids will love the
fun environment and "kid-friendly" food.

*See map p. 346. **The Kohala Coast**: In the Kawaihae Shopping Center at Kawaihae
Harbor, at Akoni Pule Highway and Kawaihae Road, Kawaihae (at the Highway 19/270
junction).* ☎ ***808-882-1031.*** *Reservations accepted for parties of 5 or more.* **Kailua-
Kona:** *75-5864 Walua Rd. (at Alii Drive, across from the Royal Kona Resort).*
☎ ***808-329-2173.*** *Reservations accepted. Main courses: $8–$22. MC, V. Open: Lunch
and dinner daily.*

Luau!

My favorite luau on the Big Island has always been the wonderful Friday-
night-only Kona Village Luau. You should make your reservations as far
ahead of time as possible (before you leave home) because it sells out
sometimes weeks in advance.

Kona Village Luau

This ultradeluxe Polynesian-style resort is the ideal place for a luau, and
you'd be hard-pressed to find a better one. The food is excellently pre-
pared and well labeled (so you know what you're eating), and the tradi-
tional *imu* (underground pig roasting) ceremony is well narrated, so you
get the cultural gist. The South Pacific revue is fast-moving and lots of fun,
if not nearly as authentic as the one you'll see at the new Traditions at
Kahaluu luau (I don't think that cowboy hulas occurred in old Hawaii). The
fire dancer is a show-stopper, of course, and everyone involved is a first-
rate entertainer. The setting isn't oceanfront, but it's lovely nonetheless;
the luau is large-scale, but it manages to feel friendly and intimate; service
is attentive and aloha friendly. Reservations are required, so book as far in
advance as possible.

*See map p. 346. At Kona Village, in the Kaupulehu resort, 7 miles north of the airport
on the Kohala Coast.* ☎ ***800-367-5290*** *or 808-325-5555.* www.konavillage.com.
*Admission: $76 adults, $46 kids 12 and under. Beer and house wine included. Included
in the rates for Kona Village guests. Time: Fri at 5:45 p.m.*

Fast Facts: Big Island

American Automobile Association (AAA)

Roadside service is availalble to members by calling ☎ 800-AAA-HELP; however, the only Hawaii office is on Oahu (see Chapter 11).

American Express

American Express has one office on the Big Island, on the Kohala Coast at the Hilton Waikoloa Village, 425 Waikoloa Beach Dr., off Highway 19 in the Waikoloa Resort (☎ 808-886-7958).

Baby Sitters and Baby Stuff

Any resort, hotel, or condo should be able to refer you to a reliable baby sitter with a proven track record. **Baby's Away** (☎ 800-996-9030 or 808-987-9236; www. babysaway.com) rents cribs, strollers, highchairs, playpens, infant seats, and the like; they'll deliver whatever you need to wherever you're staying, and they'll pick it up when you're done.

Doctors

Hualalai Urgent Care is in Kailua-Kona at 75-1028 Henry St. (behind Borders Books and Music, across the street from Safeway; ☎ 808-327-4357). In Hilo, contact **Hilo Urgent Care**, 42 Mohouli St., off Kilauea Avenue (☎ 808-969-3051), which offers walk-in service.

Emergencies

Dial **911** from any phone, just like on the mainland.

Hospitals

Kona Community Hospital, on the south Kona Coast at 79-1019 Haukapila St., off Highway 11, in Kealakekua (☎ 808-733-4020; www.kch.hhsc.org), has 24-hour emergency facilities. On the east side of the island, head to the emergency room at **Hilo Medical Center**, 1190 Waianuenue Ave. (just west of Rainbow Drive), Hilo (☎ 808-974-4700; www.hmc.hhsc.org). In Waimea, visit **North Hawaii Community Hospital**, 67-125 Mamalahoa Hwy. (☎ 808-885-4444).

Information

The **Big Island Visitors Bureau** (bigisland.gohawaii.com) has two island offices: one on the Kohala Coast at the Kings' Shops, 250 Waikoloa Beach Dr., Suite B-15, in the Waikoloa Resort (☎ 808-886-1655); and another in Hilo at 250 Keawe St., at Haili Street (across from Pescatore's restaurant), downtown (☎ 808-961-5797). Or, if you want information specifically on the island's west side, contact the **Kohala Coast Resort Association** (☎ 800-318-3637 or 808-886-4915; www.kkra.org).

For information on **Hawaii Volcanoes National Park**, contact P.O. Box 52, Hawaii National Park, HI 96718-0052 (☎ 808-965-6000; www.nps.gov/havo).

Chances are good that you'll find all the information you need even before you leave the airport. Just wander over to the information kiosks while you're waiting for your baggage and pick up copies of *This Week Big Island* and *101 Things to Do on the Big Island,* and the other free tourist publications and brochures that you'll find there. They're also available all over the island (particularly at malls and shopping centers).

Also, don't hesitate to ask the staff at your resort or condo for help or advice if you need it. These knowledgeable folks are usually more than happy to point you in the right direction and make recommendations.

Newspapers/Magazines

The Big Island has two daily papers: *West Hawaii Today* (www.westhawaiitoday.com), and the *Hawaii Tribune Herald* (www.hilohawaiitribune.com), which predominantly serves Hilo and environs. In addition, the *Hawaii Island Journal* (www.hawaiiislandjournal.com) is a free weekly newspaper that's a good source for event and entertainment listings; it's easy to find in free racks around the island.

Pharmacies

Long's Drugs (www.longs.com), Hawaii's biggest drugstore chain, has two branches on the Kona Coast: one at the Keauhou Shopping Center, 78-6831 Alii Dr, Keauhou (☎ 808-322-5122); and one in the Lanihau Shopping Center, 75-5595 Palani Rd., on the ocean side of Highway 19, Kailua-Kona (☎ 808-329-1380). In Hilo, you'll find Long's at 555 Kilauea Ave., at Ponahawai Street (☎ 808-935-3357); and in the Prince Kuhio Shopping Plaza, 111 E. Puainako St., east of Highway 11 (☎ 808-959-5881).

Police

Hawaii County Police Department headquarters is at 349 Kapiolani St. (between Kukuau and Hualalai streets), Hilo (☎ 808-935-3311). The **Kona Police Station** is at 74-5221 Queen Kaahumanu Hwy. (Highway 19), just south of Kaloko Light Industrial Park (☎ 808-326-4646). Of course, if you have an emergency, **dial 911** from any phone.

Post Offices

The Kona branch offices are at 74-7577 Palani Rd. (past Highway 11, almost to the shoreline), Kailua-Kona, and in the Keauhou Shopping Center, 78-6831 Alii Dr. (near Judd Trail), Keauhou. In Hilo, head to 1299 Kekuanaoa Ave. (past the airport; follow it as it loops around). A downtown branch is at 152 Waianuenue Ave., between Keawe and Kinoole streets. Satellite post offices are located around the island; to find the one nearest you, call ☎ 800-275-8777 or visit www.usps.com.

Taxes

Hawaii's sales tax is 4 percent. Expect taxes of about 11.42 percent to be added to your hotel bill.

Taxis

On the Kona-Kohala side of the island, call **Paradise Taxi** (☎ 808-329-1234), which serves the Kailua-Kona area, or **Luana Limousine** (☎ 800-999-4001 or 808-326-5466). In Hilo, call **Ace One** (☎ 808-935-8303).

Weather, Surf, and Volcano Reports

For the current weather, call ☎ 808-961-5582 or 808-935-8555 in Hilo. For the marine forecast, dial ☎ 808-935-9883. For volcano eruption information and weather updates for Hawaii Volcanoes National Park, dial ☎ 808-985-6000.

Chapter 16

Exploring the Big Island

*T*he Big Island's biggest attraction — indeed, the biggest attraction in all of Hawaii — is **Hawaii Volcanoes National Park,** one of the most exciting and unusual parks in the entire national parks system. But the Big Island is no one-trick pony; it boasts a wealth of wonderful and one-of-a-kind attractions that you won't want to miss.

Keep in mind that the Big Island really is a big drive — about the size of Connecticut, with virtually all the main attractions located along the island's perimeter. It takes about six hours to circle the island, which makes visiting the national park from, say, a Kona hotel, quite an arduous trip. So you may seriously want to consider dividing your stay on the island between the two coasts — a few nights on the sunny, arid Kona-Kohala coast followed by a few nights on the lush, misty Hilo-Volcano coast, or vice versa — and plan your island activities and sightseeing accordingly. For more on this subject, see Chapter 15.

Enjoying the Sand and Surf

Don't fall into the trap that so many of your fellow visitors to the Big Island do — namely, coming home complaining that the island has only ugly dark-sand beaches, not the pretty white ones that you always assumed would line the shores of paradise.

The Big Island is the youngest island in the Hawaii chain, geologically speaking; as it matures over the next few millennia, the shores will pumice into the fine white sands you're used to. But if it's unusual-looking beaches you're after, the Big Island features the most eye-popping collection you'll ever see: black-sand ones, salt-and-pepper ones, lava-covered ones, even a green-sand one. What's more, the island also happens to already boast some of the dreamiest white sands in Hawaii — it's just a matter of knowing where to find them. (Hint: Do not pass go, do not collect $200 — drive directly to Hapuna.)

Combing the beaches

Safety takes top priority at the beach, whether you're swimming, snorkeling, surfing, or even taking a stroll. Never turn your back on the ocean, because big waves can come out of nowhere in a matter of minutes. Some beaches, like the popular Hapuna on the Kohala Coast, regularly have lifeguards on duty, but others, like the Kohala Coast's Kaunaoa, have none. At beaches without lifeguards, keep an eye out for posted signs warning of dangerous currents or conditions. Winter surf is generally rough and unpredictable, although some beaches can be counted on for calm waters in any season. Others have dangerous rip currents year-round, making swimming inadvisable for all but the strongest swimmers. Do your homework: Check out the following beach descriptions and, after you're on the Big Island, make inquiries about local surf conditions.

Also, never leave valuables in your rental car while you're at the beach — not even in the glove box — or you may lose them to a thief who can be in and out of your car before you've finished slathering on your sunscreen. Remote beaches, in particular, are magnets for thieves. Be especially diligent about leaving your stuff behind at your condo or in your hotel safe when you're heading off to a remote beach.

Along the Kohala Coast

All these fabulous beaches are located on the dry leeward side of the island, along the Queen Kaahumanu Highway (Hwy. 19) north of the Kona Airport.

Hapuna Beach State Park

Wow! If forced to choose, I'd name this as my favorite beach in all Hawaii. This gorgeous stretch has it all: glorious turquoise surf, a half-mile-long crescent of powdery-fine white sand backed by green lawns that allow you to picnic without getting sand in your lunch, and the best facilities on the coast. Hapuna is simply magical, especially in the gentle seasons when the beach is widest, the ocean is calmest, and crowds — both locals and visitors — come out to swim, play, and ride the easy waves. One of the best things about this stunning beach is that it's a blast even when crowded, and even though the Hapuna Beach Prince Hotel is tucked away at the north end, you barely notice it. Venture nearer to the hotel only if you're looking to snorkel; the cove at its base is your best bet. The excellent facilities include restrooms, showers, pavilions, picnic tables, barbecues, Hapuna Harry's for snacks and beach toys, and plenty of parking. Beware the waves in winter, though, when the big surf can be very dangerous.

See map p. 366. Off Queen Kaahumanu Highway (Highway 19), about 27 miles north of Kona Airport (3 miles south of Kawaihae, where Highway 19 turns inland toward Waimea).

The Big Island's Best Beaches & Attractions

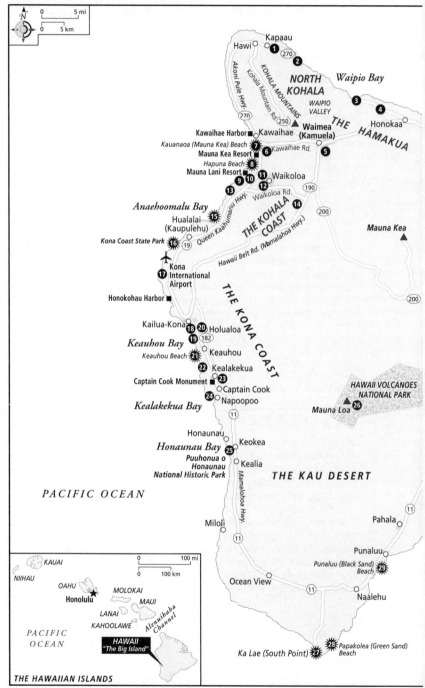

PACIFIC OCEAN

COAST

Laupahoehoe

Honomu

36 (220) (19)

35

Hilo Bay

✴ *Leleiwi Beach Park*

Hilo **33**

32 **31**

Saddle Rd.

✈ Hilo International Airport

Stainback Hwy.

Keaau

Kurtistown

Keaau-Pahoa Rd.

Mountain View

Cape Kumukahi

(130) Pahoa

Volcano Village **THE PUNA REGION**

30

Kilauea Caldera ▲

KAHAUALEA NATURAL AREA RESERVE

(130) (132)

(137)

Hawaii Belt Rd. (Mamalahoa Hwy.)

Chain of Craters Rd.

HAWAII VOLCANOES NATIONAL PARK

Airport ✈
Beach ✴
Mounatin ▲

Kaunaoa (Mauna Kea) Beach

The Mauna Kea Beach Hotel would like to keep this curving gem all to itself, no doubt. And who can blame them? Kauanoa (cow-a-NO-ah) is one of the Big Island's finest and most well-protected cove beaches. But because all Hawaii beaches are public, you can come, too, even if you're not staying at the ritzy resort. The gorgeous beige sands slope gently into the bay, where the calm, warm waters are often populated by schools of colorful tropical fish and green sea turtles, making this a wonderful snorkeling spot (especially near the rocky points). Swimming is excellent year-round. Nonhotel guests are relegated to one small section of the beach, and facilities are limited to restrooms and showers (no lifeguard). Don't be surprised if you're not warmly greeted at the gate; the hotel prefers to keep the public-access crowd small.

See map p. 366. At the Mauna Kea Resort, off Queen Kaahumanu Highway (Highway 19), 28 miles north of Kona Airport (about 2½ miles south of Kawaihae, where Highway 19 turns inland toward Waimea). To get there: Turn west at the Mauna Kea Beach Hotel entrance and ask for a beach pass from security; follow the road to the public beach parking area, at the end of the road (through the hotel and past registration).

Anaehoomalu Bay (A-Bay)

This popular beach drive — called Anaehoomalu (ah-na-ay-ho-o-MA-loo), or A-Bay for short — is the most beautiful of the Big Island's salt-and-peppery beaches. It's long, curvaceous, and boasts pretty fine-grained sand and a lovely grove of swaying coconut palms. The beach fronts the Waikoloa Beach Marriott, but it's easily accessible, and it's so nice that even locals come. The sand slopes gently from shallow to deep water; swimming, kayaking, and windsurfing are all terrific here; and the snorkeling is very good at the end nearest the hotel. At the far edge of the bay is a rare turtle-cleaning station, where snorkelers and divers can watch endangered green sea turtles line up, waiting their turn to have small fish clean them. The hotel's friendly beach boys usually have the area marked so that you can make your way out to see the action. Facilities include restrooms, showers, and plenty of parking, plus excellent beach-gear rentals at the north (hotel) end of the beach.

See map p. 366. At the Waikoloa Beach Marriott, just off Queen Kaahumanu Highway (Highway 19), 18 miles north of Kona Airport. To get there: Turn west at the stone gate marked Waikoloa, left at the stop sign, and then follow the road to the parking lot.

On the Kona-Keauhou coast

These playful beach parks are located on the sunny Kona Coast; they're all accessible from the Queen Kaahumanu Highway (Hwy. 19).

Kona Coast (Kekaha Kai) State Park

If you really want some sand to yourself, head to this remote beach park, which is separated from civilization by nearly 2 miles of vast lava fields. The road that reaches the beach is a bit rough going (see the directions that follow), but what awaits at the end is worth the drive for solitude seekers: a half-dozen long, curving, unspoiled gold-sand beaches, with well-protected coves that are great for swimming in the gentle seasons. Even if a few other folks are around, you'll find plenty of stretches of sand that you can have all to yourself. Stay out of the water in winter, when the swells come, but you may want to visit anyway to kick back on the sand and see the surfers in action. Facilities are minimal — nothing more than a few picnic tables and portable toilets — so be sure to bring your own drinking water. Word is that the road may be repaved soon, which would be a blessing.

See map p. 366. Off Queen Kaahumanu Highway (Highway 19), 2¾ miles north of Kona Airport. To get there: Turn left at the sign and follow the bumpy road 1¾ miles to the coast. The speed limit is 15 mph, but you'll find yourself going 10 mph unless you've rented a 4-wheel-drive (not necessary); take it slow and watch for potholes. Open: Thurs–Tues 8 a.m.–8 p.m.

White Sands (Magic Sands) Beach

This petite white-sand pocket of beach is an oddity on this lava-rock coast in more ways than one: Not only are darker and coarser beaches more common on this coast, but the beach itself sometimes vanishes completely, washed away by high tides or winter waves or during storms. It usually reappears in short order, just like it never went away. The small waves are great for just-learning boogie boarders and bodysurfers; on calm summer days, the water is good for swimming and snorkeling, too. Facilities include restrooms, showers, lifeguards, and a small parking lot. White Sands isn't worth traversing long distances to seek out, but it's conveniently situated for those staying in the Kailua-Kona or Keauhou areas.

See map p. 366. Adjacent to Kona Magic Sands condos, 77-6452 Alii Dr., 4½ miles south of Kailua-Kona.

Kahaluu Beach Park

Kahaluu (ka-ha-LOO-oo) isn't exactly the prettiest beach in the islands: It's narrow, salt-and-peppery, close to the road (a situation softened by a collection of coconut palms that serve as a buffer), and almost always blanket-to-blanket crowded. But don't skip it because this is one of the finest snorkeling beaches in all Hawaii, with a shore that gently slopes to shallow, well-protected turquoise pools that are so clear and rich with marine life that all you have to do is wade in and look down. If you're a first-time snorkeler, this is the place to learn, but even advanced fish-watchers will be thrilled with the schools of brilliantly colored tropical fish that weave in and out of the well-established reef. You may even spot a sea turtle or two here. (I have, more than once!) Great facilities are on hand, including a parking lot, beach-gear rentals, a covered pavilion, and a snack bar. Come early to stake out your spot. Riptides sometimes kick up in winter, though, so check the lifeguard warning flags. (Red means stay out of the water.)

See map p. 366. On Alii Drive, 5½ miles south of Kailua-Kona.

On the Hilo-Volcano coast

On the lush windward coast, the island's beaches become fewer and far between, but more breathtakingly unusual.

Leleiwi Beach Park

If you get a beautiful beach day while you're in Hilo, head to picture-perfect Leleiwi (lay-lay-EE-vee) Beach. This lovely palm-fringed cove of black-lava tidepools fed by freshwater springs and rippled by gentle waves is a photographer's delight and the ideal place to take a dip. The shallow pools are generally calm and ideal for little ones, especially in the protected inlets at the center of the park. Sea turtles make this the locals' favorite snorkel spot; playful spinner dolphins appear on occasion, too. Facilities include restrooms, showers, and picnic pavilions.

See map p. 366. On Kalanianaole Ave., 4 miles west of Hilo.

Punaluu (Black Sand) Beach Park

If you're driving the south route between Volcano and Kona, stop here if you want to set your eyes on a genuine black-sand beach, the only one that's still accessible. (The others have been blocked by lava flows.) Stay out of the water year-round because the offshore currents are strong (although you're likely to see some daredevil surfers taking on the waves), but the sands are great for sunbathing and picnicking. (Keep your distance from the turtles who often come on shore to nest.) If you do venture into the water, do it in summer and be extremely careful. Picnic pavilions and restrooms are located across the road.

See map p. 366. Off the Hawaii Belt Road (Highway 11), about 30 miles south of Volcano Village. (The turnoff is well marked.)

At Land's End

The southernmost point in the United States is Ka Lae, or South Point. There's not much down here, except some rocky cliffs and remarkable ocean views, but I love coming anyway: Standing at this dramatic, desolate, windswept place (hold on to your hat!) actually feels like you're standing at the end of the earth.

Ka Lae (South Point) and Papakolea (Green Sand) Beach

Down at South Point is Green Sand Beach, worth seeing for its olive-green sands (actually crushed olivine, a green semiprecious mineral found in eruptive rocks and meteorites). It's a bear to reach, however, so most people don't bother. You need a four-wheel-drive vehicle and a hearty constitution to traverse the 2½-mile path from the Kaulana Boat Ramp to the cliffs overlooking the beach. You can also walk it, if you wear sturdy shoes and bring water. The trail is relatively flat, but you're usually walking into the wind as you head toward the beach. After about 30 or 40 minutes, you'll see an eroded cinder cone by the water; continue to the edge, where the green sands lie below.

I highly recommend that you simply take in the view from the cliff above the beach (which is actually very good) because the trail to the sand is difficult and treacherous, requiring you to drop down (and climb back up) 4 to 5 feet in spots. If the surf's up, don't even think about it — and stay out of the water anywhere along South Point entirely.

See map p. 366. At the end of South Point Road, 12 miles south of Mamalahoa Highway (Highway 11).

Enjoying the Sand and Surf

Although some accessible beaches are on the east (Hilo-Volcano) coast (see the preceding section), the west (Kona-Kohala) coast is the exclusive domain of water sports on the Big Island.

Snorkeling

The Big Island boasts wonderful opportunities for snorkeling, possibly the best in all the islands. One of Hawaii's absolute best snorkel spots is **Kealakekua** (kay-ah-lah-kay-KOO-ah) **Bay.** The coral in this underwater marine life preserve is the most beautiful I've ever seen, and the calm, clear waters teem with a kaleidoscope of colorful reef fish, octopuses, and Moray eels; what's more, a pod of playful spinner dolphins often come by to say hi. (The bay sports a white obelisk on the North Shore, marking the spot where Captain James Cook [credited with "discovering" the Hawaiian Islands by Western-biased history books] lost his life to a group of annoyed islanders in 1778.) The bay can be reached only by snorkel cruise or kayak, however. For details on getting there, see the section "On-deck adventures — ocean cruising," later in this chapter. Fair Wind is my favorite snorkel-cruise operator.

The Kona and Kohala coasts also boast a bunch of wonderful snorkeling beaches that allow you to simply wade in and see the colorful aquatic life. The best is **Kahaluu Beach Park,** but you might also have some fish- and turtle-spotting luck at **Anaehoomalu Bay, Kaunaoa Beach, White Sands Beach,** at the north end of **Hapuna Beach,** or even right at the foot of your hotel, if you're lucky enough to be staying at a beachfront resort. (The Mauna Lani Bay Hotel, the Fairmont Orchid, and Kona Village are particularly good choices for snorkelers without budget constraints; see Chapter 15.)

All the Big Island's dive shops arrange snorkel cruises and/or take experienced snorkelers out on their dive trips. Jack's Diving Locker even takes a limited number of snorkelers out on their night dives with manta rays. See the section "Scuba diving," later in this chapter, for details.

One of the locals' favorite snorkeling spots is in South Kona, in the cove right next to the **Puuhonua o Honaunau National Historical Park.** (See the section "More attractions worth seeking out," later in this chapter.) It's not the kind of place that you'll want to set up beach camp for the day, but it is a great spot to snorkel, with an abundance of colorful reef fish and sea turtles. To get there, follow Highway 11 south from Kailua-Kona to mile marker 103 (about 22 miles); turn right at the sign onto Highway 160 and follow it 3½ miles downslope to the national park and coast. Come early in the day before the waves kick up, bring your own gear, and turn right before you get to the entrance kiosk; the road will take you down to the boat ramp and snorkel area. (The kind guard in the booth will point you in the right direction if you miss the turn.)

You can rent snorkel gear from **Snorkel Bob's** (☎ **808-329-0770**; www.snorkelbob.com) at the south end of Kailua-Kona town (see the "Kailua-Kona Town" map). The address is 75-5831 Kahakai St., but it's actually on Alii Drive (Kailua-Kona's main drag) right in front of Huggo's restaurant.

The best-quality gear — the "Ultimate Truth" — rents for $7.50 a day, or $30 a week ($22 per week for kids) for the mask/snorkel/fins set. For an additional $10, near-sighted snorkelers can opt for prescription masks (including snorkel and fins set). You can also rent boogie boards, life vests, wet suits, beach chairs, and so on. The shop is open every day from 8 a.m. to 5 p.m. You don't need to reserve gear in advance, but if it will make you feel like you're already in Hawaii if you plan ahead, you can book your gear online at www.snorkelbob.com.

Keep these **snorkel tips** in mind as you don your fins and head into the water:

- ✔ Make mornings your offshore snorkel time on Maui, because the winds often start to kick up around noon, making surf conditions rougher and less conducive to fish-spying.

- ✔ Always snorkel with a friend and keep an eye on each other.

- ✔ Look up every few minutes to get your bearings, to check your position in relation to the shoreline, and to see whether there's any boat traffic.

- ✔ Don't touch anything. Not only can your fingers and feet damage coral, but it can give you nasty cuts. Moreover, camouflaged fish and spiny shells may surprise you.

- ✔ Before you set out, check surf conditions by calling one of the local dive or snorkel shops, such as Snorkel Bob's, which can give you the latest on local conditions, and recommend alternative spots if the prime ones are too rough for snorkeling.

On-deck adventures — ocean cruising

When the Pacific humpback whales make their annual visit to Hawaii from Alaska from December to March, they swim right by the Big Island. In season, virtually all cruise boats combine whale-watching with their regular outings, which means that you can get two adventures for the price of one!

If you want to go sportfishing off the world-famous Kona Coast, see the section "Hooking the big one," later in this chapter.

Check with Maui-based activity center **Tom Barefoot's Cashback Tours** (☎ **888-222-3601;** www.tombarefoot.com), which may be able to save you a few dollars on some of the following cruises.

Body Glove Cruises

The 51-foot, 100-passenger trimaran *Body Glove* runs cruises to Pawai Bay, north of Kailua-Kona, a marine preserve with excellent snorkeling and dolphin-watching opportunities year-round. The year-round morning cruise features 2½ hours of snorkel time (total sailing time is 4½ hours), while the afternoon cruise (offered from April to November) features 1½ hours of snorkeling. Both the 15-foot water slide and high-dive board will get you into the drink immediately, and they're real kid-pleasers. Scuba upgrades with PADI-certified (Professional Association of Diving) instructors and dive masters are available as well. In winter, the afternoon sail becomes a three-hour whale-watching excursion, complete with a naturalist onboard.

See map p. 366. Cruises depart from Kailua Pier, off Alii Drive, Kailua-Kona. ☎ **800-551-8911** *or 808-326-7122.* www.bodyglovehawaii.com. *3- to 4½-hour snorkel-sails and whale-watching trips (in season): $59–$94 adults, $39–$54 kids 6–17. Scuba rates $43–$63 higher. Morning cruises include continental breakfast and buffet deli lunch; afternoon sails include snacks.*

Captain Dan McSweeney's Year-Round Whale-Watch Learning Adventures

Do you have your heart set on whale-watching, even though you missed whale season? Or maybe you're visiting in season, but you just want to spot humpbacks with the most qualified expert around? Then contact Captain Dan McSweeney, a professional whale researcher for more than 25 years, who leads excellent whale-watching tours along the Kona Coast year-round. Sure, you'll only spot the visiting humpbacks from December through April, but you can see pilot whales, sperm whales (which grow even larger than the mammoth humpbacks!), false killer and pygmy killer whales, melon headed whales, and beaked whales, as well as five kinds of dolphins, in any month. Knowledgeable and engaging, Captain Dan and his crew are experts at knowing where to look for these wonderful creatures so that you can watch them, undisturbed, in their natural habitat. (He frequently drops an underwater video camera and/or microphone into the water so that you can see them clearly and listen to their whale songs.) What's more, he professes to have a 99-percent success rate at finding humpbacks in season. But if, for some reason, you don't see any whales at all on your trip, Captain Dan will take you out again for free — not a bad guarantee! This trip is terrific for visitors of all ages.

See map p. 366. Cruises depart from Honokohau Harbor, off Queen Kaahumanu Highway (Highway 19), 2½ miles south of Kona Airport (between mile markers 97 and

98). ☎ **888-942-5376** or 808-322-0028. www.ilovewhales.com. *3-hour cruises: $60 adults, $40 kids 11 and under. Prices include snacks. No cruises May 1–July 1.*

Captain Zodiac Raft Expeditions

Captain Zodiac leads 4-hour snorkel cruises to Kealakekua Bay aboard 16-passenger, 24-foot fiberglass-bottom rubber boats (zodiacs), the inflatables pioneered by Jacques Cousteau, which have minimal environmental impact, sit low to the water, and cruise fast over the waves for a thrill-a-minute ride. On the way to Kealakekua — one of the best snorkel spots in all Hawaii and accessible only by boat (see the section "Snorkeling," earlier in this chapter) — you'll search for spinner dolphins and green sea turtles (plus humpback whales in season) and then spend more than an hour snorkeling in the bay. On the return, if conditions permit, the captain takes you exploring sea caves that only these small, easily maneuverable boats can reach. This expedition is an excellent choice for adventuresome types. Morning (8 a.m.) and afternoon (12:45 p.m.) cruises are available, as is a three-hour whale-watching trip in season (1:15 p.m.)

See map p. 366. Cruises depart from Honokohau Harbor, off Queen Kaahumanu Highway (Highway 19), 2½ miles south of Kona Airport. ☎ **808-329-3199.** www.captain zodiac.com. *4-hour tours: $85 adults, $69 kids 4–12. Deli lunch included.*

Fair Wind Snorkel Cruises & Orca Raft Adventures

Family-owned and operated since 1971, this absolutely terrific company offers my favorite sail-and-snorkel cruises to Kealakekua Bay, the best snorkel spot in all Hawaii, period. They take a hundred or so passengers out aboard their 60-foot catamaran, the *Fair Wind II*, a state-of-the-art, impeccably maintained boat complete with easy-access water stairs (so you can literally walk into the water), a 15-foot water slide (a big hit with the kids), wide-open decks (plus plenty of covered areas if you prefer to stay out of the sun), nice deck-level bathrooms (most boats require you to shimmy down narrow ladder-like stairs), a barbecue grill for lunchtime burgers, and freshwater showers. The boat (including bathrooms) is fully wheelchair accessible. The staff is friendly and knowledgable; they'll provide all manner of floaties and assistance to those who want it and leave experienced swimmers and snorkelers pretty much to do their own thing (within the established boundaries, of course). Fair Wind is also a great way to experience *Snuba*, a cross between snorkeling and Scuba diving that allows you to go as much as 20 feet below the surface of the water without getting certification or carrying cumbersome oxygen tanks.

Book ahead, because these cruises fill up fast.

See map p. 366. Catamaran cruises depart from Keauhou Bay, off Highway 11 at the end of Kamehameha III Road (between mile markers 117 and 118), 10 minutes south of Kailua-Kona. Orca cruises depart from Kailua Pier, off Alii Drive, Kailua-Kona. ☎ **800-677-9461** or 808-322-2788. www.fair-wind.com. *3- to 4½-hour Fair Wind cruises: $59–$89 adults, $35–$55 kids 6–17. Morning cruises include continental breakfast and barbecue lunch; deluxe afternoon cruises include barbecue lunch;*

regular afternoon cruises include snacks. Scuba and Snuba rates $40–$59 higher. 3- to 4-hour Orca raft cruises: $55–$77 adults, $45–$69 kids 6–12. Raft cruises include light snacks.

Kamanu Charters

If you want to snorkel in untouristed Pawai Bay but you prefer a more intimate experience than the *Body Glove* offers, go instead with the *Kamanu,* a late-model 36-foot catamaran that limits its crowds to about two dozen per sail. This route is a good choice for first-time snorkelers (instruction and all the necessary gear are provided) and nonswimmers because a wide array of alternative flotation devices is available.

Cruises depart Honokohau Harbor, off Queen Kaahumanu Highway (Highway 19), 2½ miles south of Kona Airport. ☎ 800-348-3091 or 808-329-2021. www.kamanu.com. *3½-hour cruises: $65 adults, $45 kids 12 and under. Lunch included.*

Scuba diving

With calm, warm waters (75 to 81°F), 100-plus-feet visibility, and an open drop-off that supports a wealth of colorful marine life of all shapes and sizes, the Kona-Kohala coast offers some of the best scuba diving in the world (including excellent opportunities to swim with manta rays). Conditions are so good, in fact, that scuba magazines regularly name it among the best diving destinations in the world.

One of Kona's best and most popular dive operators is **Eco Adventures,** based at King Kamehameha's Kona Beach Hotel, 75-5660 Palani Rd. (at Alii Drive) in downtown Kailua-Kona (☎ **800-949-3483** or 808-329-7091; www.eco-adventure.com). Eco Adventures offers dives to more than 75 dive sites along the coast, including one-, two-, and three-tank day dives, night dives with manta rays, and long-distance charters. It also offers a full slate of instructional courses ranging from introductory courses for beginners to instructor-certification courses. Daily two-tank dives start at $102; beach dives start at $65. The Discover Scuba Diving trip, which operates sort of like a tandem parachute jump in which you're with an instructor the entire time so you only have to learn the basics to give it a go, is ideal for beginners ($127 per person). You may be able to score a discount by booking online.

Another very highly regarded outfitter is **Jack's Diving Locker,** in the Coconut Grove Marketplace, 75-5819 Alii Dr., Kailua-Kona (☎ **800-345-4807** or 808-329-7585; www.jacksdivinglocker.com), consistently chosen by readers of *Rodale's Scuba Diving* magazine as the best dive shop in the Indo-Pacific, and one of the best in the world. Two-tank boat dives start at $95, guided shore dives start at $55, and night dives with manta rays are $105.

Jack's also offers a full slate of introductory dives and is the best dive shop on the island for kids who want to learn: Skin-diver programs are available for kids ages 8 and up, and open-water instruction is offered to kids 12 and older.

If you have little experience but a yen to learn and become certified, **Snuba Big Island** (☎ 808-324-7446; www.snubabigisland.com) is an excellent outfitter for those in need of first-time instruction and certification courses.

Kona Coast Divers, 75-5614 Palani Rd., Kailua-Kona (☎ 800-KOA-DIVE or 808-329-8802; www.konacoastdivers.com), is another good bet, especially for wallet-watching divers: Two-tank boat dives start at $89.50, and night dives with manta rays at $60.

Red Sail Sports (☎ 877-RED-SAIL or 808-886-2876; www.redsailhawaii.com), which operates watersports and dive centers from the Hapuna Beach Prince Resort and Hilton Waikoloa Village hotels, hosts two-tank dives and night dives aboard its 38-foot Delta dive boat (the *Lani Kai*) to a number of unique sites accessible from the Kohala Coast; prices run $79 to $99. Red Sail also offers a one-day introductory scuba instruction package — including pool instruction, a one- or two-tank boat dive, and all equipment — for $139 to $159 per person. A refresher course is $45.

If you want to dive from the volcano side of the island, your best choice is **Nautilus Dive Center,** 382 Kamehameha Ave., between Open Market and the Shell Gas Station, Hilo (☎ 808-935-6939; www.nautilusdivehilo.com), where dive charter prices start at $55 for certified divers, $65 for beginners.

Try-it diving for beginners: Snuba

If you've always been interested in trying Scuba but haven't gotten around to the hassles and expense of certification, you can sample a very close approximation — Snuba. I highly encourage you to try it if you're so inclined, as Snuba is a marvelous introduction to the kind of underwater exploration that Scuba offers, without any necessary preparation.

With Snuba, you wear a mask and a regulator that's connected via a 25-foot-long hose to an oxygen tank that floats on the surface, thereby allowing you to dive deep and simulate the Scuba experience without full training (or a heavy air tank attached to your back). A great place to try it is with **Fair Wind Snorkel Cruises** (see the section "On-deck adventures — ocean cruising," earlier in this chapter). All it takes is about 15 minutes of instruction, and an instructor and two or three other first-timers are usually along for the ride; you'll get about 45 minutes of underwater time. No advance booking is necessary — the Snuba instructor asks on the way out if you're interested in participating — and the charge is usually $59 extra for adults, $49 for kids. Still, you may want to call ahead to the Fair Wind office to confirm that Snuba will be offered on your cruise if your heart's set on trying it.

Also keep in mind that both Body Glove and Fair Wind offer scuba upgrades for divers aboard their cruises to Palani Bay and Kealakekua Bay, respectively; see the section "On-deck adventures — ocean cruising," earlier in this chapter.

Freshwater fluming

I'm not a huge fan of this adventure, but I seem to be alone on this score — everybody else I talk to loves it. Back in the old plantation days, North Kohala kids used to grab old inner tubes in the heat of summer and go "fluming" down the Kohala Sugar Plantation's freshwater irrigation system, past rainforests, over ravines, under waterfalls, and through cool, drippy dark tunnels. Decades later, the surreptitious fun has been legitimized as **Flumin' da Ditch — the Kohala Mountain Kayak Cruise** (☎ **877-449-6922** or 808-889-6922; www.flumindaditch.com).

The three-hour trip goes like this: You drive up to the Hawi office, at the intersection of the Akoni Pule Highway (Highway 270) and Hawi Road (Highway 250) at the north end of the North Kohala peninsula (about an hour north of Kailua-Kona), where you're outfitted with a life vest (hardly needed) and a dry jacket (the water is pretty darn cold). You'll board a four-wheel-drive van for a rough ride through the plantation fields, accompanied by knowledgeable narration on the area and irrigation system. When you reach the water, you'll board a double-hulled inflatable kayak that you may be recruited to paddle. (Two people paddle each four-person boat, with one guide dedicated to every two boats.) The local guide will "talk story" about the history, culture, and flora of the area; for the best experience, do what you can to get yourself a spot in the guide's boat.

For me, "fluming" brought to mind sitting in a fake log at Six Flags, experiencing shriek-inducing drops down steep hills and an exciting splash at the end, so perhaps it's no wonder that I was disappointed. This is more a gentle adventure than a thrill-a-minute one — no match for kayaking alongside spinner dolphins in Kealakekua Bay. But if you like your adventure easygoing and pillowy soft, or you have little ones or older folks in tow, chances are good that you'll love this trip. Prices are $89 for adults, $68 for kids ages 5 to 18. Wear a swimsuit and/or bring a change of clothes because you'll get wet.

These trips fill up fast, so book your Flumin' da Ditch trip at least three to four days in advance, more if you're a larger party. Trips leave Hawaii daily at 8:15 a.m. or 12:15 p.m.

Hooking the big one

If you want to catch fish, you've come to the right place. Big-game fish, including monster blue, black, and striped marlin; spearfish; ahi, aku, and albacore tuna, mahimahi, and ono (also known as wahoo); and other good eating fish, as well as barracuda and shark, roam the deep, warm "fish-rich" Kona waters. There are no guarantees, but few anglers come away empty-handed. More than 100 charter boats depart from four harbors along the island's west coast, but the epicenter for Hawaii sportfishing is Honokohau Harbor, located off the Queen Kaahumanu Highway (Highway 19) 2½ miles south of the Kona Airport.

The best way to arrange a charter is through a charter boat booking agency before your trip, and the best in Kona is **The Charter Desk at Honokohau Marina** (☎ 888-KONA-4-US or 808-329-5735; www.charter desk.com). The Charter Desk's booking agents are real pros; they know the best boats in Honokohau Harbor, and they'll sort through the more than 50 different available boats, fishing specialties, and personalities to match you up with the boat and crew that's right for you. When you book with the Charter Desk, you can be sure that your boat captain is licensed by the United States Coast Guard, and the boat is fully insured.

Most big-game charter boats carry six passengers maximum. Half-day and full-day charters are available, and boats supply all equipment, bait, tackle, and lures. You don't need a fishing license on a charter boat. Prices start at around $70 for a half-day share charter (where you share the boat with strangers), $170 for a full day. Private charters start at $250 for a half day, about $400 for a full day.

Understand that if you go for a share, you'll have to rotate rods, so you won't get a full four hours of fishing in on a half-day charter. If you're calculating time-for-dollars spent, you're better off booking your own boat, especially if two or three of you are along to split the costs.

One of the best charters on the coast — and an especially good option for first-timers — is the aptly named **Bite Me Sportfishing** (☎ 800-677-9461 or 808-936-3442; www.bitemesportfishing.com), operated by the terrific folks behind Fair Wind. (See the section "On-deck adventures — ocean cruising," earlier in this chapter.) Captain Brian Wargo will take you out on the *Bite Me*, a 40-foot air-conditioned turbo twin diesel uniflite vessel, in search of blue, black, and striped marlin; yellowfin tuna; mahimahi; and other impressive big-game fish. Wargo has excellent experience catching 500-plus-pound marlin. These are private fishing charters only with a capacity for up to six passengers, running five lines at a time. A full-day charter is $550, while a half day is $375.

In addition, you may also consider booking your boat through **Sportfish Hawaii** (☎ 877-388-1376; www.sportfishhawaii.com), which represents about a half-dozen boats based at Honokohau Harbor, or **Charter Services Hawaii** (☎ 800-567-2650; www.konazone.com). If you're an experienced angler and prefer to book with a boat captain directly, consider **Anxious** (☎ 808-326-1229; www.alohazone.com).

If you're interested in light-tackle sportfishing for smaller catches, contact **Reel Action Light-Tackle Fishing** (☎ 808-325-6811; www.fish kona.org/html/reel_action.html), which can take you out spinning, bottom fishing, or trolling for smaller catches. For a real thrill, try ocean fly fishing for giant tuna or marlin. Rates range from $100 to $200 per person on a shared boat, or $400 to $900 for the whole boat (up to six people) for an eight-hour trip.

Exploring Dry Land

I've said it before, and I'll say it again: Visiting Hawaii Volcanoes National Park is one of the most thrilling things that you can do not only on this trip, but also possibly in your lifetime. I know that coming within spitting distance of an active volcano was definitely one of the highlights of my life. But there's so much to see and do on the Big Island that the excitement doesn't end there. Do what you can to budget plenty of time to see at least a few faces of this wonderfully multifaceted island.

Sightseeing with a guide

If your mobility is limited, or if you're short on time and you want an introductory look at the big picture, you may want to hook up with a guided tour. But if you've rented a car and can get around easily on your own, driving yourself is definitely the way to see the island. On a guided tour, not only will you have no control over where you go and how long you stay, but if the volcano is active, you'll kick yourself for not being able to stay at the park to see the glowing red flow after dark (prime viewing time).

Big Island guided tours also tend to be way too ambitious. Trust me — there's no better way to ruin a trip to the Big Island than by spending it on a tour bus. If you're going to take a guided bus tour of Hawaii Volcanoes National Park, do yourself a favor — take the more detailed one that departs from nearby Hilo, rather than the deadly-long Circle Island tour that leaves from Kona and incorporates more than 5 hours of driving and a good half-dozen stops into an endurance-challenging 9- to 12-hour day (and ultimately short-shrifts the national park in the process). Or, better yet, if you don't mind a little hiking in your trip, book the 12-hour Volcanoes Adventure offered by conservation-minded outfitter **Hawaii Forest & Trail,** which travels full circle from the Kona-Kohala coast and offers more insight into the park and its geology and history than you're likely to glean in a three-day visit on your own. (See the section "Enjoying guide-led nature tours," later in this chapter).

Polynesian Adventure Tours (☎ **800-622-3011** or 808-329-8008; www. polyad.com) offers a range of guided tours in minivans, big-windowed minicoaches (good for small groups and big views), and full-size buses. First launched to take visitors along Maui's Heavenly Road to Hana, Polynesian Adventure's tours tend to be a little more action-oriented than those offered by competing companies. Expect to spend $50 to $68 per person ($38 to $55 for kids 3 to 11), depending on the tour that you choose and your departure point.

Roberts Hawaii (☎ **800-831-5541** or 808-539-9400; www.robertshawaii. com) is Hawaii's biggest name in narrated bus tours. Roberts offers a similar slate of tours as Polynesian Adventure, with comparable schedules and prices.

Book your Polynesian Adventure or Roberts Hawaii tour online and score a 10-percent price break.

If you do opt for a guided tour that takes you around the entire island, remember: It will be chillier on the east coast than it is on the west coast, so bring a jacket or sweater when you visit the volcano. It's also a good idea to bring along rain gear and/or an umbrella, as well as sturdy closed-toe walking shoes.

Enjoying guide-led nature tours

If you want to experience the Big Island's multifaceted natural world, I highly recommend going out with a guide. An expert guide can really help you appreciate the majesty of this fantastic island and even take you into areas that you couldn't otherwise reach on your own. Even if hiking and nature-exploring aren't parts of your daily life, don't worry; you won't be required to be in racing shape. All the following terrific tour companies offer adventures for every level of experience and ability.

My absolute favorite Big Island outfitter is **Hawaii Forest & Trail** (☎ **800-464-1993** or 808-331-8505; www.hawaii-forest.com). I first explored the Big Island with naturalist and educator Rob Pacheco way back in 1995, and it was one of the best — and most fun — nature experiences of my life, so I'm thrilled to see his first-rate business growing and widening its options for visitors. I never miss an opportunity to go out with Hawaii Forest & Trail whenever I'm on the Big Island — you just can't go wrong with these guys.

Both half-day and full-day trips are available; they're all personalized to a group's interest and ability levels and often feature easy or moderate walking. (Ask when you book if you're concerned.) Regularly scheduled half-day adventures include the **Valley Waterfall Adventure,** which takes you into private lands on the Kohala Coast to discover hidden waterfalls and killer views along a 3-mile hike. On the marvelous **Kohala Mule Trail Adventure,** island-born guide Wally Ching (one of the most genuine and generous folks I've ever met) or one of his expert muleskinner guides takes visitors on sure-footed mules to explore the crest above the stunningly pristine and history-rich Pololu Valley. During the mule ride, you'll cross two streams and visit otherwise inaccessible waterfalls.

Full-day adventures include the **Volcanoes in the Sea Adventure,** a 12-hour trip from the Kona-Kohala coast to the splendid Hamakua Coast and Hawaii Volcanoes National Park that's the best introduction to the active volcano and vulcanology that there is. If you have only one day to see the volcano, see it this way.

Another one-of-a-kind eight-hour adventure that makes lifetime memories is the **Mauna Kea Summit & Stars** trip, in which your astronomer guide takes you across Parker Ranch pastureland — gorgeous wide-open landscape that you never thought you'd see in Hawaii — to the (often snow-capped) summit of Mauna Kea (at 13,796 feet), one of the best and most famous stargazing spots in the world, dotted with a world-class array of telescopes from the world's foremost astronomical observatories. At dusk, you'll descend to 9,000 feet for an incredible lesson in astronomical observation in a night sky unlike any other you've ever seen. This trip is a total blast; everyone on ours agreed that it was the best thing they'd done in Hawaii.

Although you can visit the summit of Mauna Kea on your own, you must have a four-wheel-drive vehicle and approval from the rental company (difficult to get) in order to drive on Saddle Road and the summit road. You'll also need parkas to withstand the icy temperatures at the summit, which the guides issue. Finally, you should be accustomed to driving at high altitudes and need to know a bit about astronomy and the night sky to get anything out of your visit. For these reasons, I highly recommend just going with Hawaii Forest & Trail instead.

A number of **bird-watching adventures** to private lands are also available. Rob, from Hawaii Forest & Trail, is a birder at heart and has exclusive access to various private lands that showcase the ecological diversity of the island, so there's really no one better to go with if you're into bird-watching (or want to learn).

Call or check the Web site for details and schedules for these and other adventures. Prices for half-day trips cost $95 per person ($75 for kids ages 8 to 12), while full-day trips run $135 to $155 per person ($105 for kids under 12; not all trips are appropriate for younger ones). Rates include food and all the gear that you'll need. Prices are high, but you get your money's worth and then some. All trips depart from the Kona-Kohala coast; some include pickup and drop-off, while others have a predesignated meeting point. Reservations should be made at least a week in advance. Note that certain trips have restrictions based on age, weight, or health; be sure to confirm these with the Hawaii Forest & Trail representative when you book. After you arrive, you can also stop at the Hawaii Forest & Trail Headquarters and Outfitting Store at 74-5035B Queen Kaahumanu Highway (Highway 19, on the mountain side of the highway across from Honokahou Harbor, behind the Chevron Station), Kailua-Kona, where you can book trips and pick up outdoor equipment and nature-related gear and books.

If, for some reason, Hawaii Forest & Trail doesn't meet your needs or doesn't go where you want to go, try **Hawaiian Walkways** (☎ **800-457-7759** or 808-775-0372; www.hawaiianwalkways.com). This reliable outfitter offers a variety of regularly scheduled full- and half-day hikes led by excellent, enthusiastic guides. The Hawaii Ecotourism Association named them tour operator of the year in 2002. The Waipio Waterfall Adventure, a wonderful half-day hike that takes you along the rim of the Big Island's best-loved unspoiled valley, leaves daily at 9 a.m. You can arrange other trips in advance, including a Kona Cloud Forest Botanical Walk, a Kilauea Volcano Discovery Hike into Hawaii Volcanoes National

Park, a Saddle Road Exploration, or just about any part of the island you'd like to visit. Prices range from $75 to $175 per person, depending on the trip you choose; all gear, food, and beverages are provided.

If you can't hook up with Hawaii Forest & Trail for its Mauna Kea Summit and Stars, head to the top with **Mauna Kea Summit Adventures (☎ 808-332-2366;** www.maunakea.com), a company that has been leading Mauna Kea tours exclusively for nearly two decades. The price is $165 per person, including dinner, all necessary equipment, and parkas. You can arrange to meet your guide for your seven- to eight-hour adventure in Kailua-Kona, or at the Kings Shops at Waikoloa, or the Saddle Road junction. Reserve two weeks in advance, and you'll save 15 percent.

The folks behind Flumin' da Ditch (see the section "Freshwater fluming," earlier in this chapter) also run very fun **HMV Tours (☎ 877-449-6922** or 808-889-6922; www.flumindaditch.com/hmv.html) of the spectacular North Kohala peninsula — a hidden treasure that few visitors ever see — led by island-born locals who really know what's what. These three-hour Hummer safaris take you into unspoiled lands rife with ancient rainforests and home to secret historical sites and hidden waterfalls that were previously inaccessible to the public, mixing knowledgeable narration and off-road excitement along the way. With 30-percent banking and 60-percent slope-climbing capability, the Humvees offer a real thrill ride to boot. Prices are $99 for adults, $68 for kids. Tours leave daily at 8:15 a.m. and 12:15 p.m.

Getting a bird's-eye view — flightseeing tours

Flightseeing is a great way to explore this large, dynamic isle, which boasts sheer cliffs, pristine valleys, gorgeous waterfalls, expansive lava fields, and remote beaches that are otherwise inaccessible. And, of course, there's no better way to see that spectacular bubbling volcano, especially if the current flow is too far from civilization to see from accessible points in the national park.

Blue Hawaiian Helicopters (☎ 800-745-BLUE or 808-961-5600; www.bluehawaiian.com; 40- to 50-minute tours: $175 per person; 2-hour tour: $340 per person) is an excellent flightseeing company that's family run by David and Patti Chevalier and a loyal staff. Blue Hawaiian flies a fleet of shiny new American Eurocopter AStar 350 helicopters that carry six passengers, providing each with a 180° view and a Bose noise-canceling headset that lets you enjoy a surprisingly quiet ride. For Hilo-based travelers, Blue Hawaiian offers a 45- to 50-minute Circle of Fire volcano tour. From Waikoloa, choose between the gorgeous 45- to 50-minute Kohala Coast Adventure that shows you the secret fluted valleys, majestic peaks, and rugged coastline of the island's northernmost point; and the Big Island Spectacular, which takes you over the entire island, from rugged coast and misty peaks to rainforest and volcano, all within two hours. Tours depart from Waikoloa Heliport or Hilo Airport.

You should consider the risks of flightseeing before you sign on. Although all the companies that I recommend feature skilled pilots and helicopters with excellent safety records, the truth of the matter is that flightseeing is somewhat risky business. Twenty-eight people have died in commercial helicopter crashes in Hawaii over the last decade. Of course, just getting into your car and driving to dinner is far more dangerous than catching a 'copter ride. Still, you should make informed decisions when booking.

When reserving a helicopter tour with any company, check to make sure that safety is its first concern. The company should be an FAA-certified Part 135 operator, and the pilot should be Part 135 certified as well; the 135 license guarantees more stringent maintenance requirements and pilot training programs than those who are only Part 91 certified. And if weather conditions look iffy, reschedule.

Seeing Hawaii Volcanoes National Park

 The top natural attraction in the islands, Hawaii Volcanoes National Park is home to a rainforest in the U.S. National Park system and is the only national park that's home to a live, lava-pumping volcano. This phenomenal park stands testament to 70 million years of volcanic activity, plate tectonics, and evolution. It encompasses two volcanoes, **Mauna Loa** and **Kilauea,** and spans 217,000 acres that reach from sea level to Mauna Loa's towering summit at 13,677 feet, and has both vast fields of black lava and an ancient rainforest.

Both volcanoes are classified as active, but Mauna Loa hasn't erupted since 1984. Kilauea, on the other hand, is the most active volcano in the world. An amazing geological phenomenon, it's been erupting nonstop since January 3, 1983. Most volcanic flows last a while — several months, maybe — but 18 years is simply unheard of in the annals of scientific history. Until now, of course.

When most people think of active volcanoes, they think of Mount St. Helens: A calm mountain suddenly blowing its stack, belching out raging, destructive torrents of fire. Hawaii's volcanoes, however, are much more mellow geologic creatures: They're shield volcanoes, which erupt gradually — in a sort of gloopy, Jell-O–like fashion — rather than in one big, fiery explosion. Thus, they allow for excellent, safe viewing most of the time, giving you plenty of time to calmly move out of the way if a blob of lava starts inching toward you. Leave it to Hawaii to have such laid-back volcanoes!

The most recent lava flow — the one that you'll be able to see, if you're lucky — follows a 7-mile-long tube from the Puu Oo (POO-oo OH-oh) vent to the sea, where it spills into the ocean in a steaming stream. The hardened lava trail has extended the shoreline seaward, adding more than 560 acres of new land to the Big Island by early 2000 — and even more by the time you get here.

At press time, the lava flow was still going strong and, despite an 11-day pause in September 1999, shows no signs of stopping anytime soon, vulcanologists say. But neither Mother Nature nor Madame Pele (Pell-ay), Hawaii's volcano goddess (who is said to reside in Kilauea's steaming Halemaumau Crater), run on a fixed schedule. The volcano could be shooting fountains of lava hundreds of feet into the air, or it could be dormant on the day you arrive in the park (or the day after this book goes to press, for that matter) — there are no guarantees.

What's more, just because the lava is flowing doesn't mean that you'll be able to witness it firsthand. On many days, the lava flows right by accessible roads and within reach of hiking trails; you can get as close as the heat will allow and even watch it dump into the sea — quite a dramatic sight. At other times, the lava changes course, flowing miles away from any accessible points, visible only in the distance (or from the air via helicopter) or not at all (on occasion it sticks to underground lava tubes). If you hear that the flow is going strong and the viewing is good (word gets around quickly in Volcano), don't hesitate: Head straight to the end of the road. You won't be disappointed, I promise. And don't put it off until tomorrow, when the situation may be entirely different.

If your visit happens to land during a period when the lava isn't visible at all, don't be too disappointed — or, worse yet, consider your visit a waste. Although I've been lucky enough to have some spectacular lava-viewing experiences, my favorite day in the park was spent without even seeing a speck of red. Trust me on this — visiting Hawaii Volcanoes National Park is a one-of-a-kind, once-in-a-lifetime experience even without the lava show.

Getting ready for your visit

For information before you go, contact Hawaii Volcanoes National Park headquarters at ☎ **808-985-6000,** or visit the park's official Web site at www.nps.gov/havo, which features frequent updates on weather and lava flows. The telephone number also serves as a 24-hour eruption update and information hotline. Dial the same number (or visit the Web site) to obtain camping information.

Visit the U.S. Geological Survey's **Hawaiian Volcano Observatory** site at hvo.wr.usgs.gov for more complete information on Kilauea's recent eruption activity (including pictures!) and past history. Another excellent (albeit unofficial) site for general park information is www.hawaii.volcanoes.national-park.com.

Once you arrive on the island, you'll find that most information kiosks are stocked with a free booklet-sized official visitor's guide to the park. I recommend picking one up and reviewing it before your visit, as it's packed with practical details, historical background, and sightseeing information — way more than I am able to supply in these pages.

Hawaii Volcanoes National Park

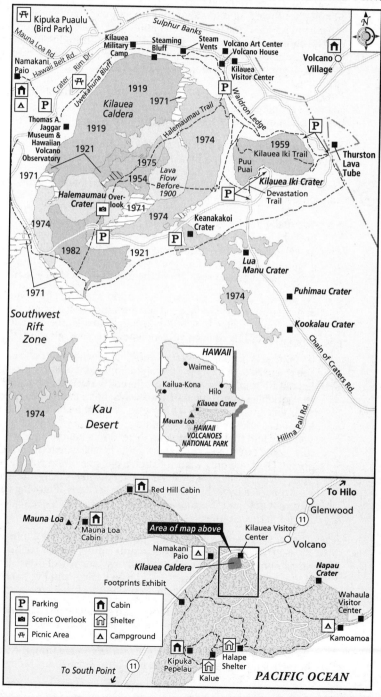

Hawaii Volcanoes National Park is on the Big Island's east side, about 30 miles southwest of Hilo along the Hawaii Belt Road (Highway 11). The drive from Kailua-Kona is about 100 miles and takes 2½ to three hours. For the shortest drive, choose the south route (around South Point) if you're staying to the south of Kailua-Kona, the north route (through Waimea) if you're staying along the Kohala Coast.

The gateway town of Volcano Village, on the north side of the park off Highway 11 just about a mile or so from the park entrance, is your best bet for accommodations and dining (Chapter 15).

Admission to the park is $10 per car ($5 for pedestrians), which allows you to come and go as you please for seven days.

Keep these tips in mind as you plan your trip to Hawaii Volcanoes National Park:

✔ You really need two or three days to explore the park thoroughly, so I recommend booking yourself a stay in Volcano Village, the park's gateway community, or the small and pretty city of Hilo, about a 45-minute drive away. But don't stay away if you can't dedicate so much time; you can see a lot of the park if a day is all you have.

✔ No matter how long you have to visit, do yourself a favor and plan on staying until after dark at least one evening. That's when, if you're lucky, you'll be able to witness nothing less than the miracle of creation as erupting Kilauea volcano spews red-hot, glowing lava.

✔ If you're staying on the west (Kona-Kohala) coast and you can only see the park on a daytrip, you might consider visiting with a guide-led nature tour, such as the one offered by **Hawaii Forest & Trail,** or the park hike that **Hawaiian Walkways** offers in order to maximize your volcano experience. Otherwise, without a knowledgeable guide at hand to show you the highlights and explain what you're seeing, you may find that you're unable to get a real handle on the park in just a day. Trust me — an expert guide is well worth the dough you'll spend. Or, if you only want to catch a glimpse of the volcano from your perch on the Kona-Kohala coast, consider taking a helicopter tour that flies over the volcano. See the sections "Enjoying guide-led nature tours" and "Getting a bird's-eye view — flightseeing tours," earlier in this chapter.

✔ The most adventurous among you may want to rent a four-wheel-drive SUV when you book your rental car on the Big Island, as a few areas of the park are accessible only by four-wheel-drive. If you don't, however, don't sweat it — I never have, and I've seen more of the park than most visitors. You won't feel limited.

✔ I just can't say it strongly enough: I've seen way too many visitors running around the park soaking wet or freezing their buns off in shorts and T-shirts. Remember: It's always colder here than it is at the beach, so dress accordingly. If you're coming from the Kona side of the island in summer, expect it to be at least 10 to 20 degrees cooler at the volcano than it is there; bring a sweater or a light jacket and long pants. It's probably even slightly cooler than it is in Hilo thanks to a higher elevation (4,000 feet), so anticipate a drop. In the cooler seasons, wear layers, and be prepared for temperatures to be in the 40s or 50s. Always have rain gear on hand, especially in winter. Sturdy close-toed shoes are a good idea year-round, and a necessity if you're going to walk on the lava flow, as sneakers sometimes melt on the lava.

✔ No matter what the weather forecast may be, always bring a hat, sunglasses, and sunscreen. Take it from me, who came away with quite a sunburn on a day that started with a downpour — the weather can change at any time. Bring drinking water, too, as it isn't readily available in most areas of the park.

✔ Pregnant visitors may want to skip the national park altogether, as it's not a good idea to expose yourself or your baby to the sulfuric fumes that are ever-present in the park. Those with heart or breathing problems may also want to stay away, although my asthmatic husband has never had a problem in four visits. Otherwise, the park is perfectly safe for visitors. Some people claim that long-term exposure to vog, the smoglike haze caused by the gases released when molten lava pours into the ocean, can cause bronchial ailments, but sulfuric fumes are actually far less dangerous than urban industrial fumes.

Getting your bearings once you arrive

Make your first stop the **Kilauea Visitor Center,** just beyond the park entrance, open daily from 7:45 a.m. to 5 p.m. Here you can get up-to-the-minute reports on the eruption and good viewing points, check out exhibits that show you how volcanoes work and introduce you to the plants and animals of the park, watch a 20-minute film on eruptions (shown hourly), and review a schedule of the day's activities (posted on the bulletin board). While you're there, impress the rangers with your knowledge of Hawaii's volcano vocabulary:

✔ The smooth, ropy lava that looks like swirls of chocolate frosting is called **pahoehoe** (pa-ho-ay-HO-ay). It results from a fast-moving flow that curls as it flows.

✔ The rough, chunky lava that looks like a chopped-up parking lot is called **aa** (AH-ah). It's caused by lava that moves slowly, pulling apart as it overruns itself.

An easy, 45-minute guided summit walk leaves from Kilauea Visitor Center daily at 9:45 p.m. It offers an excellent introduction to the park and its flora, fauna, and volcanic geology, so I highly recommend launching your first day in the park with it. I've also found that the guide is happy to make instructive recommendations on planning your time.

Be sure to use the restroom if you're heading into the depths of the park, because they're not readily available in the wild.

Exploring the park

For the best park overview, follow 11-mile **Crater Rim Drive,** which loops around the perimeter of Kilauea Crater and serves as the park's main road, passing through rainforest and lava desert and taking you past all of the park's well-marked scenic spots and points of interest. The drive takes about an hour if you don't make any stops, but what's the point in that? Allow at least three hours, plus hiking time.

If you haven't already done so on the morning guided summit walk, before you even get in your car at the visitor center to make the drive, walk across the street and through the Volcano House for a railside panoramic view of the **Kilauea Caldera** and its vast, black steaming floor. Before you enter the building, look to your right for the marked steam vents, which illustrate the underground action with a cloud of warm, wet air escaping from the earth. (Notice how all the rainforest ferns have gravitated to the moisture.)

I recommend following the Crater Rim Drive counterclockwise (west) from the visitor center about 3 miles so that you can stop at the **Thomas A. Jaggar Museum,** open daily from 8:30 a.m. to 5 p.m., early in your drive. This little museum is well worth a half-hour of your time for the insight it offers into the park's geologic complexities, island evolution, and volcano observing; there's even a great telling of the Pele legend in murals. (Jaggar was a scientist and volcano observer who arrived to head the observatory in 1912; he was instrumental in both making the Big Island's volcanoes the most closely watched volcanoes in the world and petitioning to establish the area as a national park, a status it achieved in 1916.)

Natural highlights along the Crater Rim Drive include the **Steam Vents** along the Steaming Bluff, where clouds of warmth rise from vents in the active earth. At **Halemaumau** (ha-lay-MOW-mow) **Overlook,** walk to the crater's edge and peer into the vast, still-sulfuric crater that is the legendary home of Pele, Hawaii's tempestuous goddess of volcanoes (evidenced by Halemaumau's still-wild steam vents, perhaps?). Across the road is **Keanakakoi Crater,** whose short trail leads to colorful eruption fissures — very cool! — and the backside of the Halemaumau Crater. As you drive the road, you'll see that the flows are dated (1959, 1974, 1982), which really brings home the reality of volcanic destruction.

You'll also pass numerous scenic overlooks and trailheads, and I highly recommend that you hit the trail at least once during your visit; the following offer some highlights to seek out.

The **Thurston Lava Tube** is the coolest spot in the park. This short (⅓-mile), easy, well-maintained loop trail leads you into a small rainforesty crater, luxuriant with giant ferns and native birds, and to a cave in the lava flow that hot lava once ran through. (Similar tubes are currently carrying hot lava underground closer to the current rift.) It's all drippy and cool, with naked roots hanging down. You can hike through the short tube and exit out the other side (bring your flashlight if you have one).

My absolute favorite is the **Kilauea Iki Trail,** a 4-mile, two-hour moderate hike that starts across the road from the Thurston Lava Tube and descends about 400 feet to and across the floor of the Kilauea Iki Crater, which last erupted in 1959. Crossing the black, steaming crater floor is a wild, otherworldly, magnificent trip and offers the park's best opportunity to put yourself in the heart of the matter.

Another result of Kilauea Iki's 1959 eruption is **Devastation Trail.** This brief and easy half-mile walk with the ominous name shows you what a volcanic eruption can do to a flourishing rainforest. The petrified landscape is quite astounding — it looks like a tree graveyard. Anybody can manage this walk; the trailhead is on Crater Rim Drive at Puu Puai Overlook.

If you'd like a respite from all the devastation, follow the **Kipuka Puaulu (Bird Park) Trail,** an easy 1-mile loop that takes you through a thriving forest of native trees. The trailhead is off Highway 11 to the northeast of the main park area, on the Mauna Loa Road. (The park map makes it easy to find.)

Both the Devastation and Kipuka Puaulu trails are excellent walks to take between 4 and 5 p.m., as that's when the park's resident pheasants emerge from their daytime nests to poke around and see what's going on.

The park has enough fascinating hiking trails to keep you busy and interested for days on end. Your best bet is, again, to start your day at the Kilauea Visitor Center, where you can learn about guided walks and day-hike options. Remember to always check conditions with the park rangers before you set out on any hike. If you're interested in getting a preview of accessible trails, visit www.hawaii.volcanoes.national-park.com and click Hiking Guide.

Once you circle back around to the Kilauea Visitor Center, stop in next door at the **Volcano Art Center** (www.volcanoartcenter.org), which serves as one of the top showcases for island artists. Don't miss it if you're interested in local arts and crafts — from native-wood jewelry boxes to hand-crafted jewelry to first-rate paintings and photographs — as the works you'll find here are first-rate.

More attractions worth seeking out

If you can say anything about the Big Island, it is certainly that there is an activity or interest for just about everyone. In this section, I provide some off-the-beaten-path attractions that are worth a visit.

Along the Kona-Kohala coast

In addition to these sights, you may want to head Upcountry from Kailua-Kona town on Hualalai Road to the charmingly funky gallery-lined town of **Holualoa,** which offers a nice peek at Kona's world-famous

Kailua-Kona Town

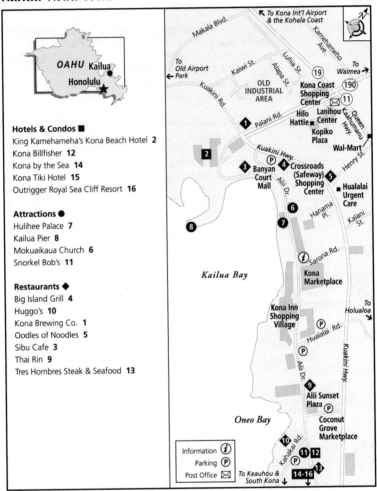

Hotels & Condos ■
King Kamehameha's Kona Beach Hotel **2**
Kona Billfisher **12**
Kona by the Sea **14**
Kona Tiki Hotel **15**
Outrigger Royal Sea Cliff Resort **16**

Attractions ●
Hulihee Palace **7**
Kailua Pier **8**
Mokuaikaua Church **6**
Snorkel Bob's **11**

Restaurants ◆
Big Island Grill **4**
Huggo's **10**
Kona Brewing Co. **1**
Oodles of Noodles **5**
Sibu Cafe **3**
Thai Rin **9**
Tres Hombres Steak & Seafood **13**

coffee-growing country; see the section "Shopping the local stores," later in this chapter, for further details on what you'll find there.

Hulihee Palace

The ancient port town of Kailua-Kona is more like a modern mall than anything else these days, lined with waterfront restaurants and tourist-friendly shopping. But if you have an interest in Hawaii's history, you may want to take 15 minutes or so to explore Hulihee Palace. Built in 1838, this beautifully restored two-story New England-style mansion of lava rock and coral mortar served as the vacation home of Hawaii's royalty. It features gleaming koa antiques as well as ancient artifacts collected by the Daughters of Hawaii. There's a cute gift shop, too.

 After you're done exploring the palace, head across the street to handsome **Mokuaikaua Church,** 75-5713 Alii Dr. (☎ **808-329-0655**), the first Christian church in Hawaii, now housing a Congregational congregation. The 112-foot steeple is still the tallest structure in Kailua-Kona. Sunday service is 10:30 a.m. and lasts about an hour.

See map p. 390. 75-5718 Alii Dr., Kailua-Kona (in the heart of town). ☎ *808-329-1877.* www.daughtersofhawaii.org. *Admission: $6 adults, $4 seniors, $1 kids under 12. Open: Daily 9 a.m.–4 p.m.*

Kalahuipuaa Fishponds

Scientists still marvel at the ancient Hawaiians' sophisticated aquaculture system, which used brackish shoreline ponds to stock, cultivate, and harvest fish for eating. This picturesque set of seven adjacent 2,000-year-old ponds are of two types: The closed ponds, inshore and closed off from the ocean, were used to raise mullet, milkfish, and shrimp, while ponds that open to the sea have rock-wall barriers and sluice gates that connect them directly to the ocean.

These beautifully preserved oceanfront ponds are a stellar example of the ancient way of life — not to mention a gorgeous place to enjoy a stroll. A palm-lined lava-rock path winds its way around the ponds; the entire walk is an easy 2½-mile loop, dotted with wooden benches that let you take frequent breaks and enjoy the vistas (or the flying mullet, which love to leap into the air). Next door is the restaurant at the Mauna Lani Beach Club, where you can enjoy a refreshing beverage after your walk.

See map p. 366. In the Mauna Lani Resort, 23 miles north of Kona Airport. ☎ *808-885-6622. To get there: Take Queen Kaahumanu Highway (Highway 19) to the Mauna Lani turnoff; ask the gate attendant to point you to the fishponds. If you're staying at the resort, the free shuttle can take you there.*

Kona Historical Society Museum

This well-organized pocket museum is housed in the historic Greenwell Store, built in 1875 by Henry Nicholas Greenwell out of native stone, with lime mortar made from burnt coral. Antiques, artifacts, and photos tell the story of the fabled Kona Coast in the heyday of coffee-growing and cattle-raising. Serious history buffs should inquire about joining one of the museum's first-rate walking tours.

See map p. 366. On Highway 11, ¼ mile south of Kealakekua town (between mile markers 111 and 112). ☎ *808-323-3222.* www.konahistorical.org. *Admission: $2. Open: Mon–Fri 9 a.m.–3 p.m.*

Puako Petroglyph Archaeological District

Petroglyphs, lava-rock carvings that tell the story of the pre-contact past (much like the paintings inside the great pyramids of Egypt), serve as a fascinating window to Hawaii's ancient history. These pictures of daily life — dancers and paddlers, families and chiefs, poi pounders and canoes — appear throughout the islands, but most of them are found on the Big Island. The largest concentration is here, at this 233-acre site just north of the Mauna Lani resort. The easy and well-marked 1½-mile **Malama Trail** leads you to rock art that's graphic and easy to see. Early morning or late afternoon is best for petroglyph viewing.

The petroglyphs are thousands of years old and can be easily destroyed, so don't walk on them or attempt to take a rubbing; stick to photos, please.

See map p. 366. At the Mauna Lani resort, 23 miles north of Kona Airport. ☎ *808-885-6622. To get there: Take Queen Kaahumanu Highway (Highway 19) to the Mauna Lani turnoff and drive toward the coast on North Kaniku Drive, which ends at a parking lot; the trailhead is marked by a sign and interpretive kiosk.*

Puuhonua o Honaunau National Historical Park

If you visit only one historic site while you're in Hawaii, make it this one. No other site better illustrates what ancient life in the islands was like — and, boy, is this place cool.

With its fierce, haunting totem-like idols, this sacred site on the ocean looks mighty intimidating. To ancient Hawaiians, though, it was a welcome sight — especially for defeated warriors and *kapu* (taboo) breakers, because Puuhonua O Honaunau (poo-oo-ho-NOO-ah oh ho-NOW-now) was a designated sanctuary. A massive rock wall defines the refuge; as long as the troubled Hawaiians made it inside the wall, they were absolved. In addition to the sanctuary itself, this visually stunning ancient site on the black-lava coast is also home to fascinating archaeological preservations and reconstructions, including royal grounds that were home to the *alii* (chiefs) of the Kona Coast in premodern times; an ancient temple re-creation; royal fishponds and burial sites (some pretty powerful chiefs called this area home); and much more. Heck, the old rock wall alone is worth a visit: Separating the royal compound from the *puuhonua* (sanctuary) and standing 10 feet high and 17 feet thick in spots, it was built entirely without mortar, by simply fitting stones together — a remarkable achievement considering that it's been standing since about 1550.

The historic site is tons of fun to explore. At the park entrance, you get a self-guided tour map that leads you to 16 important sites. The trail takes about an hour to follow and serves as a great window into precontact Hawaiian culture — not only in such fierce life lessons as war and sanctuary, but also basic living, from fish-raising and -netting to the basic rules of *konane* (ancient Hawaiian checkers). Wear shoes or sandals with good traction, and you can crawl around on the oceanfacing lava flats — fun! I highly recommend that you launch your visit, however, with a half-hour ranger-led orientation talk, held in the amphitheater periodically throughout the day. (Call for the current schedule.) All in all, allow two to three hours for your visit.

See map p. 366. At the end of Highway 160, Honaunau (about 22 miles south of Kailua-Kona). To get there: Turn off Mamalahoa Highway (Highway 11) at Highway 160, between mile markers 103 and 104, and proceed the 3½ miles to the park entrance. ☎ ***808-328-2288**, 808-328-9877, or 808-328-2326.* www.nps.gov/puho. *Admission: $5 per vehicle. Open: Park, Mon–Thurs 6 a.m.–8 p.m., Fri–Sun 6 a.m.–11 p.m.; visitor center, daily 7:30 a.m.–5:30 p.m.*

Off the beaten path: North Kohala

If you look at a map of the Big Island, you see that a mountainous peninsula protrudes from the very top of the island. That's **North Kohala,** the last bastion of plantation life on the Big Island until not too long ago. If you want to experience the old Hawaii vibe, this is the place to do it.

The hour-long drive along the Akoni Pule (ah-KO-nee POO-lay) Highway (Highway 270) from Kawaihae (at the north end of the Kohala Coast, where Highway 19 turns inland toward Waimea) to the end of the road at the island's north tip is one of my favorite drives in all Hawaii. It takes you past gorgeous rolling ranchlands with remarkable ocean vistas and through two charming old plantation towns, **Hawi** (HA-vee) and **Kapaau** (ka-PA-ow), both of which have been transformed into small but rewarding shopper's havens. (See the section "Shopping the local stores," later in this chapter, for details.)

As you drive through Kapaau, look to the mountain side of the road, where you can't miss the **Original King Kamehameha Statue** standing guard outside the New England–style courthouse-turned-senior center in the heart of town. This unspoiled territory was the birthplace of King Kamehameha the Great, the great chief who united the Hawaiian Islands as one kingdom back in 1810. This 8-foot, 6-inch bronze statue was cast in Europe in 1880 and was lost at sea before being ultimately rescued and erected here.

After you're finished browsing Hawi and Kapaau, if it's a nice day and you're enjoying your North Kohala drive, continue a few miles to the end of Highway 270, where you'll find the **Pololu Valley Lookout,** a gorgeous scenic overlook that takes in a panoramic view of foaming waves and sheer seacliffs.

After all this sightseeing, you're bound to be hungry, so don't miss retro-charming **Bamboo,** in Hawi, for lunch; see Chapter 15 for details.

If you want to explore the verdant ranchlands of North Kohala the way they were meant to be seen — from the saddle of a horse — contact **Paniolo Adventures** (☎ **808-889-5354;** www.panioloadventures.com), which offers 1½-, 2½- and 3-hour rides through 11,000 acres of still-working cattle lands. This is a spirited ride, not a nose-to-tail trailer; even brave beginners often get up to a canter. Beginning, intermediate, and advanced riders alike, ages 8 and up, will enjoy these trips. Rides are $73 to $124 per person. (You must have a group of three or more to schedule a 1½-hour ride.) Custom-designed private rides (minimum two people) are also available.

The interior: Waimea

Smack-dab in the middle of the north road between the west and east sides of the island is Waimea, the heart and soul of Hawaii's *paniolo* (cowboy) country.

As you drive along Highway 19 east from the Kohala Coast to Waimea, most of the rolling, grassy ranchland that you see is part of **Parker Ranch** (www.parkerranch.com), Hawaii's biggest ranch and one of the largest cattle ranches in the entire United States (rather remarkable, if you think about it).

If you're interested in learning just how cattle roping came to find a home in Hawaii, spend a half-hour at the **Parker Ranch Visitor Center and Museum,** in the Parker Ranch Shopping Center at the junction of highways 19 and 190 (☎ **808-885-7655** or 808-885-2303), which chronicles the ranch's history from 1847 until today, capturing the essence of day-to-day life on the ranch along the way. The museum is open daily except Sunday from 9 a.m. to 5 p.m. (the last ticket is sold at 4 p.m.). Admission is $6.50 ($4 for kids 12 and under).

The Parker Ranch also has two historic home sites that you can tour, **Mana Hale** and **Puopelu,** both open Monday through Saturday from 10 a.m. to 5 p.m. (You must arrive by 4 p.m.) These beautifully restored ranch homes (once the home of ranch founding father John Parker and his Hawaiian princess bride) are filled with gorgeous furnishings (lots of native koa in Mana Hale, European heirlooms at Puopelu). To get there, turn south at the Highway 19/190 junction in Waimea and go ¾ mile to the sign that says "Parker Ranch Historic Homes & ART Collection." Curators are available to show you around and fill you in on ranch history and gossipy lore. Admission is $8.50 per person. Allow an hour or so for your visit.

If you want to get out and see the ranch itself, a 45-minute narrated **Wagon Tour** is offered Tuesday through Saturday hourly from 10 a.m. to 2 p.m. Two large Belgian draft horses pull an old-fashioned *paniolo* wagon with seating for 20; warm blankets are on hand to keep you warm against the Upcountry temperatures. The tour rolls past 19th-century stone corrals that are still in use and miles of vast rolling hills, and it stops at a working cowboy station. If you're lucky, you may even get to see real *paniolo* herding, cutting, holding, roping, throwing, branding, or sorting the cattle. Tickets are $15 for adults, $12 for kids 12 and under. Be sure to arrive at the visitor center at least 15 minutes before your preferred tour time.

There's even more to do on Parker Ranch than I have space to discuss here. For a full list of events and activities, call ☎ **808-885-2303** or go online to www.parkerranch.com.

If you want to learn more about *paniolo* past and present and the associated activities that are available both in Waimea and around the island, point your Web browser to www.rodeohawaii.com, where you'll find a

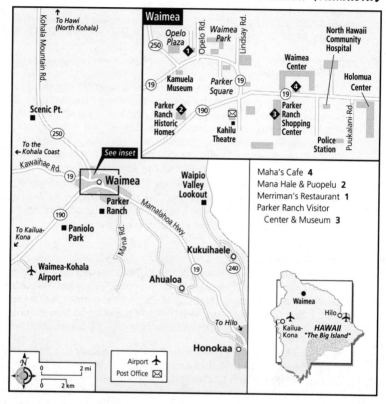

Waimea (Kamuela)

Maha's Cafe **4**
Mana Hale & Puopelu **2**
Merriman's Restaurant **1**
Parker Ranch Visitor
 Center & Museum **3**

comprehensive site detailing cowboy-related sightseeing and shopping, rodeo schedules, and more.

The Hamakua Coast

If you drive east from Waimea or north from Hilo (see the following listing), you reach more off-the-beaten-path territory: the mist-shrouded Hamakua Coast, where you find some wonderful natural attractions and the one-horse town of **Honokaa,** which still boasts a weathered old-plantation charm.

Akaka Falls

Tucked away in a misty, fragrant rainforest, this dramatic 420-footer is one of Hawaii's most scenic waterfalls. You can reach it via an easy mile-long paved loop, which takes you past bamboo and flowering ginger and down to an observation point, where you'll have a perfect view. You'll also see nearby Kahuna Falls, which is a mere 100 feet tall. Be on the lookout for rainbows.

See map p. 366. At the end of Akaka Falls Road (Highway 220), Honomu (8 miles north of Hilo). To get there: From Highway 19, turn left at Honomu and head 3½ miles inland.

Hawaii Tropical Botanical Garden

This lush, Edenlike 40-acre valley makes a magical stop for horticultural buffs, or anybody who wants to experience the extraordinary flora of the Hawaiian Islands. The spectacular collection of more than 2,000 species of tropical plants runs the gamut from delicate orchids to towering torch ginger to 100-year-old mango, coconut, and banyan trees, all of which thrive in the protected valley's rich volcanic soil. Stay for an hour or come to bask in the natural tranquility of the garden all day.

See map p. 366. On the 4-mile Scenic Route off Highway 19, Onomea Bay (8½ miles north of Hilo; look for the blue "4-MILE SCENIC ROUTE" sign on the ocean side of the highway). ☎ 808-964-5233. www.htbg.com. *Admission: $15 adults, $5 kids 6–16. Open: Daily 8:30 a.m.–5 p.m. (last admission is at 4 p.m.).*

Waipio Valley

This gorgeous tropical valley at the end of the road on the Hamakua Coast is very difficult to reach, which is precisely what makes it so spectacular. From the black-sand bay at its mouth, remote Waipio sweeps back 6 breathtaking miles, boasting green-as-can-be taro patches rustling in the wind between sheer cliffs reaching almost a mile high.

You don't have to hike down into the remote valley to admire it. Just take Highway 19 to Honokaa and then turn onto the Kukuihaele Highway (Highway 240), which leads right to the **Waipio Valley Lookout.** This grassy park on the edge of Waipio Valley's sheer cliffs has splendid views of the luxuriantly green valley below. Featuring some old redwood picnic tables and rudimentary facilities, this is the ideal spot to unpack a picnic while you take in the magnificent view.

The more ambitious among you can hike down the paved path into the valley, or catch a ride with the **Waipio Valley Shuttle** (☎ **808-775-7121**), which offers a 90-minute narrated tour. The shuttle runs Monday through Saturday at 9 a.m., 11 a.m., 1 p.m., and 3 p.m. Tickets are $40 for adults, $20 for kids 4 to 11. Get your tickets at **Waipio Valley Artworks,** in Kukuihaele Village on Highway 240, 2 miles from the lookout (☎ **808-775-0958**).

You can also explore the valley aboard a mule-drawn wagon with **Waipio Valley Wagon Tours** (☎ **808-775-9518;** www.waipiovalleywagontours.com). This touristy 1½-hour tour is also fully narrated and departs from the Last Chance Store. Tours are offered Monday through Saturday at 9:30 a.m., 11:30 a.m., 1:30 p.m., and 3:30 p.m. Tickets are $45 for adults, $23 for kids ages 3 to 12. If you want to explore the lush Waipio Valley on horseback, contact **Waipio Naalapa Stables** (☎ **808-775-0419**), which offers two-hour nose-to-tail trail rides daily (except Sunday) at 9:30 a.m.

and 1 p.m. Tickets are $78 per person, and you must be at least 8 years old. Tours leave from Waipio Valley Artworks.

 If you want to take one of the guided tours of the Waipio Valley, make advance reservations to avoid disappointment; call a week in advance to book a mule tour.

 Don't take your rental car down the steep road that leads into the Waipio Valley; you won't get back up the steeply graded hill. What's more, most rental-car contracts prevent it, so if you do get stuck, you'll also end up with a hefty tow bill (not to mention a wasted day).

Hilo

I love this pretty bayfront city and its wonderfully nostalgic atmosphere. Although Hilo is Hawaii's second-largest city (after Honolulu), it really feels like a sort of funky old plantation town. Some people, especially those who come to Hawaii to get away from gray skies, just don't understand Hilo's appeal. I've found that you have to be something of a retro-romantic to appreciate it.

Despite Hilo's reputation for rain, you may want to spend a couple of days here. Hilo is a good base from which to explore Hawaii Volcanoes National Park, which is only a 45-minute drive away (see Chapter 15 for accommodations recommendations). Hilo is also worthwhile for its interesting shopping opportunities. (See the section "Shopping the local stores," later in this chapter).

But even if you just drive through on your way to the national park, take a few minutes to cruise or stroll down **Banyan Drive,** the shady lane that curves along the waterfront, offering fabulous Hilo Bay views. (A number of the banyan trees along here were planted as saplings by such celebrities as Amelia Earhart and Babe Ruth.) If it's a clear day, take the short walk across the concrete arch bridge in front of the Hawaii Naniloa Hotel to **Coconut Island,** if only for a panoramic look at this pretty little city.

Also along Banyan Drive is **Liluokalani Gardens,** the largest formal Japanese garden this side of Tokyo. This 30-acre park, named for Hawaii's last monarch, Queen Liluokalani, is postcard-pretty, complete with bonsai, carp ponds, pagodas, and a moon gate bridge. It's free and open 24 hours, so stop by to spend a moment in old Japan.

The following are a handful of additional attractions you may want to seek out while you're in Hilo. If Hilo's charms win you over — and they just might — pick up a copy of the free *Explore Hilo* walking tour pamphlet, which is available all over town and the island. If, for some reason, you don't run across it, pick one up at the **Big Island Visitors Bureau** office at 250 Keawe St., at Haili Street, across from Pescatore's restaurant (☎ 808-961-5797; http://bigisland.gohawaii.com). You can also stop by the **Downtown Hilo Improvement Association,** 252 Kamehameha Ave., Hilo (☎ 808-935-8850; www.downtownhilo.com) for a copy of its very informative self-guided walking tour of 18 historic sites.

Hilo

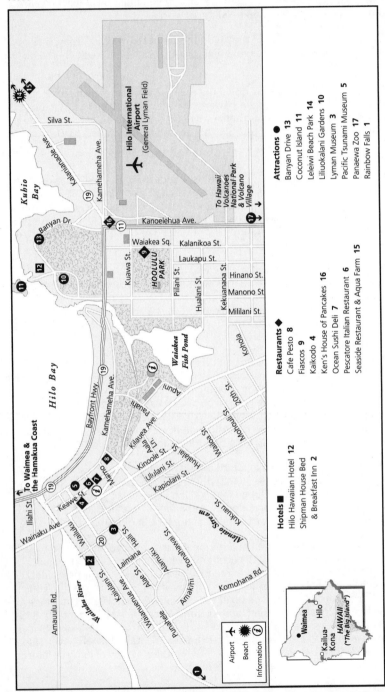

Attractions ●

Banyan Drive **13**
Coconut Island **11**
Leleiwi Beach Park **14**
Liliuokalani Gardens **10**
Lyman Museum **3**
Pacific Tsunami Museum **5**
Panaewa Zoo **17**
Rainbow Falls **1**

Restaurants ◆

Cafe Pesto **8**
Fiascos **9**
Kaikodo **4**
Ken's House of Pancakes **16**
Ocean Sushi Deli **7**
Pescatore Italian Restaurant **6**
Seaside Restaurant & Aqua Farm **15**

Hotels ■

Hilo Hawaiian Hotel **12**
Shipman House Bed
& Breakfast Inn **2**

Lyman Museum

Comprised of two major exhibit halls and a historic missionary home, this museum should be high on the priority list for culture and history buffs. The first-rate Earth Heritage and Island Heritage galleries tell the islands' native natural and cultural story; other permanent collections include notable collections of Hawaiian and Chinese art. Next door is the fully restored 1839 home of David and Sarah Lyman, a hybrid New England/ Hawaiian-style house — the oldest wooden house on the island — that perfectly exemplifies missionary times, which transformed Hawaii permanently and served as the foundation for the unique east-meets-west island culture that prevails today. No other site in Hawaii tells the story so well. Excellent guided tours of the Lyman Mission House are offered at 10 and 11 a.m. and 1, 2, and 3 p.m.

See map p. 398. 276 Haili St. (at Kapiolani Street), Hilo. ☎ *808-935-5021.* www. lymanmuseum.org. *Admission: $7 adults, $5 seniors, $3 kids. Open: Mon–Sat 9 a.m.–4:30 p.m.*

Pacific Tsunami Museum

This compelling small museum and education center chronicles the tsunamis (tidal waves) that devastated — and subsequently reshaped — Hilo in 1946 and 1960. Exhibits that tell both scientific and personal stories are on hand; some of the guides are even survivors, with their own tales to tell. The museum is well worth an hour or 45 minutes of your time.

See map p. 398. 130 Kamehameha Ave., downtown Hilo. ☎ *808-935-0926.* www. tsunami.org. *Admission: $7 adults, $6 children and seniors, $2 students. Open: Mon–Sat 10 a.m.–4 p.m.*

Panaewa Rainforest Zoo

This cute-as-a-button 12-acre rainforest zoo — the only tropical rainforest zoo in the United States — is a good bet if you have little ones in tow. Some 50 species of birds, reptiles, and mammals are on hand, from Hawaiian owls to Bengal tigers.

See map p. 398. On Stainback Highway (off Highway 11), Panaewa (just south of Hilo). ☎ *808-959-7224.* www.hilozoo.com. *Admission: Free! Open: Daily 9 a.m.–4 p.m. except Christmas and New Year's Day. Petting zoo open Saturday 1:30–2:30 p.m. Tiger feeding 3:30 p.m. daily.*

Rainbow Falls

This 80-footer isn't quite as towering or dramatic as Akaka Falls (see the section "The Hamakua Coast," earlier in this chapter), but the sight of the waterfall spilling into a pool surrounded by wild ginger is just lovely. Go in the morning, around 9 or 10 a.m., to see Rainbow Falls at its best.

See map p. 398. On Waianuenue Avenue (Highway 200), Hilo. To get there: Follow Bayfront Highway (Highway 19) to Waianuenue Avenue and turn inland; the falls are on the right past the Kaumana Drive intersection.

Hitting the links

The Kohala Coast is home to the finest golf courses on the Big Island, and among them are some of the finest golf challenges in the world. This vast island boasts far more golfing opportunities than I can list here; if you want more options, either on this coast or elsewhere around the island, contact the **Big Island Visitors Bureau** (☎ **808-886-1655** on the Kohala Coast, or 808-961-5797 in Hilo; http://bigisland.gohawaii.com).

The **Golf Hawaii Card** (www.hawaiigolfdeals.com) costs $60 annually, but can pay for itself in just one or two visits to participating courses. Nine courses on the Big Island alone offer significantly lower rates for cardholders, including Hapuna, Mauna Kea, the two Waikoloa courses, Big Island Country Club, and Waikoloa Village Golf Club.

Probably the best golf course on the Big Island is the Hualalai Golf Course at the Four Seasons Resort Hualalai. Many duffers in the know consider it the finest course in the state. Unfortunately, you have to be a resort guest to play it, but for the committed, this Jack Nicklaus–designed championship course is reason enough to pay the sky-high room rates. It also happens to be the finest contemporary luxury resort hotel in all Hawaii, if you ask me; see Chapter 15.

Book your tee times well in advance, especially in high season.

Big Island Country Club

The island's newest course is this 6,114-yard Pete and Perry Dye design, situated at 2,500 feet elevation above the Kohala Coast, offering welcome relief from the perennially hot coastal weather. Seven water features come into play along this popular, immaculately kept, dramatically situated, and justifiably popular course. The mountain and ocean views are incredible. An excellent bargain on a pricey golf coast.

See map p. 366. 71-1420 Mamalahoa Hwy. (Highway 190), near Waikoloa Road ☎ *808-325-5044. Greens fees: $85, $55 after 11 a.m. With Golf Hawaii Card, fees are $50 before 11 a.m. and $40 afterward.*

Hapuna Golf Course

This 6,029-yard links-style championship course is widely considered one of Arnold Palmer and Ed Seay's finest courses. Boasting indigenous vegetation and a design that blends seamlessly with the surrounding landscape, it has been honored as Most Environmentally Sensitive Course by *Golf Magazine* and Course of the Future by the U.S. Golf Association. The course extends from the coastline to 700 feet above sea level, with pastoral mountain scenery to one side and sweeping ocean views on the other. The elevation changes keep play challenging, as do the higher-elevation winds and a series of daunting bunkers. Facilities include a practice green, driving range, pro shop, restaurant, and fitness center.

See map p. 366. Adjacent to the Westin Hapuna Beach Prince, 62-100 Kauanoa Dr. (off Highway 19 near mile marker 69). ☎ ***808-880-3000** or 808-880-1111.* www.hapuna beachprincehotel.com. *Greens fees: $145 ($110 for hotel guests); $75 with Golf Hawaii Card. Twilight rates available seasonally for tee times after 1 p.m.*

Mauna Kea Golf Course

This 6,365-yard Robert Trent Jones, Sr., grande dame has been around since 1964, but it's still at the top of its game — just ask the editors of *Hawaii* magazine, who recently named it the second-best course in the state (after the Kiele Course at Kauai Lagoons; see Chapter 18). Its combination of breathtaking natural beauty, stunning oceanfront setting, and championship-level challenge make it one of Trent Jones' finest designs anywhere, and one of the best courses in the state. Expect undulating greens, more than 100 well-placed bunkers, and dramatic changes in elevation. The signature hole is the 3rd, a par-3 shocker with 200 yards of ocean standing between tee and green, which the legendary architect called his favorite hole of all time. Facilities include practice green, driving range, lockers and showers, pro shop, and restaurant.

See map p. 366. In the Mauna Kea resort, 62-100 Mauna Kea Beach Dr. (off Highway 19). ☎ ***808-882-5400** or 808-882-7222.* www.maunakeabeachhotel.com/ MKB/golf. *Greens fees: $195 ($130 for hotel guests). Twilight rates available seasonally for tee times after 1 p.m.*

Mauna Lani Frances H. I'i Brown Courses

Carved out of rugged black lava flows, both of these 6,335-yard championship courses are real winners. You'll really know that you're playing Big Island golf here; as a matter of fact, the dramatic oceanfront South Course is so otherworldly that it looks like it might be set on the moon. Long home to the Senior Skins Game, it's one of Hawaii's most difficult golf challenges and boasts an unforgettable ocean hole, the 221-yard, par-3 7th. The intense drama of the seasoned North Course is toned down by its rolling greens and wealth of old-growth greenery, which gives it a Scottish feel; don't be surprised if you have to wait for feral goats to clear the fairways before you take your shot. Facilities include two driving ranges, putting green, pro shop with rentals, restaurant, and on-course refreshment carts; pro-instructed golf clinics are available.

In the Mauna Lani resort, 68-150 Hoohana St. (off Highway 19). ☎ ***808-885-6655**.* www.maunalani.com. *Greens fees: $185 ($120 for resort guests); twilight rates $75 (times vary).*

Waikoloa Golf Club

You have two spectacular courses to choose from here: The beautiful, sporty par-70, 5,958-yard Beach Course is dramatically set in the lava, and it reflects designer Robert Trent Jones, Jr.'s, motto: "Hard par, easy bogey." Most golfers remember the par-5, 505-yard 12th hole, a sharp dogleg with bunkers in the corner and an elevated tee surrounded by lava. Designed by Tom Weiskopf and Jay Morrish, the par-72, 7,074-yard Kings' Course is a links-style challenge — and a real shotmaker's course — with six major lakes and about 75 bunkers that often come into play thanks to ever-present trade winds. Facilities include golf shop, restaurant, practice facility, and golf academy.

See map p. 366. In the Waikoloa Resort, 18 miles north of Kona Airport. ☎ *877-924-5656 or 808-886-7888.* www.waikoloagolf.com. *Greens fees: $165 ($115 for Waikoloa resort guests); $75 with Golf Hawaii card; twilight rates after 2 p.m.*

Waikoloa Village Golf Club

This semiprivate course on the slopes of Mauna Kea is a real gem, worth seeking out for its beautiful views, great game, and relatively affordable fees. Robert Trent Jones, Jr., designed this 5,490-yard challenge (with a par 72 for each of the three sets of tees) with his trademark sandtraps, slick greens, and great fairways. Facilities include pro shop, putting and chipping greens, driving range, locker rooms with showers, restaurant, club rentals, and private instruction.

See map p. 366. On Waikoloa Road, Waikoloa Village (off Highway 19, 28 miles north of Kona Airport). To get there: Turn toward the mountain at the Waikoloa Road traffic light; go 6 miles up the mountain and turn left at Paniolo Drive and then take another immediate left onto Lua Kula. ☎ *808-883-9621. Greens fees: $100, $55 after 2 p.m. Golf Hawaii cardholders play for $55 before 11 a.m. and $40 after 11 a.m.*

Shopping the local stores

For such a rural island, the Big Island has a shockingly good shopping scene. Because the island is home to Hawaii's greatest stores of natural materials, Big Island–based artists and artisans generate some of the best art and crafts in Hawaii, from traditional *Lauhala* weaving (rare to find) to gorgeous koa-wood gifts. But you need to know where to look, because if you don't venture past Kailua-Kona, you'll think that all this island has to sell is blatant tourism.

Kailua-Kona and South Kona

Kailua-Kona is a carnival of T-shirts, tacky trinkets, and silly souvenirs, with a little beachwear and a few quality gift items thrown into the mix for good measure. **Alii Drive** is the heart of the action; all you need to do is start at one end and browse. The best of what's to offer can be found at the **Kona Inn Shopping Village,** in the heart of town on the ocean side of the road, where one standout among the 50-plus shops is the **Honolua Surf Co.** (☎ 808-329-1001; www.honoluasurf.com), which has my favorite surf wear in the islands.

If you're looking for an offbeat beach read, head to the **Middle Earth Book Shoppe,** tucked away on the inland side of the street at 75-5179 Alii Dr. (☎ 808-329-2123).

Hilo Hattie, Hawaii's biggest name in aloha wear, has an outpost in Kailua-Kona at 75-5597A Palani Rd. (at Kuakini Highway, next to Burger King; ☎ 808-329-7200; www.hilohattie.com). Hilo Hattie is geared to the tourist market, carrying inexpensive, colorful wear that has improved in quality and style in recent years, plus a wide selection of souvenirs like macadamia nuts, Hawaii-grown coffees, and groovy Hawaiian-print seat covers. It's a good stop for gifts.

Farther south on Highway 11, in the Kealakekua area, is **Peavian Logic,** 79-7491 Mamalahoa Hwy. (☎ 808-324-4000), a worthwhile stop for unusual gifts, cards, clothing, and more.

Upcountry Kona: Holualoa

One of my favorite places to shop in all Hawaii is the artsy, funky Upcountry village of Holualoa, sitting 1,400 feet above Kailua-Kona on the slopes of Hualalai mountain. To get there, head south from Palani Road on Highway 11; turn up the mountain at the clearly marked Hualalai Road turnoff. The curving 3-mile drive up the mountain takes about ten minutes; after you reach the top, turn left on Mamalahoa Highway, the coffee country town's gallery-lined main street.

The first shop you'll reach, even before you make the turn onto Mamalahoa Highway, is **Kimura's Lauhala Shop** (☎ 808-324-0053), where the dying Hawaiian art of *Lauhala* weaving still thrives, thanks to Kimura's group of weavers. Look carefully, however, to separate the island-made crafts from the increasing number of Polynesian imports.

Farther along Mamalahoa Highway, the highlights include the **Holualoa Gallery** (☎ 808-322-8484; www.lovein.com/holualoagalleryblue. htm), which showcases original works by a bevy of local fine painters, sculptors, photographers, and jewelers. The **Ululani Gallery** (☎ 808-640-8822; www.ululani.com) specializes in top-quality original works and lithos, while the **Studio 7 Gallery** (☎ 808-324-1335), a wonderful multiroomed Japanese-style gallery, showcases prints, sculpture, multimedia art, jewelry, and gorgeous pottery and crafts, all with the signature Asian simplicity of artist Hiroki Morinoue.

Probably my favorite gallery in a sea of terrific ones is **Dovetail Gallery and Design** (☎ 808-322-4046), a gorgeous plantation-style building housing a well-curated collection of the island's most exceptional crafts, from hand-turned bowls of rare island woods and hand-painted silks to jewelry, wood cuts, and much, much more. Nearby is the **Holualoa Ukulele Gallery** (☎ 808-324-4100). Another worthwhile stop is the **Hawaii Colors Gallery** (☎ 808-324-1590; www.hawaiicolors. com), which features the bold and insightful paintings of artist Darrell Hill, plus some strikingly original print sundresses. Another notable gallery focused on the bold tropical-themed works of a local artist is the **Shelly Maudsley White Gallery** (☎ 808-322-5220; www.shelly maudsleywhite.com).

If all this top-quality shopping makes you hungry, stop into the **Holuakoa Café** (☎ 808-322-2233). This easygoing spot offers well-prepared sandwiches and salads, plus tropical smoothies made from fresh island fruit and 100 percent Kona joe grown on these local slopes.

North Kohala

If you're interested in high-quality Hawaiian crafts, especially those made of gorgeous island woods — of which native koa wood is the most highly prized — head up the Akoni Pule Highway (Highway 270) to the North Kohala towns of **Hawi** (HA-vee) and **Kapaau** (ka-PA-ow), both of which are worth browsing. All the stops are right along the highway.

As you shop around the islands, you'll see gorgeous koa wood boxes, vessels, furniture, and accessories in finer galleries. Prices are high (a small keepsake box can easily run more than $100) thanks to a quickly diminishing supply of the wood. The Big Island has the finest koa craftsmen, as it's home to the largest existing stand of koa.

If you don't mind shelling out big bucks for heirloom-quality crafts carved from koa and other woods by Hawaii's best master carvers and woodworkers, visit the **Ackerman Gallery** in Kapaau (☎ 808-889-5971; www.ackermangalleries.com). Boasting the best selection of woodcrafts in the islands, as well as Gary Ackerman's own Impressionist-style paintings, it's worth a look even if you can't buy. The second location, a little farther up the street across from the King Kamehameha Statue, is a lovely gift gallery with more affordable wood crafts, plus home accessories and jewelry. (I bought a string of Hawaii-strung Japanese black pearls on my last visit.)

Another excellent stop in Kapaau is the **Kohala Book Shop,** 54-3885 Akoni Pule Hwy. (☎ 808-889-6400; www.kohalabooks.com), Hawaii's largest used bookstore and one of the most browsable book shops in the islands, featuring everything from rare out-of-print editions to new books by Hawaii authors to gently used beach reads.

Waimea

My favorite stop in Waimea is the **Mauna Kea Galleries,** 65-1298 Kawaihae Rd., Waimea (across from Edelweiss restaurant; ☎ 877-969-HULA or 808-887-2244; www.maunakeagalleries.com), which boasts a wonderful collection of vintage Hawaiiana prints, photos, and other collectibles, many of them surprisingly affordable (expect to pay a bundle for vintage koa, however — you will anywhere).

Hilo

Boasting an appealing mix of fine and funky shops, this charming old Hawaii city is a wonderful place to browse. Shopping is centered in the wooden storefronts along oceanfront Kamehameha Avenue, on Keawe Avenue one parallel block inland, and on the side streets in between. Note that many of Hilo's shops are closed on Sunday, so plan accordingly.

If you want to come home with just one article of aloha wear, buy it at **Sig Zane,** 122 Kamehameha Ave. (☎ **808-935-7077**), whose distinctive, two-color all-cotton aloha wear is the height of simple style and good taste. The stunningly beautiful fabrics are sold in a variety of clean-lined, easy-to-wear styles, and even off the bolt if you want to take some home. Best of all, you won't look at a Sig Zane shirt or dress after you get home and say, "What was I *thinking*?" My husband and I receive regular compliments on the mainland for our Sig Zane wear; I can't recommend this marvelous shop enough.

Aloha-wear queen **Hilo Hattie** has a second Big Island outpost at Prince Kuhio Plaza, 111 E. Puainako St., at Highway 11 in Hilo (☎ **808-961-3077;** www.hilohattie.com) — but if you're going to buy aloha wear while you're in Hilo, you might as well do it at Sig Zane.

Basically Books, 160 Kamehameha Ave. (☎ **800-903-MAPS** or 808-961-0144; www.basicallybooks.com), is your stop for all kinds of Hawaii books and maps. Other Hilo favorites include **Hana Hou,** 164 Kamehameha Ave. (☎ **808-935-4555**), for an eye-catching collection of Hawaii-style gifts, both vintage and new, precious and affordable; and **Dragon Mama,** 266 Kamehameha Ave. (☎ **808-934-9081;** www.dragonmama.com), for gorgeous Asian homewares and textiles, from tatami mats to buckwheat pillows to antique kimonos (which you can wear as an elegant robe, or transform into gorgeous silk pillows and throws) — and much more, all gorgeous.

In the Volcano area

On Highway 11, the road from Hilo to Volcano, you'll find **Dan De Luz Woods** just past mile marker 12 (take the first right past the mile marker; ☎ **808-935-5587**), where the master bowl turner creates gorgeous works in koa, sandalwood, mango, and other island woods.

While you're at Hawaii Volcanoes National Park, take a few minutes to stop into the **Volcano Art Center Gallery,** next to the Kilauea Visitor Center (☎ **808-967-7565;** www.volcanoartcenter.org), a marvelous showcase for some of the island's best artists and craftspeople, and a real delight to browse.

Living It Up after Dark

This marvelous island has a wealth of stuff to see and do — more than you can take in during the course of a single vacation, as you can see from this chapter — but it all tends to come to a screeching halt at sunset.

If you're staying on the west side of the island, make sunset the highlight of your evening with a leisurely dinner at an oceanfront restaurant. The waterfront restaurants in Kailua-Kona all make great sunset perches, as do the Kohala Coast resorts, which offer beachfront spots for sunset cocktails and dinner. See Chapter 15 for recommendations. (Hint: Edward's at Kanaloa is ideal for South Kona romance, while Huggo's is the place to maximize in-town sunset fun.) The Hilton Waikoloa Beach's newly opened **Malolo Lounge** (☎ 808-886-1234; www.hiltonwaikoloavillage.com) is a wonderful setting for live Hawaiian music (5 to 9 p.m.) and jazz (9 p.m. to midnight) each night.

A top sunset draw on the Kona Coast is **Captain Beans' Polynesian Cruises** (☎ 800-831-5541 or 808-329-2955; www.robertshawaii.com). This two-hour sunset cruise sails from Kailua Pier nightly and features dinner, dancing, and a full-scale Polynesian revue aboard a 150-foot catamaran. It's really cheesy, but lots of fun nonetheless. Tickets are $52 to $62 per adult ($31 to $41 for kids 4 to 11) and include your meal, well cocktails, the show, and transportation to and from most hotels and condos on the Kona-Kohala coast. (Prices vary depending on the pickup point.)

You can save 10 percent by booking your Captain Beans cruise online.

Substantially less touristy are the sunset cruises that **Red Sail Sports** (☎ 877-RED-SAIL or 808-886-2876; www.redsailhawaii.com) operates aboard its 50-foot catamaran, the *Noa Noa,* from Anaehoomalu Bay at the Waikoloa resort on the Kohala Coast. The two-hour sail costs $53 to $59 for adults, $26 to $30 for kids 3 to 12, including appetizers and a full bar. An extra plus: You're likely to spot humpback whales in the winter whale-watching season. A Dinner Sail Cruise leaves at the same time and is a more few dollars.

For live music, a great choice is the **Blue Dolphin**, at the north end of the Kohala Coast in Kawaihae, 61-3616 Kawaihae Rd. (☎ 808-882-7771). This local favorite is a great place to hang out from Wednesday through Sunday, where the top-quality music ranges from jazz to rock, with a little karaoke and a few dance beats thrown in for good measure, depending on the evening; call to see what's on. Dinner is served.

The hottest dance club on the island is **Splash,** at the Hapuna Beach Prince Hotel, 62-100 Kaunaoa Dr. (☎ 808-880-1111), where a DJ spins hip-shaking tunes on Thursday (which is also Ladies' Night), and live bands keep the dance floor hopping on Friday and Saturday.

If you're looking for entertainment that's more culturally enriching, see what's on at the **Kahilu Theatre,** just a half-hour's drive from the Kohala Coast resorts on Highway 19 in Waimea (☎ 808-885-6868; www.kahilutheatre.org), the island's home for theater, live music, and the performing arts. Visiting artists come from all over the world to perform here, so the entertainment can range from local music masters the Brothers Cazimero (who are well worth catching) to the Aspen Santa Fe Ballet troupe to the St. Lawrence String Quartet to Bela Fleck and the Flecktones. There's also an artsy movie theater attached.

Of course, for the most animated after-dark entertainment, head to — you guessed it — a luau! The Big Island has an excellent Friday-night option; check out Chapter 15 for more information.

 If the volcano is acting up and you're staying on the east side of the island, it's the best show in town. Nighttime is the right time to see the lava pumping — so get yourself to Hawaii Volcanoes National Park and ask the rangers where's the best place for lava-watching. See the complete park section earlier in this chapter for details, including where to get the latest eruption reports.

Part VI
Kauai

THE ISLAND EXPERIENCE

Your glass of water...

In this part . . .

*W*ith its lush, tranquil landscapes, sleepy Kauai is simply one of the most beautiful places on earth. In these chapters, you discover everything this wonderful island has to offer, from pristine white sand beaches to dramatic seaside cliffs to gorgeous tropical gardens.

Chapter 17

Settling into Kauai

● ●

In This Chapter

▶ Landing at Lihue Airport and getting to your accommodations
▶ Figuring out your way around the island of Kauai
▶ Choosing among the island's top accommodations
▶ Discovering Kauai's best restaurants
▶ Arranging for a luau
▶ Using an easy-reference list of important local contacts

● ●

Kauai is an easygoing, and easily manageable, island. You'll need a rental car to get around, so plan on booking one before you arrive (see Chapter 7). No matter where you're coming from, you'll arrive at Kauai's Lihue (li-HOO-ay) Airport.

Arriving at Lihue Airport

Lihue Airport (☎ **808-246-1440** or 808-246-1448; www.hawaii.gov/dot/ airports/kauai/lih) sits on Kauai's east shore just north of Lihue town, at the end of Ahukini Road (east of Kuhio Highway). Lihue is served by four airlines: **United Airlines** and **American Airlines** from the mainland, and **Aloha Airlines** and **Hawaiian Airlines** with interisland service. In addition, some of the big packagers, such as Pleasant Hawaiian Holidays, offer direct charter service to Kauai.

Open-air Lihue Airport is very small and easy to negotiate. The major rental-car companies have counters directly across the street from the terminal (in the wooden hut), but due to increased airport security, you must now take a shuttle van offsite to pick up your car. All the rental-car agencies offer map booklets that are invaluable for getting around the island.

Getting from the Airport to Your Hotel

If you're heading to the Coconut Coast or the North Shore, turn right immediately out of the airport onto Kapule Highway (Highway 51), which eventually merges into Kuhio Highway (Highway 56) a mile down the road. Kuhio Highway leads to the Coconut Coast and the North

Kauai Orientation

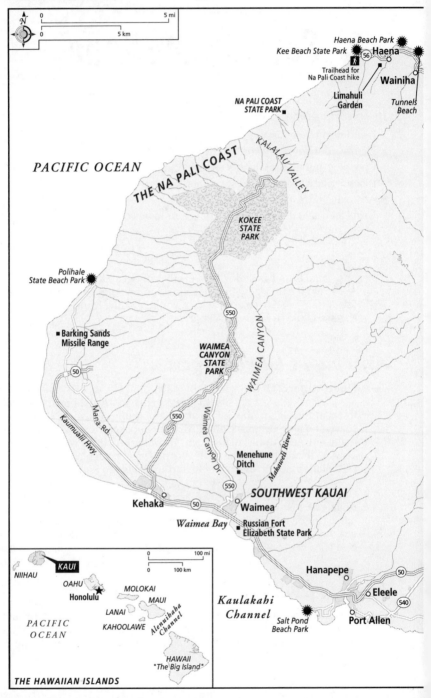

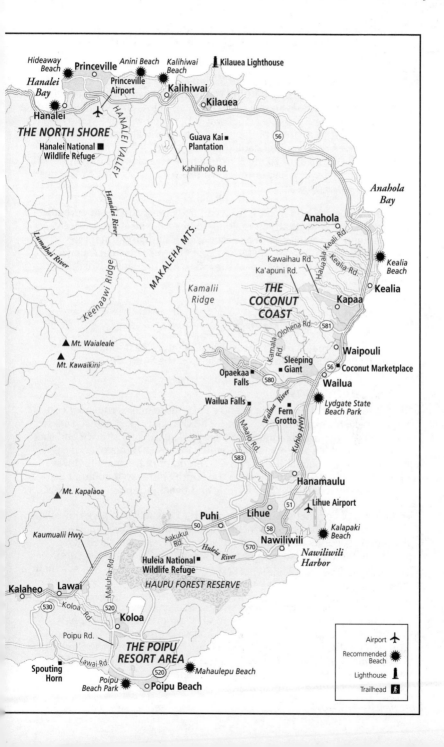

Hideaway Beach
Princeville
Anini Beach
Kalihiwai Beach
Kilauea Lighthouse
Hanalei Bay
Princeville Airport
Kalihiwai
Hanalei
Kilauea
THE NORTH SHORE
Hanalei National Wildlife Refuge
HANALEI VALLEY
Hanalei River
Lumahai River
Keenaawi Ridge
Guava Kai Plantation
Kahiliholo Rd.
56
Anahola Bay
Anahola
MAKALEHA MTS.
Kawaihau Rd.
Ka'apuni Rd.
Hauala Keali Rd.
Kealia Rd.
Kealia Beach
Kamalii Ridge
THE COCONUT COAST
Kapaa
Kealia
▲ Mt. Waialeale
▲ Mt. Kawaikini
Kamala Rd.
Olohena Rd.
581
Waipouli
Opaekaa Falls
Sleeping Giant
56
Coconut Marketplace
580
Wailua River
Wailua
Wailua Falls
Fern Grotto
Kuhio Hwy
Lydgate State Beach Park
Maalo Rd.
583
Hanamaulu
▲ Mt. Kapalaoa
51
Lihue Airport
Puhi
Lihue
50
58
Kalapaki Beach
Kaumualii Hwy.
Aakukui Rd.
570
Nawiliwili
Huleia River
Nawiliwili Harbor
Huleia National Wildlife Refuge
Maluhia Rd.
HAUPU FOREST RESERVE
Kalaheo
Lawai
530
Koloa Rd.
520
Koloa
Poipu Rd.
THE POIPU RESORT AREA
Lawai Rd.
Spouting Horn
520
Mahaulepu Beach
Poipu Beach Park
Poipu Beach

Airport ✈
Recommended Beach ✴
Lighthouse 🕯
Trailhead 🚶

Shore. Expect the trip to take 10 to 15 minutes if you're headed for the Coconut Coast, and about an hour if you're staying in Princeville or Hanalei on the North Shore.

If you're heading to Poipu Beach or Waimea, follow Ahukini Road out of the airport and turn left onto Kuhio Highway (Highway 56), which will take you through Lihue. Stay in the right lane; in less than a mile, merge right onto Kaumualii Highway (Highway 50), which will take you to the south and southwest areas of the island. The highway doesn't follow the coast, however, so if you're heading to Poipu, turn left on Maluhia Road (Highway 520); it's about 10 miles from where you picked up Highway 50. You can expect about a half-hour trip to reach Poipu; getting to Waimea takes 45 minutes or so.

If, for some reason, you don't have a car, taxis are available at curbside; however, if you know that you're going to need a taxi when you arrive, I recommend arranging one in advance with **Kauai Taxi Company** (☎ **808-246-9554**). Expect the fare to cost $32 to $37 to reach Poipu, $13 to $20 to reach the Coconut Coast, or $65 to $85 to reach a North Shore destination.

Choosing Your Location

Kauai has three major resort areas: The Coconut Coast, on the East Shore; the North Shore; and Poipu Beach, on the South Shore.

The Coconut Coast

Of all Kauai's resort areas, the island's East Shore makes the most convenient base for exploring the island. The Coconut Coast is just a 10- to 15-minute drive north of Lihue (li-HOO-ay), Kauai's largest town and the center of island life and commerce, which means that lots of conveniences are right at hand. It's also at the midpoint of the main highway, which connects the North Shore to the South Shore, so it couldn't be more centrally located for sightseeing and beach-hopping.

The groves of coconut trees that pepper the area lend it a nice Hawaiian vibe — some compensation for the minimalls that line the highway along here. A gorgeous mountain backdrop and leftover island-style plantation buildings also help to make what could have been a suburban-generic resort coast actually rather charming. And the region's main beach, Lydgate State Beach Park, is a winner.

This area is geared toward value-conscious travelers. Your accommodations choices here are mostly mid- and budget-priced family-friendly condos, so it's a good bet if you're in the market for a deal. However, although the East Shore doesn't get as much rain as the North Shore, it's not as consistently dry and sunny as the South Shore, either; in winter, you should expect a bit more rain than you might get in Poipu. Also expect more traffic and noise than what you'd find in Poipu.

The North Shore

Kauai's North Shore is as breathtaking as Hawaii gets. It boasts a string of stunning beaches; two charming towns for exploring, Hanalei and Kilauea; a sophisticated and well-manicured resort, Princeville, tucked away on a peninsula bluff so that you can enjoy it or ignore it as you see fit; lush fields of taro as far as the eye can see; and cliffs so beautiful that they starred as Bali Hai in the film version of *South Pacific*. Spend as much time up here as you can. No place on the island is as soothing to the spirit as this verdant, almost magical coast.

So why don't I tell everyone to stay up here, you ask? First of all, the North Shore is quite removed; Lihue is a full hour's drive away. Second, the number of accommodation choices is limited. Third, the North Shore gets lots of rain, especially in winter. The rain is what keeps this coast so lush and stunning, but it can really put a damper on your vacation. Another turnoff is the winter surf, which can be too turbulent for most swimmers.

Still, the North Shore's stunning natural beauty more than makes up for its shortcomings, and I highly recommend staying up here. Your best bet is to come in summer or autumn, when the weather is usually excellent. Choose Princeville if you like world-class golf, spa offerings, and other modern amenities. But if you're turned off by manicured resort living, skip Princeville in favor of a B&B or vacation rental in island-charming Hanalei, Kileauea Anini Beach, or Haena.

The South Shore: Poipu Beach

Excellent year-round weather, great beaches, a wealth of ocean activities, terrific golf and tennis, and an easy-access location for both sight-seeing and airport convenience make Poipu Beach an excellent place to stay, and Kauai's all-around best choice in terms of convenience, climate, activities, and natural beauty. You can't go wrong here, no matter what your budget or what kind of accommodations you're looking for — whether luxury resort, oceanfront B&B, multibedroom vacation home, or bargain-priced condo.

The beach is particularly family-friendly, and the whole area is surprisingly relaxing considering its popularity. It's one of Hawaii's best resort developments, simply because it hasn't been overdeveloped — there's still plenty of open space to enjoy. And although Poipu may not be quite as breathtaking as the North Shore (what is?), its sunny, vibrant setting — red earth, lush greenery, turquoise waves, blond sand, clear blue skies — can hold its own in any natural-beauty category. The only marks in the negative column are the 1½-hour drive to the North Shore, and tiny Koloa, a one-horse plantation town that's a bit too ticky-tacky for its own good; still, it's so small that you can easily ignore it.

Farther afield: Kalaheo and Waimea

Just about a ten-minute drive inland and west from Poipu is Kalaheo, a nondescript but pleasantly quiet town offering some wallet-friendly accommodations for budget travelers who will also enjoy a more locals-only, nonresort location and affordable restaurants.

The southwest town of Waimea is a good 45 minutes from Lihue and nearly two hours from the North Shore. But it's worth mentioning not only because Waimea is sunny nearly year-round, but also because it's home to one of my favorite places to stay, a charming group of fully restored plantation-era beachfront cottages that will charm the pants off even the most committed modernist. These cottages are great for a family reunion or a get-away-from-it-all vacation. You should know, however, that you'll have to drive to the beach (the surf is rough at Waimea and isn't suitable for swimming), and you'll spend a lot of time in the car if you plan on exploring the island thoroughly. But one of the most beautiful spots on the island, Waimea Canyon, is nearby, as well as the departure point for most Na Pali cruises.

Getting Around Kauai

You pretty much have to drive yourself around Kauai. The island has a public transportation system, **Kauai Bus** (☎ **808-241-6410;** www.kauai gov.org/kauaibus.htm), but it operates a minimal fleet and is geared to serving locals, not visitors. It doesn't serve any of the resort areas, and you're not allowed to carry anything larger than a shopping bag onboard. Taxis are available (see Kauai Taxi, in the section "Getting from the Airport to Your Hotel," or the Fast Facts at the end of this chapter), but they're not really a viable means for regular transport, either.

Kauai is a compact island — only 25 miles long by 33 miles wide — and easy to negotiate. Still, it does take some time to get around because no roads cut through the middle of the island, and no road goes all the way around, thanks to the impassable Na Pali Coast at the northwest corner of the island.

The island has two major highways, each beginning in Lihue, Kauai's biggest town and commercial hub. They each run basically around the perimeter of the island — one north, one south — dead-ending at the Na Pali Coast on each side. The entire drive, from end to end, takes about three hours.

The two major highways are

✔ **Kuhio Highway** (Highway 56), which follows the coast north from Lihue, leading through the Coconut Coast communities of Wailua, Waipouli, and Kapaa (ka-PA-ah) to the North Shore, where it passes by charming Kilauea (turn at the Shell Station, where the sign says

"Kilauea Lighthouse," if you want to explore) and, 5 miles beyond, the carefully manicured Princeville resort. Then (31 miles and about an hour's drive beyond Lihue) Kuhio Highway runs directly through Hanalei (probably my favorite little town in all Hawaii) and Haena (less a town than a collection of homes and vacation rentals tucked away in the tropical brush) before dead-ending at Kee (KEH-eh) Beach, where the Na Pali Coast begins.

✔ **Kaumualii** (cow-moo-a-LEE-ee) **Highway** (Highway 50) heads south from Lihue, passing through the undistinguished towns of Kalaheo (ka-la-HAY-oh) and Hanapepe (ha-na-PAY-pay) before reaching the little cowboy town of Waimea (where you can pick up the road that climbs inward and upward to Waimea Canyon; see Chapter 18 for details); at this point, you will have traveled 23 miles, or about 45 minutes, west of Lihue. After Waimea, the road curves north again before winding up in the far west at Polihale (po-lee-HA-lay) Beach, dead-ending at the other side of the Na Pali Coast.

Highway 50 doesn't hug the coast like its northern counterpart — it runs roughly 4 miles inland until Hanapepe — so Maluhia Road (Highway 520) cuts south to reach Poipu (po-EE-poo) Beach, Kauai's most popular resort, about 10 miles west of Lihue.

Kauai doesn't have what you'd call traffic, especially compared with places like Los Angeles (or even Honolulu, for that matter). Still, because the main highways have only one lane traveling in each direction, traffic can bottleneck in certain spots, especially along the Coconut Coast, largely from drivers turning in and out of the minimalls and shops that line that stretch of highway.

What's more, the roads are curvy (especially after you start heading toward the North Shore), and the speed limit doesn't top 50 mph anywhere on the island. So don't let the short distances fool you; it *will* take a full hour to reach the North Shore from Lihue, and 20 minutes or so longer if you're traveling the additional 8 miles beyond Hanalei. Allow 1½ hours to reach Hanalei from Poipu.

Kauai boasts fewer accommodations choices than its three big-sister islands, and only a handful of full-fledged resorts. But it does offer condos in every price range, some fine B&Bs (including one of Hawaii's very few oceanfront B&Bs), and even a complex of historic plantation cottages that are ideal for both families and lovers of vintage style.

Rates tend to be pretty reasonable on Kauai; in fact, this island features some of Hawaii's best lodging values. Still, Kauai is an increasingly popular destination, and travelers are booking rooms earlier and earlier each year. So try to reserve your accommodations as soon as possible to avoid missing out on your first choice.

Staying In Style

Remember that you almost never need to pay the asking price for a hotel room. Check out Chapter 8 for details on how to avoid paying for full-price hotel rooms. Also see Chapter 6 for advice on how to score an all-inclusive package that can save you big bucks on both accommodations and airfare, and sometimes car rentals and activities, too.

Also, don't forget that pesky 11.42 percent in taxes that the state adds to your hotel bill.

You may also want to check with **Hawaii Beachfront Vacation Homes** (☎ **808-247-3637;** www.hibeach.com).

Kauai's best accommodations

In the following listings, each property is followed by a number of dollar signs, ranging from one ($) to five ($$$$$). Each represents the median rack-rate price range for a double room per night, as follows:

$	Super-cheap — less than $100 per night
$$	Still affordable — $100 to $175
$$$	Moderate — $175 to $250
$$$$	Expensive but not ridiculous — $250 to $375
$$$$$	Ultraluxurious — more than $375 per night

Aloha Beach Resort
$$$ Coconut Coast

With a wonderful beachfront location, pleasantly outfitted rooms, lots of amenities (including a minifridge, coffeemaker, and Sony Playstation in every room), and a well-rounded kids' program, this former Holiday Inn resort is under new management. It remains a good choice for families, or anybody looking for a reasonably priced vacation, for that matter. What the resort lacks in personality it makes up in moderate prices and excellent amenities. It fronts Lydgate Beach, the best beach on the Coconut Coast, which has a playground and a protected natural pool that's ideal for young swimmers and first-time snorkelers. On-site extras include two pools, a Jacuzzi, and a coin-op laundry. The regular doubles are on the small side, so book a suite (with pullout sofa), or a freestanding family-size villa (with queen sleeper sofa in the living room and a kitchenette with a microwave and a toaster) if you're traveling with the kids; if you need to stick with a standard room to meet your budget, one with two queens (rather than two doubles) gives you more elbow room. Children under age 19 stay free, and kids under 12 eat dinner free — that's right, free — when dining with Mom and Dad and ordering off the *keiki* menu.

See map p. 420. 3-5920 Kuhio Hwy., Kapaa. ☎ ***800-HOLIDAY**, 888-823-5111, or 808-823-6000. Fax: 808-823-6666.* www.alohabeachresort.com. *Parking: Free! Rack rates: $198–$230 room for up to 4; $260 suite for up to 4; $365 2-room cottage.*

Deals: Family, romance, and other promotional packages regularly available (at press time, an oceanview room for 2 was $150 per night, including breakfast). Discounts available for AAA and AARP members and government employees. AE, DC, DISC, MC, V.

Aston Islander on the Beach
$$ Coconut Coast

This pleasant, recently renovated plantation-style beachfront hotel complex is a great choice for value-minded travelers, especially if you can score one of the many packages and discounts that are usually offered. (They're pretty easy to come by.) The rooms are motel-like, but they're fresh, attractive, and boast pretty textiles, firm beds, minifridges, and coffeemakers. (The oceanfront rooms have microwaves, too.) The nicely maintained property has a good swimming beach, a smallish pool and a hot tub, barbecue grills, and a coin-op laundry; the Coconut Marketplace is just a stone's throw away. The only downside? Bad lanai furniture. And some of the rooms labeled "oceanview" are a stretch, so beware.

See map p. 420. 484 Kuhio Hwy., Kapaa. ☎ *800-922-7866 or 808-822-7417. Fax: 808-822-1947.* www.aston-hotels.com. *Parking: Free! Rack rates: $151–$208 double, $255 junior suite. Deals: Excellent opportunities for discounts. Internet-only ePriceBreaker rates as low as $99 at press time. Ask for AAA, senior (50-plus), and corporate discounts, and other special rate programs, plus packages that include airfare. AE, DC, DISC, MC, V.*

Classic Vacation Cottages
$ Kalaheo

If you don't mind staying a bit off the beaten path, you'll love the incredible value that these five lovely units offer. They're located in the perfectly nice suburban town of Kalaheo, ten minutes from Poipu Beach, and range in size from a basic studio to a spacious house that can accommodate six. Each features hardwood floors, stained-glass windows, attractive furnishings, full kitchen facilities (with microwave, coffeemaker, toaster, and so on), a lanai, and cable TV (no phones in units, though). My favorites are the two one- and two-bedroom garden cottages, although the studios are fine for two. On-site is a Jacuzzi, plus all the free beach gear and recreational equipment that you may need (even snorkel gear, coolers, tennis rackets, and golf clubs). Many fans consider the tranquil and pretty location to be a boon rather than a disadvantage. Guests have unlimited access to the Kiahuna Tennis and Swim Club in Poipu, and $7 greens fees and spectacular ocean views make the nearby Kukuiolono Golf Course a real hidden gem. Hiking trails begin right at the end of the driveway.

See map p. 420. 2687 Onu Place, Kalaheo. ☎ *808-332-9201. Fax: 808-332-7645.* www.classiccottages.com. *Parking: Free! Rack rates: $50–$90 studio, $75–$120 1- or 2-bedroom cottage, $100–$150 house. All rates based on double occupancy; $10 for each extra person. Deals: Ask about discounted rental-car rates. No credit cards.*

Kauai's Accommodations

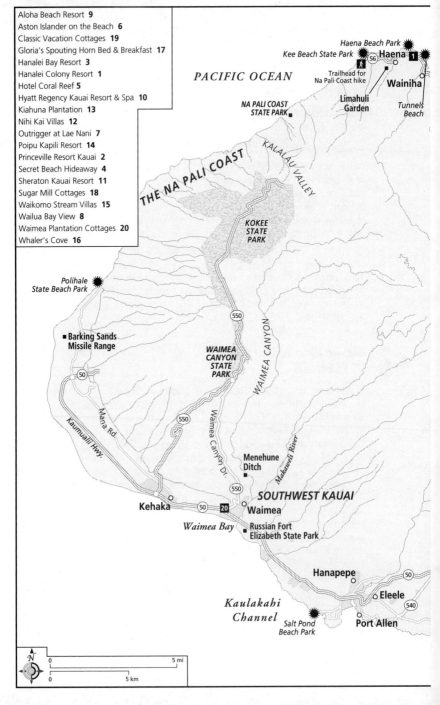

Aloha Beach Resort **9**
Aston Islander on the Beach **6**
Classic Vacation Cottages **19**
Gloria's Spouting Horn Bed & Breakfast **17**
Hanalei Bay Resort **3**
Hanalei Colony Resort **1**
Hotel Coral Reef **5**
Hyatt Regency Kauai Resort & Spa **10**
Kiahuna Plantation **13**
Nihi Kai Villas **12**
Outrigger at Lae Nani **7**
Poipu Kapili Resort **14**
Princeville Resort Kauai **2**
Secret Beach Hideaway **4**
Sheraton Kauai Resort **11**
Sugar Mill Cottages **18**
Waikomo Stream Villas **15**
Wailua Bay View **8**
Waimea Plantation Cottages **20**
Whaler's Cove **16**

PACIFIC OCEAN

Haena Beach Park
Kee Beach State Park
Haena
Wainiha
Trailhead for
Na Pali Coast hike
56
1
NA PALI COAST
STATE PARK
Limahuli
Garden
Tunnels
Beach

THE NA PALI COAST
KALALAU VALLEY

KOKEE
STATE
PARK

Polihale
State Beach Park

550

Barking Sands
Missile Range

WAIMEA
CANYON
STATE
PARK

WAIMEA CANYON

50

550

Mana Rd.

Kaumualii Hwy.

Waimea Canyon Dr.

Makaweli River

Menehune
Ditch

550

SOUTHWEST KAUAI

Kehaka
50
20
Waimea

Waimea Bay
Russian Fort
Elizabeth State Park

Hanapepe

Eleele
540

Kaulakahi
Channel

Salt Pond
Beach Park

Port Allen

50

N
0   5 mi
0   5 km

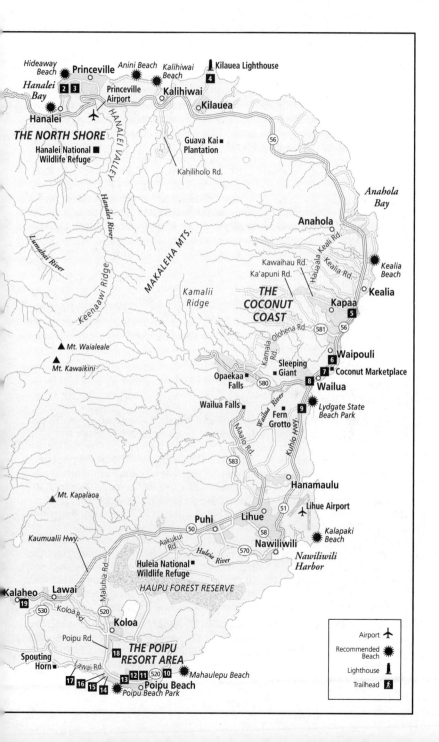

Hideaway
Beach

Princeville

Anini Beach

Kalihiwai
Beach

Kilauea Lighthouse

*Hanalei
Bay*

2 3

Princeville
Airport

Kalihiwai

4

Hanalei

Kilauea

THE NORTH SHORE

Hanalei National ■
Wildlife Refuge

HANALEI VALLEY

Guava Kai ■
Plantation

Kahiliholo Rd.

56

Hanalei River

Lumahai River

*Anahola
Bay*

Anahola

Hauala Keali Rd.

Kawaihau Rd.

Ka'apuni Rd.

*Kamalii
Ridge*

Kealia
Beach

Kealia Rd.

**THE
COCONUT
COAST**

Kapaa

Kealia

5

Keenaawi Ridge

MAKALEHA MTS.

▲ Mt. Waialeale

▲
Mt. Kawaikini

Kamalii Rd.

Olohena Rd.

581

56

6 Waipouli

7 Coconut Marketplace

Sleeping
■ Giant

Opaekaa ■
Falls

580

8 Wailua

Wailua River

Wailua Falls ■

Maalo Rd.

Fern
Grotto

9

Lydgate State
Beach Park

Kuhio Hwy.

583

Hanamaulu

51

Lihue Airport

Mt. Kapalaoa ▲

Puhi

50

Lihue

58

Kalapaki
Beach

Kaumualii Hwy.

Aakukui
Rd.

Huleia River

570

Nawiliwili

*Nawiliwili
Harbor*

Huleia National ■
Wildlife Refuge

HAUPU FOREST RESERVE

Kalaheo

19

Lawai

530

Koloa Rd.

Maluhia Rd.

520

Koloa

Poipu Rd.

18

Spouting
Horn ■

Lawai Rd.

**THE POIPU
RESORT AREA**

17 **16** **15** **14**

13 **12** **11** 520 **10** Mahaulepu Beach

Poipu Beach

Poipu Beach Park

Airport ✈

Recommended ✴
Beach

Lighthouse 🅸

Trailhead 🚶

Gloria's Spouting Horn Bed & Breakfast
$$$$ Poipu Beach

Attention, romance-seeking couples: You'll be hard-pressed to do better than Gloria's, one of Hawaii's very few oceanfront B&Bs — and among its finest. The inn is located right at water's edge, on a simply stunning stretch of Kauai's sunny South Shore: Red earth, lush greenery, golden sand, white-capped waves, and brilliant blue sky all come together in a perfect marriage of nature's most vivid hues. The very friendly and accomplished innkeepers, Gloria and Bob Merkle, welcome guests (mostly youngish, active couples) into their attractive and comfortable home, which offers three well-stocked, well-furnished, and ultraromantic guest rooms. Each has a wet bar with fridge, coffeemaker, and blender; a VCR; a private lanai overlooking the surf and the solar-heated pool at ocean's edge; and a Japanese-style soaking tub in the bath. Breakfasts are elaborate buffet affairs, sunset is celebrated nightly with an open bar and *pupu* (appetizers), and snacks are out all day — you won't go hungry here. Other appealing perks include a video library, an oceanfront hammock for lazy days, and a lava-rock outdoor shower beneath a leafy mango tree. It's worth every penny, and people know it, so book as far in advance as possible.

See map p. 420. 4464 Lawai Beach Rd. (just before Spouting Horn Park), Koloa. ☎/Fax: 808-742-6995. www.gloriasbedandbreakfast.com. *Parking: Free! Rack rates: $325 double ($400 at Christmas holidaytime, with 7-night minimum). Rates include full breakfast and afternoon drinks and all-day snacks. 3-night minimum. No credit cards.*

Hanalei Bay Resort
$$$ North Shore

This first-rate condo resort is an excellent North Shore choice. It overlooks the same fabled Bali Hai cliffs and gorgeous golden beach as the ritzy Princeville Resort (see the listing later in this chapter), but for a substantial savings, especially if you have the family in tow. The apartments are nicely done and boast plenty of room to spread out, plus rattan furnishings and big lanais. All but the most basic units are between 1,100 and 2,100 square feet and come with all the extras, including a fully outfitted kitchen, a washer/dryer, a VCR in the living room, an extra TV in every bedroom, and a nicely outfitted bathroom (with hair dryer, of course). The super-lush, terraced grounds feature two terrific freshwater pools, Jacuzzis, and tennis courts, plus easy beach access. The restaurant is just fine, and the lounge is a stellar place to sip a sunset cocktail. The solicitous staff will ferry you around via golf cart if the steep pathways are too much for you. The property is part timeshare, so beware, you will be invited to an "orientation" (read: sales) meeting, but you can easily ignore it.

See map p. 420. 5380 Honoiki Rd., Princeville. ☎ 800-827-4427 or 808-826-6522. Fax: 808-826-6680. www.hanaleibaykauai.com. *Parking: Free! Rack rates: $190–$285 double, $225–$250 studio with kitchenette, $360–$400 1-bedroom suite, $430–$735 2- or 3-bedroom suite. Suite rates include full breakfast and afternoon cocktails. Deals: Always ask about packages or other special offers (from $119 at press time). Also inquire about discounted greens fees at Princeville area golf courses. AE, DC, DISC,*

MC, V. **Aston Resorts units:** ☎ *800-922-7866.* www.aston-hotels.com. *Rack rates: $190–$285 double, $225–$250 studio with kitchenette, $360–$400 1-bedroom. Deals: Internet-only ePriceBreaker rates as low as $149 at press time. Ask for AAA, senior (50-plus), and corporate discounts, and other special rate programs, including packages with airfare. AE, DC, DISC, MC, V.*

Hanalei Colony Resort
$$$ North Shore

This small, quiet, low-rise condo resort is a pleasant and affordable place to stay if you're looking to experience Kauai's pristine North Shore in all its lush, end-of-the-road glory. It's well past Hanalei town, near the very end of the North Shore highway — perfect if you're looking to get away from it all, less than ideal if you're planning to do lots of exploring. The golden beach that fronts the property is okay, but some of Hawaii's best beaches and most celebrated stretches of sand are close by. Each of the spacious two-bedroom, one-bath apartments is simply but pleasantly furnished in island style and has a lanai, a complete kitchen, ceiling fans (air-conditioning isn't necessary), and mountain views that are just as fab as the ocean views. Twice-a-week maid service is included, and a coin-op laundry is on the premises. The atmosphere is quiet and relaxing — no TVs or phones to interfere with the waves and birdsong. Even the kids won't miss the TV; the resort has plenty of beach gear at hand, plus a pool, lawn and board games, and more to keep them happy. Beware: The nearest grocery store or restaurant is a 15-minute drive away, so stock up on staples. Not my absolute favorite place to stay on Kauai, but the accommodations are comfortable for families, and the price sure is right. The property is undergoing a big renovation, so ask whether any work will be underway when you plan to visit and expect a rate increase when fresh new amenities are in place.

See map p. 420. 5-7130 Kuhio Hwy., Haena (2 miles past Hanalei town, near the end of the road). ☎ *800-628-3004 or 808-826-6235. Fax: 808-826-9893.* www.hcr.com. *Parking: Free! Rack rates: $180–$225 2-bedroom/1-bath, $215–$335 2-bedroom/2-bath. 5-night minimum stay during summer and during Christmas holidays. Deals: Seventh night free; also ask about car-and-condo, honeymoon, and other package deals. AAA, government, senior, and return guests qualify for discounts. AE, MC, V.*

Hotel Coral Reef
$ Coconut Coast

If your wallet's thin but you're committed to staying right on the beach, here's your best choice. The Coral Reef is older and basic — nothing fancy — but the simple rooms are well maintained, the service is gracious, and the white-sand beach out front is gorgeous. The rooms in the main building are cheapest, but spend a bit more to stay in the oceanfront wing, which offers the kind of views that usually come with a much, much higher price tag. Rooms have most of the basics: private bath, TV, ceiling fans, daily maid service, but no phones. Oceanfront rooms also have minifridges. On-site amenities include barbecue grills and picnic tables, a coin-op laundry, complimentary morning coffee, and beach mats and coolers for your use. There's good snorkeling out front, plus an 8-mile bike path that leaves right from the grounds. You'll be within walking distance of shops and restaurants.

See map p. 420. 1516 Kuhio Hwy., Kapaa. ☎ *800-843-4659 or 808-822-4481. Fax: 808-822-7705.* www.hotelcoralreef.com. *Parking: Free! Rack rates: $59–$110 double or suite. Deals: Ask about room/car packages and discounted senior rates. MC, V.*

Hyatt Regency Kauai Resort & Spa
$$$$$ Poipu Beach

I have one big complaint about this hotel: I never get to stay here. It's always too full of contented vacationers who adore the high plantation style, the easygoing vibe, the big and beautiful rooms, the excellent service, and the pleasingly sunny South Shore location. The facilities are first-rate — especially the sigh-inducing, open-air 25,000-foot Anara Spa, one of the two best spas in the state, which is looking better than ever following a million-dollar facelift in 2003. One of Hawaii's best luxury hotels, the Hyatt is fabulous in an understated way; everyone feels comfortable here. The most distant guest rooms are a good five-minute hike from the lobby, but are oversized, elegant rooms with rich wood furnishings, well-chosen tropical fabrics, luxurious marble baths, and spacious lanais (most with ocean views). Every unit was renovated in 2003, with brand-new bedding and linens, new lanai furniture, and lovely new bathroom fixtures. Because the ocean is rough here, the gorgeously landscaped grounds boast a mega-pool complex that's a total blast without being over the top, plus five acres of swimming lagoons (with islands and a man-made beach) that are perfect for learning to kayak.

The restaurants and lounges are elegant and satisfying across the board, particularly Dondero's for Italian, Tidepools for romantic open-air Pacific Rim-style dining, and the first-rate cafe for stellar morning smoothies. The kids' program is terrific, including evening "camp" sessions that allow Mom and Dad to enjoy a romantic dinner alone. The fitness center offers a good selection of equipment, plus an array of free classes. Next door is the Robert Trent Jones, Jr.-designed Poipu Bay Golf Course, home to the PGA Grand Slam of Golf (and one of Tiger's favorites, judging by how many times he's won here). You won't want for anything here. It's perfect for honeymooners, families, everybody. Needless to say, book well ahead.

See map p. 420. 1571 Poipu Rd., Koloa. ☎ *800-55-HYATT or 808-742-1234. Fax: 808-742-1557.* www.kauai-hyatt.com *or* www.hyatt.com. *Parking: $8 for valet, $6 for self-parking. Rack rates: $425–$650 double, $1,200–$3,500 suite. Mandatory "resort fee" of $15 per day for "free" local calls, access to the fitness center, and other amenties. Deals: Multiple packages almost always on offer; ask about sixth night free; golf, spa, and romance packages; and other special deals, including discounts for AAA members, seniors, and government employees. AE, DC, DISC, MC, V.*

Kiahuna Plantation
$$$–$$$$ Poipu Beach

The only Poipu condos that sit right on the sand, this low-rise complex maintains an air of privacy and retro Hawaiian style. Two- and three-story plantation-style buildings pepper 35 spacious, gardenlike acres fronting a wonderful stretch of swimmable beach. The individually decorated one- and two-bedroom apartments feature fully outfitted kitchens with microwave and dishwasher, daily maid service, cooling ceiling fans, and private lanais. A coin-op laundry, barbecues, and a pleasant restaurant and bar are on-site, and a first-class tennis center with pool, championship golf at the Poipu Bay Course, and Poipu Shopping Village are just across the street. Rack rates are too high, especially for the oceanview units, but discounts abound; go with whichever of the two reliable management companies can score you the best rate.

See map p. 420. 2253 Poipu Rd., Poipu Beach. **Outrigger Resorts:** ☎ *800-688-7444 or 808-742-6411. Fax: 808-742-1698.* www.outrigger.com. *Parking: Free! Rack rates: $225–$460 1-bedroom, $365–$505 2-bedroom. 2-night minimum. Deals: Better-than-average discounts for AAA and AARP members and seniors (50-plus), plus corporate, government, and military discounts. First-night-free, bed-and-breakfast, room-and-car, and other packages regularly on offer. AE, DC, DISC, MC, V.* **Castle Resorts:** ☎ *800-367-5004 or 808-545-3511. Fax: 808-477-2329. Internet:* www.castleresorts.com. *Parking: Free! Rack rates: $235–$490 1-bedroom, $395–$575 2-bedroom. Deals: Check Web site for special Internet rates and Hot Deals (1-bedrooms as low as $139 at press time). AE, MC, V.*

Nihi Kai Villas
$$ Poipu Beach

This beautifully maintained Mediterranean-style condo complex, just a block from the finest stretch of Poipu Beach, is an excellent choice on all fronts. It's lovingly and meticulously run by Grantham Resorts, a Poipu-based company about whom I've heard nothing but praise, and the tropical-style apartments are gorgeous. Each boasts a full kitchen (with microwave), ceiling fans, washer/dryer, full cable (most have VCRs), lots of windows, and at least one lanai (usually two). Everything is top-notch, from the big, comfy furniture to the plush carpet underfoot. The grounds are well landscaped and quiet, boasting two tennis courts, paddleball, barbecues, and two nice pools. No daily maid service, but I actually enjoyed it on my last stay; I didn't mind rinsing my own breakfast dishes, and I thoroughly enjoyed not having to worry about the intrusion.

 In addition to the highly recommendable Nihi Kai Villas and the more budget-oriented Waikomo Stream Villas (later in this chapter), Grantham Resorts manages a wealth of other excellent condo properties in the Poipu Beach area — including the spectacularly located **Lawai Beach Resort** (**$$**), whose tidy one-bedroom apartments overlook one of the best snorkel beaches on the island; **Poipu Crater Resort** (**$ to $$**), one of the best two-bedroom bargains in Hawaii for families; and the gorgeous blufftop **Makahuena** condos (**$$$**), most of which command spectacular ocean views — as well as full-scale vacation homes. For more information, see the section "Home, sweet vacation home," later in this chapter.

See map p. 420. 1870 Hoone Rd., Poipu Beach. ☎ *800-325-5701, 800-742-1412, or 808-742-2000. Fax: 808-742-9093.* www.grantham-resorts.com. *Parking: Free! Rack rates: $135–$165 1-bedroom, $169–$375 2- or 3-bedroom. 5-night minimum.*

Deals: Discounts on stays over 30 days. Also inquire about discounted rates on rental cars. MC, V (accepted for deposit only).

Outrigger at Lae Nani
$$$ Coconut Coast

I just love this pleasant and unpretentious tropical condo complex. It's quiet, easygoing, and situated on a wonderful stretch of beach (and located near the shops and restaurants of the Coconut Marketplace). The individually decorated one- and two-bedroom apartments are comfortable and spacious, with large living rooms, adjacent dining areas, complete kitchens, cooling ceiling fans, and well-furnished lanais. The two-bedroom/two-baths can easily accommodate six, as long as two don't mind sleeping in the living room; even my one-bedroom unit had a second bath. The property has a pool, tennis courts, barbecues, and a coin-op laundry, and daily maid service makes it feel like real vacation.

See map p. 420. 410 Papaloa Rd. (next to the Coconut Marketplace), Kapaa. ☎ *800-688-7444 or 808-822-4938. Fax: 808-822-1022.* www.outrigger.com. *Parking: Free! Rack rates: $207–$230 1-bedroom, $225–$295 2-bedroom. 2-night minimum. Deals: Better-than-average discounts for AAA and AARP members and seniors (50-plus), plus corporate, government, and military discounts. First-night-free, bed-and-breakfast, room-and-car, and other packages regularly on offer. AE, DC, DISC, MC, V.*

Poipu Kapili Resort
$$$ Poipu Beach

This quiet, upscale cluster of condos is outstanding in every way but one: The ocean is across the street and the nearest sandy beach is a block away, even though the waves are right out your window. Still, I love the home-away-from-home amenities and comforts in the very nice apartments, as well as the beautifully manicured grounds with an especially lovely pool, barbecues, tennis courts (lit for night play), and an herb garden (you're welcome to take samples to cook with). The tropical-style apartments are extra-large (one-bedrooms are 1,120 square feet, two-bedrooms are a massive 1,900 to 2,600 square feet). All the one-bedrooms have two bathrooms, and most of the two-bedrooms have three baths, making this an ideal place for family gatherings. The oceanfront two-story, two-bedroom townhouse-style units are my favorites because they catch the trade winds. All units have full kitchens, ceiling fans, private lanais, VCRs, and CD players; the two-bedrooms also have washer/dryers (a coin-op laundry is on the grounds). Towels are changed three times a week, and weekly maid service is offered for longer stays. It's a very nice choice, especially if you want a tranquil, residential-style ambience.

See map p. 420. 2221 Kapili Rd., Koloa. ☎ *800-443-7714 or 808-742-6449. Fax: 808-742-9162.* www.poipukapili.com. *Parking: Free! Rack rates: $210–$300 1-bedroom, $280–$575 2-bedroom. Ask about minimum-stay requirement (usually 5 nights in winter). Your seventh night is free May through mid-Dec. Deals: Ask about discounts for longer stays and discounted car-rental rates. Seventh-night-free, car-and-condo ($237 at press time), golf, romance, senior, and other special packages often available. MC, V.*

Princeville Resort Kauai
$$$$$ North Shore

This stunning North Shore resort is among Hawaii's very best; in fact, it's nearly faultless. The setting is breathtaking (you won't be surprised to learn it's the most popular site on Kauai for weddings), and the tiered hotel steps down the cliffs above Hanalei Bay to take spectacular advantage of the views. A subdued color palette and natural fibers strike the perfect note of comfortable island elegance. Grand and gorgeous public spaces lead to universally sizable rooms that come outfitted with eye-catching original art, oversized windows (no lanais, though), and bedside control panels for everything. Your oversized green-marble bath features double sinks and a huge soaking tub, plus a "magic" shower window that you can switch in an instant from opaque to clear, allowing you to take in those awesome views even as you shampoo. The infinity pool is one of the state's best and comes complete with a swim-up bar and always-attentive service. Just steps away is a golden-sand beach with a wonderful snorkel reef for beginners and well-practiced snorkelers alike; it remains well protected even when the winter waves kick up. Additional perks include world-class golf (the Prince Course is regularly named best in Hawaii by *Golf Digest*), a first-rate spa and fitness center, a kids' program, a resort shuttle, and excellent dining options. Service is impeccable. It's one of my all-time favorites; needless to say, you'll want for nothing here.

See map p. 420. 5520 Ka Haku Rd., Princeville. ☎ *800-325-3589, 800-826-4400, or 808-826-9644. Fax: 808-826-1166.* www.princeville.com. *Parking: $15. Rack rates: $450–$675 double, $775–$4,800 suite. Deals: Package deals are usually available — sometimes including such perks as full breakfast, room upgrades, and unlimited golf — so be sure to ask. Also inquire about AAA-member and senior discounts. AE, DC, DISC, MC, V.*

Secret Beach Hideaway
$$$$$ North Shore

If you want Kauai's most romantic lodgings, and money is no object, pick up the phone now and book one of these exquisite cottages overlooking magical Sunset Beach on Kauai's fabled North Shore. Built with celebrating couples in mind, these three intimate cottages are spread over 11 lush tropical acres; you're guaranteed privacy, gorgeous ocean views, and faultless appointments. Each is tiny — about 500 square feet — but boasts the finest of everything: polished maple furnishings, granite countertops, fine linens and china, full-size SubZero fridges in the gourmet kitchens, TV with VCR, CD stereo, gas barbecue grill, washer/dryer, deck furniture, and outdoor private hot tub for soaking in the spectacular views, plus two phone lines, in case you just can't leave your laptop at home. Each is perfect, but the jewel of the property is Japanese-style Hale Lani. A private path leads from each cottage to Secret Beach, which is only swimmable from May to October. One word of warning: This place is a vacation rental, not a hotel or B&B, so it's best for independent travelers rather than those who need a guiding local hand.

See map p. 420. Next to Kilauea Lighthouse, Kilauea. ☎ *800-820-2862 or 808-828-2862.*
www.secretbeachkauai.com. *Parking: Free! Rack rates: $395–$425 double, plus
one-time $175 cleaning fee, and $500 security deposit. 2-night minimum; 7-night minimum at Christmas holidays. Deals: Always inquire about possible discounts. No
credit cards.*

Sheraton Kauai Resort
$$$$$ Poipu Beach

This very nice Sheraton is an excellent choice for visitors who like the
advantages that a resort hotel can offer, but who don't care for the forced
formality that often goes along with it. The resort brims with aloha spirit
and an easygoing style that's reminiscent of old Hawaii. You have a choice
of three buildings: one nestled in tropical gardens with koi-filled ponds;
one facing a fabulous stretch of palm-fringed, white-sand beach (my
favorite, of course); and one ocean-facing wing that boasts great sunset
views. Whichever you choose, you'll get a spacious, comfortably decorated room with minifridge; most in the Ocean Wing have sofa beds,
making them suitable for small families. Amenities include an oceanfront
pool, a kids' pool, and Jacuzzi; a fitness center; tennis courts; a handful of
restaurants (one child 12 or under eats free for each paying grown-up in
Shells, the signature restaurant); and a glass-walled lounge featuring live
Hawaiian music and sunset views. Rack rates are ridiculous, but specials
abound.

See map p. 420. 2440 Hoonani Rd., Poipu Beach. ☎ *800-782-9488 or 808-742-1661.
Fax: 808-742-4041.* www.sheraton-kauai.com *or* www.sheraton.com. *Valet
parking: $6; free self-parking. Rack rates: $325–$595 double, $595–$1,100 suite.
Mandatory "resort fee" of $23 for "free" breakfast buffet, "free" local and 800-access
phone calls, use of the fitness center, and more. Deals: Promotional rates and/or
package deals are almost always available, so be sure to ask (from $125 at press
time). Also ask for AAA-member and senior discounts. AE, DC, DISC, MC, V.*

Sugar Mill Cottages
$–$$ Poipu Beach

These 12 studio apartments are some of my favorite cheap sleeps on
Kauai. The simple plantation-style complex sits on a pleasant residential
parcel just a five-minute stroll from Brennecke's Beach, everybody's
favorite stretch of Poipu sand. Each brand spanking-new studio for two
boasts pretty textiles, cooling slate floors, an attractive bath (shower
only), a kitchenette with all the tools to prepare a full meal, dining table,
and TV and VCR. Three have phones (the others share), so request one
when you book if you want it. Also request the kitchen that's right for you
because they vary from petite to nearly full-size. Every three units share a
free laundry room, and each unit has its own beach cooler, towels, chairs,
mats, and toys, plus access to a swimming pool and tennis courts. This is
an excellent place to stay, but with no on-site manager, the cottages are
best for independent types.

See map p. 420. 2391 Hoohu Rd. (at Pe'e Road), Poipu Kai. ☎ *877-742-9369, 800-367-8020, or 808-742-7400. Fax: 818-742-9121.* www.kauai-rent.com/sugar-mill-poipu/sugar-mill-poipu.htm. *Parking: Free! Rack rates: $80–$153 double (rates change based on length of stay; single-night stay $153). AE, DC, DISC, MC, V.*

Waikomo Stream Villas
$$ Poipu Beach

Here's another excellent deal, this one perfect for families or anyone hoping for all the comforts of home at bargain-basement prices. These huge (1,100 to 1,500 square feet), well-managed, and attractive one- and two-bedroom apartments have everything that you could possibly need — fully equipped kitchen, VCR, CD player, ceiling fans, a king or queen bed in the master bedroom and a sofa bed in the living room, washer/dryer, and private lanai, plus a second bath and cathedral ceilings in the two-bedrooms — at *very* affordable prices. The beautifully landscaped complex boasts both adults' and kids' pools, tennis courts, and a barbecue area; right next door is the Kiahuna Golf Course, designed by Robert Trent Jones, Jr., so pack your irons and woods. The beach is a five- to seven-minute walk away — a worthy sacrifice for the kind of savings you'll realize here. Value-conscious travelers who need their space can't do better for the dough. No daily maid service, but for the savings that you get here, you won't mind pulling the blanket up on the bed or washing your own breakfast dishes.

See map p. 420. 2721 Poipu Rd., Poipu Beach. ☎ *800-325-5701, 800-742-1412, or 808-742-2000. Fax: 808-742-9093.* www.grantham-resorts.com. *Parking: Free! Rack rates: $99–$165 1- or 2-bedroom. 5-night minimum. Deals: Discounts on stays over 30 days. Also inquire about discounted rates on rental cars and low-season stays. MC, V (accepted for deposit only).*

Wailua Bay View
$$ Coconut Coast

These one-bedroom, one-bath apartments on the beach aren't fancy, but they offer good value if your budget is tight. Every apartment has at least a partial ocean view, plus a complete kitchen (with microwave and dishwasher), ceiling fans, washer/dryer, TV with VCR, air-conditioning in the bedroom, and a large furnished oceanview lanai. A sleeper sofa in the living room makes each unit spacious enough for a budget-minded family of four who don't mind sharing. Facilities include a small pool and barbecues. Apartments closest to the road can be noisy, so book oceanview for maximum quiet. All in all, it's an excellent value if you want cheap, comfortable sleeps. You'll have to make your own bed, but at these prices, who cares?

See map p. 420. 320 Papaloa Rd., Kapaa. ☎ *800-882-9007. Fax: 425-391-9121.* www.wailuabay.com. *Parking: Free! Rack rates: $110–$120 double. $70 cleaning fee charged for stays of less than 5 nights. Deals: Seventh night free mid-Apr to mid-June and Sept to mid-Dec; tenth night free during summer. MC, V.*

Waimea Plantation Cottages
$$–$$$ Waimea

Choose one of these historic 1930s plantation workers' cottages, set among a beachfront grove of coconut palms in perpetually sunny Waimea, and you'll feel as if you've stepped back to a time when the island living was easy. These beautifully restored bungalows are authentically outfitted with tropical-style furniture and fabrics; each has a furnished lanai, ceiling fans, a full kitchen, and oodles of period charm. On-site is a pool, tennis courts, a coin-op laundry, an intimate full-service spa, and a nice restaurant, the Waimea Brewing Company. Maid service is offered every third day. The only downsides are the black-sand beach, which is lovely but not swimmable (the water is too rough), and the remote location. Still, it's a real retro delight and an ideal place to get away from it all. It's ideal for every occasion, from vintage-romantic honeymoons to multigenerational family reunions.

See map p. 420. 9400 Kaumualii Hwy., Waimea. ☎ *800-992-7866 or 808-338-1625. Fax: 808-338-2338.* www.waimea-plantation.com *or* www.aston-hotels.com. *Parking: Free! Rack rates: $135–$150 studio, $185–$240 1-bedroom, $230–$300 2-bedroom, $295–$385 3-bedroom. Deals: Excellent opportunities for discounts. Internet-only ePriceBreaker rates as low as $120 at press time. Ask for AAA, senior (50-plus), and corporate discounts, and other special rate programs. AE, DC, DISC, MC, V.*

Whaler's Cove
$$$$$ Poipu Beach

Condo living hardly gets better than this. The individually decorated apartments are elegant, oversized, and held to a high standard; each has a full modern kitchen, a large furnished lanai, washer/dryer, and ceiling fans throughout. Most have Jacuzzi tubs in the master bath (what's with the lack of hair dryers at these prices, though?). One of my favorites is no. 230, a two-bedroom duplex done in a beautiful Asian bamboo style. The contemporary and stylish water's-edge complex was smartly designed to give each unit a spectacular view of the crashing surf. Hotel-like amenities include bell service, concierge, and daily housekeeping; an elevator (uncommon in condo complexes) is another nice luxury touch. A very nice oceanside pool is on-site, plus a hot tub, sauna, and barbecues. You'll have to drive to the beach, but there's good swimming and snorkeling (often with sea turtles) from a rocky cove.

See map p. 420. 2640 Puuholo Rd., Poipu Beach. ☎ *800-225-2683, 800-367-7052, or 808-742-7571. Fax: 808-742-1185.* www.whalers-cove.com. *Parking: Free! Rack rates: $349–$469 1-bedroom, $479–$619 2-bedroom. "Resort fee" of $5 per night. 2-night minimum; longer requirement over holidays. Deals: Ask about seventh-night-free, honeymoon, car-and-condo, and other package deals (weekly rates from $1,900 at press time). AE, MC, V.*

More B&Bs worth writing home about

Tropically tranquil Kauai makes the ideal place to hide away in a B&B. If you're a fan, also consider these enticing, and quite affordable, options.

If you want a Poipu-area B&B, but Gloria's (reviewed earlier in this chapter) is just too darn expensive, consider the **Bamboo Jungle House** ($$; ☎ 888-332-5115 or 808-332-5515; www.kauai-bedandbreakfast.com), an exotic choice for left-of-center romantics, with three beautifully outfitted suites hidden away in an impeccably restored old plantation house on a tropical gated estate in Kalaheo, less than ten minutes from the beach. Rates are $110 to $130 per night, plus cleaning fees.

You might consider **Hale Manu Bed & Breakfast** ($; ☎ 888-828-6641 or 808-828-6641; www.bnbweb.com/HaleManu.html), which boasts a delightful one-bedroom unit ($95 per night) with a private entrance attached to the owners' charming plantation-style home. It's nestled on a lush and fragrant flower farm in Kileauea, on the verdant North Shore. (The owners supply arrangements to the fabulous Princeville Resort.) The magical gardens, which have been featured on HGTV, are reason enough to stay.

On the Coconut Coast sits another romantic gem, **Alohilani Bed & Breakfast** ($$; ☎ 800-533-9316 or 808-823-0128; www.hawaiilink.net/~alohila), with three guest suites and a private cottage, all impeccably decorated and tucked away on six tranquil acres at the end of a country road (but within minutes of dining, shopping, and beaches). Rates are $99 to $119 per night.

Golfers — or anybody who prefers home-style touches over anonymous conformity — will enjoy **Hale 'Aha** ($$; ☎ 800-826-6733 or 808-826-6733; www.haleaha.com), a lovely home fronting 500 feet of world-class fairway in the North Shore's Princeville Resort. Three guest rooms ($115 to $125 per night) and two suites ($185 or $275 per night) are all comfortably outfitted and impeccably maintained, and the generous breakfast boasts baked dishes and fresh fruit smoothies. If you dislike manicured resort areas, pastels, or personal attention, don't bother; otherwise, you'll be very happy here.

 Another North Shore B&B that budget travelers will enjoy is **Hale O'O Maha** ($; ☎ 800-851-0291 or 808/828-1341; www.aloha.net/~hoomaha), with four guest rooms (two with shared bath) tucked into a suburban ranch-style house filled with *South Pacific* artifacts and surrounded by gorgeous Eden-like grounds. Nearby is Kalihiwai Beach, one of Kauai's best-kept secrets. Rates run $75 to $95 double.

If you want more options, contact **Hawaii's Best Bed & Breakfasts** (☎ 800-262-9912 or 808-885-4550; www.bestbnb.com). The staff can book a room for you in a Kauai inn that they have personally inspected and approved, and they offer vacation home rentals, too.

Home, sweet vacation home

Kauai has lots of fabulous apartments, condos, and full homes that can be rented by the day, the week, or the month, and many are just steps from the ocean. Vacation rentals can be a fabulous deal. They often cost no more than your average resort room, but for your money, you get a whole house brimming with conveniences and privacy. Sometimes it's even cheaper to rent a home, especially after you factor in the extra bucks you inevitably hand out at resorts for room service, poolside cocktails, and the like. Vacation rentals are also the only available option if you want to base yourself in the North Shore's most appealing residential communities, such as Anini Beach, Hanalei, or Haena. Make sure that you understand payment policies (including any cleaning fees and security deposits) and minimum-stay requirements.

Two darling North Shore cottages, **Aloha Sunrise Inn** and **Aloha Sunset Inn** ($$; ☎ 888-828-1008 or 808-828-1100; www.kauaisunrise.com or www.kauai-sunset.com), are ideal for independent-minded travelers with a yen for natural beauty and seclusion. Hidden away near Kilauea on seven farmlike acres blooming with fruit trees and flowers, each vacation rental is a beautifully outfitted tropical-style home, complete with full kitchen, washer/dryer, VCR with video library, barbecue, and more. An ideal choice if Secret Beach Hideaway (reviewed earlier in this chapter) is simply out of your price range, but these cottages aren't appropriate for families with children. Rates are $875 or $910 per week.

I've had great luck renting through **Kauai Vacation Rentals** (☎ 800-367-5025 or 808-245-8841; www.kauaivacationrentals.com), which handles top-quality vacation rentals all over the Garden Isle. It has a particularly fab selection on the lush North Shore; renting a home on this quiet coast is a great way to commune with nature, especially for those who favor being on their own over the sometimes smothering atmosphere of a big resort. KVR has something for everybody; prices start at about $650 a week for a cozy cottage for two ($500 for a studio condo) and reach into the thousands for luxurious multibedroom beachfront homes. Check out the complete list of options on the extensive Web site. One of my favorites is the ultracharming Ursula Taylor home, a modern two-bedroom done in traditional plantation style; it's perfectly located, just across the street from idyllic Hanalei Bay and a walk from charming Hanalei town, and it goes for $1,500 a week.

Another agency that represents an extensive collection of North Shore vacation rentals is **Hanalei North Shore Properties** (☎ 800-488-3336 or 808-826-9622; www.kauai-vacation-rentals.com). You might also check with **Hanalei Paradise Vacation Rentals** (☎ 808-826-6111; www.bestofhawaii.com/hanalei).

For the best deal in sunny Poipu Beach, either on a condo or a full vacation home, call **Grantham Resorts** (☎ 800-325-5701, 800-742-1412, or 808-742-2000; www.grantham-resorts.com). In addition to managing the Nihi Kai Villas and Waikomo Stream Villas (both reviewed earlier in this chapter), Grantham handles Poipu-area rental units in eight other condo developments as well as dozens of Poipu-area houses (including some beachfront homes that turned me pea-green with envy on my visit to Poipu). Owner Nancy Grantham sets exacting standards for all her rentals; when you rent a Grantham apartment or home, you know that you're getting high quality and top value for your dollar. You can peruse its full list of properties on the Web.

Gloria Merkle, the innkeeper behind magical Gloria's Spouting Horn B&B (reviewed earlier in this chapter), also offers an excellent selection of vacation-rental cottages, condos, and homes in Poipu and around the island. Contact **Gloria's Vacation Rentals** (☎ **888-742-6995** or 808-742-2850; www.gloriasvacationrentals.com).

Hawaii's Best Bed & Breakfasts (see the section "More B&Bs worth writing home about," earlier in this chapter) also represents some excellent vacation homes on Kauai.

Dining Out

The gorgeous Garden Isle has used its not-so-subtle charms to woo some of Hawaii's top chefs over to its shores, so prepare to dine well. For reasons that escape me, Kauai has an excess of quality Italian, zesty island-style Mexican, and great burgers — not that I'm complaining, mind you. Your options won't be limited here. Whether you're looking for a romantic candlelit dinner, quality seafood in an oceanfront setting, or just a great island-style pizza, terrific choices abound.

In the following restaurant listings, each restaurant review is followed by a number of dollar signs, ranging from one ($) to five ($$$$$). The dollar signs are meant to give you an idea of what a complete dinner for one person — including appetizer, main course, dessert, one drink, tax, and tip — is likely to set you back. The price categories go like this:

$	Cheap eats — less than $15 per person
$$	Still inexpensive — $15 to $25
$$$	Moderate — $25 to $40
$$$$	Pricey — $40 to $70
$$$$$	Ultraexpensive — more than $70 per person

Of course, it all depends on how you order, so stay away from the surf and turf or the north end of the wine list if you're on a tight budget. To give you a further idea of how much you can expect to spend, I also include the price range of main courses in the listings.

 The state adds 4 percent in sales tax to every restaurant bill. A 15- to 20-percent tip is standard in Hawaii, just like on the mainland.

Beach House Restaurant
$$$$ Poipu Beach   Hawaii Regional

The open-air, on-the-ocean setting makes this place my favorite special-occasion restaurant on Kauai. The long, Japanese-inspired room is lined

Kauai's Restaurants

Beach House Restaurant **23**
Brennecke's Beach Broiler **20**
Brick Oven Pizza **24**
Bubba Burgers **1** & **9**
Cafe Hanalei **3**
Caffè Coco **12**
Casa Blanca **21**
Casa di Amici **19**
Dali Deli **21**
Dondero's **18**
Duane's Ono-Char Burger **6**
Duke's Canoe Club **15**
Hamura's Saimin Stand **16**
Hanalei Dolphin **2**
Hanalei Gourmet **1**
Joe's on the Green **22**
Keoki's Paradise **22**
La Playita Azul **10**

Lemongrass Grill Seafood
  & Sushi Bar **11**
Lighthouse Bistro **4**
Mango Mama's **5**
Mema Thai Chinese Cuisine **13**
Norberto's El Cafe **7**
Ono Family Restaurant **8**
A Pacific Cafe **10**
Pau Hana Pizza & Kilauea Bakery **4**
Plantation Gardens Restaurant **22**
Postcards Cafe **2**
Roy's Poipu Bar & Grill **22**
Sushi Blues **1**
Waimea Brewing Company **26**
Wrangler's Steakhouse **25**
Zelo's Beach House **1**

Luaus
Drums of Paradise Luau **4**
Kauai Coconut Beach Luau **14**
Luau Kilohana **17**

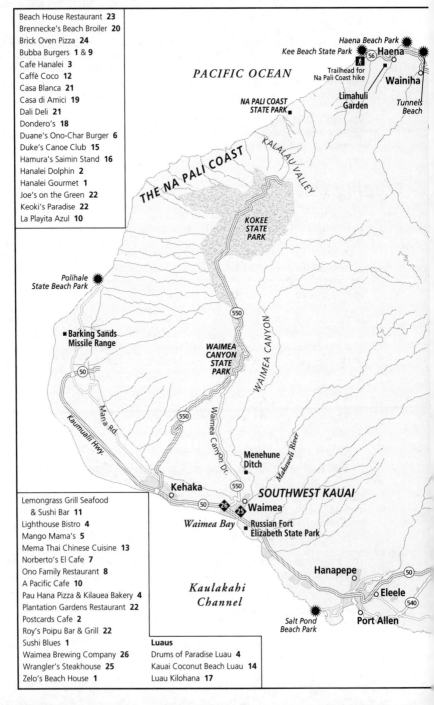

PACIFIC OCEAN

Haena Beach Park
Kee Beach State Park
Trailhead for
Na Pali Coast hike
Haena
56
Wainiha
Limahuli
Garden
Tunnels
Beach

*NA PALI COAST
STATE PARK*

THE NA PALI COAST

KALALAU VALLEY

KOKEE
STATE
PARK

Polihale
State Beach Park

WAIMEA CANYON

550

■ **Barking Sands
Missile Range**

*WAIMEA
CANYON
STATE
PARK*

50

Mana Rd.

550

Waimea Canyon Dr.

Makaweli River

Kaumualii Hwy.

Menehune
Ditch

Kehaka

50

550

26

25

SOUTHWEST KAUAI

Waimea

Waimea Bay

Russian Fort
Elizabeth State Park

*Kaulakahi
Channel*

Hanapepe

50

○ **Eleele**

540

Salt Pond
Beach Park

Port Allen

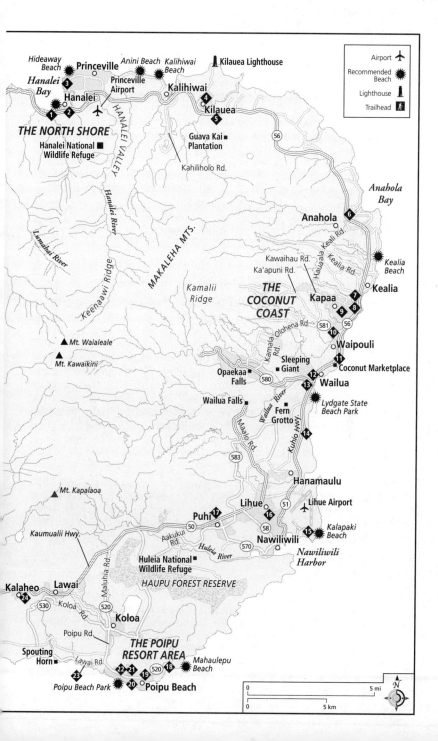

Hideaway Beach
Hanalei Bay
THE NORTH SHORE
Princeville
Anini Beach
Kalihiwai Beach
Princeville Airport
Kalihiwai
Hanalei
Hanalei National Wildlife Refuge

Airport ✈
Recommended Beach ✺
Lighthouse 🗼
Trailhead 🚶

Kilauea Lighthouse
Kilauea
Guava Kai Plantation
Kahiliholo Rd.

Anahola Bay
Anahola
Kawaihau Rd.
Ka'apuni Rd.
Kamalii Ridge
THE COCONUT COAST
Kealia Beach
Kealia
Kapaa
Hauaala Keali Rd.
Kealia Rd.

Mt. Waialeale
Mt. Kawaikini
Keenaawi Ridge
MAKALEHA MTS.
Lumahai River
Hanalei River
HANALEI VALLEY

Olohena Rd.
Kamalu Rd.
Waipouli
Coconut Marketplace
Sleeping Giant
Opaekaa Falls
Wailua
Wailua Falls
Fern Grotto
Lydgate State Beach Park
Wailua River
Maalo Rd.
Kuhio Hwy.

Mt. Kapalaoa
Hanamaulu
Lihue
Lihue Airport
Puhi
Nawiliwili
Kalapaki Beach
Nawiliwili Harbor
Kaumualii Hwy.
Aakukui Rd.
Huleia River
Huleia National Wildlife Refuge
HAUPU FOREST RESERVE
Maluhia Rd.

Kalaheo
Lawai
Koloa Rd.
Koloa
Poipu Rd.
Spouting Horn
Lawai Rd.
THE POIPU RESORT AREA
Mahaulepu Beach
Poipu Beach Park
Poipu Beach

0   5 mi
0   5 km

with shojilike windows that make sunset a celebration every night and let in a symphony of surf after dark. The first-rate food lives up to the setting nicely. Even though star chef Jean-Marie Josselin (of A Pacific Cafe fame; see the listing later in this chapter) has sold the restaurant, the new owners have wisely decided not to change the original formula for success. Under the steady hand of chef Scott Lutey, the kitchen turns out creative island dishes that feature the best of the land and sea, from fresh-caught fish and island-raised beef to locally harvested organic greens and salt. The menu changes nightly, but count on such winners as macadamia nut–crusted mahimahi in citrus miso sauce or mint-coriander marinated rack of lamb roasted with a goat cheese–garlic crust — yum! Feel free to come strictly for the first-rate cocktails if you don't want to splurge on dinner; strong on California labels, the wine list is equally pleasing.

See map p. 434. 5022 Lawai Rd. (off Poipu Road, toward Spouting Horn), Koloa. ☎ *808-742-1424.* www.the-beach-house.com. *Reservations highly recommended. Main courses: $22–$29. AE, MC, V. Open: Dinner nightly.*

Brennecke's Beach Broiler
$$–$$$ Poipu Beach   American/Seafood

"Right on the Beach, Right on the Price." If you have kids in tow, skip the Beach House in favor of this fun, casual restaurant, which boasts ocean views galore. The fresh fish specials attract locals and visitors alike — always a good sign of consistent quality. Well-priced and well-prepared seafood and prime rib dinners (all of which include the creamy New England–style chowder or the appealing salad bar) are guaranteed to make Mom and Dad fans, while the best burgers in Poipu will keep the kids wanting to come back every night. This long-time favorite is so welcoming and laid-back that you can come in straight off the beach for baby-back ribs, kiawe-broiled (mesquite-broiled) seafood kebabs, or surprisingly good veggie selections. Kids even have a menu to themselves. The restaurant has great sunset mai tais, too, plus a full menu of island-style munchies at happy hour (2 to 5 p.m.).

See map p. 434. 2100 Hoone Rd. (across the street from Poipu Beach Park), Poipu Beach. ☎ *888-384-8810 or 808-742-7588.* www.brenneckes.com. *Reservations recommended for dinner. Main courses: $5–$14 at lunch. Complete sunset dinners (including salad bar or chowder) $17–$31 at dinner (most under $24). AE, DC, DISC, MC, V. Open: Lunch and dinner daily.*

Brick Oven Pizza
$ Kalaheo   Pizza

Just a ten-minute drive from Poipu Beach, this mom-and-pop pizza joint has been serving up Kauai's best pies for a quarter of a century. It's the real thing: traditional or whole-wheat crust topped with homemade sauces, high-quality cheeses, and your choice from the long toppings menu, and then baked in a real brick oven. You can choose standard-size pies to share or smaller individual ones á la California Pizza Kitchen if you and the kids just can't agree. A decent beer selection that includes Gordon Biersch and Kona brews is available to wash it all down. The setting is pizzeria-standard, but the terrific pies make it worth the drive west from Poipu.

See map p. 434. 2-2555 Kaumualii Hwy. (Highway 50), Kalaheo (inland from Poipu Beach). ☎ *808-332-8561. Reservations not taken. Pizzas: $9.50–$29. MC, V. Open: Tues–Sun lunch and dinner.*

Bubba's Hawaii
$ Coconut Coast/North Shore American

"Bubba refuses to serve any burger costing less than a can of dog food." "The food is hot, the service is cold, and the music's TOO DAMN LOUD." Quick wit and commercial appeal aside, Bubba serves up one mean hamburger. It's served on a toasted bun with mustard, relish, diced onions, and lots of attitude — and boy, is it yummy. Bubba burgers are plump and juicy, so have a pile of napkins ready and waiting. Chicken, ginger-teriyaki tempeh, and fish burgers are also available, plus variations on the standard Bubba: the Slopper (served open-faced and smothered in Budweiser chili), the three-patty Big Bubba, and the Hubba Bubba (with a scoop of rice *and* a hot dog, all smothered in chili and onions). Come to Bubba for your burger fix — boy, you'll be glad you did!

*See map p. 434. **The Coconut Coast:** 4-1421 Kuhio Hwy., Kapaa.* ☎ *808-823-0069.* www. bubbaburger.com. *Open: Lunch and early dinner (to 8 p.m.).* **The North Shore:** *On Kuhio Highway (across from the Ching Young Center), Hanalei.* ☎ *808-826-7839. Open: Lunch and early dinner (to 8 p.m.). Everything under $8. MC, V.*

Cafe Hanalei
$$$$ North Shore Eclectic

Most people think of La Cascata, Princeville's elegant Mediterranean-Italian dining room, as the resort's premier special-occasion restaurant. But I just love Cafe Hanalei's perfect Bali Hai mood. A romantic indoor-outdoor setting makes the most of breathtaking Hanalei Bay and Na Pali views. The marvelously modern seafood-rich menu features Asian and Mediterranean accents (and includes plenty of selections to satisfy steak-lovers, too). Add in first-rate service, and you've got an ideal dining experience. Book a table on the casually elegant terrace for the ultimate dinner for two. The Friday-night seafood buffet adds an elegant all-you-can-eat spread to the à la carte menu. The bounteous Sunday champagne brunch boasts sushi and raw bars (all the peel-and-eat shrimp and crab legs you can put away!) as well as hot carving stations and made-to-order omelettes and crepes. The food is satisfying through and through.

If you're in the mood for Italian instead, the resort's intimate and romantic **La Cascata** ($$$$) fits the bill.

See map p. 434. At Princeville Resort Kauai, 5520 Ka Haku Rd., Princeville. ☎ *800-325-3589 or 808-826-9644.* www.princeville.com. *Reservations highly recommended. Main courses: $7–$13 at breakfast, $12–$21 at lunch, $21–$35 at dinner; 3-course fixed-price dinner $52 nightly; Sunday brunch $37; Friday seafood buffet $48. AE, DC, DISC, MC, V. Open: Breakfast, lunch, and dinner daily.*

Caffè Coco
$$ Coconut Coast   Eclectic/International

The left-of-center alfresco cafe-cum-art gallery is an ideal spot for a low-budget romantic dinner with a bring-your-own bottle of Merlot. The inventive cuisine spans the globe for ideas; everything is made from scratch and simply wonderful. You can dine casually on healthful soups, salads (including an excellent Greek), and sandwiches or opt for something more substantial. The beautifully prepared main plates include seared fresh ahi, crusted in delicate panko and served with a cilantro pesto and papaya salsa; Arista pork, slow roasted with garlic and herbs and served South American style, with black beans, rice, and tortillas; and a couple of creative, healthful pastas. The kitchen prepares all its own breads, baked goods, juices, salsas, curries, and chutneys. Dining is in the fragrant flower-and-fruit garden, under flickering tiki torches that set an idyllic island mood. The restaurant is an excellent choice for vegetarians, especially, but I recommend it for everyone else, too. Service is Hawaiian style, so dine elsewhere if you're in a hurry (this is Kauai — what's your rush?). Live entertainment on Thursday, Friday, and Saturday nights adds to the already-winning ambience. A $5 corkage is charged if you bring your own beer or wine.

See map p. 434. 4-369 Kuhio Hwy., next to Bambulei (on the inland side of the street, behind the green storefront across from Kintaro Restaurant), Wailua (just south of the Coconut Marketplace). ☎ *808-822-7990. Reservations recommended. Main courses: $15–$21; sandwiches, salads, and lighter fare $4–$14. MC, V. Open: Lunch Tues–Fri, dinner Tues–Sun.*

Casa Blanca
$$$ Poipu Beach   Mediterranean/Island

This all-day restaurant from chef/owner Liz Foley is an absolutely delightful addition to Kauai's open-air dining scene. The garden setting is casually sophisticated — all cool tile, warm colors, fresh flowers, and refreshing breezes — and the extensive menu is always pleasingly prepared. Start the day with *Basque piperrada* (Spanish scrambled eggs) or crepes dressed with fresh island fruit. Midday brings a creative selection of sandwiches, salads, soups, and Mediterranean brochettes, plus a menu of small tapas dishes for grazers and family-style sharing. Both the island ambiance and the culinary sophistication get a boost at dinner, when the beautifully presented plates shine with such flavorful dishes as *zarzuela* (Spanish seafood and saffron stew) and New Zealand lamb with ricotta mashed potatoes. It's a real winner!

If you'd like equally fabulous food to take home or to the beach, try Liz's winning **Dali Deli** ($), across the street from the Old Post Office at 5492 Koloa Rd. in old Koloa town, just inland from Poipu Beach (☎ **808-742-8824**). This casual daytime spot specializes in healthy gourmet fare, from morning muffins to lunchtime subs and salads — all fresh made, of course — and always-friendly service.

See map p. 434. At Kiahuna Swim & Tennis Club, 2290 Poipu Rd., Poipu Beach.
☎ *808-742-2929. Reservations recommended for dinner. Main courses: $6–$13 at breakfast and lunch, $12–$21 at dinner. DC, DISC, MC, V. Open: Breakfast, lunch, and dinner Mon–Sat; closed for dinner Sun.*

Casa di Amici
$$$ Poipu Beach   Eclectic Italian

Mediterranean accents abound in chef Randall Yates's hearty cooking, but he often reaches farther afield for inspiration: Witness such specialties as New Zealand spring lamb dressed in orange-hoisin-ginger sauce and Japanese mahogany-glazed salmon matched with grilled black tiger prawns. Yates virtually never disappoints, but I love the straight Italian/Mediterranean fare best, particularly the porcini-crusted chicken breast in a sundried cherry, port, and mushroom sauce, bolstered by an almost-creamy parmesan-basil polenta. Traditionalists will love the rich-as-it-should-be linguine alfredo. The setting is lovely and comfortable, with twinkling lights and cordial service. A pianist accents the ambience on Friday and Saturday evenings.

See map p. 434. 2301 Nalo Rd. (off Hoone Road, the road that fronts Poipu Beach Park), Poipu Beach. ☎ *808-742-1555. Reservations requested. Main courses: $19–$25. DC, MC, V. Open: Dinner nightly.*

Dondero's
$$$$ Poipu Beach   Regional Italian

The menu changes seasonally at this elegant Italian restaurant, but you can always count on a practiced, beautifully prepared regional menu with an emphasis on the classics. Dishes are prepared with homegrown herbs picked fresh from the kitchen garden. The setting is sublime, whether you choose to dine indoors in a beautiful marble-tiled setting reminiscent of Tuscany with exquisite Franciscan artwork or on an outdoor patio that says "only in Hawaii." You'll pay too much, but the food, wine list, ambience, and service are top-notch, making this a winner for those evenings when you're in a celebratory mood.

See map p. 434. At the Hyatt Regency Kauai Resort & Spa, 1571 Poipu Rd., Koloa.
☎ *808-742-1234. Reservations highly recommended. Main courses: $18–$36. AE, DC, DISC, MC, V. Open: Dinner nightly.*

Duane's Ono-Char Burger
$ North Shore   Burgers

Bubba (see the listing earlier in this chapter) would just cringe if I called him "establishment," but compared with Duane's, Bubba's the Wal-Mart of Kauai burgers. Little more than a roadside stand with a few picnic tables and some resident wild chickens, Duane's sets the standard for island-style burgers. I dream about the Local Girl, a juicy patty topped with teriyaki, Swiss cheese, pineapple, mayo, and lettuce on a bun — a perfect packet of juicy goodness. Sublime fries, shakes, and floats round out the lunchtime experience. Stop by on the way to the North Shore or pick up a takeout beach lunch. (Kealia Beach in Kapaa is just a few minutes' drive to the south.)

See map p. 434. 4-4350 Kuhio Hwy. (next to Whaler's General Store, on the ocean side of the street), Anahola. ☎ *808-822-9181. Burgers: $4–$7. MC, V. Open: Lunch daily.*

Duke's Canoe Club

$–$$$ Lihue   Steaks/Seafood (American/Hawaii Local in the Barefoot Bar)

The Kauai Duke's isn't as magical as the Waikiki branch, but it's appealing nonetheless. Thanks to a wide-ranging menu and a wonderful beachfront setting, this big, bustling, tropical restaurant is appealing to families and cuddly couples alike. The dependable menu has something for everyone, from fresh-caught fish prepared a half-dozen ways to finger-lickin'-good ribs dressed in mango barbecue sauce. Come for sunset if you can and ask for a beachfront table when you reserve; the view over Kalapaki Beach is fabulous, but some of the tables miss out. The Barefoot Bar, which spills out onto the sand and boasts its own waterfall (fake, of course), is the island's best spot for tropical noshing at reasonable prices. Live music completes the ambience.

See map p. 434. At the Kauai Marriott Resort & Beach Club, 3610 Rice St. (on Kalapaki Beach, near Nawiliwili Harbor), Lihue. ☎ *808-246-9599.* www.hulapie.com. *Reservations recommended for dinner. Main courses: $11–$20 at dinner (salad bar included). Barefoot Bar menu (served all day): $7–$11. AE, DC, DISC, MC, V. Open: Lunch and dinner daily.*

Hamura's Saimin Stand

$ Lihue   Local Hawaiian

I've eaten lots of memorable gourmet meals in Hawaii, but this nondescript lunch counter is the place that makes me yearn for a repeat visit. Located on an industrial side street just off Lihue's main drag, Hamura's serves up Hawaii's best *saimin* (ramen-style noodle soup). Cozy up to one of the U-shaped counters and order off the posted menu. The *saimin* here comes in a variety of sizes and with a variety of extras, like veggies and a hard-boiled egg. Other offerings include succulently broiled beef and chicken skewers (a steal at $1 a stick) and Chinese pretzels, which are like hard funnel cakes. (I like to put them in my *saimin* — a cultural travesty, I'm sure.) Don't be put off by the brisk service; you'll feel right at home — and you'll be done eating — in no time. You can also get your *saimin* to go in Chinese food containers — perfect if you need a hearty bite on the way to the beach (or the airport). This cultural adventure is a culinary marvel.

See map p. 434. 2956 Kress St. (1½ blocks off Rice Street; turn at the Aloha Furniture Warehouse), Lihue. ☎ *808-245-3271. Reservations not taken. Most soups and other items under $6. No credit cards. Open: Lunch and dinner daily.*

Food shopping tips

If you're staying in a house or condo equipped with a kitchen, visit Hanalei Dolphin's adjacent **Hanalei Dolphin Fish Market** (☎ **808-826-6113**), where you can choose from a wide range of unprepared fresh catches to grill back at your vacation rental. Barbecue-ready steaks are on hand, too. The market is open daily from 10 a.m. to 8 p.m.; look for its entrance at the back of the building.

Hanalei Dolphin
$$$ North Shore   Seafood

Fresh-off-the-boat seafood and a nicely romantic tropical-garden setting on the banks of the Hanalei River make the Hanalei Dolphin a very pleasing choice for cocktails and dinner. This isn't sophisticated fare; rather, it's refreshingly simple. Choose from a wide selection of the day's catches, which come charbroiled or Cajun-style, with salad and rice, pasta, or steak fries on the side. Alaskan king crab is always on hand, but why bother? Go with one of the stellar island catches, such as ruby-red ahi, moist and tender *onaga* (red snapper), or mackerel-like *ono* (wahoo). Starters include such retro classics as shrimp cocktail and stuffed mushroom caps, while sweet finishes include old-fashioned delights like strawberry cheesecake and ice-cream pie. Steak and chicken are available for nonfish eaters.

See map p. 434. 5-5016 Kuhio Hwy., Hanalei. ☎ *808-826-6113.* www.hanalei dolphin.com. *Reservations not taken. Sandwiches and salads: $7–$14 at lunch. Complete dinners: $15–$34. MC, V. Open: Lunch and dinner daily.*

Hanalei Gourmet
$$ North Shore   American

This unpretentious restaurant in the heart of Hanalei town is a great choice for an informal bite at any time of day. Breakfast standards and lunchtime burgers, sandwiches, and salads give way to dinner specialties like pan-fried Asian-style crab cakes, macadamia-nut fried chicken, and charbroiled pork chops (deliciously seasoned with locally harvested salt that has its own hearty, wonderfully distinct flavor). Service is super-friendly and super-easygoing — but the North Shore isn't the place to be in a hurry, anyway. Choose a table on the veranda if the TV set over the bar interferes with your Hanalei reverie. There's live music most evenings.

See map p. 434. In the Old Hanalei School at Hanalei Center, 5-5161 Kuhio Hwy., Hanalei. ☎ *808-826-2524. Main courses: $6–$11 at lunch, $11–$24 at dinner. AE, DC, DISC, MC, V. Open: Breakfast, lunch, and dinner daily.*

Joe's on the Green
$ Poipu Beach   American

Facing the greens of the Kiahuna Golf Course, this patio restaurant is a lovely and relaxing place to start the day. The small but satisfying morning menu features first-rate huevos rancheros (with a terrific fresh-made salsa), fluffy banana-macadamia nut pancakes, and corned beef hash and scrambled eggs served in crisp potato skins — an anti-dieter's delight. Lunchtime brings bountiful salads of island-grown greens and burgers, sandwiches, and the like. Clad in an aloha shirt, Joe works this modest indoor-outdoor restaurant as if it were the main dining room at Caesar's Palace; it's not, but the food's well prepared, the setting is lovely, and the prices are low, low, low.

See map p. 434. At the Kiahuna Golf Club, 2545 Kiahuna Plantation Rd. (turn inland from Poipu Road, next to the Poipu Shopping Village), Poipu Beach. ☎ 808-742-9696. Reservations not necessary except for Thurs dinner. Main courses: $5–$9 at breakfast, $7–$11 at lunch. MC, V. Open: Breakfast, lunch, and afternoon cocktails and pupus daily; dinner Thurs.

Keoki's Paradise
$–$$$ Poipu Beach   Steaks/Seafood (American/Local in the Cafe)

Keoki's offers buckets of alfresco allure, with flickering tiki torches, aloha-friendly ambience and service, and live Hawaiian music on weekends. It isn't on the oceanfront like its sister restaurant, Duke's Canoe Club (see earlier in this chapter), but it boasts a similarly lively tropical vibe and a lengthy menu highlighted by top-quality fresh fish prepared at least a half-dozen ways. Plenty of carnivore-friendly options are on hand, too, plus a decadent Hula Pie to finish. All dinners come with Keoki's surprisingly good Caesar salad, which makes meals a very good deal. The bar-area cafe, where there's live music on weekend nights, serves cheaper, more casual fare all day, including fish tacos, island-style ribs, and quesadillas, plus the requisite fruity cocktails.

See map p. 434. In the Poipu Shopping Village, 2360 Kiahuna Plantation Dr. (at Poipu Road), Poipu Beach. ☎ 808-742-7534. www.hulapie.com. Reservations recommended. Cafe menu: $6–$12. Main courses: $14–$25 at dinner (with salad). AE, DC, DISC, MC, V. Open: Lunch and dinner daily (cafe menu served all day).

La Playita Azul
$–$$ Coconut Coast   Mexican

This simple storefront restaurant serves up fabulously authentic Pacific regional Mexican cooking, including heaping plates of nachos bigger than your head. Portions are universally huge, and dishes are beautifully prepared across the board. The welcome basket of home-baked tortilla chips comes with two sauces, a zesty traditional red salsa and a fresh, piquant pico de gallo; I love to augment with the dense, well-seasoned guacamole. Things only get better from there: Pork is slow-baked in a rich tomato sauce for fork-tender chile colorado; chimichangas are stuffed with shredded beef until bursting and then deep-fried until golden; and fish tacos and burritos are stuffed with the fresh-grilled catch of the day. Expect zero ambience, and you won't be disappointed — but the fare never disappoints. No alcohol is served, but you're welcome to bring in your own brews. (An ABC store is just a few doors down in the same shopping center.)

See map p. 434. In the Kauai Village Shopping Center, 4-831 Kuhio Hwy., Kapaa. ☎ *808-821-2323. Reservations not taken. Main courses: $10–$20 (most less than $15). No credit cards. Open: Lunch Tues–Sat, dinner daily.*

Lemongrass Grill Seafood & Sushi Bar
$$$ Coconut Coast   Thai-Seafood

Designed pagoda style and glowing with tiki torches in the evening, this Asian seafooder is a winner for fresh, beautifully prepared fish. Skip the downstairs sushi bar in favor of the high-ceilinged, wood-paneled dining room, where chef Wally Nishimura shows off his best Thai-influenced dishes, such as ahi pole *poke* (a Southeast Asia spin on the local marinated-ahi favorite, seasoned with sambal, shiso leaf, and shredded daikon) and seafood stew in a fresh lemongrass broth. On my last visit, I enjoyed a beautifully presented fresh seafood and shellfish sampler that included a delectable spiny lobster tail and purple island sweet potato. Plenty of nicely prepared dishes are on hand for the nonseafood eaters in your party, including guava-glazed BBQ ribs served with garlic mashed potatoes. Considering the highway views, the ambience is quite pleasant and lovely, and service is attentive.

See map p. 434. 4-885 Kuhio Hwy. (next to Kauai Village Shopping Center), Kapaa. ☎ *808-821-2888. Reservations recommended. Main courses: $13–$21. AE, DC, DISC, MC, V. Open: Dinner nightly.*

Lighthouse Bistro
$$–$$$ North Shore   Mediterranean/Eclectic

This island-style bistro keeps improving with age; it has matured into a terrific place to enjoy a casual and well-prepared North Shore dinner. The menu is a tad generic — pastas, salads, island fish — so I was pleasantly surprised with the high quality and tastiness of the burrito-like ahi wrap. My fellow diners were equally pleased with selections that ranged from a bounteous Caesar salad to a fresh grilled mahi sandwich. At dinner, the coconut shrimp in a sweet chili sauce or the char-grilled pork medallions topped with pineapple chutney are tropical delights, while the broiled sirloin steak topped with a gorgonzola cheese and Burgundy sauce will appeal to classic tastes. An extensive and pleasing wine list is also on hand at dinner.

See map p. 434. In the Kong Lung Center, 2484 Keneke St., Kilauea. ☎ *808-828-0480.* www.lighthousebistro.com. *To get there: From Kuhio Highway, turn right at the sign for Kilauea Lighthouse (at Shell gas station) and then right onto Keneke Street. Reservations recommended at dinner. Main courses: $5–$11 at lunch, $18–$30 at dinner. MC, V. Open: Lunch and dinner daily.*

Mango Mama's
$ **North Shore** **Smoothies**

This charming roadside takeout cafe is housed in an old plantation-style building that's been painted a cheerful, rosy pink. Place your order at the window for a divine fresh-fruit smoothie; you'll have a good two dozen to choose from, all bursting with fresh tropical flavor. My favorite is the Kauai Crème, made with banana, coconut, and guava juice. Baked goods, power bars, fresh whole fruit, fresh-squeezed juices, bagels, and coffee and espresso round out the morning offerings, and sandwiches join the party for lunchtime. You can take a seat on the cute-as-a-button covered patio, pony up to a picnic table, or take your order to go.

See map p. 434. 4660 Hookui St. (off Kuhio Highway, near mile marker 23, ⁹⁄₁₀ mile east of turnoff for Kilauea Lighthouse). ☎ *808-828-1020. All items under $8. No credit cards. Open: Breakfast and lunch daily.*

Mema Thai Chinese Cuisine
$$ **Coconut Coast** **Thai/Chinese**

Tucked away in a nondescript minimall, Mema is well worth seeking out thanks to a mammoth, culturally cross-bred menu and a dining room that's much prettier and more appealing than most at this price level. The menu leans heavily toward the Thai classics, including a satisfyingly spicy lemon-grass soup, a fresh island papaya salad, a better-than-average pad thai, and rich coconut milk curries that border on the sublime. Best is the house specialty: panang curry made with kaffir lime leaves, garlic, and other seasonings, and spiced mild, medium, or hot to suit your palate. Service is thoughtful, too, making Mema a winner with well-rounded appeal. Mema is an ideal place for an affordable date.

See map p. 434. In the Kinipopo Shopping Village, 4-369 Kuhio Hwy. (just north of Haleilio Road on the mountain side of the street), Wailua. ☎ *808-823-0899. Reservations accepted. Main courses: $9–$19. AE, DC, DISC, MC, V. Open: Lunch Mon–Fri, dinner daily.*

Norberto's El Cafe
$–$$ **Coconut Coast** **Mexican**

This cool, dark Mexican restaurant marries fresh-grown island greens and fish with traditional south-of-the-border recipes, resulting in Mexican fare that's both top-quality and pleasingly authentic. Vegetarians and carnivores alike will enjoy the Hawaiian taro leaf enchiladas — corn tortillas stuffed with the spinach-like island staple, dressed in a zesty Spanish sauce, and baked to cheesy perfection. The rellenos and the fresh fish enchiladas are excellent choices, and the crisp corn chips are accompanied by a fresh-made salsa that will make your taste buds sit up and take notice. I've never been disappointed with any of Norberto's eats. Service is attentive and friendly, and Mexican beers are on hand.

See map p. 434. 4-1373 Kuhio Hwy., downtown Kapaa. ☎ *808-822-3362. Reservations accepted, recommended for larger parties. A la carte items and complete dinners: $3.25–$18. AE, MC, V. Open: Dinner Mon–Sat.*

Ono Family Restaurant
$ Coconut Coast   American/Local

Service isn't exactly what I'd call friendly at this colorfully rustic, local-style restaurant in the heart of Kapaa, but the hearty homestyle breakfasts make Ono's a fortifying place to launch a day of beachgoing or sightseeing. The coffee is strong, and the home cooking is indeed *ono* (Hawaiian for "delicious"). The menu features a full slate of fluffy omelets, pancakes, and other breakfast standards, including several variations on eggs Benedict, all of which come topped with a perfectly puckery hollandaise. Classic burgers and crispy fries are midday standouts.

See map p. 434. 4-1292 Kuhio Hwy. (on the ocean side of the street), downtown Kapaa. ☎ *808-822-1710. Everything less than $10. AE, DC, DISC, MC, V. Open: Breakfast and lunch daily.*

A Pacific Cafe
$$$$ Coconut Coast   Hawaii Regional

Jean-Marie Josselin was one of the forces behind Hawaii's culinary revolution. He spent the 1990s expanding throughout the islands, but he's back down to a single restaurant — and his original showcase is still one of the state's finest for haute Hawaii Regional cooking. Josselin may be a Frenchman, but he's captured the island style perfectly. Tucked away in a Coconut Coast shopping center, the pretty, unassuming room bustles with energy and verve, just like Josselin's cooking. The menu changes daily, but expect a bold fusion of Asian flavors and Mediterranean techniques, plus lots of choices from the kiawe-fired (mesquite-fired) grill. Don't miss such signature dishes as light-as-air tiger-eye ahi tempura with soy wasabi and Chinese mustard dipping sauces, and "firecracker" salmon on a Thai chile sauce bed — a perfect marriage of hot and sweet. On the dessert menu, the "toasted Hawaiian" (white chocolate cake with white chocolate macadamia nut mousse and caramel sauce) is a guaranteed happy ending. It's a sublime and thoroughly enjoyable dining experience every time. Don't miss it if you can help it.

See map p. 434. In the Kauai Village Shopping Center, 4-831 Kuhio Hwy., Kapaa. ☎ *808-822-0013. Reservations highly recommended. Main courses: $21–$29. AE, DC, DISC, MC, V. Open: Dinner nightly.*

Pau Hana Pizza & Kilauea Bakery
$ North Shore   Pizza/Baked Goods

Some declare the pizza that issues forth from this unassuming closet to be the best in the state, and they just might be right. Fresh-from-scratch dough lays the chewy foundation for this near-perfect pie, while top-flight olive oil, whole-milk cheeses, homemade marinara, and a host of high-quality toppings serve as the culinary building blocks. You're welcome to order standard pepperoni, but even traditionalists will be tempted by such innovations as the Billie Holiday, topped with house-smoked ono, Swiss chard, roasted onions, and gorgonzola-rosemary sauce; the Provencal, a symphony of sun-dried tomatoes, garlic, roasted onions, fresh-basil pesto, and Asiago cheese; or the Classic Scampi, adorned with giant tiger prawns. The stellar bakery also churns out a wealth of to-die-for breads, pastries, and bagels — not to mention potent coffee and espresso — making this a great place to start your North Shore day. The plain-Jane dining room has a few tables, and you can find some umbrella-covered tables out of doors; if you prefer, place your order to go. Slices are also available for a lunch on the run (and why not throw in a macadamia nut butter cookie or a white chocolate scone while you're at it?).

See map p. 434. In the Kong Lung Center, Keneke Street and Kilauea Road, Kilauea. ☎ *808-828-2020. To get there: From Kuhio Highway (Highway 56), turn right at the sign for Kilauea Lighthouse and then right at Kong Lung onto Keneke Street; it's behind the Lighthouse Bistro. Baked goods: $1.50–$5. Whole pizzas: $11–$26. MC, V. Open: Breakfast, lunch, and dinner Mon–Sat.*

Plantation Gardens Restaurant
$$$ Poipu Beach   Hawaii Regional-Mediterranean

Housed in a former plantation house that stands on lush tropical grounds, this lovely restaurant of gleaming woods, rattan, and bamboo is a bit too bright to be really called romantic; book a seat on the garden-facing patio for maximum ambience. The top-notch gourmet island fare is prepared with a Mediterranean flair, using herbs, greens, and sweet tropical fruits grown out in the back garden, and seafood harvested from local waters. You can keep the bill down by sticking with an array of starters and island-style pizzas or go all out with lovingly prepared entrees like sugarcane-crusted pork; macadamia lamb chops; miso-shiitake risotto; fettucine dressed with giant prawns and asparagus; and seafood lau lau (wrapped in taro leaves and steamed) served with chutney made from homegrown mangoes.

See map p. 434. In the Kiahuna Plantation, 2253 Poipu Rd. (across from Poipu Shopping Village), Poipu Beach. ☎ *808-742-2216. Reservations recommended. Main courses: $14–$29. AE, DC, MC, V. Open: Dinner nightly.*

Postcards Cafe
$$$ North Shore   International

This historic plantation house on the edge of Hanalei wears two hats: one as a hugely popular vegetarian-minded breakfast place, the second as a globe-hopping seafood restaurant. Choose a seat in the schoolhouse-simple but exceedingly charming dining room or out on the wide veranda for alfresco dining. The kichen uses no meat, poultry, refined sugar, or foods with chemical additives; many of the offerings are vegan or can be customized to meet special needs. But healthy doesn't mean bland — not by any means. The creative kitchen pulls out the pan-cultural stops, from yummy taro fritters topped with tropical salsa to Indian-spiced potato-phyllo pockets (much like samosas) to blackened fresh-caught fish in macadamia butter or peppered pineapple sage. I've always loved

Postcards for its innovative yet unfussy preparations and the freshness of the local ingredients; the friendly service doesn't hurt, either. Postcards doesn't have a wine list, but you're welcome to BYOB for a minimal corkage fee.

See map p. 434. 5-5075A Kuhio Hwy., Hanalei. ☎ ***808-826-1191.*** www.postcards cafe.com. *Reservations recommended. Main courses: $13–$22. AE, DC, MC, V. Open: Dinner daily.*

Roy's Poipu Bar & Grill
$$$–$$$$ **Poipu Beach** **Hawaii Regional**

More casual than the other Roy's throughout Hawaii, Roy's Poipu is my favorite of the famous chain. Star chef Roy Yamaguchi's take on Hawaii Regional Cuisine is more overtly Asian than what you'll find at the Mediterranean-accented A Pacific Cafe (see the listing earlier in this chapter). Thanks to an extensive grazing menu of dim sum, appetizers, and imu-baked pizzas, you can easily eat inexpensively here; my husband and I got no guff at all from the waitstaff for building a meal from the starter menu (love those spinach-shiitake ravioli). Signature dishes include luscious Szechuan baby-back ribs (better than dessert!) and blackened ahi with a delectable soy mustard butter. The service is friendly and easygoing, in keeping with the ambience, and the wines bottled under Roy's own label are affordable and surprisingly good. In sum, Roy's is a winner that lives up to its reputation in every way.

See map p. 434. In the Poipu Shopping Village, 2360 Kiahuna Plantation Dr. (at Poipu Road), Poipu Beach. ☎ ***808-742-5000.*** www.roysrestaurant.com. *Reservations highly recommended. Appetizers and pizzas: $6–$13. Main courses: $20–$28. AE, DC, DISC, MC, V. Open: Dinner nightly.*

Sushi & Blues
$$$ **North Shore** **Japanese/Island Eclectic**

The name may be awkward, but neither raw fish nor live entertainment gets any better on Kauai than what you'll find at this loftlike second-floor restaurant and sushi bar. The first-rate sushi chef is a master with ultrafresh fish, much of it caught in island waters or flown in from Japan. There's also a big bar with an extensive vodka, gin, martini, sake, and beer list; a kitchen that prepares very good island-style seafood and steaks for sushi-phobes; and gorgeous Bali Hai views. The restaurant hosts live music — generally jazz and blues — Thursday through Sunday; call for the schedule. It's very chic for Kauai (in fact, this spot wouldn't be out of place in L.A. or Manhattan), but feel free to come in your shorts and Ts — everybody does.

See map p. 434. In Ching Young Village, 5-8420 Kuhio Hwy., Hanalei. ☎ ***808-826-9701*** *or 808-828-1435.* www.sushiandblues.com. *Reservations recommended. Sushi: $4–$8. Combos and main courses: $18–$23. MC, V. Open: Dinner Tues–Sun.*

Waimea Brewing Company
$$ Waimea Island Eclectic

This casual restaurant on the sunny west side is an ideal spot for a late lunch or early dinner after a day spent at Waimea Canyon or Kokee State Park (see Chapter 18). Housed in an attractively restored 1940s plantation house, the restaurant is easygoing and kid friendly; live music adds to the island ambience Wednesday through Sunday evenings. Order up a micro-brewed Na Pali Pale Ale or a Pakala Porter along with a slate of munchies to share, family style. The accents are international, from buffalo wings and quesadillas to island-favorite noodle dishes, jerk-seasoned Jawaiian chicken, and honey-mango-glazed barbecue ribs. Burgers, sandwiches, and foods that go well with brew fill out a surprisingly satisfying menu.

See map p. 434. At Waimea Plantation Cottages, 9400 Kaumualii Hwy. (Highway 50), Waimea. ☎ *808-338-9733.* www.wbcbrew.com. *Reservations recommended for large parties. Main courses: $7.50–$12 at lunch, $14–$21 at dinner. MC, V. Open: Lunch and dinner daily.*

Wrangler's Steakhouse
$$$ Waimea Steaks

This popular Tex-Mex/Hawaii-style steakhouse has "cowboy" written all over it. It's a rustically charming place with good food, good service, and pleasant veranda seating. The menu leans toward hearty burritos, meaty sandwiches, and substantial salads at lunch, and good-value complete steak dinners at day's end. The lil' pardners will love the Wild West setting and the finger-friendly food, including juicy flame-broiled burgers served with steak-cut fries. The menu also has a few fish and chicken options (like ahi with penne pasta) for non-red-meat eaters.

See map p. 434. 9852 Kaumualii Hwy. (Highway 50), Waimea. ☎ *808-338-1218. Reservations recommended for large parties. Main courses: $8–$13 at lunch, $17–$30 at dinner (soup and salad bar included). AE, MC, V. Open: Lunch Mon–Fri, dinner Mon–Sat.*

Zelo's Beach House
$$ North Shore Steaks/Seafood/California

Despite its location blocks from the ocean, Zelo's is the embodiment of North Shore beach culture. This hip, happy spot bursts with life and surfer-dude charm. Don't expect anything approaching gourmet fare, but the large, appealing menu of seafood, pastas, steaks, burgers, fresh fish tacos, and California-style eats is uniformly pleasing. The casual vibe and the lovely views from the outdoor deck make Zelo's a great place to just hang out between meals, too: Choose from a huge selection of coffee concoctions, frosty tropical drinks, microbrews, and martinis.

See map p. 434. 5-8420 Kuhio Hwy. (at Aku Road), Hanalei. ☎ *808-826-9700.* www.zelosbeachhouse.com. *Reservations recommended for parties of six or more. Main courses: $8–$13 at lunch, $10–$30 at dinner (most less than $23). MC, V. Open: Lunch and dinner daily.*

Ice cream, Garden-Island style

For the best ice cream in the islands, hop in the car and head to southwest Kauai to **Lappert's Ice Cream** on Kaumualii Highway (Highway 50), at Puolo Road, just past the turnoff for the town of Hanapepe (☎ **808-335-4045**). This storefront parlor doles out some of the best ice cream I've ever tasted. The secret to Lappert's success is the 16 to 18 percent butterfat in every scoop — yum!! (Most ice cream contains a parsimonious 10 percent butterfat, max.) Lappert's also uses only premium local ingredients in every yummy flavor, from good old-fashioned vanilla to Kauai Pie (Kona coffee ice cream with coconut, chunky macadamia nuts, and chocolate fudge). And these folks never skimp — the Chocolate Chip Cookie Dough is the densest, cookie-doughiest, divinest version ever made. Lappert's also makes tropical-fruity sorbets, justifiably famous cookies, and its own rich and flavorful estate-grown coffees.

I like this original Kauai location best, but you can also find outposts in Koloa, near Poipu Beach and at the Princeville Shopping Center; in a handful of Maui locations, including downtown Lahaina and the Shops at Wailea; and at the Hilton Hawaiian Village in Waikiki. The chain keeps growing — it has even expanded to California and Nevada — so new locations are always popping up. Call ☎ **800-356-4045** or visit www.lapperts.com to find the Lappert's nearest you or to place a mail order and have Lappert's sweet treats shipped right to your door!

Luau!

When it comes to luaus, Kauai excels in quantity rather than quality. Not one is in the ballpark with Maui's Old Lahaina Luau or Feast at Lele (see Chapter 13), or the Big Island's Kona Village Luau (Chapter 15). Still, if you want to join an island-style party on the Garden Isle, the following are your best bets.

Reservations are almost always required for luaus, so be sure to call in advance (a few days ahead if you want to guarantee admission).

At press time, you could save up to 10 percent on the price of admission by booking your Kauai Coconut Beach or Drums of Paradise luau tickets through **Tom Barefoot's Cashback Tours** (☎ 888-222-3601; www.tombarefoot.com).

Drums of Paradise Luau

This lively Poipu Beach luau is the most sophisticated among the Kauai choices, and my favorite. The tropical garden setting is lovely; the bountiful spread, which includes a full *imu* ceremony, is the best of the luau feasts; and the lively floor show features Hawaiian and Tahitian dances as well as Samoan fire dancers in a loosely threaded narrative that tells the story of ancient Polynesian history and migration to the islands.

See map p. 434. At the Hyatt Regency Kauai Resort & Spa, 1571 Poipu Rd., Koloa.
☎ *808-742-1234.* www.kauai-hyatt.com. *Reservations essential. Admission: $65 adults, $50 teens (13–20), $33 kids (6–12). Prices include open bar. Times: Sun and Thurs at 5:45 p.m.*

Kauai Coconut Beach Luau

This Coconut Coast luau (run by packager Pleasant Hawaiian Holidays) loves to tout its Kahili Award, presented by the Hawaii Visitors and Convention Bureau for authenticity. Don't put *too* much stock in that, however; come instead for the family-friendly fun. Set among a grove of coconut palms, the tiki-torchlit luau grounds are attractive, and the hula-focused production numbers are entertaining. A nightly *imu* ceremony is performed (in which the luau pig is unearthed from an underground oven), but the rest of the food is middlin' at best.

See map p. 434. At the Kauai Coconut Beach Resort, Kuhio Hwy., Kapaa. ☎ *808-822-3455.* www.kcb.com/kcb/kcb_luau.htm. *Reservations highly recommended. Admission: $57 adults, $52 seniors over 60, $38 teens (13–18), $26 kids (3–11). Prices include open bar. $5 extra for premium seating. Times: Sun and Tues–Fri at 5:30 p.m.*

Luau Kilohana

This all-you-can-eat buffet of both traditional luau foods and familiar favorites, such as teriyaki beef and chicken, is prepared by Gaylord's, an elegant restaurant that I like but no longer recommend because the kitchen is inconsistent and I've received too many complaints about it. Still, Gaylord's seems to excel at this kind of food preparation, so the luau fare is pretty good. The party is held on the lovely grounds of a historic 1930s plantation house in the lush heart of the island, and it prides itself on celebrating the island's vintage sugar-plantation era. It features a traditional *imu* ceremony starring a kalua-roasted pig, plus a full-on Polynesian Revue. It's not the most authentic presentation, but it's fun, and the kids will love the fire-knife dancer. Expect lots of silly audience participation.

See map p. 434. Kilohana Carriage House at Kilohana Plantation, Kaumualii Hwy. (Highway 50) 1 mile west of Lihue. ☎ *808-245-9593.* www.luaukilohana.com. *Reservations required. Admission: $58 adults, $52 seniors over 55 and teens 13–18, $30 kids 5–12, free for kids 4 and under. Prices include all-you-can-drink mai tais. Times: Tues and Thurs at 5 p.m.*

Fast Facts: Kauai

American Automobile Association (AAA)

Roadside service is availalble to members by calling ☎ 800-AAA-HELP; however, the only Hawaii office is on Oahu (see Chapter 11).

American Express

Sorry, Kauai doesn't have a branch office. Be sure to do your business while you're on one of the other islands.

Baby Sitters and Baby Stuff

Any hotel, and most condo management offices, should be able to refer you to a reliable baby sitter with a proven track record.

Doctors

Walk-ins are accepted at the **Kauai Medical Clinic**, 3420-B Kuhio Hwy. (next to Wilcox Hospital; see "Hospitals"), Lihue (☎ 808-245-1500 or 808-245-1831; www. wilcoxhealth.org/kauai_ medical_clinic.html). Or head to Kauai Medical Clinic's North Shore Clinic at Kilauea and Oka roads, Kilauea (☎ 808-828-1418) on the North Shore, and its Koloa Clinic, 5371 Koloa Rd., 3 miles from Poipu in Koloa town (☎ 808-742-1621).

Emergencies

Dial **911** from any phone, just like on the mainland.

Hospitals

Wilcox Memorial Hospital, 3420 Kuhio Hwy., Lihue (☎ 808-245-1100; www. wilcoxhealth.org), has a 24-hour emergency room located at the north end of Lihue next to Wal-Mart.

Information

The **Kauai Visitors Bureau** is located at 4334 Rice St., Suite 101, Lihue, HI 96766 (☎ 800-262-1400 or 808-245-3971; www. kauaivisitorsbureau.org). Call before you leave home to order the free *Kauai Vacation Planner* or check the Web site for lots of good information. You can also stop in while you're in town to pick up information, but chances are you won't have to; plenty of information is available right at Lihue Airport. Just meander over to the information kiosks while you're waiting for your baggage and pick up a copy of *This Week Kauai, 101 Things to Do on Kauai,* and other free tourist publications; they're packed with good area maps. If you forget, don't worry — they're available from magazine racks all over the island.

Another organization worth contacting for useful islandwide information is the **Kauai Chamber of Commerce,** at 2970 Kele St., Suite 112, Lihue, HI 96766 (☎ 808-245-7363; www.kauaichamber.org); its Web site is especially useful.

The **Poipu Beach Resort Association** (☎ 888-744-0888 or 808-742-7444; www. poipuadventure.com) can send you a Poipu area vacation planner, including a full index of lodging options, before you leave home, or answer specific questions after you arrive. Its innovative Web site lets you book accommodations online and offers an excellent interactive guide to the full range of Poipu area activities.

Internet Service

If your accommodation doesn't offer e-access and you need a fix, visit one of two **Akamai Computer Centers**: on the Coconut Coast at 4-1286 Kuhio Hwy. (behind the Ono Family Restaurant), Kapaa (☎ 808-823-0047); and on the North Shore in the

Princeville Shopping Center (upstairs from Bank of Hawaii), 5-4280 Kuhio Hwy. (☎ 808-826-1042).

Newspapers/Magazines

The daily island paper is *The Garden Island,* available online at www.kauai world.com. The *Kauai Beach Press* is a free biweekly, available around town, that focuses on arts, entertainment, and dining.

Pharmacies

Long's Drugs (www.longs.com), Hawaii's biggest drugstore chain, has a branch in Lihue at the Kukui Grove Shopping Center, 3-2600 Kaumualii Hwy. (☎ 808-245-7771); and on the Coconut Coast next to Safeway in the Kauai Village Shopping Center, 4-831 Kuhio Hwy., Kapaa (☎ 808-822-4915). There's also a pharmacy just north of downtown Lihue at **Wal-Mart**, 3-3300 Kuhio Hwy. (☎ 808-246-1599).

Police

Kauai's main headquarters is at 3060 Umi St. (at Rice Street) in downtown Lihue (☎ 808-241-6711). If you have an emergency, dial **911** from any phone.

Post Office

The main post office is at 4441 Rice St., downtown Lihue (just off Kuhio Highway, near the Kauai Museum; ☎ 808-245-1628).

Satellite post offices are all around the island; to find the branch nearest you, call ☎ 800-275-8777 or go online to www.usps.com.

Taxes

Hawaii's sales tax is 4 percent. Expect taxes of about 11.42 percent to be added to your hotel bill.

Taxis

For islandwide service, call **Kauai Taxi Company** (☎ 808-246-9554), which has sedans, six- and seven-passenger vans, or limos available. You can also call **City Cab** (☎ 808-245-3227). For service in and around Princeville and Hanalei, call **North Shore Cab** (☎ 808-639-7829), or **Kauai North Shore Limousine and Tours** (☎ 808-826-6189 or 808-634-7260) for a limousine, town car, or multipassenger van. For Poipu area service, dial up **Poipu Taxi** (☎ 808-639-2044). Always arrange for pickup well in advance.

Weather and Surf Reports

For current weather, call ☎ 808-245-6001. For marine conditions, call ☎ 808-245-3564.

Chapter 18

Exploring Kauai

. . . .

In This Chapter

▶ Finding Kauai's best beaches

▶ Enjoying the waves

▶ Seeing Kauai's top attractions

▶ Scoping out the shopping scene

▶ Having fun on the quiet isle after sunset

. . . .

*I*f any island was made for kicking back, Kauai is it — so don't knock yourself out trying to stay busy on this idyllic, easygoing island.

That said, you can find plenty of wonderful things to do on Kauai, especially if you're the type of traveler who prefers communing with nature over seeking out man-made attractions and entertainment.

Enjoying the Sand and Surf

Kauai is the oldest of the Hawaiian Islands, geologically speaking — which means that it's had plenty of time to fashion some world-class beaches. Lined with powdery white sands and dotted with swaying palms, the island's stunning shoreline is skirted by crystal-clear waters and numerous well-developed reefs for snorkeling.

Combing the beaches

Safety takes top priority at the beach. Always check on the local surf conditions before you head out. And *never* leave valuables in your rental car while you're at the beach. Thieves prey on tourists, and they can get inside your car quicker than you can spread out your beach towel. Leave good stuff behind at the condo or in the hotel safe if you're heading off to the beach.

On the Coconut Coast

These beaches are located along the Kuhio Highway (Hwy. 56) north of Lihue.

Kauai's Beaches & Attractions

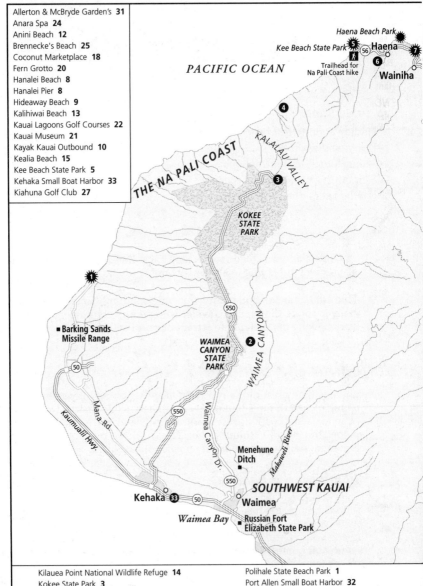

Allerton & McBryde Garden's **31**
Anara Spa **24**
Anini Beach **12**
Brennecke's Beach **25**
Coconut Marketplace **18**
Fern Grotto **20**
Hanalei Beach **8**
Hanalei Pier **8**
Hideaway Beach **9**
Kalihiwai Beach **13**
Kauai Lagoons Golf Courses **22**
Kauai Museum **21**
Kayak Kauai Outbound **10**
Kealia Beach **15**
Kee Beach State Park **5**
Kehaka Small Boat Harbor **33**
Kiahuna Golf Club **27**

Haena Beach Park
Kee Beach State Park **5**
56 **Haena**
Trailhead for
Na Pali Coast hike
6
7
Wainiha

PACIFIC OCEAN

4

KALALAU VALLEY

THE NA PALI COAST

3

KOKEE
STATE
PARK

1

■ Barking Sands
Missile Range

550

WAIMEA
CANYON
STATE
PARK

2

WAIMEA CANYON

50

Kaumualii Hwy.

Mana Rd.

550

Waimea Canyon Dr.

Menehune
Ditch ■

Mahaweli River

550

SOUTHWEST KAUAI

Kehaka **33** 50

Waimea

Waimea Bay ■ Russian Fort
Elizabeth State Park

Kilauea Point National Wildlife Refuge **14**
Kokee State Park **3**
Lawai (Beach House) Beach **29**
Limahuli Garden **6**
Lydgate State Beach Park **19**
Mahaulepu Beach **23**
Na Pali Coast State Park **4**
Poipu Bay Golf Course **24**
Poipu Beach Park **26**
Poipu Shopping Village **27**

Polihale State Beach Park **1**
Port Allen Small Boat Harbor **32**
Princeville Health Club & Spa **11**
Princeville Resort Golf Courses **11**
Princeville Tennis Club **11**
Sleeping Giant **17**
Snorkel Bob's **16** & **28**
Spouting Horn **30**
Tunnels Beach **7**
Waimea Canyon **2**

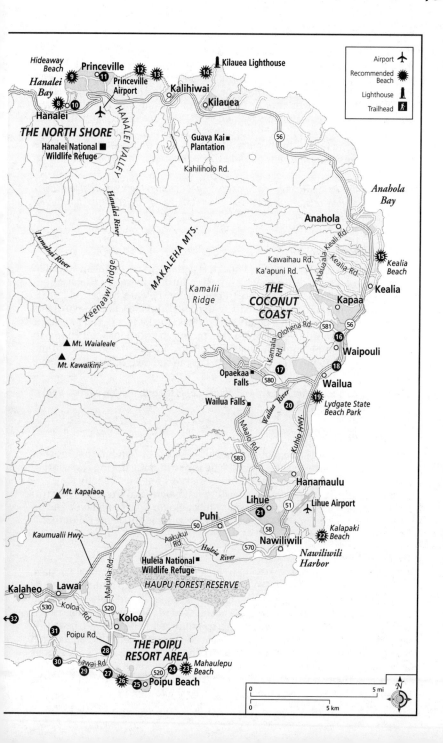

The North Shore

Hideaway Beach
Princeville
Hanalei Bay
Hanalei
THE NORTH SHORE
Hanalei National Wildlife Refuge

Princeville Airport
Kalihiwai
Kilauea
Kilauea Lighthouse

Guava Kai Plantation
Kahiliholo Rd.

Anahola Bay

Anahola

Kawaihau Rd.
Ka'apuni Rd.

Hanalei Valley
Hanalei River
Lumahai River

THE COCONUT COAST
Kamalii Ridge

Kealia Beach
Kealia
Kapaa

Mt. Waialeale
Mt. Kawaikini

Keenaawi Ridge

MAKALEHA MTS.

Olohena Rd.
Kamala Rd.

Waipouli

Opaekaa Falls
Wailua Falls

Wailua River
Maalo Rd.

Wailua
Lydgate State Beach Park

Kuhio Hwy.

Hanamaulu

Mt. Kapalaoa

Lihue
Puhi
Nawiliwili

Lihue Airport
Kalapaki Beach
Nawiliwili Harbor

Kaumualii Hwy.
Aakukui Rd.
Huleia River

Huleia National Wildlife Refuge

HAUPU FOREST RESERVE

Kalaheo
Lawai
Koloa Rd.
Maluhia Rd.
Koloa

THE POIPU RESORT AREA
Poipu Rd.
Lawai Rd.
Poipu Beach
Mahaulepu Beach

Airport
Recommended Beach
Lighthouse
Trailhead

0   5 mi
0   5 km

N

Lydgate State Beach Park

My favorite beach on the Coconut Coast offers the safest swimming and the best snorkeling on the eastern shore and makes an all-around great place to hang out for a day. A rock wall breaks the open ocean waves, forming a protected natural pool that's perfect for kids and first-time snorkelers. Wide, grassy lawns that are ideal for picnicking and kite-flying lead downhill to an expanse of fine-grained sand, with dramatic vistas in either direction. Among the nice facilities are a pavilion, restrooms, outdoor showers, picnic tables, barbecues, lifeguards, and plenty of parking. Note that the waves can be rough outside the protected pool, even in summer, so beware.

See map p. 454. At the Holiday Inn Sunspree Resort, Kuhio Highway (Highway 56) 5 miles north of Lihue (just south of Wailua River State Park). To get there: Look for the turnoff at Leho Road.

Kealia Beach

This long, wide, crescent-shaped beach is a great place to play in summer. Gorgeous golden sands fringe white-crested turquoise waters that are suitably calm, particularly at the north end — but beware winter and year-round late-day swells, which can really kick up. This local favorite is particularly popular with casual bodysurfers. Kealia is a perfect spot for those seeking solitude because it has plenty of room for everybody to spread out, even on summer weekends. Bring a blanket and a lunchtime picnic because no facilities are on-site. Park in the dirt lot and don't leave any valuables in your car.

See map p. 454. On Kuhio Highway (Highway 56) just north of Kapaa town, across from the Kealia Country Store.

On the North Shore

Welcome to the finest beaches in Hawaii — but bear in mind that most of Kauai's North Shore beaches aren't safe for swimming during the winter months. The swells come just before Christmastime and usually stay through March, turning up the waves to full height and the undertow to unmanageable levels for most regular folks. So do yourself a favor and head to the South Shore if you want to take a dip in the winter months.

Kalihiwai Beach

This best-kept secret of North Shore beaches is a favorite of local families, who come to enjoy the wide and gorgeous white sands and the shallow brackish ponds that remain safe for little ones to play in even when the ocean surf kicks up. You actually get two beaches here: The main beach, which offers plenty of sand for everybody to enjoy; and the second beach — actually the shoreline of the Kalihiwai Stream (accessible via the Anini Beach Road fork; see the upcoming directions), from which you can wade across freshwater shallows to the wide main beach "island" in the middle. (The main beach is actually a wide sandbar separating the tranquil stream from the ocean; the ocean and river meet at one very shallow end.)

I suggest using the first set of directions that I give in the next paragraph so that you don't have to wade across the stream to reach the beach. (The water is waist-deep for most adults at its deepest point.) In the warm-weather seasons, the surf is usually calm enough for swimming and easy wave jumping, while the brackish stream water is tranquil, shallow, and warm as a bathtub. Preschoolers love to toddle in the extreme shallows, and bigger kids jump off the lava rocks into the deep freshwater pool at the beach's west end (to your left as you face the waves). The shallows usually stay calm, but stay out of the surf if it begins to kick up — and stay out altogether in winter. The beach has no facilities, so bring everything that you may need; a grove of ironwood trees offers shade for an afternoon picnic. The crowd runs the gamut from local families to construction workers on their lunch break, but it tends to be friendly and easygoing across the board.

See map p. 454. Off Kuhio Highway (Highway 56) past the turnoff for Kilauea. To get there: As you head toward the North Shore, take the first exit called Kalihiwai Road, near mile marker 24; follow it to the parking lot. Or, follow the directions for Anini Beach (coming up next); take a right at the Anini Beach Road fork (the sign says "Dead End"), and then park at the makeshift lot just before the "No Trespassing" sign.

Anini Beach

Tucked away in a million-dollar residential neighborhood, this secret beach is one of the most beautiful — and safest — swimming beaches on Kauai. The 3-mile-long gold-sand beach is shielded from the open ocean by the longest, widest fringing reef in the islands. With shallow water less than 5 feet deep, it's the very best beach on Kauai for beginning snorkelers, and it boasts the most well-protected North Shore waters in winter. The grassy park has picnic and barbecue facilities, restrooms, and a boat-launch ramp. A real gem!

See map p. 454. Off Kuhio Highway (Highway 56) past the turnoff for Kilauea. To get there: As you head toward the North Shore, ignore the first exit called Kalihiwai Road (the turnoff for Kalihiwai Beach) and turn right at the second exit (west of mile marker 25); at the fork, follow Anini Beach Road (left) to beach park.

Hideaway Beach

Reaching this super-secret spot may take a little work, but this beach is well worth the effort, especially for romance-seeking couples. The perfectly named Hideaway Beach is a gorgeous pocket of beach in the Princeville Resort where the snorkeling is great, the sand is powder-fine, and the atmosphere is as tranquil as it gets. Even if a few other souls find their way there, everyone is happily content to keep to themselves. Fair warning: Getting to Hideaway is not for the faint of heart. From the parking lot, walk down the dirt path that runs between the two chain-link fences on the right; the path will take you to a steep staircase that leads down to the beach. It has no facilities, of course, so bring what you need. You shouldn't visit this beach at night; the staircase isn't appropriate at night, and there are no lights.

See map p. 454. In the Princeville Resort off Kuhio Highway (Highway 56), just east of Princeville Shopping Center. To get there: Go 2 miles to the entrance of the hotel; just before the gatehouse, turn into the public parking lot on your right.

Hanalei Beach

Half-moon Hanalei Bay has to be one of the loveliest beaches on earth. Gentle waves roll up the wide, golden sand; towering coco palms sway to the rhythm of the trade winds; waterfalls vein volcanic ridges in the distance, some 3 miles inland. Like the tab of a giant jigsaw-puzzle piece, the bay takes a sizeable bite out of the coastline a full mile inland. It's an excellent spot for swimming in summer; in winter, stick to the westernmost curve of the bay, where the water usually stays calm even when winter swells hit. Facilities include a pavilion, restrooms, picnic tables, and parking. This beach is always packed with both local residents and visitors, but the bay is big enough for everyone to enjoy; you can usually find a spot to yourself just by strolling down the shoreline.

See map p. 454. Off Kuhio Highway (Highway 56), Hanalei. To get there: Turn right on Aku Road (just after Tahiti Nui), which leads to Weke Road and the main parking lot.

Tunnels Beach

If I had to pick one beach above all others on Kauai, it would have to be Tunnels. Postcard-perfect, with swaying palms, a shelter of ironwoods, and gold sand rimming a curving shore, Tunnels is one of the most beautiful stretches of beach in all Hawaii. Go at sunset, when golden rays butter a wide-open blue sky and bounce off the green steepled ridges. The sand here is rougher and more pumice-textured than elsewhere (but somehow all the more luxurious for it). The ironwoods provide welcome shade in the heat of the tropical summer. Protected by a fringing coral reef, Tunnels is excellent for swimming and snorkeling — one of my best snorkeling days ever was here — but beware the winter waves, of course. No facilities mar the pristine scene, so bring whatever supplies that you think you may need.

You must park on the dirt access road — if you park on the shoulder of the main road, you *will* get a ticket. Heed the "No Parking Anytime" signs. If no parking's available along the access road, go ⅗₀ mile down, park at the Haena Beach Park, and walk back.

See map p. 454. Off Kuhio Highway (Highway 56) beyond Hanalei, ⅗₀ mile past Hanalei Colony Resort, down an unmarked drive. To get there: Turn right down the sandy access road across the street from the green house; it's just after the yellow "Narrow Bridge" sign and the two-story light green house. Park in the alley or along the highway with everybody else, walk down the alley, and turn left at the "Beach Path" sign.

Kee (KAY-eh) Beach State Park

At the end of Kuhio Highway is a real dandy of a beach — a small crescent of golden-brown sand nestled between soaring volcanic cliffs and an ironwood grove. This remote little spot isn't quite as lovely as Tunnels, but it comes close — and it boasts easier access and facilities and is equally terrific for swimming and snorkeling (although a friend I recently brought here — a bonafide city girl — despised the hippie vibe). You'll really feel as if you're at the end of the world out here, even if you're not alone (which you probably won't be). A well-developed reef keeps the water shallow and calm, making the inlet great for kids and snorkelers of all levels; nobody should venture out beyond the reef, though. Facilities include some rustic restrooms, showers, and lots of parking, but no lifeguard. Don't be surprised if you see a substantial clutch of Kauai's infamous wild chickens pecking and cock-a-doodle-doing their way around the parking lot.

Kee is where you pick up the trailhead to the Na Pali Coast. It takes about three hours to hike the first 2 miles in (that's as far as I suggest you go) and back, so the heartier among you may want to plan on it; see the section called "Exploring on Dry Land," later in this chapter, for further details.

See map p. 454. At the end of Kuhio Highway (Highway 56), about 7½ miles past Hanalei.

In the Poipu area

To reach these beaches, Maluhia Road (Hwy. 520) from the Kaumualii Highway (Hwy. 50) toward Poipu Beach.

Poipu Beach Park

Nobody should miss this big, wide beach park. It's the perfect beach playground, where grassy lawns with leafy shade trees skirt abundant white sand at the water's edge. It's actually a series of crescents, with the two most prominent ones divided by a sandbar: On the left, a lava-rock jetty protects a sandy-bottom pool that's perfect for small kids; on the right, the open bay is great for more advanced swimmers, snorkelers, and surfers. The swimming is excellent, with small tidepools for exploring and great reefs for snorkeling and diving. Amenities include lots of top-notch facilities — including nice bathrooms, outdoor showers, picnic pavilions, plenty of parking, and a good restaurant and snack bar (Brennecke's Beach Broiler; see Chapter 17) just across the street. Poipu attracts a daily crowd of visitors and local residents, but the density seldom approaches Waikiki levels, except on holidays.

See map p. 454. To get there: From Kaumualii Highway (Highway 50), turn south on Maluhia Road and follow it to Poipu Road. Go past Poipu Shopping Village and turn right on Hoowili Road, which will take you to the beach.

Lawai Beach (Beach House) Beach

This small, rocky white-sand beach just to the west of the Beach House Restaurant isn't the most beautiful on the South Shore, but snorkelers will love it. The water is warm, shallow, clear, and delightfully populated with clouds of tropical fish. Plenty of streetside parking is available, plus some nice restrooms and showers just across the street and a grassy lawn in front of the Beach House.

See map p. 454. On Lawai Road next to the Beach House Restaurant, Poipu Beach. To get there: From Kaumualii Highway (Highway 50), turn south on Maluhia Road (Highway 520) and continue south on Poipu Road. At the "WELCOME TO POIPU BEACH" sign, go to the right, toward Spouting Horn; it's a mile or two down, across from the Lawai Beach Resort (look for the restaurant on your left).

Mahaulepu Beach

Here is one of the finest stretches of untouched sands in Hawaii. With 2 miles of grainy, red-gold sand tucked among rocky cliffs, sand dunes, and a forest of casaurina trees, this idyllic stretch is perfect for beachcombing, sunbathing, or just cuddling up with your cutie and watching the endless waves roll in. Swimming and snorkeling are risky, except in the reef-sheltered shallows about 200 yards west of the sandy parking lot. No facilities are on-site — just lots of pristine natural beauty. Best of all, you're likely to have it all to yourselves. Mahaulepu makes a wonderful place to get away from it all and discover Hawaii at its natural best. Bring a picnic for maximum romance.

See map p. 454. Off Poipu Road, 3 miles past the Hyatt Regency Kauai Resort and Spa and 2 miles from the end of Poipu Road (the unpaved stretch is called Weliweli Road). To get there: Turn right at the T intersection; stop and register at the security hut, drive 1 mile to the big sand dune, turn left, and drive a ½ mile to the small lot under the trees.

On the west shore

If it's raining everywhere else on Kauai, just get in your car and head west. Keep going to the end of the road, and you'll find a mini-Sahara where the sun (almost) always shines.

Polihale State Beach Park

Polihale is a wonderful place to get away from it all. It holds Hawaii's biggest beach — 17 miles long and as wide as three football fields. The golden sands wrap around Kauai's northwestern shore from just beyond Waimea all the way to the edge of the Na Pali Coast. Some of the stretches of sand are accessible from the highway, but I like the remote area past the cane fields best. The safest place to swim is Queen's Pond, a small, shallow, sandy-bottomed protected inlet that's usually calm, except when the high winter surf washes over the reef — stay out of the water altogether then. Restrooms, showers, picnic tables, and pavilions are scattered throughout the park, but no lifeguards are on hand.

 Be careful at Polihale year-round because this is open ocean, and swimming is dangerous. Strong swimmers can bodysurf with caution in summer, but everybody should stay out of the water in winter. And here are a few more tips for visiting Polihale State Beach Park:

- Don't leave any valuables in your car. Rental cars are burgled on occasion out here.

- Always wear flip-flops or reef shoes. The midday sand can be hotter than a griddle.

- Don't attempt to drive the unpaved cane road out to the beach if recent rains have left the road muddy. It's easy to get stuck, and this beach is far from civilization.

See map p. 454. At the end of Kaumualii Highway (Highway 50), a 40-minute drive west of Poipu. To get there: Drive past the Barking Sands Missile Range and follow the signs through the sugarcane fields to Polihale. The road isn't paved, but it's flat and well graded, so just take it slow; it's about a 5-mile drive. Queen's Pond is at the 3¼-mile mark along the cane road, where the road curves near a large monkeypod tree; take the fork to the left and park almost immediately and then walk north along the beach until you come to a hollow in the rock; pass through it to the beach.

Playing in the surf

If you want to rent boogie boards, snorkel gear, kayaks, and other beach toys, Kauai has a number of reliable outlets — all of which can book organized activities for you, too.

My favorite place to rent snorkel gear is **Snorkel Bob's** on the Coconut Coast at 4-734 Kuhio Hwy. (on the ocean side of the street), Kapaa (☎ **808-823-9433**); and at Poipu Beach at 3236 Poipu Road, just south of Old Koloa Town (☎ **808-742-2206**). Snorkel Bob's rents the best-quality snorkel gear. The best-quality gear — the "Ultimate Truth" — rents for $7.50 a day, or $30 a week ($22 per week for kids) for the mask/snorkel/fins set. If you're nearsighted, you can even rent a prescription mask for $10 more (so you can actually see while you're underwater), plus boogie boards, life vests, wetsuits, beach chairs, and so on. The people at Bob's shop can also sign you up for select activities — snorkel cruises, helicopter rides, bike tours, and luaus — with their favorite vendors. (Their choices are, in general, very good ones.) Both shops are open every day from 8 a.m. to 5 p.m. You don't need to reserve in advance, but advance bookings are available online at www.snorkelbob.com.

 You can rent a set of snorkel gear from Snorkel Bob's at the start of your trip, carry it with you as you travel throughout the islands (you get attached to this stuff, you know), and then return it to another Snorkel Bob's location on Oahu, Maui, or the Big Island. (All shops offer 24-hour gear return service.) I suggest renting equipment, even if you intend to go on snorkel cruises or kayak trips that provide gear. Free gear is almost always awful — and I don't want you to miss out on spotting sea turtles and other groovy critters because you're fussing with a clogged snorkel or a leaking mask.

On the North Shore, rent your gear from the friendly folks at **Kayak Kauai Outbound,** a mile past Hanalei Bridge on Highway 56 (look for them on the ocean side of the road, the third building on the right as you enter Hanalei, across from Postcards Cafe) in Hanalei (☎ **800-437-3507** or 808-826-9844; www.kayakkauai.com). They have a second shop on the Coconut Coast, in the south parking lot of the Coconut Marketplace, on Kuhio Highway (Highway 56) in Wailua (☎ **808-822-9179**). Kayak Kauai rents snorkel gear, body- and surfboards, river and ocean kayaks (the Coconut Coast shop is just a half-mile from the Wailua River), and even camping and backpacking gear. (See the kayaking section later in this chapter for details on their guided kayak trips.)

Snorkeling

Kauai does offer a number of snorkel cruises, but unless you're going to combine snorkeling with a Na Pali sightseeing trip (see the following section), I say save your money. Kauai is best known for its offshore snorkeling, which anybody can do — it only requires that you have a small amount of swimming ability and some good gear (see the preceding section for rental locations). You can rent snorkel gear from **Snorkel Bob's** (see the preceding section for rental locations).

My absolute favorite offshore snorkeling in Hawaii is off Kauai's North Shore. **Anini, Hideaway, Tunnels,** and **Kee beaches** are all world-class, boasting crystal-clear water and a mind-boggling abundance of colorful fish.

Although placid throughout the summer months, most of Kauai's North Shore beaches become too rough for swimming during the winter, when swells kick up, and the undertow starts churning. Anini Beach is well-protected enough to stay calm year-round. Kee Beach is the second-most reliable in terms of calm winter waves.

For little ones or first-time snorkelers, head to the Coconut Coast's **Lydgate State Beach Park,** where a lava-rock wall forms a natural pool that stays calm even as the waters churn around it. The calm coves at **Poipu Beach Park** make another excellent choice for beginners, whether they're 6 or 60. Of the North Shore beaches, Kee is the best protected. **Lawai Beach** isn't picture-postcard pretty, but it's my favorite place to snorkel in the Poipu area. You may even spot some little critters darting in and out of detritus left by Hurricane Iniki, such as concrete blocks and spare tires, the remnants of nearby hotels devastated by the 1992 storm.

For details on all the beaches that I discuss here, see the section "Combing the beaches," earlier in this chapter.

Keep these **snorkel tips** in mind as you don your fins and head into the water:

- ✔ Make mornings your offshore snorkel time on Maui, because the winds often start to kick up around noon, making surf conditions rougher and less conducive to fish-spying.

- ✔ Always snorkel with a friend and keep an eye on each other.

- ✔ Look up every few minutes to get your bearings, check your position in relation to the shoreline, and see whether there's any boat traffic.

✔ Don't touch anything. Not only can your fingers and feet damage coral, but it can give you nasty cuts. Moreover, camouflaged fish and spiny shells may surprise you.

✔ Before you set out, check surf conditions by calling one of the local dive or snorkel shops, such as Snorkel Bob's, which can give you the latest on local conditions, and recommend alternative spots if the prime ones are too rough for snorkeling.

Cruising the Na Pali Coast and other on-deck adventures

There are three ways to see the most spectacular coastline in all Hawaii, Kauai's remote Na Pali Coast: by helicopter tour (see "Taking a flightseeing tour," later in this chapter), by hiking in (see "Sightseeing with a guide," later in this chapter), or by catching a boat ride around the bend. I like the approach from sea best; it's simply breathtaking. Most cruises combine snorkeling with sightseeing.

Kauai serves as an excellent vantage from which to see the Pacific humpback whales make their annual visit to Hawaii from Alaska between December and April. In season, most cruise operators combine whale-watching with their regular adventures.

The water can be very choppy as you cruise the North Shore — especially in winter, but not exclusively so. Mornings are usually calm, but the surf tends to kick up later in the day. Those of you with sensitive tummies should take Dramamine or other motion-sickness meds *well before* you set out on one of these expeditions — when you're out on the sea, it's too late for the drugs to have any benefit. You won't enjoy yourself, and a perfectly good (and expensive) trip will be ruined. Also available are nausea-prevention wristbands, which you can find at any drugstore, that seem to benefit many users.

 You may be able to save a few bucks on your Na Pali Coast or other cruise by booking it through Maui-based **Tom Barefoot's Cashback Tours** (☎ **888-222-3601;** www.tombarefoot.com), which also books activities on Kauai. Tom Barefoot is a very reliable activities center that's willing to split its commissions with you so that everybody comes out ahead. You'll save 7 to 15 percent on trips with select outfitters — which could add up to big savings, especially if you're bringing along the entire family.

Capt. Andy's Sailing Adventures

Capt. Andy runs the *Spirit of Kauai,* a late-model 55-foot, 49-passenger Gold Coast catamaran, on a number of regular trips to the glorious Na Pali Coast. The boat is sleek and comfy, excelling at both speed and stability, and the staff is friendly, extremely knowledgable about the Na Pali Coast, and attentive. Choose from morning, afternoon, and full-day Na Pali Coast trips, which include sailing, snorkeling, dolphin-watching, and usually lunch. You also have the option of a sunset cruise, which includes cocktails, to either

Na Pali or Poipu. Call or check the Web site for the current schedule because the Na Pali schedule is truncated in winter (but whale-watching compensates).

Most cruises depart Port Allen Small Boat Harbor, Highway 541 (off Highway 50 halfway between Poipu and Waimea). Poipu sunset cruises depart from Kukuiula Harbor, Poipu Beach. ☎ *800-535-0830 or 808-335-6833.* www.capt-andys.com. *Prices: $59–$129 adults, $40–$89 kids 5–12. At press time, you could book online for a 10 percent discount.*

Captain Sundown

Captain Sundown is the only operator to offer cruises year-round from the North Shore, which is much closer to the Na Pali Coast but has a severe limitation on permits. Its 40-foot sailing catamaran carries only 15 passengers, so this cruise is an excellent choice for those looking for an intimate trip. Options include year-round Na Pali sails. From April through December, you have two options: a six-hour morning tour that includes snorkeling, plus a three-hour afternoon sightseeing-only sunset tour. Whale-watching is the raison d'etre on the three-hour winter outing. All trips include an exciting short paddle out to the boat in a Hawaiian Outrigger canoe. This is a small family-owned and family-run business, and they're committed to making sure that you're happy, well informed, and seeing the best of Kauai. Reserve well in advance because these small-capacity trips often book up a week or more ahead of time.

Trips depart from Hanalei Beach, Hanalei. ☎ *808-826-5585.* www.captainsundown. com. *Prices: $110–$138 adults, $75–$115 kids.*

Liko Kauai Cruises

This Hawaiian-owned and -operated company offers four-hour combination Na Pali Coast/snorkel/dolphin-watching/cave tours, with lunch. It all happens on a comfortable 49-foot twin-hulled catamaran (with padded seating, a nice plus). In addition to seeing whales in season, you'll peek into sea caves and lush valleys, glimpse waterfalls and miles of white-sand beaches, and make stops along the way for snorkeling. The narration is in-depth, culturally as well as naturally oriented, and very good. Prices include a deli-style lunch and sodas to wet your whistle throughout the tour.

Cruises depart from Kehaka Small Boat Harbor, Waimea. ☎ *888-SEA-LIKO or 808-338-0333.* www.liko-kauai.com. *Prices: $110 adults, $75 kids 4–12.*

Ocean and river kayaking

Kauai is an excellent place for kayaking, whether you're a beginner, an expert, or fall somewhere in between. First-timers don't have to brave the open ocean; rather, they can paddle down the Huleia River into Huleia National Wildlife Refuge, the last stand of Kauai's endangered birds (it's the only way the nature refuge can be explored), or follow the winding Hanalei River out to beautiful Hanalei Bay. More skilled kayakers can set out for the majestic Na Pali Coast for some real excitement. Here are the best outfitters:

✔ **Kayak Kauai Outbound,** a mile past the Hanalei Bridge on Highway 56 (look for them on the ocean side of the road, across from Postcards Cafe) in Hanalei (☎ **800-437-3507** or 808-826-9844; www.kayakkauai.com), offers guided tours (starting at $115 for an all-day outing, including transportation and lunch) plus lessons and equipment rentals if you want to set off on your own. A second shop is on the Coconut Coast, in the south parking lot of the Coconut Marketplace, on Kuhio Highway (Highway 56) in Wailua (☎ **808-822-9179**).

✔ **Outfitters Kauai,** on the South Shore, at Poipu Plaza, 2827A Poipu Road, just before the turnoff to Spouting Horn (☎ **888-742-9887** or 808-742-9667; www.outfitterskauai.com), has its own full slate of guided kayaking trips. It offers sea tours for skilled kayakers (including a kayak trip along the Na Pali Coast), as well as a guided paddle along the Huleia and Wailua rivers for less experienced folks just looking for some fun. Kayak rentals are also available.

✔ **Kayak Wailua** (☎ **808-822-3388;** www.kayakwailua.com) offers well-priced rentals and guided river kayak tours from the Wailua Marina.

✔ You can also book guided jungle and Hanalei kayak adventures with **Princeville Ranch Hike & Kayak** (☎ **888-955-7669** or 808-826-7669; www.kauai-hiking.com).

Catching a wave

If you've always wanted to surf the ocean waves, now's your chance — Poipu Beach is a great place to learn the moves. Contact **Margo Oberg's Surfing School** (☎ **808-742-8019** or 808-639-0708; www.surfonkauai.com), the domain of seven-time world-champion surfer Margo Oberg. One of Margo's accredited instructors will teach you the basics — yep, including how to stand up — on dry land, so by the time you hit the water, you'll have some idea of what you're doing! These guys swear that they can get anybody up and riding a wave by the end of a lesson. The price is $50 for the two-hour beginner group lesson, including equipment; book at least a day in advance. Lessons are also available for more advanced surfers.

If you already know some basic moves, you can rent a surfboard from the **Nukumoi Surf Co.,** across the street from Poipu Beach at Brennecke's Beach Center (☎ **808-742-8019**). Nukumoi also rents boogie boards, which come in handy at the Brennecke's section of Poipu Beach. (See "Combing the beaches," earlier in this chapter.)

If you want to learn to surf on the North Shore, reach out to **Windsurf Kauai** (☎ **808-828-6838**), which offers surfing lessons in Hanalei Bay as well as windsurfing lessons from Anini Beach, an excellent — and beautiful — place to learn the basics, whether you're 6 or 60. A 1½-hour surf lesson is $60, and a three-hour windsurf lesson is $75. You can book windsurf lessons a day in advance; surf lessons require further notice, and they depend on conditions.

On the North Shore, surfboards and boogie boards are available for rent at the **Hanalei Surf Company,** in the heart of Hanalei at the Hanalei Center (directly across from Zelo's), 5-5161 Kuhio Hwy. (☎ **866-HANALEI** or 808-826-9000; www.hanaleisurf.com). To arrange for a surf lesson with Hanalei Surf's own surf champ and accredited coach Russell Lewis, call ☎ **808-826-1900,** 808-826-9000, or 808-828-0339. Group lessons are $50 for 1½ to 2 hours (four people max), while private instruction is $100 an hour.

Hanalei Bay is the island's most popular surf spot in winter, but it's strictly for experts — so stay out of the water when the waves are up unless you *really* know what you're doing.

Hooking the big one

You simply can't find a better place in the world to sportfish than off the Big Island's Kona Coast, often called the Sportfishing Capital of the World — but if you're not going to the Big Island, you don't have to miss out. Contact **Sportfish Hawaii** (☎ **877-388-1376** or 808-396-2607; www.sportfishhawaii.com), which can book a first-class charter for you on the Garden Isle. Prices range from $795 to $995 for a full-day exclusive charter (your group of up to six gets the entire boat to yourselves) down to as little as $119 for a share charter (you share the boat with five other people).

I always book with Sportfish Hawaii first, but you might also try **Lahela Ocean Adventures** (☎ **808-635-4020;** www.sport-fishing-kauai.com), which takes groups as large as 14 out aboard the *Lahela,* a 34-foot Radon sport fisher, in search of marlin, ahi, mahimahi, amberjack, and other sultans of the sea.

For scuba divers (and those who want to be)

Diving on Kauai is dictated by the weather. In winter, when heavy swells and high winds hit the island, diving is generally limited to the more protected South Shore. When the winter swells disappear and the easygoing summer conditions move in, the magnificent North Shore opens up for divers, where you'll find a kaleidoscopic marine world that's one of the most diverse in Hawaiian waters. I recommend booking a two-tank dive off a dive boat. Here are the best scuba charters:

✔ **Bubbles Below Scuba Charters** (☎ **808-822-3483** or 808-332-7333; www.bubblesbelowkauai.com) specializes in highly personalized small-group dives, with an emphasis on marine biology. It offers up to two dives daily, plus one night dive, with most trips departing from Port Allen Small Boat Harbor on the South Shore. The daytime dives usually feature two locations, depending on conditions. The night dive is particularly awesome, often featuring octopus and other nocturnal sea creatures. Prices are $105, with all equipment and snacks. Instruction, from beginner to refresher courses, is also offered.

✔ If you want to explore a wider range of dive sites — including those off the north, east, and west shores — contact **Dive Kauai Scuba Center,** 976 Kuhio Hwy., Kapaa (☎ **800-828-3483** or 808-822-0452; www.divekauai.com). In fact, it offers so many different dives that you should call for options and prices, which range from $78 to $118 for one- and two-tank shore and boat dives. Dive Kauai also offers a "Discover Scuba" introductory program for $98 to $135, as well as a full slate of PADI (Professional Association of Diving Instructors) certification and refresher courses.

✔ If you've never scuba-dived before but want to learn while you're on Kauai, **Fathom Five Divers,** 3450 Poipu Rd., Koloa (☎ **808-742-6991;** www.fathomfive.com), is the company to call. In business for more than 15 years, this PADI (Professional Association of Diving Instructors) five-star IDC facility offers charters for experienced divers and first-timers alike. It offers no-experience-necessary introductory trips — both tank boat and shore dives — for $80 to $140 per person, including class, dives, and all gear. It also offers full-on four- or five-day certification courses, as well as a range of dives — two-tank boat, night, and shore dives — for experienced divers at reasonable prices.

Exploring on Dry Land

The most enticing thing about Kauai is its natural beauty — so get in your car and explore. Take Kuhio Highway up to the North Shore — my favorite drive in all Hawaii — just surveying the beauty as you go. Stop to take in the beautiful vistas along the way, have lunch and explore laid-back Hanalei town, kick back at one of the fabulous beaches along this shore (see "Enjoying the Sand and Surf," earlier in this chapter), and watch the sunset at the end of Kilauea Lighthouse Road (23 miles north of Lihue, 7 miles east of Hanalei; turn off at the Menehune Mart). It's the best sightseeing you can do on Kauai.

Sightseeing with a guide

If you're a movie buff — or if you just want a local to show you this gorgeous island — call **Hawaii Movie Tours** (☎ **800-628-8432** or 808-822-1192; www.hawaiimovietour.com), which offers the finest guided sightseeing tour of Kauai, hands down. The $95 land tour ($76 for kids 11 and under) shows you more of Kauai in the course of a day (including private areas and estates not open to the public) than you could take in on your own if you toured the island yourself for a whole week. (The four-wheel-drive tour, priced at $113 for adults, $103 for kids, takes you to gorgeous private preserves where the company has exclusive rights.) And the movie angle serves as great context — you'll realize that you've been seeing Kauai on the silver screen for years without knowing it! Remember Blue Hawaii, Honeymoon in Vegas, Jurassic Park, and Fantasy Island? Yep — all Kauai! (Even *Lilo & Stitch* — cartoon Kauai!)

Hawaii Movie Tours also arranges for full-day sightseeing extravaganzas that add a one-hour flightseeing tour to your itinerary. Priced at $255 (including the Land Tour) or $274 (including a four-wheel-drive off-road tour) at press time, this sightseeing value pack is a steal.

The movie tours sell out regularly, so call well in advance to book your spots and avoid disappointment. (A month in advance isn't too early in the high season.) Also, do yourself a favor and schedule a Hawaii Movie Tour for early in your trip. That way, you can go back to that hidden beach or lush garden you fell in love with for some quality time on another day. You can book tickets for specific dates right on the Web site. (Check for Internet specials, which are sometimes offered.)

If you want a more general sightseeing tour of the island, or you don't want to drive yourself to destinations like Waimea Canyon or the North Shore, contact **Polynesian Adventure Tours** (☎ **800-622-3011** or 808-246-0122; www.polyad.com), which offers a range of guided tours in minivans, big-windowed minicoaches (good for small groups and big views), and full-size buses. Only go with these folks if you have no other way to get around; otherwise, they're not going to show you anything that you can't show yourself without the high price tag. In fact, they'll show you less, because these tours are only designed to give you an overview at each of the stops. You'll have to go back on your own if you want to really explore or take time to commune with nature — which is why I suggest that you guide yourself around in the first place.

Book your Polynesian Adventure Tour online to get a 10 percent price break.

Taking a flightseeing tour

If you're going to choose one island on which to take a flightseeing tour, do it on Kauai. Kauai is the helicopter capital of Hawaii. So much of the Garden Isle's pristine natural world — hidden waterfalls, lush valleys, mist-shrouded peaks, the rugged interior of the thrilling Na Pali Coast, the spectral hues of Waimea Canyon's deepest ravines — is inaccessible by any other means. Helicopter rides are expensive, but they're worth the splurge if you want to take home memories above and beyond those of less adventuresome visitors. Most companies can even make a videotape of your ride for you to take home and relive again and again in the comfort of your living room.

There are, however, some considerations. Although all the companies I recommend feature skilled pilots and helicopters with excellent safety records, the truth of the matter is that flightseeing is risky business. Twenty-eight people have died in commercial helicopter crashes in Hawaii over the last decade, six of those in a 1998 Kauai accident. Of course, just getting into your rental car and driving to dinner — or even getting into the shower in your condo with a renegade bar of soap — is many times more dangerous than catching a 'copter ride. Still, you should make informed decisions when booking.

When reserving a helicopter tour with any company, check to make sure that safety is its first concern. The company should be an FAA-certified Part 135 operator, and the pilot should be Part 135 certified as well; the 135 license guarantees more stringent maintenance requirements and pilot-training programs than those who are only Part 91 certified. And if weather conditions look iffy, reschedule.

Be sure to book your flight in advance (at least a week before in high season). All flights depart from Lihue Airport.

✔ **Island Helicopters** (☎ 800-829-5999 or 808-245-8588; www.island helicopters.com. 55-minute island tour: $220 per person): Owner Curt Lofstedt has more than 25,000 hours of flying under his belt, and he personally selects and trains professional pilots with an eye to both their flying skills and their ability to show you Kauai. All flights are in either the four-passenger Bell Jet Ranger III or the six-passenger American Eurocopter AStar, both with extra-large windows, all forward-facing seats, and stereo headsets to hear the pilot's personal narration, which is strong on island culture and history. You'll get a free preproduced video of the tour highlights, but custom videos aren't available. You can usually snag substantial discounts by booking online via its Web site.

✔ **Jack Harter** (☎ 888-245-2001 or 808-245-3774; www.helicopters-kauai.com. one-hour tour: $199 per person; 90-minute tour: $269 per person): A Kauai pioneer, Jack personally started the sightseeing-via-helicopter trend — so, needless to say, he knows this island well. He flies four-passenger Bell Jet Rangers, which give everybody a great forward view and lots of leg and shoulder room, plus windows that open (great for the photographers among you), as well as six-passenger Eurocopter AStars. Jack's signature 90-minute tour hovers over the sights a bit longer than the one-hour flight, so you can get a good look, but the 60-minute tour pretty much covers the island without whizzing by the big attractions in a blur. If you're a shutterbug who's counting on getting some good shots from above, though, go with the longer flight. Be sure to check the Web site for online discounts ($30 off the regular price for the hour-long tour at press time).

✔ **Ohana Helicopter Tours** (☎ 800-222-6989 or 808-245-3996; www.ohana-helicopters.com. 50-minute tour: $175 per person; 65-minute tour: $225 per person): Founded and run by part-native-Hawaiian, Kauai-born pilot Bogart Kealoha, Ohana flies three six-passenger American Eurocopter 350BA AStar 'copters, all with forward-facing seats and colorful pilot narration via individual headsets. This tour is a wonderful choice for an insider's view of the Garden Isle. At press time, you could realize a substantial savings by booking your Ohana helicopter adventure through **Tom Barefoot's Cashback Tours** (☎ 888-222-3601; www.tombarefoot.com).

✔ **Will Squyres Helicopter Tours** (☎ 888-245-4354, 808-245-8881, or 808-245-7541; www.helicopters-hawaii.com. one-hour tour: $199 per person): Will flies a six-passenger American Eurocopter AStar 350 BA helicopter, which has custom bubble windows to allow for maximum views and side-by-side seats (so nobody sits backwards and everybody gets a window seat). Squyres and his pilots have each flown several thousand hours over Kauai since 1984. They're experts on the island, and it shows in their colorful, in-depth commentary. At press time, online bookings made at least seven days in advance garner you a 10 percent price break.

Exploring Kauai's top attractions

For such a small, laid-back island, Kauai boasts a wealth of attractions that are worth seeking out. The Allerton and McBryde Gardens and the Kilauea Point Wildlife Refuge are my favorites of a fine bunch.

Allerton & McBryde Gardens

A former turn-of-the-century private estate that's been transformed into a nationally chartered research facility for the study and conservation of tropical botanics, the 300-acre **Allerton Garden** is simply amazing. It's home to an extraordinary collection of tropical fruit and spice trees, rare introduced and native Hawaiian plants, hundreds of varieties of flowers, a marvelous palm collection, a series of Green Giant-sized Moreton Bay fig trees that were featured in *Jurassic Park,* and some prime examples of landscape gardening featuring outdoor "rooms" and gravity-fed fountains that would have turned William Randolph Hearst green with envy. You can visit the garden only on a docent-led guided tour; it's a fascinating, well-spent 2½ hours for serious green thumbs and novices alike (really — I loved it, and I can't identify common house plants), and it's well worth the price tag. The secret beach you'll visit is worth the trip alone — the view of it from above at the start of the tour was one of the most awe-inspiring views that I've ever seen.

McBryde Garden is a gorgeous research garden that focuses on the conservation and cataloguing of the plants of Hawaii and the Pacific. It's home to the largest collection of native Hawaiian plants in the world (many of them rare and endangered) in a much more natural setting than what you'll see at Allerton. Offered on Mondays only, McBryde tours are led by Dean Jamieson, a fascinating and simply lovely man who also practices the beautiful art of traditional Hawaiian quilting, an art that he weaves into his tour narrative as well. McBryde tours are often conducted aboard a historic open-air red 1950s sampan, which is part of the fun.

You can also tour the well-signed McBryde Garden on a 1-mile self-guided walk Monday through Saturday (a tram will take you into the garden; allow about 1½ hours). You also can tour for free a gorgeous native plant garden located at the departure point.

I suggest starting with the Allerton tour first and then coming back for a McBryde tour if you want more (which you very well may). You may also want to consider visiting **Limahuli Garden,** another National Tropical Botanical Garden on the North Shore (see the listing later in this chapter).

Reservations are required for the guided tours through the Allerton and McBryde gardens. Reserve your tour at least a week in advance, especially in the peak months of July, August, and September. Wear comfortable walking shoes and long pants and bring insect repellent (you'll need it).

See map p. 454. On Lawai Road (across the street from Spouting Horn), Poipu Beach.
☎ **808-742-2623.** www.ntbg.org. *2½-hour guided tours: $30. Kids under 5 not allowed (they wouldn't enjoy it anyway). Tour times: Allerton Garden, Mon–Sat at 9 a.m., 10 a.m., 1 p.m., and 2 p.m.; McBryde Garden, Mon 9 a.m. 1½-hour self-guided McBryde tours: $15. Tour times: Mon–Sat 9:30 a.m., 10:30 a.m., 11:30 a.m., 12:30 p.m., 1:30 p.m., and 2:30 p.m.*

Fern Grotto

One of Kauai's oldest ("since 1947") and most popular attractions is this tacky-touristy trip filled with Hawaiian song and hula — but it's a good bit of fun nonetheless. Flat-bottomed boats take visitors up the Wailua River to a natural amphitheater filled with ferns that's the source of many Hawaiian legends (and a popular site for weddings). Mark my words: Within ten minutes of the launch, you'll be on your feet doing the Hukilau (Hawaii's version of the Hokey Pokey) along with everybody else. The Fern Grotto is lovely, but you'll see more stunning natural beauty just by heading to the North Shore, so you have to be in the mood for the cheeky laughs as well as the ferns. It doesn't matter which boat operator you take; both offer just about the same experience for the same price. Allow 90 minutes for the entire trip.

See map p. 454. Wailua Marina, at the mouth of the Wailua River. To get there: Turn off Kuhio Highway (Highway 56) into Wailua Marine State Park. **Smith's Motor Boats:** ☎ **808-821-6892. Waialeale Boat Tours:** ☎ **808-822-4908.** *Tickets: $15 adults, $7.50 kids 2–12. Reservations recommended. Open: Daily 9 a.m.–3:30 p.m.*

Kauai Museum

The biggest and best museum on the neighbor islands is housed in an attractive Greco-Roman-style building in downtown Lihue. If you're interested in the history of Kauai and neighboring Niihau (or if you just have a rainy day), it's definitely worth a stop. Among the holdings is a wealth of artifacts tracing the Garden Island's history from the beginning of time through contact — when Capt. James Cook "discovered" Kauai in 1778 — and the present. A short video presentation sets the context for what you'll see. The main room houses well-curated rotating exhibitions; I saw a fascinating photo exhibit documenting the reclamation of Kahoolawe, a Hawaiian island used as a U.S. military bombing target until it was returned to the Hawaiian people in the 1990s, a couple of years back. You won't need more than an hour to see the entire museum — maybe 90 minutes if you're really interested. The gift shop is one of the island's top stops for Kauai-made crafts. Guided tours are offered Monday, Wednesday, and Thursday for $10; reservations are required.

See map p. 454. 4428 Rice St. (across from the post office), Lihue. ☎ *808-245-6931.* www.kauaimuseum.org. *Admission: $7 adults, $5 seniors, $3 students 13–17, $1 kids 6–12. Open: Mon–Fri 9 a.m.–4 p.m., Sat 10 a.m.–4 p.m.*

Kilauea Point National Wildlife Refuge

I just love this place. Sitting at the northernmost tip of the Hawaiian Islands and jutting out 200 feet above the deep blue surf, this nationally protected 203-acre headland habitat is a magnet for magnificent seabirds and land-birds alike. Park your car, pay your entrance fee, and walk an easy ⁹⁄₁₀ mile to the rocky headland, whose only structure is the Kilauea Lighthouse, serving as a beacon for ships arriving from Asian and South Pacific waters since 1913. Year-round you can spot red-footed boobies, Kauai's most visible seabird, which roost in the surrounding trees; the magnificent great frigatebird, with 7½-foot wings; and the endangered nene, or Hawaiian goose, the state bird of Hawaii. Depending on the time of year, you might also spot red- and white-tailed tropicbirds; Laysan albatross, famous for their elaborate courtship rituals; or wedgetailed shearwaters, which like to winter at sea. Informative placards make identification easy, even for novices. Look out to sea for spectacular views; if you get lucky, you might also spot sea turtles, spinner dolphins, and Hawaiian monk seals in the waters below. Call for the schedule of interpretive programs and guided hikes. The refuge is well worth a half-hour of your North Shore time.

The wildlife refuge closes its gate at 4 p.m. daily, but don't let that stop you from parking along Kilauea Lighthouse Road to watch one of Hawaii's most magnificent sunsets. No doubt you'll have company, both locals and in-the-know visitors, as you look west to watch the sun sink into the horizon beyond Hanalei Bay, brilliantly illuminating the luxuriant Bali Hai cliffs with its warm orange rays in the process.

See map p. 454. At the end of Kilauea Lighthouse Road, 1 mile north of Kilauea. To get there: From Kuhio Highway (Highway 56), turn right at the sign for Kilauea Lighthouse (at Menehune Mart and gas station, 23 miles north of Lihue). ☎ *808-828-1413.* http://pacificislands.fws.gov/wnwr/kkilaueanwr.html. *Admission: $3. Open: Daily 10 a.m.–4 p.m.*

Kokee State Park

Keep going upland and inland through Waimea Canyon, known as the Grand Canyon of the Pacific (see the listing later in this section), all the way to the top, where you'll find a high-altitude treat: Kokee (ko-KAY-eh) State Park. It's a whole different world up here at 4,000 feet: Kokee is a cloud forest at the edge of an upland bog known as the Alakai Swamp, where the breeze has a bite and trees look like the ones on the mainland. Days are cool, wet, and mild, with intermittent bright sunshine — sort of like the Oregon Coast on a good day. The forest is full of beautiful native plants and imports, like *ohia,* rare stands of koa, hibiscus, eucalyptus, and redwoods. Pigs, goats, and black-tailed deer thrive in the forest, as do a wealth of native birds.

Before you get out of the car, head 2 miles above Kokee Lodge to Kalalau Lookout, the spectacular climax of your drive through Waimea Canyon and Kokee. The panoramic view is simply breathtaking. Then head back down to the park itself. Before you explore, stop at the Kokee Natural History Museum, a small, vital museum where you can learn about the forest and bog before you see it. If you want a bite to eat, Kokee Lodge is open for continental breakfast and lunch right next door. After your museum visit, pick up the nature trail that starts behind the building at the rare Hawaiian koa tree. (You'll see lots of expensive gifts, such as boxes and bowls, made out of this gorgeous wood in shops throughout the islands.) The easy, self-guided walk is your best introduction to this rainforest, and it's great for those who'd rather not take on a tougher trail. The ⅒-mile walk takes about 20 minutes if you stop and look at all the plants that are identified along the way.

Here are a few tips to keep in mind when preparing for a visit to Kokee:

✔ No matter how hot and dry it is down at the beach, bring a jacket with you up to Kokee. Average daytime temperatures range from 45°F in January to 68°F in July. Also bring rain gear and an umbrella if you have it — especially if you're visiting between October and May — as the annual rainfall up here is 70 inches. You can call the museum to check current conditions.

✔ Wear good shoes, as it can be damp and muddy — hiking boots are preferable (if you don't have them, sneakers will do).

✔ The best time to visit Kokee is early in the morning. That's when you have the best chance of seeing the panoramic view of Kalalau Valley from the lookout, before clouds obscure the valley and peaks. Early morning is also the best time to spot native birds.

✔ If you're going to hike, check trail conditions (posted on a bulletin board at the museum) before you set out. Stay on established trails, as it's easy to get lost here. Get off the trail well before dark. Carry water and rain gear and wear sunscreen.

See map p. 454. At the end of Kokee Road, 16 miles north of Waimea; from Kaumualii Highway (Highway 50), turn north on Highway 550, Waimea Canyon Drive, which eventually becomes Kokee Road. ☎ *808-335-9975.* www.aloha.net/~kokee. *Admission: Free! Open daily 24 hours; museum, daily 10 a.m.–4 p.m.*

Limahuli Garden

If you've already visited the gorgeous Allerton Garden on the South Shore (see the listing earlier in this section) and you want more botanical experiences, head to this North Shore branch of the National Tropical Botanical Garden, where you'll find 17 lush, Edenlike acres featuring lava-rock terraces of taro and other native and introduced species. This small, almost secret garden is eco-tourism at its best. You're welcome to explore the garden on your own along a ¾-mile loop (be prepared — it's steep in some areas), which takes about 1½ hours. Or you can schedule a 2½-hour guided tour if you want botanical insight into what you're seeing. Wear comfortable walking shoes; umbrellas are available for your use in case it rains.

See map p. 454. Near the north end of Kuhio Highway (Highway 56), ¼ mile before Kee Beach (look to your left, toward the mountain), Haena. ☎ *808-826-1053.* www. ntbg.org. *Reservations required for guided tours. Admission: $10, or $15 for the guided tour. Open: Tues–Fri and Sun 9:30 a.m.–4 p.m.*

Na Pali Coast State Park

Na Pali Coast State Park is the most spectacular place in the Hawaiian Islands. This 22-mile stretch of green-velvet fluted cliffs wraps around the northwest shore of Kauai. Seven valleys crease the soaring cliffs; hidden within are waterfalls, remote beaches, and other wonders of nature that are too beautiful to be real — and more than difficult to reach. You can see it one of three ways: on a commercial cruise for a from-the-sea perspective (see "Cruising the Na Pali Coast and other on-deck adventures," earlier in this chapter); via a helicopter ride for an on-high view (see "Taking a flightseeing tour"); or by trekking in on your own two feet from the end of the road on the North Shore (park at the lot at Ke'e Beach; you'll see the trailhead on the north side of the road, marked by a large sign). If you reach the 2-mile mark and you want to go farther, you must have a permit (permits are $10 per night and are issued in person at the **Kauai State Parks Office,** 3060 Eiwa St., Room 306, Lihue; ☎ **808-274-3444**). The total length of the trail is 11 miles, and it's a serious challenge. Visit the park's Web site for details and advice before you consider a trip longer than the 2-mile segment I describe.

Without a permit, you can also hike another 2 miles inland from the beach to Hanakapiai Falls, a 120-foot cascade. This part of the trail is more difficult, however, and it shouldn't be tackled if it's muddy. (I saw people coming out who had been literally knee-deep in mud.) Allow another three hours round-trip to the falls.

If you're planning to hike the Kalalau Trail, keep these tips in mind as you plan your adventure:

- ✔ Wear good, supportive shoes (tennis shoes or hiking boots).

- ✔ Don't attempt even the first half-mile if the trail is too muddy.

- ✔ If you're going any farther than the first half-mile, bring plenty of water, plus a hat and sunscreen; snacks and insect repellent are a good idea, too.

- ✔ Use the porta-potties at the parking lot before you hit the trail, because you'll find no facilities along it.

- ✔ If you get as far as Hanakapiai Beach, try to resist taking a dip, as currents are strong year-round, and drownings occur here regularly. Don't even think about entering the water in winter.

See map p. 454. Kalalau trailhead at the end of Kuhio Highway (Highway 56) at Kee Beach, about 7½ miles past Hanalei. ☎ **808-274-3444.** www.hawaii.gov/dlnr/ dsp/NaPali/na_pali.htm.

Sleeping Giant

If you squint your eyes as you drive down Kuhio Highway past the 1,241-foot-high Nounou Ridge, which forms a dramatic backdrop to the Coconut Coast towns of Wailua and Waipouli, you just may see the fabled Sleeping Giant. At the 7-mile marker, look toward the mountain. It's easy to spot: The geologic giant lies on his back, with his head pointing north and slightly east, his feet south and slightly west, and he's got his great mouth open in a mammoth yawn. As island legend goes, he's a giant named Puni who fell asleep after a great feast, but he reminds me of Gulliver and the Liliputians. You're welcome to climb the big guy if you like; the Sleeping Giant Trail offers an easy-to-moderate family hike to a fabulous panoramic view. From the parking lot, posted signs lead you over the 1¾-mile trail, which ends at a picnic table and shelter. Wear sunscreen and bring water — and a picnic, if you like.

See map p. 454. Trailhead on Haleilio Road, off Kuhio Highway (Highway 56) between Wailua and Kapaa. To get there: At the Kinipopo Shopping Village traffic light (there's also a Shell Station here), turn toward the mountain off Kuhio Highway and follow Haleilio Road for just over a 1 mile to the parking area at telephone pole no. 38; look for sign at trailhead that says "NouNou Mt. Trail E."

Spouting Horn

Sort of like an ocean version of Yellowstone's Old Faithful, this *puhi* — blowhole — is quite a natural phenomenon. Big waves hit Kauai's South Shore with enough force on a constant basis to propel a spout of funneled saltwater skyward like a dramatic natural fountain, 10 feet or more in the air. An additional hole blows air that makes a loud moaning sound, ascribed by Hawaiian legend to a giant female lizard, Mo'o, who once guarded this coastline, gobbling up any intruders that came along. Along came Liko, who wanted to fish in this area, and Mo'o rushed out to eat him. Quickly, Liko threw a spear right into the giant lizard's mouth, who then chased Liko into a lava tube. Liko escaped, but legend says Mo'o is still in the tube; the moaning sound, they say, is her cry for help (or her toothache, I'd say). You can stop by for a few minutes to admire Spouting Horn or bring a picnic and enjoy the view as you munch; the grassy little oceanfront park features picnic tables and restrooms. This spot is a popular hangout with Kauai's wild chickens, who apparently can't read the posted "No Animals Allowed" sign.

See map p. 454. On Lawai Rd., Poipu Beach. To get there: From Kaumualii Highway (Highway 50), turn south on Maluhia Road (Highway 520) and continue south on Poipu Road. At the "WELCOME TO POIPU BEACH" sign, go to the right; after you pass Prince Kuhio Park, Spouting Horn Park will be on your left (across from the entrance to the National Tropical Botanical Garden).

Waimea Canyon

The great gaping gulch that Mark Twain dubbed the "Grand Canyon of the Pacific" is quite a sight — no other island offers anything like it. The nickname is apt, for the valley and its reddish lava beds remind everyone who sees it of Arizona's Grand Canyon. Kauai's version is bursting with ever-changing color, just like its namesake, but it's much smaller — only a mile wide, 3,567 feet deep, and 12 miles long. You can stop to take in the view (a great stop on your way to Kokee State Park; see the previous section), hike down, and swoop through in a helicopter. (See the section "Taking a flightseeing tour," earlier in this chapter). As you climb north — and up in elevation — the first good vantage point that you'll reach is Waimea Canyon Lookout, located between the 10- and 11-mile markers on Waimea Canyon Road. Take a peek; you'll see why the canyon got its nickname. A few more lookout points dot the route, each offering spectacular views; Puu Hina Hina Lookout, located between the 13- and 14-mile markers at 3,336 feet in elevation, is a particular jewel.

If you want to hike in, your best bet is the Canyon Trail, which leads to the east rim for a breathtaking view into the canyon. Park your car at the top of Halemanu Valley Road, located between the 14- and 15-mile markers on Waimea Canyon Road, about a mile down from the Kokee Natural History Museum. Walk down the not-very-clearly marked trail on the 3½-mile round-trip, which takes about two to three hours and leads to Waipoo Falls and back. I suggest going in the afternoon — following your visit to Kokee is best — when the late afternoon light illuminates the canyon magnificently.

See map p. 454. About 11 miles north of Waimea; turn north from Kaumualii Highway (Highway 50) onto Waimea Canyon Drive (Highway 550).

Hitting the links

 Always book your tee times well in advance — before you leave home, preferably — especially in high season.

 Be sure to ask about afternoon and twilight rates, which can save you a bundle. Some courses also offer discounted rates to select hotels and condos; check with your concierge or call the course directly to inquire.

Kauai Lagoons Golf Courses

Kauai Lagoons often appears on lists of top resort courses in the United States; in 2000, *Golf Digest* awarded Kauai Lagoons its gold medal, calling the Kiele Course "one of the four finest courses in the country." Both of the Jack Nicklaus-designed courses are excellent: The Mokihana Course is an 18-hole Scottish-style links course that's ideal for recreational golfers, while the Kiele Championship Course offers an exciting blend of tournament-quality challenge and high-traffic playability — perfect for low handicappers. The Kiele winds up with one of Hawaii's most difficult — and rewarding — holes, a 431-yard, par-4 played straightaway to an island green surrounded by water; but the signature is the par-4, 330-yard 16th, a short but demanding ocean cliff shot whose green isn't even visible from the tee. (The trick is to hit your tee shot toward the coconut trees on the right side of the fairway.) The two courses share one of the largest practice facilities in the islands; facilities include a driving range, lockers, showers, restaurant, snack bar, pro shop, practice greens, golf clubhouse, and golf club and shoe rental. Duffers looking to work on their game can arrange for individual instruction or sign up for one of the daily clinics.

3351 Hoolaulea Way (off Rice Street), Lihue (turn at the sign for the Kauai Marriott Resort and Beach Club). ☎ ***800-634-6400** or 808-241-6000.* www.kauailagoons golf.com. *Mokihana course greens fees: $75–$120. Kiele Course greens fees: $125–$170 (includes on-cart beverages). Rates depend on where you're staying (Kauai Marriott guests get the best prices).*

Kiahuna Golf Club

This par-70, 6,353-yard Robert Trent Jones, Jr.–designed course is a real only-in-Hawaii gem, awarded four stars by *Golf Digest*. As we went to press, the course was being fully renovated; the back nine was already completed and looks better than ever. The challenging layout plays around four large archaeological sites, ranging from an ancient Hawaiian temple to the remains of a Portuguese home and crypt built in the early 1800s. The Scottish-style links course has rolling terrain, undulating greens, sand bunkers galore, near-constant winds, a swath of rainbow-colored vegetation, and terrific ocean and island views. A good mix of locals and visitors man the tees. Facilities include driving range, practice greens, and a terrific breakfast-and-lunch restaurant, Joe's on the Green (see Chapter 17).

2545 Kiahuna Plantation Dr. (at Poipu Road), Poipu Beach. ☎ ***808-742-9595.*** www. kiahunagolf.com. *Greens fees: $75; $65 after 11 a.m., $45 after 2 p.m.*

Poipu Bay Golf Course

Home to the PGA's Grand Slam of Golf, this 6,959-yard, par-72 oceanfront links-style course designed by Robert Trent Jones, Jr., is already a favorite among avid golfers — including, no doubt, Tiger Woods, who has won numerous Grand Slams here. *Golf Digest* named the course one of the top ten in all of Hawaii. Fairways and greens are undulating, and water hazards are located on eight holes; the prevailing trade winds add an extra challenge. The champs play this rugged beauty, often referred to as "the Pebble Beach of the South Pacific," like a British Isles links course — smart and low. Facilities include an excellent pro shop, plus a restaurant, driving range, and putting greens.

2250 Ainako St. (across the street from the Hyatt Regency Kauai), Poipu Beach. ☎ ***800-858-6300** or 808-742-8711.* www.kauai-hyatt.com, *or* http://poipubay. ezlinks.com *for online reservations. Greens fees: $185 ($125 for Hyatt Regency guests); $120 noon to 3 p.m. ($110 for hotel guests); $65 after 3 p.m.*

Princeville Resort Golf Courses

Nestled in the glorious environs of Kauai's North Shore, these two much-heralded Robert Trent Jones, Jr., designs are the real stars of the Kauai show. One of the most breathtaking — and toughest — golf courses in all

Hawaii, the Prince sits on 390 acres carefully sculpted to offer ocean views from every hole. Golfers in the know often name it the best layout in the state, and *Golf Digest* lauded it as the No. 1 course in Hawaii. Some holes have a waterfall backdrop to the greens, others shoot into the hillside, and the famous par-3 seventh requires that you tee off over a stunning wide-mouthed gorge — dead against the wind, no less. Needless to say, accuracy is key here; if you miss the fairway, chances are good that your ball's in the drink. The Makai is more forgiving, but don't kick back just yet. It's actually three nine-hole courses in one — the Ocean, the Woods, and the Lakes — with the Lakes being the most spectacular and the Ocean being the most thrilling, thanks to a seventh hole that requires you to shoot from one ocean promontory to the other, with the blue Pacific roiling below. Facilities include a health club and spa, a restaurant and bar, clubhouse, golf shop, and driving range.

Check the Web site www.princeville.com/play and click "Promotional Packages" for value-priced three- and seven-round packages.

In the Princeville Resort, off Kuhio Highway (Highway 56) at mile marker 27. ☎ *800-826-1105 or 808-826-5070. www.princeville.com/play. Prince course greens fees: $175 ($130–$150 for Princeville guests); $120 after noon; $85 for 9 holes after 2 p.m. Makai course greens fees: $125 ($105–$110 for Princeville guests); $85 after 1:30 p.m.; $47 after 4 p.m.*

Horseback riding

There's no better way to admire Kauai's remarkable natural scenery than from high in the saddle. In the Poipu area, **CJM Country Stables** (☎ **808-742-6096;** www.cjmstables.com) offers a number of guided 2- to 3½-hour rides along the beach, some of which work in a break for a swim and a picnic. Prices run $75 to $95 per person, and all levels of riders are accepted.

Personally, I think that the spectacular North Shore makes even better quarter-horse stomping grounds. **Princeville Ranch Stables** (☎ **808-826-7777** or 808-826-7473; www.princevilleranch.com) can take you out on a whole host of guided rides, from a casual yet magical three-hour waterfall picnic ride ($110) to horsemanship lessons for serious riders. Prices range from $65 to $120 for 1½ hours in the saddle. (The higher price lets you participate in a full-on cattle drive.) The company also offers guided hikes, plus sunset dinner and wagon rides that are a great adventure for the entire family.

Always book horseback adventures with plenty of advance notice — before you leave home is best — and inquire about age, height, weight, and other restrictions.

Getting pampered at the spa

The 25,000-square-foot, state-of-the-art **Anara Spa** at the Hyatt Regency Kauai Resort & Spa, 1571 Poipu Road, Poipu Beach (☎ **808-742-1234;** www.kauai-hyatt.com), is Kauai's finest spa, and one of the best in all

Hawaii. "Anara" is an acronym for "A New Age Restorative Approach," which sets the tone for Anara's touchy-feely, homeopathic-minded mission — and God bless 'em for it. This phenomenal indoor/outdoor facility — a lush paradise of fragrant gardens, open-air treatment rooms, lava-rock showers, and therapists with the magic island touch — is the perfect place to spend the day. The spa's masterminds know it, which is why they designed a full slate of spa packages that run anywhere from 1½ hours to a complete day of head-to-toe pampering. You'll spend an arm and a leg here, but it's worth every penny. Stand-alone services are available as well. This place is always booked, so reserve well ahead.

On the North Shore, **Princeville Health Club & Spa** (☎ 808-826-5030; www.princeville.com/play) isn't quite so extensive, mission-oriented, or eye-catching, but its facilities are comfortable, its spa menu appropriately lengthy, and its technicians first-rate. (I enjoyed a sublime Aveda facial here on my last visit.) Prices are a bit lower, too.

Shopping the Local Stores

The Garden Isle isn't exactly what you'd call a shopper's destination, so don't come expecting to give your credit card an aerobic workout. That said, a few hidden gems make the Garden Isle sparkle, especially for those in search of gifts with a Hawaiian flair.

In Lihue

One of the best resources for Kauai-made crafts and gifts is the shop at the **Kauai Museum,** across from the post office at 4428 Rice St., downtown Lihue (☎ 808-245-6931; www.kauai-museum.org). In addition to astonishing native-wood bowls that have been carved and polished to a high sheen, the shop boasts a nice collection of budget-friendly koa gifts like barrettes, bracelets, and key rings, all made from the gorgeous native wood. The little shop also has a good selection of books, *Lauhala* bags, coconut products, and more. You can reach the shop only through the museum entrance, but the door attendant will let you in for free if you want to skip the permanent collection and head straight for the saleable stuff. Hours are Monday to Friday 9 a.m. to 4 p.m., Saturdays 10 a.m. to 4 p.m.

The Kauai outpost of **Hilo Hattie,** Hawaii's biggest name in aloha wear, is at 3252 Kuhio Hwy., at Ahukini Road (the turnoff for the airport; ☎ 808-245-3404; www.hilohattie.com). Geared to the tourist market, Hilo Hattie carries inexpensive, colorful wear that has substantially improved in quality and style in recent years. It's right by the airport, so this is a good spot to stock up on last-minute gifts before you head home.

On the Coconut Coast

Kuhio Highway is dotted with minimalls boasting practical stops and familiar shops, from Safeway to the Sunglass Hut. Most prominent is the **Coconut Marketplace,** 484 Kuhio Hwy., between the Wailua River and

Kapaa (☎ 808-822-3641; www.coconutmarketplace.com). This open-air mall features a largely unimpressive collection of 70 or so shops, mostly of the gift variety. Highlights include **Ship Store Galleries,** which features a compelling collection of 19th-century nautical antiques among the contemporary art; the **Happy Kauaian** for its unabashed collection of tacky souvenirs; **Elephant Walk** for quality Hawaii-themed gifts; and Kauai's own **Lappert's Ice Cream,** a must-stop for ice-cream lovers. Free entertainment, either hula or live music, is offered at the centerstage daily at 5 p.m.

If it's a rainy day and you want to kill some time by catching a flick, see what's on at the **Coconut Marketplace Cinemas** by calling ☎ 808-821-2324.

One of my favorite shopping stops in all Hawaii is **Bambulei** (☎ 808-823-8641), which takes a little effort to find — but stick with it, especially if you're a retro buff, because you're bound to come away with a prize. It's on the inland side of Kuhio Highway just south of the Coconut Marketplace, behind the green storefront across from Kintaro Restaurant. Watch for the multicolored sign just past the Wailua intersection (where Sizzler is). Little Bambulei is home to a charmingly displayed collection of vintage Hawaii collectibles, from salt-and-pepper shakers and '50s fiberglass-shade lamps to aloha shirts and vintage bamboo furniture, plus a small but quality selection of new aloha wear. It's a real joy to browse. Next door is Caffe Coco, an equally appealing spot for a light snack or a full meal (see Chapter 17).

Boasting an attractive blend of old-time retailers and newer fashion boutiques, sweet old **Kapaa** town has really blossomed as a boutique row of late. All you need to do is park along Kuhio Highway and stroll the plantation-style storefronts along the few blocks, and you're sure to come away with an island treasure. **Vicky's,** 1326 Kuhio Hwy. (☎ 808-822-1746), boasts Hawaii's best collection of on-the-bolt fabrics. **Jim Saylor Jewelers,** 1318 Kuhio Hwy. (☎ 808-822-3591), specializes in elegant custom jewelry designs and fine gems. **Hula Girl,** at 1340 Kuhio Hwy. (☎ 808-822-1950), specializes in the most stylish lines of aloha wear for men, women, and kids. Nearby at 1312 Kuhio Hwy. is **dondi ho** (☎ 808-822-3513), which sells T-shirts, sundresses, and other casual wearables printed with the bright floral watercolor paintings of artist Dondi Ho (daughter of island crooner Don Ho).

On the North Shore

The simple town of **Kilauea** is home to the North Shore's premier shopping stop: **Kong Lung Company,** housed in a historic stone building on Kilauea Road and Keneke Street, a few blocks from Kuhio Highway (☎ 808-828-1822). This airy and gorgeous Asian-accented gallery of design brims with beautiful homewares and gifts from Hawaii and around the world, all artfully displayed. The collections of women's wear and aloha shirts in back are the height of casual island fashion. The shop is expensive, but not overpriced; this is beautiful stuff. Upstairs is a delightful loft filled with well-chosen women's fashions on consignment. Out back is the **Lotus Gallery of Fine Art** (☎ 808-828-9898; www.jewelof thelotus.com), a pan-Asian gallery (with an emphasis on works from India, Nepal, and Tibet) that's something of an oddball but nonetheless boasts some incredible gold and talismanic jewelry as well as antique artifacts and carpets. To reach Kilauea from Kuhio Highway (Highway 56), turn right at the sign for Kilauea Lighthouse (at the gas station, 23 miles north of Lihue); a few blocks down on your right is Keneke Street and Kong Lung.

Hanalei boasts more great shopping. Two of the town's finest shops are at the entrance to Hanalei town, on the ocean side of Kuhio Highway just after the bridge and Kayak Kauai Outbound: **Ola's** (☎ 808-826-6937), a top stop for high-quality island crafts, including a gorgeous collection of jewelry and koa pieces; and **Kai Kane's** (☎ 808-826-5594), which is great for hip aloha and surf wear. (Its groovy collection of surfboards alone is worth a peek.)

In the heart of Hanalei on the ocean side of the street, **Ching Young Village** covers the basics, from supermarket to pizza joint. Unrepentant shoppers should instead head across the street to **Hanalei Center,** which boasts a small but satisfying collection of boutiques. The standout is the **Yellowfish Trading Company** (☎ 808-826-1227), which features an eye-popping assemblage of vintage and contemporary Hawaiiana and gifts with wide-ranging appeal (read: you don't have to be a retro nut to love this place), plus vintage bark-cloth fabrics, in case you want to give your home that tropical touch. The **Hanalei Surf Company,** in the old school building at the Hanalei Center (☎ 866-HANALEI or 808-826-9000; www.hanaleisurf.com), is the place to go for surf gear and beach goodies.

In the Poipu Beach area

Poipu has few notable shopping opportunities. On your way to Poipu Beach, you'll pass **Old Koloa Town,** a block-long collection of less-than-exciting storefronts.

Boutique lovers can find a good mix of sportswear, sandals, and the like at **Poipu Shopping Village,** 2360 Kiahuna Plantation Drive (at Poipu Road). The standouts are **Honolua Surf Co.** (☎ 808-742-9152; www.honoluasurf.com), a Maui-based company that makes terrific quality casual wear whose appeal reaches well beyond the surf crowd; and **Hale Mana** (☎ 808-742-1027), a gorgeous boutique with a beautiful mix of vintage Orientalia, smartly designed jewelry, and new Asian-themed clothing and gifts.

My favorite stop for Hawaii-made crafts — even more so than the Kauai Museum Shop — is the visitor center at the **National Tropical Botanical Garden**, on Lawai Road across the street from Spouting Horn (☎ 808-742-2623), where the simply displayed collection is small but high-quality. The emphasis is on smallish, affordable items such as koa accessories,

Lauhala hatboxes, botanical prints, and Hawaii-made paper goods, although a few excellent examples of koa calabashes and jewelry boxes are always on display.

Living It Up after Dark

Things really couldn't get much quieter than they already are on Kauai. This island is made for daytime fun — so my advice is to make sunset the highlight, enjoy a leisurely dinner, and call it a night.

If you want a bit more action, Poipu Beach is your best bet. Of course, for the most animated after-dark entertainment, head to — you guessed it — a **luau.** Kauai has some good options that increase the appeal of just-okay food with an open bar and surprisingly good island-style entertainment; for my recommendations on the island's best, see Chapter 17.

Another fine way to celebrate the end of another day in paradise is to set sail on a sunset cruise. **Capt. Andy's Sailing Adventures** and **Captain Sundown** — both recommended earlier in this chapter, under "Cruising the Na Pali Coast and other on-deck adventures" — offer regularly scheduled sunset sails.

The Hyatt Regency Kauai Resort & Spa, 1571 Poipu Road (☎ **808-742-1234**), has two lovely spots worth mentioning. The **Seaview Terrace** makes a lovely spot for sunset cocktails and live Hawaiian entertainment. After sunset, head indoors to **Stevenson's Library,** a cozy library-like lounge offering live soft jazz and a noteworthy menu of after-dinner drinks, including respectable single-malt and vintage port lists.

Even if you don't dine at the **Beach House Restaurant,** 5022 Lawai Road, off Poipu Road, toward Spouting Horn, Poipu Beach (☎ **808-742-1424**), stop at the lounge for tropical cocktails and a glorious view of the sun setting over the Poipu surf.

Keoki's Paradise, at the Poipu Shopping Village, at Poipu Road and Kiahuna Plantation Drive (☎ **808-742-7534**), features a lengthy tropical drinks menu in the relaxing tiki-style bar, plus live music (usually a trio performing a mix of Hawaiian standards and contemporary hits) Thursday and Friday nights.

For a similar scene in Lihue, head to Keoki's sister restaurant, **Duke's Canoe Club,** on the beach at the Kauai Marriott and Beach Club, 3610 Rice St. (near Nawiliwili Harbor; ☎ **808-246-9599**), which also features live Hawaiian music on Thursday and Friday.

My favorite hangout on the North Shore is **Sushi & Blues,** in Ching Young Village, 5-8420 Kuhio Hwy., Hanalei (☎ **808-826-9701** or 808-828-1435), a cavernous and casual-chic sushi bar and restaurant that features great food (see Chapter 17), a big bar with extensive vodka, gin, martini, sake, and beer lists, and live jazz and blues or dance music Thursday through Sunday. When the music's on, this is one of the liveliest scenes on the island.

Just a stone's throw down the block from Sushi Blues is **Zelo's Beach House,** at Kuhio Highway and Aku Road in the heart of Hanalei (☎ **808-826-9700**), a hip, happy spot that brims with friendly energy and beachy charm. The welcoming tropical-style bar boasts a `lengthy` menu of tropical cocktails, martinis, and microbrews.

Just down the road, Princeville has several night spots. My favorite is the open-air **Happy Talk Lounge** at the **Hanalei Bay Resort,** 5380 Honoiki St. (☎ **808-826-6522**, `www.hanaleibayresort.com`), which offers some of the finest sunset views in all of the islands. Come for cocktails at any time of day — the lounge is open from 11 a.m. to 10 p.m. daily for cocktails and munchies — or come to enjoy a side of live island music with your sunset Monday through Saturday from 6:30 to 9:30 p.m. and Sunday from 3 to 7 p.m.

Part VII
The Part of Tens

The 5th Wave   By Rich Tennant

"Pssst - Philip! It's not too late to fly back to a more civilized island."

In this part . . .

This wouldn't be a *For Dummies* book without an ending that's pure fun. In Chapter 19, you find insider tips on how to ditch the tourist trappings and fit in like a local. And what's more entertaining than good food? In Chapter 20, I give you the lowdown on island dining and traditional Hawaiian eats and tell you how to decipher the local culinary lingo.

Chapter 19

Ten Ways to Lose the Tourist Trappings and Look Like a Local

. . . .

In This Chapter

▶ Fitting in on the islands

▶ Making yourself at home in paradise

. . . .

*H*awaii may be the 50th U.S. state, but it's an ocean — and a world — apart from its mainland brethren. In fact, because it didn't join the star-spangled party until 1959, Hawaii came into the Union as an adopted adult, complete with its own unique personality, fully formed (indeed, ancient) culture, and distinct worldview.

Honolulu sits closer to Tokyo than it does to Washington, D.C. — and that makes a big difference, creating a further divide between the islands and the Eurocentric perspective that many Americans have on the world.

Even the population is dramatically different. Unlike in the rest of the United States, no one ethnic group forms a majority in Hawaii. Although Caucasian and Japanese are the two largest ethnic groups (each account for roughly 22 percent of the population), nearly 35 percent of islanders consider themselves of mixed ethnicity. Hawaii's residents, as a group, don't consider race a factor in marriage; they're just as likely to marry someone from a different race as not.

The fact that Hawaii is both exotic and familiar is one of its greatest appeals. It's also one of the biggest pitfalls for visitors, however: Because Hawaii is part of the good ol' U.S. of A., many first-time visitors think that they have it all figured out. What could they possibly have to know?

 You need to know a few things, it turns out. If you'd rather come across as an *akamai* (smart) traveler instead of advertising your status as a *Malihini* (newcomer), then this chapter is for you.

Mastering the Two Most Important Words in the Hawaiian Language

Everyone in Hawaii speaks English, of course. A few Hawaiian words and phrases have made their way into the common vernacular, though, and regularly pop up in everyday conversation.

You probably already know the Hawaiian word *aloha* (a-LO-ha), which serves as an all-purpose greeting — hello, welcome, or goodbye. It's a warm and wonderful word, full of grace and compassion and good feeling, so use it liberally; there's no better way to get caught up in the true spirit of Hawaii.

A second word that every visitor should learn is *mahalo* (ma-HA-low), which means "thank you" and is used extensively throughout Hawaii. If you want to say "Thanks very much!" or "Thank you *so* much," say *mahalo nui loa* (ma-HA-low NOO-ee LOW-ah). Not only will the locals be impressed with your efforts to learn, but they'll be flattered by your graciousness, too.

Adding a Few More Hawaiian Words and Phrases

If you only master *aloha* and *mahalo,* you'll do just fine. But if you want to put yourself ahead of the curve by knowing some additional useful words, take a few minutes to read the following list. That way, when you're in a restaurant and the waiter offers your little ones a *keiki* menu, describes today's lunch special as particularly *ono,* or asks you whether you're *pau* when he comes to clear your plate, you'll feel like a regular *kamaaina:*

- ✔ **Alii** (ah-LEE-ee): Hawaiian royalty

- ✔ **Halau** (ha-LAU): School

- ✔ **Hale** (HA-lay): House

- ✔ **Haole** (HOW-lee): Foreigner or Caucasian (literally "out of breath" — pale, or paleface); a common reference, not an insult (usually)

- ✔ **Heiau** (heh-EE-ow): Hawaiian temple

- ✔ **Hui** (HOO-ee): A club, collective, or assembly (for example, an artists' collective is an artists' hui)

- ✔ **Hula** (HOO-lah): Native dance

- ✔ **Imu** (EE-moo): Underground oven lined with hot rocks that's used for cooking the luau pig

- ✔ **Kahuna** (ka-HOO-nah): Priest or expert

- ✔ **Kamaaina** (ka-ma-EYE-nah): Local person

- **Kapu** (KA-poo): Anything that's taboo, forbidden
- **Keiki** (KEH-kee): Child
- **Kupuna** (koo-POO-nah): An elder, leader, grandparent, or anyone who commands great respect
- **Lanai** (LAH-nigh): Porch or veranda
- **Lei** (lay): Garland (usually of flowers, leaves, or shells)
- **Luau** (LOO-ow): A celebratory feast
- **Malihini** (ma-li-HEE-nee): Stranger or newcomer
- **Mana** (MA-na): Spirit, divine power
- **Muumuu** (moo-oo-MOO-oo): A loose-fitting dress, usually in a tropical print
- **Ono** (OH-no): Delicious
- **Pau** (pow): Finished or done
- **Pali** (PAH-lee): Cliff
- **Pupu** (POO-poo): Starter dish, appetizer

Pronouncing Those Pesky Hawaiian Words and Place Names

Because the Hawaiian language has only 12 characters to work with — the five vowels (*a, e, i, o,* and *u*), plus seven consonants (*h, k, l, m, n, p,* and *w*) — Hawaiian words and names tend to be long and difficult, with lots of repetitive syllables that can really get your vocal chords into a twist. Master just a few basic rules, however, and "Honoapiilani Highway" and "Haliimaile" will be rolling off your tongue like "Main Street" and "Anytown, USA" in no time.

Half the letters in the Hawaiian language — *h, k, l, m, n,* and *p* — sound out just like they do in English. The one consonant that sounds different in Hawaiian is *w*. W usually carries the "v" sound when it follows "i" or "e"; for example, the Oahu town of Haleiwa is "Ha-lay-EE-vah." At the beginning of words and after "a," "u," and "o," though, it's usually your standard "w" — hence Wailea (why-LAY-ah) and Makawao (mah-KAH-wow), two Maui destinations.

The vowels are pronounced like this:

a	*ah* (as in father) or *uh* (as in above)
e	*eh* (as in bed) or *ay* (as in they)
i	*ee* (as in police)
o	*oh* (as in vote)
u	*oo* (as in too)

Almost all vowels are sounded separately, although some are pronounced together, as in the name of Waikiki's main thoroughfare, Kalakaua Avenue, which is pronounced "Kah-lah-COW-ah".

Here's the most important tip to remember when trying to pronounce a Hawaiian word or name: Don't be overwhelmed by length. Get into the habit of seeing long words or names as a collection of short syllables, and you'll find them much easier to say. (Accents almost always fall on the second-to-last syllable.)

The trick is knowing where to put on the breaks. That leads me to important tip No. 2: All syllables end with vowels, so a consonant will always indicate the start of a new syllable. One of the best examples of this is the tongue-twisting Kealakekua Bay (the famous marine preserve off the Big Island's Kona Coast), which throws nearly everyone for a loop. Break the syllables down by reading the consonants as red flags, though, and see how easy it becomes: "Kay-ah-lah-keh-KOO-ah."

The Hawaiian language actually has a 13th character: the glottal stop, which looks exactly like a single opening quotation mark (') and is meant to indicate a pause. I've chosen not to use the glottal stop throughout this book; it's often omitted in printed Hawaiian and on things like store and street signs. Although serious Hawaiian-language students learn volumes about the glottal stop and its equal importance to its fellow consonants and vowels, you don't need to worry about it for your purposes; you can basically ignore it when you see it.

I've laid out these basics so that you can understand how the language works, but no one expects you to become an expert at pronouncing Hawaiian words. Whenever I return to Hawaii, I always feel as if it takes me a day or two to get my tongue back in working order — and I *know* this stuff. Still, practicing is fun, and with these basic tools under your

If you want to tackle more

If the vocabulary list and pronunciation key in this chapter whet your appetite for the Hawaiian language, a few Web sites can help you learn more. Probably most comprehensive — and the best place to start — is the **Hawaiian Language** Web site (www.hawaiianlanguage.com).

If you want to translate specific words or terms, try the searchable online **Coconut Boyz' Hawaiian Dictionary** (www.hisurf.com/hawaiian/dictionary.html).

If you prefer a hard-copy Hawaiian-language reference or dictionary, a number are available at the online bookstores, including Arthur Schultz's pocket-size *All About Hawaiian,* and the comprehensive *New Pocket Hawaiian Dictionary,* published by the University of Hawaii and generally considered the standard; you can order it online at www.uhpress.hawaii.edu.

belt, you'll quickly get the hang of it. Practice with the first two examples at the start of this chapter, and you'll really impress the locals when you get to Maui: Honoapiilani Highway (ho-no-ah-pee-ee-LA-nee) and Haliimaile (ha-lee-EE-MY-lee).

Knowing How to Give and Take Directions

Leave your compass at home — islanders have a different sense of direction than mainlanders do. Although locals do think of the islands as having north shores and south shores, west coasts and east coasts, seldom will anybody direct you by using the most common directional terms.

Instead, they'll send you either **makai** (ma-KAI), a directional meaning toward the sea, or **mauka** (MOW-kah), meaning toward the mountains. Because each island is basically a volcano with a single coastal road circling it, those two terms are often enough to do the trick.

When they don't suffice, locals are likely to invoke relative terms rather than "north," "south," "east," or "west." If you're standing in Kapaa on Kauai's east shore, for example, locals tell you to head toward Lihue if they want you to go south. In Honolulu, people use **Diamond Head** when they mean to the east (in the direction of the world-famous crater called Diamond Head), and **Ewa** (EE-va) when they mean to the west (in the direction of the town called Ewa, beyond Pearl Harbor).

So if you ask an islander for directions on Oahu, you're likely to hear something like this: "Turn left and go 2 miles Diamond Head (east), turn at the light and go two blocks *makai* (toward the sea), and then turn at the stop light. Go two more blocks and turn Ewa (west); the address you want is on the *mauka* (mountain) side of the street."

If you're on the Big Island at a luxury Kohala Coast resort and you're heading out to catch a snorkel cruise, for example, you're more likely to hear something like this: "Go 8 miles past Kailua-Kona (south) to mile marker 109. Turn *makai* (toward the ocean) on King Kam Road and then left at the bottom of the hill."

Remembering that You're in the United States

If you're from the continental United States, don't say "back home in the U.S." when you're talking to folks in Hawaii. This tip seems like a real no-brainer, but that long flight across the Pacific and the one-of-a-kind Hawaiian ambience and culture can really play tricks with your mind. Islanders are, by and large, a patriotic bunch, so they don't take kindly to being left off the national map. Refer to the continental United States as the *mainland,* which is what they do.

Another very important point in the same vein: Locals are always called "islanders," never Hawaiians, unless they have native blood, which not that many islanders do. (Hawaiian is an ethnic label.)

Wearing Sunscreen

You don't need a trained eye to spot the newest arrivals a mile away — they're the ones with the excruciating sunburns. *Way* too many newcomers fry themselves on the first day of their vacations in an overzealous quest to tan, putting a major damper on their trip — and sometimes their long-term health — in the process. The sun's rays are much stronger in Hawaii than on the mainland.

Hawaii's sun-loving population has achieved the dubious distinction of having the highest incidence of skin cancer in the United States, and as a result, has developed quite an attachment to sunscreen. The deep-tanning Coppertone days are a thing of the past, even among the most zealous sun worshippers — so people will merely look on in horror rather than admiration if you whip out a bottle of SPF 8 to spread on your just-flown-in virgin skin.

Most locals I know use SPF 25 or 30 sunscreen on a daily basis. It's wise not to go out in the sun, even for ten minutes, wearing anything less than SPF 15; those of you with light complexions should stick with SPF 30 or 45.

I always make a special effort to apply sunscreen under bathing suit straps, on the tops of my feet, on the back of my neck, and on my ears and lips — all spots that are the easiest to forget but the most sensitive to painful burns. (In fact, I usually slather up before I get dressed in the morning. It's easier to be thorough when you're not worrying about being modest on the beach; you'll be protected from the moment you leave your hotel room; and you won't get sandy right off the bat.) To prevent sunscreen from dripping into your eyes, use a waxy sunscreen stick around your eyes and a high-SPF lip balm; both are available at just about any Hawaii convenience store.

Sunglasses and a hat are two more good weapons for fending off the sun's rays. Throw away those $5 shades and splurge on a decent pair with UV filters to protect your corneas from sunburn and to prevent cataracts. Wear a hat with a wide brim that goes all the way around; baseball caps leave some of your most vulnerable areas — your ears and neck — exposed to the sun's harsh rays.

Attention, Mom and Dad: Infants under 6 months should not be directly exposed to the harsh Hawaiian sun. Older babies need zinc oxide to protect their fragile skin, and kids should be slathered with high-SPF sunscreen every hour. They also need shades, hats, and other protective gear.

Dressing the Part

There's nothing more tacky-touristy than a bold tropical-patterned aloha shirt, right? Wrong!

Invented by an enterprising Honolulu tailor looking for a new way to drum up business in 1936, the aloha shirt has since spawned a whole wardrobe of bright, tropical-print wearables for men, women, and children, collectively known as aloha wear — and, in the process, it has developed into a way of life in the Hawaiian islands. Spirited, beautiful, easy to wear, and comfortable, aloha wear is the embodiment of the Hawaiian lifestyle.

Aloha wear is acceptable just about anywhere in Hawaii, from the beach to the boardroom to the best table at a four-star restaurant. (A tiny handful of Hawaii's most expensive resort restaurants do require men to wear a jacket, but I don't recommend those places. Go to Europe if you want to pack a blazer.) Of course, the key to wearing aloha wear well is understanding the line that separates sublime from goofy — or, in plainer terms, how to tell good aloha wear from bad aloha wear.

Look for beautiful, well-designed prints with strong colors and no bleeding. Look for quality buttons (coconut or wood are best, but not a must) and pattern matching at the seams and pockets. Excellent brands that offer consistently top-quality aloha wear include **Kahala Sportswear, Kamehameha Garment Co.,** and the **Paradise Found** and **Diamond Head** labels, all of which have revived vintage designs; **Reyn's,** which boasts beautiful patterns in a range of flattering styles, especially for women; **Tommy Bahama's,** whose top-quality clothing lines are generically tropical but suit the Hawaii mood perfectly; and, one of my all-time favorites, **Tori Richard,** which employs some of Hawaii's finest artists to design its patterns. If you visit Maui or the Big Island, **Sig Zane's** all-cotton aloha wear is the height of subdued sophistication and nature-inspired beauty, while on Oahu, **Mamo Howell** has elevated the muumuu to haute couture status. **Hilo Hattie** is the largest manufacturer and distributor of aloha wear (producing more than 300,000 shirts annually); although its stuff isn't the height of aloha fashion, it has increased substantially in quality in recent years while remaining very affordable.

 The cardinal rule of wearing aloha wear like a local rather than a tourist? *No matching.* No themed husband-and-wife shirts, no mom-and-daughter muumuus, no two garments on one person in the same pattern. Period.

Remembering Your Island-Style Manners

As in many Eastern cultures, removing your shoes when you enter a private home is common practice in Hawaii — which is one reason why flip-flops and other slip-on-style shoes are so common in the islands.

Islanders pride themselves on their laid-back manner and friendliness, and they really show it in their driving habits — so leave your need for speed at home. Take it easy. Don't be in a hurry. And don't honk your horn to chastise other drivers, which is considered the height of rudeness. If the car in front of you isn't moving quickly enough, or someone cuts you off, just let it slide. Car horns are used to greet friends in Hawaii.

Leaving Your Laptop at Home and Turning Off Your Cellphone

Even the newly minted mainland millionaires who are buying up Hawaii real estate left and right understand the meaning of Hawaii. Don't cart your business worries halfway around the world; an island vacation is far too precious for that. Conveniently forget to give your boss your itinerary. Hawaii is the place to leave work behind and *relax*.

And don't just leave the work behind — dump the rat-race attitude, too. The quickest way to label yourself a "tourist" in Hawaii is to be pushy, aggressive, or demanding. Islanders tend to take things nice and easy. They're not ruled by the clock and don't like to rush. It's called "island time." Take things as they come, don't stress if things don't happen with the utmost timeliness, and leave plenty of space in your day to do nothing but appreciate the beauty that surrounds you.

Smiling a Lot and Saying "Aloha" to Strangers

Who knows? You may even get yourself mistaken for a local.

Chapter 20

Ten Easy Steps to Island Dining

. . . .

In This Chapter

▶ Knowing what you're eating and how to eat it
▶ Maximizing your dining experiences

. . . .

*E*ating well in the islands isn't a problem. Hawaii has lured some of the world's finest chefs to its kitchens and managed to cultivate some stars of its own in the process. If you love quality seafood, fresh-grown veggies, and sweet tropical fruits, you'll think that you've died and gone to heaven.

But that's far from the end of the bounty. Hawaii's melting-pot society sets a global table. Although Asian flavors and cooking styles are most prevalent, island menus travel the globe, from old-world European culinary classics to good ol' ranch-raised, fire-grilled steaks. Hawaii's cooks have even managed to put their own spin on some of the world's most revered foods — pizzas, burgers, and burritos — with rousing success.

You may, however, want to know a few things about island dining before you sit down to a meal — the first being that Hawaii has two brands of homegrown cuisine: local food (the unpretentious, hearty fare that islanders traditionally eat on an everyday basis) and Hawaii Regional, or Hawaii Island, Cuisine (the gourmet version). If you want to find out more on the culinary front, then this chapter is for you.

Fresh-Caught and Island-Raised

To say that Hawaii's seafood may be the best in the world is no stretch — in fact, some of the world's finest chefs think so. And the selection is generally much more diverse than what you'll find in your average mainland supermarket. But Hawaii's bounty isn't limited to the sea. A wealth of fresh-grown vegetables, including leafy lettuces and vine-ripened tomatoes, thrives in the lava-rich soil. But fruits are Hawaii's real forte. All you need to do is head to the local supermarket to discover a whole new world of citrus and more varieties of banana than you ever knew existed.

Tropical fruit comes as no surprise, of course, but who knew that Hawaii offered so much island-raised meat? In fact, the island called Hawaii is home to the largest privately owned cattle ranch in the United States: Parker Ranch, covering 225,000 acres, including more than 50,000 cattle, and serving as the heart of Hawaii's *paniolo* (cowboy) country.

Traditional Island Eats

Local food is a casual, catch-all cuisine, mirroring Hawaii's melting-pot soul. Outsider influences on the local cuisine arrived in Hawaii from all over the map, from Portugal to Japan and just about everywhere in between. *Lomilomi* salmon is the perfect example of local food as a hybrid cuisine: Islanders didn't have natural access to the cold-water fish, but they accepted it in trade from globe-trotting explorers and traders. Learning to prepare it ceviche-style for short-term preservation, they quickly became accustomed to accepting it in trade and incorporated it into their diet as a staple.

Local food is generally starch-heavy and high in calories, so don't expect it to have a positive impact on your waistline. The most quintessential element of local food is the plate lunch, which usually consists of a main dish (anything from fried fish to teriyaki beef), "two scoops rice," an ice-cream-scoop serving of macaroni salad, and brown gravy, all served on a paper plate. Plate lunches are cheap and available at casual restaurants and beachside stands throughout the islands.

A great place to try local food is at a *luau*. For more on luaus, see the section "What to Expect at a Luau" at the end of this chapter.

The Gourmet Side of the Island Stove

About a dozen or so years ago, Hawaii's kitchens underwent a culinary revolution that went with its cultural renaissance, and *voilà!* Hawaii Regional Cuisine was born. Island chefs were tired of living up to a continental standard that was unsuited to Hawaii living, so they created their own brand of gourmet fare, using fresh local ingredients in creative combinations and preparations.

This type of cuisine is often disguised under other names, such as Euro-Asian, Pacific Rim, Indo-Pacific, Pacific Edge, Euro-Pacific, and Island Fusion, but it all falls under the jurisdiction of Hawaii Regional Cuisine. Although there are variations, you can expect the following keynotes: lots of fresh island fish, many Asian flavorings (ginger, soy, wasabi, seaweed, and so on) and cooking styles (searing, grilling, panko crust, wok preparations), and fresh tropical fruit sauces (mango, papaya, and the like).

A Translation List for Seafood Lovers

Even savvy seafood eaters can become confused when confronted with a Hawaiian menu. Although the mainland terms are sometimes included, many menus only use the Hawaiian names to tout their daily catches. What's more, some types of seafood that make regular appearances in Hawaii's kitchens simply don't show up on mainland menus at all.

You're likely to encounter many of the following types of seafood while you're in Hawaii:

- ✔ **Ahi:** This dense, ruby-red bigeye or yellowfin tuna is a Hawaiian favorite; it may already be one of yours, too, as its popularity grows on the mainland. Ahi is regularly served raw, as sushi and sashimi, or panko-crusted and seared in Hawaii Regional Cuisine. Yellowfin is the beefier of the two.

- ✔ **Aku:** This meaty, robust skipjack tuna is also known as bonito (which may be familiar to you sushi fans out there). Aku is best as raw sushi because it can get too dry if not expertly cooked.

- ✔ **Au** (ow): This firm-fleshed marlin or broadbill swordfish sometimes stands in for ahi in local dishes. Pacific blue marlin is sometimes called *kajiki,* and striped marlin often shows up as *nairagi.*

- ✔ **Hebi** (HEH-bee): This mildly flavored, almost lemony, spearfish is sometimes the day's catch in upscale restaurants.

- ✔ **Mahimahi:** Like ahi, this white, sweet, moderately dense fish is likely to also be familiar to you; it's Hawaii's most popular fish, and it shows up regularly on mainland menus.

- ✔ **Monchong** (MON-chong): This exotic fish boasts a flaky, tender texture and a simple flavor. It's best served broiled, sauteed, or steamed.

- ✔ **Onaga** (o-NA-ga): This mild, moist, and tender ruby-red snapper is served in many fine restaurants; be sure to sample it if it's available.

- ✔ **Ono** (OH-no): "Ono" means "good to eat" in Hawaiian, and this mackerel-like fish sure is. Also called *wahoo,* it's similar to snapper, but firmer and drier. You should have multiple opportunities to try this popular, distinctly flavored fish; it's often served grilled and in sandwiches.

- ✔ **Opah** (OH-pa): This rich, almost creamy moonfish is good served just about any way, from sashimi to baked.

- ✔ **Opakapaka** (oh-pa-ka-PA-ka): Either pink or crimson snapper, this light, flaky, elegant fish is very popular on fine-dining menus.

- ✔ **Shutome** (shuh-TOE-me): This is what mainlanders call swordfish. It's a sweet and tender steaklike fish that's great grilled or broiled.

- ✔ **Tombo:** This is albacore tuna — but this firm, flavorful whitefish surpasses the canned stuff by miles when prepared appropriately.

- **Uku** (OO-koo): This gray — pale pink, really — snapper is flaky, moist, and delicate.

- **Ulua** (oo-LOO-ah): Ulua is large jack trevally, a firm-fleshed, flavorful fish also known as *pompano*.

More Everyday Hawaiian Food Terms

All the following foods are common in plate lunches and at luaus. A number of them also pop up on gourmet menus — usually with expensive ingredients and prepared with a twist, of course:

- **Bento:** A Japanese box lunch.

- **Haupia** (how-PEE-ah): Creamy coconut pudding, usually served in squares.

- **Kalua pork:** Pork slow-cooked in an *imu,* or underground oven; listed on menus as "luau pig" on occasion. Sometimes, it's served in a pulled kalua pork sandwich, much like barbecue pork might be in the southeast United States or Texas.

- **Kiawe** (kee-AH-vay): An aromatic mesquite wood often used to fire the wood-burning ovens.

- **Laulau:** Pork, chicken, or fish wrapped in ti leaves and steamed.

- **Lilikoi** (lil-EE-koy): Passion fruit.

- **Lomilomi** (low-mee-LOW-mee) **salmon:** Salted salmon marinated, ceviche-like, with tomatoes and green onions.

- **Lumpia** (lum-PEE-ah): The Portuguese version of a spring roll, but spicier, doughier, and deep-fried (and usually stuffed with pork and veggies).

- **Malassada** (mah-lah-SAH-da): The Portuguese version of a doughnut, usually round, deep-fried, and generously sprinkled with powdered sugar.

- **Manapua** (man-ah-POO-ah): A bready, doughy bun with sweetened pork or sweet beans inside, like Chinese bao.

- **Ohelo** (oh-HAY-low): A berry very similar to a cranberry that commonly appears in Hawaii Regional sauces.

- **Panko:** Japanese bread crumbs, most commonly used to prepare *katsu* (a deep-fried pork or chicken cutlet). Creative chefs often use it for other purposes, most commonly as a tempura-like crust on sushi-grade ahi rolls.

- **Poi:** The root of the taro pounded into a purple, starchy paste; a staple of the island diet, but generally tasteless to most outsiders.

- **Poke** (PO-kay): Cubed raw fish — usually ahi or marlin — seasoned with onions, soy, and seaweed.

- ✔ **Ponzu:** A soy-and-citrus dipping sauce popular with Hawaii Regional Cuisine chefs.

- ✔ **Pupus:** Appetizers or hors d'oeuvres.

- ✔ **Saimin** (SAI-min): A brothy soup with ramenlike noodles, topped with bits of fish, chicken, pork, and/or vegetables. Saimin is served almost everywhere in Hawaii, from plate-lunch stands to museum cafes to McDonald's.

- ✔ **Shave ice:** The island version of a snow cone, best enjoyed with ice cream and sweet *azuki* (red) beans at the bottom.

- ✔ **Taro:** A green leafy vegetable grown in Hawaii; the root is used to make poi (mentioned earlier in this list), and the leafy part of the vegetable is often steamed like spinach.

Other Local Favorites

Lest all this unfamiliar food talk makes you think otherwise, remember that the majority of Hawaii islanders are red-blooded, flag-waving Americans — and they love a good burger just as much as your average mainlander. Hawaii has also co-opted Mexican cuisine and made the burrito its own.

Ethnic Eats

Thanks to Hawaii's proximity to the Eastern Hemisphere and its large, multifaceted Asian population, the islands boast a wealth of fabulous Asian restaurants, including Chinese, Thai, Vietnamese, and Japanese. With the exception of Japanese (of course), most Asian restaurants tend to be very affordable. What's more, because island palates are much more used to dining Asian-style, the dishes aren't gringo-ized for a mainland population. Flavors are bold and strong, and ingredients are fresh and crisp. Dining out in Hawaii, you may just find yourself enjoying the finest ethnic food you've ever eaten.

The Joys and Sorrows of the Supermarket

Hawaii supermarkets offer a number of treats that you won't find at your average mainland supermarket. Poi, for example, comes in instant, pre-made, and make-your-own forms (I defy you to find poi in *any* form in your hometown supermarket!). The bounty in the seafood case is much more diverse than what you see at home; Hawaii refrigerator cases regularly contain such taste treats as sushi-grade tuna, fresh Pacific octopus, and whole squid (insert "yum!" or "yuck!" here, depending on your taste buds).

Just about any Hawaii supermarket will have multiple aisles devoted to Asian foods, from noodles to bizarre candies. The juice refrigerator case is also a treat, so don't be afraid to try something new. My husband never misses an opportunity to chug *POG* (passion fruit-orange-guava juice) when he's in the islands.

Java lovers, rejoice. Every Hawaiian island except Lanai has a coffee plantation, and the local brew is available in just about any average market. All Hawaii-grown coffees are delicious, but the world-famous Kona coffee, grown on the Big Island, is the top of the heap. Kauai's beans are probably the second-best of Hawaii's caffeinated crop.

The greatest bounty appears among the fresh fruits, where you'll find such fresh tropical treats as mangoes, guava, star fruit, lychee, lilikoi (passion fruit), and much more. Pineapples are another Hawaii taste treat; the small white pineapples are sweetest, and you'll usually find them clearly labeled at the market. The Big Island's lava-rich soil produces extra-flavorful citrus fruits; Kau oranges, for example, are legendary for their sweetness. Even watermelon is an extra-special treat; Molokai-grown watermelons are the best in the world — full of seeds, but fabulous.

Among Hawaii-grown vegetables, Maui onions are the ultimate treat. They're very sweet, like Vidalias, but with a distinctive flavor all their own. Slice 'em thick, and you'll find that you can throw them right on the barbecue grill. Dense, purple Molokai-grown sweet potatoes are another of my favorites.

Don't shy away from tropical fruits or other foods just because you're unfamiliar with them. Islanders are friendly and talkative folks. Supermarket attendants — or even your fellow shoppers — will be happy to advise you on how to cut or clean island fruits. Just ask, and you're likely to find yourself on the receiving end of some friendly conversation.

Shopping in Hawaii does, however, have a downside — namely, high prices. Although you'll save quite a few bucks over three-meals-a-day restaurant dining by stocking up and cooking for yourself back at the condo, be prepared to pay more for staples than you will back home. The general rule is this: Expect anything that has to wing its way across the Pacific to be more than you usually pay.

Another Island Tradition: Tropical Cocktails

In Hawaii, the mai tai is practically the official state cocktail. The classic mai tai is a magical sweet-tart concoction of Jamaican rum, fresh lime juice, and chunky ice, generally served in a tumbler and topped with a fresh sprig of mint. It's a simple blend, and any bar worth its salt in Hawaii can mix you a well-balanced mai tai.

Of course, mai tais may not be your thing. If that's the case, don't worry. You'll find plenty of other ways to toast your time in paradise. Personally, I'm a big fan of the piña colada — okay, okay, I know it's not a Hawaiian cocktail, but it never fails to put me in the tropical mood, especially when a colorful paper umbrella and a generous slice of pineapple are included in the picture.

What to Expect at a Luau

A luau is the ideal place to experience island traditions — but only to a degree, of course. Any commercial luau (read: any luau that you're likely to attend) will be tainted by its commercialism. But a few luaus do a great job of bringing genuine island culture into the mix.

You can find the best luaus — offering the best mix of good food, amenities, setting, and authentic culture — on Maui. The **Old Lahaina Luau** and the **Feast at Lele** are the best luaus that Hawaii has to offer, hands down. If you're going to be on the Valley Isle, be sure to book your spots now; see Chapter 13.

If you're not visiting Maui, don't despair. Each island offers its own versions of the luau feast, with the Big Island garnering second-runner-up awards for its very respectable feast and top-quality entertainment at **Kona Village** (see Chapter 15). In Waikiki, book your spot at the oceanfront **Royal Hawaiian Luau** (see Chapter 11). On Kauai, your best choice is probably the **Luau Kilohana** (Chapter 17).

When you attend a luau, all you need to bring is your appetite and aloha spirit. Dress for the festivities in bright, bold colors, even if you don't own any aloha wear — bright colors really suit the mood. Other than that, just wear what's comfortable to you, and bring a sweater if the weather is expected to cool down after dark. (All luaus take place out-of-doors, and most in breezy oceanfront settings.)

Upon arrival, you're likely to be greeted with a lei, made of either fresh flowers or shells, and a cocktail, often a mai tai (or fruit juice, if you're too young or a teetotaler). You'll be led to your assigned seat, usually at a communal table with chairs (although the Old Lahaina Luau now features some traditional seating, on cushions facing low-slung tables).

 Cocktails are usually included in the pay-one-price admission fee to a luau. Open bars are common, but some luaus limit you to a certain number or kind of drink. If it matters to you, be sure to ask when booking.

After the luau pig is unearthed from the imu, everyone is usually asked to take their seats. You'll be invited to fill your plate from the buffet luau spread; the best luaus clearly mark the dishes so that you know what you're sampling. In addition to the kalua pork (shredded from the bone after the luau pig is unearthed), you can expect such traditional dishes as poi, the tasteless purple paste that's the staple starch of Hawaii. Poi is worth trying just so that you can say you sampled it, but you're unlikely to become a fan. It's not usually eaten alone, but with other starches; ask an attendant what's best in the night's feast for poi-dipping. You're more likely to prefer such dishes as lomilomi salmon, *poke,* and haupia (see the section "More Everyday Hawaiian Food Terms," earlier in this chapter). If you're not an adventurous diner, don't worry — you'll find plenty of familiar dishes on hand, including chicken teriyaki, long rice, and salad. You'll be allowed to refill your plate as often as you like. After dinner comes the evening's entertainment, usually a hula show that lasts an hour or so before the evening winds down.

Appendix

Quick Concierge

● ●

Fast Facts

American Automobile Association (AAA)

Although roadside service is available to members on the four major islands — Oahu, Maui, the Big Island, and Kauai — the only local AAA office is on Oahu at 1130 Nimitz Hwy., Honolulu (☎ 808-593-2221 from Oahu, or 800-736-2886 from neighboring islands; www.aaa-hawaii.com). The office is open Monday through Friday from 9 a.m. to 5 p.m. and Saturday from 9 a.m. to 2 p.m. For roadside assistance or information on becoming a member, call ☎ 800-AAA-HELP or point your Web browser to www.aaa.com, where you'll be linked to your regional club's home page by entering your zip code. See the sidebar "The AAA advantage" in Chapter 5 for details on the many benefits of AAA membership.

American Express

American Express has branch offices on Oahu at 677 Ala Moana Blvd., Honolulu (☎ 808-585-3200); two offices at Hilton Hawaiian Village, 2005 Kalia Rd., at Ala Moana Boulevard, Waikiki (☎ 808-947-2607 or 808-951-0644); and at the Hyatt Regency Waikiki, 2424 Kalakaua Ave. (☎ 808-926-5441).

There are two AmEx offices on Maui: one in Kaanapali at the Westin Maui, 2365 Kaanapali Pkwy. (☎ 808-661-7155); and in Central Maui at 355 Hukilike St., Suite 207 (☎ 808-893-0388).

AmEx has one office on the Big Island: on the Kohala Coast at the Hilton Waikoloa Village, 425 Waikoloa Beach Dr., off Highway 19 in the Waikoloa Resort (☎ 808-886-7958).

Kauai has no AmEx office at this time.

Not all services are offered at all offices, so call before you go.

Cardholders and traveler's check holders should call ☎ 800-221-7282 for all money emergencies. To make inquiries with the American Express Travel Agency or to locate other branch offices, call ☎ 800-AXP-TRIP. For more information, visit www.americanexpress.com.

Area Code

All the Hawaiian Islands are in the **808** area code. When dialing, you can leave the area code off if you're calling someone on the same island that you're on. If you're calling someone on a different island, though, you must dial 1-808 before the seven-digit phone number.

If you're calling from one island to another island, the call will be billed as a long-distance call, which can be more expensive than calling the mainland from Hawaii. Be sure to use your long-distance calling card when calling between islands to avoid adding inflated phone charges to your hotel bill.

ATMs

All the islands, except Molokai and Lanai, have plenty of ATMs in the major resort areas. Branches of Hawaii's most popular banks are plentiful, and all are connected to all the global ATM networks. Most supermarkets also have ATMs inside, as do many convenience stores. Do yourself a favor, though, and stock up on cash before heading off to remote areas such as the north shore of Kauai, say, or the Big Island's North Kohala peninsula or Volcano area. These areas do have ATMs, but why waste precious vacation time tracking them down and risking that they won't be on your network?

One of Hawaii's most popular banks, with branches throughout the state, is **Bank of Hawaii,** which is linked with all the major worldwide networks. To find the one nearest you, call ☎ 888-643-3888 or point your Web browser to www.boh.com/locations/atmdir.asp. You can also find ATMs on the **Cirrus** network by dialing ☎ 800-424-7787 or going online to www.mastercard.com; to find a **Plus** ATM, call ☎ 800-843-7587 or visit www.visa.com and then click the ATM locator at the bottom of the start page.

Credit Cards

If your Visa card is lost or stolen, call ☎ 800-847-2911. MasterCard holders should call ☎ 800-307-7309. American Express cardholders should call ☎ 800-221-7282 for all money emergencies.

Emergencies

No matter where you are in Hawaii, dial **911** from any phone, just like you do on the mainland. To locate doctors and hospital emergency rooms on the specific islands, see the "Fast Facts" sections in Chapter 11 (Oahu), Chapter 13 (Maui), Chapter 15 (the Big Island), and Chapter 17 (Kauai).

Liquor Laws

The legal drinking age in Hawaii is 21. Bars are allowed to stay open daily until 2 a.m.; places with cabaret licenses are able to keep the booze flowing until 4 a.m. Grocery and convenience stores are allowed to sell beer, wine, and liquor seven days a week.

Mail

To find the U.S. Postal Service branch nearest you, call ☎ 800-275-8777 and give the operator the local zip code. This number also serves as an all-purpose national info line, so call it if you have any questions about postage, zip codes, or shipments back home. You can also locate post office branches by going online to www.usps.com and clicking "Locate A Post Office." To locate convenient local branches, see the "Fast Facts" sections in Chapter 11 (Oahu), Chapter 13 (Maui), Chapter 15 (the Big Island), and Chapter 17 (Kauai).

Maps

All the rental-car companies hand out very good free map booklets on each island, which are all that you need to navigate your way around.

If you want more complete topographic maps of each island, the best are printed by the **University of Hawaii Press.** They're available from just about any bookstore in the islands. If you want to order them before you leave home, contact **Basically Books,** 160 Kamehameha Ave., Hilo, HI 96720 (☎ 800-903-MAPS or 808-961-0144; www.basicallybooks.com). Or go straight to the source and order them directly from the UH Press: www.uhpress.hawaii.edu.

AAA members should note that excellent maps of Hawaii are available free of charge. (See the earlier listing for the American Automobile Association (AAA).)

Newspapers/Magazines

The *Honolulu Advertiser* (www.honolulu advertiser.com) and the *Honolulu Star-Bulletin* (www.starbulletin.com) are the two statewide dailies. The main weekly entertainment rag is Oahu's *Honolulu Weekly* (www.honolulu weekly.com). Daily neighbor island newspapers include the *Maui News* (www.mauinews.com), the Big Island's *West Hawaii Today* (www.westhawaii today.com), the *Hawaii Tribune Herald* (www.hilohawaiitribune.com), and Kauai's *The Garden Island* (www.kauai world.com).

Hawaii magazine is a glossy monthly that's targeted to visitors; it offers a good introduction to the islands. You can usually find the current issue in the travel magazine sections at your local branch of the big chain bookstores, such as Borders and Barnes & Noble. Subscriptions are available by calling ☎ 800-365-4421.

Pharmacies

Long's Drugs, Hawaii's biggest drugstore chain, has convenient locations on all the major islands. To locate the nearest branch, point your Web browser to www.longs.com and click "Store Locator." To locate convenient branches on each island, see the "Fast Facts" sections in Chapter 11 (Oahu), Chapter 13 (Maui), Chapter 15 (the Big Island), and Chapter 17 (Kauai).

Smoking

In Hawaii, smoking is against the law in just about all public buildings. In Honolulu County and Kauai, all restaurants have a complete smoking ban, except for outdoor seating; you can, however, smoke in bars. On Maui and the Big Island, you can't smoke in any part of a restaurant (even in the bar, although stand-alone bars can allow smoking). Hotels have nonsmoking rooms available, and most bed-and-breakfasts prohibit smoking altogether inside their buildings. Car-rental agencies also have smoke-free cars.

Taxes

Hawaii's sales tax is 4 percent. Expect taxes of about 11.42 percent to be added to your final hotel bill.

Time Zone

Hawaii standard time is in effect year-round. Hawaii is two hours behind Pacific standard time and five hours behind eastern standard time — so when it's noon in Hawaii, it's 2 p.m. in California and 5 p.m. in New York.

Hawaii doesn't observe daylight saving time, however, so when daylight saving time is in effect on the mainland — April through October — Hawaii is three hours behind the West Coast and six hours behind the East Coast (making it noon in Hawaii when it's 3 p.m. in California and 6 p.m. in New York).

For the exact local time, call ☎ 808-245-0212.

Weather and Surf Reports

For statewide marine reports, call ☎ 808-973-4382. For statewide coastal wind reports, call ☎ 808-973-6114.

For local conditions and forecasts, call the following:

Oahu: ☎ 808-973-4380 or 808-973-5286; marine forecast ☎ 808-973-4382.

Maui, Molokai, and Lanai: ☎ 808-877-5111; marine forecast ☎ 808-877-3477 or 808-877-3949.

Big Island: ☎ 808-961-5582 or 808-935-8555; marine forecast ☎ 808-985-9883.

Kauai: ☎ 808-245-6001; marine forecast ☎ 808-245-3564.

To check the weather forecasts online, go to www.hawaiiweathertoday.com. I like to compare forecasts, so you might also check the Weather Channel's site at www.weather.com or CNN's weather page at www.cnn.com/weather, both of which offer multiday forecasts for hundreds of destinations around the globe. You can find the official National Weather Service forecast for the Hawaiian Islands online at www.prh.noaa.gov/pr/hnl. Toll-Free Numbers and Web Sites

Toll-Free Numbers and Web Sites

Airlines

Air Canada
☎ 888-247-2262
www.aircanada.ca

Air New Zealand
☎ 800-262-1234 in the U.S.
☎ 800-663-5494 in Canada
☎ 0800-737-000 in New Zealand
www.airnewzealand.com

Alaska Airlines
☎ 800-252-7522
www.alaskaair.com

Aloha Airlines
☎ 800-367-5250
www.alohaair.com

American Airlines
☎ 800-433-7300
www.americanair.com

American Trans Air
☎ 800-435-9282
www.ata.com

Continental Airlines
☎ 800-525-0280
www.continental.com

Delta Air Lines
☎ 800-221-1212
www.delta.com

Hawaiian Airlines
☎ 800-367-5320
www.hawaiianair.com

Island Air
☎ 800-323-3345 from North America
☎ 800-652-6541 from Hawaii
www.islandair.com

Northwest Airlines
☎ 800-225-2525
www.nwa.com

Pacific Wings Airlines
☎ 888-575-4546
www.pacificwings.com

Qantas
☎ 800-227-4500 in the U.S.
☎ 13-13-13 in Australia
www.qantas.com

United Airlines
☎ 800-864-8331
www.ual.com

Major hotel and motel chains

Aston Hotels and Resorts/ResortQuest
☎ 800-997-6667
www.aston-hotels.com

Best Western International
☎ 800-780-7234
www.bestwestern.com

Castle Resorts and Hotels
☎ 800-367-5004
www.castleresorts.com

Clarion Hotels
☎ 877-424-6423
www.hotelchoice.com

Comfort Inns
☎ 877-424-6423
www.hotelchoice.com

Doubletree Hotels
☎ 800-222-8733
www.doubletree.com

Four Seasons Hotels and Resorts
☎ 800-819-5053
www.fourseasons.com

Hilton Hotels
☎ 800-HILTONS (445-8667)
www.hilton.com

Holiday Inn
☎ 800-HOLIDAY (465-4329)
www.ichotelsgroup.com

Hyatt Hotels and Resorts
☎ 800-591-1234
www.hyatt.com

Marc Resorts Hawaii
☎ 800-535-0085
www.marcresorts.com

Marriott Hotels
☎ 888-236-2427
www.marriott.com

Ohana Hotels
☎ 800-462-6262
www.ohanahotels.com

Outrigger Hotels and Resorts
☎ 800-OUTRIGGER (688-7444)
www.outrigger.com

Premier Resorts
☎ 888-774-3533
www.premier-resorts.com

Prince Resorts Hawaii
☎ 800-944-4491
www.princeresortshawaii.com

Quality Inns and Resorts
☎ 877-424-6423
www.hotelchoice.com

Radisson Hotels International
☎ 800-333-3333
www.radisson.com

Renaissance Hotels and Resorts
☎ 800-468-3571
www.renaissancehotels.com

Ritz-Carlton
☎ 800-241-3333
www.ritzcarlton.com

Sheraton Hotels and Resorts
☎ 888-625-5144
www.sheraton-hawaii.com

Starwood's Luxury Collection
☎ 888-625-5144
www.luxurycollection.com

W Hotels
☎ 888-625-5144
www.whotels.com

Westin Hotels
☎ 888-625-5144
www.westin.com

Car-rental agencies

Alamo
☎ 800-462-5266
www.alamo.com

Avis
☎ 800-230-4898 in U.S.
☎ 800-272-5871 in Canada
www.avis.com

Budget
☎ 800-527-0700
www.budget.com

Dollar
☎ 800-800-4000
www.dollarcar.com

Enterprise
☎ 800-261-7331
www.enterprise.com

Hertz
☎ 800-654-3131
www.hertz.com

National
☎ 800-CAR-RENT (227-7368)
www.nationalcar.com

Thrifty
☎ 800-THRIFTY (847-4389)
www.thrifty.com

Where to Get More Information

Hawaii Visitors and Convention Bureau (HVCB)
2270 Kalakaua Ave., 7th Floor
Honolulu, HI 96815
☎ 800-464-2924 or 808-923-1811
www.gohawaii.com

Planet Hawaii
737 Bishop St., Suite #1900
Honolulu, HI 96813
☎ 877-91-ALOHA
www.planet-hawaii.com

Maui Visitors Bureau (also issues information on Molokai and Lanai)
1727 Wili Pa Loop
Wailuku, Maui, HI 96793
☎ 800-525-6284 or 808-244-3530
www.visitmaui.com

Kaanapali Beach Resort Association
2530 Kekaa Dr., Suite 1-B
Lahaina, HI 96761
☎ 800-245-9229 or 808-661-3271
www.maui.net/~kbra

Kapalua Resort
800 Kapalua Dr.
Kapalua, HI 96761
☎ 800-KAPALUA (527-2582)
www.kapaluamaui.com

Wailea Resort
161 Wailea Ike Place
Wailea, HI 96753
☎ 800-332-1614
www.kapaluamaui.com

Haleakala National Park
P.O. Box 369
Makawao, HI 96768
☎ 808-572-4400
www.nps.gov/hale

Maui.net
www.maui.net

Molokai Visitors Association
P.O. Box 960
Kaunakakai, HI 96748
☎ 800-800-6367 or 808-553-3876
www.molokai-hawaii.com

Destination Lanai
☎ 800-947-4774
www.visitlanai.net

Island of Lanai/Castle & Cooke Resorts
P.O. Box 630310
Lanai City, HI 96763
☎ 800-321-4666
www.lanai-resorts.com

Index

BUSINESS, CAREERS & PERSONAL FINANCE

0-7645-5307-0   0-7645-5331-3 *†

Also available:
- Accounting For Dummies †
  0-7645-5314-3
- Business Plans Kit For Dummies †
  0-7645-5365-8
- Cover Letters For Dummies
  0-7645-5224-4
- Frugal Living For Dummies
  0-7645-5403-4
- Leadership For Dummies
  0-7645-5176-0
- Managing For Dummies
  0-7645-1771-6

- Marketing For Dummies
  0-7645-5600-2
- Personal Finance For Dummies *
  0-7645-2590-5
- Project Management
  For Dummies
  0-7645-5283-X
- Resumes For Dummies †
  0-7645-5471-9
- Selling For Dummies
  0-7645-5363-1
- Small Business Kit For Dummies *†
  0-7645-5093-4

HOME & BUSINESS COMPUTER BASICS

0-7645-4074-2   0-7645-3758-X

Also available:
- ACT! 6 For Dummies
  0-7645-2645-6
- iLife '04 All-in-One Desk Reference
  For Dummies
  0-7645-7347-0
- iPAQ For Dummies
  0-7645-6769-1
- Mac OS X Panther Timesaving
  Techniques For Dummies
  0-7645-5812-9
- Macs For Dummies
  0-7645-5656-8
- Microsoft Money 2004 For Dummies
  0-7645-4195-1

- Office 2003 All-in-One Desk
  Reference For Dummies
  0-7645-3883-7
- Outlook 2003 For Dummies
  0-7645-3759-8
- PCs For Dummies
  0-7645-4074-2
- TiVo For Dummies
  0-7645-6923-6
- Upgrading and Fixing PCs
  For Dummies
  0-7645-1665-5
- Windows XP Timesaving
  Techniques For Dummies
  0-7645-3748-2

FOOD, HOME, GARDEN, HOBBIES, MUSIC & PETS

0-7645-5295-3   0-7645-5232-5

Also available:
- Bass Guitar For Dummies
  0-7645-2487-9
- Diabetes Cookbook For Dummies
  0-7645-5230-9
- Gardening For Dummies *
  0-7645-5130-2
- Guitar For Dummies
  0-7645-5106-X
- Holiday Decorating For Dummies
  0-7645-2570-0
- Home Improvement All-in-One
  For Dummies
  0-7645-5680-0

- Knitting For Dummies
  0-7645-5395-X
- Piano For Dummies
  0-7645-5105-1
- Puppies For Dummies
  0-7645-5255-4
- Scrapbooking For Dummies
  0-7645-7208-3
- Senior Dogs For Dummies
  0-7645-5818-8
- Singing For Dummies
  0-7645-2475-5
- 30-Minute Meals For Dummies
  0-7645-2589-1

INTERNET & DIGITAL MEDIA

0-7645-1664-7   0-7645-6924-4

Also available:
- 2005 Online Shopping Directory
  For Dummies
  0-7645-7495-7
- CD & DVD Recording For Dummies
  0-7645-5956-7
- eBay For Dummies
  0-7645-5654-1
- Fighting Spam For Dummies
  0-7645-5965-6
- Genealogy Online For Dummies
  0-7645-5964-8
- Google For Dummies
  0-7645-4420-9

- Home Recording For Musicians
  For Dummies
  0-7645-1634-5
- The Internet For Dummies
  0-7645-4173-0
- iPod & iTunes For Dummies
  0-7645-7772-7
- Preventing Identity Theft
  For Dummies
  0-7645-7336-5
- Pro Tools All-in-One Desk
  Reference For Dummies
  0-7645-5714-9
- Roxio Easy Media Creator
  For Dummies
  0-7645-7131-1

* **Separate Canadian edition also available**
† **Separate U.K. edition also available**

Available wherever books are sold. For more information or to order direct: U.S. customers visit www.dummies.com or call 1-877-762-2974.
U.K. customers visit www.wileyeurope.com or call 0800 243407. Canadian customers visit www.wiley.ca or call 1-800-567-4797.

SPORTS, FITNESS, PARENTING, RELIGION & SPIRITUALITY

0-7645-5146-9   0-7645-5418-2

Also available:
- ✔Adoption For Dummies
  0-7645-5488-3
- ✔Basketball For Dummies
  0-7645-5248-1
- ✔The Bible For Dummies
  0-7645-5296-1
- ✔Buddhism For Dummies
  0-7645-5359-3
- ✔Catholicism For Dummies
  0-7645-5391-7
- ✔Hockey For Dummies
  0-7645-5228-7

- ✔Judaism For Dummies
  0-7645-5299-6
- ✔Martial Arts For Dummies
  0-7645-5358-5
- ✔Pilates For Dummies
  0-7645-5397-6
- ✔Religion For Dummies
  0-7645-5264-3
- ✔Teaching Kids to Read
  For Dummies
  0-7645-4043-2
- ✔Weight Training For Dummies
  0-7645-5168-X
- ✔Yoga For Dummies
  0-7645-5117-5

TRAVEL

0-7645-5438-7   0-7645-5453-0

Also available:
- ✔Alaska For Dummies
  0-7645-1761-9
- ✔Arizona For Dummies
  0-7645-6938-4
- ✔Cancún and the Yucatán
  For Dummies
  0-7645-2437-2
- ✔Cruise Vacations For Dummies
  0-7645-6941-4
- ✔Europe For Dummies
  0-7645-5456-5
- ✔Ireland For Dummies
  0-7645-5455-7

- ✔Las Vegas For Dummies
  0-7645-5448-4
- ✔London For Dummies
  0-7645-4277-X
- ✔New York City For Dummies
  0-7645-6945-7
- ✔Paris For Dummies
  0-7645-5494-8
- ✔RV Vacations For Dummies
  0-7645-5443-3
- ✔Walt Disney World & Orlando
  For Dummies
  0-7645-6943-0

GRAPHICS, DESIGN & WEB DEVELOPMENT

0-7645-4345-8   0-7645-5589-8

Also available:
- ✔Adobe Acrobat 6 PDF
  For Dummies
  0-7645-3760-1
- ✔Building a Web Site For Dummies
  0-7645-7144-3
- ✔Dreamweaver MX 2004
  For Dummies
  0-7645-4342-3
- ✔FrontPage 2003 For Dummies
  0-7645-3882-9
- ✔HTML 4 For Dummies
  0-7645-1995-6
- ✔Illustrator CS For Dummies
  0-7645-4084-X

- ✔Macromedia Flash MX 2004
  For Dummies
  0-7645-4358-X
- ✔Photoshop 7 All-in-One Desk
  Reference For Dummies
  0-7645-1667-1
- ✔Photoshop CS Timesaving
  Techniques For Dummies
  0-7645-6782-9
- ✔PHP 5 For Dummies
  0-7645-4166-8
- ✔PowerPoint 2003 For Dummies
  0-7645-3908-6
- ✔QuarkXPress 6 For Dummies
  0-7645-2593-X

NETWORKING, SECURITY, PROGRAMMING & DATABASES

0-7645-6852-3   0-7645-5784-X

Also available:
- ✔A+ Certification For Dummies
  0-7645-4187-0
- ✔Access 2003 All-in-One Desk
  Reference For Dummies
  0-7645-3988-4
- ✔Beginning Programming
  For Dummies
  0-7645-4997-9
- ✔C For Dummies
  0-7645-7068-4
- ✔Firewalls For Dummies
  0-7645-4048-3
- ✔Home Networking For Dummies
  0-7645-42796

- ✔Network Security For Dummies
  0-7645-1679-5
- ✔Networking For Dummies
  0-7645-1677-9
- ✔TCP/IP For Dummies
  0-7645-1760-0
- ✔VBA For Dummies
  0-7645-3989-2
- ✔Wireless All In-One Desk Referenc
  For Dummies
  0-7645-7496-5
- ✔Wireless Home Networking
  For Dummies
  0-7645-3910-8

HEALTH & SELF-HELP

0-7645-6820-5 *†   0-7645-2566-2

Also available:

- ✔Alzheimer's For Dummies
  0-7645-3899-3
- ✔Asthma For Dummies
  0-7645-4233-8
- ✔Controlling Cholesterol For Dummies
  0-7645-5440-9
- ✔Depression For Dummies
  0-7645-3900-0
- ✔Dieting For Dummies
  0-7645-4149-8
- ✔Fertility For Dummies
  0-7645-2549-2

- ✔Fibromyalgia For Dummies
  0-7645-5441-7
- ✔Improving Your Memory For Dummies
  0-7645-5435-2
- ✔Pregnancy For Dummies †
  0-7645-4483-7
- ✔Quitting Smoking For Dummies
  0-7645-2629-4
- ✔Relationships For Dummies
  0-7645-5384-4
- ✔Thyroid For Dummies
  0-7645-5385-2

EDUCATION, HISTORY, REFERENCE & TEST PREPARATION

0-7645-5194-9   0-7645-4186-2

Also available:

- ✔Algebra For Dummies
  0-7645-5325-9
- ✔British History For Dummies
  0-7645-7021-8
- ✔Calculus For Dummies
  0-7645-2498-4
- ✔English Grammar For Dummies
  0-7645-5322-4
- ✔Forensics For Dummies
  0-7645-5580-4
- ✔The GMAT for Dummies
  0-7645-5251-1
- ✔Inglés Para Dummies
  0-7645-5427-1

- ✔Italian For Dummies
  0-7645-5196-5
- ✔Latin For Dummies
  0-7645-5431-X
- ✔Lewis & Clark For Dummies
  0-7645-2545-X
- ✔Research Papers For Dummies
  0-7645-5426-3
- ✔The SAT I For Dummies
  0-7645-7193-1
- ✔Science Fair Projects For Dummies
  0-7645-5460-3
- ✔U.S. History For Dummies
  0-7645-5249-X

Get smart @ dummies.com®

- **Find a full list of Dummies titles**
- **Look into loads of FREE on-site articles**
- **Sign up for FREE eTips e-mailed to you weekly**
- **See what other products carry the Dummies name**
- **Shop directly from the Dummies bookstore**
- **Enter to win new prizes every month!**

* Separate Canadian edition also available
† Separate U.K. edition also available

Available wherever books are sold. For more information or to order direct: U.S. customers visit www.dummies.com or call 1-877-762-2974.
U.K. customers visit www.wileyeurope.com or call 0800 243407. Canadian customers visit www.wiley.ca or call 1-800-567-4797.